COMPENSATION AND REWARD PERSPECTIVES

COMPENSATION AND REWARD PERSPECTIVES

THOMAS A. MAHONEY
Industrial Relations Center
University of Minnesota

1979

RICHARD D. IRWIN, INC.
Homewood, Illinois 60430

Irwin-Dorsey Limited
Georgetown, Ontario L7G 4B3

ISBN 0-256-02229-1
Library of Congress Catalog Card No. 78-72060
Printed in the United States of America

1 2 3 4 5 6 7 8 9 0 ML 6 5 4 3 2 1 0 9

To Ursula, Charles, and John

PREFACE

This book is about theories of employee motivation and performance as related to employee compensation and rewards. Administrative practices for compensating employees have evolved largely through experimentation and independent of theoretical considerations, although successful practices have been consistent with relevant theory. Given this empirical approach, one might well question the need for a theory of compensation. While not necessary for the development and application of administrative practice, knowledge of theory provides an understanding of why certain practices are useful and others are less useful. It also provides a basis for the development of improved practices more efficiently than through ad hoc experimentation. A theory for employee compensation also ought to provide the understanding needed to adapt practice to changed circumstances and to develop improvements in practice.

Theories and models relevant to employee compensation are found in the related social sciences of economics, psychology, and sociology. Developed within the context of these disciplines, the social science theories and models focus upon specific elements of motivation and behavior and are not integrated into consistent theories that address specific issues of employee compensation. This book integrates relevant theories and models of employee motivation and performance as they bear upon the compensation issues of attracting a labor force, occupational choice, joining and staying with an employer, job performance, and job satisfaction.

This book grew out of ten years of teaching compensation administration. Lacking textual sources for an integrated theory, readings from journals and texts were used in the presentation of various theoretical models and related research findings relevant to a theory of compensation. The readings presented here have been culled from experimentation in different classes and represent the most successful packaging found to date. Integration of the diverse readings was developed in examination of the readings in class discussions. The extensive discussions presented in the introduction of and commentary upon readings in the book provide a guide to integration, yet sufficient freedom remains for differing interpretations and innovative restructuring of the theory presented.

I believe that good theory will outlive any specific application of that theory in practice. Practice will change with varying circumstances, yet good theory is independent of those circumstances and ought to guide changes in practice. Thus the readings and commentary in the book are oriented primarily toward theory and models relevant to employee compensation, and references to compensation practice illustrate the applications of theory. Supplementary materials concerning compensation practices might be employed with this book in teaching both compensation theory and practice.

Alternatively, someone more oriented toward compensation practice might employ this book as a supplement to primary materials concerning compensation practice, a supplement rationalizing and explaining the practices.

The book was developed with classes of students interested in employee performance, motivation, and compensation, and will apply most directly in similar classes. It also has been used fruitfully in executive seminars, particularly where the aim was to provide understanding of compensation and the motivation of employee performance rather than familiarity with the wide range of compensation practices available. Additionally, the book has been used in an earlier form in organizational behavior courses with a focus upon employee behavior in work organizations.

Acknowledgments are due to the many students who contributed over the years to the development of this book. Their responses to various readings determined which selections were discarded and which were retained, and their challenges and insights contributed significantly to the development of the integrative commentary presented here. This current stage of integration of compensation and reward theory would not have been achieved without their contributions. Further integration and development of compensation theory is desirable, and current students and readers are invited to contribute to this development.

May 1979   ***Thomas A. Mahoney***

CONTENTS

9. MOTIVATION, COMPENSATION, AND ORGANIZATIONAL BEHAVIOR 335

10. TOWARD AN INTEGRATED THEORY OF COMPENSATION 367

CHAPTER 7

COMPENSATION PERSPECTIVES

Essay 1-1

Morris and other fat cats*

Melvin Maddocks

According to informed sources, Morris, the finicky cat in that TV ad for pet food, earned $10,000 last year, not to mention residuals.

Which is about twice the income of the average American actor.

Well, there you are. What makes money so fascinating a subject, after all, is the magnificent lack of justice with which it gets distributed. Salaries constitute comedy as the dictionary defines it: instances of "incongruity," "exaggeration carried to the point of the ridiculous."

Who can help rolling in the aisles at the thought that Johnny Carson (at $1 million per year) makes nearly 100 times the salary of a typical schoolteacher, who has all he or she can do to edge out Morris?

It would simplify one's sense of humor (or moral indignation, as the case may be) if money were distributed with consistent injustice. But consider:

A professional woman tennis player can make $32,000 in a week by winning a single tournament. A professional man squash player, performing in a racquet sport equally demanding of skill and more

exhausting, will win $1,500 tops for a tournament and, by giving lessons, selling equipment, etc., earn perhaps $18,000 to $22,000 a year.

Singing for supper

Still—to return to Morris and friends— the most mysterious, the most inexplicable pay scale may exist among the arts. Once the fiscal rewards for the arts were nothing if not predictable—that is to say, minimal. Neglected by the public, denied even social status, the artist characteristically was a vagabond singing (or sketching or scribbling) for his supper.

The one connecting theme in artists' lives, it seemed, was the legend of poverty. What did Rembrandt and Beethoven, Mozart and William Blake have in common? Money trouble.

Things have changed. Take the case of Chaucer. Presumably that jolliest of poets —moonlighting as a government clerk on the side—walked the road to Canterbury for little more reward than his pilgrims. Inward satisfaction, as they say. The traditional pay-off for artists.

Then a couple of weeks ago a 15th-century manuscript of "Canterbury Tales" was auctioned in London for $216,000.

It's enough to make an artist subscribe to cyrogenics: be frozen now, be paid later.

Financial chasms

Nowadays there are at least two kinds of artists: the very rich and the very poor. The financial distance between, say, Marlon Brando or Robert Redford or Paul Newman and an Off-Broadway, Equity-scale actor may be nearly as vast as that between Henry Ford and a nut-tightener on the Pinto assembly line.

If one is to believe what one reads, certain rock musicians can command $150,000 for a single night's work.

Are very rich artists different from very poor artists, as Fitzgerald might have argued? Or, to paraphrase Hemingway's side of that famous dialogue, do they simply have more money? Norman Mailer, who is reported to have signed a $1-million contract with his publisher, claims that writing for profit, a lot of profit, brings out the best in an author. He *has* to write well so that cynics cannot say: "He just did it for the money." Money is an artist's ultimate risk; and the more money, the more stimulating the risk.

Spoken like a true capitalist.

The temptation of the rich artist is to regard his wealth as merited. The temptation of the poor artist is to regard his poverty as confirmation of his integrity. Both assumptions are dangerous. Money, in terms of being "deserved" or even "earned," is a treacherous subject.

Zeus is known to have turned himself into a shower of gold, and probably this is the safest way to think of money—as a kind of meteorological accident which falls, like other sorts of rain, upon the just and the unjust, from J. Paul Getty to Morris the cat.

Commentary: Theory and practice of compensation

The questions raised about the income of Morris the cat in 1974 appear repeatedly throughout the ages. The toilers in the vineyard cited in the gospel questioned the equity of paying those hired in the afternoon the same wages as those who worked all day. Sports fans question the magnitude of contracts negotiated with baseball stars, and the salaries of corporate executives are frequent objects of jealous comparison. Wage and salary income, employee compensation, is a subject of concern to almost everyone. We are concerned about our personal compensation because it is a major determinant of our standard of living, level of consumption, social status, and sense of personal worth and achievement. The compensation of others is of concern since relative compensation reflects upon our status and worth, and also since we, as consumers, bear the cost of others' incomes. We question the logic and justice of the distribution of wage and salary income and are reluctant to view the determination of salaries as a "meteorological accident." We demand a more logical and defensible explanation of the relative salaries paid different occupations and individuals working in those occupations.

Explanation of the wages and salaries paid different occupations and individuals can be sought in the actions of employing organizations, corporations, universities, hospitals and governmental agencies, for these employers establish rates of compensation and provide the payment of compensation. As employers, their concerns are to provide compensation payments adequate to secure necessary labor services at costs which permit profit making or are consistent with efficient budget operations. Employers also question wage and salary determination wondering what rates of compensation ought to be provided different occupations and individuals. Like us, they are reluctant to view the determination of salaries as a "meteorological accident" and seek a logical and defensible explanation of their actions in wage and salary determination. We seek more than a description of the policies and practices of wage determination in employing organizations, however; we seek an explanation of, and a rationale for, these policies and practices. We seek a theory capable of explaining compensation practices and capable of serving as the base from which improved practices might be developed.

An observation made some years ago to the effect that "economists develop wage theories, managers pay wages" characterizes much of the development of theory and practice in the administration of compensation. Employee compensation has been the subject of considerable speculation and theorizing in economics, psychology, and sociology, each discipline typically addressing somewhat different issues. In consequence, various theories of compensation have developed rather than a single integrated theory, and compensation administration has proceeded to develop clinically, experimenting and building a body of accepted practice based upon results of this experimentation. Compensation practice does possess an integrity and rationale broader than the criterion of "it works," however. Much of current practice can be explained and rationalized in terms of various theoretical models of the social sciences, although not developed from knowledge of those models. The fact that something "works" is hardly accidental and ought to be explainable in a broader perspective of knowledge.

One might well question the need for a theory of compensation since much of current practice was developed on the basis of experimentation in the absence of accepted theory. Explanation of the income of Morris the cat or the salaries of Henry Ford II or a police officer in Minneapolis is difficult lacking a theory of compensation. One of the major purposes of a theory is to explain observed phenomena in such a way that one can develop reasonable answers to "what if" kinds of questions. What if, for example, everyone were to receive equal compensation? Or, what if carpenters were paid twice what attorneys are paid? Experimentation to answer such questions is costly and a difficult way to learn; an accepted theory would provide a more efficient way of learning why observed rates of compensation are paid and predicting consequences of change.

All of us, knowingly or not, apply theories, however crude, when we make predictions about the consequences of different actions or select among alternative actions. Proposals to raise the level of minimum wages, provide dental insurance to employees, or restrict the compensation of physicians are all based upon assumptions about motivation and performance. These assumptions and reasoning based upon them constitute a theory, however loosely structured and developed. Much of the conflict about such proposals stems from conflict over the appropriate assumptions and theory to apply in analysis of specific compensation issues. Understanding* and integration of theoretical contributions to the explanation of compensation issues should contribute to informed analysis and policy decisions regarding employee compensation.

No comprehensive theory of employee compensation exists at present. Rather, there exists a number of segmented theories or models of compensation and employee behavior as well as numerous empirical observations focusing upon limited aspects of compensation and employee behavior. These segmented approaches to analysis and understanding of compensation issues largely reflect the fact that each is directed toward answering a relatively specific question, a question different from the questions addressed by other approaches. Consider, for example, the diagram in Figure 1. Employee

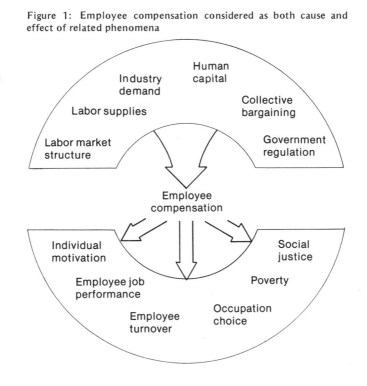

Figure 1: Employee compensation considered as both cause and effect of related phenomena

compensation might be addressed as an observable phenomenon to be explained, a dependent variable in a conceptual formulation. Thus, for example, theories of labor economics are directed toward explanation of observed wage differentials among occupations, industries, and employee groups differentiated in terms of gender and race; other wage phenomena of interest to the labor economist include rates of change in compensation. Various influences of compensation phenomena have been considered and are indicated at the top of Figure 1; influences such as public policy and government regulation of wages, collective bargaining between unions and employers, variations in human capital of individuals expressed in the form of education and skill, industry demands for labor services, unemployment and the availability of labor supplies, and the structure of labor market processes in the allocation of labor among different employments. Specific models in labor economics relate to the effects of one or more of these influences upon wage phenomena.

Compensation is of more concern to the behavioral scientist as a cause of other relevant phenomena than as something to be explained. The industrial psychologist interested in the explanation of job performance or employee turnover considers employee compensation as one of a number of independent influences upon employee behavior. Employee compensation, in this context, is viewed as a manipulable or controllable variable rather than as a dependent variable to be explained. Similarly, compensation is viewed as an independent variable in the explanation of individual motivation, occupational choice, social poverty and living standards, and social justice obtained in the distribution of income. Again, specific models or theories in the behavioral sciences relate to the influence of compensation upon one or more of these individual and social phenomena.

Like the chicken and the egg, aspects of employee compensation are both cause and consequence of individual and social behavior. Occupational choice, for example, is influenced by existing occupational wage differentials and those choices, once made, influence occupational labor supplies which in turn impact upon occupational wage differentials. Thus models or theories focused upon one specific question regarding compensation often make assumptions about relationships addressed in other models. Models regarding the influence of labor supplies upon compensation differentials, for example, make assumptions about the influence of compensation upon individual motivation and choice, assumptions which are the direct object of inquiry in another model. There is opportunity for the integration of related models in the development of a more comprehensive theory of compensation.

An attempt to integrate compensation theories must begin with a central issue or concept which can serve as the focus for integration. We choose the focus of employment exchange or employment contract; the exchange of labor services and compensation between the employee and employing organization. This conceptualization, elaborated in Chapter 2, considers compensation as an instrument to secure desired labor services, an instrument which is varied as necessary to elicit desired employee behaviors. Later chapters examine specific elements of, and influences upon, the employment exchange and elaborate the general model developed in Chapter 2.

A major concern in the design of compensation offers by employing organizations is the behavioral response of employees. Compensation offers are intended to elicit specific employee behaviors and are based upon assumptions regarding employee motivation and behavior. Chapter 3 examines employee behavior in terms of decisions about work and employment opportunities. Models of individual decision making are presented, and models of aggregate labor supply behavior based upon the individual decision making models are examined. Chapter 3 integrates models of individual decision making from psychology and economics and models of labor supply from labor economics.

Different concepts and measures of compensation are examined in Chapter 4. Compensation is a multi-faceted concept as employed within the context of the employment exchange, at broadest including all aspects of the exchange found attractive to an individual. Different aspects of work and employment including monetary compensation are considered as potential rewards and compared with each other. Aspects of monetary compensation including varied meanings to the individual, ways of varying amount and form of compensation, and measures of compensation level, rate, and structure are examined in some detail. Potential motivational and cost implications of different aspects of monetary compensation are indicated.

Chapter 5 examines compensation in terms of employer valuation of labor services, a major concern of economic analysis. The concept of employment exchange implies that the level of compensation provided for the labor services exchanged must be mutually acceptable to both employer and employee. Readings in this chapter identify economic constraints upon the employer's ability to pay compensation, and examine specific influences upon the wage level offered by an employer within the economic constraints of ability to pay. The level of compensation offered by the employer is considered as a function of both labor supply considerations developed in Chapter 3 and employer ability to pay considered in Chapter 5.

A second major concern of compensation administration, the structuring of compensation differentials among jobs within an organization, is examined in Chapter 6. The concept of an internal labor market to allocate employees among jobs within the organization is developed and combined with models of social comparison and equity to explain the consequences of compensation structures within organizations. Employee motivations to accept job assignments, to perform as directed, and to terminate employment are related to compensation structure decisions.

Chapter 7 examines specifically task motivation, performance, and compensation. Reinforcement and expectancy models from psychology are examined as well as experiments in their application in work settings. Other related models which are examined include the role of goals in performance and the role of social setting upon the application of compensation for individual task performance.

Later chapters, 8 and 9, consider more general aspects of compensation and reward systems as related to job satisfaction and organizational behavior. Chapter 10 attempts an integration of the full set of readings and considerations into a more complete theory or model of employee compensation and performance. This integration is incomplete at this stage and readers are encouraged to test it against the earlier readings. Ambitious students are urged to read Chapter 10 first and challenge the attempted integration as they read other chapters; curious students are invited to read it also for a more complete introduction to the chapters which follow this chapter. Readers are encouraged to attempt their own integrations of the concepts and ideas presented in later chapters. An integrated theory based upon these conceptual approaches to employee compensation and reward should help provide understanding of observed compensation phenomena and of the likely consequences of alternative compensation practices. The reader ought to be able to provide a better explanation of the income of Morris the cat when finished than provided by the appeal to a meteorological accident.

A careful reader may observe the various publication dates of reading selections in the later chapters. The selection from Adam Smith's *Wealth of Nations* dates from 1776 and other publication dates range from 1955 through 1977. There are several reasons for including what may appear to the youthful reader as old, possibly dated, approaches to the analysis of compensation issues. As any field of inquiry develops over time, the topics and issues of concern become more and more specific. Although the approach applied in the analysis of these topics reflects past conceptualization and research, those past conceptualizations often are not as easily perceived as in earlier statements of them. Thus, for example, expectancy models of motivation underlie much current research, but current research reports do not present or rationalize basic expectancy models as clearly as Vroom did in 1964. Readings have been selected without regard to the date of original publication to provide the clearest available statement of models and conceptualizations which have been found useful. A second reason for including original statements of conceptualizations is that many of these statements tend to become distorted with retelling. A notable example is the selection from Adam Smith, often associated with the concept of "economic man" motivated solely by pecuniary gain. You will note as you read Chapter 3 the striking similarity between Smith's model and the expectancy model by Vroom in 1964. The fact that some selections were published a number of years ago does not mean they are dated and inapplicable today; rather, these are statements of conceptualizations and research which have influenced considerably the development of theory and practice in compensation and which have passed the test of time. These are the selections most likely to aid you in understanding and explaining the phenomenon of Morris the cat's income.

CHAPTER 2

WORK AND COMPENSATION: THE EMPLOYMENT CONTRACT

One is paid wages for working. Issues and concerns regarding wages, how much one should be paid, hinge upon the relationship between wages or pay and work. We must begin with an examination of work if we are to understand the arguments made concerning wages or to make satisfactory decisions about compensation. Work is a simple four-letter word which has been the subject of philosophical examination. Work has been viewed alternatively as drudgery to be avoided insofar as possible and as the means of expressing a person's unique abilities, interests, and values; as a means to some desired goals and as an end in itself; as painful to the individual and as a source of joy and fulfillment. All of these descriptions of work are valid in one situation or another for work serves a multitude of purposes for different persons and at different times. Work can be a source of self-identity and meaning to an individual and at the same time a painful irritant preventing that individual from enjoying the first snowfall of winter. Nevertheless, the concept of work most common to wage and compensation issues regards work as a means to other desired ends. While other interpretations of work vary among individuals, work is for most people something undertaken for outcomes associated with working, outcomes such as wages or other monetary compensation.

A definition of work as an activity in which one engages as a means to achieving desired ends is far too broad for our purposes. Such a definition would include practicing the piano or swimming as means of winning a competition, preparing a picnic for oneself, and studying in order to pass an examination. While the reader may class all of these activities as work, they are not activities with which we normally associate wage payments. Elliot Jaques, in Essay 2-1, terms these activities noneconomic work. Other examples of noneconomic work would include cleaning one's house, changing the oil in one's car and raising vegetables for personal consumption. Such activities are productive but are directed toward personal consumption of the outputs. Economic work is productive of a good or service offered for exchange in the network of economic markets; the immediate output of economic work is offered for exchange rather than consumed directly by the producer. House cleaning as a domestic employee, changing oil for others for a fee, and raising vegetables for sale in the farmers market would qualify as economic work.

Wage payments are associated with a specific class of economic work activities, activities we call employment work. Employment work is a set of activities performed by an individual under the direction of someone else who acquires title to, or ownership of, any output resulting from these efforts. The individual engaged in employment work agrees to perform services at the direction of the employer and never, in fact, holds title to the output of these services. Employment work, with which we associate wage payments, excludes many types of work and productive activities in our society. The evening newspaper carrier, the truck farmer selling produce at a roadside stand, and the free-lance short story writer work and produce for sale but receive payments based solely upon customer valuations of their produce and not upon the effort expended in work; they are not engaged in employment work.

Jaques describes employment work in terms of the content or nature of the tasks performed. Employment work involves performance of prescribed tasks or activities to the satisfaction of the employer. The exercise of discretion in performance of tasks is constrained to greater or lesser degree depending upon the specific job. Employment work, in this context, involves submission of oneself to the authority of another in that work role. This authority relationship is central to the analysis of the "employment contract" by March and Simon (Essay 2-2). An individual, accepting employment with an organization, enters into an employment contract in which he explicitly or implicitly accepts an authority relationship and agrees to perform as directed. The employer acquires the services of the employee through this relationship, services which may be used however the employer desires within certain constraints (termed the zone of indifference). The employee "contributes" services to the organization and in return receives what March and Simon term "inducements," typically, payments for those services. Wage payments or inducements thus characterize employment work and are analyzed meaningfully only in the context of an employment relationship and an employment contract.

The concept of employment contract and an exchange of contributions and inducements underlies all analyses of compensation for employment work. A contract may be explicit as in collective bargaining between an employer and a labor union or in the negotiation of individual employment contracts with key executives; alternatively, the concept of employment contract is implicit in individual acceptance of a job offer specifying the type of work to be performed and the wage rate for that work. In each instance, work is exchanged for some form of payment. Jaques's conceptualization of employment work in terms of prescribed and discretionary elements of work behavior also illustrates a generally accepted belief that the wages provided in return for employment work ought to vary depending upon the nature or content of that work. Determination of the appropriate compensation for work performed under the employment contract is a central issue in all wage and compensation analyses.

Essay 2-1

The nature of economic work*

Elliott Jaques

Two broad categories of work may be separated—economic and noneconomic. By economic work is meant all work whose designated goal is part of the social network connected with the creation and distribution of goods and services. Under the rubric of noneconomic work are included all other types of work in connection with which labor services are not offered for sale—as, for example, family, recreational, and some charitable work. By way of illustration, and not detailed description, the work of the housewife comprises such matters as judgment in the upbringing of children, choices in the running arrangements for the house, and for meals. She operates within the limits of the family financial means, cultural custom and practice, and a variety of other geographical, social, and psychological constraints.

Our main endeavor being the exploration of the nature of economic work, however, we need be diverted no further into considering other forms of noneconomic activities. Economic work aimed toward the production and distribution of goods and services comprises the manifold activities broadly encompassed within the field of economics—primary production of food and raw materials, manufacturing and processing, transportation, distribution including wholesaling and retailing, and the planning and organization and administration of economic work, including governmental planning and administration, accounting, supply, technical, per-

sonnel, and other specialized functions essential to the running of the economic process.

An obvious feature of work in the economic sphere is that those so employed are participating in the production and supply of the material requirements of living. In more primitive economies—where exchange is at a minimum and is carried on by barter—the material fruits of a person's labor are reaped and handled by himself, and hence are directly and tangibly apparent to him. Differences in standard of living among different members of the community are more immediately relatable to individual differences in capacity to produce—to farm, to fish, to build, to hunt. By comparison with the relative directness of perception of rewards in primitive production, there is an absolute quality to the intangibility of the appropriateness of individual economic reward in our own society. In an industrial economy based on large-scale organization of production and distribution in which individuals are deployed on more or less detailed aspects of the total process of production and distribution, and with money excluding for all practical purposes the trading of goods as a means of exchange, the relationship between the material outcome of one's own work and the material value of one's reward is totally obscured from conscious assessment.

There are two main forms of economic work, each generating its own form of economic return—entrepreneurial work (including shareholding and directing work), and contractual employment work. It is contractual employment work with which the present study is mainly con-

*Reprinted from Elliott Jaques, *Equitable Payment* (New York: John Wiley and Sons, 1961), pp. 48-51 (abridged). Copyright © 1961 John Wiley and Sons, Inc. Reprinted by permission.

cerned. In order to define the problems of employment work, however, it is necessary to define entrepreneurial work as well. It is within the total setting of entrepreneurial work that the full character of contractual employment work may be made manifest. I shall briefly set out the main features of each type of work with particular emphasis upon the type of discretion which must be exercised.

Entrepreneurial work is that of deciding which kinds of economic enterprise are likely to prove profitable by virtue of the demand for the particular goods and services which they provide, investing appropriate amounts of capital in the establishment or purchase of such an enterprise, employing an organization to carry out the work, and directing how it shall be operated by its employees in order to fulfill its objectives. The amount and character of the shareholding of the entrepreneur—be he an individual or a financial combine—if he attracts capital other than his own, must be such that he retains effective financial control of the enterprise.

Employment work, by contrast with entrepreneurial work, is that of carrying out designated tasks within the executive organization of an enterprise with which the person has a contract to work, the contract ordinarily not having a specified time limit for which it holds good. Employment work does not carry responsibility for setting goals or objectives. Although it may not always be obvious, what an employee is to do and the results to be achieved by his work are *always* set for him. This fact need not be obscured by the fact that there are employees in managerial positions who set the results to be achieved by their subordinates. Every manager has had his own objectives set for him, and is authorized to allocate to his subordinates only that work which will enable him to discharge his own responsibilities. That is to say, he is limited to allocating work consistent with the objectives and goals of the enterprise.

Employment work is that type of work, then, carried out by every single member of an executive organization established by a company to do its work. It includes the work of the chief executive employed by the company, and of all the managers, technicians, specialists, and workers employed by him or by his subordinates. In this regard it is useful to keep firmly in mind the true distinction between a company—the legal entity whose members are the shareholders—and executive organizations established by a company to do its work, whose members are *employees* of the company and not *members* of it.

The discretionary content of employment work has to do with deciding what steps to take to achieve the results prescribed—how best to do the jobs allocated —within the resources provided, company policies and regulations, set methods, administrative procedures and routines, and other prescribed limits. In return for discharging the responsibilities which he was employed for and which he has contracted to carry out, each employee is paid a wage or salary which is ordinarily the greater the more the responsibility carried in a job.

Essay 2-2

Theory of organizational equilibrium*

James G. March and Herbert A. Simon

The Barnard-Simon theory of organizational equilibrium is essentially a theory of motivation—a statement of the conditions under which an organization can induce its members to continue their participation, and hence assure organizational survival. The central postulates of the theory are stated by Simon, Smithburg, and Thompson (1950, pp. 381-82) as follows:

1. An organization is a system of interrelated social behaviors of a number of persons whom we shall call the *participants* in the organization.
2. Each participant and each group of participants receives *from* the organization *inducements* in return for which he makes *to* the organization *contributions*.
3. Each participant will continue his participation in an organization only so long as the inducements offered him are as great or greater (measured in terms of *his* values and in terms of the alternatives open to him) than the contributions he is asked to make.
4. The contributions provided by the various groups of participants are the source from which the organization manufactures the inducements offered to participants.
5. Hence, an organization is "solvent"—and will continue in existence—only so long as the contributions are sufficient to provide inducements in large enough measure to draw forth these contributions.

The theory, like many theoretical generalizations, verges on the tautological. Specifically, to test the theory, and especially the crucial postulate 3, we need independent empirical estimates of *(a)* the

behavior of participants in joining, remaining in, or withdrawing from organizations; and *(b)* the balance of inducements and contributions for each participant, measured in terms of his "utilities."

The observation of participants joining and leaving organizations is comparatively easy. It is more difficult to find evidence of the value of variable *(b)* that does not depend on the observation of *(a)*. Before we can deal with the observational problem, however, we must say a bit more about the concepts of inducements and contributions.

Inducements. Inducements are "payments" made by (or through) the organization to its participants (e.g., wages to a worker, service to a client, income to an investor). These payments can be measured in units that are independent of their utility to the participants (e.g., wages and income can be measured in terms of dollars, service to clients in terms of hours devoted to him). Consequently, for an individual participant we can specify a set of inducements, each component of the set representing a different dimension of the inducements offered by the organization. Thus, each component of the inducements can be measured uniquely and independently of the utilities assigned to it by the participants.

Inducement utilities. For each component in the set of inducements there is a corresponding utility value. For the moment we will not be concerned with the shape of the utility function; but we do not exclude from consideration a step function. The utility function for a given individual reduces the several components of the inducements to a common dimension.

Contributions. We assume that a participant in an organization makes certain "payments" to the organization (e.g., work from the worker, fee from the client, capital from the investor). These payments, which we shall call contributions, can be measured in units that are independent of their utility to the participants. Consequently, for any individual participant we can specify a set of contributions.

Contribution utilities. A utility function transforming contributions into utilities of the individual contributor can be defined in more than one way. A reasonable definition of the utility of a contribution is the value of the alternatives that an individual foregoes in order to make the contribution. As we shall see below, this definition of contribution utilities allows us to introduce into the analysis the range of behavior alternatives open to the participant.

These definitions of inducements and contributions permit two general approaches to the observational problem. On the one hand, we can try to estimate the utility balance directly by observing the behavior (including responses to pertinent questions) of participants. On the other hand, if we are prepared to make some simple empirical assumptions about utility functions, we can make predictions from changes in the amounts of inducements and contributions, without reference to their utilities.

To estimate the inducement-contribution utility balance directly, the most logical type of measure is some variant of individual satisfaction (with the job, the service, the investment, etc.). It appears reasonable to assume that the greater the difference between inducements and contributions, the greater the individual satisfaction. However, the critical "zero points" of the satisfaction scale and the inducement-contribution utility balance

are not necessarily identical. The zero point for the satisfaction scale is the point at which one begins to speak of degrees of "dissatisfaction" rather than degrees of "satisfaction." It is, therefore, closely related to the level of aspiration and ... is the point at which we would predict a substantial increase in search behavior on the part of the organism.

The zero point on the inducement-contribution utility scale, on the other hand, is the point at which the individual is indifferent to leaving an organization. We have ample evidence that these two zero points are not identical, but, in particular, that very few of the "satisfied" participants leave an organization, whereas some, but typically not all, of the "unsatisfied" participants leave (Reynolds, 1951).

How do we explain these differences? The explanation lies primarily in the ways in which alternatives to current activity enter into the scheme (and this is one of the reasons for defining contribution utilities in terms of opportunities foregone). Dissatisfaction is a cue for search behavior. Being dissatisfied, the organism expands its program for exploring alternatives. If over the long run this search fails, the aspiration level is gradually revised downward. We assume, however, that the change in aspiration level occurs slowly, so that dissatisfaction in the short run is quite possible. On the other hand, the inducement-contribution utility balance adjusts quickly to changes in the perception of alternatives. When fewer and poorer alternatives are perceived to be available, the utility of activities foregone decreases; and this adjustment occurs rapidly.

Consequently, we can use satisfaction expressed by the individual as a measure of the inducement-contribution utility balance only if it is used in conjunction with an estimate of perceived alternatives available. Speaking roughly, only the desire to move enters into judgments of satisfaction; desire to move *plus* the perceived ease of movement enters into the inducement-contribution utility measure. Many students of mobility (particularly those concerned with the mobility of workers) have tended to ignore one or the other of these two facets of the decision to participate (Rice, Hill, and Trist, 1950; Behrend, 1953).

Direct observation of the inducement-contribution utilities, however, is not the only possible way to estimate them. Provided we make certain assumptions about the utility functions, we can infer the utility balance directly from observations of changes in the inducements or contributions measured in nonutility terms. Three major assumptions are useful and perhaps warranted. First, we assume that the utility functions change only slowly. Second, we assume that each utility function is monotonic with respect to its corresponding inducement or contribution. Although we may not know what the utility of an increase in wages will be, we are prepared to assume it will be positive. Third, we assume that the utility functions of fairly broad classes of people are very nearly the same; within a given subculture we do not expect radical differences in values. Also, we can expect that if an increase in a given inducement produces an increase in utility for one individual, it will produce an increase for other individuals.

There are other reasonable assumptions about individual utility functions; some will be indicated below when we relate individual participation to other factors. These three assumptions, however, in themselves lead to a variety of estimation procedures. Under the first assumption the short-run effect of a change in inducements or contributions will be uncontaminated by feedback effects. By the second assumption (particularly in conjunction with the third) a host of ordinal predictions can be made on the basis of knowledge of changes in the inducements and contributions. The third assumption permits us to estimate some of the cardinal

properties of the inducements-contributions balance, avoiding the problem of interpersonal comparison of utilities.

Assumptions such as those listed have some a priori validity, but it is more important that much of the evidence currently available on the behavior of participants is consistent with them. Thus, predictions are frequently and often successfully made by businessmen as to the feasibility of proposed organizational plans.

Consider the analysis of a businessman exploring the feasibility of a business venture. His first step is to construct an operating plan showing what activities and facilities are required to carry on the proposed business, including estimates of the quantities of "inputs" and "outputs" of all categories. In the language of economics, he estimates the "production function." In the language of organization theory, the production function states the rates of possible conversion of contributions into inducements (Simon, 1952-53).

His second step is to estimate the monetary inducements that will be needed to obtain the inputs in the amounts required, and the monetary contributions that can be exacted for the outputs—i.e., the prices of factors of production and of product. In estimating these monetary inducements, predictions are being made as to the inducements-contributions balances of various classes of participants. Let us give some hypothetical examples:

Salaries and wages

Information is obtained on "going rates of wages" for similar classes of work in other companies in the same area. An implicit *ceteris paribus* assumption is made with respect to other inducements, or (if the work, say, is particularly unpleasant, if proposed working conditions are particularly good or bad, etc.) the monetary inducement is adjusted upward or downward to compensate for the other factors.

If the problem is to attract workers from other organizations, it is assumed that a wage differential or other inducement will be required to persuade them to change.

The same procedure is followed for the inducements to other participants. In each case, information is required as to the alternative inducements offered by other organizations, and these establish the "zero level" of the net inducement-contribution balance. If nonmonetary factors are not comparable among alternatives, an estimated adjustment is made of the monetary inducements by way of compensation. Of course, the adjustment may just as well be made in the nonmonetary factors (e.g., in product quality).

If the planned inducements, including the monetary inducements, give a positive balance for all groups of participants, the plan is feasible. If the plan is subsequently carried out, a comparison of the actual operations with the estimates provides an empirical test of the assumptions and the estimates. If the outcomes fail to confirm the assumptions, the businessman may still choose which of the two sets of assumptions he will alter. He may interpret the result as evidence that the basic inducements-contributions hypothesis is incorrect, or he may conclude that he has estimated incorrectly the zero points of one or more of the inducements-contributions balances. The fact is, however, that such predictions are frequently made with substantial success.

The testing of the theory is not confined to predicting the survival of new enterprises. At any time in the life of an organization when a change is made—that (a) explicitly alters the inducements offered to any group of participants; (b) explicitly alters the contributions demanded from them; or (c) alters the organizational activity in any way that will affect inducements or contributions—on any of these occasions, a prediction can be made as to the effect of the change on participation. The effects may be measurable in terms of turnover rates of employees, sales, etc., as appropriate.

Most obvious in any catalog of organizational participants are the employees, including the management. Ordinarily, when we talk of organizational participants what we mean are workers, and membership in a business organization is ordinarily treated as equivalent to employment. Employees receive wages and other gratuities and donate work (production) and other contributions to the organization. As will become obvious below, employment is the area of participation in organizations in which the most extensive research has been executed.

In one respect an employee's relation to the organization is quite different from that of other participants. In joining the organization he accepts an authority relation; i.e., he agrees that within some limits (defined both explicitly and implicitly by the terms of the employment contract) he will accept as the premises of his behavior orders and instructions supplied to him by the organization. Associated with this acceptance are commonly understood procedures for "legitimating" communications and clothing them with authority for employees. Acceptance of authority by the employee gives the organization a powerful means for influencing him—more powerful than persuasion, and comparable to the evoking processes that call forth a whole program of behavior in response to a stimulus.

On the assumption that employees act in a subjectively rational manner, we can make some predictions about the scope of the authority relation from our knowledge of the inducements and contributions of the employees and other organization members (Simon, 1952-53). An employee will be willing to enter into an employment contract only if it does not matter to him "very much" what activities (within the area of acceptance agreed on in the contract) the organization will instruct him to perform, or if he is compensated in some way for the possibility that the organization will impose unpleasant activities on him. It will be advantageous for the organization to establish an authority relation when the employee activities that are optimal for the organization (i.e., maximize the inducement utility to other participants of the employee's activity) cannot be predicted accurately in advance.

These propositions can be restated in a form that permits them to be tested by looking at terms of the employment contract. A particular aspect of an employee's behavior can be *(a)* specified in the employment contract (e.g., as the wage rate usually is), *(b)* left to the employee's discretion (e.g., sometimes, but not always, whether he smokes on the job), or *(c)* brought within the authority of the employer (e.g., the specific tasks he performs within the range fixed by the job specification). The conditions that make it advantageous to stipulate an aspect of behavior in the contract are sharp conflict of interest (e.g., as to wage level) and some uncertainty as to what that interest is. It is advantageous to leave to the employee's discretion those aspects that are of little interest to the employer but great interest to the employee; and to subject the employee to the organization's authority in those aspects that are of relatively great interest to the employer, comparatively unimportant to the employee, and about which the employer cannot make accurate predictions much in advance of performance.

REFERENCES

Behrend, J. "Absence and Labour Turnover in a Changing Economic Climate." *Occupational Psychology* 27 (1953), 69-79.

Reynolds, L. G. *The Structure of Labor Markets.* New York: Harper and Row, 1951.

Rice, A. K.; Hill, J. M. M.; and Trist, E. L. "The Representation of Labour Turnover as a Social Process." *Human Relations* 3 (1950), 349-72.

Simon, H. A. "A Comparison of Organization Theories." *The Review of Economic Studies* 20 (1952-53), 40-48.

Simon, H. A.; Smithburg, D. W.; and Thompson, V. A. *Public Administration.* New York: Alfred A. Knopf, 1950.

Commentary

The preceding essays call out several issues which recur in later analyses of compensation, reward, and motivation. Employment work involves exchange—exchange of work for compensation according to Jaques, and exchange of contributions for inducements according to March and Simon. In both cases, the exchange is voluntary and symbolized in either a formal or a psychological contract between employer and employee. Both parties to any voluntary exchange must evaluate the exchange favorably and view it as fair, equitable, or beneficial if the exchange is to be effected. Each party to a voluntary exchange, whether it involves the purchase of a used car, the acceptance of employment, or the sale of a house, is free to reject the exchange, so any exchange which is effected implies the consent of both parties and favorable evaluation by both parties. The employment exchange for most employees is more analogous to the sale of milk in large supermarkets than to the sale of a house; work, like milk, is priced and the individual may accept or reject the proffered exchange without the individual haggling and negotiation which characterizes the sale of a house. The pricing of work in such a way that both employer and employee accept the proposed exchange as desirable is the central issue underlying compensation theory and administration. How should be, or is, employment work priced?

Paradoxically, both parties to any voluntary exchange must perceive that they benefit from that exchange. Such an outcome is made possible because the parties to the exchange apply different values to the inducements and contributions being exchanged. The five dollars I pay a neighbor boy to shovel the snow from my walk is more valuable to him relative to the effort he will expend than it is to me relative to the effort I would otherwise expend. March and Simon indicate that inducements are evaluated in terms of utility or value to the individual and that valuations will vary among individuals. Thus five dollars appears more valuable to the child saving for a bicycle than to the adult owning two cars. Similarly, certain forms of inducements (e.g., dental insurance, pension, wages) have more value or appeal to some individuals than to others, and it is unlikely that all individuals will value a specified set of inducements equally. Limited research into employee preferences for alternative forms of compensation reveals that preferences indicative of relative utility vary among individuals and, in fact, need not reflect directly economic cost to the employer. While not stated explicitly by March and Simon, their conceptualization of inducements would include any characteristic of employment valued as rewarding by the employee whether or not it also occasioned a cost to the employer. Jaques, on the other hand, limits his examination of the employment exchange to consideration of monetary compensation and related forms easily translated into monetary terms.

The valuation of contributions by employees is, according to March and Simon, more complex. They suggest that contribution or work is valued indirectly in terms of the value of foregone opportunities. In this context, inducements "compensate" for the imbalance occasioned by work contributions. The value of an hour spent at work thus depends upon the foregone inducements of alternatives; thus the value of an hour spent shoveling snow relates to my valuation of a foregone hour of skiing while it relates to valuation of a foregone hour of television to my neighbor's boy. Jaques, on the other hand, argues that the valuation of work is not relative to the individual and that this valuation varies directly with the amount of discretion required in the work. The criteria appropriate for the valuation of work is a very unsettled issue and one to which we shall return in later chapters.

Both Jaques and March and Simon analyze the employment exchange from the standpoint of the individual rather than from the standpoint of the employing organization. Both propose frameworks which they suggest employees apply in the valuation of employment work, valuations presumably predictive of employee behavior and/or performance. An employing organization, interested in securing work from employees, attempts to design a work-compensation or inducements-contributions exchange which will be viewed favorably by the individuals upon whom it is dependent for work. Alternative employment exchange offers will be more or less successful in securing work contributions and the validity of assumptions about individual responses to these offers is a critical factor in the success of a compensation program. Models of individual valuation and choice among alternative employment exchanges are examined in more detail in the following chapter. March and Simon distinguished between the concept of employee satisfaction and employee willingness to accept an inducements-contributions exchange. They suggested, but did not elaborate, that satisfaction is a function of valuation of the inducements-contributions exchange relative to one's aspirations and that willingness to accept the exchange is a function of alternative opportunities. Thus an individual might accept a particular inducements-contributions exchange as the best available and yet be dissatisfied with that exchange. We return to this distinction in a later chapter when we examine job satisfaction; we are concerned only with the willingness to accept an employment exchange in the chapters immediately following.

The theories of Jaques and of March and Simon focus upon valuation of the employment exchange by individuals and do not consider explicitly the valuation by the employing organization. We noted above that both parties to a voluntary exchange must view the exchange as desirable for it to be effected, and employer valuation of the employment exchange is equally critical to compensation decisions. Work, or labor services, are of value to an employing organization to the extent that these services are productive of some product or service which the organization in turn sells to customers. The output of work rather than work itself is valued. Labor services or work, not outputs, are exchanged in the employment exchange, however, and the employing organization must estimate the ultimate value of these labor services when determining employee compensation. The uncertain link between labor services and the ultimate valuation of outputs of those services by consumers introduce complexities into employer valuations of labor services which are considered in Chapter 5. Influences of employer demand for labor, employer valuation of work contributions, are examined in detail in Chapter 5.

Because of differences in individual valuations of inducements-contributions exchanges, the amount of contributions or labor services forthcoming varies with the inducements offered. More people will be willing to shovel snow at ten dollars an hour than at five dollars an hour. Some of those people would have been willing to shovel snow at less than ten dollars and receive inducements greater than would have been necessary; others are unwilling to shovel snow at less than ten dollars. The supply of work contributions or labor services available for employment varies along several dimensions. We can view this supply abstractly as a number of standardized labor inputs but, in fact, these inputs vary with the number of persons seeking employment, the hours they are willing to expend at work, the skills applied to tasks, and the diligence of application or effort expended at work. We measure these dimensions of labor supply in behavioral terms such as labor force participation, turnover, unemployment, absenteeism, and hours of work. Each of these measures, whether applied within a single labor market, an employing organization, or an occupation, is the summary consequence of a number of individual behaviors or decisions to seek work, train for a given occupation, accept employment in a given organization, appear for work each day, and accept overtime work assignments. Analyses of labor supply behavior are conducted on at least two levels of analysis:

(1) summary measures of numbers of persons behaving in a particular manner (e.g., number of persons seeking employment), and (2) measures of individual behavior (e.g., individual occupational choices). The broader analysis identifies factors predictive of mass behavior from which models of individual behavior might be inferred, and the individualized analysis identifies influences of individual behavior from which models of mass behavior might be inferred. The two approaches ought to be complementary but, due to methods of analysis, may not always appear to yield consistent results. One of our tasks as we review the analyses of compensation and behavior presented here will be to search for links between analyses employing different levels of analysis and to search for bridges between the two sets of observations.

Labor supply concepts, whether they relate to individual or population behavior, can be structured in terms of specificity of the supply dimension. We distinguish, for example, between labor supply of persons seeking employment (labor force) and the level of effort and productivity realized in job performance. Typical compensation issues also can be related to these different dimensions of supply, each such compensation issue usually being considered relative to one of these dimensions of labor supply. Figure 1

Figure 1: Relationships between dimensions of labor supply and compensation issues

Dimensions of labor supply		
Population concepts	Individual concepts	Compensation issues
Labor force, labor force participation	Decision to seek employment	Market wage level
Occupational supply	Occupational choice	Occupational wage structure
Supply of labor to the firm	Attractiveness of employing organization	Industry wage structure, wage level of employer
Turnover	Decision to terminate employment	Market wage structure, wage structure of employer
Hours of work	Tardiness, absenteeism, overtime decisions	Contingency compensation, employer wage structure
Productivity of job performance	Level of effort and diligence in performance	Contingency compensation

presents a general framework of dimensions of labor supply with the related population and individual supply concepts and the relevant compensation issues. Population concepts of labor force and labor force participation are reflective of individual decisions to seek employment, concepts often analyzed relative to the general wage level of the economy or labor market. We might expect, for example, that the supply of labor varies directly with the general wage level, more people seeking work as wages rise. Occupational supply is reflective of individual decisions to seek training and experience to qualify for specific occupations, decisions presumably related to the occupational wage structure. Other things being equal, we might expect the occupational wage structure to reflect relative scarcities of labor supply to different occupations, and expect occupational choices to respond to changes in this wage structure. The supply of labor to an individual firm is reflective of individual decisions regarding the relative attractiveness of that organization as an employer, decisions presumed reflective of industry and labor market wage structures, the higher paying employer being judged more attractive. Turnover rates are reflective of individual decisions to terminate specific employments and seek alternative employment, decisions usually presumed reflective of the employer's wage rate relative to market rates and/or the wage structure within the employing organization. Hours of work are reflective of individual decisions to appear for work and to accept over-time assignments, decisions presumed reflective of contingency relationships between compensation and hours of work, higher rates of compensation eliciting additional hours of work. Finally, productivity in job performance is reflective of the level of effort and diligence expended in individual job behavior, behavior presumably influenced by contingency compensation such as incentives and merit increases. Thus the typical compensation issues of general wage level, occupational and industrial wage structures, wage level of the employing organization, wage structure of jobs within the employing organization and alternative forms of contingency compensation are each related more or less directly to specific dimensions of labor supply behavior. The general framework outlined in Figure 1 underlies the analyses which follow; we proceed from analysis of labor force behavior and general wage levels through analysis of job performance and contingency compensation. We shall be concerned in each instance with influences of the particular dimension of labor supply behavior, compensation influences as well as other influences. We seek to determine the influence of compensation relative to other influences, not merely the direction of the relationship between compensation and the particular dimension of labor supply behavior.

March and Simon's concept of the employment contract suggests conscious, rational decision-making processes of individuals deterministic of behavior; a similar model underlies economic models of choice behavior, and certain motivation models are consistent with, and supportive of, this concept of an employment contract. Having differentiated labor supply behaviors along different dimensions in Figure 1, we must question whether or not the same motivational model explains all behaviors equally well. While a rational decision-making model such as implied in the concept of the employment contract may be predictive of behavior in accepting employment in an organization, other behaviors such as overstaying a coffee break or applying extra effort to meet a production deadline are not obvious consequences of rational decision making. Different motivation models may be more applicable in the analysis of one form of behavior than another; our later analyses consider different motivation models as they relate most clearly to the different dimensions of behavior.

A variety of different perspectives of compensation issues are presented in the readings which follow. We begin with an examination of the determinants of employer valuations of labor services, the determination of demand for labor services, and then examine different aspects of dimensions of labor supply, particularly as related to the compensation issues of wage level, wage structure, and compensation schedules. An integration of these various perspectives is presented in Chapter 10 which is intended as a summary. Curious readers may wish to read that chapter first in order to learn in advance the integrative framework implicit in the organization of topics and readings; rationales for the conclusions presented in Chapter 10 will be developed in the following chapters.

CHAPTER 3

SUPPLY OF LABOR SERVICES: DECISIONS AND BEHAVIOR

How do individuals evaluate employment offers? How do suppliers of labor services respond to different opportunities for employment? While the concept of employment exchange suggests a contract between employer and employee, the contractual process cannot be perceived in most cases as a process of mutual negotiation. Typically, an employing organization offers specified compensation in return for labor services, and individual acceptance of the contract is implied with acceptance of the employment offer; individual rejection of the contract is signified in refusal to accept employment and/or termination from employment. Collective agreements between an employing organization and a labor organization, although the outcomes of a negotiating process, merely specify the terms and conditions of the employment exchange offered to individuals; an employment exchange is effected only as individuals accept employment under the terms specified. Employing organizations seeking labor services try to offer compensation which will induce or elicit those labor services from individuals. Compensation and other inducements offered in the employment contract reflect employer assumptions about individual behavior and reactions to the inducements offered. This chapter examines in more detail how individuals evaluate and respond to offers of employment exchange. The first section of the chapter examines models of individual choice and behavior from which inferences can be drawn concerning the summed behavior of the labor force; the second section examines models of labor supply or aggregate behavior.

A: Individual choice and behavior

Essays in this section present models of individual choice and behavior and provide a basis for prediction of relationships between labor supplies and offers of compensation. Three of the essays abstract all dimensions of labor supply behavior to a single concept analyzed as a function of a single decision-making process; the decision to seek employment, the choice of occupation and/or industry, the choice of employer, the determination of hours worked, and the choice of level of effort to be expended are all considered as results of the same general decision process. The fourth essay differentiates among these different aspects of labor supply behavior and considers each individually.

Essay 3-1 was written by Adam Smith over 200 years ago and underlies much of economic reasoning about labor supplies. Smith observed different wage rates paid for different jobs and explained these differences in terms of individual decisions concerning work. He identifies various aspects of employment which individuals consider in their valuations of labor services sought by employers, characteristics of specific employments which individuals consider advantageous or disadvantageous. Smith reasons that individuals consider "the whole of the advantages and disadvantages of the different employments of labour" in making decisions about work and employment, and are most attracted to those opportunities which offer the greatest "net advantage." Monetary compensation is an advantage associated with employment, an advantage which may be counterbalanced by other, less attractive characteristics of employment. Other relevant characteristics of employment considered by Smith include agreeableness of employment, difficulty and expense of learning the job, security or constancy of employment, trust or responsibility, and the probability of success. Observed differentials in compensation were attributed by Smith to counterbalancing differentials in these other characteristics of employment, compensation varying directly with the perceived level of disadvantages associated with specific employments.

The more recent Essay 3-2 by Rottenberg elaborates Smith's thesis and defends it against modern critics, but the basic analysis is the same; individuals evaluate the employment exchange in terms of the net advantage of inducements relative to contributions, and increased levels of inducements are required to overcome the disadvantages of increased levels of contributions. Rottenberg explains a common tendency to focus upon compensation as the primary determinant of labor supply decisions since a direct function can be inferred more easily between compensation and job attractiveness than between attractiveness and other job characteristics. The statement that "more is always better" can be more easily attributed to compensation than to other job characteristics.

Vroom's analysis (Essay 3-3) was written in 1964 employing psychological theories of motivation, yet it is strikingly similar to the earlier analysis by Smith; individuals evaluate employment opportunities in terms of anticipated rewards and costs associated with the opportunities. Vroom reviews briefly several motivation theories and then develops what he terms a "cognitive" model of motivation; motivation is viewed as a process of rational choice and decision making by individuals. He defines a concept of "valence" which is used to indicate the attractiveness of an outcome or condition; outcomes which are more attractive than others possess more valence and are preferred to other outcomes. Outcomes may be attractive and possess valence as ends (e.g., fun) or as means to other ends (e.g., compensation is valued as a means of buying fun). Outcomes valued as means to other outcomes are termed "instrumental" by Vroom, the valence of such an outcome varies directly with the valence of the ultimate outcome and the instrumentality relationship (correlation) between the two outcomes. Individuals evaluate specific acts or behavioral choices in terms of generalized expectations of valence associated with those acts. While much more elaborate than Smith's analysis, the models of Vroom and Smith share many aspects in common.

Finally, Essay 3-4 by Katz challenges the applicability of a single general model of decision making to all labor-supply behaviors. Katz specifies different types of labor-supply behavior, behaviors which he suggests are subject to different motivational influences. Katz distinguishes among the behaviors of joining and maintaining membership in the organization, dependable role performance, and innovative and spontaneous behaviors beyond role specifications and suggests that the nature of inducements relevant to each are different. These distinctions among different labor supply behaviors are particularly relevant to an employer seeking to influence different dimensions of labor supply and are considered in more detail in later sections.

Essay 3-1

On wage differentials*

Adam Smith

The whole of the advantages and disadvantages of the different employments of labour and stock must, in the same neighbourhood, be either perfectly equal or continually tending to equality. If in the same neighbourhood, there was any employment evidently either more or less advantageous than the rest, so many people would crowd into it in the one case, and so many would desert it in the other, that its advantages would soon return to the level of other employments. This at least would be the case in a society where things were left to follow their natural course, where there was perfect liberty, and where every man was perfectly free both to chuse what occupation he thought proper, and to change it as often as he thought proper. Every man's interest would prompt him to seek the advantageous, and to shun the disadvantageous employment.

Pecuniary wages and profit, indeed, are everywhere in Europe extremely different according to the different employments

of labour and stock. But this difference arises partly from certain circumstances in the employments themselves, which, either really, or at least in the imaginations of men, make up for a small pecuniary gain in some, and counterbalance a great one in others; and partly from the policy of Europe, which nowhere leaves things at perfect liberty.

Inequalities arising from the nature of the employments themselves

The five following are the principal circumstances which, so far as I have been able to observe, make up for a small pecuniary gain in some employments, and counterbalance a great one in others: first, the agreeableness or disagreeableness of the employments themselves; secondly, the easiness and cheapness, or the difficulty and expence of learning them; thirdly, the constancy or inconstancy of employment in them; fourthly, the small or great trust which must be reposed in those who exercise them; and fifthly, the probability or improbability of success in them.

First, the wages of labour vary with the

*Reprinted from Adam Smith, *The Wealth of Nations: Inquiry into the Nature and Causes of the Wealth of Nations* (New York: Random House, 1937), pp. 99-107 (abridged).

ease or hardship, the cleanliness or dirtiness, the honourableness or dishonourableness of the employment. Thus in most places, take the year round, a journeyman taylor earns less than a journeyman weaver. His work is much easier. A journeyman weaver earns less than a journeyman smith. His work is not always easier, but it is much cleanlier. A journeyman blacksmith, though an artificer, seldom earns so much in twelve hours as a collier, who is only a labourer, does in eight. His work is not quite so dirty, is less dangerous, and is carried on in daylight, and above ground. Honour makes a great part of the reward of all honourable professions. In point of pecuniary gain, all things considered, they are generally underrecompensed, as I shall endeavour to show by and by. Disgrace has the contrary effect. The trade of a butcher is a brutal and an odious business; but it is in most places more profitable than the greater part of common trades. The most detestable of all employments, that of public executioner, is, in proportion to the quantity of work done, better paid than any common trade whatever.

Hunting and fishing, the most important employments of mankind in the rude state of society, become in its advanced state their most agreeable amusements, and they pursue for pleasure what they once followed from necessity. In the advanced state of society, therefore, they are all very poor people who follow as a trade, what other people pursue as a pastime. Fishermen have been so since the time of Theocritus. A poacher is everywhere a very poor man in Great Britain. In countries where the rigour of the law suffers no poachers, the licensed hunter is not in a much better condition. The natural taste for those employments makes more people follow them than can live comfortably by them, and the produce of their labour, in proportion to its quantity, comes always too cheap to market to

afford anything but the most scanty subsistence to the labourers.

Disagreeableness and disgrace affect the profits of stock in the same manner as the wages of labour. The keeper of an inn or tavern, who is never master of his own house, and who is exposed to the brutality of every drunkard, exercises neither a very agreeable nor a very creditable business. But there is scarce any common trade in which a small stock yields so great a profit.

Secondly, the wages of labour vary with the easiness and cheapness, or the difficulty and expence of learning the business.

When any expensive machine is erected, the extraordinary work to be performed by it before it is worn out, it must be expected, will replace the capital laid out upon it, with at least the ordinary profits. A man educated at the expence of much labour and time to any of those employments which require extraordinary dexterity and skill, may be compared to one of those expensive machines. The work which he learns to perform, it must be expected, over and above the usual wages of common labour, will replace to him the whole expence of his education, with at least the ordinary profits of an equally valuable capital. It must do this too in a reasonable time, regard being had to the very uncertain duration of human life, in the same manner as to the more certain duration of the machine.

The difference between the wages of skilled labour and those of common labor, is founded upon this principle.

Education in the ingenious arts and in the liberal professions, is still more tedious and expensive. The pecuniary recompence, therefore, of painters and sculptors, of lawyers and physicians, ought to be much more liberal: and it is so accordingly.

Thirdly, the wages of labour in different occupations vary with the constancy or inconstancy of employment.

Employment is much more constant in some trades than in others. In the greater part of manufactures, a journeyman may be pretty sure of employment almost every day in the year that he is able to work. A mason or bricklayer, on the contrary, can work neither in hard frost nor in foul weather, and his employment at all other times depends upon the occasional calls of his customers. He is liable, in consequence, to be frequently without any. What he earns therefore, while he is employed, must not only maintain him while he is idle, but make him some compensation for those anxious and desponding moments which the thought of so precarious a situation must sometimes occasion. Where the computed earnings of the greater part of manufacturers, accordingly, are nearly upon a level with the day wages of common labourers, those of masons and bricklayers are generally from one half more to double those wages. Where common labourers earn four and five shillings a week, masons and bricklayers frequently earn seven and eight; where the former earn six, the latter often earn nine and ten, and where the former earn nine and ten, as in London, the latter commonly earn fifteen and eighteen. No species of skilled labour, however, seems more easy to learn than that of masons and bricklayers. Chairmen in London, during the summer season, are said sometimes to be employed as bricklayers. The high wages of those workmen, therefore, are not so much the recompence of their skill, as the compensation for the inconstancy of their employment.

A house carpenter seems to exercise rather a nicer and more ingenious trade than a mason. In most places, however, for it is not universally so, his day-wages are somewhat lower. His employment, though it depends much, does not depend so entirely upon the occasional calls of his customers; and it is not liable to be interrupted by the weather.

Fourthly, the wages of labour vary according to the small or great trust which must be reposed in the workmen.

The wages of goldsmiths and jewellers are everywhere superior to those of many other workmen, not only of equal, but of much superior ingenuity; on account of the precious materials with which they are intrusted.

We trust our health to the physician; our fortune and sometimes our life and reputation to the lawyer and attorney. Such confidence could not safely be reposed in people of a very mean or low condition. Their reward must be such, therefore, as may give them that rank in the society which so important a trust requires. The long time and the great expence which must be laid out in their education, when combined with this circumstance, necessarily enhance still further the price of their labour.

Fifthly, the wages of labour in different employments vary according to the probability or improbability of success in them.[1]

The probability that any particular person shall ever be qualified for the employment to which he is educated, is very different in different occupations. In the greater part of mechanic trades, success is almost certain; but very uncertain in the liberal professions. Put your son apprentice to a shoemaker, there is little doubt of his learning to make a pair of shoes: But send him to study the law, it is at least 20 to 1 if ever he makes such proficiency as will enable him to live by the business. In a perfectly fair lottery, those

---

[1] The argument under this head, which is often misunderstood, is that pecuniary wages are (on the average, setting great gains against small ones) less in trades where there are high prizes and many blanks. The remote possibility of obtaining one of the high prizes is one of the circumstances which "in the imaginations of men make up for a small pecuniary gain" (p. 99). Cantillon, *Essai*, p. 24, is not so subtle, merely making remuneration proportionate to risk. Cantillon, *Essai sur la nature du commerce en général*, 1755.

who draw the prizes ought to gain all that is lost by those who draw the blanks. In a profession where 20 fail for 1 that succeeds, that 1 ought to gain all that should have been gained by the unsuccessful 20. The counsellor at law who, perhaps, at near 40 years of age, begins to make something by his profession, ought to receive the retribution, not only of his own so tedious and expensive education, but of that of more than 20 others who are never likely to make anything by it. How extravagant soever the fees of counsellors at law may sometimes appear, their real retribution is never equal to this.[2] Compute in any particular place, what is likely to be annually gained, and what is likely to be annually spent, by all the different workmen in any common trade, such as that of shoemakers or weavers, and you will find that the former sum will generally exceed the latter. But make the same computation with regard to all the counsellors and students of law, in all the different inns of court, and you will find that their annual gains bear but a very small proportion to their annual expence,

even though you rate the former as high, and the latter as low, as can well be done. The lottery of the law, therefore, is very far from being a perfectly fair lottery; and that, as well as many other liberal and honourable professions, is, in point of pecuniary gain, evidently underrecompenced.

Those professions keep their level, however, with other occupations, and, notwithstanding these discouragements, all the most generous and liberal spirits are eager to crowd into them. Two different causes contribute to recommend them. First, the desire of the reputation which attends upon superior excellence in any of them; and, secondly, the natural confidence which every man has more or less, not only in his own abilities, but in his own good fortune.

To excel in any profession, in which but few arrive at mediocrity, is the most decisive mark of what is called genius or superior talents. The public admiration which attends upon such distinguished abilities, makes always a part of their reward; a greater or smaller in proportion as it is higher or lower in degree. It makes a considerable part of that reward in the profession of physic; a still greater perhaps in that of law; in poetry and philosophy it makes almost the whole.

---

[2] *Lectures on Justice, Police, Revenue and Arms,* delivered in the University of Glasgow by Adam Smith. Reported by a student in 1763, and edited with an Introduction and Notes by Edwin Cannan, 1896, p. 175.

Essay 3-2

On choice in labor markets*

Simon Rottenberg

THE CLASSICAL THEORY

Criteria for choice among alternatives in labor markets and the consequences of choice were discussed by Adam Smith in some detail in a classic chapter, "Of Wages and Profit in the Different Employments of Labour and Stock."[1]

The theory has two parts. One relates to the nature of occupational choice: "every man" will pursue his interest and this will "prompt him to seek the advantageous, and to shun the disadvantageous employment." The other relates to the consequences of this behavioral choice system: "the whole of the advantages and disadvantages" of all employments will be equal or will tend toward equality. Any disparity in net advantage will cause persons to redistribute themselves. Greater numbers in the relatively more advantaged employments, and fewer in the relatively disadvantaged, will tend to restore equality of net advantage in all.

Inequalities may occur in the short run, while the process of adjustment works itself out; in this period, net advantage will be only "tending to equality." Inequalities may also occur when things are not left at perfect liberty and men are not free to choose among alternative employments. Otherwise, in Smith's system, net advantage will be equal in all employments.

It is of primordial importance to understand that the early economists said that it was "the whole of the advantages and disadvantages" in all employments that would be equal. This is so apparent from their writings that there should be no confusion about it. They did not say wages are equal in all employments. Smith, who knew the economy of his time in remarkable detail, despite the rudimentary state of the statistical arts, knew that wages were different in various employments and explicitly enumerated the causes of difference. Wages would vary, he said, with the ease or hardship, the cleanliness or dirtiness, the honorableness or dishonorableness of the employment; with the easiness and cheapness or the difficulty and expense of its learning; with its constancy or inconstancy; with the small or great trust which is reposed in the worker; and with the probability or improbability of success in the employment.

Occupations equal in other respects would tend to be equal in price, but occupations unequal in other respects would be unequal in price. Just as price differentials compensate for differentials in other qualities; so differentials in other qualities compensate for differentials in price. Thus occupational choice was understood by the economists to be made with reference to the total complex of attributes which attach to jobs.

Labor market of classical economics

In the labor markets of Adam Smith and the economists who followed him, workers made occupational choices in

*Reprinted with permission from Simon Rottenberg, "On Choice in Labor Markets," *Industrial and Labor Relations Review* 9 (1956), pp. 183-99 (abridged). © 1956 by Cornell University. All rights reserved.

[1] Adam Smith, *The Wealth of Nations: Inquiry into the Nature and Causes of the Wealth of Nations*, Modern Library edition (New York: Random House, 1937), Book I, chap. 10.

terms of comparative total net advantages, not in terms of comparative wages. McCulloch saw, for example, that some workers might prefer low-wage, healthful employment to high-wage, unhealthful employment. "The agreeableness and healthiness of their employments," he said, "seem to be the principal cause of the redundant numbers, and consequent low wages, of workmen in ordinary field labor."[2] Adam Smith said that the price of labor in inconstant employments must compensate for the "anxious and desponding moments" which the casual worker suffers when he thinks of the instability of his situation. This is the same as saying that workers consider instability as well as price in making choice. Nassau Senior, on the other hand, maintained that steady, regular labor is disliked by workers and that "the opportunities for idleness afforded by an occupation of irregular employment" will cause the long-period earnings of irregular employment to be less than the common average of regular employments. Though Smith and Senior pursued the principle to opposite judgments, what is relevant for us is that neither saw workers choosing solely in terms of relative price. For one, choice was made in terms of relative price and relative instability; for the other, it was made in terms of relative opportunity for idleness. For neither was choice made in terms of relative price, standing alone.

Thus, it is clear that total net advantage and not price alone is the touchstone of occupational choice and change in the theory of the economists, and it is total net advantage and not price alone that is said to be equal in all employments.

Price-quantity curves

Latter-day economists, who have developed more elegant systems of analysis

than the classicists, *do* use price as the instrument for allocating labor among alternative uses, and their supply curves are drawn to relate quantity to price. Price-quantity curves are drawn, however, upon other-things-equal assumptions, but since economists are not repetitively explicit about this, it is sometimes forgotten.

Quantity is related to price in formal economic analysis for several reasons. First, price is continuously quantifiable; other qualities which attach to occupations may not be quantifiable at all or may be discontinuous. Second, preference patterns related to price are consistent; preference patterns related to other qualities are not. Other things being equal, all persons prefer a higher price for their services to a lower one; but all individuals do not, for example, prefer security to risk. Some are timid and others are gamblers by nature. Third, the analytical model which assumes that behavioral choices are related to price, *ceteris paribus*, gives tolerably good predictive results. Everywhere there is massive aggregative evidence that people move from low-income areas to high, and from areas of thin opportunity, where long-run earnings are likely to be low, to thick opportunity areas, where long-run earnings are likely to be high. Irishmen move to Scotland, Mexicans to the United States, Southerners to the North, rural people to the towns, and Europeans to the New World; net flows are not in the opposite directions.

Despite this, it is not inconsistent with the classical model for another attribute than price to operate as an allocating instrument. If, for example, an employer finds that he is losing his workers to other employers because, given the structure of other differentials, the difference between the wage he pays and the wage paid by the others draws the workers away, he has a variety of tactics open to him to induce them to stay. He may offer more wages, or better housing, or superior schooling for the workers' children, or less obnoxious foremen, or more security, or a more

[2] J. R. McCulloch, *A Treatise on the Circumstances Which Determine the Rate of Wages and the Condition of the Labouring Classes*, 2d ed. (London: G. Routledge and Co., 1854), p. 55.

acceptable system of advancement to better jobs. But, though tactical choices are open in great variety, there is only a single strategy and this is to reduce the differential of total net advantage between employment with others and employment with him. This is all the classical economists said; they did not say the price differential itself must be changed. Any choice of method made by an employer is consistent with their understanding of the system by which workers are distributed among occupations.

While the employer may contrive any tactic to make employment in his enterprise relatively more attractive, he will usually find that the supply of labor is more elastic to a money price than to a nonmoney price and that it will be usually cheaper, therefore, to increase the wage he pays than to improve the quality of the employment in some other way. This is so because preferences are diverse among men, and money is a more efficient instrument of exchange than any other commodity. Consider, for example, the employer who wants to attract workers to an occupation. Assume two choices are open to him: he may pay more wages or he may "pay" free gifts of spirituous beverages. Those who have a strong preference for spirits over other commodities may be indifferent to the "currency" in which they are paid; if they received money payments, they would, in any case, exchange it for spirits. Others, who prefer liquor less, will seek to exchange it for other things which they prefer more. The latter persons will suffer some inconvenience in seeking out others willing to make an exchange, and it will be necessary to compensate for this inconvenience by paying more in spirits than would have been necessary to pay in money. The inconvenience effect applies especially to the class of cases where nonmoney payments are made in commodities which workers can acquire easily through normal purchase. It applies somewhat less to cases where payments are made in nonmarketed "com-

modities" like plant ventilation, for which only imperfect substitutes (such as respiratory masks which filter out dust fragments) are purchasable. It is inapplicable only for nonmarketed "commodities" which are not at all substitutable by marketed goods, such as decent and compassionate supervisors.

Complexity of motivation

Real life is complex, and the behavior of men has diverse motivations. If many variables affect a result, however, it does not mean that a particular one is without influence. As Lionel Robbins has remarked, the thermometer reading in his room in winter is affected by the opening of his window, as well as by the intensity of the fire in the grate. It may be uncomfortably cold in the room with the window open, but Robbins is surely right to say that the room will be warmer if there is a fire. For some purposes, it is useful to hold other things constant and examine the consequences of differentiation in a single variable. This is what Robbins does when he remarks that his room will be warmer if the fire is high. It is what the economist does when he says workers will choose a high wage in preference to a low one. Robbins does not say that the temperature of the room is a unique function of the efficiency of the fire; the economists do not say that occupational choice is a unique function of relative price.

Complex motivation in real life does not destroy the truism of simple motivational behavior in the abstract neoclassical model of the labor market. Other things equal, it can be a correct description of real life behavior to say that workers make job choices with reference to relative prices.

Elements in job attractiveness

Some of the recent literature takes the position that wage differentials have little to do with job choice. Workers are asked why they leave jobs, why they take jobs, why they change jobs. They reply that a constellation of considerations influences their decisions, that alternative wages are only one component of that constellation, and that other factors than alternative wages weigh more heavily on choice. Such choice criteria are consistent, however, with conventional doctrine, which permits choice to be made in terms, let us say, of the cleanliness or dirtiness of jobs. In the classical system, a worker may choose a job because it is clean and reject another because it is dirty. The classicists only argue that other things equal, the clean job will carry a lower wage than the dirty job and that the difference in the wage will be only enough to compensate for the cleanliness properties of the two jobs, if workers are permitted to move freely between jobs.

Occupational choice in terms of relative wages is made only in a framework in which other job properties are given. If a dirty occupation is expanding and must attract workers from a clean occupation, then the wage differential between the two must be, for a time, larger than when the distribution of workers between the two is in equilibrium. It can be seen that given other job properties, choice will be made in terms of relative wages, if one asks whether workers can be attracted to otherwise unattractive employments by offering very, very high wages. There surely is some wage high enough to move workers. The principle that relative wages are meaningful in job choice can be proved by arguing the case of the extremely high wage. The economists' position is simply this: that workers will be indifferent between clean and dirty occupations, if the wage differential is just sufficient to compensate for differential cleanliness; that they will prefer the clean job, if the wage differential is less than this; that they will prefer the dirty job, if the wage differential is more than this. It

does not matter whether we say that they choose jobs in terms of cleanliness properties, *wages being given,* or that they choose jobs in terms of relative wages, *cleanliness properties being given.* In either case, we say the same thing.

The money wage becomes the determinant of choice only when other attributes are compared. This does not say that choice is made only in terms of relative prices.

Comparisons by unemployed workers

It seems to be a plausible proposition that even unemployed workers assess alternatives and choose among them. Consider a worker who is unemployed and who is offered a job with properties x, y, and z. Is comparison possible here? It is, and it is comparison with a dual facet.

The worker makes, first, a comparison between a continued status of unemployment and the job offered. He would not, under all circumstances, accept the job. If it were offered, for example, at a wage of one penny per year, he would prefer unemployment. A "job" with full leisure at zero income would be preferred to a job with less leisure at a one-penny-per-annum wage. The wage differential would not be sufficient to compensate for the relatively less advantageous nonwage properties of the penny-per-annum job.

The worker makes, secondly, a comparison between the net advantages of the job offered and the net advantages of other jobs not offered and not known in any specific sense, but which are known in some expectational sense. This only says that the choice is made in conditions of uncertainty. Most economic choices are made in conditions of uncertainty; we have only to look at business mortality rates to verify this fact. But this does not mean that choice cannot be made in any other way than randomly. The worker knows the properties of the job offered to him; he estimates the properties of other jobs which he expects may become available; and he compares the two and chooses whether to accept the first or wait for another.[3] Assume that the worker quits his job (about whose properties he has knowledge) but has no other job immediately available to him. He may move to unemployment, but still be available for other employment. In the same way as has already been discussed, there is a comparison made and choice is possible. The choice here is between a known job and an unknown, expected job whose properties are estimated. If the worker moves from a known job to "out-of-the-labor-force status" and is not available for work, again he compares and chooses. Here, the properties of the known job were not sufficiently advantageous to compensate for the attractions of leisure.

The notion that when unemployed workers take jobs "because they are unemployed," (choice is made by them outside a framework of comparison) is, thus, not correct. An unemployed worker can be expected to reject work at a very low wage or, what is the same thing, work at a very high wage which is so hazardous that he has perfect certainty that it will cause his death. Unemployed workers, thus, do not take "any" job or "the first job offered." Persistent unemployment will be preferred to some jobs. If the "first job offered" is taken, it is because the worker, having made an estimate, decides that all things considered, he is better off with it than he would be if he continued to be unemployed and waited for a next offer.

"Pushes" and "pulls"

Some writers have attempted to distinguish between "pushes" and "pulls" to explain worker behavior in the labor market.[4] If a worker is discharged or demoted, or if something else distasteful to him transpires in his present place, he is said to be "pushed" to make a change. If he is offered or becomes aware of a higher wage or otherwise superior job elsewhere, he is said to be "pulled" to make a change.

Because "pushed" workers move to other jobs more frequently and because a disproportionately large number of new job-takers are of this class, they may appear to be more actively engaged in calculating net advantage among alternatives than those who are "pulled." But appearance may be deceptive. It may be only that differential rates of movement for "pushed" and "pulled" workers reflect different magnitudes for the two classes in the net advantages of present and new situations. The average difference between the net advantage of their present position and that of a new situation may be very much larger for "pushed" workers than the average difference between the two for workers who are merely "pulled." If this is so, we should expect a higher rate of movement between jobs by "pushed" workers, even if the propensity to calculate and compare were equal for the two classes.

If choices are rational, they are made in terms of the worker's assessment of differ-

---

[3] By omitting the possibility of estimation in uncertainty, I think that Professor Reynolds underestimates the number of alternatives by which workers consider, in some implicit sense, that they are confronted. He says of New Haven workers, "The decision to take or to keep a job usually depends on a comparison between the characteristics of the job and the worker's minimum standards, rather than on a comparison of the job with other known alternatives." Lloyd G. Reynolds, *The Structure of Labor Markets* (New York: Harper and Row, 1951), p. 212.

[4] See, for example, Clark Kerr. "There is some real question how effective a wage structure can be in distributing labor in any event. Wages are only one of several important considerations which repel workers from some jobs and attract them to others. The push of unemployment, for example, is often more effective than the pull of higher wages." "Labor Markets: Their Character and Consequences," *American Economic Review*, May 1950, p. 288.

ence between two situations. It is not the fact that he is badly off, by any absolute measure, in his present place that causes him to move; it is rather that he is badly off relative to what he estimates his position will be after moving. If he believes that he can improve his lot by going elsewhere, he will go; if he does not, he will stay. What is important to his decision is difference; to understand the nature of choice in labor markets, we must look at response to difference.

The comparison of estimated alternatives is made in a context of more or less correct understanding of the "going rate" in different employments, of the "worth" of the worker's services, or of the availability of alternative opportunities. There is verification of this behavioral pattern in the empirical studies themselves, which show that quits are more frequent in times and places of expanding employment than in those of constant or diminishing employment.

The unemployed worker who sets a minimum standard for jobs which he will find acceptable is making a choice with respect to the comparative attractiveness of alternatives. In substance, the worker is saying, "For work of this kind, I shall not accept a wage of less than X cents per hour; because I believe that if I wait, I shall find this price." Seen in this way, the case of the minimum standard turns out to be a specific variation of the general case of calculation and choice on the basis of comparative net attractiveness. Even if, as the empirical studies have found, "workers' knowledge of job alternatives is fragmentary and imperfect,"[5] movement of workers can equalize earnings in equal employments. Some will overestimate the relative value of a new job and will move more rapidly and frequently than they would if they had full knowledge. Some

---

[5] George P. Schultz, "Recent Research on Labor Mobility," in *Proceedings, Industrial Relations Research Association*, Boston, 1951, p. 116.

will underestimate and will move less rapidly and frequently than they would if they had full knowledge. If over and underestimation is randomly distributed among workers, the differences will cancel, and movement will tend to be just that required to equalize net advantage. This may be a sensible expectation of what happens in the labor market.

Uncertainty and job selection

Estimates made in uncertainty may lead, of course, to some wrong directional movement. Even if the cancelling-out process which is here suggested does operate in labor markets, therefore, and appropriate allocation of labor among uses is finally achieved, economists will still be interested in enlarging knowledge and diminishing uncertainty, because the more certain are the conditions within which choice is made, the smaller will be the number of moves necessary to reach the optimum.

Empirical research has found that workers who leave a present employment with another specific employment already arranged move to higher gross weekly earnings positions more often than do workers who leave without a specific alternative arranged. From this the conclusion has been drawn that the classical understanding of the nature of worker behavioral choice is more consistent with reality in the former case than in the latter. In both cases, however, workers may well be searching for greater advantage. The conclusion we can appropriately draw from the evidence is that choice in a context of less uncertainty is more successful than choice in a context of more uncertainty. This is only like saying that the incidence of mortality of firms with certain futures is less than the incidence of mortality of firms with uncertain futures. We cannot infer from differential mortality rates differential motivations or differential behavioral patterns.

DESIRE OF WORKERS FOR SECURITY

Surely, workers give attention to security, along with price, in making job decisions. The security attribute is one of the comparative components, along with price, upon which workers make choices. Workers who have acquired security of tenure or who are employed by firms which are expected to be successful in the future may prefer to stay at a lower wage, rather than moving to other employments at a higher wage. But this is no proof that actual behavior of workers is at variance with the classicists' perception. The economists realized that workers *do* give weight to the expected duration of employment in making behavioral choices.

Choice is not made by workers in terms of instantaneous earnings differences, and it was not understood by the economists that it would be. It was "obvious" to Senior that "the labourer's situation does not depend on the amount which he receives at any one time, but on his average receipts during a given period—during a week, a month, or a year; and that the longer the period taken, the more accurate will be the estimate."[6] He saw,

too, that the number of competitors in the medical and legal professions was diminished, not only by the high cost of learning these arts, but also because, for a period of some years of apprenticeship or study, the earnings of practitioners are very low.[7]

Thus it is consistent with the theory that in periods of less than full employment, the relative hourly wage should be less important in motivating job changes than in periods of full employment. A sensible worker accepts a "low" wage in present employment, at the trough of the cycle, because he has a low estimation of his future earnings prospects if he should leave to search for an alternative. A comparison of long-run earnings in different employments (one known and others estimated) diminishes the influence of hourly wages upon choice in trough periods. In periods of cyclical peak, on the other hand, when opportunities for work elsewhere are many, the expectation of long-run earnings in other employment is high, and hourly wage rates weigh more heavily upon choice.

It is even consistent with the theory that in conditions of layoffs in particular labor markets, workers move from "better" previous employment to a "worse" present one. The worker who makes a job choice must be thought to calculate net advantage in long-run rather than instantaneous terms. He may, therefore, choose a secure employment at a lower wage over an insecure employment at a higher wage, even in periods of full employment. Just so, in times of unemployment he accepts a job with reference to his calculation of

---

[6] Nassau W. Senior, *Three Lectures on the Rate of Wages* (London: John Murray, 1830), p. 7. Professors Reynolds and Shister wrote, "Economists have tended to assume that even when a worker has a job he will keep his eyes continuously open for something better and will be willing to switch to a superior job at the drop of a hat." Lloyd G. Reynolds and Joseph Shister, *Job Horizons* (New York: John Wiley and Sons, Inc., 1919), p. 45.

If a "superior job" means merely a job paying a higher wage, then two things need to be said. (1) The classical economists did not assume such behavior; and (2) the neoclassical economists may have assumed such behavior, but this assumption was not intended to be descriptive of real life. The usefulness of the abstraction from the real world in which the assumption appears depends not upon its "realism" but upon the degree of conformity of predictions derived from the abstraction with observable experience. If, on the other hand, "superior

job" means one which is, on balance, superior, *all things considered*, then it seems indeed to be sensible to assume that a worker "*will* be willing to switch." Any other assumption has the worker making choices according to the rule that he shall be disadvantaged. It is doubtful that many workers are guided by such a rule.

[7] Nassau W. Senior, *An Outline of the Science of Political Economy*, Library of Economics edition (London: George Allen and Unwin Ltd., 1938), p. 207.

long-run prospects, and this may lead him to conclude that a lower wage job than he has held is still for him the more advantageous one.

Meaning of rational choice

When we assume that workers choose rationally among employment alternatives, we mean that they make choice decisions which are consistent with their goals. If the goal is A, choice which leads to the achievement of A is rational; choice which leads to the achievement of B, when the chooser believes it leads to A, is also rational. Choice is irrational, if the goal is A, and the choice leads to B, when the chooser believes it leads to B. Choice is random, when there is no goal (when there is indifference among ends) and selection is made as though it depended upon the turn of a coin.

If, therefore, workers' goals are to maximize net advantage and if they make choices which they believe will maximize net advantage, they are making rational choices. They may miscalculate and come to wrong decisions, but wrong decisions are not irrational decisions and do not destroy the classical thesis.

It may be said that the qualities which attach to jobs are so large in number and so diverse that calculated comparison of jobs is not possible. To this there are two answers. First, though comparison is difficult, comparison occurs; we know this because we know that choices are made and that the pattern of choice does not distribute people randomly in the economy but puts them more or less where they are wanted. Second, comparison is diverse among individuals. The qualities of an employment do not attach to it in any intrinsic, objective sense. An occupation has qualities only as workers perceive them, and their perceptions are diverse. Some will think dirtiness very disagreeable; others will think it only somewhat disagreeable. Some will have a preference

for security; others for risk. If John Doe believes that, wages aside, job A is only slightly preferable to B, Richard Roe may believe it is preferable by far. Doe, who, let us say, was on the margin of moving to B, can be induced to move by a small differential in wages; a large differential will be necessary to move Roe.

It is because there is variation among workers in the evaluation of jobs that we have an upward sloping supply curve of labor of a craft and the possibility of equalization of net advantage by adjusting relative wages, with only fractional response by workers to a changing wage structure.

Habit and calculated comparison

The apparent persistence of wage differentials in similar employments in a labor market does not necessarily mean that calculated comparison does not occur. What seem to be similar employments may not be similar at all in the worker's perception of them, and there also may be errors in observation. What appears to be "the same kind of work" may really be different when account is taken of all the qualities considered by workers in making occupational choices. Some of these are surely so subtle that they escape detection.

The distinction between choice from habit and choice based upon calculation is not clear-cut, and what seems to be habitual behavior may be consistent with calculated behavior. Senior remarked, for example, that "ten [English mechanics] go to America for one who will venture to France," although their wage gain would be greater, if they went to France.[8] This can be interpreted as pursuit of the habitual idiom, but it can also be seen as calculated avoidance of the real cost of assimilating an unhabitual one.

If there are persistent price differentials

---

[8] *An Outline of the Science of Political Economy,* p. 222.

in truly similar employments, it may only be because adjustment is not quickly brought about. McCulloch said on this point:

It often happens that, owing to an attachment to the trade, or the locality in which they have been bred, or the difficulty of learning other trades, individuals will continue, for a lengthened period, to practice their peculiar trades, or will remain in the same district, when other trades in that district and the same trades in other districts, yield better wages to those engaged in them. But how slowly soever, wages, taking everything into account, are sure to be equalized in the end.[9]

CONCLUSIONS

If we accept the argument that workers

make employment choices without respect to wages, or in ignorance or randomly, we are then confronted with some questions. How shall we explain, for example, the massive evidence that the geographical movement of workers is from low, long-run earnings opportunities to high? Or how shall we explain why occupations requiring rare talent or long and arduous training for their successful performance carry a higher price than those requiring talents possessed by many and skills that are come by easily?

Can we sensibly believe that gross behavior which is consistent with the conventional theory is the result of accidental circumstance and random choice? It seems unlikely that this should be so. The economic theory of the labor market is logically defensible and gives good gross predictive results, if allowance is made for the time necessary for the allocational process to work itself out.

[9] J. R. McCulloch, *A Treatise on the Circumstances Which Determine the Rate of Wages and the Condition of the Labouring Classes*, 2d ed. (London: G. Routledge and Co., 1854), pp. 67-68.

Essay **3-3**

Motivation: A point of view*

Victor H. Vroom

THE NATURE OF MOTIVATION

There are two somewhat different kinds of questions which are typically dealt with in discussions of motivation. One of these is the question of the arousal or energizing of the organism. Why is the organism active at all? What conditions instigate action, determine its duration or persistence and finally its cessation? The

phenomena to be explained include the level of activity of the organism and the vigor of amplitude of its behavior. The second question involves the direction of behavior. What determines the form that activity will take? Under what conditions will an organism choose one response or another or move in one direction or another? The problem is to explain the choices made by an organism among qualitatively different behaviors.

The latter question—concerning direction or choice—is probably the more important of the two to the psychologist.

*From Victor H. Vroom, *Work and Motivation* (New York: John Wiley and Sons, 1964), pp. 8-19. Copyright © 1964 by John Wiley and Sons, Inc. Reprinted by permission.

Research on conditions affecting the choices made by organisms among alternative acts or responses constitutes a large part of the psychology of learning and of motivation. Furthermore, there are some psychologists (Estes, 1958; Logan, 1956) who have seriously questioned whether differences in level of activity and response amplitude cannot be explained in the same terms as the direction of activity.

Is all behavior motivated? The answer to this question depends somewhat on the range of processes which are subsumed under the heading of motivation. We will follow the relatively common practice of viewing as motivated only the behaviors that are under central or voluntary control. Accordingly, we would not apply the term in explanations of reflexes or tropisms, where responses are strictly determined by external stimuli. It is not necessary to look to motivation to account for the contraction of the pupils of the eye in response to light, or the jerk of the knee in response to a tap.

It is also questionable to treat, as motivated, responses mediated by the autonomic nervous system, such as heart rate and adrenalin secretion. As well as being governed by a different neural and muscular system, such responses are not under voluntary control and appear to become attached to new stimuli by a process of classical conditioning rather than by operant conditioning.

To sum up, we view the central problem of motivation as the explanation of choices made by organisms among different voluntary responses. Although some behaviors, specifically those that are not under voluntary control, are defined as unmotivated, these probably constitute a rather small proportion of the total behavior of adult human beings. It is reasonable to assume that most of the behavior exhibited by individuals on their jobs as well as their behavior in the "job market" is voluntary, and consequently motivated.

HISTORICAL APPROACHES: THE INFLUENCE OF HEDONISM

Most contemporary conceptions of motivation have their origins in the principle of hedonism. This principle can be traced back to the Greek philosophers as well as to the writings of the English utilitarians like Jeremy Bentham and John Stuart Mill. Its central assumption is that behavior is directed toward pleasure and away from pain. In every situation people select from alternative possibilities the course of action which they think will maximize their pleasure and minimize their pain.

The influence of hedonism on the writings of early psychologists is clear. In his monumental *Principles of Psychology*, William James wrote:

But as present pleasures are tremendous reinforcers, and present pains tremendous inhibitors of whatever action leads to them, so the thoughts of pleasures and pains take rank amongst the thoughts which have most impulsive and inhibitive power (1890, v. 2, p. 550).

Freud also assumed a hedonistic position in his early writings, and Troland (1928) proposed a theory of human motivation which clearly reflects the influence of the English utilitarians. Despite its simplicity and widespread appeal, the philosophical doctrine of hedonism presented many problems for those who saw in it the foundation for a theory of behavior. There was in the doctrine no clear-cut specification of the types of events which were pleasurable or painful, or even how these events could be determined for a particular individual; nor did it make clear how persons acquired their conceptions of ways of attaining pleasure and pain, or how the sources of pleasure and pain might be modified by experience. In short the hedonistic assumption had no empirical content and was untestable. Any form of behavior could be explained, after the fact, by postulating particular sources of pleasure or pain, but no form of behavior could be predicted in advance.

The study of motivation by psychologists has largely been directed toward filling in the missing empirical content in hedonism. As in the hedonistic doctrine, people are assumed to behave in ways which maximize certain types of outcomes (rewards, satisfiers, positive reinforcements, etc.) and to minimize other outcomes (punishments, dissatisfiers, negative reinforcements, etc.). However, some of the circularity of hedonism has been overcome by the development of more precisely stated models and by the linking of the concepts in these models to empirically observable events.

CONTEMPORARY APPROACHES

Two groups of psychologists each carrying out important work have helped to translate the hedonistic doctrine from the realm of philosophical discourse to that of testable psychological theory. These two groups have focused on different problems and have developed different types of models to guide their research and interpret their findings. The first group has focused on the problem of *learning* and has approached this problem with a strong behavioristic emphasis. The theories which they have constructed are *historical* in the sense that they assert lawful relations between the behavior of organisms at one point in time and events which have occurred at earlier points in time. The empirical foundation for much of their work is the law of effect, which Thorndike originally stated as follows:

Of several responses made to the same situation, those which are accompanied or closely followed by satisfaction to the animal will, other things being equal, be more firmly connected with the situation, so that, when it recurs, they will be more likely to recur; those which are accompanied or closely followed by discomfort to the animal will, other things being equal, have their connections with that situation weakened, so that when it recurs, they will be less likely to occur. The greater the satisfaction or discomfort, the greater is the strengthening or weakening of the bond (1911, p. 244).

The significance of the law of effect and its modern counterpart, Hull's principle of reinforcement (Hull, 1943, 1951) for the doctrine of hedonism, has been noted by Postman (1947). The experiments on which the law was based provided tangible evidence that behavior was directed *toward* certain outcomes and *away* from other outcomes. Those outcomes increasing the probability of responses which lead to them were often referred to as satisfiers or rewards, terms implying that their attainment was pleasurable. Similarly, outcomes decreasing the probability of responses which lead to them were referred to as dissatisfiers or punishments.

Gordon Allport (1954) has noted that theories based on the law of effect or on the principle of reinforcement imply a "hedonism of the past." They assume that the explanation of the present choices of an organism is to be found in an examination of the consequences of his past choices. Responses to a stimulus which have been rewarded in the past will be repeated in the present, whereas those which have not been rewarded or have been punished in the past will not be repeated.

Although the law of effect helped to answer one of the classical problems of hedonism (i.e., how behavior came to be directed toward pleasure and away from pain), it was silent in regard to the question of which outcomes are pleasurable and which are painful. Unless one was willing to rely on the subject's report of his experience of pleasure or pain, there was, in the statement of the law, no mention of an independent criterion by which one could distinguish in advance the class of outcomes which would strengthen responses and those which would weaken them. Without such a criterion the law of effect was difficult to test conclusively and was accused of circularity.

A number of attempts have been made to define more completely the classes of outcomes which act as rewards and as punishments. Hull's conception of need, as a condition in which "any of the commodities or conditions necessary for individual or species survival are lacking" (p. 17), represented an early attempt in this direction. Satisfaction, or reinforcement to use Hull's term, occurred when a condition of need was reduced. This use of changes in states of physiological needs was justly criticized on a number of grounds, and subsequently Hull (1951) and many of his associates changed their conception of the basis for reinforcement from changes in tissue conditions to changes in aversive states called drives. Reinforcement resulted not from the reduction of a biological need but from drive reduction. Although Hull was never very explicit about the defining properties of a drive, Miller and Dollard (1941) have anchored it in the intensity of stimulation. A drive was "a strong stimulus which impels action" (p. 18) on the part of the organism. Increases in stimulation, e.g., from an electric shock or loud noise, constituted increases in drive and were predicted to decrease the probability of responses preceding them. On the other hand, decreases in stimulation constituted drive reduction and were predicted to increase the probability of responses preceding them.

The concept of drive reduction as the basis of reinforcement has achieved greater currency than that of need reduction, but it too has been criticized. There is considerable evidence that organisms, under many conditions, do not seek to avoid stimulation but to attain it. The optimal state does not appear to be the absence of stimulation as drive reduction theory would imply. Sensory deprivation studies indicate that humans find very low levels of stimulation highly unpleasant and disruptive (Bexton, Heron, and Scott, 1954). Work by Harlow on manipulation (1953), by Berlyne on curiosity (1960), and by Montgomery on exploration (1954) indicates that, at least under some circumstances, stimulation is rewarding and can strengthen responses. A similar conclusion is suggested by everyday observations of the frequency with which people engage in highly stimulating activities such as riding roller coasters, driving sports cars, and reading detective stories.

In an attempt to account for such observations, Hebb (1949) and McClelland et al. (1953) have suggested that the satisfying and dissatisfying properties of any stimulus are dependent on the size of the discrepancy between the stimulus and a hypothetical neural organization or adaptation level, which has been acquired as a result of past stimulation. If the stimulus is mildly different from the adaptation level, it is pleasant; if it is highly different from the adaptation level or very similar to the adaptation level, it is unpleasant. Since these theories shift the basis for affect from tissue conditions or stimulation to central processes, which are by their nature difficult to observe, it is hard to subject them to a critical test. There is as yet no way of predicting in advance for a particular organism how much pleasure or pain will be generated with a particular event.

Although there are clearly many unsolved problems in explaining behavior in terms of reinforcement principles, definite progress has been made. The empirical validity of the proposition that the probability of occurrence of a wide range of behaviors can be altered by the outcomes of those behaviors has been supported by a wealth of research using both animals and humans as subjects. Without a doubt the law of effect or principle of reinforcement must be included among the most substantiated findings of experimental psychology and is at the same time among the most useful findings for an applied psychology concerned with the control of human behavior.

A second group of psychologists has accepted the empirical evidence underlying the law of effect but has asserted that the stimulus-response reinforcement theories of Hull and his followers are not sufficient to account for the more complex aspects of choice behavior. Tolman (1932) and Lewin (1938) were among the early advocates of *cognitive* theories of behavior. Although Tolman's work was mainly with animals and Lewin's was with humans, they both attributed to their subjects internalized representations of their environment. The organism was assumed to have beliefs, opinions, or expectations concerning the world around him. To Tolman, learning consisted not of changes in the strength of habits (i.e., stimulus-response connections) but of changes in beliefs (i.e. stimulus-stimulus or stimulus-response-stimulus connections). He attributed the results of reinforcement studies to learning, but he did not regard reinforcement as a necessary condition for learning to take place.

Although reinforcement was accorded a much less central role, the models of Lewin and Tolman also reflect the influence of hedonism. Both investigators viewed behavior as purposeful or goal-directed, with organisms striving to attain positively valent objects or events and to avoid negatively valent objects or events.

Lewin (1935) distinguished between historical and ahistorical explanations of behavior. He pointed out that the former had its roots in Aristotelian thinking and the latter in Galilean thinking. From an ahistorical point of view behavior at a given time is viewed as depending only on events existing at that time. The problem is one of accounting for the actions of a person from a knowledge of the proper-

ties of his life space at the time the actions are occurring. From an historical standpoint, behavior is dependent on events occurring at an earlier time. The historical problem is to determine the way in which the behavior of a person at one point in time is affected by past situations he has experienced and the responses he has made to them. Freud's constant emphasis on the dependence of adult behavior on events which occurred in childhood and Hull's stress on reinforcement of previous responses provide us with good examples of historical explanations.

Lewin's own theorizing was ahistorical, but he noted the complementary nature of ahistorical and historical approaches. Past events can only have an effect on behavior in the present by modifying conditions which exist in the present. If a particular childhood experience is to have any effect on adult behavior, it must do so by changing some property of the person which persists through adulthood. Historical explanations are consequently explanations of the process of change, i.e., of the ways in which properties of persons are modified by events. Ahistorical explanations, on the other hand, concern the effects on behavior of conditions existing at the time the behavior is occurring, and say nothing about how these conditions were established.

Ahistorical models of choice behavior bypass many of the problems that concern the psychologist interested in learning. The choices made by a person in a given situation are explained in terms of his motives and cognitions at the time he makes the choice. The process by which these motives or cognitions were acquired is not specified nor is it regarded as crucial to a consideration of their present role in behavior.

Although bypassing the problem of the origins of psychological properties, an ahistorical approach to motivation is confronted with another set of problems, i.e., problems of operational definition or measurement. In order to test ahistorical models, we must develop methods of measuring or experimentally manipulating these variables. The strategy of the learning theorist, creating carefully controlled training conditions, is supplanted by the use of psychometric assessment devices or the manipulation of situational conditions which are assumed to have some relationship to the constructs in the model.

AN OUTLINE OF A COGNITIVE MODEL

In the remainder of this essay, we outline a conceptual model .... The model to be described is similar to those developed by other investigators including Lewin (1938), Rotter (1955), Peak (1955), Davidson, Suppes, and Siegel (1957), Atkinson (1958), and Tolman (1959). It is basically ahistorical in form. We assume that the choices made by a person among alternative courses of action are lawfully related to psychological events occurring contemporaneously with the behavior. We turn now to consider the concepts in the model and their interrelations.

The concept of valence

We shall begin with the simple assumption that, at any given point in time, a person has preferences among outcomes or states of nature. For any pair of outcomes, x and y, a person prefers x to y, prefers y to x, or is indifferent to whether he receives x or y. Preference, then, refers to a relationship between the strength of a person's desire for, or attraction toward, two outcomes.

Psychologists have used many different terms to refer to preferences. The terms, valence (Lewin, 1938; Tolman, 1959), incentive (Atkinson, 1958), attitude (Peak, 1955), and expected utility (Edwards, 1954; Thrall, Coombs, and Davis, 1954; Davidson, Suppes and Siegel, 1957) all

refer to affective orientations toward outcomes. Other concepts like need (Maslow, 1954), motive (Atkinson, 1958b), value (Allport, Vernon, and Lindzey, 1951), and interest (Strong, 1958) are broader in nature and refer to the strength of desires or aversions for large classes of outcomes.

For the sake of consistency, we use the term valence throughout this essay in referring to affective orientations toward particular outcomes. In our system, an outcome is positively valent when the person prefers attaining it to not attaining it (i.e., he prefers x to not x). An outcome has a valence of zero when the person is indifferent to attaining or not attaining it (i.e., he is indifferent to x or not x), and it is negatively valent when he prefers not attaining it to attaining it (i.e., he prefers not x to x). It is assumed that valence can take a wide range of both positive and negative values.

We use the term motive whenever the referent is a preference for a class of outcomes. A positive (or approach) motive signifies that outcomes which are members of the class have positive valence, and a negative (or avoidance) motive signifies that outcomes in the class have negative valence.

It is important to distinguish between the valence of an outcome to a person and its value to that person. An individual may desire an object but derive little satisfaction from its attainment—or he may strive to avoid an object which he later finds to be quite satisfying. At any given time there may be a substantial discrepancy between the anticipated satisfaction from an outcome (i.e., its valence) and the actual satisfaction that it provides (i.e., its value).

There are many outcomes which are positively or negatively valent to persons, but are not in themselves anticipated to be satisfying or dissatisfying. The strength of a person's desire or aversion for them is based not on their intrinsic properties but on the anticipated satisfaction or dissatisfaction associated with other outcomes to which they are expected to lead. People may desire to join groups because they believe that membership will enhance their status in the community, and they may desire to perform their jobs effectively because they expect that it will lead to a promotion.

In effect, we are suggesting that means acquire valence as a consequence of their expected relationship to ends. Peak (1955) has discussed this relationship in some detail. She hypothesizes that attitudes, i.e., affective orientations toward objects, are "related to the ends which the object serves" (p. 153). From this general hypothesis it is possible for Peak to distinguish two types of determinants of attitudes: (1) The cognized instrumentality of the object of the attitude for the attainment of various consequences; and (2) the intensity and the nature of the affect expected from these consequences. If an object is believed by a person to lead to desired consequences or to prevent undesired consequences, the person is predicted to have a positive attitude toward it. If, on the other hand, it is believed by the person to lead to undesired consequences or to prevent desired consequences, the person is predicted to have a negative attitude toward it.

General support for these predictions is provided by a number of studies and experiments conducted by Peak and her associates. Rosenberg (1956) showed that it is possible to predict subjects' attitudes toward free speech for communists and desegregation in housing from their reported goals and their judgments of the probability that free speech and segregation will aid or block attainment of these goals. In a follow-up experiment, Carlson (1956) changed subjects' attitudes toward desegregation by modifying their beliefs regarding the consequences of desegregation for the attainment of their goals. Peak (1960) has also shown that students'

attitudes toward conditions believed to hinder the attainment of good grades are more negative on the day of the quiz, when their motivation for attaining good grades was presumably strongest.

We do not mean to imply that all the variance in the valence of outcomes can be explained by their expected consequences. We must assume that some things are desired and abhored "for their own sake." Desegregation may be opposed "on principle" not because it leads to other events which are disliked, and people may seek to do well on their jobs even though no externally mediated rewards are believed to be at stake.

Without pretending to have solved all of the knotty theoretical problems involved in the determinants of valence, we can specify the expected functional relationship between the valence of outcomes and their expected consequences in the following proposition.

Proposition 1. *The valence of an outcome to a person is a monotonically increasing function of the algebraic sum of the products of the valences of all other outcomes and his conceptions of its instrumentality for the attainment of these other outcomes.*

In equation form the same proposition reads as follows:

$$V_j = f_j \left[\sum_{k-1}^{n} (V_k I_{jk}) \right] (j = 1 \ldots n)$$

$$f_j' > 0; \; i I_{jj} = 0$$

where

V_j = the valence of outcome j

I_{jk} = the cognized instrumentality $(- 1 \leqslant I_{jk} \leqslant 1)$ of outcome j for the attainment of outcome k

The concept of expectancy

The specific outcomes attained by a person are dependent not only on the choices that he makes but also on events which are beyond his control. For example, a person who elects to buy a ticket in a lottery is not certain of winning the desired prize. Whether or not he does so is a function of many chance events. Similarly, the student who enrolls in medical school is seldom certain that he will successfully complete the program of study; the person who seeks political office is seldom certain that he will win the election; and the worker who strives for a promotion is seldom certain that he will triumph over other candidates. Most decision-making situations involve some element of risk, and theories of choice behavior must come to grips with the role of these risks in determining the choices that people do make.

Whenever an individual chooses between alternatives which involve uncertain outcomes, it seems clear that his behavior is affected not only by his preferences among these outcomes but also by the degree to which he believes these outcomes to be probable. Psychologists have referred to these beliefs as expectancies (Tolman, 1959; Rotter, 1955; Atkinson, 1958) or subjective probabilities (Edwards, 1954; Davidson, Suppes, and Siegel, 1957). We use the former term throughout this essay. An expectancy is defined as a momentary belief concerning the likelihood that a particular act will be followed by a particular outcome. Expectancies may be described in terms of their strength. Maximal strength is indicated by subjective certainty that the act *will* be followed by the outcome while minimal (or zero) strength is indicated by subjective certainty that the act *will not* be followed by the outcome.

The differences between the concepts of expectancy, discussed in this section, and instrumentality, discussed in the previous section, should be noted.

Expectancy is an action-outcome association. It takes values ranging from zero, indicating no subjective probability that an act will be followed by an outcome, to 1, indicating certainty that the act will be followed by the outcome. Instrumentality, on the other hand, is an outcome-outcome association. It can take values ranging form −1, indicating a belief that attainment of the second outcome is certain without the first outcome and impossible with it, to +1, indicating that the first outcome is believed to be a necessary and sufficient condition for the attainment of the second outcome.

The concept of force

It remains to be specified how valences and expectancies combine in determining choices. The directional concept in our model is the Lewinian concept of force. Behavior on the part of a person is assumed to be the result of a field of forces each of which has direction and magnitude. The concept of force as used here is similar to Tolman's performance vector (1959), Atkinson's aroused motivation (1958), Luce's subjective expected utility (1962), and Rotter's behavior potential (1955).

There are many possible ways of combining valences and expectancies mathematically to yield these hypothetical forces. On the assumption that choices made by people are subjectively rational, we would predict the strength of forces to be a monotonically increasing function of the *product* of valences and expectancies. Proposition 2 expresses this functional relationship.

Proposition 2. *The force on a person to perform an act is a montonically increasing function of the algebraic sum of the products of the valences of all outcomes and the strength of his expectancies that the act will be followed by the attainment of these outcomes.*

We can express this proposition in the form of the following equation:

$$F_i = f_i \left[\sum_{j=1}^{n} (E_{ij}V_j) \right] (i = n + 1 \ldots m)$$

$$f_i' > 0; \quad i \cap j = \Phi, \quad \Phi \text{ is the null set}$$

where

F_i = the force to perform act j
E_{ij} = the strength of the expectancy $(0 \leqslant E_{ij} \leqslant 1)$ that act i will be followed by outcome j
V_j = the valence of outcome j

It is also assumed that people choose from among alternative acts the one corresponding to the strongest positive (or weakest negative) force. This formulation is similar to the notion in decision theory that people choose in a way that maximizes subjective expected utility.

Expressing force as a monotonically increasing function of the product of valence and expectancy has a number of implications which should be noted. An outcome with high positive or negative valence will have no effect on the generation of a force unless there is some expectancy (i.e., some subjective probability greater than zero) that the outcome will be attained by some act. As the strength of an expectancy that an act will lead to an outcome increases, the effect of variations in the valence of the outcome on the force to perform the act will also increase. Similarly, if the valence of an outcome is zero (i.e., the person is indifferent to the outcome), neither the absolute value nor variations in the strength of expectancies of attaining it will have any effect on forces.

Our two propositions have been stated in separate terms, but are in fact highly related to one another. Insofar as the acts and outcomes are described in different terms the separation is a useful one. We have in the first proposition a basis for predicting the valence of outcomes, and in the second proposition a basis for predicting the actions that a person will take

with regard to the outcome. The distinction between acts and outcomes is not, however, an absolute one. Actions are frequently described in terms of the particular outcomes which they effect. For example, a person may be described as having chosen a particular occupation only when he successfully attains it, or he may be described as having chosen to perform effectively in that occupation only when he succeeds in doing so. In such cases the derivations from the two propositions become identical. The conditions predicted to affect the valence of the occupation or of effective performance in it are identical to those predicted to affect the relative strength of forces toward and away from these outcomes.

In practice we will find it useful to maintain the separation between the two propositions by defining sets of actions and sets of outcomes independently of one another. We will use the term action to refer to behavior which might reasonably be expected to be within the repertoire of the person, e.g., seeking entry into an occupation, while the term outcomes will be reserved for more temporally distant events which are less likely to be under complete behavioral control, e.g., attaining membership in an occupation.

REFERENCES

Allport, G. "The Historical Background of Modern Social Psychology." In G. Lindzey (ed.), *Handbook of Social Psychology*. Cambridge, Mass.: Addison-Wesley, 1954, pp. 3-56.

Allport, G. W.; Vernon, P. E.; and Lindzey, G. *Study of Values*, Rev. ed. Boston: Houghton Mifflin, 1951.

Atkinson, J. W. "Towards Experimental Analysis of Human Motivation in Terms of Motives, Expectancies, and Incentive." In J. W. Atkinson (ed.), *Motives in Fantasy, Action and Society*. Princeton: Van Nostrand, 1958, pp. 288-305.

Berlyne, D. E. *Conflict Arousal and Curiosity*. New York: McGraw-Hill, 1960.

Bexton, W. H.; Heron, W.; and Scott, T. H. "Effects of Decreased Variation in the Sensory Environment." *Canadian Journal of Psychology* 8 (1954), pp. 70-76.

Carlson, E. R. "Attitude Change through Modification of Attitude Structure," *Journal of Abnormal and Social Psychology* 52 (1956), pp. 256-61.

Davidson, D.; Suppes, P.; and Siegel, S. *Decision Making: An Experimental Approach.* Stanford: Stanford University Press, 1957.

Edwards, W. "The Theory of Decision Making." *Psychological Bulletin* 51 (1954), pp. 380-417.

Estes, W. K. "Stimulus-Response Theory of Drive." In M. R. Jones (ed.), *Nebraska Symposium on Motivation.* Lincoln: University of Nebraska Press, 1958, pp. 35-69.

Harlow, H. F. "Mice, Monkeys, Men and Motives." *Psychological Review* 60 (1953), pp. 23-32.

Hebb, D. O. *The Organization of Behavior.* New York: Wiley, 1949.

Hull, C. L. *Principles of Behavior.* New York: Appleton-Century, 1943.

Hull, C. L. *Essentials of Behavior.* New Haven: Yale University Press, 1951.

James, W. *The Principles of Psychology.* New York: Holt, 1890.

Lewin, K. *A Dynamic Theory of Personality.* New York: McGraw-Hill, 1935.

Lewin, K. "The Conceptual Representation and the Measurement of Psychological Forces." *Contributions to Psychological Theory.* Durham, N.C.: Duke University Press, 1938, p. 1.

Logan, F. A. "A Micromolar Approach to Behavior Theory." *Psychological Review* 63 (1956), pp. 63-73.

Luce, R. D. "Psychological Studies of Risky Decision Making." In G. B. Strother (ed.), *Social Science Approaches to Business Behavior.* Homewood: Dorsey, 1962, pp. 141-61.

Maslow, A. H. *Motivation and Personality.* New York: Harper, 1954.

McClelland, D. C.; Atkinson, J. W.; Clark, R. A.; and Lowell, E. L. *The Achievement Motive.* New York: Appleton-Century-Crofts, 1953.

Miller, N. E.; and Dollard, J. *Social Learning and Imitation.* New Haven: Yale University Press, 1941.

Montgomery, K. C. "The Role of the Exploratory Drive in Learning," *Journal of Comparative Physiological Psychology* 47 (1954), pp. 60-64.

Peak, Helen. "Attitude and Motivation." In M. R. Jones (ed.), *Nebraska Symposium on Motivation.* Lincoln: University of Nebraska Press, 1955, pp. 245-68.

Peak, Helen. "The Effect of Aroused Motivation on Attitudes." *Journal of Abnormal and Social Psychology* 61 (1960), pp. 463-68.

Postman, L. "The History and Present Status of the Law of Effect." *Psychological Bulletin* 44 (1947), pp. 489-563.

Rosenberg, M. J. "Cognitive Structure and Attitudinal Affect." *Journal of Abnormal and Social Psychology* 53 (1956), pp. 367-72.

Rotter, J. B. "The Role of the Psychological Situation in Determining the Direction of Human Behavior." In M. R. Jones (ed.), *Nebraska Symposium on Motivation.* Lincoln: University of Nebraska Press, 1955, pp. 245-68.

Strong, E. K., Jr. "Satisfactions and Interests." *American Psychologist* 13 (1958), pp. 449-56.

Thrall, R. M.; Coombs, C. H.; and Davis, R. L. (ed.). *Decision Processes.* New York: Wiley, 1954.

Thorndike, E. L. *Animal Intelligence: Experimental Studies.* New York: Van Nostrand, 1928.

Tolman, E. C. *Purposive Behavior in Animals and Men.* New York: Century, 1932.

Tolman, E. C. "Principles of Purposive Behavior." In S. Koch (ed.), *Psychology: A Study of a Science.* vol. 2. New York: McGraw-Hill, 1959, pp. 92-157.

Troland, L. T. *The Fundamentals of Human Motivation.* New York: Van Nostrand, 1928.

Essay 3-4

The motivational basis of organizational behavior: I*

Daniel Katz

The basic problem to which I shall address myself is how people are tied into social and organizational structures so that they become effective functioning units of social systems. What is the nature of their involvement in a system or their commitment to it?

The major input into social organizations consists of people. The economist or the culturologist may concentrate on inputs of resources, raw materials, technology. To the extent that human factors are recognized, they are assumed to be constants in the total equation and are neglected. At the practical level, however, as well as for a more precise theoretical accounting, we need to cope with such organizational realities as the attracting of people into organizations, holding them within the system, insuring reliable role performance, and in addition stimulating actions which are generally facilitative of organizational accomplishment. The material and psychic returns to organizational members thus constitute major determinants, not only of the level of effectiveness of organizational functioning, but of the very existence of the organization.

The complexities of motivational problems in organizations can be understood if we develop an analytic framework which will be comprehensive enough to identify the major sources of variance and detailed enough to contain sufficient specification for predictive purposes. The framework we propose calls for three steps in an analysis process, namely, the formulation of answers to these types of questions: (1) What are the types of behavior required for effective organizational functioning? Any organization will require not one, but several patterns of behavior from most of its members. And the motivational bases of these various behavioral requirements may differ. (2) What are the motivational patterns which are used and which can be used in organizational settings? How do they differ in their logic and psycho-logic? What are the differential consequences of the various types of motivational patterns for the behavioral requirements essential for organizational functioning? One motivational pattern may be very effective in bringing about one type of necessary behavior and completely ineffective in leading to another. (3) What are the conditions for eliciting a given motivational pattern in an organizational setting? We may be able to identify the type of motivation we think most appropriate for producing a given behavioral outcome but we still need to know how this motive can be aroused or produced in the organization (Katz, 1962).

BEHAVIORAL REQUIREMENTS

Our major dependent variables are the behavioral requirements of the organization. Three basic types of behavior are essential for a functioning organization: (1) People must be induced to enter and remain within the system. (2) They must carry out their role assignments in a dependable fashion. (3) There must be innovative and spontaneous activity in achiev-

*Reprinted from Daniel Katz, "The Motivational Basis of Organizational Behavior," *Behavioral Science*, vol. 9, no. 2 (1964), pp. 131-33, by permission of James G. Miller, M.D., Ph.D., Editor.

ing organizational objectives which go beyond the role specifications.

Attracting and holding people in a system

First of all, sufficient personnel must be kept within the system to man its essential functions. People thus must be induced to enter the system at a sufficiently rapid rate to counteract the amount of defection. High turnover is costly. Moreover, there is some optimum period for their staying within the system. And while they are members of the system they must validate their membership by constant attendance. Turnover and absenteeism are both measures of organizational effectiveness and productivity, though they are partial measures. People may, of course, be within the system physically but may be psychological absentees. The child may be regular and punctual in his school attendance and yet daydream in his classes. It is not enough, then, to hold people within a system.

Dependable role performance

The great range of variable human behavior must be reduced to a limited number of predictable patterns. In other words, the assigned roles must be carried out and must meet some minimal level of quantity and quality of performance. A common measure of productivity is the amount of work turned out by the individual or by the group carrying out their assigned tasks. Quality of performance is not as easily measured and the problem is met by quality controls which set minimal standards for the pieces of work sampled. In general, the major role of the member is clearly set forth by organizational protocol and leadership. The man on the assembly line, the nurse in the hospital, the teacher in the elementary school all know what their major job is. To do a lot of it and to do it well are, then, the most conspicuous behavioral requirements of the

organization. It may be, of course, that given role requirements are not functionally related to organizational accomplishment. This is a different type of problem and we are recognizing here only the fact that some major role requirements are necessary.

Innovative and spontaneous behavior

A neglected set of requirements consists of those actions not specified by role prescriptions which nevertheless facilitate the accomplishment of organizational goals. The great paradox of a social organization is that it must not only reduce human variability to insure reliable role performance but that it must also allow room for some variability and in fact encourage it.

There must always be a supportive number of actions of an innovative or relatively spontaneous sort. No organizational planning can foresee all contingencies within its operations, or can anticipate with perfect accuracy all environmental changes, or can control perfectly all human variability. The resources of people in innovation, in spontaneous cooperation, in protective and creative behavior are thus vital to organizational survival and effectiveness. An organization which depends solely upon its blueprints of prescribed behavior is a very fragile social system.

Cooperation

The patterned activity which makes up an organization is so intrinsically a cooperative set of interrelationships, that we are not aware of the cooperative nexus any more than we are of any habitual behavior like walking. Within every work group in a factory, within any division in a government bureau, or within any department of a university are countless acts of cooperation without which the system would break down. We take these everyday acts for granted, and few, if any, of them form the role prescriptions for any job. One man will call the attention of his companion on the next machine to some indication that his machine is getting jammed, or will pass along some tool that his companion needs, or will borrow some bit of material he is short of. Or men will come to the aid of a fellow who is behind on his quota. In a study of clerical workers in an insurance company one of the two factors differentiating high-producing from low-producing sections was the greater cooperative activity of the girls in the high-producing sections coming to one another's help in meeting production quotas (Katz, Maccoby, and Morse, 1950). In most factories specialization develops around informal types of help. One man will be expert in first aid, another will be expert in machine diagnosis, etc. We recognize the need for cooperative relationships by raising this specific question when a man is considered for a job. How well does he relate to his fellows, is he a good team man, will he fit in?

Protection

Another subcategory of behavior facilitative of organizational functioning is the action which protects the organization against disaster. There is nothing in the role prescriptions of the worker which specifies that he be on the alert to save life and property in the organization. Yet the worker who goes out of his way to remove the boulder accidentally lodged in the path of a freight car on the railway spur, or to secure a rampant piece of machinery, or even to disobey orders when they obviously are wrong and dangerous, is an invaluable man for the organization.

Constructive ideas

Another subcategory of acts beyond the line of duty consists of creative suggestions for the improvement of methods of production or of maintenance. Some

organizations encourage their members to feed constructive suggestions into the system, but coming up with good ideas for the organization and formulating them to management is not the typical role of the worker. An organization that can stimulate its members to contribute ideas for organizational improvement is a more effective organization in that people who are close to operating problems can often furnish informative suggestions about such operations. The system which does not have this stream of contributions from its members is not utilizing its potential resources effectively.

Self-training

Still another subcategory under the heading of behavior beyond the call of duty concerns the self-training of members for doing their own jobs better and self-education for assuming more responsible positions in the organization. There may be no requirement that men prepare themselves for better positions. But the organization which has men spending their own time to master knowledge and skills for more responsible jobs in the system has an additional resource for effective functioning.

Favorable attitude

Finally, members of a group can contribute to its operations by helping to create a favorable climate for it in the community, or communities, which surround the organization. Employees may talk to friends, relatives, and acquaintances about the excellent or the poor qualities of the company for which they work. A favorable climate may help in problems of recruitment, and sometimes product disposal.

In short, for effective organizational functioning many members must be willing on occasion to do more than their job prescriptions specify. If the system were to follow the letter of the law according to job descriptions and protocol, it would soon grind to a halt. There have to be many actions of mutual cooperation and many anticipations of organizational objectives to make the system viable.

Now these three major types of behavior, and even the subcategories, though related, are not necessarily motivated by the same drives and needs. The motivational pattern that will attract and hold people to an organization is not necessarily the same as that which will lead to higher productivity. Nor are the motives which make for higher productivity invariably the same as those which sustain cooperative interrelationships in the interests of organizational accomplishment. Hence, when we speak about organizational practices and procedures which will further the attainment of its mission, we need to specify the type of behavioral requirement involved.

REFERENCES

Katz, D. "Human Interrelationships and Organizational Behavior." In S. Mailick and E. H. Van Ness (eds.), *Concepts and Issues in Administrative Behavior.* New York: Prentice-Hall, 1962, pp. 166-86.

Katz, D.; Maccoby, N.; and Morse, Nancy. *Productivity, Supervision and Morale in an Office Situation.* Ann Arbor, Mich.: Institute for Social Research, Univ. of Michigan, 1950.

Commentary

The essays by Smith, Rottenberg, and Vroom are amazingly similar in treatment of choice decision making despite the span of 200 years. Smith argues that the sum of the advantages and disadvantages of an opportunity is evaluated and that choices favor that opportunity offering the greatest net advantage. Rottenberg, elaborating Smith's analysis and defending it from critics of the "economic man" concept, points out that compensation is only one of the many elements considered in labor supply choices; all of the advantages and disadvantages of an employment exchange are taken into account in evaluations of net advantage, a concept strikingly similar to Vroom's concept of force. Smith, Rottenberg, and Vroom concur in noting that individuals assign different utilities or valences to different job characteristics or outcomes. While individual decisions vary with individual perceptions and utility or valence functions, all three authors would expect general tendencies in the valuation of employment opportunities, choices, and labor supply behaviors for large numbers of people. Rottenberg notes in this regard that compensation is one element of an employment opportunity where all would agree that "more is better" while there might be disagreement in the valuation of other elements such as responsibility and steadiness of employment. Thus Rottenberg would argue that relative wage rate tends to be more predictive of labor supply behavior than are other elements associated with employment opportunities; increasing the level of compensation offered is the most direct way of increasing labor supply according to Rottenberg's analysis.

One difference among the three treatments of decision making concerns the nature of the standard employed in the final judgment of an employment opportunity. Each employment opportunity is evaluated first in terms of relative advantages and disadvantages, net advantage or valence. Smith and Vroom imply that the net advantage of any opportunity then is compared with the net advantage associated with other alternative opportunities and that the opportunity with the largest valence or net advantage is selected; Rottenberg, on the other hand, indicates that a single alternative is evaluated relative to some generalized concept of the "going rate," a generalized concept of other alternatives, rather than relative to each alternative. March and Simon, if you recall, conceived of the evaluation of employment opportunities as a single, rather than double, stage process; the inducements of other foregone alternatives were conceptualized as contributions of the employment opportunity being considered. The two stage models of Smith, Rottenberg, and Vroom call explicit attention to the assessment of individual alternatives and then comparison with other alternatives. In all models, however, the choice is relative, alternatives are compared one with another or with a single generalized concept of alternatives and are not compared with some absolute standard for choice. Individuals cannot be aware of the full range of employment opportunities available and must compare any alternative with some limited set of known alternatives. This standard for comparison will tend to be impressionistic and will vary with recent experiences of the individual, and the relevant alternatives will vary with the particular decision. The student considering part-time employment will tend to view full-time study as a relevant alternative while a carpenter considering a change of employers will tend to view the current employment exchange as a relevant alternative. Thus relevant comparisons will vary among decisions to seek work, choice of occupation, attraction to an employer and decisions about task performance.

Another difference among the three treatments concerns the role of expectancies or probabilities. Smith and Rottenberg consider the probability of success as one of many elements considered in evaluation of an opportunity and, presumably, combined in an additive fashion with valuations of other elements to obtain some overall valuation. Vroom, on the other hand, employs the concept of expectancy or probability in a multiplicative model to obtain an overall evaluation. Vroom can now argue that expectancy of employment, like wages, is an element of choice where all will agree that "more is better." The expectancy of employment in the multiplicative model also conditions the influence of other choice elements rather than merely compensating for them as in the additive model; the difference in attractiveness of two employment opportunities associated with difference in an element such as wages can be easily reversed when the probability of employment is considered. Vroom's model, emphasizing the expectancy of employment, probably is more explanatory of labor supply choices than alternative models which emphasize wage differentials. Relative wages in employment tend to be reasonably stable over time, more stable than expectancies of employment. Traditional wage differentials among occupations, industries, and employers are rarely altered despite significant changes in demand and supply of labor resources. One might thus argue that labor supply is more a function of job opportunities than of relative wages, particularly in the short run. Significant shifts in the occupational distribution of employment have occurred over time despite the relative stability of occupational wage rates, consistent with the role of expectancy of employment in labor supply decisions. Analyses of labor force participation suggest that this measure of labor supply also is more sensitive to changes in job opportunities than to changes in wage rates. Decisions of students, housewives, and retirees to seek employment probably can be viewed as a direct function of job opportunities influencing expected income, employment being sought as jobs become more readily available rather than solely as a function of wage rates. This observation would apply particularly to decisions to seek employment by members of the secondary labor force, individuals with attractive alternatives to working, who account for much of the short-run fluctuation in size of the labor force.

The decision-making model implies that job opportunities and expectancy of employment influence attraction to an employer as well as decisions to work and occupational choices, individuals are attracted to apply for employment with an organization known to be seeking employees and are disinclined to terminate employment when alternative opportunities are scarce. Organizations seeking employees rely first upon advertisements and recruiting efforts to create awareness of the opportunities for employment and do not resort immediately to increasing wage rates in order to attract labor services. Labor supply to the organization probably is more directly a function of perceived opportunities for employment than it is a function of wage rates.

The decision-making or choice models of Smith, Rottenberg, and Vroom appear particularly appropriate in the analysis of individual decisions to apply for and accept employment within an occupation or firm, the "joining" behavior specified in Katz's analysis. They are less clearly appropriate in the analysis of other behaviors identified by Katz, particularly the innovative and spontaneous behavior beyond specified task performance. For the present we shall limit our consideration of labor supply to a single dimension, the number of individuals seeking employment and apply the choice models within that constraint. Later sections consider different labor supply behaviors and the choice models will be examined then in the analysis of those behaviors.

B: Aggregate supplies of labor services

Aggregate supplies of labor services to an industry, occupation, and employing organization reflect the summed choices of individuals, and assumptions about the behavior of aggregate supplies are based upon inferences from the models of individual behavior reviewed in the previous section. Questions of major interest concerning aggregate labor supplies relate to the magnitude of supply and change in the magnitude of supply, questions such as why the number of people seeking employment in an occupation or an organization increases or decreases. Knowledge about the determinants of aggregate labor supplies is useful in making predictions about future labor supplies and in trying to influence employment decisions. Employers attempting to recruit a labor force, for example, must decide what is most likely to attract the desired applicants for employment. Models of aggregate labor supply behavior attempt to explain change in the magnitude of labor supplies and to indicate the variables most predictive of change.

Models of individual choice and decision making which indicate that individuals seek to maximize net advantage, subjective expected utility or valence, are operationally predictive only when advantage, utility or valence can be identified and measured. A principle that individuals act so as to maximize net advantage becomes tautological in the absence of a means for defining and measuring net advantage. While it is true that the definition and measurement of utility or valence is idiosyncratic and varies among individuals, a model of aggregate labor supply requires that we identify general tendencies in valuations of employment opportunities by individuals which might be predictive of aggregate behavior. Adam Smith identified six characteristics of employment including monetary compensation which he argued influence individual employment decisions and are predictive of aggregate labor supplies. Monetary compensation was presented as a variable inducement balancing other advantages and disadvantages in the equalization of net advantage among jobs; monetary compensation is manipulated to change the net advantage associated with a job and redirect labor supplies among jobs. Accepting Smith's model of individual decision making, Rottenberg went on to present a rationale for viewing aggregate labor supplies as a function primarily of monetary compensation.

Rottenberg argues that aggregate labor supplies can be viewed best as a function of price or monetary compensation for several reasons. First, monetary compensation is continuously quantifiable while other employment characteristics such as status or security are not as easily quantified and may also be discontinuous. Second, preference patterns related to monetary compensation are consistent whereas preferences related to other employment characteristics often are not consistent. All will agree that more compensation is better than less, whereas the same is not true for employment characteristics such as responsibility or seasonality of employment. Preferences related to characteristics other than compensation may be discontinuous, more responsibility may be preferred up to a point after which less responsibility is preferred to more responsibility. Rottenberg's third reason is that price or monetary compensation is predictive of aggregate labor supply behaviors, that aggregate labor supplies do in fact flow from lower paying to higher paying employment opportunities. In consequence, Rottenberg proposes that aggregate labor supplies are most reasonably viewed as a function of monetary compensation as indicated in Figure 3-1, increasing magnitudes of labor services are attracted to an industry, occupation or employer at higher levels of monetary compensation.

The relationship between magnitude of labor services and monetary compensation depicted in Figure 3-1 implies a cause-effect relationship, but is not meant to imply that monetary compensation is the sole determinant of the magnitude of labor services offered for employment. Rather, the upward sloping relationship is derived from assumptions that other factors also influence employment decisions and that monetary compensation is varied as a

Figure 3-1: Labor supply as a function of compensation

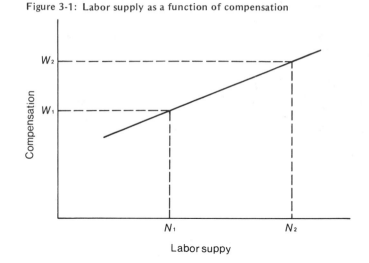

means of overcoming other influences. The variation in magnitude of labor services with rate of compensation reflects the fact that individuals have alternatives, some more attractive than others. The labor services offered by individuals at any specific rate of compensation include some labor services which would have been offered at lower rates of compensation and others which would not have been offered at lower rates; labor services ON_1 in Figure 3-1 would have been offered at wage W_1 while the additional labor services $N_1 N_2$ were forthcoming only at wage W_2. The individuals providing the additional $N_1 N_2$ labor services presumably view other alternatives as more attractive at wage rates below W_2. The schedule of labor supplies indicated in Figure 3-1 depicts the magnitude of labor services which would be made available at different rates of compensation and thus the rate of compensation necessary to elicit any specific quantity of labor services.

The slope of the function relating magnitude of labor services to rate of compensation indicates the relative change in labor services associated with relative change in rates of compensation and is termed elasticity of labor supply. A relatively elastic function has a low degree of slope and indicates considerable change in labor supplies relative to minor change in rates of compensation; an inelastic function has a high degree of slope and indicates relatively little change in labor supplies compared with relatively large change in rates of compensation. The elasticity of the function assumed between labor supplies and compensation is critical to the formulation of compensation policies. Assumption of a highly elastic function implies that labor supplies are quite responsive to changes in rates of compensation, and assumption of an inelastic function implies the reverse, that labor supplies are not very responsive to changes in rates of compensation.

Assuming that individuals seek employment opportunities offering the greatest net advantage and that rate of compensation is a significant component in the calculation of net advantage, the elasticity of labor supplies is determined by the ease with which individuals can make their labor services available, and the magnitude of labor services occupied in other alternatives. Any significant expansion or contraction of specific labor supplies requires that there be alternatives from which supplies can be drawn or to which labor supplies can turn. Consider, for example, the number of persons seeking employment in a particular locality, say, Denver, Colorado. An increase in compensation rates in Denver would make employment opportunities there more attractive and, other things being equal, some persons now attending school, keeping house, or retired in Denver could be expected to seek employment; additionally, we might expect employment in Denver to become more attractive to persons now working in Boulder, Colorado or even Chicago and migration of these persons to Denver to increase the supply of labor services. Similarly, an increase in rates of compensation for short-order cooks, other things being equal, would make that employment more attractive and should attract individuals not now working or working in alternative, less attractive employment. The ease with which individuals can vary labor supply decisions thus influences significantly the elasticity of labor supplies relative to rates of compensation. It is easier to commute from Boulder to Denver or to abandon retirement for employment than it is to move from Chicago to Denver. Thus the elasticity of labor supply in a particular locality ought to vary directly with the size of the surrounding population; the labor supply in the Denver metropolitan area ought to be more elastic than the labor supply in Ketchikan, Alaska. Similarly, the ease of acquiring employment skills influences the elasticity of labor supplies to specific occupations; the supply of short-order cooks ought to be more elastic than the supply of nuclear physicists because of the significantly higher educational requirements for the latter occupation. In a similar manner, we might expect the elasticity of supply of persons to a given employer to vary inversely with the relative size of the employer within the labor market; a small employer in a large labor market can attract individuals from many more alternatives than can a large employer who dominates the particular labor market. All factors influencing the ease of movement of persons among employment alternatives and the magnitude of alternatives relative to the particular supply considered influence the elasticity of labor supplies or the responsiveness of labor supplies to change in rates of compensation. Size of the surrounding community, ease of commuting, and barriers to movement such as educational requirements, licensing, or certification requirements all determine the elasticity of labor supplies to local, occupational, or employer organization labor markets. The assumed elasticity of labor supplies indicates responsiveness to change in rates of compensation, an assumption critical to the determination of compensation policy.

A confusing issue in the analysis of elasticity of labor supplies which was outlined earlier relates to the appropriate unit for analysis of labor supplies. The employing organization is interested primarily in the output of labor services, not the labor services themselves. Dimensions of labor services relevant to the determination of resulting output include number of persons available for employment, number of hours worked, level of skill or capability, and intensity of application of effort. The latter three dimensions vary from person to person and may vary from day to day for a single person making it difficult to infer levels of output associated with number of individuals employed. Models of aggregate labor supplies often abstract from the varying dimensions of labor supply to a concept of a standardized unit of labor, units of labor which are equally productive under identical circumstances. It is difficult to relate such standardized units of labor to individual behavior since any two standardized units of labor may incorporate quite different labor inputs. In practice, employing organizations hire individuals of specified capabilities to perform according to terms in the employment contract and then attempt to influence the productivity of these labor services through training, supervision, and motivation on the job. It is conceptually easier to separate different dimensions of labor supply for analysis, and so we consider here the supply of individuals and hours of work postponing until later consideration of the supply of effort and intensity of application. The typical employment exchange specifies minimal contributions of hours, skill, and intensity of effort; aggregate labor supply is considered here as the number of persons seeking or responding to such offers of employment exchanges.

Labor supply and employer wage policy

Assumptions regarding the elasticity of labor supplies to the employing organization are critical in the determination of compensation policy as can be seen most clearly in the analysis of the relatively common principle to "pay the market rate." This fairly common principle of employee compensation is based upon a relatively complex set of assumptions and a particular model of labor markets, a model implicit in Adam Smith's conceptualization of behavior of labor supplies. This model assumes that individuals seek employment opportunities which offer greatest net advantage and will move rather quickly from one employer to another who offers opportunities with greater net advantage. Workers are assumed to be competitive one with another, and employers are assumed to be competitive one with another, no single employer dominating the labor market. For the reasons outlined by Rottenberg, competition centers upon the wage rate, employers bidding against each other in terms of wage offered and employees bidding against each other in terms of wage accepted. If all workers were the same and all job opportunities were the same, a single wage rate for the labor market would emerge from this competitive process, a wage rate at which market demand and supply would be equated. Individual employers in the labor market would be confronted with perfectly elastic supplies of labor at that market rate, they could employ all the labor sought at that rate and would be unable to hire any persons at lower rates. The principle of paying the market rate thus emerges from this model as a requirement for individual employers; employer wage policy is dictated by competitive forces in the labor market and any exercise of discretion in the determination of wage rates poses the risk of being unable to obtain or retain employees.

The relevance of the principle of paying the market rate obviously varies with the validity of the assumptions of a competitive labor market upon which the assumption of an elastic supply of labor to the employer at the market rate of wages is based. The first qualification to this principle mentioned in Adam Smith's analysis lies in recognition that the concept of a market rate is an abstraction not realized in practice. Smith observed that wage rates vary among employment opportunities to balance other characteristics of jobs; net advantage rather than wage rates would be equated through competitive processes in the labor market. Thus Smith would anticipate higher wage rates associated with employment opportunities with low security of employment and harsh, disagreeable tasks or working conditions, characteristics which might vary from one employer to another as well as from one occupation to another. Every labor market is, in fact, characterized by an array of wage rates, wage rates which vary among industries, occupations, employers, and localities. These differences in wage rates may be attributed in part to barriers to employee mobility among employment opportunities, either natural barriers such as differences in qualifications of individuals and differences in job characteristics other than wages or artificial barriers such as discriminatory hiring practices. In either event, the result is that individual employers encounter supplies of labor with varying elasticities of supply which imply different wage policies. Assumptions about the elasticity of labor supply to the employing organization thus are important in estimating the wage rate which ought to be offered in an employment exchange.

Employer size relative to the labor market was mentioned earlier as an influence of elasticity of supply of labor to the employing organization. Variation in the number of persons attracted to an employer at different wage rates requires alternatives from which persons can be attracted and to which they can be attracted, and we would expect that elasticity of the labor supply would vary directly with the number of relevant alternatives. An employer who dominates the labor market (a monopsonist or single buyer market) has relatively few alternatives from which prospective employees can be attracted. Any significant expansion in employment by the organization requires that individuals must be induced to enter the labor market either from school, retirement, or more distant labor markets. Similarly, current employees have relatively few alternative employment opportunities available and must either withdraw from the labor force, or migrate to another labor market for employment if they reject employment by the dominant employer. The labor supply to the organization thus will be relatively inelastic, the entire labor force in the community being available for employment at a wide range of wage rates. The employing organization would possess relatively wide latitude in the establishment of rates of compensation, there being relatively few alternatives for employment, yet increases in rates of compensation would be relatively ineffective in attracting labor supplies beyond those available in the immediate labor market. By the same logic, relatively small employers in the labor market would encounter relatively elastic labor supplies and considerable upward pressure on rates of compensation; they would be unable to attract labor supplies at rates below those available in alternative employment, yet could attract significant increases in labor supplies at rates slightly above those of alternative employers.

The elasticity of labor supplies can be expected to vary with the specificity of skill requirements for employment and with the level of skills required. The more specific the job requirements for hiring, the smaller the available labor force from which the employing organization can draw and the less elastic labor supplies to the organization. The labor supply eligible for employment in jobs requiring only average physical health and a high school education will be larger than the supply eligible for jobs requiring very specific physical and/or skill characteristics. The labor supply for jobs with stringent educational, experiential, or skill requirements also will be less elastic than the supply for jobs with lower requirements; persons with skill capabilities can easily shift to jobs with lower requirements whereas considerable lead time may be required for lesser skilled persons to acquire higher skill capabilities.

Contrary to the assumptions of the labor market model, wage rates are not very flexible downwards as unemployed persons bid for jobs. Consequently, unemployment is present to greater or lesser degree at all times in every labor market, and the elasticity of labor supplies to the organization varies with the degree of unemployment in the labor market. Interestingly, the effects of unemployment upon the elasticity of labor supplies are different depending upon whether an increase in labor supply or a decrease in rates of compensation is considered. Consider, for example, an employer paying wage rates W and employing N people as indicated in Figure 3-2A. Given high unemployment in the labor market, relatively large numbers of additional persons are attracted to employment at wage W and the supply of labor for expansion is elastic at the current wage. Also, given high unem-

Figure 3-2: Labor supply relative to current wage *(W)* and current employment *(N)* under conditions of (A) unemployment and (B) full employment

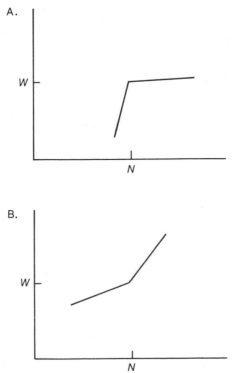

ployment, there are relatively few alternatives available for persons currently employed and relatively few current employees might be expected to leave if wage rates were lowered; the supply of labor is inelastic for wage decreases. Opposite relationships would be expected during periods of full employment, the labor supplies for expansion are inelastic as wages must be raised to attract people and supplies are inelastic for wage decreases as individuals leave for alternative employment (Figure 3-2B).

The discontinuity of the labor supply functions in Figures 3-2A and B at the point of current wage-employment relationships indicates that the relationship of labor supplies to wage rates may well vary depending upon whether one is "looking up" the supply function or "looking down" the supply function, whether one is analyzing the addition of new employees or the retention of current employees. Currently unemployed persons and persons actively seeking alternative employment are more likely to be aware of alternatives and more mobile in response to employment advantages than are persons satisfactorily employed. Those persons actively engaged in seeking employment opportunities are more likely to respond to changes in rates of compensation than are persons who are currently satisfied with their employment. Satisfactorily employed individuals have developed routines and ties to their current employment (which vary directly with tenure) and are not likely to be aware of or to change employers for relatively minor wage differentials. These individuals have acquired tenure rights, pension rights and other privileges which they would forego with a change of employers; they are aware of the full range of outcomes associated with that employment and have relatively certain expectancies regarding those outcomes. In consequence, we would expect that the supply of labor to an employer will tend to be relatively inelastic with respect to wage decreases, the degree of inelasticity varying with the tenure of employees, the rate of unemployment, and the number of readily available alternatives. We might reason also that current employees of an organization are more responsive to employment advantages or inducements other than compensation, employment characteristics such as closeness of supervision, working conditions, work pace and friendliness of co-workers, characteristics which the prospective employee cannot be aware of. Prospective employees normally are only aware of rate of compensation and general nature of the work, and will be more responsive to compensation differentials since this characteristic constitutes relatively more of the set of inducements known and considered. We consider later in more detail the different behaviors of joining and leaving an organization and reasons why the supply of prospective employees is likely to be more elastic with respect to compensation than is the supply of current employees.

Introduction to readings

Another approach to analysis of the elasticity of labor supplies conceives of wage rates in terms of cost of employment inducements to the employer regardless of the nature of these costs. Wage rate, in this context, reflects the cost of direct wages, fringe benefits, training, and the loss of productivity occasioned through employment of lesser skilled persons. Conceived in this manner, wage rate is not the cause of variation in labor supplies, it merely indexes the cost of whatever cause is considered. This approach is illustrated in the short reading from Cartter (Essay 3-5) where he analyzes the labor cost implications of alternate ways of varying labor supplies. He compares, for example, the cost of expanding labor supplies through scheduled over-time hours and through hiring additional employees. A similar type of analysis might be applied in comparing the labor costs associated with increasing relatively low cost employment inducements which reduce turnover and the labor costs associated with recruitment and training of new employees. The analytical approach illustrated in the Cartter reading can be usefully employed in a decision-making context, although it provides little guidance for assumptions concerning the responsiveness of labor supplies to change in rates of compensation.

Essay 3-6 by Lester Thurow in this section challenges the traditional model of aggregate labor supply behavior sketched above, what Thurow terms the "wage competition" model. Thurow characterizes the traditional model as one in which prospective workers compete with each other in terms of the wage they are willing to accept, and develops instead what he terms a "job competition" model in which individuals compete with each other based upon their relative costs of being trained to fill whatever job is considered. Briefly, Thurow argues that individuals are rarely hired fully qualified into jobs; rather, they acquire the necessary skills for job performance after being hired. Prior education, skill training, and employment experience as well as intelligence, values, and aptitude may facilitate development of the required job skills but do not serve as a substitute for skill development through performance. Prospective employees can be viewed as ordered in a "labor queue" based upon background and personal characteristics rather than willingness to accept lower wages for employment. Job opportunities also are ordered in terms of skills and presumably wages. Individuals are allocated to job opportunities depending upon ordering of the labor queue and the distribution of job opportunities. In this conceptualization, wages are attached to job opportunities but are not influenced by specific labor supplies for those job opportunities. Labor supplies are not differentiated into very specific skill groupings associated with related jobs. Rather, the background characteristics of persons allocated into specific jobs vary with the distribution of opportunities in the job queue and the qualifications of persons in the labor queue. Individuals seek high paying jobs and are employed in the highest paying job to which their position in the labor queue qualifies them. Practically speaking, this means that the qualifications of workers available for employment with an organization, not the number of persons, vary with the relative position of the employer's jobs within the job queue and the distribution of qualifications in the labor queue. An employer might face a very elastic supply of individuals seeking employment with the organization, but the qualifications of these workers and their capacities for learning the required skills vary with the relative wages of the employer and the distribution of worker qualifications in the labor queue. Thurow's analysis highlights two points. First, the elasticity of labor supplies conceived in terms of number of persons and conceived in terms of implied productive capabilities may be quite different; a large number of persons may offer themselves for employment at a single wage rate while the per unit labor cost of production may vary considerably among these persons because of different levels of capacity for production. Whether it is more profitable to raise wage rates and compete for higher qualified persons or to maintain wage rates and pay higher labor costs because of lower productivity is problematic and will vary with specific circumstances. Later readings suggest that the adjustment of hiring qualifications probably is more frequent than adjustment of wage rates. Another point brought out in Thurow's analysis relates to the responsiveness of labor supplies to variation in job opportunities. Thurow argues that since job skills are largely acquired through employment, supplies of job skills expand and contract in response to employment opportunities rather than in response to changes in wage rates. Thurow observes elsewhere that relative occupational wage rates have remained unchanged for the past 20 years despite significant changes in the occupational structure of the labor force. Aggregate labor supplies appear to respond to change in the number of employment opportunities available regardless of the wage structure.

Thurow's attribution of elasticity of labor supplies to number of employment opportunities parallels the importance attributed to expectancy in Vroom's model where the attractiveness of an employment opportunity depends critically upon the expectancy of employment. Significant change in the expectancies of employment without change in rates of compensation would alter considerably labor supply decisions predicted by the expectancy model. While Thurow and Vroom reason from different conceptual bases, they both conclude that opportunities for employment probably are a more relevant and easily manipulated cause of change in labor supplies to the firm than are wage rates. Both consider labor supplies in terms of number of persons attracted to an employment opportunity, not the quality or productivity of those persons. The relative cost of labor services of more and less qualified employees can be approached with an analysis similar to Cartter's and will depend critically upon the nature of tasks involved and the amount of training provided after employment.

Essay **3-5**

*Supply of labor to the firm**

Allan M. Cartter

The slope of the labor supply curve may be affected under certain types of wage payments by differences in the efficiency of workers. For example, assume that we arrange the available workers in order of their efficiency, so that, beginning at the left on a graphic supply function the first labor units are those of the most efficient workers, the units of less efficient workers falling further to the right. The labor supply curve measured in terms of "efficiency

*Reprinted from Allan M. Cartter, *Theory of Wages and Employment* (Homewood, Ill.: Richard D. Irwin, 1959), pp. 54-59. © 1959 by Richard D. Irwin, Inc.

units," would therefore be upward sloping. If the same wage is paid to two workers, one of whom is the equivalent of, say,
three labor (efficiency) units and one of
whom is the equivalent of only two efficiency units, then the wage rate per labor
(efficiency) unit will be 50 percent higher
for the less efficient worker. This upward-
sloping supply curve would also be true
for "decreasing piece rates"; while straight
piece-rate payment would not affect the
slope of the curve.

If an employer is going to successfully
hire workers in direct order of their efficiency, there are, as Reynolds has pointed
out,[1] at least three necessary conditions:
he must be free to hire without restrictions (such as seniority rules, closed shop,
etc.), he must have access simultaneously
to all available workers in the market, and
he must have some satisfactory means of
predicting performance. While these conditions are never perfectly fulfilled, it
must be presumed that in these days of
large personnel departments with batteries
of testing devices, employers on the average do at least a little better than chance
in selecting the most efficient available
workers. Since better than four fifths of
production workers are paid on a time or
decreasing piece-rate basis, it therefore
seems reasonable to assume that the labor
supply curve to the individual firm has a
slight positive slope for all additions to
the labor force, the slope becoming much
steeper the nearer the firm comes to exhausting the available supply of unemployed labor.

But what of decreases in employment?
What is the shape of the supply curve for
lower levels of employment than the current one? Two different shapes seem most
probable. If an employer were to lay off
workers in reverse order of efficiency,
then the positive slope of the labor supply
curve would be applicable throughout its

length. If, however, a firm takes seniority
into account, the shape may be quite different. Assume, for example, that an employer follows a strict seniority rule in
layoffs. Assume, also, that jobs in this
particular firm require a certain amount
of skill and experience, that a substantial
amount of physical exertion and mental
alertness is required, and that all workers
are paid the same hourly rate (although
possibly there are moderate supplements
based on seniority). If this is the case, the
most efficient workers in the firm's employ are most likely to be those who have
been employed for more than a year or
two, but who are still relatively young in
age. This kind of labor supply curve for
declining levels of employment is indicated in Figure 1. OK is the original level
of employment. As employment declines
from K to J, workers of increasingly
higher efficiency are laid off, as indicated
by the lower wage cost per unit of labor.
As employment declines further, successively older workers are laid off until, at
G, we are left only with a handful of
laborers who are just ready for retirement.
Note that at the original wage level, OW,
units HK were being underpaid for their
services, while units OH were overpaid. If
there are substantial training costs of new
employees, it is possible that both the old-
est and newest employees will be overpaid

Figure 1

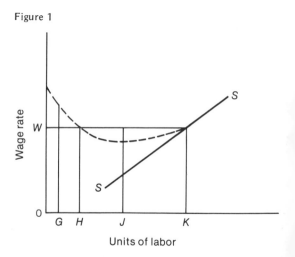

[1] L. G. Reynolds, "Some Aspects of Labor Market
Structure," in R. A. Lester and J. Shister (eds.), *Insights
into Labor Issues* (New York: The Macmillan Co., 1949).

for their services, at the expense of the young-but-experienced workers. Professor Bronfenbrenner, from whom I have borrowed this concept,[2] suggests that this may be a reason why industry is tending to hire more vocationally trained persons from the high schools and colleges (shifting backwards the incidence of training costs) and at the same time tending to lower the age of retirement.

For the general case of labor supply it seems most logical, in view of the preceding, to assume a gently upward-sloping curve for the individual employer (assuming other wages constant), the function becoming considerably less elastic as the margin of full employment is reached. We would also expect the function to be less elastic the larger the share of total employment in the area accounted for by the particular firm, since the greater the monopsonistic element, the more the individual employer would see the wage effects of an increase in employment.

SOME VARIANTS OF THE SHORT-RUN WAGE-EMPLOYMENT EQUILIBRIUM

In the usually illustrated case of a labor market free of monopoly and monopsony elements, with smooth and continuous supply and demand functions, the determination of wages is a simple matter. In Figure 2, for example, the equilibrium price would be at *OW*, with employment *OA*. . . . In the short run, a firm would be minimizing its losses if it shut down when the wage rate was above the average revenue product curve; this is the same as saying that a firm would minimize its short-run losses if it shut down when the price of the product fell below average variable (operating) costs.

Critics of the marginal productivity principle often point to the short-run sta-

Figure 2

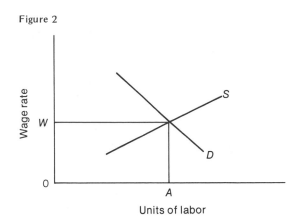

Units of labor

bility of employment in many firms despite changes in labor supply or demand as evidence that the real labor market does not look like that portrayed in Figure 2. We have already suggested two reasons why an employer may not make a small marginal adjustment in the rate of employment in response to a shift in labor supply or demand, and it may be useful to repeat these and add to them a third possibility.

1. In many instances the technical production function is such that a firm has, in the short run, almost fixed labor requirements. Thus, the demand for labor may be almost perfectly inelastic at technical capacity, the demand rising vertically up to the point where it would pay the employer to shut down completely. In this case, shifts in labor supply would tend to have only a wage effect, and shifts in the demand for the firm's product would be reflected only in the rising or lowering of the shutdown point at the top of the firm's MRP function. This would be the case where there was a single indivisible process, capable of operating only at a single rate of output.

2. If a firm sells in a market characterized by oligopoly (with a homogeneous product), the demand for its product may appear kinked for the familiar reasons of different anticipated price responses by competitors for price increases and price

[2] "Potential Monopsony in Labor Market," *Indust. and Labor Rel. Rev.* (July 1956), pp. 577-88.

decreases. ... the discontinuity in the firm's marginal revenue function will also be reflected in the derived demand for the factors of production. Thus a shift in the supply schedule, if it still cut through the "gap" in the labor demand, would result in no change in employment. If this is a logical explanation of short-run oligopolistic behavior in the product market, then there is logic in the conclusion of a zero short-run employment effect. If the firm is restrained from making a price change, then *ceteris paribus* there will be no change in quantity demanded, and therefore no change in the amount of labor needed to produce that level of output in the short run. It is only when we forget that the wage-employment relationship is really a four-cornered wage-price-output-employment relationship that the lack of response of employment to a wage change seems anomalous.

3. A third possible reason for the lack of marginal adjustment in employment in response to a small change in labor supply or demand is the existence in some kinds of employments of substantial training costs for new employees. Let us imagine a hypothetical case where the wage rate is $1.00 per hour, but the hiring of a new worker involves the employer in a training cost over a period of three months of, say, $300. (Since an employee would earn approximately $600 in this period, we may assume that for the first three months he produces at only 50 percent of the output expected of him at the end of the training period.) Training costs will discourage an employer from expanding his labor force unless he is relatively certain that the increased demand is going to be more than a brief occurrence. If, for example, he thought that he would only need the additional employee for a period of six months, the training costs, spread over this period, would raise the average hourly wage cost of this worker from $1.00 to approximately $1.20. If the employer anticipated a need for this marginal worker of approximately a year, his average hourly wage cost for this year would appear to be approximately $1.10, etc. Only if the need for the extra man appeared to be permanent would the training cost appear insignificant. Thus the cost of the added worker would be not merely a function of his wage rate and the training cost involved, but would appear also as a function of the degree of certainty as to the permanency of the need.

Diagrammatically we might illustrate this as in Figure 3. Employment is currently *OA*, and the wage rate *OW*. The relevant supply schedule to the right of *P*, however, would depend upon the assumed permanency of the demand for labor, when it shifted from *D* to *D'*. If this level of demand were thought to be of a quite temporary nature (say, six months), then the relevant supply schedule would appear to be that denoted by *S''*. If the increase in demand were thought to be for a year, then *S'* would be the relevant supply function for added workers. If the increase were thought permanent, then *S* would continue unbroken to the right of *P*. In the example illustrated in Figure 3, only if the new level of demand could be counted on for more than a year would it be profitable to expand employment beyond level *OA*. Substantial training costs are obviously a deterrent to the expansion of employment when there is a high degree of uncertainty concerning the future level of demand, and thus some employers may appear quite unresponsive to short-run variations in demand.

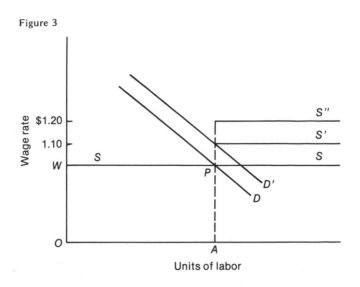

Figure 3

Essay 3-6

Supply of job skills*

Lester C. Thurow

In the job-competition model, instead of competing against one another based on the wages that they are willing to accept, individuals compete against one another for job opportunities based on their relative costs of being trained to fill whatever job is being considered. Hence the new model will be called "job competition" to distinguish it from the old "wage competition" forms of marginal productivity.

To make the presentation as clear as possible and to highlight the differences between wage competition and job competition, the job-competition model will be developed *as if* it exists in isolation and is the sole market clearing mechanism. This is a pedagogical device and not meant to imply that wage competition

*Excerpted from Lester C. Thurow, *Generating Inequality: Mechanisms of Distribution in the U.S. Economy* (New York: Basic Books, 1975), pp. 75-81. © 1975 by Basic Books, Inc., Publishers, New York.

never exists. Wage competition and job competition are not mutually exclusive. Both could, and probably do, coexist as alternative mechanisms for clearing labor markets. In some labor markets wage competition may dominate; in other labor markets job competition may dominate. Over time, the mixture of one or the other may change. The author believes that there is a continuum between wage competition and job competition and that the American economy lies somewhere between these two extremes. The "as if" assumption is used to clarify the role of job competition by separating its impacts from those of wage competition.

The key ingredient in the job-competition model is the observation that most cognitive job skills are not acquired before a worker enters the labor market but after he has found employment through on-the-job training programs (see below). Thus, the labor market is not primarily a bidding market for selling existing skills but a training market where training slots must be allocated to different workers. The distribution of training slots and the allocation of individuals among these slots depend upon two sets of factors.

One set of factors determines an individual's *relative* position in the labor queue; another set of factors, not mutually exclusive of the first, determines the actual distribution of job opportunities in the economy. Wages are paid based on the characteristics of the job in question, and workers are distributed across job (training) opportunities based on their relative position in the labor queue. The most preferred workers get the best jobs. In this context a job is best thought of as a lifetime sequence of jobs rather than as a specific job with a specific employer. The labor queue is competitive, but workers compete for position based upon their background characteristics rather than on their willingness to accept low wages. As we shall see, the training function of the labor market makes the repression of direct wage competition profitable.

To some extent the job-competition model reverses the normal assumptions about short-run and long-run market clearing mechanisms. In the wage-competition model, wages fluctuate in the short run to clear markets, and these wage changes then induce shifts in the long-run supply and demand curves. In the job-competition model, supply and demand curves shift in the short run to clear markets. Markets clear by altering hiring requirements and the amount of on-the-job training they provide. Changes in relative wages occur only after a substantial period of disequilibrium in relative wages, if at all.

If you like to think in marginal-productivity terms, the marginal product resides in the job and not in the man. The individual's earnings depend upon the job he acquires and not directly upon his own personal characteristics. Since the individual is trained into the productivity of the job he holds, the job allocation procedure assumes a much greater importance than it does in wage competition, where an individual's skills automatically place him in some particular job market.

Given the factors that determine an individual's position in the labor queue and given the factors that determine the distribution of jobs or lifetime income ladders, it is possible to see how earnings are allocated across the work force or, more accurately, to see how individuals are allocated across the job or earnings opportunities that exist in the labor market. This is one of the key inversions of the job-competition model. People are allocated across earnings or job opportunities; there are no equilibrium wages that should be paid people based on their personal qualifications as workers upon entry into the labor force.

THE SUPPLY OF SKILLS

In neoclassical theory the labor market exists to match labor demands with labor supplies. In the matching process, or in the mismatching process, various signals are given. Businesses are told to raise wages and redesign jobs in sectors with skill shortages. In surplus sectors they are told to lower wages. Individuals are told to acquire skills in high wage areas and discouraged from acquiring jobs and skills in low wage areas. In the process each skill market is cleared with increases or reductions in wages in the short run and by a combination of wage changes, skill changes, and production process changes in the long run.

The key ingredient in this view of the world is the assumption that workers acquire laboring skills exogenously in formal education and/or training and then bring these skills into the labor market. Possessing skills, they bid for the jobs that use these skills. Unfortunately, the underlying assumption does not seem to be correct for the American economy. Workers do not bring fully developed job skills into the labor market. Most cognitive job skills, general or specific, are acquired either formally or informally through on-the-job training after a worker finds an entry job and the associated promotion ladder.

The evidence for this is very clear for the American economy. In the 1960s the President's Automation Commission undertook extensive surveys on how workers learned the actual cognitive job skills they were using.[1] Their surveys found that only 40 percent of the work force reported that they were using any skill that they had acquired in formal training programs or in specialized education. Most of this 40 percent reported that some of the skills they were using had been acquired in informal, casual, on-the-job training. The remaining 60 percent acquired *all* of their job skills through informal, casual, on-the-job training. Even among college graduates, over two-thirds reported that they had acquired cognitive skills through informal, casual processes on the job.

Perhaps the most convincing evidence in this direction came when the survey asked workers to list the form of training that had been the most helpful in acquiring their current job skills. Only 12 percent of the work force listed formal training and specialized education. (Some of this was also done at their place of work and was directly dependent upon their already having been selected for the job in question.)

Although initially surprising, the results are not without an easy explanation. Most job skills are best taught in conjunction with the job in question, since training and production are complementary pro-

ducts. Goods and services produced in the process of training can be sold to lower training costs. Only actual production generates the degree of realism necessary to polish production skills. It is also the only way to guarantee that the worker will know everything he needs to know without having to learn lots of things he does not need to know. On-the-job training from one worker to another is simply the cheapest method of training.[2]

As a result, the labor market is not a market where fully developed skills bid for jobs. Rather, it is primarily a market where supplies of trainable labor are matched with training opportunities that are in turn directly associated with the number of job openings that exist. Training opportunities only occur when there is a job opening that creates the demand for the skills in question.

This situation has a profound effect on the labor market, since it means that the supply and demand curves for different types of workers are not independent. Because most skills are acquired on the job, skills are only created when there is a demand for labor with that skill. People are only trained when a job opening exists. This leads to a situation where the supply of trained labor depends upon the demand for trained labor. Thinking in terms of simple supply and demand curves (Chart 1), the supply curve lies along the demand curve as long as the wage rate is above some opportunity wage and high enough to attract trainable labor to this particular job opportunity. If the actual wage for a particular job happens to be above the opportunity wage, training will not proceed down to the level dictated by the opportunity wage (q_0) but will stop at the level dictated by the actual wage (q_1).

Given identical supply and demand curves, it is obviously impossible to deter-

---

[1] U.S. Department of Labor, *Formal Occupational Training of Adult Workers*, Manpower Automation Research Monograph No. 2 (Washington, D.C.: Government Printing Office, 1964), pp. 3, 18, 20, 43.

[2] At the extreme, the two may be joint products and inseparable. This is clearly the case when unique equipment exists.

mine an equilibrium wage rate at the intersection of the relevant supply and demand curves. They do not intersect; they coincide. Thus, there is no supply curve in the normal sense of that word. For every exogenously given wage, the demand (and supply) curve determines how many jobs openings will exist and how many workers will be trained. The demand curve cannot, however, determine a wage by itself. The wage must come from elsewhere in the economic system (see below). It is also not determined by a process of competive bidding between potential suppliers and demanders—there are few, if any, independent potential suppliers of the desired skills.

In the process of normal job turnover or as the result of business cycles, individuals may acquire cognitive job skills and be unemployed, but, as we shall see later, even this limited supply of trained labor is restricted in its ability to bid back into their old job categories. To allow them to bid back into their old job categories at lower wages would bring on-the-job training to a halt and be counterproductive in the long run.

4
COMPENSATION AND REWARD
CONCEPTS AND MEASURES

E mployee compensation is the primary inducement offered in exchange
for the contributions of labor services in the employment contract; it
is the single characteristic of an employment exchange upon which all
will agree that "more is better." Other characteristics of the employment
exchange such as hours worked, location, responsibility, and nature of the
task may be valued or disliked, perceived as inducements or contributions,
depending upon the utility or valence function of the individual. These other
characteristics of the employment exchange may prove to be more powerful
than compensation as influences of behavior in any specific instance, but
behavioral responses to compensation are more predictable over a range of
individuals and situations. These other characteristics of the employment
exchange must be taken into account in the design and administration of
compensation, but the primary focus of our attention will be the influence
of compensation upon behavior.

Employee compensation is viewed alternatively as an inducement to elicit
labor services and as a reward for services performed, two related concepts
with subtle and significant differences. An inducement is an incentive to
behavior, a proferred reward, receipt of which is contingent upon some
specified occurrence. Inducements or incentives are meaningful in terms of
ex ante analysis of the employment exchange such as implied in the analyses
of decision making in the earlier section. Decisions, in those analyses, were
based upon anticipated rewards or inducements to behavior. Rewards, on the
other hand, are experienced and influence the individual's *post hoc* evaluation of the employment exchange rather than the prior evaluation and
decision making. Rewards and incentives clearly are related in the sense that
experienced rewards serve as a source of anticipations of future rewards,
anticipations which also are related to experiences of others and promises
of future rewards. Rewards experienced yesterday, condition expectations
of incentives for tomorrow. However, rewards and incentives serve different
functions in the employment exchange; only incentives or reward anticipations can influence labor supply behavior dependent upon individual decision making, while experienced rewards influence directly satisfaction
resulting from the exchange.

Incentives influence decision making and behavior to the extent that
anticipated rewards are perceived to be contingent upon some prior event or
qualification. Rewards, on the other hand, may be gratifying whether experienced as contingent upon prior qualification or not. Perception of a contingency relationship between anticipated rewards and some prior qualification serves to direct attention and behavior toward achievement of that
qualification as means to experiencing the anticipated reward. The expec-

tancy model presented by Vroom relies heavily upon these contingency relationships; the motivational force to behave in a particular way varies directly with expectancy of desired outcomes associated with that behavior. In this context, contingency relationships between incentives and prior qualifications are as critical as the form and amount of inducement provided in the employment exchange. We can differentiate among rewards contingent solely upon membership in the organization, upon job or task performed, and upon specific behaviors or outcomes of behavior within the job. Compensation for membership would include benefits such as insurance, vacations, and anniversary awards provided all employees and varying only on the basis of tenure with the organization; the concept of wage level developed later in this chapter also typifies the amount of compensation provided on the basis of membership. Job or task compensation includes special rates of compensation which vary with job assignments, compensation such as shift differentials and skill differentials. Piece-rate incentives, performance awards, bonuses, and attendance awards typify rewards contingent upon individual performance within the job assignment. Variations in these contingency relationships presumably serve to motivate the different types of performance upon which rewards are contingent.

Another aspect of rewards which figures in many analyses relates to the extrinsic or intrinsic nature of the reward. Extrinsic rewards are conceived as rewards where the contingency relationship between performance and reward is mediated by some person or process not involved directly in the performance; intrinsic rewards are contingent upon some performance but are not mediated by an external influence, they are experienced directly by the individual. Commonly cited examples of extrinsic rewards include monetary compensation, awards, promotion, and praise; intrinsic rewards would include sense of accomplishment and pride of achievement, exhileration, and fun of task performance. The relevance of the distinction between extrinsic and intrinsic rewards relates to the role of mediation between performance and reward. Extrinsic rewards require careful administration of the mediating relationship in order to be effective, intrinsic rewards require no such mediation. Both intrinsic and extrinsic outcomes of behavior can be punishing as well as rewarding, however, and extrinsic rewards provide the opportunity to manipulate contingencies not permitted with intrinsic rewards. Finally, the conceptual distinctions between extrinsic and intrinsic rewards are not always easy to operationalize in practice; sense of accomplishment and pride of achievement, for example, may be as much a function of mediated recognition of task performance as a function of the performance itself. We return to consideration of intrinsic rewards later in Chapter 9.

While the concepts of reward and incentive are relatively straightforward, application of these concepts is more involved. Any characteristic of the employment exchange is potentially rewarding depending upon individual perceptions and valuations of the characteristic, and given the diversity of individual differences, it is difficult to generalize about specific rewards. Even the distinction between inducement and contribution becomes confusing in application; anything associated with work and employment is potentially a contribution or an inducement to the individual. Employment itself may be a source of status and gratification to one individual and a symbol of oppression and dependency to another. Various theories of motivation have attempted to identify the sources of gratification which give meaning to different reward characteristics. One well-known formulation of human needs and motivations is Maslow's need hierarchy theory. The human being is conceived as "wanting," as desirous of satisfying certain innate needs. Any characteristic of the employment exchange which serves to satisfy one of these needs is rewarding. Maslow posits five categories of need which he attributes to most individuals, (1) physiological needs, (2) safety needs, (3) needs for belongingness, (4) esteem needs, and (5) needs for self-actualization. An unsatisfied need creates tension in the individual leading to behavior designed to reduce tension. Any satisfied need loses potency as a motivating force until that satisfaction is dissipated or need aspiration levels increase creating renewed tension. Maslow also hypothesizes that needs are structured in a hierarchical fashion, higher order needs achieving potency only as the more basic, lower order needs are satisfied. Thus hunger can serve as a motivating force only for a hungry person, other needs achieving prominence as hunger is satisfied. Employee compensation and other characteristics of the employment exchange influence individual behavior only as they relate to these basic human needs and individual levels of need satisfaction. While Maslow's model has influenced much writing about motivation, it lacks empirical validation and remains an interesting, speculative model of motivation.

An analysis somewhat more to the point of work motivation and compensation is presented in Essay 4-1 from Vroom. Vroom identifies five properties of employment opportunities and examines the motivational implications of these properties. Wage income, expenditure of energy, production of goods or services, social interaction, and social status are the five properties considered. Vroom argues that although wage income is an important property of employment opportunities, the importance of wage income varies among individuals and work provides rewards other than income which are important. The properties of work considered by Vroom are analogous to the advantages and disadvantages of work considered by Adam Smith in the sense that the properties are conceptually additive in the determination of overall net advantage or motivational force associated with employment.

Essay 4-2 by Opsahl and Dunnette focuses more specifically upon financial compensation as a source of employee motivation. They examine a number of dimensions of employee compensation in relation to motivation theories. One such dimension concerns the form of compensation and the role of money in motivation. They observe that money possesses no intrinsic reward characteristics but may have achieved meaning as a generalized conditioned reinforcer, as an anxiety reducer or as an instrument for gaining desired rewards. The instrumental interpretation of money probably is more commonly accepted (one works to achieve a desired standard of living) but money can also be observed to serve as a generalized conditioned reinforcer when individuals work to achieve "more" despite a lack of specific intentions for the instrumental use of the money achieved. Employee compensation takes forms other than money, forms such as pension rights, medical and life insurance, and related fringe benefits. One rationale for providing

compensation in forms other than money relates to cost, greater amounts
of certain fringe benefits can be purchased with pretax dollars by the employer than could be purchased with equivalent monetary compensation by
the employee. Another rationale concerns employee valuations of different
forms of compensation, employees often value different forms of compensation in ways other than indicated by economic cost or value. These differences in employee valuation of forms of compensation have led many to
advocate "cafeteria" styles of compensation permitting employee choice
among compensation forms as a means of achieving greatest motivational
impact from any given expenditure of funds. Opsahl and Dunnette also
examine other characteristics of compensation, particularly compensation
policies, contingencies and schedules of payment, as they relate to individual
motivation. They suggest that these characteristics of compensation influence motivation independently of the amount of compensation involved,
issues which we examine in more detail in later chapters.

The selection from Ross (Essay 4-3) examines concepts and measures of
compensation which figure importantly in economic analyses of compensation and which serve to structure decisions concerning the determination
and administration of compensation. These concepts are wage rate, wage
level, and wage structure.

Wage rate refers to the basis for determination of earnings or compensation and typically is stated in terms of a specified amount per unit of time
worked (hour, week, month) or in terms of a specified amount per unit of
output produced (commission, piece-rate). The compensation due the individual at any point is determined by applying this rate to either the time
worked or the production achieved. The most common form of wage rate
currently is based on time worked rather than production achieved; even
employment which is compensated as some function of production (typically sales employment) often is guaranteed some minimum time rate with
compensation related to production provided as a supplement. Wage rates
may vary from employer to employer, job to job, and among persons within
the same job.

Wage level is an abstraction of wage rate referring usually to the concept
of average or typical wage rate for persons in a job, jobs within an organization, or employers within a labor market. The concept of wage level
typically is not applied to an individual except in those instances where the
individual's earnings vary over time. When applied to a broader grouping,
wage level refers to some average of the group and, since there are various
ways of computing averages, there is no single definition of wage level always
employed in these computations.

Wage structure is a concept applied when referring to a number of wage
rates or wage levels and it focuses upon relationships and differentials among
these rates or levels. Rather than averaging to obtain a single measure, the
concept of wage structure identifies differentials as a primary characteristic
of concern and interest. Differentials may be stated in either absolute dollars
or percentage terms depending upon custom as, for example, in wage policies
dictating payment of 5 percent more than the market level or payment of
supervisors at $100 a month more than subordinates.

The concepts of wage rate, level, and structure differ in relevance to the employer and employee as do the most appropriate measures of each. Wage rate, for example, is of direct and immediate relevance to the employee since it is the basis for determining earnings and rewards for employment. In most instances, it is difficult for an employer to assess the specific economic worth or value of a job or an individual. Thus, while wage rate measures the cost of the job or individual, the employer cannot easily compare that cost with a corresponding measure of value. Rather, the concept of wage level relates more closely with labor cost of production which has direct relevance in comparison with product price. The most appropriate measure of wage level conceptualized as labor cost is an average job wage rate weighted by the number of persons employed at each wage rate. A concept of wage level also characterizes the general employment opportunities of an organization to prospective applicants who are unlikely to be familiar with specific wage rates paid in that organization; the appropriate measure of wage level in this instance is likely to be an arithmetic average of job wage rates, however, characterizing the range of wage rates paid. While the wage structure reflects specific wage rates paid in an organization and influences the measurement of wage level, consideration of wage structure characteristics is more relevant to current employees of an organization than to potential applicants; wage structure characteristics influence employee valuations of wage rate relative to others in the same organization. Each of these concepts is elaborated in later chapters as it relates to motivation, behavior, and compensation administration.

Essay *4-1*

Motivational bases of work*

Victor H. Vroom

At some time during their lives virtually every man and about four out of every five women are members of the labor force (Bancroft, 1958). Working by both men and women is so commonplace that the question why people work is seldom asked. We are much more likely to wonder why people climb mountains, drive sports cars, or commit suicide than to question the motivational basis of the decision to work. If asked directly why they

*From Victor H. Vroom, *Work and Motivation* (New York: John Wiley and Sons, 1964), pp. 29-44 (abridged). Copyright © 1964 by John Wiley and Sons, Inc. Reprinted by permission.

work, most individuals would probably give a simple answer. They work because there is work to be done, because they like work, or because they need to earn a living. Although these answers contain a grain of truth, their apparent simplicity obscures what is, on close examination, an extremely complex and basic problem. In the balance of this essay we deal with this problem in more detail, drawing on any research findings which bear on its solution.

When the scientist asks why a phenomenon occurs, he typically means "under what conditions does it occur." Consequently when we ask "why do people work," we mean "under what conditions do they work." There are two types of conditions that affect the likelihood that people will work. One is economic in nature. In order for people to work there must be some opportunity to work. There must be a demand on the part of members of a society for goods and services and a demand on the part of employers for people to produce these goods and perform these services. The second type of condition is motivational. People must prefer working to not working. Our model leads us to predict that given the opportunity a person will choose to work when the valence of outcomes which he expects to attain from working are more positive than the valence of outcomes which he expects to attain from not working.

These two types of conditions—economic and motivational—may vary independently from one another. There may be a larger number of job vacancies than there are people seeking work, or there may be a larger number of people who prefer to work than there are job vacancies. Both sets of conditions must exist to the same degree in order for there to be full employment.

It is the motivational aspect of this problem which is of interest to us here. In the remainder of this essay we will seek an answer to the question "why people work" by looking at the motivational significance of outcomes which are attained through working.

There are two ways in which we can approach this problem. We can start with some conception of the motives or needs of man and then ask in what ways these motives are gratified or frustrated by working; or we can begin with some conception of the consequences of participation in work roles and then ask what motivational implications these consequences have. In view of the difficulty in formulating a meaningful list of motives

which are common to all persons, the latter would appear to be the more parsimonious approach and will be used here. In the remainder of this essay we discuss the motivational implications of the following properties of employment work roles.

1. They provide *wages* to the role occupant in return for his services.
2. They require from the role occupant the *expenditure of mental or physical energy.*
3. They permit the role occupant to contribute to the *production of goods or services.*
4. They permit or require of the role occupant *social interaction* with other persons.
5. They define, at least in part, the *social status* of the role occupant.

WAGES

One indisputable source of the desire of people to work is the money they are paid for working. Although we may disagree with the monolithic conception of the classical "economic man," few people would dispute the importance of anticipated economic consequences in the guidance of human conduct. Despite the old saw that "money can't buy happiness," it can be exchanged for many commodities which are necessary for survival and comfort.

It would be incorrect to link the importance of money in our society strictly to the satisfaction of biological needs. The goods and services that are purchased with money go far beyond insuring survival. They serve, among other things, as an indicator of social status of the purchaser.

The weekly or monthly paycheck by no means represents the only form of financial remuneration. Originally restricted to wages, the economic outcomes derived from the occupancy of work roles now include a wide range of fringe benefits including retirement programs, life and health insurance plans, free meals, and free recreational and educational programs.

Although economic factors undoubtedly play an important part in the decision to work, it is highly improbable that they are the only inducements.

THE EXPENDITURE OF ENERGY

All work roles require some energy expenditure. This energy may be expended in physical activity, in mental activity or, as is true for most work, in both. Any discussion of "why men work" would be incomplete without some mention of the affective consequences of energy expenditure.

Virtually all general theories of behavior postulate that dissatisfaction results from energy expenditure. Hull (1943), for example, postulated that making any response in the presence of a stimulus results in an increase in a drive-like state called reactive inhibition which reduces the strength of the response. Reactive inhibition is an increasing function of the amount of work involved in the performance of the response in question and is hypothesized to decrease with the passage of time according to a simple decay or negative growth function.

Some writers, however, have suggested exactly the opposite notion. They propose that the expenditure of effort is basically satisfying rather than dissatisfying.

In support of such an idea it has been customary to point to the reports of many persons concerning the feeling of physical well-being that they derive from hard physical labor. Some recent experimental evidence with animals provided a stronger empirical basis for this notion. Hill (1956) reports that rats will run in an activity wheel in proportion to the amount of time their activity has been restricted. The confinement cages contained food and water making it difficult to explain the behavior in terms of these tissue needs and related drive stimulation. In interpreting these findings, Hill suggests that there is an activity drive which is related in strength to the amount of activity deprivation.

The problem of the affective consequences of energy expenditure is central to the relationship between work and motivation, but its solution appears rather complex and probably entails both innate and learned mechanisms. It does seem safe to conclude that the physical and mental effort which is involved in work is not solely a source of negative affect. There are probably conditions, e.g., continued inactivity and certain early socialization conditions, under which people derive satisfaction from energy expenditure. Some industrial studies lend support to such a notion. Friedmann and Havighurst's study of coal miners (1954) and Morse and Weiss' study of a national sample of employed workers (1955) indicate that a large proportion of workers state that they like their work because it keeps them busy and active and would dislike not working because they would have nothing to do with their time and dislike being idle. There may be important individual differences in the affective consequences of energy expenditure or in the specific forms of energy expenditure which are sources of satisfaction. So far we can only speculate concerning possible answers to these problems. Their solution awaits further research.

THE PRODUCTION OF GOODS AND SERVICES

Work roles involve not only the expenditure of energy but energy expenditure for some purpose. The mental and physical effort is directed toward the production of goods or services—to the assembly of transistors, or the growing of food, or the curing of the sick. Our interest here is in the motivational implications of these functional properties of work roles. To what extent and in what ways do the particular functions involved in a work role represent a source of satisfaction or dissatisfaction to the worker?

A great deal has been written about the pleasures and frustrations associated with different kinds of jobs. Historians have described the enjoyment that the craftsman during the Middle Ages obtained from plying his trade, novelists have described the dedication of the scientist and the artist, and social critics have assailed the plight of the modern industrial worker. Although such observations lack the objectivity and rigor demanded by the scientist, they do underscore the difficulty of drawing any firm conclusions on this problem without at least specifying the form of work being considered, if not the person who carried it out.

Beginning about 1950, research in experimental psychology using animal subjects has contributed a new perspective to the problem. Since that date there have been numerous references to rewarding properties of outcomes which are not easily reducible to physiological needs or drives and suggest a motivational system which is more akin to the self-actualization tendencies proposed by Goldstein (1940) and Maslow (1955). In brief, the data suggest that higher organisms are rewarded by the opportunity to explore and manipulate their environment.

This development, along with parallel trends in psychoanalytic theory and general psychology, has led White (1959) to propose the concept of effectance motivation:

Effectance motivation must be conceived to involve satisfaction—a feeling of efficacy—in transactions in which behavior has an exploratory, varying, experimental character and produces changes in the stimulus field. Having this character, the behavior leads the organism to find out how the environment can be changed and what consequences flow from these changes (p. 329).

White argues convincingly that effectance motivation is not learned through association with primary drive reduction. The feeling of efficacy is innately satisfying. He does suggest, however, that learning results in the differentiation of effectance motivation and makes it profitable in adults "to distinguish various motives such as cognizance, construction, mastery, and achievement" (p. 323).

Working may also serve a moral purpose for the worker. Many work roles provide their occupants with an opportunity to contribute to the happiness and well-being of their fellow man. The physician reduces the pain and prolongs the life of his patients; the teacher broadens the intellectual horizons of his students; the policeman protects members of the community against those who would break its laws; and the minister enriches the spiritual life of his congregation. Even when the actual value of a worker's contribution to society is more problematic, it may not be so viewed by the worker. People seem to cognitively structure their world so as to provide moral justification for their labors. Members of the armed forces charged with wholesale destruction of the enemy may view themselves as preservers of freedom; lawyers, hired to defend clients whom they believe to be guilty, may view themselves as defenders of the judicial system; and scientists involved in the development of weapon systems of frightening destructive power may stress their role in extending the frontiers of knowledge.

There is no doubt that the magnitude or nature of these satisfactions may vary greatly from one job to another or that the sources of satisfaction from jobs are different for different people. We still have much to learn about the nature of the interaction between the task or functional properties of work roles and the motivational systems of their occupants.

SOCIAL INTERACTION

Social psychologists typically emphasize the fact that work is a social activity. Virtually all work roles require social interaction with other people. The salesman interacts with his customers, the doctor with his patients, the supervisor with his subordinates, and the teacher with his students. Furthermore, most workers are members of one or more work groups, with whom they may interact more frequently than with members of their immediate family.

It has frequently been suggested that the social outcomes provided by the work role may constitute an important factor in the decision to work. Miller and Form (1951) state

> The motives for working cannot be assigned only to economic needs, for men may continue to work even though they have no need for material goods. Even when their security and that of their children is assured, they continue to labor. Obviously this is so because the rewards they get from work are social, such as respect and admiration from their fellow men.... For all, work activity provides fellowship and social life (p.115).

The tendency to gain satisfaction from social relationships has long been recognized as a human attribute.

The complexity of the relationship between social motivation and work becomes apparent when we attempt to specify the kinds of social outcomes which provide satisfaction. Clearly, it is not social interaction in any general sense that is satisfying to a given person, but specific kinds of socially derived outcomes, e.g., having influence over other people, being liked by other people, being cared for by other people, etc. Undoubtedly, there are extensive individual differences in the amount of satisfaction afforded by these particular kinds of outcomes. One person may derive satisfaction from one type of outcome, whereas a second may derive satisfaction from a very different kind of outcome. Furthermore, there are variations in the degree to which different kinds of social outcomes are provided by different work roles. A complete explanation of the role of social interaction in the motivation to work must be based on both individual differences in the strength of tendencies to derive satisfaction from particular kinds of social interaction as well as differences in the amount and kind of social interaction permitted or required by work roles.

SOCIAL STATUS

Sociologists have emphasized the importance of the work role in determining social status. A person's occupation greatly influences the way in which other people respond to him outside the work situation. Members of a high-status occupation (e.g., physicians) are accorded greater respect and have greater freedom in choosing leisure activities than those of lower-status occupations receiving comparable economic rewards.

The source of satisfaction represented by social status is very similar to that discussed in the preceding section, i.e., rewards derived from interaction with other persons. Here, however, we are concerned not only with persons with whom one interacts within the context of the work role but also with those with whom one interacts in other situations, such as family, friends, neighbors, and relatives.

A person may desire to work because he expects that doing so will affect his social status or, to be more precise, because he believes that others will be more likely to accept him if he does so. Working may be perceived to be instrumental to social acceptance and respect, whereas not working may be anticipated to result in social rejection and disapproval.

The effects of employment on social status depend on the norms of the culture or subculture of which the person is a member. Conceivably there are some segments of the population in which not working has no detrimental effects on status, or may even enhance one's status.

DISCUSSION AND SUMMARY

Our concern in this essay was, "Why do people work at all?" Virtually every man and almost every woman at some point in the course of their lifetimes engage in remunerated employment. By examining the rather simple-minded and yet seldom raised question of why people work, we have tried to set the stage for later consideration of the more specific and more easily researched aspects of the work-motivation relationship.

We have assumed that the probability that a person will work is dependent both on the availability of work and on his preference between working and not working. In an attempt to specify what some of the determinants of this preference are, we have examined five properties of work roles:

1. They provide financial remuneration.
2. They require the expenditure of energy.
3. They involve the production of goods and services.
4. They permit or require social interaction.
5. They affect the social status of the worker.

We have no basis for judging the relative influence of these different properties of work roles on the strength of preference for working. To study this question adequately we would have to systematically vary the outcomes provided by work, e.g., eliminate economic remuneration, and observe the effects on the number of people in the labor force. Such research is obviously impossible so we have had to rely on other more indirect sources of data. With the possible exception of expenditure of energy, there is reason to believe that each of these properties is satisfying to most persons. The desire to work is not to be explained solely in terms of its instrumental relationship to the attainment of money but also in terms of its consequences for the use and devel-opment of skills, the attainment of acceptance and respect by others, and the opportunity to contribute something useful to society.

Although we have said little in this essay about individual differences, there is no reason to believe that working serves the same purpose for different individuals. People differ in their desires and aversions, and for this reason simple generalizations about why people work are meaningless. We should also not lose sight of the extensive differences existing among work roles. All work roles may provide financial remuneration, but some provide more than others. Similarly, work roles differ in the amount and kind of energy expenditure they require, in the content of the functions performed, in the social interaction they permit or require, and in the social status they afford. These work role differences are exceedingly important for a consideration of satisfaction and performance.

REFERENCES

Friedmann, E. A., and Havighurst, R. J. *The Meaning of Work and Retirement.* Chicago: University of Chicago Press, 1954.

Goldstein, K. *Human Nature in the Light of Psychopathology.* Cambridge: Harvard University Press, 1940.

Hill, W. F. "Activity as an Autonomous Drive." *Journal of Comparative Physiological Psychology* 49 (1956), pp. 15-19.

Hull, C. L. *Principles of Behavior.* New York: Appleton-Century, 1943.

Maslow, A. H. "Deficiency Motivation and Growth Motivation." In Jones, M. R. (Ed.) Nebraska Symposium on Motivation. Lincoln: University of Nebraska Press, 1955, pp. 1-30.

Miller, D. C., and Form, W. H. *Industrial Sociology.* New York: Harper, 1951.

Morse, Nancy C., and Weiss, R. S. "The Function and Meaning of Work and the Job." *American Sociological Review* 20 (1955), pp. 191-98.

White, R. W. "Motivation Reconsidered: The Concept of Competence." *Psychological Review* 66 (1959), pp. 297-333.

Essay 4-2

The role of financial compensation in industrial motivation*

Robert L. Opsahl and Marvin D. Dunnette

THEORIES OF THE ROLE OF MONEY

Does money serve to stimulate job effort? If so, why does it do so? How does it take on value in our industrial society? There are at least five theories or interpretations of the role of money in affecting the job behavior of employees.

Money as a generalized conditioned reinforcer

One widely held hypothesis is that money acts as a generalized conditioned reinforcer because of its repeated pairings with primary reinforcers (Holland and Skinner, 1961; Kelleher and Gollub, 1962; Skinner, 1953). Skinner (1953) has stated that such a generalized reinforcer should be extremely effective because some deprivation will usually exist for which the conditioned reinforcer is appropriate. Unfortunately, solid evidence of the behavioral effectiveness of such reinforcers is lacking, and what evidence there is has been based almost entirely on animal studies.

Money as a conditioned incentive

According to this hypothesis, repeated pairings of money with primary incentives[1] establish a new learned drive for money (Dollard and Miller, 1950). Presumably, money could become a generalized conditioned incentive in the same manner that it is presumed by some to become a generalized conditioned reinforcer—that is, by many pairings with many different types of incentives. Perhaps the main difference between the conditioned reinforcer and conditioned incentive interpretations is the introduction of drive reduction in the incentive hypothesis. In contrast, no such drive need be hypothesized under empirical reinforcement principles.

Money as an anxiety reducer

Brown (1953, 1961) also utilized the concept of drive in an effort to explain how money affects behavior. He suggested that one learns to become anxious in the presence of a variety of cues signifying the absence of money. Presumably, anxiety related to the absence of money is acquired in childhood through a process of higher-order conditioning. The first stage consists of pairings of pain with cues of warning or alarm provided by adults. For example, before a child actually touches a hot stove, a nearby adult may provide facial gestures of alarm and warnings such as "Look out, you'll get hurt!" These cues eventually elicit anxiety without the unconditioned stimulus. In the second stage, anxiety-arousing warnings are conditioned to a wide variety of cues indicating lack of money. After such learning, the child becomes anxious upon hearing phrases such as "That costs too much money," or "We can't afford to buy you that." The actual presence of money produces cues for the

---

*From Robert L. Opsahl and Marvin D. Dunnette, "The Role of Financial Compensation in Industrial Motivation," *Psychological Bulletin* (66, 1966), pp. 95-116 (abridged). Copyright 1966 by the American Psychological Association. Reprinted by permission.

[1] Incentive: "an object or external condition, perceived as capable of satisfying an aroused motive, that tends to elicit action to obtain the object or condition (English and English, 1958)."

cessation of anxiety. This concept of anxiety as a learned motivating agent for money-seeking responses in no way contradicts the possible action of money according to the two previous hypotheses; money as an anxiety-reducer could operate jointly with them as an additional explanatory device.

Harlow (1953), however, has taken issue with Brown's thesis, stating: "It is hard to believe that parental expression at the time a child suffers injury is identical with or highly similar to a parent's expression when he says 'we have no money' [p. 22]." Harlow pointed out further that an infant's ability to recognize emotional expression when suffering pain has not been reliably demonstrated. Unfortunately, Brown presented no experimental evidence bearing on his theory.

Money as an instrument for gaining desired outcomes

Vroom's (1964) cognitive model of motivation has implications for understanding how money functions in affecting behavior. According to Vroom's interpretation, money acquires valence as a result of its perceived instrumentality for obtaining other desired outcomes. The concept of valence refers simply to affective orientations toward particular outcomes and has no direct implications for behavioral consequences. However, the "force" impelling a person toward action was postulated to be the product of the valence of an outcome and the person's expectancy that a certain action will lead to attainment of the outcome. Thus, for example, if money is perceived by a given person as instrumental to obtaining security, and if security is desired, money itself acquires positive valence. The probability, then, of his making money-seeking responses depends on the degree of his desire for security *multiplied* by his expectancy that certain designated job behaviors lead to attaining money. Although Vroom summarized studies giving general support to his theory, the specific role of money in his theory was not dealt with in any detail.

Gellerman's (1963) statement of how money functions in industry also stressed its instrumental role. According to him, money in itself has no intrinsic meaning and acquires significant motivating power only when it comes to symbolize intangible goals. Money acts as a symbol in different ways for different persons, and for the same person at different times. Gellerman presented the interesting notion that money can be interpreted as a projective device—a man's reaction to money "summarizes his biography to date: his early economic environment, his competence training, the various nonfinancial motives he has acquired, and his current financial status [p.166]." Gellerman's evidence was largely anecdotal, but nonetheless rather convincing.

Summary of theoretical speculations

Much remains to be learned before we will understand very well what meaning money has for different persons, how it affects their job behaviors, which motives it serves, and how its effectiveness may come about. It is probably doubtful that there will ever be a "theory of money" in the sense that money will be given a unique or special status as a psychological variable. It is true that money functions in many ways, depending upon the setting, the antecedent conditions, and the particular person involved. According to Brown, money must be present to avoid anxiety. For Herzberg et al., it serves to avoid feelings of being unfairly treated or economically deprived. Reinforcement theories, on the other hand, seem to treat money either as a generalized entity, functioning independently of specific deprivations, or as a general incentive that has been coupled with variously valued goals during a person's total learning history. Obviously, the answers are not yet available, and it is probably best to view money symbolically, as Vroom and Gellerman do, and to begin to learn and measure the personal, situational, and job parameters that may define more fully what it is the symbol of and what its attainment is instrumental to. Only by mapping the domain in this way will we come to know the relevant factors associated with money as a "motivator" of behavior in industry.

BEHAVIORAL CONSEQUENCES OF COMPENSATION

The major research problem in industrial compensation is to determine exactly what effects monetary rewards have for motivating various behaviors. More specifically, we need to understand more precisely how money can be used to induce employees to perform at high levels. Relevant research centers around two major groupings: studies related to the job or the job content and studies related to personal characteristics—preferences, perceptions, opinions, and other responses—made by the job incumbent. The first of these, the job or task variables, include primarily the policies and practices constituting the "compensation package" for any given job or job setting. The personal or subject variables influence not only the way a job holder responds to the specific policies and practices in any given situation, but they also vary as a function of these task or job variables. Thus, it is necessary to give careful attention to the interaction between job and personal variables which is frequently overlooked in research designs and has an important bearing on the interpretations to be attached to the results of such research studies.

JOB AND TASK VARIABLES

Compensation policies

Our assumption is that the manner in which financial compensation is administered may account for a large amount of the variation in job behavior. The particular schedule of payment, the degree of secrecy surrounding the amount of pay one receives, how the level of salary or pay is determined, and the individual's long-term or career pay history all have important potential effects on how the employee responds to any specific amount of money.

Schedules of pay. In this review we shall be concerned solely with "incentive" payment systems[2] which are based on behavioral criteria (usually amount of output) rather than biographical factors such as education, seniority, and experience. Incentive pay schemes of various sorts are believed to function primarily to "increase or maintain some already initiated activity or ... to encourage some new form of activity ... [Marriott, 1957, p. 12]."

There is considerable evidence that installation of such plans usually results in greater output per man-hour, lower unit costs, and higher wages in comparison with outcomes associated with straight payment systems (e.g., Dale, 1959; Rath, 1960; Viteles, 1953). However, the installation of an incentive plan is not and can never be an isolated event. Frequently, changes in work methods, management policies, and organization accompany the changeover, and it is difficult to determine the amount of behavioral variance that each of these other events may contribute. This would seem to constitute a persuasive argument for placing workers in a controlled laboratory situation and analyzing the effectiveness of different methods of payment, isolated from the usual changes accompanying their installation. Unfortunately, there have been few studies of this nature.[3]

---

[2] We will not attempt to evaluate all the evidence on incentive plans. For an excellent review and evaluation of these, see Marriott (1957).

[3] Marriott (1957) mentioned only three experimental studies, all in an industrial setting and all conducted at least 30 years ago: Burnett (1925); Roethlisberger and Dickson (1939), and Wyatt (1934).

SUBJECT VARIABLES

Perceived relations between performance and pay

According to Vroom's (1964) theory of work motivation, the valence of effective performance increases as the instrumentality of effective performance for the attainment of money increases, assuming that the valence of money is positive. Vroom cited supporting evidence from experiments by Atkinson and Reitman (1956), Atkinson (1958), and Kaufman (1962) showing a higher level of performance by subjects who were told that their earnings were contingent on the effectiveness of their performance. Georgopoulos, Mahoney, and Jones' (1957) Path-Goal Approach theory similarly states that if a worker has a desire for a given goal and perceives a given path leading to that goal, he will utilize that path if he has freedom to do so. Georgopoulos et al. found that workers who perceived higher personal productivity as a means to increased earnings performed more effectively than workers who did not perceive this relationship.

The effectiveness of incentive plans in general depends upon the worker's knowledge of the relation between performance and earnings. The lack of this knowledge is one cause of failure in incentive schemes. Campbell's (1952) study showed that one of the major reasons for lower productivity in large groups under group incentive plans is that the workers often do not perceive the relation between pay and productivity as well as they do in smaller groups. In the Georgopoulos et al. (1957) study, only 38 percent of the workers perceived increased performance as leading to increased earnings. More amazingly, 35 percent perceived *low* productivity as an aid to higher earnings in the long run. Lawler (1964) recently found that 600 managers perceived their training and experience to be the most important factors in determining their pay—not how well or how poorly they performed their jobs. Since Lawler found that the relation between their pay and their rated job performance also was low, their perceptions were probably quite accurate. A separate analysis of the most highly motivated managers, however, indicated that they attached greater importance to pay and felt that good job performance would lead to higher pay.

These studies confirm the importance of knowing how job performance and pay are related. The relation between performing certain desired behaviors and attainment of the pay-incentive must be explicitly specified. The foregoing statement seems so obvious as hardly to warrant mentioning. Unfortunately, as we have seen, the number of times in industry that the above *rule* is ignored is surprising. Future research must determine how goals or incentives may best be presented in association with desired behaviors. Practically nothing has been done in this area—especially for managers. In fact, programs for the recognition of individual merit are notoriously poor. Methods for tying financial compensation in with management-by-results (Schleh, 1961) or with systematic efforts to set job goals and methods of unambiguously outlining what the end result of various job behaviors will be should be developed and studied.

Personality-task interactions

Under some conditions, it appears that even specifying the relation between performance and pay is not sufficient. Early studies (Wyatt and Fraser, 1929; Wyatt, Fraser, and Stock, 1929; Wyatt and Langdon, 1937) conducted on British factory workers showed that feelings of boredom are associated with reduced output even under a carefully developed program of incentive pay.

One possible method of alleviating feelings of boredom is suggested by Wyatt and Fraser's (1929) finding that piece-rate systems lead to fewer symptoms of boredom than does straight hourly pay. This is in keeping with Whyte's (1955) contention that, in addition to money, there are three other sources of reward in a piece-rate situation: escape from fatigue, because the worker has a meaningful goal to shoot at; escape from management pressure and gain of control over one's own time; and "playing the game" of trying to attain quota.

The net conclusion from these studies is that repetitive tasks, destructive tasks, boring tasks, and disliked tasks are apparently much less susceptible to monetary incentives. Little has been done, however, to explore other possible interactions in this area. What little data we do have suggest that nonmonetary incentives are more effective for subjects who have high ability on the task being measured. Thus, Fleishman (1958) found that subjects high in ability on a complex coordination task increased their performance under incentive conditions significantly more than did low ability subjects. However, we do not know if such findings would generalize to situations in which monetary incentives are used or how the effectiveness of incentives varies as a function of other important variables such as the type of task, the amount of physical effort demanded, or the degree of interpersonal interaction involved, to mention but a few examples. Without knowledge of the range of behaviors susceptible to incentives or the degree to which they are susceptible, we cannot make optimal use of them in any specific situation. Should we use incentives for maintaining or improving leadership behavior? And how about jobs which are highly challenging and intrinsically rewarding? Are incentives in this situation a cause of mercenary feelings which detract from the main source of reinforcement—the job itself—and ultimately lower job effectiveness? Or do they spur the employees on to yet greater

heights? Of course, we do not know; and, even more unfortunately, little research seems to be under way to test assumptions implicitly made by many firms' present compensation policies.

Perceived importance of pay

It seems obvious that employees must regard money as a highly desirable commodity before increased amounts of it motivate increased behavior. Results of studies in this area are extremely confusing because of the almost exclusive dependence on self-reports to estimate the relative importance of pay.

While most self-report surveys place salary in a position of only moderate importance, it is easy to find people in industry who *behave* as if they value money highly. Executives strive mightily to advance to high-paying jobs; entertainers work toward more and more lucrative arrangements; bankers embezzle; robbers rob; university professors publish to win increased salary and to enjoy royalty checks.

It is not implied that bankers embezzle *only* for money or that university professors publish *only* for money or that executives strive *only* for money. Money plays a role in all these—a role probably far greater than that suggested by the self-report studies. The self-report studies are based on oversimplified notions tending to ignore the complexities and multidetermined aspects of human behavior. In sum, the question, "How do people value money?" will not be answered accurately simply by asking them.

Pay preferences

Although money *per se* is usually accorded a middle position in any ranking of job factors, different ways of making salary payments are differentially preferred. Mahoney (1964) found that managers prefer straight salary over various types of management incentive payments (such as stock options, deferred compensation, etc.). This is in keeping with the results of other surveys. Jaques, Rice, and Hill (1951), for example, reported that the majority of both workers and management in an English factory were in favor of a change from individual piece-rates to hourly wages. Likewise, Davis (1948) found that 60 percent of a sample of building operatives were opposed to incentive schemes, with only 21 percent expressing definite or conditional approval. The main arguments against incentive systems, as reported by Davis, include the fear that the incentive would inhibit other strong and pleasurable motives for working, such as the pleasure of work for its own sake and the solidarity and good fellowship of the working group.

Mahoney (1964, p. 144) concluded that preferences for alternative forms of compensation are relatively uniform and that "fine distinctions among alternative forms of compensation probably are considerably less important in managerial motivation than is often suggested." Such preferences should not be the sole criterion for assessing the effects of compensation on motivation if we are mainly interested in actual job behavior, not satisfaction,[4] since the relation between the two is complex and, in many instances, unknown. From stated preferences one cannot easily infer that the compensation program is optimally motivating.

Although there has been a fair amount of research done in determining the pay preferences of managers and other em-

ployees, no work has been done on the relation between preference for a particular plan and the actual incentive value of that plan. The implicit, but unwarranted, assumption in all the above-mentioned studies is that if a person has a pay plan he likes, this plan will motivate behavior more than one that he does not like. Although this is an appealing assumption, future studies, in addition to determining employees' pay-plan preferences, should seek to map the relation between such preferences and the incentive value of different plans. The motivation of behavior, *not* the preference for compensation policies, is the prime goal of company pay plans, and research strategies should be directed toward this end.

FUTURE RESEARCH

Although it is generally agreed that money is the major mechanism for rewarding and modifying behavior in industry, we have seen that very little is known about how it works. Haire remarked at a recent symposium on managerial compensation that, in spite of the tremendous amount of money spent and the obvious relevance of behavioral theory for compensation practices, there is less research and theory in this area than in almost any other field related to management (Haire, 1965). Similarly, Dunnette and Bass (1963), in a critique of current personnel management practices, pointed out that personnel men have relied on faddish and assumptive practices in administering pay which lack empirical support. One reason for this is the dearth of sound research upon which to base practices. The following are some suggested directions for research which may help to remedy these current deficiencies.

The principal research problem is to discover in what way money motivates employees and how this, in turn, affects their behavior. For this, we must know more about the motives of employees—

---

[4] There is correlational evidence that amount of pay is positively associated with satisfaction with pay (Andrews and Henry, 1963; Lawler and Porter, 1963), job satisfaction (Barnett, Handelsman, Stewart, and Super, 1952; Centers and Cantril, 1946; Marriott and Denerly, 1955; Miller and Form, 1951; Smith and Kendall, 1963; Thompson, 1939; all as reported in Vroom, 1964), and with need satisfaction (Lawler and Porter, 1963; Porter, 1962). However, it is not known to what degree the satisfaction is a result of the level of pay or the changes in job status, duties, and privileges that so often accompany higher pay.

which motives are dominant, and how employees differ from one another in the configuration of their motives. We must also determine which of these motives can be linked to money as an incentive. Can money be linked with insatiable needs so goal attainment does not cause cessation of behavior? Can money act as an incentive for the "higher order" needs? The two main hypotheses here—that money can serve only "lower order" needs, and that it can serve essentially all needs—have very different implications for compensation practices. Investigation of this question requires not only the discovery of the motives for which money has instrumental value but also the extent to which money can serve to fulfill or satisfy these needs. Quite obviously, money serves to satisfy needs for food, clothing, and shelter, but it is much less obvious how money may be related to such other areas as need Achievement or need Power. It seems obvious that money serves these needs too, but solid evidence of a relationship is lacking. To what extent may money be a primary way of dispensing feelings of achievement, competence, power, and the like? In other words, what needs are currently served by money, and what needs, not now perceived as associated with money, may it be called upon to serve?

As this review shows, very little is known about the behavioral laws regulating the effectiveness of incentives. We continue to dole out large sums of money under the guise of "incentive pay" without really knowing much about its incentive character. We do not know, for instance, the nature of the effect of a pay raise or the length of time before that effect occurs; or, for that matter, how long the raise may be effective. Nor do we know the optimal reinforcement schedule to be used in giving salary increases for obtaining desired changes in job behavior. A simple monitoring of work outputs on jobs where amount of production is under

the direct control of the employee and where it is easily assessed, may provide valuable information here. Such knowledge would have important implications for how often and in what amounts incentive raises should be built into the compensation package.

We also need to investigate the relation between amount of money and the amount of behavior money motivates. Is there some point beyond which increases in compensation are no longer related to increases in relevant behavior? That is, do humans show the same negatively accelerated relation between amount of reward and number of responses that lower organisms display? Or do increases in money "whet the appetite" and lead to behavior that follows some exponential or positively accelerated function?

If we are to effectively manipulate incentives, more information is needed about how they function. Money's incentive character, to be fully understood, must also take account of the perceptions of money by the recipient. For example, if it is assumed that the amount of extra pay needed in a raise before it assumes incentive character is partly determined by the value of a just noticeable difference of money, recent evidence (Haire, 1965) shows that not only the amount of money but also how a person perceives his work role are vital factors. Presidents apparently need a larger percentage increase than vice presidents before they see it as constituting an incentive raise. Is this difference a function of the work role alone? Or do anticipations of future earnings, differences in abilities and dominant motives, and past earning history account for a good share of the variance? So far, these research questions are virtually untapped.

We have seen from Wyatt (1934) that money can be cheapened or lowered in value by the behavior demanded to attain it. To understand more about this relationship, it would be helpful to scale money values against behaviors demanded for money's attainment. This could best be done in a laboratory setting and by using actual workers. Such controlled laboratory experiments have been utilized *almost not at all* with actual employees as subjects. So far, we have depended heavily on rats and psychology sophomores to build a psychology of motivation. We sorely need studies in which real workers are brought into the laboratory and the effects of incentives under different conditions studied.

A very important variable influencing money's effectiveness is the schedule by which it is administered. Of the simple reinforcement schedules, the fixed interval—reinforcement following a fixed period of time after the last reinforced response—leads to notoriously poor performance in lower organisms (Ferster and Skinner, 1957). Yet this is the present pay schedule of most industrial employees. Lower organisms on this schedule tend not to respond very rapidly until just before their "payday." The notable exception to this type of pay schedule in industry occurs for commission salesmen (e.g., life insurance selling) and for entrepreneurs. It is probably worth noting that these two groups contain "workers" who must certainly be viewed as being among the most highly motivated persons in our industrial society.

Although more is known about the simple schedules of reinforcement, the complex schedules—composed of both interval and ratio elements—may be applicable in an industrial setting. In particular, the effects of alternative, conjunctive, and interlocking schedules are worth investigating. With these schedules, it would be possible to follow the suggestion of Haire, Ghiselli, and Porter (1963); that is, divide the paycheck into several parts: so much for tenure, so much for minimum services rendered, so much for excellent performance, etc. For example, about 70 percent of the total available might be given on a fixed interval for minimum services.

The rest of the potential pay could be divided and incorporated into different variable ratio schedules, made contingent on outstanding performance.

Finally, evidence seems to indicate that, at various times, employees seek to maximize the amount of their reward, the fairness of their reward, and their acceptance by the group in which they work. The research question is: in which situations, and in what ways is behavior directed toward maximizing one or more of these goals? Which goals are maximized at the expense of others? What are the relative saliencies of each goal in differing situations? What are the functional relationships between goals? Which goals account for most of the variance in productivity, and under what conditions? These are vital questions that must be answered before we can effectively utilize incentives.

As research on the role of financial compensation in industrial motivation becomes more and more prevalent, answers to many of the questions posed above should be forthcoming. Increased knowledge should be accompanied by more effective use of money in industry. It is hoped that the firm of the future will be able to establish compensation policies and practices based on empirical evidence about the behavioral effects of money as an incentive rather than on the nontested assumptions, hunches, and time worn "rules-of-thumb" so common in industry today.

REFERENCES

Andrews, I. R., and Henry, M. M. "Management Attitudes toward Pay." *Industrial Relations* 3 (1963), 29-39.

Atkinson, J. W. (ed.). *Motives in Fantasy, Action, and Society.* Princeton: Van Nostrand, 1958.

Atkinson, J. W., and Reitman, W. R. "Performance as a Function of Motive Strength and Expectancy of Goal Attainment." *Journal of*

Abnormal and Social Psychology 53 (1956), 361-66.

Barnett, G. J.; Handelsman, I.; Stewart, L. H.; and Super, D. E. "The Occupational Level Scale as a Measure of Drive." *Psychological Monographs* 66 (1952), (10, Whole No. 342).

Brown, J. S. "Problems Presented by the Concept of Acquired Drives." In, *Current Theory and Research in Motivation: A Symposium.* Lincoln: University of Nebraska Press, 1953, pp. 1-21.

Brown, J. S. *The Motivation of Behavior.* New York: McGraw-Hill, 1961.

Burnett, F. *An Experimental Investigation into Repetitive Work.* (Industrial Fatigue Research Board Report No. 30) London: His Majesty's Stationery Office, 1925.

Campbell, H. "Group Incentive Payment Schemes: The Effects of Lack of Understanding and Group Size." *Occupational Psychology* 26 (1952), 15-21.

Centers, R., and Cantril, H. "Income Satisfaction and Income Aspiration." *Journal of Abnormal and Social Psychology* 41 (1946), 64-69.

Dale, J. "Increase Productivity 50 Percent in One Year with Sound Wage Incentives." *Management Methods* 16 (1959), 38-42.

Davis, N. M. "Attitudes to Work among Building Operatives." *Occupational Psychology* 22 (1948), 56-62.

Dollard, J., and Miller, N. E. *Personality and Psychotherapy.* New York: McGraw-Hill, 1950.

Dunnette, M. D., and Bass, B. M. "Behavioral Scientists and Personnel Management." *Industrial Relations* 2 (1963), 115-30.

English, H. B., and English, C. A. *A Comprehensive Dictionary of Psychological and Psychoanalytical Terms.* New York: McKay, 1958.

Ferster, C. B., and Skinner, B. F. *Schedules of Reinforcement.* New York: Appleton-Century-Crofts, 1957.

Fleishman, E. A. "A Relationship between Incentive Motivation and Ability Level in Psychomotor Performance." *Journal of Experimental Psychology* 56 (1958), 78-81.

Gellerman, S. W. *Motivation and Productivity.* New York: American Management Association, 1963.

Georgopoulos, B. S.; Mahoney, G. M.; and Jones, N. W. "A Path-Goal Approach to Productivity." *Journal of Applied Psychology* 41 (1957), 345-53.

Haire, M. "The Incentive Character of Pay." In R. Andrews (ed.), *Managerial Compensation.* Ann Arbor: Foundation for Research on Human Behavior, 1965, pp. 13-17.

Haire, M.; Ghiselli, E. E.; and Porter, L. W. "Psychological Research on Pay: An Overview." *Industrial Relations* 3 (1963), 3-8.

Harlow, H. F. Comments on Professor Brown's paper. In, *Current Theory and Research in Motivation.* Lincoln: University of Nebraska Press, 1953, pp. 22-23.

Herzberg, F.; Mausner, B.; and Snyderman, B. *The Motivation to Work.* (2d ed.) New York: Wiley, 1959.

Holland, J. G., and Skinner, B. F. *The Analysis of Behavior.* New York: McGraw-Hill, 1961.

Jaques, E.; Rice, A. K.; and Hill, J. M. "The Social and Psychological Impact of a Change in Method of Wage Payment." *Human Relations* 4 (1951), 315-40.

Kaufman, H. "Task performance, expected performance, and responses to failure as functions of imbalance in the self-concept." Unpublished doctoral dissertation, University of Pennsylvania, 1962.

Kelleher, R. T., and Gollub, L. R. "A Review of Positive Conditioned Reinforcement." *Journal of the Experimental Analysis of Behavior* 5 (1962), 543-97.

Lawler, E. E., III. "Managers' job performance and their attitudes toward their pay." Unpublished doctoral dissertation, University of California, Berkeley, 1964.

Lawler, E. E., III, and Porter, L. W. "Perceptions regarding Management Compensation." *Industrial Relations* 3 (1963), 41-49.

Mahoney, T. "Compensation Preferences of Managers." *Industrial Relations* 3 (1964), 135-44.

Marriott, R. *Incentive Payment Systems: A Review of Research and Opinion.* London: Staples Press, 1957.

Marriott, R., and Denerley, R. A. "A Method of Interviewing Used in Studies of Workers' Attitudes: II. Validity of the Method and Discussion of the Results. *Occupational Psychology* 29 (1955), 69-81.

Miller, D. C., and Form, W. H. *Industrial Sociology.* New York: Harper, 1951.

Porter, L. W. "Job Attitudes in Management: I. Perceived Deficiencies in Need Fulfillment as a Function of Job Level." *Journal of Applied Psychology* 46 (1962), 375-84.

Rath, A. A. "The Case for Individual Incentives." *Personnel Journal* 39 (1960), 172-75.

Roethlisberger, F. J., and Dickson, W. J. *Management and the Worker.* Cambridge: Harvard University Press, 1939.

Schleh, E. C. *Management by Results: The Dynamics of Profitable Management.* New York: McGraw-Hill, 1961.

Skinner, B. F. *Science and Human Behavior.* New York: Macmillan, 1953.

Smith, P. C., and Kendall, L. M. "Cornell Studies of Job Satisfaction: VI. Implications for the Future." Unpublished manuscript, Cornell University, 1963.

Thompson, W. A. "Eleven Years after Graduation." *Occupations* 17 (1939), 709-14.

Viteles, M. S. *Motivation and Morale in Industry.* New York: Norton, 1953.

Vroom, V. H. *Work and Motivation.* New York: Wiley, 1964.

Whyte, W. F. *Money and Motivation: An Analysis of Incentives in Industry.* New York: Harper, 1955.

Wyatt, S. *Incentives in Repetitive Work: A Practical Experiment in a Factory.* (Industrial Health Research Board Report No. 69) London: His Majesty's Stationery Office, 1934.

Wyatt, S. and Fraser, J. S. *The Comparative Effects of Variety and Uniformity in Work.* (Industrial Fatigue Research Board Report No. 52) London: His Majesty's Stationery Office, 1929.

Wyatt, S.; Fraser, J. A.; and Stock, F. G. L. *The Effects of Monotony in Work.* (Industrial Fatigue Research Board Report No. 56) London: His Majesty's Stationery Office, 1929.

Wyatt, S., and Langdon, J. N. *Fatigue and Boredom in Repetitive Work.* (Industrial Health Research Board Report No. 77) London: His Majesty's Stationery Office, 1937.

Essay *4-3*

Concept of the wage structure*

Arthur M. Ross

The concept of the wage structure is not without subtleties and complexities. In the first place, wage structure has no independent reality, nor does it exist in a state of nature. It is an intellectual construct which is useful in thinking about wages and arriving at decisions about them. Economic behavior in general is too various and disorganized to deal with in raw form and needs to be ordered and simplified before much can be said of it. Organizing concepts are therefore indispensable and are free from objection so long as they are not mistaken for veritable entities.

The reality of wages is that millions of employees each receive some rate of pay and accumulate certain earnings per hour, per week, and per annum. For some purposes it is useful to conceive of a general wage level, and for other purposes it is necessary to envisage a structure of wages; but we should not suppose that either one really exists, any more than a marginal product, a competitive price, or a natural rate of interest really exists.

*Reprinted from Arthur M. Ross, "The External Wage Structure," in *New Concepts in Wage Determination,* ed. George W. Taylor and Frank C. Pierson, pp. 174-83 (abridged). Copyright © 1957 by McGraw-Hill, Inc. Used with permission of McGraw-Hill Book Company.

Significant relationships

Although every wage rate is related to every other from a strictly statistical standpoint, some relationships are more significant than others. Suppose that a window washer in St. Louis earns $1 per hour and that a cotton picker in the San Joaquin Valley of California picks 250 pounds in 10 hours, receives $4 per hundredweight, and therefore averages $1 per hour. Here is a statistical equality between the wages of the window washer and the cotton picker, but one which creates little excitement because it is fortuitous and meaningless. Suppose, on the other hand, that printing pressmen employed on New York and Chicago newspapers each receive $2.65 per hour. Here is another statistical equality, but one which is arresting and important. Both of these equalities are part of the wage structure; yet the second clearly shows more "relatedness" than the first.

A relationship is important for one or both of two reasons: first, because it has significant economic effects; and second, because it has considerable influence in the making of wage decisions. A large disparity between the wage rates in Northern and Southern cotton mills may cause a shift of orders and production to the South. It may therefore be the weightiest factor in a decision to reduce the rates in the Northern mills. A 2-cent differential between the wage increases granted to AFL and CIO unions at the Oak Ridge atomic energy installation may impel one of the unions to go on strike. For this reason the differential would have to be eliminated in order to prevent an untenable situation.

Much is written of different "types" of relationships—intraindustry, interindustry, interarea, etc. These are conventional groupings of the innumerable relationships which are found in the industrial world. They may be thought of as the dimensions of the wage structure, or the lines along which a wage rate is related to other rates. We might begin with a senior stenographer earning $60 per week in the office of a small Los Angeles furniture factory. For one purpose or another, it might be important to compare this rate with that of the senior stenographer in a large Los Angeles furniture plant (intraindustry), or in the motion picture firms (interindustry), or in a small San Francisco furniture plant (geographical); or with the rate of a junior stenographer in the same plant (occupational); or with the rate of senior stenographers represented by a different union in the same industry (interunion).

To avoid misunderstanding, it would be emphasized again that these "types" of differentials are merely mental aids and not real phenomena. Often it is impossible to classify a differential as falling in one class or another or to factor out the respective contributions of the various bases of differentiation. We may know, for example, that a janitor receives an average of $1.05 per hour in cotton textiles and $1.80 in automobile manufacturing. We may associate this 75-cent disparity with differences in job content, geographical location, and the character of the two industries. The last-named factor may encompass differences in typical size of the firm, degree of competition in the product market, rate of growth and profitability. Thus we may regard the differential as the resultant of numerous forces, but nonetheless it is all one and the same differential.

Labor economists have often concerned themselves with the question of whether some differentials merely represent others in disguise. It is said, for instance, that the so-called sex differential is a statistical illusion reflecting the concentration of women in low-wage occupations. At the same time, certain occupational differentials are explained by the fact that some of the jobs are staffed with men and some with women. The alleged rural-urban differential is attributed to the fact that large plants are located in cities and many small plants are found in the countryside. But the differential between large and small plants is sometimes accounted for by stating that the latter are frequently situated in rural areas, where surplus farm population is available. Similarly, are Southern wages low because low-wage industries are located there, or does the textile industry pay low wages because it is centered in the South?

These dilemmas cannot be resolved unequivocally and actually are not real; for every differential has its own set of causes, and these are not changed or affected by the labels which may be attached to them.

WAGE DECISIONS AND THE WAGE STRUCTURE

For practical purposes the distinction between internal and external wage structures is virtually synonymous with the distinction between intraplant and interplant structures. The terminology employed here has been chosen because it seems to dramatize certain differences between wage relationships in the two situations. These differences pertain to the degree of control over wage relationships enjoyed by the decision makers and to the relative importance of factors intrinsic or extraneous to the decision-making unit.

An internal wage structure is established within a single area of decision. The decision makers can apply formal criteria and utilize systematic procedures. They have it within their power to create, maintain, or revive some desired differentials; they can eliminate others by equalizing the wage rates. As E. Robert Livernash shows, many of the principal considerations are interior to the unit. This is not to say, however, that the decision makers are insulated from exterior forces. The determination of "key rates" in particular is often governed by craft rates in the area, labor-market pressures, and similar influences.

It is more difficult to characterize the external wage structure in these respects. Some external relationships are not the result of conscious or integrated decisions. Average wages are higher in the North than in the South, for example, but not because of any specific adjudication that this should be so. Similarly, there was a time when office workers received higher wages than lathe operators; today the positions are reversed. Once again no one has decided that the stenographer is less deserving than she used to be or that the lathe operator was relatively underpaid. The changing relationships between Northern wages as a whole and Southern wages as a whole is the resultant of separate sets of causes; likewise the changing relationship between clerical and manual wages.

Many specific external relationships, on the other hand, are deliberately fashioned. Some decision makers can control only one end of the relationship. For example, employers and union leaders in the electrical industry may decide to match wage increases awarded in the auto industry. They can follow the auto industry, but they cannot govern what it will do. (But the auto decision makers may be influenced by the knowledge that the electrical industry will follow their lead; and the largest auto company has several plants in the electrical industry.)

The degree of control is further attenuated when several relationships are involved. A manufacturer may find that his local employer association is endeavoring to hold wage adjustments below 5 cents per hour; the major firms in his industry, who are located elsewhere, have renewed their contracts without change; while neighboring locals of his union, which operates throughout a broad jurisdiction, have received 10-cent increases. Try as he may, he cannot maintain all three connections simultaneously. At least two will necessarily be altered.

Some interplant relationships are encompassed within a single unit of decision, however, so that both ends of the relationship are under control. One example is found in the multiplant company which must decide whether or not to pay identical rates in its several establishments. Another example is the multiemployer or "industry-wide" bargaining agreement, which again may provide either for uniform or diversified wages. Strict adherence to logic might suggest that wage relationships between plants in the same company, or companies in the same multiemployer group, be classified as internal if subject to central determination. But notwithstanding this fact, there are sound reasons for regarding them as part of the external wage structure. It is customary to associate them with other interplant relationships for analytical and statistical purposes. Moreover, certain influences are active which are germane to interplant wage determination but not relevant in the development of an intraplant structure. Of these the most significant are diversities in local wage levels and disparities in technology and profit position as between plants and companies.

Level and structures

Thus there are clear differences between the general wage level, the internal wage structure, and the external wage structure in their relation to wage decisions. These differences are as follows:

1. The general wage level in the United States is beyond the control of individuals, except perhaps control by government boards in periods of national emergency. In certain countries, such as Sweden, where bargaining procedures have become highly centralized, groups at the top of the pyramid are in a position to govern general wage movements. But in the United States not even the most important pattern-setting groups have any significant proportion of total employment within their own grasp. Admittedly, some bar-

gaining decisions are more significant than would be indicated by the percentage of the labor force involved. But when all is said and done, there is no such thing as a nationwide pattern; and as it will appear later, the pattern-setting decisions are strongly influenced by the trend of settlements at the time. For these reasons a theory of the general wage level must deal broadly with economic and institutional influences affecting wages in general. A grass-roots approach is entirely out of place for this kind of problem.

2. Internal wage structures, as already noted, are encompassed within a single area of decision and are within the control of decision makers. Therefore a theory of internal wage structures may address itself single-mindedly to the task of explaining the choices that have been made.

3. It is more difficult to characterize the external wage structure in this respect. The broad outlines of the external wage structure are often the product of uncoordinated decisions and the resultant of separate sets of causes. Thus the differentials between clerical and manual workers, Northern and Southern regions, or textile and steel industries have not been established by anybody in particular, but by decision makers in general. Some specific relationships, as pointed out in the previous section, are accidental and without any particular significance. But many are organically interrelated and consciously coordinated. They may be controlled at one end, as in the case of one industry following the lead of another, or at both ends, as in the case of a company with two establishments. In either case they are marked with "relatedness."

It is the nature of this "relatedness"—the extent and means of coordination—with which this essay is largely concerned.

Putting it differently, external forces in the market determine the rough contours of the external wage structure, but they are ordinarily loose enough to leave a margin of choice. Within this margin employers and unions make their decisions as to desired relationships—to establish or eliminate a differential, to abandon or follow a leader, and so on.

It follows that a complete theory of the external wage structure must accomplish three tasks: (1) it must explain how the larger outlines of the wage structure, which are beyond the reach of individual decisions, are drawn; (2) it must account for the fact that a substantial range of discretion remains available; and (3) it must explain the decisions made by employers and unions within the range of discretion.

STATIC AND DYNAMIC ASPECTS OF THE WAGE STRUCTURE

Another complication is that the wage structure has both a static and a dynamic aspect. The static aspect consists of significant equalities and differentials at one point of time. The dynamic comprises relative movements over the course of time. These are clearly distinguishable matters. The question of why wages were higher in railroads than in coal mining as of 1935 is essentially different from the question of why coal-mining wages have gone up more rapidly since 1935. The two aspects have not always been clearly distinguished in the literature, however, and it is sometimes difficult to know whether a writer is referring to comparative levels or to comparative movements.

Movement versus level

Wage determination is probably a unique form of pricing in the degree of importance which is often attached to the movement as compared to the level. Very seldom do the parties have an occasion to establish a schedule of wages *de novo*. The opening of a new plant would furnish such an occasion; and perhaps the negotiation of a first contract in a formerly unorganized plant, since the new rates may be bargained with little or no reference to the previous nonunion rates. With these exceptions, the parties play their roles on a set stage: the changes in rates as well as the rates themselves are integrally involved. The negotiators generally communicate with each other in terms of change rather than level; the union refers to the change in announcing its gains to the membership; and the newspapers and reporting services emphasize the amount of change. It cannot be said in the abstract that change is more important than level, or vice versa; and this is not the place to analyze the concrete circumstances lending weight to one or the other. It is sufficiently clear, however, that the degree of movement is often a crucial consideration.

One of the traditional criteria of collective wage determination has been designated "the going rate," and one of the purposes of the trade union has been the establishment of what is called "the standard rate." In view of what has been said above, we should recognize "the going increase" as the touchstone in many cases and "the standard increase" as the union objective under many circumstances.

Measurement problems

When comparative movements are important, it is necessary to measure them. Here we come face to face with one of the more subtle problems of wage analysis. Are comparative movements to be measured in cents per hour or in percentages? Wage rate A rises from 50 cents to 80 cents. Wage rate B advances from $1 to $1.40. Which has gone up the more? Has the differential between the two rates become narrower or wider? Should an arbitrator consider that workers receiving A or those receiving B have been more "underprivileged"? What should be the employer's response if the union seeks to increase or reduce the gap?

Of course, the arithmetical results can be characterized in either fashion. A's relative increase has been 60 percent and

B's has been 40 percent. On the other hand, A's absolute increase has been 30 cents per hour and B's has been 40 cents. The percentage differential between the two rates has dropped from 100 percent to 75 percent. The cents-per-hour differential has risen from 30 cents to 40 cents. When percentage increases are equal, the relative differential is maintained and the absolute differential is enhanced; but when cents-per-hour increases are equal, the absolute differential is maintained and the relative differential is reduced. All this is clear enough. But it provides no answer when a choice must be made, as it often must.

An appealing argument can be made out that the percentage measurement is more significant. Such an argument would stress that the monetary unit is only a *numeraire* and that the relations are what count. Returning to our example, suppose the cost of living had advanced 50 percent. A's real wages have improved, while B's have deteriorated. Under these circumstances, it would not seem to make sense if one should assert that B's wage rate had gone up faster. Or suppose that all values in the economy were simultaneously doubled. Cents-per-hour wage differentials would also be doubled while percentage differentials would be unaffected. Since the real position of all individuals would be unaltered, it would seem illogical to claim that their comparative position had changed.

But no matter how persuasive these logical exercises, the fact remains that exclusive reliance on the percentage method often yields unsatisfactory results. In selecting an appropriate measure of comparative change, particular attention must be paid to the character of the underlying movement which has taken place during the period involved. If percentage differentials in general have been maintained during a given period, then the percentage basis is more suitable for comparing particular movements. If percentage differen-

tials have been continuously compressed, then a comparison of cents-per-hour changes may be more revealing and significant. Between 1933 and 1946, for example, absolute increases were much more nearly uniform between industries than were percentage increases, and the magnitude of absolute change was not related in any systematic way to the original level. For this reason comparisons covering this period are more meaningful if stated in terms of cents-per-hour changes.

Admittedly, the degree of percentage compression between 1933 and 1946 was unusual. A more common development is that percentage differentials decline while cents-per-hour differentials spread apart over the course of time. Under these circumstances both types of measurement are strongly affected by the original level of wages. A low-wage occupation, area, or industry will tend to show larger percentage increases and smaller cents-per-hour increases than a high-wage occupation, area, or industry; and allowance should be made for this general tendency when particular comparisons are made.

That percentage differentials are inclined to narrow and cents-per-hour differentials to spread apart is not being stated as a natural law but only as an empirical observation of what appears to be true more often than not. No good explanation suggests itself, but the tendency is there nonetheless. Failure to recognize it is responsible for a great many pointless arguments and comparisons in collective bargaining and wage arbitration. It also accounts for the fact that so many studies of movements in the wage structure arrive at inconclusive results.

WAGE RATES AND FRINGE BENEFITS

Further complications arise when we ask what is meant by "wages" in connection with the structure of wages. There are numerous questions involved, but the most interesting and important is whether fringe benefits are included along with wage rates or segregated for separate comparison. This question is of the greatest practical importance in contract negotiation, arbitration, and government-control programs. Recurrently in arbitration cases, for example, the union will seek to justify its generous wage demand by showing that its members do not enjoy some of the standard fringe benefits. Employers frequently argue that a comparative deficiency in wage levels can be explained and exonerated by a comparative surplus in fringes. Emergency wage-control agencies must decide whether to impose a single "ceiling" for wage and fringe benefits combined or to set separate standards and limits instead.

No categorical answer can be given to the question of whether wage comparisons should include or exclude fringes. "Relatedness" is a social rather than a natural phenomenon and depends on the thought patterns of labor and management officials and others who participate in the wage-setting process.

The issue is really whether wages and fringes are substitutable for each other as part of the aggregate "price of labor" and as components of a total "package" adjustment. In principle it might be argued that they are. Clearly the fringes *are* part of the price of labor: they are forms of income to the worker and elements of cost to the employer. Although sometimes difficult to evaluate, they make up a significant and growing proportion of the employer's labor bill, often exceeding 20 or 25 percent.[1] Certainly the individual worker takes the fringe benefits into account in weighing the relative attractiveness of jobs, and increasingly as he be-

comes older.[2] Just as he may select the lower-paid job because of steadier employment opportunity, he may also be influenced by a generous vacation allowance or an advantageous retirement plan. Finally, wages and fringes are negotiated together, and great attention is usually paid to the size of the total package.

Wage differentials are sometimes justified by countervailing fringe differentials when otherwise they would be deemed inequitable. For instance, longshoremen receive a lower hourly rate on the West Coast than on the East Coast. Overtime begins after 8 hours on the West Coast, however, and an 8-hour day is prescribed, so that the daily earnings of the West Coast longshoreman approximate those of the East Coast worker. And in a number of public jurisdictions in California, construction unions have accepted wage rates 11 or 12 percent below what is prevailing, for the reason that exceptional fringe benefits, beyond those provided in the area contracts, are available. The unions at the University of California at Berkeley, however (influenced perhaps by some of the literature produced there) have insisted on maintaining the standard rate at the expense of sacrificing the extra fringe benefits.

Thus a respectable argument can be made on behalf of an inclusive concept of "wage" for comparative purposes; and examples of substitution between wages and fringes are not lacking. Nevertheless there are important ways in which wages and fringes are not strictly equivalent.

First, a union is concerned not only with the size of a bargaining package but also with its components. An 8-cent package consisting of 6 cents in wages and 2 cents in insurance might be more acceptable than a 10-cent package of 4 cents in wages and 6 cents in insurance. Similarly,

---

[1] See *Fringe Benefits, 1953* (Chamber of Commerce of the United States, 1954); A. M. Fisher and J. F. Chapman, "Big Costs of Little Fringes," *Harvard Business Review*, vol. 32 (September-October, 1954), pp. 35-44.

[2] Richard A. Lester, *Hiring Practices and Labor Competition* (Princeton, N.J.: Princeton University Press, 1954).

an employer may feel easier about granting a wage increase than granting two extra holidays, in the belief that he would find it more difficult to withdraw fringe benefits and because he is reluctant to cause embarrassment to other employers in the form of holiday demands.

A few cents per hour may "look better" to workers in the form of a fringe benefit than as an addition to the hourly rate. A worker already receiving $2.25 per hour, for example, will not become unduly excited by the announcement of a 5-cent wage increase; but he will regard the adoption of a new retirement plan or health and welfare program as a substantial and impressive development. Furthermore, both parties have a motive to exaggerate the cents-per-hour cost of fringe adjustments in reporting the results of their bargaining.

Frequently more is involved than appearances. Assume that an employer and a union agree, during their 1956 negotiations, that 6 cents per man-hour will go into a fund to finance the payment of supplementary unemployment compensation (guaranteed wages). More important than the amount involved is acceptance of the principle. The employer has assumed a new responsibility which may eventually cost considerably more. Probably he would have paid more than 6 cents to avoid embracing the principle of guaranteed wages. Certainly the union would be unwilling to trade the agreement for merely 6 cents on the wage rate.

There are other circumstances where the cost of fringe benefits to the employer is not commensurate with their meaning to the employee. The most common circumstance is that insurance is made available to the employee which he could not obtain as an individual except at a much greater monetary cost. Even the imperfect health and welfare plans which are currently in effect are much more advantageous than the available individual health insurance policies. These considerations tend to show that wages and fringes are separate matters not to be mixed in the same bowl.

CHAPTER 5

EMPLOYER VALUATION OF LABOR SERVICES: WAGE LEVEL

The employment exchange of inducements and contributions must be acceptable to both parties, employer and employee, to be effectuated. This is possible since both parties value the contributions of labor services differently; the employee values these contributions in terms of the benefit of foregone alternatives, and the employer values them in terms of consumer revenue anticipated from sale of the output of these services. We examined earlier some of the factors influencing employee evaluations of employment opportunities and responses to compensation (labor supplies). Employer evaluations of labor supplies are equally important in the determination of compensation and are the subject of this chapter.

Labor services constitute a primary resource in the production of goods and services ranging from automobiles to kites, health care, wine, newspapers, grand opera, and telephone communications. These services are provided in a variety of forms ranging from the efforts of the physician to the efforts of the professional athlete, the advertising account executive, the stockbroker, carpenter, and teacher. Human resources in the form of labor services are combined with other resources such as coal, iron ore, stamping presses, computers, and typewriters to produce goods and services purchased for consumption. Unlike employee valuations of employment opportunities which vary with individual utility functions, all productive resources can be valued in terms of consumer valuation of the output of the resource, the consumer revenue associated with employment of the resource. This relationship between employer valuation of labor services and consumer valuation of the output of the employer is illustrated in the concept of derived demand. An employer's demand for labor is derived from consumer demand for the employer's product. Labor services possess no innate value for the employer and are valued only insofar as they permit the employer to obtain sales revenue from the output of labor services.

The level of compensation provided in the employment exchange reflects both employer and employee valuation of labor services. Determination of the level of compensation (wage level) to be offered by an employer is influenced both by what is economically feasible and by anticipated responses to the compensation offer by potential employees. The first influence can be characterized as "ability to pay" reflective of economic constraints upon the employer, constraints which determine the maximum wage level at which the employer can operate profitably. Analysis of these economic constraints and influences of employer ability to pay different levels of compensation is the topic of the first section of this chapter. The second section examines constraints on the minimum wage level which might be offered and considerations which influence an employer to offer higher levels of compensation in the employment contract.

A: Economic constraints and ability to pay

Essay 5-1 by Hicks develops a traditional economic model of wage determination based upon the interaction of labor supplies and employer demands for labor in a competitive labor market. The concept of marginal revenue product is critical to Hicks's analysis of employer demand for labor and thus the determination of wages in the labor market. The concept of marginal revenue product is a joint function of the physical productivity of labor services and consumer valuation of the product, and it indicates the maximum worth of labor services to the employer. Considered in simplest form, assume that hiring an additional employee would permit an employer to produce two more units of output each day, output sold to the consumer for $10 each. If no additional expenses other than compensation for labor services were involved, the employer could afford to pay the additional employee up to $20 a day for labor services; payment at lower rates of compensation would be even more profitable for the employer. For purposes of simplicity, Hicks assumes in his analysis that all factors of production other than labor services are held constant so that he can attribute any change in total revenue associated with additional employees to the marginal productivity of labor. Given a fixed investment in capital, plant, and equipment, as well as raw materials, increasing units of labor will yield an increasing marginal revenue product as the plant and technology are utilized more efficiently. Beyond some point associated with capacity production, however, increasing units of labor will yield a decreasing marginal revenue product as efficiency declines. Other things being equal, a profit maximizing employer will operate at the level of employment where the marginal revenue product of labor is decreasing and equal to the additional cost (marginal cost) of the most recently hired units of labor. The number of employees sought by an employer thus varies with the marginal revenue product of labor and the wage rate for employees, fewer persons being hired at higher wage rates.

Wage rates in the Hicksian model are determined in the labor market through competitive bidding among employers for labor services and among employees for jobs; wage rates are not determined individually by employing organizations. The relevant demand for, and supply of, labor services in the competitive labor market model are market phenomena, not the demand and supply of labor services associated with individual employing organizations. The supply of labor services to an employing organization implied by this model is perfectly elastic at the prevailing market wage and, as noted in Chapter 3, provides the theoretical rationale for the compensation principle of paying the market rate for labor. The employer's demand for labor in this model is relevant in determining the amount of labor services it is profitable to hire at the market rate, not the rate to be offered for labor services.

Dunlop (Essay 5-2) calls for a reformulation of wage theory to answer questions different from those addressed by Hicks. Whereas Hicks generalized to a single market wage rate, Dunlop focuses upon the array of wage rates observed in any labor market and seeks an explanation for these observed differences. Dunlop notes that employers in the same labor market pay different wage rates to the same occupation (wage contours) and that these differences persist over time rather than converging as Hicks would argue. These observations, Dunlop reasons, cannot be explained by the Hicksian model of competitive labor markets and require different explanations. While he describes some of the forces influencing the payment of differential wage rates, Dunlop does not develop a complete explanation. We'll return to Dunlop's observations in later chapters as we develop attempts to explain them.

Essay 5-1

The theory of wage determination*

J. R. Hicks

The theory of the determination of wages in a free market is simply a special case of the general theory of value. Wages are the price of labour; and thus, in the absence of control, they are determined, like all prices, by supply and demand. The need for a special theory of wages only arises because both the supply of labour, and the demand for it, and the way in which demand and supply interact on the labour market, have certain peculiar properties, which make it impossible to apply to labour the ordinary theory of commodity value without some further consideration.

The demand for labour is only peculiar to this extent: that labour is a factor of production, and is thus demanded (as a general rule) not because the work to be done is desired for and by itself, but because it is to be used in the production of some other thing which is directly desired.

*Reprinted from J. R. Hicks, *The Theory of Wages* (New York: St. Martin's Press, Macmillan & Co., Ltd., 1963), pp. 1-22 (abridged). Reprinted with permission of Macmillan, London and Basingstoke.

Personal services are indeed an exception to this rule; but apart from this exception, the demand for labour is a derived demand, and the special properties of derived demand may thus reasonably be considered a part of the general theory of wages. It is true that these properties are important, not only in the theory of wages, but also in other departments of economics; most of what has to be said about the demand for labour applies equally to the demand for other factors of production. Yet the matter is so important for an understanding of wages that it has to be given serious attention here.

The supply of labour raises issues of an altogether different character. Most of the special difficulties of labour supply arise from the fact that "labour" is a two-dimensional quantity, depending both on the number of labourers available, and upon their "efficiency"—the amount of labour each is able and willing to provide. It is the task of manipulating these two dimensions simultaneously which has at times caused some confusion.

However, the very nature of this difficulty suggests at once the way in which we had best deal with it. We shall assume the amount of work each man is prepared to do—the individual supply of labour—to be given. It will be found that we can explain most of the more important phenomena of the labour market without reference to the complication introduced by these variations.

This assumption does not altogether remove the difficulties of the supply side, but it very substantially reduces them. For the question of the total number of labourers available in a community is one which modern economists are content to treat as lying outside the theory of wages (differing in this from their predecessors of a century ago). It may be regarded as belonging to the theory of population. For our purposes the total number of labourers available is given.

One difficulty of the supply side does, however, still remain. Unless our theory is to remain very unreal for an unduly large part of the process of its construction, we have to take into account the fact that the efficiencies of different men differ. We can continue for some time to neglect differences in the efficiency of the same man under different circumstances, without thereby making it impossible for us to grasp the more obviously important phenomena of the labour market. But we cannot neglect the differences in the efficiency of different men under the same circumstances without much more serious trouble.

However, ... we shall do even this, though the deficiency must be repaired as soon as possible. Most current theories of the demand for labour do work under the simplifying assumption that "all men are equal"; and while we are examining the demand for labour, it is therefore best to proceed under that assumption.

The interaction of supply and demand

on the labour market is a problem which will have to occupy a good deal of our attention. All buying and selling has some features in common; but nevertheless differences do exist between the ways in which things are bought and sold on different markets. Organised produce markets differ from wholesale trade of the ordinary type; both of these differ from retail trade, and from sale by tender or by auction. The labour market is yet another type. It has been the usual practice of economists to concentrate their attention on those features of exchange which are common to all markets; and to dismiss the differences between markets with a brief reminder that markets may be more or less "perfect." There is little doubt that in doing so they did seize on the really significant thing; the general working of supply and demand is a great deal more important than the differences between markets. But this course meant the almost complete neglect of some factors which appear at first sight very important indeed; the fact that they are really less important than those aspects which were discussed was rarely demonstrated clearly.

When an attempt is made to apply to the labour market the ordinary principles of price determination—without making allowance for the type of market—the result appears at first sight very odd. Wages, say the text-books, tend to that level where demand and supply are equal. If supply exceeds demand, some men will be unemployed, and in their efforts to regain employment they will reduce the wages they ask to that level which makes it just worthwhile for employers to take them on. If demand exceeds supply, employers will be unable to obtain all the labour they require, and will therefore offer higher wages in order to attract labour from elsewhere.

Now this, as I hope to make abundantly clear, is quite a good simplified model of the labour market. So far as general tendencies are concerned, wages do turn out on the whole very much as if they were determined in this manner. It is therefore not in the least surprising if valuable results have been attained by this sort of reasoning. But, since it is a simplified model, it is extremely likely to be misconstrued by those who take it to be an account of how the real labour market works. One of the most obvious features of the real labour market is the fact that at all times there is a certain amount of unemployment. Now it is easy to say—and of course it has often been said—that this means that there is a permanent excess of supply over demand; and that in consequence wages have a permanent tendency to fall. The answer which is most frequently given to this line of argument is a mere appeal to facts. Facts certainly do disprove it; unemployment is undoubtedly sometimes coexistent with rising wages; but such an appeal is surely insufficient. If the conclusion to which an argument leads is false, then it is our business to show just at what point the reasoning was fallacious.

The problems of the nature of the market are almost entirely problems of change. If no one was ever dismissed, and if no one ever had an incentive to change his employment, there would be no problem here. And this suggests a way by which we can postpone consideration of these questions—just as we decided above to postpone the problem of labour supply. We can begin by confining our attention to a labour market in equilibrium. Let us suppose that a level of wages is fixed so that demand and supply balance, and thus there is no tendency for wages to rise or to fall. Let us suppose, further, that this balancing of demand and supply is brought about, not by compensating fluctuations of the demand from particular firms, but by the demand from each firm being stationary, because no employer has any incentive to vary the number of men he takes on. It is necessary for us to adopt this abstract and rigorous conception of equilibrium, since otherwise we should not be effectively ruling out the difficulties of change, but should still be faced with very much the same kind of problem which confronts us in the case of a rise or fall in wages.

We have thus to examine the conditions of full equilibrium in the labour market, assuming the supply of labourers given, and their efficiencies given and equal. This enables us finally to isolate the pure problem of demand. It is true that we only achieve this isolation at the expense of a series of highly artificial assumptions; but in economics, as in other sciences, abstraction is usually the condition of clear thinking. The complications created by the things we have left out can be reintroduced later.

The first of the necessary conditions of equilibrium is that every man should receive the same wage—subject at any rate to allowances for "other advantages" and possibly for costs of movement (but these things also we neglect at present). If wages are not equal, then it will clearly be to the advantage of an employer who is paying a higher level of wages to dismiss his present employees, and to replace them by other men who had been receiving less. If he offers a wage somewhere between the two previously existing levels, he will both lower his own costs (and consequently improve his own situation) and successfully attract the new men, since he is offering them a higher wage than they received before. So long as such transfers can be made advantageously to both parties entering upon the new contract, there is no equilibrium; since someone can always disturb it to his own advantage. Equal wages are a necessary condition of equilibrium in a market governed by our present assumptions.

The second condition is much more critical. The only wage at which equilibrium is possible is a wage which equals the value of the marginal product of the labourers. At any given wage it will pay employers best to take on that number of labourers which makes their marginal product—that is to say, the difference between the total physical product which is actually secured and that which would have been secured from the same quantity of other resources if the number of labourers had been increased or diminished by one—equal in value to the wage. In this way the demand for labour of each employer is determined; and the total demand of all employers is determined from it by addition. Since in equilibrium it is necessary that the total demand should equal the total supply, the wage must be that which just enables the total number of labourers available to be employed. This must equal the value of the marginal product of the labourers available.

The conventional proof of the marginal productivity proposition is simple enough. It follows from the most fundamental form of the law of diminishing returns that an increased quantity of labour applied to a fixed quantity of other resources will yield a diminished marginal product. Thus if the employer were to take on a number of labourers so large that their marginal product was not worth the wage which has to be paid, be would soon find that the number was excessive. By reducing the number he employed, he would reduce his total production, and therefore (under competitive conditions) his gross receipts. But at the same time he would reduce his expenditure; and since the wage was higher than the marginal product, he would reduce his expenditure more than his receipts, and so increase his profits. Similarly, he would not reduce his employment of labour to such a point as would make the wage less than the marginal product; for by so doing he would be reducing his receipts more than his expenditure, and so again diminishing his profits. The number of labourers which an employer will prefer to take on is that number which makes his profits a maximum, and that number is given by the

equality of wages to the marginal product of the labour employed.

It is thus clear that the wage at which equilibrium is possible will vary in the opposite direction to changes in the total number of labourers available. If the number of labourers available on the market had been larger, the wage must have been lower; since the additional product secured by the employment of one of these extra labourers would be worth less than the previously given wage, and consequently it would not pay to employ these men unless the wage-level was reduced. If the number had been less, employers would have had an incentive to demand more labourers at the given wage than would actually have been available, and their competition would therefore force up the level of wages. The only wage which is consistent with equilibrium is one which equals the value of the marginal product of the available labour.

The number of men employed by a firm depends directly upon two things: the quantity of product it desires to turn out, and the method it decides to adopt in production. Some methods use a large amount of one factor, some use less of that and relatively more of another; and though no entrepreneur in his senses would ever use a method which needed a large amount of all factors, when a method which needed a smaller quantity of each of them was available, a very real choice does arise between methods, one of which uses relatively more of factor A and relatively less of factor B, while the other uses less of A and more of B. If the method of production is given, then the quantity of labour employed varies directly with the output; the larger the output, the more men will be employed. If the output is given, then a variation in method will still vary the quantity of labour employed to some extent, since some methods need more labour than others.

In equilibrium, both the scale of production and the method of production must be chosen in such a way that no opportunity remains open for employers to benefit themselves by a change. Thus if for the present we work under the assumption that the methods of production are fixed, the amount produced in each firm (and consequently the demand for labour) is determined by the condition that the price of the product should equal its cost of production—including an allowance for "normal profits." These normal profits are genuinely an element in costs; for they are simply the price which has to be paid for the resources—the capital and managerial skill—which are contributed by the employer himself, in order just to induce them to stay in the branch of production in question. If the wages which have to be paid in a particular industry were higher, costs of production would be raised relatively to selling prices, and the profits of employers would consequently be reduced. These employers would therefore find that the employment of their own resources in the industry in question had become less advantageous relatively to the employment of similar resources in other industries, so that they would tend to turn their attention to other industries, and production in the first industry would contract. And under our present assumptions, the contraction of production would lead to a roughly proportional contraction of the demand for labour in that industry.

In exactly the same way, a fall in wages, other things remaining equal, would make the industry concerned a relatively profitable one for the investment of other resources; new capital would flow in, new firms would set up, and the demand for labour would expand. If the industry is to be in equilibrium, there must be no tendency for an expansion of this kind, or for a contraction; the cost of production must equal the selling price.

When an entrepreneur has to choose between two different methods of produc-

ing a given output, he may be expected to choose that which costs least. For, at any rate in the first place, anything which reduces his costs will raise his profits. If employers are not using the cheapest method of production available to them, they have an incentive to change; and so there is no equilibrium.

It is this condition of minimum cost of production per unit of output which leads us directly to the law of marginal productivity. For if we suppose the prices of all the factors of production to be given, the "least cost" combination of factors will be given by the condition that the marginal products of the factors are proportional to their prices. If the

$$\frac{\text{Marginal product of factor A}}{\text{Price of A}}$$

is greater than

$$\frac{\text{Marginal product of B}}{\text{Price of B}},$$

then this means that it will be to the advantage of the entrepreneur to use a method of production which uses a little more of A and a little less of B, since in that way be will get a larger product for the same expenditure, or (what comes to the same thing) he will get an equal product at a lower cost.

This condition of the proportionality of marginal products is simply another means of expressing the necessity that the method employed in a position of equilibrium should be the cheapest method of reaching the desired result. No new principle whatever is introduced; so that in practical applications we can work with the condition of minimum cost, or with the condition of the proportionality of marginal products—whichever seems more significant in the particular case.[1]

[1] The proportionality of marginal products is simply the mathematical condition for minimum cost of production—or maximum production from a given expenditure. It is thus easy to see why it takes the same form as the law of equi-marginal utilities—the condition for maximisation of satisfactions.

It must, however, be observed that the above condition only states that the marginal products are proportional to the prices of the factors—it does not say that the prices *equal* the values of the marginal products. So far as the choice of methods of production is concerned, it appears that the prices of the factors might all exceed, or all fall short of, the values of the marginal products—so long as they do it in the same proportion. But if this were to be the case, it would be possible for the entrepreneur to increase his profits by expanding or contracting production without changing his methods. The condition of equality between price and cost of production would not be satisfied.

When we allow for the variability of methods of production, there is thus another way in which changes in wages may affect the demand for labour. A rise in wages will make labour expensive relatively to other factors of production, and will thus encourage entrepreneurs to use methods which employ less labour and more of these other factors. And this evidently applies in exactly the same way to industry as a whole, as it does to particular industries. The more extensive the rise in wages, the more substitution will take place. For exactly the same reason, a fall in wages will lead to substitution in the reverse direction.

The law of marginal productivity, in its usual form, is simply a convenient means whereby the statement of the two tendencies we have been discussing can be combined. On the one hand, the returns to other resources than labour tend to equality in their different applications (the tendency which alone is taken account of in the formulation of "net productivity"); on the other hand, employers can modify the methods which they employ in their businesses, and the relative profitability of different methods depends on the relative prices of the factors of production. For some purposes it is convenient to use the conventional formulation, which brings together the two tendencies, and enables us to manipulate them together; but for a good many other purposes it is convenient to treat them separately.

There can be no full equilibrium unless the wages of labour equal its marginal product; since, if this equality is not attained, it means that someone has open to him an opportunity of gain which he is not taking. Either employers will be able to find an advantage in varying the methods of production they use, or investors and other owners of property will be able to benefit themselves by transferring the resources under their control from one branch of production to another. But we cannot go on from this to conclude that this equality of wages and marginal products will actually be found in practice; for the real labour market is scarcely ever in equilibrium in the sense considered here. In actual practice changes in methods are continually going on; and resources are continually being transferred from one industry to another, or new resources being put at the disposal of industry, which are not uniformly distributed among the various branches of production. This ceaseless change is partly a consequence of changes in the ultimate determinants of economic activity—those things which we have to take as the final data of economic enquiry—changes in tastes, changes in knowledge, changes in the natural environment, and in the supply and efficiency of the factors of production generally. As these things change, so the marginal product of labour changes with them; and these changes in marginal productivity excert pressure, in one direction or the other, upon the level of wages.

Essay 5-2

Suggestions toward a reformulation of wage theory*

John T. Dunlop

PRELIMINARY OBSERVATIONS

All wage theory is in a sense demand-and-supply analysis. A wage is a price, and the wage structure is a subsystem of prices. Prices and price systems are fruitfully to be interpreted in terms of demand and supply. There is no special or peculiar "demand-and-supply" theory of wages.

The notion of a "political" theory of wages involves confusion. In the absence of unions, firms or groups of managements make wage decisions; and under conditions of collective bargaining, the parties reach agreement on wage scales. It is indeed appropriate to study the processes, procedures, and influences which determine decisions in these organizations and the techniques which they employ in agreement making. Both parties ordinarily have some discretion, particularly in the short run and depending on whether they are wage leaders or wage followers, concerning the amount and the form of the wage settlement. But it does not advance understanding of decision making in organizations to label the process as either "political" or "economic." The decision-making process internal to a management organization or a union is an appropriate area of research, but this subject does not preempt the theory of wages. Moreover, a large part of the institutional study of

*Reprinted from John T. Dunlop, "The Task of Contemporary Wage Theory," in *New Concepts in Wage Determination*, ed. George W. Taylor and Frank C. Pierson, pp. 127-39. Copyright © 1957 by McGraw-Hill, Inc. Used with permission of McGraw-Hill Book Company.

decisions should seek to show the impact of external events, including market developments, on internal decisions.

Wage theory has tended historically to disintegrate on the supply side. As has been noted, in the course of refinement of the wage-fund theory and the supply function associated with marginal productivity, the supply function tended to be pushed outside the analytical system. The amount of labor supplied and the wage rate came to be determined by social custom or institutional considerations. For purposes of economic analysis the wage rate came to be regarded as a given. In a sense the pivotal task of wage theory is to formulate an acceptable theory on the supply side.

It is not satisfactory to treat wage determination in terms of a single rate. In the past there have been various devices to reduce wage setting to the problem of a single rate. A single unskilled or common-labor rate has been envisaged into which all skilled labor may be translated as consisting of so many "units" of unskilled labor. This classical convention was followed by both Marx and Keynes. A single wage rate, out of the whole structure, is regarded as an index or barometer for all other rates. But all wage rates do not move together, either in the short run or in the long run. The wage structure is not rigid throughout a period of time. Moreover, the determination of the wage level and the determination of wage structure are closely interrelated.

Wage theory must operate with the concept of *wage structure*—the complex of rates within firms differentiated by occupation and employee and the complex of interfirm rate structures. The concept of wage structure, for the purpose of the present analysis, is a central concept; the analysis of wage determination will be approached through the wage structure. Indeed, the task of analyzing wage determination is not the problem of setting a single rate but rather the problem of setting and variation in the whole structure or complex of rates. While the general level of wage rates can be thought of as changing apart from variations in structure, they are not actually dissociated. Changes in the wage level, associated with changes in output levels in the system, are necessarily associated with changes in wage structure. The interrelation between the wage level and the wage structure is itself a major area of inquiry.

The wage structure within a bargaining unit, plant, firm, association, or other grouping in which wage differentials are set by the same authorities must be distinguished from the complex of interfirm or group structures each set by different agencies. From the point of view of the individual decision makers, the first wage structure is internal while the second is external. One of the central problems of wage analysis is to indicate the interrelations between the internal and external wage structure.

The analysis that follows utilizes two concepts which require explanation: *job clusters* and *wage contours.*

JOB CLUSTERS AND WAGE CONTOURS

A job cluster is defined as a stable group of job classifications or work assignments within a firm (wage-determining unit) which are so linked together by (1) technology, (2) the administrative organi-

zation of the production process, including policies of transfer, layoff and promotion, or (3) social custom that they have common wage-making characteristics.[1] In an industrial plant which may have literally thousands of jobs, each wage rate is not equally related and dependent upon all other wage rates. The internal wage structure, the complex of differentials, is not rigidly fixed for all time. Neither do relative rates change in random relation to each other. The internal wage-rate structure is to be envisaged as divided into groups of jobs or job clusters. The wage rates for the operations and jobs within a cluster are more closely related in their wage movements and wage-making forces than are rates outside the cluster.

Thus a tool room in a plant would ordinarily constitute a job cluster. The training and skill of the machinists who operate the various specialized machines—lathes, shapers, cutters, and so on—are similar. Their work is closely interrelated in the productive process. They may work together apart from others. They may have a common promotion, transfer, and layoff pattern. The wage rates within the tool room are more closely related to each other than they are to the rates for other employees in the power plant—on production lines, in the maintenance crew, in the office, or in the sales force. The wage structure of the ordinary plant is to be envisaged as comprised of a limited number of such job clusters, each with a number of rates.

From the analytical point of view these job clusters are given in the short period by the technology, the managerial and administrative organization of the wage-determining unit, and the social customs of the work community. Thus the em-

---

[1] See [Essay 6-3] by E. Robert Livernash for a further development of the concept of job clusters and for much rich illustrative material. This concept has been developed in joint discussion and in common or similar administrative experience over the years.

ployees on a furnace or a mill and the crew of a train or plane may constitute a job cluster (technology); so also may employees in a department (administrative organization), or the salesgirls in a department store or the stenographers in an office (social custom). These factors may reinforce each other in describing a job cluster, as in the instance of technological and administrative consideration defining the cluster of trucking rates in a department store or plant. In turn, certain job clusters may be more closely related to some rather than to other clusters. In this sense, clerical rates as a whole may be more closely related to other clerical rates than to managerial or factory rates. Wage theory, for the short period, does not seek to explain the configuration of particular job clusters. For the longer period, it is essential to show that the scope of a job cluster within a wage-rate structure may be expanded, restricted, or divided as a consequence of changes in the technology, administrative organization, or social customs, including union organization, in the plant.

The job cluster can be examined in more detail. Ordinarily a job cluster will contain a key rate, or in some cases several. The cluster consists of the key rate(s) and a group of associated rates. The key rate may be the highest paid, or the rate paid at the top step in a promotion ladder, or the rate paid for a job at which a large number of workers are employed. The rates set for a one-man streetcar or bus operator, a reporter at the top automatic step of advancement, a pilot of an airplane, a toolmaker, and a meat boner are illustrations of key rates. There may be several key rates in a single cluster and a number of clusters in one internal rate structure. Typically, the key-rate jobs show relatively less change in job content over a period of time and are often relatively more standardized among firms than are other jobs. The key rates are

those which managements and unions typically have in mind and explicitly discuss in considering the internal wage structure.

The smallest building block in the wage structure is thus the job cluster comprised of a key rate, or several such rates in some cases, and a group of associated rates. The internal wage structure of the plant (wage-determining unit) consists of a number of these job clusters. Such is the anatomy of the internal wage structure.

The forces which determine the wage rates for the key jobs and the rates for associated jobs in a cluster are not confined within a firm. The "exterior" plays a very important role. The "exterior" consists of labor-market influences, including union and government wage policies, and forces in the markets for products. The "exterior" cannot operate directly on a thousand slightly differentiated jobs. The key rates play a decisive role in relating the exterior to the internal rate structure. Indeed, the key rates are affected by the exterior, and adjustments in these rates are transmitted to other rates within the plant, cluster by cluster.

NATURE OF WAGE CONTOURS

A wage contour is defined as a stable group of wage-determining units (bargaining units, plants or firms) which are so linked together by (1) similarity of product markets, (2) resort to similar sources for a labor force, or (3) common labor-market organization (custom) that they have common wage-making characteristics. The wage rates for particular occupations in a particular firm are not ordinarily independent of all other wage rates; they are more closely related to the wage rates of some firms than to others. A contour for particular occupations is to be defined in terms of both the product market and the labor market. A contour thus has three dimensions: (1) particular occupations or job clusters, (2) a sector of industry, and (3) a geographical location. The firms which comprise a contour constitute a particular product market; also, they may either be located in one labor market or scattered throughout a region or the country as a whole. The level of wage rates by occupations within the contour need not be equal, but changes in compensation are highly interrelated.

In the United States the basic steel contour for production jobs consists of the producers of basic steel products scattered in various communities throughout the country. The wage rates of the jobs in these firms—in their blast furnaces, steel works, and rolling mill operations—are closely interrelated. Some other operations of the same companies, such as cement mills or shipping, are typically excluded from the basic steel contour. While there are a variety of submarkets, and each basic steel producer may have specialized features resulting from its particular product market or from the particular locality in which it hires labor, nonetheless the basic steel wage contour is sharply defined and clearly distinguishable from others.

The meat-packing and rubber contours are further illustrations. But a contour is not to be identified with an industry. Many broad industrial groups of firms have such specialized submarkets that they are decisive for wage setting. In the paper industry, for example, kraft paper, newsprint, tissue paper, quality writing paper, and bank-note paper firms have such distinctive products markets, with some distinctive production and labor-cost problems, that they have separate wage-setting processes.

A contour should not be regarded as necessarily having a sharp boundary line. Some firms have such unique product markets that they fall among several wage contours. Specialized markets and competitive conditions may result in some

firms "at the the edge of the contour" being only slightly influenced by wage developments "at the center." The meat-packing pattern may spread from the major packers to other packing plants, then to some cutting plants for the hotel and restaurant trade, but not necessarily to all sausage makers. Indeed, in some localities such small plants may even constitute a separate wage contour.

Some major contours may constitute limits to the wage settlements within less significant wage-setting groups of firms. Thus, the flat-glass contour has been influenced both by the basic steel and the automobile contours. These larger patterns have provided limits conditioning the amount and the form of the flat-glass settlements.

A contour may be confined to a locality in its labor-market dimension. Thus newspapers in New York City constitute a contour for wage-setting purposes. The rates for various occupations in one newspaper are closely related to those in other newspapers in that city. Specialized product markets, for other types of printing or publishing, are a part of still other wage contours. In some localities, wages in one group of firms may be so dominant as to spread that contour to firms which would ordinarily be in a different contour. The roles played by auto rates in Detroit, steel rates in Pittsburgh, and, traditionally, textile rates in Fall River are illustrative. Similarly, the role of some unions may be so significant in a locality as to expand a contour to include companies which ordinarily would be in separate contours or which would be relatively isolated.

A contour is confined to particular ranges of skill, occupations, or job clusters of the constituent firms. Not all types of labor hired by a firm will have wage rates determined in the same contour. Thus, a firm employing a professional chemist, a patternmaker, and a clerk may be expected to be part of three quite different contours. A construction firm hiring boilermakers, operating engineers, and laborers will be a part of the construction product market in each instance, but three separate wage contours are involved. The boilermaker's rate is set over the largest geographical area, while the laborer's rate is likely to be confined to a single locality.

A wage contour can be explored in further detail. In the ordinary case a wage contour contains one, or in some instances, several key settlements. The contour is comprised of the rates for the key firm(s) and a group of associated firms. The key settlement may be set by the largest firm, the price leader, or the firm with labor-relations leadership. Thus in the basic steel contour, the wages determined by the United States Steel Corporation generally have been followed by all other firms in the contour. The other basic steel producers have customarily followed the "pattern" immediately. In the meat-packing contour, the wage leader has been Swift, or in some instances Armour. In the rubber industry each of the "big four" has been the leader on occasion. In these cases, more time elapses between a change by the leaders and a change by the followers. Some firms may follow only at a distance, altering even the terms of the key settlement in some respects. The American Motors contract in 1955 provided such an illustration in the automobile contour.

A wage contour, then, can be envisaged as a grouping of firms, for a given range of occupations, in which some firms are very closely related to the leaders. Other firms are less directly associated. At the exterior of the contour, furthest from the key settlement, the firms may follow the leadership only remotely.

A variety of devices have been developed which relate wages determined by the key settlement to those of other firms in the contour. The existence of a common expiration date for the wage agreements in several firms or the sequence of anniversary dates is reflective of the rela-

tions within a wage contour. Some firms commit themselves in advance to pay the wages set by other companies; many commit themselves to consider a wage change when a "wage movement" has developed in the industry (contour). Specialized product markets or sources of labor supply or skill requirements or union organization may mean that a particular firm, remote from the "center" of the contour, will modify in some respects the "pattern" established at the key bargain.

The firms which comprise a wage contour may be organized into a formal employers' association rather than appear to make wage decisions without a common organization. In an association not all firms actually have equal weight in making decisions; wage leaders exercise the same functions within an organization as they would without one, although an association may mean that all wages are changed at the same time. In many instances, an association constitutes only a formal difference from the wage-leadership conditions that would be evident without an employers' organization.[2]

Wage-making forces are envisaged as concentrated on the key rates in the job clusters. These rates "extend" out from the internal structure of the firm to the "exterior" and constitute the focal points for wage-setting forces among firms within the contour. The key rates in the job clusters constitute the channels of impact between the exterior developments in the contour (and through the contour the larger developments in the economy) and the interior rate structure of the firm. Moreover, in an analogous way, the key bargains constitute the focal point of wage-setting forces within the contour and constitute the points where those

---

[2] While the impact of labor organization upon wage rates is frequently discussed in current literature, the question of the effect of employer organization upon wage rates is seldom explored. Frequently a formal employer organization merely sharpens relations already apparent.

wage-making forces converge that are exterior to the contour and common to the total economy.

A theory of wages is not required to treat each wage rate in the system as of equal importance. The view of the wage structure outlined above singles out a limited number of key job rates and key wage settlements or bargains for analysis. These particular rates are selected, at least in the short run, by the anatomy of the wage structure which is given by (1) the technology and administrative arrangements of firms, (2) competitive patterns in product markets, and (3) the sources of labor supply. Long-run forces affecting technology and competitive conditions in the product or labor market change both job clusters and contours given in the short run. Thus the spreading of large firms or unions with established wage policies into different product markets may change the anatomy of clusters or contours.

The concepts of job cluster and wage contour are analogous. In each case a group of rates surrounds a key rate. The concepts seek to relate the internal and the external wage structure; they focus attention on the mechanics by which the internal structure through job clusters is influenced by external developments in the wage contour. Wage theory cannot reduce all structure to a single rate; the limited number of strategic rates depicted by the job clusters and wage contours are to be the focus of wage theory.[3]

WAGE STRUCTURE IN THE SHORT RUN

The concepts developed in the preceding discussion can now be applied to a

particular case. Table 1 shows the union scale for motortruck drivers in Boston for July 1953. Each rate shows the wage scale established between the union and an association or group of employers engaged in selling transportation services. Each rate is to be interpreted as the key rate for truck drivers in a series of contours. Some small part of the differences in wages may be attributed to variations in the skill or work performed; some may be related to differences in the length of the work week and the timing of contract expiration during a year, and some may arise from differences in methods of wage payment. The teamsters who work at these various rates are essentially similar and substitutable. Essentially the same disparity in rates is found in most other cities, with a high similarity in the relative ranking of rates for various branches of the trade.

In a significant sense, the case constitutes a kind of critical experiment. One type of labor performing almost identical work, organized by the same union, is

Table 1: Union scale for motortruck drivers, Boston, July 1, 1953

Transportation service	Hourly rate
Magazine.	$2.494
Newspaper, day	2.393
Oil	2.215
Paper handlers, newspaper.	2.062
Building construction	2.00
Beer, bottle and keg	1.905
Railway express, 1½–5 tons	1.869
Meatpacking house, 3–5 tons	1.83
Grocery, chain store	1.819
Garbage disposal	1.725
Bakery, Hebrew	1.71
General hauling, 3–5 tons	1.685
Rendering	1.675
Coal	1.65
Movers, piano and household	1.65
Armored car	1.64
Ice	1.56
Carbonated beverage	1.54
Linen supply.	1.537
Wastepaper	1.44
Laundry, wholesale.	1.28
Scrap, iron and metal	1.27

Source: *Union Wages and Hours: Motortruck Drivers and Helpers,* U.S. Bureau of Labor Statistics Bulletin 1154 (July 1, 1953), pp. 9-10.

[3] For an imaginative discussion on the concept of labor market, see Clark Kerr, "The Balkanization of Labor Markets," *Labor Mobility and Economic Opportunity: Essays by E. Wight Bakke and Others* (New York: Wiley, 1954), pp. 92-110. The present discussion would add to that of Professor Kerr the emphasis that the scope of product markets is reflected back into the labor market, thus defining the scope of wage setting.

paid markedly different rates by different associations of employers in the truck transportation industry. Why the wide range in wage rates? Are the disparities temporary? Do they arise from "friction" or "immobilities" in the labor market? Are they primarily the consequence of a monopolistic seller of labor discriminating among types of employers? I believe the answer to these several questions is largely in the negative.

Basically each rate reflects a wage contour. Each is a reflection of the product market. Within any one contour the wage rates among competing firms will tend to be equal. Among individual beer distributors, construction firms, ice deliverers, or scrap iron and metal haulers there tend to be few differences in rates. But there are sharp differences in rates among contours. Fundamentally the differences in the product market are reflected back into the labor market.

But what are the mechanics? Why do not all teamsters move to the higher-paying contours? Or why do not the employers in the higher-paying contours set a lower wage rate, since similar labor seems to be available to other contours at lower rates? In a perfect labor market (a bourse) such changes toward uniformity would tend to take place.

Part of the explanation is to be found in the historical sequence of growth of the trucker's wage scale. Newer and expanding industries or contours, such as oil, have had to pay higher wages to attract labor in the evolution of wage scales. Part of the explanation is derived from the fact that this historical structure of wages has conditioned the labor supply so that the relative rates among contours are regarded as proper. A minor part of the explanation lies in the fact that these wage rates are influenced by the wages of the group of workers these employees tend to be associated with in work operations. Teamsters hauling oil and building materials come in contact with high-paid employees in their work operations, while laundry and scrap

drivers have more direct contact with lower-paid employees. A larger emphasis is to be placed on the fact that competitive conditions permit higher pay at the top end of the list. Demand is less elastic and wages tend to be a lower proportion of the sales revenue. But do the firms pay more simply because they can afford to do so? If the union is considered a decisive factor, then an explanation can be made simply in terms of the union acting as a discriminating seller in dealing with different industries. While union influence may be significant in some cases, this type of wage spread is so general, apart from the union, that the principal explanation should lie elsewhere.

When the labor market is tight, the various contours are able to bid for labor so that a differentiated structure of rates reflecting the product-market contours and competitive conditions tends to be established. For a variety of reasons these differentials are not readily altered in a looser labor market. Making a wage change or changing a differential among sectors involves costs. Newer and expanding employers using the same type of labor have to pay more to attract a labor force, and a differential once established by a contour is not easily abolished.

For these various reasons the product market tends to be mirrored in the labor market and to determine the wage structure. The differentials are not transitory; they are not to be dismissed as imperfections. The differentials are not basically to be interpreted as a range of indefinite or random rates, although a community with a wide variety of firms in different product markets may present the impression of random rates. The wage contours and their relative rates reflect the basic nature of product and labor markets.

These arguments can be applied to most of the cases of interfirm wage differentials that have been reported. There are some differences in wage rates which reflect differences in job content; there are differences in costs and earnings in the way firms administer the same wage structure, and there are differences in methods of compensation (incentive and time rates). These factors account for some of the statistically observed variations in wage rates. However, the theoretically significant differences for similar grades of labor are those which reflect different product-market competitive conditions.

THE LONG-TERM DEVELOPMENT OF WAGE STRUCTURE

The structure of wage rates of a country reflects to some extent the course of its industrialization and economic development. The supply of labor and the rate and pattern of industrialization are the crucial factors. A country with a scarcity of labor will probably require and establish larger wage differentials for skill than one with an abundant labor supply. A rapid rate of industrialization will produce larger skill differentials than will a slow rate. The sequence in the development of industries in the industrialization process will affect to some degree the structure of wage rates as differentials are used to attract a labor force to these industries from agriculture or from other industrial activities. A comparative study of the wage structures of various countries today reflects the imprints of the path of economic development.[4]

In an agrarian society, relatively small differentials are required to attract a labor force away from agriculture to industry. The first industries historically required simpler skills, and the levels of rates over agriculture were only slightly higher. As successive industries developed, higher rates were required to draw a work force, not primarily directly from agriculture, but from lower-paid industries. Successive industries appear to require more special-

ized skills, and higher wages result. The structure of wages thus reflects the pattern of industrialization.

Some of the same phenomena can be seen today when new plants are introduced into a particular community. There are a variety of circumstances which may result in new employers setting higher rates. The higher the general level of employment, the stronger these factors will be. The new industries may require higher standards of skill. The new plants may need several thousand employees as a minimum work force. A higher rate is needed to attract that number than if the plant were to grow gradually from a small figure. Labor costs are frequently a small fraction of total costs, and the product markets are often oligopolistic. These factors permit or encourage the enterprise to set a higher rate for the key jobs than would be paid for a comparable level of skill in other jobs in the community. The oil, chemical, atomic, and television industries provide current examples. All this suggests that there is a tendency for new industries to push the wage level upward.

The wage structure is to be approached as a reflex of the larger pattern of industrialization. The wage structure of an agricultural economy is largely undifferentiated by skill or product-market divisions. Increasing industrialization creates increasing differentiation by skill, creating many new occupations and job operations. Some of these occupations or jobs are key jobs and provide the basis for interfirm comparisons. Increasing industrialization also creates new groupings of products within which are unique types of competition. These product-market characteristics, combined with some features of the labor market, create wage contours within which wages tend to move under common forces, as opposed to wages outside the contour.

When a wage structure has been established, the labor supply tends to adapt itself to the relative structure of rates, as

---

[4] See John T. Dunlop and Melvin Rothbaum, "International Comparisons of Wage Structures," *International Labour Review*, vol. 71 (April 1955), pp. 347-63.

reflected in key rates, in a variety of ways. Preferences and relative ratings given to jobs by workers are not autonomous; they reflect the broad outlines of the established wage structure. The long-established rate structure, created as envisaged in this discussion, influences the choice of workers and may even take on normative elements. The labor force, for most occupations, would appear to be highly pliable over a generation. The established wage structure comes to shape labor supply over the long run. This is not to deny that supply may not adapt readily in the short period to changes in relative demand. Nor does it deny that relative wage rates may affect long-run supply for some occupations within some limits. The point is that the labor supply over a generation is clearly highly adaptable to the great variety of jobs created by modern industrialization and that the work force tends in important respects to adapt itself to the long-established rate structure for key jobs.

Commentary

Hicks explains wages as a result of interacting market forces, employer demand for, and employee supply of, labor services. Employer demand is based upon the productivity of labor and the marginal revenue realized by the employer in the sale of the resulting products, the marginal revenue product of labor. An employer will seek to hire more labor as long as the marginal revenue product exceeds the wage rate and will offer wage rates up to the level of marginal revenue product to elicit a larger supply of labor. Wage rate is the price of labor, and the labor services offered by employees vary directly with this price. Employers bidding to secure labor services and workers bidding to secure employment tend to force the market wage to that level which equates supply and demand; a higher wage would elicit more job seekers and reduce the number of jobs available and a lower wage would restrict the number of job seekers and expand the number of jobs available. Wage determination in this model is a market phenomenon, not an employer decision. Hicks also argues that labor resources are substituted one for another as differentials in wage rates exceed differentials in marginal revenue product, low wage occupations are substituted for high wage occupations if the difference in marginal revenue product is less than the wage differential. Thus any observed wage differentials should, according to Hicks, reflect compensating differentials in marginal productivity among occupations.

Evidence supportive of Hicks's reasoning can be observed in the increased employment of para-professionals as professional salaries increase; the bidding up of wage rates for computer programmers as demand increases faster than the supply of programmers; and in the introduction of containerized shipping as wage rates for longshoring increase. Contradictory evidence also appears in the maintenance of relative wages for teachers as demand declines relative to supply and in Dunlop's observations of wage contours, interemployer wage differentials within a single occupation. Dunlop explicitly rejects the concept of a single occupational wage rate and focuses attention upon the structure of wage rates or wage differentials. He notes that one of the major characteristics of employers associated with different wage contours is industry or product market, employees in a single occupation are paid higher or lower wage rates depending upon the industry in which employed. Wage rates in a job cluster and in a wage contour traditionally are compared one with another and tend to change in concert; a change in wage rate for a "key job" occasions comparable change in the wage rates of other jobs in the cluster or contour. Dunlop does not develop an explicit rationale or explanation for the behavior of wage contours, and implies that wage contours reflect institutionalized tradition whatever the original cause of the behavior.

Despite seeming contradictions, the concepts presented in Hicks's analysis can be elaborated and developed to provide an explanation for the behavior observed by Dunlop. We should note first that the determination of wage rates in the Hicks model is a function of competition in the labor market rather than individual employer decisions. This conclusion results from assumptions about the supply of labor services to the market and to the employer, assumptions challenged later. The supply of labor services to the labor market is assumed to be relatively inelastic in the short run. The size of the potential labor force is determined by population and age and can change only slightly in the short run as individuals migrate to the market or forsake alternative activities such as education, retirement, or homemaking. Individuals within the labor force, however, are assumed to be competitive in job seeking and highly mobile among alternative employers in the labor market. A market wage rate is determined by bidding among employers and employees, a wage rate which balances demand for, and supply of, labor services within the market. The resulting supply of labor services to an employing organization is very elastic at this wage rate due to the assumed mobility and competition among workers. An individual employer in the competitive labor market model is constrained to payment of the market wage rate and can exercise discretion only in the determination of the number of persons to hire at that rate, he cannot exercise discretion in the determination of the wage rate to be offered. We noted in Chapter 3 that the compensation principle of payment of the market wage rate is based upon assumptions of a highly elastic supply of labor to the employing organization, and then challenged these assumptions noting various factors influencing the elasticity of labor supplies. Depending upon these factors, an individual employer is more or less constrained to payment of a market rate of wages. Labor supplies differentiated among employers would permit variation of wage rates for a single occupation within a labor market as would Thurow's hypothesis of a labor queue, workers gaining access to high- and low-wage employment opportunities based upon order in the queue. The opportunity for variation in wage rates offered by employers indicated in Dunlop's wage contours is provided by relaxing the assumptions of highly elastic supplies of labor to employing organizations, but this provides no explanation of how employers could afford to pay different wage rates or why they would be motivated to pay them. The analysis of demand for labor by the employing organization can be elaborated and the concept of marginal revenue product refined as an influence of employer valuations of labor services to provide partial explanation of Dunlop's wage contours and to develop guides for employer determination of wage rates to offer in the employment exchange.

Marginal revenue product

The value of labor services to an employer is represented in the concept of marginal revenue product (MRP) and is equivalent to the additional revenue accruing to the employer from employment of those labor services. At most, an employer can afford to pay an employee the amount of sales revenue obtained from the worker's production, assuming no additional costs other than labor were involved in this production. Marginal revenue product thus varies as a joint function of physical productivity and demand for the product, and differences in either or both of these factors influence the amount feasible for payment of labor services.

Consider first the influence of physical productivity upon marginal revenue product. The additional production realized through employment of an individual, marginal physical productivity (MPP), depends critically upon the technology employed in the production process and the level of operations relative to capacity of the process. Certain production processes require the addition of teams of individuals for operation and total production is a step function of labor rather than a continuous function; marginal physical productivity varies with teams of employees, not with individual employees. Physical productivity also varies with the level of technology employed, often reflected in the capital-labor ratio; an individual working with a calculator typically completes more arithmetic calculations than one working without such assistance. Technology and capital investment typically are fixed in the short run and are not variable with additional units of labor. We might expect that marginal physical productivity of labor varies with the level of operations relative to capacity operations; marginal physical productivity increases significantly with the initial employment of workers, may continue to increase due to efficiency realized through expanded operations, and then declines rapidly with increases in labor beyond the level of capacity operations. These relationships are illustrated in Figure 5-1 where C indicates employment associated with capacity level of operations. Since the marginal physical productivity curve *MPP* indicates the additional produc-

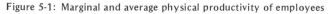
Figure 5-1: Marginal and average physical productivity of employees

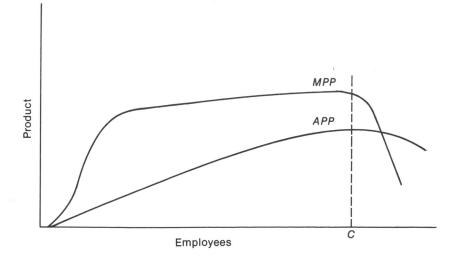

tion associated with each additional employee, total production at any level of employment is illustrated by the area under the curve up to that level of employment, the sum of marginal products to that point. Average physical production for each level of employment might be calculated as total production divided by number of employees and is indicated in Figure 5-1 as *APP*. Note that average physical productivity increases more slowly than marginal productivity and reaches a maximum value when marginal productivity is declining and is equal to marginal productivity at that level of employment. This relationship results from the fact that average productivity will continue to increase as long as the marginal product of an additional employee is greater than the average product achieved to date; average productivity will reach a maximum when the marginal product of an additional employee is equal to the average product realized for the labor force, and average productivity will decline as marginal additions to output are smaller than the previously achieved average productivity.

The general nature of relationships illustrated in Figure 5-1 can be inferred for many work organizations although specifics may vary considerably from one organization to another depending upon the nature of the technology employed, capital-labor ratio, size of operations, and organizational influences upon productivity. Thus, for example, marginal and average productivity relationships might be higher in one organization than another due to newer or more efficient technology, or due to better training, motivation, or supervision of employees. The level of employment corresponding to capacity production will vary depending upon the nature of technology and size of operations. Finally, the continuity of relationships and slopes of the relationships will vary with the nature of technology as well. Both marginal and average productivity also will vary over time in a single organization as capital investment increases, more efficient technologies are employed, and as more capable and effective individuals are employed. Major differences in productivity relationships can be associated with different industries which produce different products involving different technologies and raw materials. Organizations in a single industry, however, will tend to employ similar technologies and to experience similar relationships between productivity and labor.

The concept of marginal revenue product also reflects valuation of the product as well as physical productivity. Marginal revenue productivity is realized only through sale of the marginal physical product of labor. The additional sales revenue generated by a specific amount of marginal physical product depends upon the nature of the demand for output of the organization. In the simplest case, the organization can sell all additional output at the same price as obtained for previous output and marginal revenue product is a constant function of marginal physical product. This situation, illustrated in Figure 5-2A, suggests that the organization assumes an elastic demand for output at a constant price; marginal revenue *(MR)*, the increased revenue resulting from sale of an additional unit of output, is constant and equal to the product price. The marginal revenue product *(MRP)* associated with different amounts of labor reflects, in this instance, the marginal physical productivity *(MPP)* of labor converted to monetary terms with a constant marginal revenue *(MR)*.

Figure 5-2: The determination of revenue productivity of labor in organizations with (A) elastic and (B) inelastic product demand.

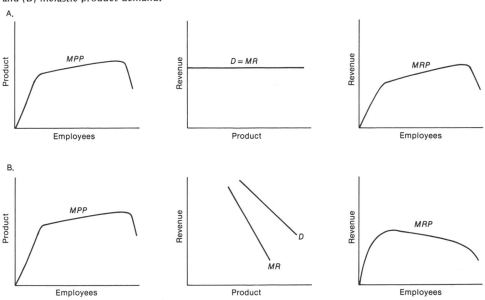

The concept of marginal revenue product is somewhat more complex when applied to an organization with a less elastic demand for its output. This situation, illustrated in Figure 5-2B, requires that the organization lower the price of the product in order to sell more units of output. While the price of additional units of output may occasionally be reduced without affecting the price of previously produced units (a special sale, for example), an organization planning for the sale of anticipated output typically must price all of the output identically. Thus the sale of additional units of output typically requires a reduction in price for all units of output sold. The marginal revenue *(MR)* associated with the additional output will be less than the sales revenue realized directly from the additional output; that revenue must be decreased by the reduced revenue from all other units of output now sold at the lower price. Marginal revenue in this instance will be a decreasing function of demand as indicated in Figure 5-2B, and marginal revenue product will be a decreasing function of marginal physical productivity. The marginal revenue product associated with labor thus reflects both technological influences (physical productivity) and product market influences (elasticity of product demand).

Constraints on ability to pay

Both marginal revenue product and average revenue product of labor have implications for the valuation of labor services and determination of the amount the organization can afford to pay for labor. An organization operating at any level of employment and production must receive enough in revenue to cover the costs of the associated labor as well as other costs of production. Figure 5-3 illustrates this concept. Marginal revenue product

Figure 5-3: Revenue productivity of labor functions

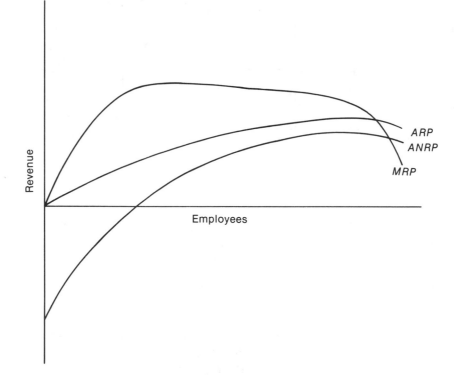

(MRP) and average revenue product (ARP) are depicted as before; average net revenue product (ANRP) represents average revenue product minus all costs other than labor costs. The organization in this instance can afford to operate only at wage rate–employment combinations indicated in the area under the average net revenue product function; other combinations are unprofitable. Just as average net revenue product represents the average value of labor at any level of employment, average wage level represents the average cost of labor and the organization might be able to afford a wage level equivalent to the average net revenue product of labor.

The analysis by Hicks focused upon long-run tendencies which may never be realized. The profit maximizing employer in Hicks's analysis would attempt to employ labor and operate at the level of employment and production where the marginal revenue product and marginal cost of labor are equal; he would attempt to expand production and employment as long as the marginal revenue product realized from an additional unit of labor is greater than or equivalent to the marginal cost of that labor. Such an employer would always operate near capacity level in our model where marginal revenue product is declining. Under the framework of assumptions in Hicks's competitive model, the only relevant portion of Figure 5-3 is the extreme right-hand portion where marginal revenue product is declining and that portion of the marginal revenue product function would represent the organization's demand for labor. The amount of labor services employed by an organization would be equivalent to the amount of labor at which marginal revenue product is equal to the wage rate paid labor. The assumptions of Hicks's model are quite restrictive, however, and are not accurate descriptions of employer behavior in many sectors of the economy. For one thing, many factors in production are variable only in the long run and cannot be varied with any frequency; investments in plant and technology, for example, are based upon a planning period of the productive life of these investments and once undertaken cannot be altered to any significant degree. Similarly, many of the factors can be varied only by relatively large, fixed amounts; a new plant has a minimum economic size and smaller, more frequent additions are uneconomical. Thus plant capacity, core technology, and equipment are varied relatively infrequently and, when changed, typically provide for excess capacity to be utilized only at some future date as product demand expands. Other variables such as product price and wage rates are more variable, but even these variables tend to be considered as fixed for the term of the organization's planning period; the distribution of price catalogs, for example, requires a minimum period during which prices are relatively fixed. Thus many employers will, in fact, often operate at levels of production and employment below those levels indicated by Hicks's marginal analysis. Marginal revenue product of labor cannot in those instances be interpreted as determining the organization's demand for labor. Demand for labor is more realistically viewed in these instances as a function of the organization's estimated level of sales and plans for production; an employer's demand for labor thus is a function of wage rates only in those instances where organizations are operating near capacity production and could sell additional production.

While an employer's demand for labor may not be a direct function of marginal revenue product, the concept of average net revenue product developed in Figure 5-3 is of direct relevance in the determination of wage rates and the understanding of differences in wage rates among organizations such as observed by Dunlop. Wage level was defined earlier as some sort of average of specific wage rates, an average which typifies the total array of wage rates. The concept of wage level is applied most commonly to characterization of wage rates of an employing organization, and the organization is characterized as a high, average, or low wage employer based upon comparisons of wage levels. The wage concept most appropriate for analysis relative to average net revenue product is wage level, not wage rate. Wage level, in this instance, characterizes labor cost to the employing organization and an average wage level can be calculated as an average of wage rates weighted by the number of persons or jobs paid at each rate. This conceptualization of wage level characterizes average cost of labor and is directly comparable to the concept of average net revenue product of labor.

The concept of average net revenue product of labor indicates, for each level of employment considered, the maximum profitable average cost of labor or wage level. Further, it can be operationalized to serve as a guide to determination of this maximum wage level for an organization. Consider, for example, an organization with fixed plant and technology, an established product and market, which is planning production and employment for the future six months. Product price is estimated based on positioning of the organization's product in the market, anticipated inflation, and prices of competitors. Thus, for the planning period, price and average revenue per unit of sales are considered constant as indicated in Figure 5-4 *(P and AR)*. Average net revenue per unit of sales can be estimated sequentially by deducting from average revenue variable product costs, fixed costs, and targeted profit for the six-month period. Variable costs such as raw materials costs are variable with total production and constant for each unit of production and deduction of these costs from average revenue produces the

Figure 5-4

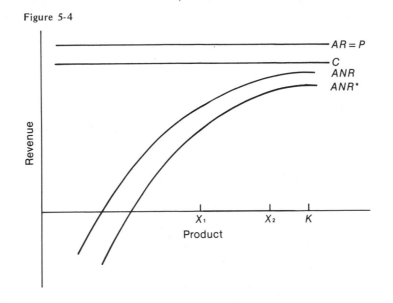

curve *C*. Fixed costs such as overhead and capital charges, when deducted from *C* result in the function *ANR;* fixed costs per unit of production decline as the number of units produced increases. Similarly, targeted profit for the planning period can be deducted as a fixed charge against revenues resulting in the average net revenue function *(ANR*)* in Figure 5-4. Note that the relationships described in Figure 5-4 describe average revenue concepts relative to number of units produced, not relative to number of units of labor employed.

The concepts of average revenue relative to units produced in Figure 5-4 can be transformed into concepts of average revenue relative to units of labor employed as illustrated in Figure 5-5. The average net revenue product of labor depicted in Figure 5-5 is based upon an assumption of a relatively constant marginal physical productivity of labor until the level of capacity operations indicated at *K*. Conceptually, the average net revenue product of labor *(ANRP*)* can be derived by dividing the average net revenue per product *(ANR*)* by the amount of labor resources or employment required at each level of production. The *ANRP** function mirrors the *ANR** function until capacity operations are reached at which point it declines due to the increasing number of units of labor required per unit of expanded output due to declining marginal physical productivity. The relationships depicted

Figure 5-5

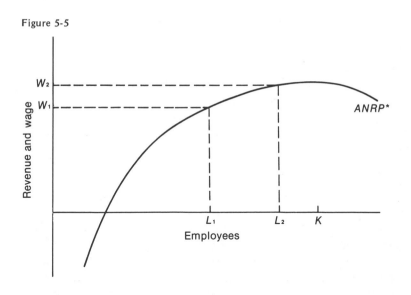

in Figures 5-4 and 5-5 are conceptual and it is unlikely that an employing organization would calculate the full range of measures implicit in these relationships. What is more likely is that the analysis implicit in these figures would be conducted for specific estimates of production and sales targets for the planning period, X_1 and X_2 in Figure 5-4. For purposes of illustration, assume that employment of L_1 and L_2 would be required at these levels of production and that estimates of average net revenue product at these levels of employment are as indicated in Figure 5-5. The maximum wage level consistent with the profit target used in estimating average net revenue product varies with the level of employment and production and is indicated as W_1 and W_2. The wage level W_1 would permit the organization to operate profitably at the lower estimate of sales and production (X_1) and would permit increased profits if the higher estimate (X_2) were realized. Average net revenue product, both as a concept and as an operational guide to decisions, indicates the maximum profitable wage level which might be paid for employment in an organization.

Wage contours

Dunlop's observation of high wage and low wage employers operating in different industries can be explained in terms of our analysis of average net revenue product. Employers within an industry tend to employ similar technologies and raw materials and tend to price their products similarly for sale within the product market; thus the average net revenue product associated with employment tends to be similar for organizations in a single industry. Quite different relationships can be expected, however, when comparing organizations in different industries and the ability of employers to pay high wage levels characterized by average net revenue product will vary from industry to industry. Whether or not estimates of average net revenue product are calculated by employers in an industry, any employer might well reason that all organizations in the industry encounter similar constraints of technology, raw materials, product demand, and pricing and that payment of wage levels above those of competitors would be unprofitable. Wage levels paid by competitors in the product market thus provide another operational constraint upon employer ability to pay high wages and we would anticipate that industry groupings characterize Dunlop's different wage contours.

The influence of product market also appears in the structure of collective bargaining observed in different industries, the structure of collective bargaining tending to parallel the structure of product market competition. Organizations competing in a single product market tend to negotiate comparable collective agreements through formal bargaining associations and through less formal practices of patterning agreements after key settlements. Thus we find that collective bargaining in industries with a national product market is characterized by negotiations between a national union and either formal or informal industry associations of employers; collective bargaining in the steel and coal mining industries particularly exemplifies this approach to bargaining. A relatively uniform wage level for all employers in the single national product market results from this bargaining. Collective bargaining and wage level determination is quite different for employers competing in restricted local or regional product markets, local building contractors, for example, where bargaining is conducted by local or regional employer associations. The resulting wage level is relatively uniform for all employers in the local or regional product market, but may differ considerably from the wage level in another region. For example, wage levels paid by building contractors in Chicago are relatively uniform yet relatively independent of wage levels paid by building contractors in another market such as Atlanta. With few exceptions, the constraint of maximum wage level appears to be the wage level paid by product market competitors and surveys of these wage levels provide key benchmarks for employers in the determination of wage level.

The elasticity of product demand and the degree of competition in the industry also influence wage level and wage behavior over time. Price and marginal revenue of the product were key determinants of average revenue product of labor, and the ability of employers to finance higher wage levels by raising average revenue product through price increases depends upon the elasticity of demand for the product. Employers in a highly competitive product market with a very elastic product demand will feel incapable of raising prices without significant loss of sales. At the other extreme, monopolists of a product with a very inelastic product demand will feel far more capable of raising prices and thus average revenue product without significant loss of sales. Thus both assumed elasticity of product demand and degree of competition in the product market influence employer ability to pay high wage levels through ability to alter the average revenue product of labor, and ability to pay high wage levels will vary from industry to industry.

Wage levels vary from industry to industry as Dunlop observed. An employer's ability to pay high wage levels, conceptualized as average net revenue product of labor, is influenced critically by the physical productivity of labor, a function of technology and level of production relative to capacity, average revenue, a function of price and elasticity of demand, and by the amount of nonlabor costs. Product demand in the industry and degree of competition among producers also determine the ability of employers to change prices as a means of covering higher wage levels through increased average net revenue product. The tendency for employers within a single industry to rely upon industry surveys in the determination of wage levels as noted by Dunlop thus has a sound basis in the economics of wage determination and is not merely ritual without purpose.

B: Labor force attraction and wage level

The analysis of average net revenue product of labor provided a rationale for determination of maximum wage level or the average cost of labor to an employing organization. The analysis of average net revenue product does not, however, provide any motivation for determination of the minimum wage level to be paid. The explanation of differences in ability to pay wage levels does not explain actual differences in wage levels unless one assumes that all employers pay the maximum wage level affordable. In this section we analyze additional influences of wage level decisions, influences which constrain the minimum wage which an employer might consider.

Wage level represents both cost to the employer and return to the employee, an inducement offered in exchange for employment contributions. Wage level is an average reflecting the array of wage rates offered by an employer, and a weighted average indicating average cost of labor is the characterization of wage level of most relevance to the employer. Some modal wage rate or an average of wage rates paid jobs for which workers are recruited from the labor market more likely characterizes the concept of wage level relevant to workers seeking employment. This characterization of wage level may be higher or lower than the average labor cost characterization depending upon the distribution of employment among different wage rates and upon the relative rates paid jobs into which workers are recruited. Recognition of the difference between the two characterizations permits manipulation of one characterization while holding the other constant.

Viewed as an inducement in the concept of employment exchange, the purpose of wages is to attract and retain employees. An employing organization must offer a wage level sufficiently high to attract and retain the desired number of employees. The competitive labor market model, assuming a perfectly elastic supply of labor to the organization, implies an identifiable market wage level as the minimum wage level for all employers in the labor market. Observation indicates that no such single wage level prevails in the labor market, wage rates vary among occupations and employing organizations. It also appears from our analysis of labor supply behavior that the supply of labor to an organization relative to wage rates is unlikely to be perfectly elastic. There undoubtedly exists some minimum wage level below which the organization will be unable to attract and retain the desired number of employees, but it is by no means a simple matter to ascertain that wage level.

Certain minimum wage level constraints are specified in federal and state minimum wage legislation. This legislation specifies either absolute minimum wage levels to be paid or prevailing wage level minima. The absolute minimum specifies a minimum rate to be paid per hour, and the prevailing wage minimum specifies that the minimum shall be some amount established through wage surveys of employers of a particular occupation in a particular geographic location. The logic of minimum wage legislation implies that competitive forces in the labor market are not sufficient to establish a minimum market wage and that employing organizations possess at least limited monopsonistic power to establish wage levels, that the supply of labor to an employer is so inelastic that he is free to force extremely low wage levels upon employees. Minimum wage legislation constrains employer exploitation of the lack of competition in the labor market.

Another potential constraint upon employer exploitation of monopsonistic power in the labor market is found in the institution of collective bargaining where employees represented by a labor union negotiate the wage level to be offered in the employment exchange. Through the threat of strike, employees organized in a union attempt to control the supply of labor to the organization so that it becomes perfectly elastic at the wage level demanded, no workers offer themselves for employment at a lower wage level. Certainly the negotiation of a collective agreement regularizes the employment contract and makes explicit the specific inducements and contributions that might otherwise be only implicit in the offer of an employment exchange. It is not as clear, however, that collective bargaining results in a higher wage level than would otherwise exist. Studies of the interindustry wage structure, for example, have identified various influences of industry wage level differences, influences such as capital-labor ratio, degree of concentration of producers in the product market, changes in productivity, occupational mix and skill level of employees in the industry. Given these varying influences of industry wage levels, it is difficult to attribute specific cause to collective bargaining. The threat of work stoppages through collective bargaining would appear to push wage levels upward, however, just as would turnover experienced due to relatively low wage levels.

Essay 5-3 from Ross focuses upon the structure of interorganization wage levels (Dunlop's wage contours) and develops a rationale for observed patterns of differentials as well as changes over time. Ross views the organizational wage level as the result of a decision, often a negotiated decision, subject to a variety of influences. He labels one set of influences "ability to pay," determinants of the maximum feasible wage level. These influences relate to industry classification (hard goods and soft goods industries), specific technology employed (labor cost relative to total cost), and competition in the product market (concentration). These descriptive characteristics of high and low wage level employers correlate with Dunlop's earlier descriptions and are interpretable in terms of the analysis of marginal and average revenue product above. Physical productivity of labor will tend to be comparable among employers in a single industry and relatively higher in those industries with advanced technology and high capital-labor ratio, hard goods industries with relatively low labor cost compared with total cost. The assumed elasticity of product demand, and thus ability to raise average revenue product through price increases, will vary from industry to industry and with degree of competition in the product market. The set of influences Ross identifies as "comparisons" also relate to considerations of ability to pay since the primary comparisons are with competitors in the product market. These comparisons provide operational measures of ability to pay in the absence of specific measures of average revenue product. Ross does not develop any specific labor supply pressures upon wage levels other than the expectations of employees and labor unions exemplified in the wage comparisons put forward for wage level decision making. Wage level, in Ross's analysis, appears to be more a function of ability to pay than a function of labor supply considerations.

Essay 5-4 by Bronfenbrenner provides a rationale for employer determination of wage levels. Bronfenbrenner begins with the observation that every employing organization possesses at least limited monopsonistic power, that the supply of labor to the organization is less than perfectly elastic. Due to attachments of workers to organizations as a result of tenure rights, ignorance of alternatives, inertia due to habit, and attraction to nonwage characteristics of employment, it is assumed that many workers would remain attached to the employer even at relatively low wages. Bronfenbrenner argues that various advantages accrue to an employer paying wage levels above the minimum required to attract and retain labor, advantages such as attracting more employees than required, thus permitting selection among the applicants, reduced turnover contributing to higher skill levels due to knowledge of specific organizational practices, avoidance of pressure for collective bargaining, and the capability to maintain a specified wage level over time without having to adjust for changes in the labor market or expansion of the organization's labor force. All in all, payment of a wage level above the minimum required makes life easier for the employer and may, in fact, contribute to higher productivity of the labor force at no greater labor cost per unit of product. Payment of relatively high wage levels buffers the employer from pressures of the labor market and permits greater stability in policy and practice. Employers thus seek to pay wage levels higher than their competitors in the labor market, not as a prerequisite for the attraction of desired labor supplies, but as a means of buffering themselves against labor market pressures. Employers are inclined to offer wage levels more in accord with their ability to pay wages than to exploit their monopsonistic position. Observed differentials in wage levels thus might be expected to reflect differences in employer ability to pay higher wages and to be the cause of differential benefits such as lower turnover, a larger pool of applicants, and consequent higher capability of employees. As suggested by Thurow's concept of the labor queue, high wage employers are able to attract workers from the top end of the queue, lesser qualified workers remaining in the queue for selection by lower paying employers.

Bronfenbrenner also develops a rationale for a compensation phenomenon observed in practice, the problem of wage compression where the compensation of newly recruited workers advances at a greater rate than the compensation of longer tenured employees. The cost of wage level is constrained to the average revenue product of labor or more commonly the wage level paid by competitors in the industry. The characterization of wage level of most relevance in the attraction of labor supplies probably is more reflective of wage rates offered in the recruitment of workers than it is reflective of the full range of wage rates in the organization. An employing organization can appear to be a high wage employer in the labor market by offering relatively high wages to new recruits and yet constrain wage level costs for longer tenured employees in jobs filled through promotion rather than recruiting. In this sense, the employing organization exploits its monopsonistic position with regard to tenured employees who are less mobile than active participants in the labor market. We'll return to this consideration in Chapter 6 where we consider more explicitly issues in the determination of the structure of wage rates in the organization.

Empirical evidence supportive of Bronfenbrenner's analysis is available from several different studies. Burton and Parker, for example, report that industry rates of voluntary employee terminations vary inversely with industry wage rates, low wage industries being subjected to greater turnover (1969). Relatively lower turnover rates for high wage industries are evidence of the buffering of high wage employers against labor market pressures, the buffering effect hypothesized by Bronfenbrenner. A study of variation in interindustry wage structure by Wachter provides complementary evidence of the buffering effects of high wages (1970). Wachter analyzed the wage differential between high and low wage industries during 1947-55 and reported that the differential narrows during periods of low unemployment. This narrowing occurs as low wage industries are forced to raise wages in competition for scarce labor resources; high wage industries, buffered from labor market pressures, do not raise wages as quickly, thus narrowing the wage differential. High wage industries, Wachter observes, are more inclined to vary wage rates in response to changes in cost of living or inflation in some regular pattern than to vary wage rates with change in scarcity of labor resources. This evidence, coupled with Ross's observation that wage rates tend to vary by industry, is supportive of Bronfenbrenner's hypothesis that employers prefer to establish relatively high wage rates as a buffer against labor market pressures and our hypothesis that this buffering capability is constrained by ability to pay, a function of industry or product market characteristics.

In summary, it appears that employers attempt to set wage levels which serve to attract and retain a pool of labor resources attached to the organization, a pool from which employees may be selected as needed. Wage levels must be economically feasible, however, and permit the organization to operate profitably. Thus the primary constraint upon wage levels will be the average revenue product associated with labor, or the organization's ability to pay. Wage surveys of competitors provide an operational measure of this ability to pay. To the extent possible, the organization strives to buffer itself from pressures of the labor market, and voluntary terminations or difficulty in the recruitment of employees indicate that wage levels ought to be adjusted upward if economically feasible; wage surveys of competitors in the labor market may also provide warning of anticipated labor market pressures. Wage levels of entry jobs into which employees are recruited are of most concern in this regard and ought to be viewed as attraction inducements; other wage levels in the organization are more appropriately analyzed as labor costs.

REFERENCES

Burton, John F. Jr., and Parker, John E. "Interindustry Variations in Voluntary Labor Mobility." *Industrial and Labor Relations Review* 22 (1969), pp. 199-216.

Wachter, Michael L. "Cyclical Variation in the Interindustry Wage Structure." *American Economic Review* 60 (1970), pp. 75-84.

Essay 5-3

The external wage structure*

Arthur M. Ross

It was pointed out previously that a full-blown theory of the external wage structure would have to accomplish three tasks. The first is to explain how the larger outlines of the wage structure, which are beyond the reach of individual decisions, are drawn. For this purpose, supply and demand in their full quantitative sense are entirely relevant. The analytical problem is to isolate the specific influences affecting the supply and demand for particular groups of workers and accounting for the wage variations which obtain. At this level, a wage differential is a residual or a statistical difference, and a wage equality is an accident.

The second task is to account for the fact that supply and demand control particular wage rates only roughly or loosely, leaving a margin of choice in ordinary cases. The impediments to mobility and the weaknesses of competition in the labor market have been systematically described in recent years, particularly in the writings of Lester, Reynolds, and Myers and Shultz.[1]

Space will permit extended discussion only of the third problem, which is to explain the decisions made by employers and unions within the range of discretion. Here are the differentials and equalities which are willed into existence and do not merely happen. Why do the parties decide to maintain an existing differential as historically valid or to eliminate it as a gross inequity? Why do they choose to accept the leadership of another major producer or to strike off on their own? What is the true significance of the so-called national patterns? Why are there considerable wage variations between one region and another in the construction industry and not in the coal industry?

The wheel has turned full circle since Adam Smith's day. Then it was deemed important to explain why all workers did

---

---

[1] See Richard A. Lester, "A Range Theory of Wage Differentials," *Industrial and Labor Relations Review*, vol. 5 (July 1952), pp. 483-500; Lloyd G. Reynolds, *The Structure of Labor Markets* (New York: Harper, 1951); and Charles A. Myers and George P. Shultz, *The Dynamics of a Labor Market* (Englewood Cliffs, N.J.: Prentice-Hall, 1951).

not receive the same wage; the theory of equal net advantage and the later doctrine of noncompeting groups were addressed to that question. Today it is more interesting to inquire why some workers *do* receive the same wage as others. When all petroleum companies raise their prices simultaneously and to the same extent, they hold this to be the result of vigorous competition in the product market; but one suspects that a better explanation is available. In the same way, it is generally recognized that competitive forces in the labor market are not sufficiently strong to produce a single rate even for a single "grade" of labor.

It is true that a few employments are so rudimentary and unstructured that a single rate prevails even though no one has decreed that this must be so. Cleaning women in a metropolitan area employed casually by the day, cotton pickers in a particular county at a particular stage of the harvest, shoeshine boys operating around a railroad terminal—such groups are the salvation of the economics instructor who wishes to demonstrate the mechanics of a competitive labor market, but are impressive chiefly for their quaintness and singularity. Generally the single rate is a reliable token of combination rather than competition at work. Thus it is probably true that most of the remaining random-rated firms are nonunion (although the converse is certainly not correct). Local wage variations are greater in poorly organized communities, such as New Orleans and Dallas, than in centers of unionism, such as Detroit and Pittsburgh. Likewise intraindustry variations are greater in chemicals and furniture than in aircraft, rubber, and steel.

Wage comparisons and ability to pay

In dealing with centrifugal and centripetal tendencies in wage determination, a convenient point of departure is to examine the customary standards of equity which are almost universally invoked around the bargaining table and before arbitrators and government boards. These include changes in the cost of living, comparative rates and comparative adjustments, the employer's wage-paying capacity, the budgetary requirements of a living wage, and trends in productivity. These criteria have changed little since before World War I, except that in recent years some unions have stressed the need for adequate purchasing power and employers have dwelt upon the evils of inflation. Experienced negotiators and arbitrators will probably agree that in most cases the living-wage, productivity, full-employment, and inflation arguments have little or no weight in the decision. Cost of living, wage comparisons, and ability to pay are generally of great significance, however, either singly or in combination with each other.

The problem at hand can be analyzed by watching the interplay between two of the three more significant wage-determining standards: wage comparisons and ability to pay. Comparisons exert a centripetal force, pulling separate wage bargains together into a system. Ability to pay is often centrifugal, since no two employers are situated exactly alike from the standpoint of financial capacity.

If comparisons were unlimited and unrestricted, then rates of pay would be equal everywhere (except for occupational differentials) and would be equally adjusted. There are two reasons why this does not happen: first, comparisons run in limited orbits; and second, even within a customary orbit they are sometimes superseded by more compelling considerations, especially differences in ability to pay. There are times, of course, when the economic position of most employers is changing in the same direction. These are also likely to be times in which the cost of living, which affects all workers more or less equally, is moving rapidly. During such periods, the pressure of equitable comparison is particularly strong because it is subject to unusually little interference.

The importance of comparisons to all parties concerned is self-evident. They tell the employer whether he is "staying in line," neither allowing his employees to become disgruntled nor embarrassing his fellow employers. They serve as a measure of fairness to the worker and indicate whether he has obtained what is coming to him. They are the crucial test of performance in the union world. To the arbitrator they are a shining candle in the black night of conflicting claims and statistics. The ready-made settlement is administratively convenient, mutually face-saving, and simple to defend.

The importance of ability to pay to the employer is even more obvious. The term should not be taken literally, of course, as indicating that the employer is paying the highest wage of which he is capable and that anything higher would be attended with catastrophic results. Doubtless many firms could pay higher wages if absolutely required to, without going out of business, changing their methods of production, or substantially reducing their volume of employment. But there are many legitimate claimants on the income of a firm, and their competing claims must be balanced. What is ordinarily involved is a rough relationship between the level of profits and the willingness to make wage adjustments.

When comparisons are difficult to ignore but ability to pay also presents problems, there are ways of carrying water on both shoulders. One of the most interesting examples is found in the Brockton shoe industry, which has been carefully studied by George Shultz. On the one hand, "the statements and actions of rival leaders, rival unions and 'radicals' within the Brotherhood have created pressure for general wage movements, pressure acting primarily through the medium of 'institutional' and 'personal' objectives."[2] On the other hand, there has been severe non-union competition in this rather unprofitable industry; and "both the rank and file and the officials of the Brotherhood have been greatly concerned over the volume of work available in the Brockton district."[3] The solution for this dilemma has been to negotiate general wage increases but to adjust the "grade system," under which piece rates depend on the grading or classification of shoes.

There are other methods of dampening the real effect of a general wage increase. The parties can decide not to adjust incentive rates correspondingly. Fringe benefits can be traded off for part of the wage increase. Workers can be classified more stringently. Time studies and labor standards can be tightened up. In these ways, labor cost can be insulated to a greater or lesser extent from the impact of a nominal general wage increase.

Soft- and hard-goods industries

It is instructive to note the large differences among industries with respect to the prominence of the ability-to-pay standard. In some industries it is generally a crucial issue. Wage reductions are frequently negotiated, although arbitrators are sometimes engaged to fix the amount of a reduction which both parties recognize to be inevitable. These are the same industries in which unions give most explicit consideration to the "employment effect" of wage bargains. They are likewise the industries in which "national patterns" have the smallest influence. Hosiery, apparel, shoes, and textiles come to mind most readily.

The hard-goods industries present an

[2] George P. Shultz, *Pressures on Wage Decisions* (Cambridge, Mass.: Technology Press, 1951), pp. 131-32.
[3] Ibid., p. 132.

altogether different picture. These include basic steel, autos, farm equipment, rubber, glass, nonferrous metals, shipbuilding, aircraft, electrical goods, and similar activities. The "national patterns" are played out on these grounds. Employers resent and resist any reference to their financial position and reject ability to pay as a legitimate standard of wage determination. With one exception, there have been no significant wage reductions for over 20 years.

The following differences between these two groups of activities can be noted, the most pertinent of which are the last two listed: (1) in soft goods, labor cost tends to be a somewhat larger component of selling price; (2) piecework is more common, so that wage rates are closely and mechanically linked to labor cost; (3) the firms are typically smaller and have lesser financial reserves; (4) the product market is more competitive in the soft-goods industries, so that prices are cut when demand falls off; whereas in steel, autos, etc., prices are maintained and production curtailed;[4] and (5) the heavy industries are almost completely organized, whereas there is a substantial nonunion sector in shoes, hosiery, and many branches of the textile industry.

LOCUS OF DIRECT RATE COMPARISONS

Now, what is the locus of the "standard rate"? According to Dunlop wage rates are equal within "wage contours." He defines a wage contour as a stable group of firms (wage-determining units) "so linked together by (1) similarity of product markets, (2) resort to similar sources for a labor force, or (3) common labor-market

organization (custom) that they have common wage-making characteristics." The first of these linkages appears to be the crucial one, so that for practical purposes it is competition in the same product market which produces equality of wage rates. Conversely, "the theoretically significant differences for similar grades of labor are those which reflect different product-market competitive conditions."

Certainly the product-market link is a basic one, but a full statement requires that other complications be noted.

The plant and company

The simplest application of the standard rate is, of course, within a plant. Under collective bargaining and modern personnel administration, jobs are classified and uniform rates are established even though many products selling in different markets are produced. Moreover, unions are generally unenthusiastic about merit ranges, except in the case of skilled trades, and tend to insist on single rates or length-of-service ranges. The gradual elimination of merit ranges from the lower labor grades in the airframe industry serves as an interesting example.

The next stage consists of the multi-plant company. Where the plants are located in a single area, generally uniform rates and benefits are offered. Where they are geographically dispersed, however, there are pressures for both uniformity and diversity.

On the one hand, it is administratively convenient to have standard terms of compensation, particularly welfare and the insurance programs which can be operated on a company-wide basis. Interchange of labor is facilitated. If a single union with centralized wage policies enjoys bargaining rights throughout the company, interplant differentials will be attacked as irrational and inequitable. Moreover, the union will be concerned lest work be transferred to the lower-wage

---

[4] "Declines in product prices and not unemployment constitute the effective downward pressure on wage structures. . . . Wages fell last (and probably least) . . . in the sector of the economy in which unemployment was clearly relatively greatest." From John T. Dunlop, *Wage Determination under Trade Unions* (New York: A. M. Kelley, 1950), pp. 146, 148.

plants at the expense of its members in the older metropolitan areas.

On the other hand, the company may dislike offending the local business and financial interests in the low-wage communities. It may resist the notion of paying wage rates considerably higher than what is prevalent in these communities. The various plants may compete in separate and unrelated product markets, and their wage-paying capacity may differ so widely as to override equitable comparisons. If a decentralized union holds bargaining rights, or different unions which are not engaged in active organizational rivalry hold them, wage differentials may persist solely for the reason that no one is making an issue of them. Or the differentials may continue because the union chooses to take all wage increases in the form of company-wide adjustments, in order to avoid creating internal political stresses.

Thus the outcome depends on numerous variables which defy generalization. A few observations can be noted, however:

1. Uniform wages regardless of location are more probable if the enterprise is unionized.

2. Fringes are likely to be equalized more readily than wage rates. In fact, fringe benefits and general wage increases may be dealt with in company-wide agreements, while occupational wage schedules are covered by separate local agreements.

3. Frequently the parties will eliminate geographical differentials in several bites as an alternative to swallowing a single indigestible lump. A good many years may pass before full equalization is achieved. Perhaps the plants will be grouped into categories, such as the "metropolitan," "river," and "Southern" plants in the meat-packing industry. Equalization can then proceed by the reclassification of plants as well as by negotiating larger increases for the lower-paid categories. This more leisurely approach has certain advantages to both parties: the company's cost structure is adjusted gradually, and the union

is able to devote part of its gains to general wage increases rather than pass over part of its membership altogether as might otherwise be necessary.

4. Although the situation is mixed, clearly the trend is in the direction of company-wide equalization. Differentials are being reduced or eliminated in many firms, while few are being increased or established for the first time, so far as the evidence discloses.[5]

The industry

When an industry is dominated by a relatively small number of firms, each having numerous plants, company-wide and industry-wide equalization tend to coalesce as one process. Uniformity of hourly rates in bituminous coal and of labor costs in men's clothing has been accomplished through multiemployer bargaining. In meat packing, rubber, and steel the same result has been achieved or is being approached on a company-by-company basis. In general it may be said that formal employer organization and industry-wide negotiations do not necessarily produce different results from those achieved by the more informal bargaining structures such as "wage leadership." In either case there are pressures for uniformity and for diversity. In either case the union can present a solid front, although differences in expiration dates may create difficulties. In either case the besetting problem for the employers is whether they can hold together. Disruption may develop despite formal organization, and the most impregnable unity may be achieved in its absence. Mine operators have their associations, but the United Mine Workers have easily split them apart

[5] One qualification to this statement should be noted. Some firms, which heretofore have operated in one location, have installed branch plants in widely separated communities. Such firms are not all observing company-wide wage schedules. They can therefore be described as establishing interplant differentials for the first time.

on numerous occasions. Steel companies consult informally with each other but generally maintain solidarity.

Certainly the intraindustry comparison is the weightiest one insofar as equalization of rates is concerned.

It should not be supposed that the wage rates for even a single occupation in a single industry and area are "naturally" uniform owing to some equilibrium of market forces. They are often made uniform by conscious decision, usually in the collective-bargaining process. But unless measures of this type are taken, substantial disparities are almost certain to be found.

The definition of "industry" presents a complication. Where the goods or services are sold in a local market (as in building construction, cemeteries, and the culinary trades), the pressure for equalization may not extend beyond the locality. Where they compete in a national market (as in coal), wages may be equalized on a national basis. The geographical orbit of product competition and of wage equalization are not necessarily the same, however. Soaps compete in a national market, but sizable wage differentials prevail in the soap industry. Presumably the structure and intensity of union organization have not been such as to anticipate interarea wage comparisons. Longshoring is a local service, but a rigid wage parity exists between the East and West Coasts, rival unionism providing the energy.

Furthermore, there is a distinct tendency for unions to extend their wage rates from metropolitan centers into suburban areas and smaller communities in the vicinity. Still, the product market may be as localized as the neighborhood butcher shop. On the other hand, a local industry may be subdivided for the purpose of collective bargaining if there are substantial differences in wage-paying capacity. Thus there will be Class A, Class B, and Class C hotels; chain and local radio stations; and so on.

The classification of new enterprises and activities is often the subject of controversy between employers and unions. One of the most troublesome issues in atomic energy labor relations has arisen in this way. Is there an atomic energy industry? The unions insist that there is; the operating contractors contend that their respective plants are to be classified in the chemical, petroleum, and electrical industries. What is principally at stake is whether certain advantageous fringe benefits established in the original installations are to be extended more widely, or whether the employers may "bring in" their own fringes. The situation is anomalous in that the establishments do not compete with chemical plants, oil refineries, etc., but neither do they compete with each other.

Cross-industry comparisons

When we pass beyond the boundaries of the industry, direct rate comparisons lose much of their force. Certainly there is no likelihood that wage rates will be equalized regardless of industry, although percentage differentials have declined greatly. Dunlop's definition of a "wage contour" as generally coterminous with a single product market has considerable merit therefore. Contrary tendencies must be noted, however:

1. Some craft unions have been able to establish uniform rates in some of their communities. In the San Francisco-Oakland area, for example, tool- and diemakers are employed in numerous manufacturing industries; but practically all of them receive the wage rate negotiated by the machinist's union and the metal-trades association. The same is true of warehousemen under the contract between the longshore union and the distributors' association, who are employed in such diverse enterprises as mayonnaise plants, coffee-roasting houses, steel distributors, and paint warehouses.

2. Some multi-industrial unions en-

deavored to extend wage rates negotiated in the original centers of their jurisdiction into the more recently organized activities. The rate structure and job-evaluation plan developed in the steel industry have had a great deal of influence in aluminum, iron ore, and even nonferrous metals. The auto workers have attempted to establish "Detroit rates" in airframe plants, but with very little success up to now.

3. The major industries in an area often exert an upward or downward pull on the wage level of other industries. This does not result in full equalization, of course; but it should not be thought that the various "wage contours" are independent of each other. Thus, there is one lonely textile mill in Oakland, California, with rates which are low by area standards but high by industry standards. Examples of this type, and of the converse situation, could be reiterated without end.

COMPARATIVE MOVEMENTS

Normally the orbit of direct wage comparisons is confined within an industry, but relative movements in wage rates are subject to broader comparisons. There are four influences in particular which encourage the diffusion of wage movements throughout a wider range: (1) centralization in union bargaining policy, (2) common ownership of establishments, even in separate product markets, (3) active government participation in determining wages, and (4) organizational and leadership rivalries within the labor movement.

Social and economic influences

Other significant factors which influence the diffusion of wage patterns are the business cycle and the force of custom. The range of uniform adjustments is wider in periods of prosperity and inflation than in periods of depression, and for two reasons. First, increases in the cost of living affect all workers more or less equally and

generate more or less equal pressure for relief throughout the labor market. Second, when most employers are operating at a satisfactory profit level, differences in ability to pay do not obstruct the flow of uniform adjustments. At the other end of the cycle, however, the shadow of uneven financial capacity is thrown across the bargaining table and produces irregular results.

The influence of custom in sanctifying established relationships (and therefore in promoting uniform adjustments) is embodied in the concept of the "historical differential." Established wage relationships have great force, not only within plants, but also between plants. Within a plant, workers and managers come to take it for granted that the higher paid jobs require more skill and carry more status.[6] Attitudes and sentiments regarding the relative worth of jobs develop as part of the "social structure" of the plant. If excessive violence is done to these attitudes and sentiments by the installation of a job-evaluation plan, demoralization can result.

Between plants, customary relationships seem to have considerable strength, whether or not the employees are organized.

Certainly the rationale of many estab-

---

[6] "The factor which has been somewhat neglected in the discussion of industrial wage administration we may call, for want of a more precise term, custom. There are two ways in which this factor operates. Whenever wages are altered—either by administrative determination or negotiation—the new figure is determined by reference to the wages previously paid for that kind of work.... The other way in which custom affects wage rates is the determination of differentials between jobs in the same plant. Warner and Low have shown very lucidly in their study of shoe manufacturing in Yankeetown that wages are roughly correlated with the degree of skill *assumed* necessary for each job. On close examination these assumptions are often found to be spurious. The rank order of skill attached to jobs is a derivation from the original rank order which existed in the days when the boot and shoe industry was on a handicraft basis, but intervening events have stripped it of all validity." From Theodore Caplow, *The Sociology of Work* (Minneapolis: University of Minnesota Press, 1954), pp. 159, 160.

lished relationships which command the attention and respect of negotiators, arbitrators, and wage-control authorities is found mainly in the fact that they are established. The difference between a "historical differential" which must be preserved and a "gross inequity" which must be eliminated is frequently that one is sanctioned by habitual usage while the other is not.

But just as the logical foundation of ideas may crumble, so may a wage relationship built on custom. A change in the size of a firm, in its product line, in the economic condition of its industry, or in the union representing its workers may be sufficient to move it out of one customary relationship and into another. In other words, wage patterns acquire considerable inertia as time goes on but are not invulnerable to changes in the economic and institutional environment.

CONCLUSIONS

The principal purpose of this essay has been to explore the nature and the determinants of interplant, or external, wage relationships. A brief summary may be in order at this point.

The rough outlines of the external wage structure are fixed by economic forces which are beyond the control of individual decision makers. This refers to broad aggregative relationships such as between Northern and Southern regions, textile and metalworking industries, or manual and clerical employees. The economic forces are sufficiently loose in their operation, however, to leave an area of discretion within which choices can be made. Choices to equalize or not to equalize wages, to create or eliminate differentials, constitute the decision-making aspect of the external wage structure. The bulk of the present essay has been concerned with the rationale of such choices.

One of the initial problems is to define the unit of choice or comparison. Are choices made in terms of a gross concept of "wages" including hourly rates plus fringe benefits, or are there separate comparisons of wage rates and of the several fringe benefits? We have seen that although wages and fringes are bargained together and are substitutable for each other under some circumstances, basically they are subject to separate comparison.

In discussing interplant relationships, it was found useful to distinguish between centripetal pressures, which pull separate decisions together into a system, and centrifugal pressures, which hold them apart. Equitable comparison tends to make wages (and wage adjustments) equal, while differences in financial capacity tend to make them vary. The interaction between these major centripetal and centrifugal pressures was illustrated by cases in which one was dominant over the other and in which the two have been reconciled.

The pressure of equitable comparison is buttressed by the importance of custom in sanctifying established relationships. "What has been, should be." However, uniformity is more easily preserved in periods of prosperity, when increases in the cost of living are affecting all workers more or less equally and most employers are making satisfactory profits, than in periods of depression, when uneven financial capacity produces irregular results.

It was shown that, if the analysis of equitable comparison is to be carried further, another distinction has to be made between direct wage-rate comparisons and comparative adjustments. The simplest application of the "standard rate" was seen to lie within a plant. Pressures for equalization in the multiplant company were discussed, along with some counteracting tendencies which are generally weaker. The importance of interplant comparisons within the industry was stressed, but problems of industry definition and classification should be kept in mind. Finally, it was indicated that although direct wage comparisons operate primarily within an industry, cross-industry comparisons are influential in some circumstances.

Relative wage *movements* are subject to broader comparisons, which are sharpened by organizational alignments and rivalries in the labor movement. Here again differences must be noted, however. A large group of heavy industries characterized by oligopolistic market structure tends to move up more or less as a unit, while other activities (particularly those which are only partially organized) go their own way insofar as wage adjustments are concerned.

Essay 5-4

Potential monopsony in labor markets*

Martin Bronfenbrenner

RESEARCH FINDINGS ON LABOR MARKETS

The task of modification and reformulation of wage theory is too great for a single essay or even for a single volume, although interesting beginnings have been made, as for example by Mr. K. W. Rothschild from the formal economic side and by Professor Lloyd G. Reynolds from the labor market side.[1] I shall limit my discussion here to labor markets which are unorganized by trade unions—although the threat of organization may be present—and I shall further limit to five the particular factual results of labor market research which I shall try to incorporate into wage theory.

1. The typical employer in an unorganized labor market is by no means a pure competitor facing market wage rates which he cannot alter. The mobility of the labor force, even between firms located close together, is low by reason of the inability of workers to wait for employment or risk unemployment, plus the inadequacy of the information usually available to them regarding alternative employment opportunities. This low mobility permits each employer to set his own rates and form his own labor market within limits which at some times may be quite wide. As a result of each firm forming its own labor market, it is often quite impossible to identify any overall standard rates for unorganized workers in what one would imagine to be geographical labor market areas.

2. At the same time that he possesses monopsony power, the typical employer in an unorganized labor market is not striving to maximize anything so easily quantifiable as his short-run monopsony profit, so that the conventional theory of monopsony pricing (centering about equalizing marginal factor cost and revenue product)[2] is likewise only imperfectly applicable.

This employer may not be maximizing anything whatever, being able to satisfy

*Reprinted with permission from Martin Bronfenbrenner, "Potential Monopsony in Labor Markets," *Industrial and Labor Relations Review* 9 (1956), pp. 577-88 (abridged). © 1956 by Cornell University. All rights reserved.

[1] K. W. Rothschild, *The Theory of Wages* (New York: Macmillan, 1954), chaps. 6-9, 15; Lloyd G. Reynolds, *The Structure of Labor Markets* (New York: Harper & Brothers, 1951), chaps. 8-9.

[2] Joan Robinson, *Economics of Imperfect Competition* (London: Macmillan, 1933), chaps. 17-18; Rothschild, op. cit., pp. 94-99.

what is called in psychological shorthand his "aspiration levels" significantly short of maximizing behavior. Alternatively, he may be seeking to maximize some complex function combining profits, liquidities, degrees of control over his enterprise, public relations with consumers, workers, governmental bodies, etc., all in an environment of fragmentary and erroneous information. If "he" is a person only legally and a corporate entity in fact, choice of the variable to be maximized may involve political controversies between numerous officers and department heads. It may involve the power and status of each officer within the general organization, as well as the economic interests of the organization as a whole.[3]

Such variations upon, or retreats from, maximizing behavior often lead in practice to situations in which the employer's monopoly or monopsony power is largely "potential," in the sense that it is not exercised actively. Hence the title of the present essay. The common trait of potential monopsony or monopoly is the use of rules, rituals, and routines to solve problems which would be solved by the market mechanism in a competitive economy or by judicious marginal-type calculations in an overtly monopsonistic or monopolistic one. These various rules, rituals, and routines may be peculiar to the firm or common to its entire industry or community. They may have been tested by experience, meaning that they have been followed for some years or even generations with generally satisfactory results. They have the further advantages of reducing stresses, conflicts, uncertainties, and ulcers, while keeping "enterprise" safe for "supply sergeants" and other notoriously nonenterprising types. Yet this is hardly adequate to permit their equation with maximizing behavior in any sense.

Rituals, rules, and routines are apt to

play an even larger role in employers' dealings with employees on the labor market than in their dealings with customers on product markets, since personnel managers are by and large less addicted to enterprise and innovation than are production or merchandising managers.

3. Within each category of labor, however finely drawn (first-class carpenters, apprentice machinists, or what have you), there is a wide range of "factor differentiation." Within each category, even the finest, workers may differ in productivity and other factors which influence their desirability to employers. Rather than setting "equilibrium" wage rates low enough to clear their labor markets and requiring acceptance of all applicants with minimal qualifications, monopsonistic employers usually set "disequilibrium" rates somewhat higher. This gives personnel officers leeway to pick and choose among applicants and eliminates any need to raise wages whenever employment increases. (This sort of procedure has its analogy in commodity markets, in production for inventory rather than directly for the market and in permitting inventory fluctuation prior to price change.) The choice among workers on the labor market may be related directly to anticipated productivity, or it may be based entirely on "prejudices" connected with age, sex, race, or religion.

4. In addition, changes in the firm's monopsony power, which under received theory might be expected to reflect themselves mainly in wage rates, are reflected in fact primarily in the standards enforced by personnel officers, i.e., in changes of factor qualities. Here again, this is no peculiar characteristic of labor markets. There is obvious analogy with the problem of varying the product versus varying its price in monopolistic competition. It is at any rate factually clear that the mechanism of monopolistic competition harbors a built-in bias toward product rather than price changes, for institutional reasons difficult to incorporate in theoretical treat-

---

[3] These matters have been spelled out particularly clearly in M. W. Reder, "A Reconsideration of the Marginal Productivity Theory," *Journal of Political Economy*, October 1947, pp. 450-58.

ment. In the case of price increases, consumer resentment is aroused, an occurrence which can be avoided, at least in part, by quality or service deterioration at a constant price. In the case of price declines, consumer expectations of further reductions are engendered, but these can be avoided almost completely by quality or service improvement at a constant price. Furthermore, competitors usually find it more difficult and more costly to meet a quality or service change than they do to meet a change in price. Something similar, we shall maintain, occurs on labor markets in potential competition, i.e., hiring standards are often lowered (raised) in preference to increasing (decreasing) wages.

5. In most concerns, promotion from within seems to be the rule, and contact with any general labor market is limited largely to the bottom rungs of one or at most of a few job ladders. (This is clearly a further factor reducing labor mobility.) As a result, differentials for skill, experience, or hardship above basic rates are largely insulated from market forces or from other factors operating outside of individual firms. The supply of "labor" to a particular firm should therefore not be related to any specific rung of any particular job ladder—least of all the bottom one at which the worker is ordinarily being hired on the market—but to a series of jobs to be held at different times and at different rates of compensation. The same principle should also hold on the demand side. Whatever relation may exist between a worker's pay and his marginal productivity is probably closer between his lifetime earnings and lifetime marginal productivity than between his earnings and productivity in any one year or on any one job.

FIRM WITH FIXED LABOR REQUIREMENTS

Let us consider the simplest case, which unlike some "simplest cases" is also fairly realistic. We have a monopsonistic employer whose requirements of labor of some sort are fixed over a wide range of possible wage rates. They are fixed with reference to his output of some product, by his fixed plant capacity, or by the limited availability of complementary variable factors of production. These "complementary variable factors of production" may be either raw materials or other types of labor. The relative fixity of labor requirements, or rather their apparent independence of wage rates, makes this case perhaps an ideal type of the "bargaining theory of wages," of which potential monopsony can in turn be treated as a subspecies.

The fixed labor requirements are indicated on Figure 1 as a vertical line, labeled *RR*, between wage rates *OA* and *OB*. The supply of labor minimally qualifying for the job description and offering itself to this employer is some function of the wage rate (among other variables). It is indicated in Figure 1 by *SS*, which is drawn as a smooth curve, although in practice it is likely to be a discontinuous step function.[4] Departure of *SS* from the horizontal measures the imperfection of labor mobility as it affects this employer. In the extreme case of immobility, *SS* may be vertical throughout its length, denoting complete insensitivity of the labor supply to wage rate changes. Further, it may never intersect *RR*, but rather lie entirely to one side, thereby implying an *absolute* labor shortage or labor surplus as the case may be. We need not go quite so far in reacting against conventional theory, but rather draw *SS* (to the employer) as sloping upward and intersecting *RR* at *P*, which may in practice be a zone rather than a single point.

In the conventional theory of wages under monopsony, there is an immedi-

---

[4] Compare Richard A. Lester, *Hiring Practices and Labor Competition* (Princeton: Princeton University, 1954), p. 87. "Managements have in mind some range of tolerance ... beyond which mobility will be an important wage-determining influence. The idea of a

Figure 1

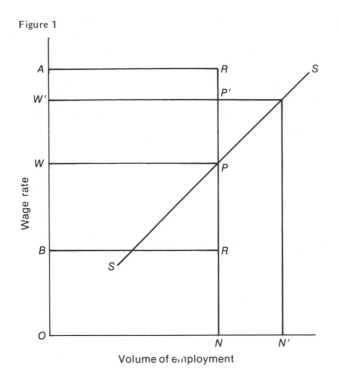

Volume of employment

ate solution for this fixed-requirements model. The monopsonistic employer will set a wage of OW where SS crosses RR. His "demand curve" for labor will not be RR but WP. Employment will be ON. These same ON men could have been employed at any wage up to OA, so that we may treat the differential WA as a measure of monopsonistic exploitation per unit of labor and the rectangle $WAPR$ as a measure of total monopsony or exploitation profit.

This would mean that wages would of necessity be raised whenever this employer's requirements increased or whenever his labor supply fell off, and conversely that wages would of necessity be lowered in the opposite situations. Such wage-rate sensitivity, labor market analysts assure

us, corresponds to nothing in the actual world. A more realistic treatment of this case is to suppose that the employer does not exercise all his monopsony power, but leaves some portion of it latent or potential. (Whence our term, "potential" monopsony.) Rather than the sweatshop wage OW, he is apt to select some higher wage OW' within the range AB. This selection is made with reference to what other firms are paying in similar jobs, to what unions are demanding of employers with less monopsony power, and (primarily, we suggest) to the percentage of minimally qualified applicants which the firm must employ at the rate selected. (At OW', ON are employed out of ON' applicants. The rejected fringe NN' presumably remain unemployed or take less desirable jobs. The quantity ON includes existing employees, some of whom might lack minimal qualifications but are kept on regardless.)

Too low a rate (too near OW) would require the hiring of nearly all minimally qualified workers, regardless of any spe-

---

no-reaction range or nonfunctioning zone does, however, eliminate the possibility of any simple relationship between wages and labor supply." We cannot accept, however, Lester's next sentence, "Thus, it makes the use of labor-supply curves for the firm inappropriate . . . ," unless he restricts "labor-supply curves" to such smooth and continuous functions as SS (in Fig. 1).

cial standards of skill, experience, education, etc. which the firm might wish to impose, and regardless also of any personnel office prejudices regarding age, sex, race, nationality, religion, and so on. In the extreme case of a wage below *OW*, the firm would have some percentage of jobs unfilled in any event. Too high a wage rate (too near *OA*), on the other hand, involves paying a premium for qualifications not immediately required for the job at hand (as when an electrical engineer is hired as an electrician, or a secretary as a typist). On the other hand, it gives in general a wider scope to the special crotchets of the firm's employment office, since so small a proportion of applicants are hired.

The potential monopsony wage rate *OW'* and the monopsony "demand curve" *W'P'* involve a disequilibrium and not an equilibrium situation. They leave a fringe of *NN'* individuals as an excess supply to the firm, which excess is eliminated at the conventional monopsony wage *OW*. As for exploitation, potential monopsony does not generally eliminate it in the fixed-requirements case, but reduces it from *AW* to *AW'* per worker, as compared with the standard monopsony presentation.

Further, if *RR* moves to the right (as by expansion of the employing firm), or *SS* to the left (as by entrance of new firms into the geographical area), the employer is left with a range of maneuver in which he may either raise wages or revise employment standards (in a downward direction). The firm is not limited to raising wages, as in the conventional model, and studies suggest the short-run path of least resistance to be primarily along quality-dilution rather than wage-raising lines.[5] Similar arguments hold in reverse, when the firm contracts or otherwise reduces

its labor requirements, and when the supply of labor to the firm increases.

OCCUPATIONAL PROGRESSION

Men are hired less frequently for specific jobs than taken in at the bottom of industrial job ladders, up which they are expected to clamber by seniority throughout their working lives. Furthermore, men are seldom hired directly from the market for the higher rungs of the manual job ladders—nor, for that matter, of clerical or executive ladders either. "Promotion from within" is the general rule. Under these circumstances, a man is hired, not for one job at one wage rate, but for a roughly envisioned *sequence* of jobs at an equally roughly estimated *sequence* of wage rates. This is perhaps more true for clerical than for manual workers.

In the decision to hire or not to hire an *n*th worker, the comparison between his pay and productivity on his first job, or indeed on any individual job, should be of much less importance to the employer than the comparison between his expected lifetime productivity and his expected lifetime earnings. If this is true, it should occasion no surprise to find wide disparities between statistical estimates of productivity on particular jobs and earnings on these jobs. The productivity theory of demand for labor should be modified or reformulated to refer to lifetime productivities and earnings, even if its basic presumption of profit maximization is retained as a first approximation. What follows is an attempt at such modification and reformulation. It is inspired primarily by the criticisms levied by labor economists and industrial relations specialists at the conventional model; it is presented primarily for their consideration and criticism.

As a compromise between literary and mathematical formulation, we again have recourse to a diagram, in this case Figure 2. On this diagram, the horizontal axis refers to time, while the vertical axis mea-

---

[5] Most clearly in point is Lester, *Adjustments to Labor Shortages* (Princeton: Princeton University, 1955), p. 71. Studying the reaction of 70-odd firms in and near Trenton, New Jersey, to a labor shortage introduced by the establishment of four steel and defense plants in the area, Lester found that approximately half lowered their hiring standards for new employees, while only 12 firms raised starting wages.

Figure 2

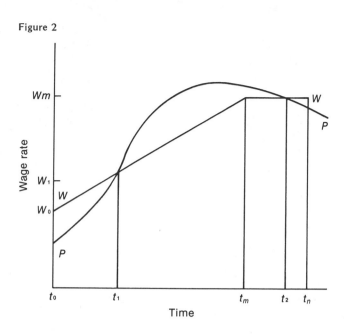

sures both wage rates and marginal net products in money terms. Our analysis runs in terms of anticipated wage functions (WW) and anticipated productivity functions (PP), to be derived in the succeeding paragraphs.

A man employed at time t_0 at wage W_0 is expected, we suppose, to progress normally by a series of conventional promotions from lower- to higher-paid jobs within the firm, until at t_m he attains a maximum rate W_m, which he holds until his retirement at t_n. Since we deal in this essay with a monopsonistic employer, we suppose him to determine each separate wage rate more or less as discussed in the previous analysis. Connecting the various points (t_1, W_1) gives us our wage function WW, which we have drawn smoother than it can ever be in practice.[6]

Based as it must be upon anticipations held only vaguely and imprecisely at the

time of hiring, t_0, WW may be thought of as a locus of expected values of wage rates at different points in time, that is to say, as some sort of average points in possible wage ranges. At any point of time t_1, these ranges could be measured vertically above and below the corresponding W_1. Inclusion of these limits would transform the wage function from a line to a broad band or ribbon, with WW itself moving down the middle like the central vein in a blade of grass.

If we take the area under WW (Figure 2) over the interval $t_0 t_n$, by integration or otherwise, and then discount for futurity, the result is the present value of the expected lifetime earnings of the worker whose employment is being considered.

His net marginal productivity, on the other hand, may be expected equally imprecisely to follow a path somewhat like the one we have indicated by PP. It begins close to zero or perhaps even below it, when one considers materials wasted by novices and the lost time of other workers in teaching them and correcting their blunders. Then it rises steadily as the new man "catches on" to more and more dif-

---

[6] In practice, WW is in the first place a step function rather than a smooth curve. In the second place, even the smoothed approximation to WW may bend sharply above or below particular points at which there is more competition from other firms and therefore closer approximation to the conditions on organized commodity markets.

ficult aspects of his work, or acquires more and more facility at the routine aspects. Normally, it reaches a peak, then falls gradually at first and then more sharply before retirement at t_n. The area under PP, between t_0 and t_n, again discounted for futurity, is the present value of the expected lifetime productivity of the worker being considered for a job.

Over the intervals $t_0 t_1$ (training) and $t_2 t_n$ (senescence), WW may be expected to exceed PP. The worker may be expected to receive more than he is worth. Over the interval $t_1 t_2$, the most productive period of his working life, the reverse should normally be true.

If in general (ignoring the discounting factor) the area by which PP exceeds WW between t_1 and t_2 exceeds the area by which WW exceeds PP between t_0 and t_1 and again between t_2 and t_n, it will pay to employ additional labor at the going wage rates. If the reverse is true, it does not pay to employ additional labor; indeed, the work force may be overexpanded. But for any one job (even under conditions of long-run profit maximization) the wage may be above, below, or equal to the marginal productivity. We are not here considering the substantial and significant possibilities collected and presented, by Reder for example,[7] in which nonprofit considerations lead to employment of either more or less labor than it would pay the employer to hire.

Our diagram, and the shapes of the functions presented therein, may appear arbitrary, even for a theoretical model; and in some respects such criticism is quite justified. We may point out, however, certain features which make contact with reality and are consistent with some of the facts of the labor market. First is the resentment which management shows toward the "floater." A floater is a man who quits at approximately time t_1 to go to another job. Employment offices avoid

hiring him whenever possible. How explain this, beyond laziness of personnel people, if his wage and productivity have been equal during the period of his employment? It is more simple and reasonable to suppose that over the interval $t_0 t_1$ this worker's productivity has been substantially less than the wages he has been paid. The employer loses money if the man quits at t_1. The employer may be thought of as having paid at t_0 higher wages than he might otherwise have done to induce the worker to remain with the company for a long period. If he quits anyway, a black mark on his record may go with him.

A second and not unrelated contact with reality is to be found in the mixed attitude of many employers toward much vocational training in high schools, the armed services, and even in colleges of commerce and engineering. On the one hand, employers denounce the inferior quality of the training and the waste of time involved in what they consider academic irrelevancies. It is indeed a common complaint that six months on the job is worth two years in the army or four years of commerce school. On the other hand, the same employers support appropriations for such training and hire the end products with far more alacrity than other products of the educational assembly lines. Why? In terms of Figure 2, we suggest that it is because vocational training raises the lower reaches of functions like PP at public or philanthropic expense. Usually, the increase is not all the way to WW, where the employers would like to see it, but a good part of the way. At the same time, the breakeven point t_1 is moved closer to the origin t_0, although again not usually so close as the employer might desire. A cruder way of putting the matter is that the businessman prefers four years (or any other amount) of what is from the social viewpoint wasted or unnecessary training time at public expense to six months efficient training at

[7] See footnote 3, above.

his own expense. This is a neglected example of conflict between social and private concepts of efficiency, with the academic profession and the business community sharing the benefits of a socially questionable status quo.

A third contact with reality may be the resentment felt toward employers who pension workers too soon after the second break-even point at t_2, unless indeed the pensions are unusually generous.[8] These older workers have given the best years of their working lives to their employers for what is (up to time t_2) considerably less than those years were normally worth. It is not only unfortunate for them to be pensioned early, in itself a sufficient cause for a certain amount of resentment. It is likewise "unfair" or even "exploitative" in that they have not yet drawn the full value of their prior services. In Marxian terms but with a modern twist, these workers have deposited "surplus value" with the employer and are deprived by early retirement of the chance to draw it back.

This analysis appears to apply to the lower and middle reaches of management, for which indeed it was developed originally,[9] as well as to the subordinate classes of manual and clerical labor. It does not, however, apply to the higher reaches of the executive stratosphere, and it is therefore not presented as a contribution to this central problem of executive compensation theory.

------

[8] It would be possible to allow in Figure 2 for the possible existence of pension systems by extending WW to the right beyond t_n, where PP falls to zero, albeit at a low level and with a large discontinuity at t_n. (The rightward extension of WW would represent the pension payments.) Our literary analysis would also have required minor complications at a few points.

------

[9] I wish to express indebtedness to a former colleague, David R. Roberts, now dean of Butler University, for stimulating conversations, manuscripts, and suggestions on the relations between wage theory and the executive compensation problem, which combined to arouse my interest in the subject.

CHAPTER 6

WAGE STRUCTURE CONSIDERATIONS

The concept of wage structure refers to the array of wage rates paid different jobs within an organization and focuses attention upon the differential compensation paid these jobs. The highest paid job in some organizations receives 100 times the compensation of the lowest paid job, and the differential may be considerably less (9 or 10 times) in other organizations. We examine in this chapter the influences and consequences of the structure of rates of compensation within an organization, what determines the structure of compensation differentials in an organization and what are the implications of different structures?

The relationship between compensation structure and wage level is the relationship between a distribution of values and the average value of the distribution; wage level was defined earlier as some average value characterizing the rates of compensation paid by an employing organization. As an average, wage level might be viewed as a summary statistic descriptive of wage rates determined individually for specific jobs, or as a policy parameter constraining those decisions. There is some validity in both views although we have emphasized the conceptualization of wage level as a policy parameter, a measure of average labor cost to be controlled by the organization and not merely a summary statistic derived from decisions about compensation for individual jobs. As a policy parameter, wage level constrains but does not determine the structure of rates of compensation within an organization. The same wage level can be associated with widely different wage structures. It is common practice in many breweries, for example, to pay the identical wage rate to all plant personnel regardless of job assignment, there are no wage differentials among jobs. Another employer might pay the same wage level with a wide distribution of differentials among jobs. We pointed out in the previous chapter the importance of control of wage level as a measure of average cost of labor and the influence of perceptions of wage level in the labor market in the attraction of labor supplies. The determination of appropriate differentials among wage rates in the organization can be approached as a relatively independent set of decisions subject only to the constraints of the wage level parameter.

It is not clear from the concept of the employment exchange or the decision making models of Smith, Rottenberg, and Vroom whether the organization or the specific job is the more appropriate unit for analysis, whether individuals accept employment in the organization or accept employment in specific jobs. The decision-making models suggest that decisions are made about employment in specific job assignments, although they might also be applied to acceptance of employment in an organization with an implied willingness to accept a variety of job assignments. The competitive labor market model developed from Adam Smith's decision-making

model indicates that individuals make decisions about specific job employments and that a structure of market wage differentials emerges which tends
to equalize the net advantages of these different job employments. Any
structure of wage differentials within an organization would be derived from
the structure of wage differentials in the broader labor market and vary
inversely with individuals' perceptions of the nonwage advantages associated
with employment in those jobs.

We observed in our examination of labor supply behavior that employees
are not as mobile as assumed in the competitive labor market model and that
they become attached to employers through tenure. Studies of employee
mobility indicate, for example, that the most common form of mobility—
job change—occurs without change of employers. Our analysis based upon
the model of Bronfenbrenner implied that employers seek to attract workers
to the organization through wage levels of hiring jobs, retain the workers
within the organization, and to make specific job assignments from the pool
of tenured employees. Just as payment of a relatively high wage level is
intended to attract a pool of applicants and buffer the organization against
labor market pressures, the confinement of hiring to specific entry jobs and
the staffing of other jobs through promotion and assignment of tenured
employees also buffers the majority of jobs from labor market pressures. The
supply of labor to specific jobs within the organization thus is more appropriately viewed as a function of the wage structure and the pool of employees within the organization than as a function of wage level and the labor
market. The supply of labor to the organization and supplies of labor to
specific jobs, while related, can be differentiated conceptually and analyzed
as different functions of compensation characteristics, the one influenced by
wage levels and the other influenced by wage structure considerations.

The essays by Doeringer, Thurow, and Livernash in this section employ
explicitly a conceptualization of an "internal labor market." The external
labor market is viewed in the traditional manner as the processes through
which persons seeking employment are allocated among organizations
bidding for their services; the internal labor market refers to those processes
within the employing organization through which employees are allocated
among alternative jobs. In Essay 6-1, Doeringer describes the processes giving
rise to the internal labor market, the ways in which organizations recruit and
maintain a pool of employees, and the structure and processes for allocation
of employees within the organization. Individuals typically are recruited into
the employing organization only for selected entry jobs or a labor pool from
which later assignments will be made. As suggested by Bronfenbrenner, the
wage rates paid these entry jobs characterize employer wage levels to prospective employees, and employers strive to offer relatively high wages for
these jobs in order to attract a pool of applicants. Nonentry jobs are staffed
through assignment and/or promotion of current employees and not by
bidding for applicants in the external labor market. Although not considered
explicitly by Doeringer, the structure of wages for nonentry jobs must serve
to secure and retain employee willingness to perform these jobs, but it is less
subject to influence from the external labor market than wage rates paid
entry jobs.

Essay 6-2 by Thurow elaborates upon the "job competition" model he introduced earlier. He argues that marginal productivity is essentially a job characteristic, not a person characteristic, and that employees qualify for jobs through training and development in prior jobs of the organization. Employees develop job qualifications through employment in the organization, they do not bring essential qualifications with them. Thurow rationalizes the rigid structure of the internal labor market as a means of furthering employee training and development both through the sequencing of career experiences and through the encouragement provided more highly skilled employees for the training of lesser qualified employees; individuals are protected from wage competition of lesser qualified employees through positioning in the labor queue within the organization on the basis of seniority and related criteria employed for advancement within a career sequence. The wage structure of an organization thus may very well parallel the sequencing of jobs in a career ladder but it is clearly not determined by wage competition among workers bidding for these jobs. Thurow thus provides a further rationale for a structured internal labor market, but he does not explain the emergence of a complementary structure of wage rates.

Livernash (Essay 6-3) accepts implicitly the description of the internal labor market of Doeringer and Thurow and examines specifically the determinants of wage structure within the internal labor market. He describes job evaluation, an approach to wage structure determination, as evolving from the social context of the workplace rather than from the influences of the external labor market. According to Livernash, employees desire "fair" rates of compensation and judge the fairness of their wage rates through comparison with wage rates paid other jobs related in some fashion to their own jobs (job clusters). The clustering of jobs for comparative purposes obeys no single rule; jobs in a cluster simply are those jobs which the incumbents consider when judging the fairness of their own compensation. Jobs in a cluster may share skill characteristics, similar function in the production process, proximity of location, administrative reporting relationships, or career ladder sequencing, anything which makes them visible to one another and provides some bond or other basis for comparison. In a similar fashion, key jobs representing different job clusters are compared with one another and with similar jobs in other firms in judgments of equity of compensation. While Livernash reviews certain operational criteria employed in job evaluation (skill level, working conditions, responsibility), he asserts that the central criterion in determination of an internal wage structure is acceptability to the employees involved. Departures from an acceptable wage structure occasion turnover, grievances, and other dysfunctional behavior, all elements of labor supply, particularly the supply of effort and diligence of performance on the job. Unfortunately, Livernash provides little guidance for the achievement of equity or acceptability; we have only the empirical test of acceptability. Wage structure is, however, a phenomenon of the internal labor market and explanation of wage structure characteristics is to be sought in analysis of the internal labor market rather than in analysis of external labor market influences.

Essay *6-1*

The structure of internal labor markets*

Peter B. Doeringer

In the classical competitive labor market model, the market for labor is perceived as a bourse, a place where the buyers and sellers of labor meet to transact their business and where every job in the economy is continuously open to all workers on the same terms and conditions. In a dynamic market environment, the work relationship between employer and employee in such a system must be, perforce, of a nonpermanent nature; each worker is subject to being underbid and each employer faces the exodus of his employees if he fails to pay the current, market-determined wage. Such is the way the forces of competition are envisioned to operate in the classical model to produce the efficient allocation of labor resources and the concomitant marginal equalities required in a competitive equilibrium.

For the *cognoscenti* of labor market operation, however, the descriptive or predictive usefulness of this classical model, as characterized by (1) reliance upon wage rates to produce adjustments to changing market conditions, and (2) assumptions of frictionless mobility and "open" job structures, is vitiated by the realities of the employment relationships and wage-setting procedures observed in the manufacturing sector. The need for a viable alternative to the classical labor market model, similar to those developed in the product market by E. H. Chamber-

lin[1] and Joan Robinson,[2] has been demonstrated by the assaults upon the validity of the classical model,[3] by the development of institutional models of wage determination, and by the market models and case studies dealing with both interplant and intraplant labor allocation.[4]

THE KERR MODEL

In one such institutional model, formulated by Clark Kerr,[5] the labor market is not viewed as operating like an open and competitive bourse, but rather as a series

---

*Reprinted from Peter B. Doeringer, "Determinants of the Structure of Industrial Type Internal Labor Markets," *Industrial and Labor Relations Review* 20 (1967), pp. 206-20.

[1] E. H. Chamberlin, *The Theory of Monopolistic Competition*, 8th ed. (Cambridge: Harvard University Press, 1962).

[2] Joan Robinson, *The Economics of Imperfect Competition*, 2d ed. (London: Macmillan, 1942).

[3] See, for example, Richard A. Lester, "Shortcomings of Marginal Analysis for Wage-Employment Problems," *American Economic Review*, vol. 36, March 1946.

[4] Some of the works in this area are John T. Dunlop, "The Task of Contemporary Wage Theory," and E. Robert Livernash, "The Internal Wage Structure," both of which appear in George W. Taylor and Frank C. Pierson, eds., *New Concepts in Wage Determination* (New York: McGraw-Hill, 1957); J. L. Meij, "Wage Structure and Organization Structure," and G. H. Hildebrand, "External Influences and the Determination of the Internal Wage Structure," in J. L. Meij, ed, *Internal Wage Structure* (Amsterdam: North-Holland Publishing Co., 1963); Clark Kerr, "The Balkanization of Labor Markets," in E. Wight Bakke et al., *Labor Mobility and Economic Opportunity* (Cambridge: Technology Press of M.I.T., 1954); John T. Dunlop, "Job Vacancy Measures and Economic Analysis," in National Bureau of Economic Research, *The Measurement and Interpretation of Job Vacancies* (New York: Columbia University Press, 1966), pp. 28-47; and Lloyd Reynolds, *The Structure of Labor Markets: Wages and Labor Mobility in Theory and Practice* (New York: Harper and Brothers 1951).

[5] Kerr, loc. cit.

of distinct markets, reminiscent of the "noncompeting groups" of Cairnes and Mill,[6] each with boundaries determined by geographical, occupational, and most important, institutional factors. While the boundaries of these markets touch or overlap in places, for purposes of labor mobility they are largely separate. The existence of these market boundaries creates a distinction, in terms of employment preferences, between workers included within a bounded market and those without. As Kerr describes it,[7]

Labor markets are of two broad types: (1) the Structureless and (2) the Structured. In the structureless market there is no attachment except the wage between the worker and the employer. No worker has any claim on a job and no employer has any hold on any man. Structure enters the market when different treatment is accorded to the "ins" and to the "outs." In the structured market there always exists (1) the *internal market* and (2) the *external market.* The internal market may be the plant or the craft group, and preferment within it may be based on prejudice or merit or equality of opportunity or seniority, or some combination of these. The external market consists of clusters of workers actively or passively available for new jobs lying within some meaningful geographical and occupational boundaries, and of the port or *ports of entry* which are open or are potentially open to them.

The theoretical construct of the internal labor market, as introduced by Kerr, may be more precisely defined as an administrative unit within which the market functions of pricing, allocating, and often

training labor are performed.[8] It is governed by a set of institutional rules which delineate the boundaries of the internal market and determine its internal structure.[9] These institutional or administrative hiring and work rules define the "ports of entry" into the internal market, the relationships between jobs for purposes of internal mobility, and the privileges which accrue to workers within the internal market. A single or multiplant enterprise, a union hiring hall providing manpower for a number of different enterprises, and a branch of the military services are all examples of such administrative units. In many instances, these broadly defined internal labor markets are further divided into internal submarkets for different occupational categories, such as managerial, clerical, maintenance, production, and the like, each of which is governed by its own specific set of rules. These may in turn be divided into smaller units for purposes of hiring, upgrading, downgrading, lateral transfer, and layoff. An example of such an internal labor market is shown in Chart 1.

INTERNAL LABOR MARKET STRUCTURES IN MANUFACTURING

This analysis will concentrate upon the allocative mechanism for production and maintenance labor in what is probably the

[6] See J. S. Mill, *Principles of Political Economy,* vol. 1, book 2, chap. 14 (London: Longmans Green, 1909), pp. 480-81; and J. E. Cairnes, *Some Leading Principles of Political Economy Newly Expounded,* Part 1, chap. 3, sec. 5 (New York: Harper and Brothers, 1874), pp. 62-65.

[7] Kerr, loc. cit., n. on p. 101 (emphasis added).

[8] See Dunlop, "Job Vacancy Measures and Economic Analysis," loc. cit., pp. 7-15. Dunlop defines the internal labor market as the complex of rules which determines the movement of workers among job classifications within administrative units such as enterprises, companies, or hiring halls. These movements may be transfers, promotions, demotions, or layoffs to the exterior labor market. These movements may be temporary or permanent, which may affect the operation of the rules . . . (ibid, n. on p. 32).

[9] The internal labor market of the manufacturing plant, for example, may be more broadly viewed as a complex equilibrium system composed of the following internal variables which are, at least to some degree, interdependent: (1) the job structure of the plant; (2) the administrative rules defining the patterns and

Chart 1: Internal labor market, chemical plant

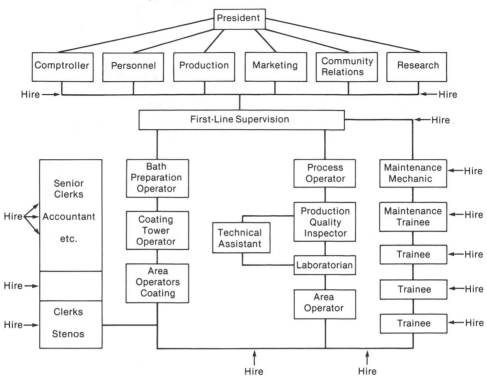

most familiar type of structured internal labor market, the manufacturing plant. The allocative structure found within the internal labor markets of such enterprises may be characterized by a threefold classification scheme: (1) the degree of openness to the external labor market as determined by the number and location of the ports of entry (hiring job classifications); (2) the dimensions, both horizontal and vertical, of the units for internal movement (i.e., upgrading, downgrading, lateral transfer, and layoff); and (3) the rules which determine the priority in which workers will be distributed among the jobs within the internal market.[10]

For purposes of exposition, two polar types of production and maintenance internal submarket structures may be postulated, closed and open. The closed internal submarket has only a single-entry job classification, all other jobs in the plant being filled internally through upgrading. Some plants, notably in steel and petroleum, exhibit such closed structures since they prefer to hire almost exclusively into low-skilled job classifications and to develop most of their blue-collar skills, including maintenance and mechanical skills, internally.[11]

At the opposite end of the classifica-

---

priorities of internal movement; (3) the location of the "entry ports" and recruitment and selection procedures; (4) training procedures; (5) compensation; and (6) employee pressures and union and employer bargaining objectives.

[10] Movement within the internal labor market of the plant is typically of three types: (1) a secular trend

as a result of upgrading, (2) vertical and lateral movement in response to output fluctuations, and (3) temporary assignments due to absent employees. This analysis will consider only the first two types which are the most predictable.

[11] For a study of an internal labor market which develops all of its operating and maintenance skills through internal training and upgrading, see U.S. Bureau of Labor Statistics, *A Case Study of a Modernized Petroleum Refinery* (Washington: G.P.O., 1957), Report no. 120.

tion spectrum is the open internal labor submarket, in which vacancies in all job classifications are filled directly from the external labor market. In men's clothing, for example, a considerable degree of openness is found; vacancies in most stitching and pressing job classifications being typically filled directly from the external market.

In most industrial plants, however, the proportion of job classifications which serve as interfaces between the plant and the external market lies somewhere between these extremes. Typically, the hiring ports into production and maintenance jobs are located at the low-skilled level—such as maintenance trainee, sweeper, machine cleaner, packer, assembler, and the like—and at the high-skilled, journeyman level, while most semiskilled and high-skilled production jobs are closed to the external market.[12]

The entry ports into the internal labor market of the manufacturing plant are typically connected to clusters of jobs within the plant which constitute the districts within which an employee may be upgraded, downgraded, transferred, or laid off.[13] The contours of these districts may vary with the type of movement (i.e., promotion, layoff, and so forth), and are de-

termined by economic variables such as the technology of the production process, predictable fluctuations in product demand, external labor market conditions, and also by such factors as equity and custom. The dimensions of these districts for internal movement are defined by the vertical range of the grades of job content within the district and by the number and the degree of specialization of the job classifications contained within any job grade.[14]

DISTRICTS UNDER REVIEW

In the study on which this article is based the broadest district for upgrading in the production internal submarket was plantwide. Plantwide districts are typically associated with production job structures with a relatively small range of variation in levels of job content and a low proportion of specialized jobs, such as occurs in food products manufacturing. A narrower district for upgrading involves the division of production jobs into departments based upon the production process, the nature of the occupations, the product type, or the administrative organization of the plant. In some plants—steel, chemicals, and petroleum, for example—the districts for upgrading are even more narrow, consisting of specific lines of progression within each department. These progression lines may be only one job classification wide or may consist of several branches. When upgrading districts are narrow and interjob mobility linkages are carefully defined, upgrading sequences usually reflect a skill or experience development sequence. The range of job content and the proportion of specialized jobs, moreover, is usually greater in those plants with narrow upgrading districts than in plants with broad districts.

---

[12] Formal in-plant training programs may also constitute ports of entry, albeit rather specialized ones. Some companies provide such training entry ports to prepare entrants for particular jobs or progression patterns, usually of a skilled nature. Formal production and maintenance training programs of this type, usually for such skills as drafting, production planning, computer programming, and computerized equipment maintenance, are designed to (1) provide the plant with the needed skills more quickly and efficiently than through alternative routes in the internal labor market, such as on-the-job training of current employees, and (2) to provide a special entry port enabling the plant to hire a select group of employees with higher educational and aptitude qualifications than are required of most unskilled entrants.

[13] These forms of internal labor market structuring bear an implicit relationship to the constructs of "job clusters" used by Dunlop and Livernash (Dunlop, *The Task of Contemporary Wage Theory*, loc. cit., p. 129, and Livernash, loc. cit., pp. 148-49) to describe the process of the determination of the intraplant wage structure.

---

[14] See Sumner H. Slichter, James J. Healy, and E. Robert Livernash, *The Impact of Collective Bargaining upon Management* (Washington: Brookings Institution, 1960), pp. 154-58 for a discussion of the types of seniority districts found in manufacturing.

The extreme type of narrow internal labor market district consists of a single job classification and emphasizes the uniqueness or independence of each type of job, in contrast to multiclassification districts which recognize the skill and experience relationships among the jobs in the internal market. These single job classification districts appear when the jobs in the plant are highly specialized, as in the production submarkets in men's garments referred to above—in which, despite the existence of some common skill elements, most pressing and stitching job classifications are not related through internal transfer linkages.

PRIORITY OF MOVEMENT

The final dimension of the classification system for industrial type internal labor markets involves the rules governing the priority of movement within the internal market. Relying primarily upon the factors of ability and seniority, these·rules define the order in which employees within the relevant internal grouping of job classifications—seniority district, progression ladder, department, or the like—will receive promotions, transfers, downgradings, and layoffs. They may also be supplemented by rules governing bumping rights and the type of choice permitted employees in selecting or accepting internal reassignment.[15]

The exclusive reliance upon either seniority or ability for determining all internal movement priorities constitutes the limit of the range of types of movement priority systems. Most plants, however, employ some combination of criteria, although the particular combination will often vary with the type of movement (i.e., promotion, layoff, and so forth).

The rules governing the priorities for internal movement may be supplemented with additional arrangements by which workers may select or accept internal movements and the way in which bumping rights can be exercised during reductions in forces. Job vacancies, for example, may frequently be "posted" within a particular promotion district. Workers in the district can then express their desire to be assigned to the vacancy by filling out an application or "bid" for the job. The employer would then fill the vacancy from among these bids on the basis of the criteria described above. An alternative method requires workers to file bids in advance of job vacancies, so that a list of applicants for any job is always available. If no one applies for a vacancy, some plants may expand the area of internal selection to permit a broader group of employees to apply, while other plants might assign the least senior worker in the department or plant to the job or else seek to fill the vacancy from the external market.

During downgrading, an employee's bumping rights also constitute a component of the internal selection process. Within the district in which a surplus employee is allowed to exercise his bumping rights, several types of bumping patterns may occur. Chain bumping, in which a bump by one employee may lead to a number of consecutive bumps before a layoff results, produces the greatest number of moves per surplus employee. Alternatively, rules may exist which curtail the number of bumps by using narrow downgrading districts, by requiring that a surplus employee bump directly into a low-skilled labor pan, or by establishing arbitrary seniority limits upon bumping. Frequently, the scope of the downgrading district is balanced by the rules limiting

---

[15] The scope of the district and the rules determining the priority for internal movement are not functionally separable. Especially in the case of layoffs and downgradings, where the equity of employment and earnings security is important, the internal movement district, the rules governing movement priorities, and employees' bumping rights must be viewed simultaneously in order to understand completely the operation of the internal labor market. (See Slichter, Healy, and Livernash, op. cit., pp. 157-58.)

bumping in order to reduce the costs of the disruptions which accompany the internal movement of workers.[16]

DETERMINANTS OF THE MARKET STRUCTURE

In a static internal labor market the most important variables shaping its structure, excluding the influence of noneconomic market forces such as custom, are the technology of production and the work methods within the plant. The plant may be perceived as an administrative unit which contains a set of tasks. The technology of the capital equipment and the product mix which must be produced on this equipment define, within certain limits, the skill mix and the proportion of specialized jobs in the plant at any point in time. Whatever flexibility exists in the plant's job structure results from the discretionary fashion in which tasks may be combined to produce broadly or narrowly skilled jobs (i.e., job design) and decisions regarding the division of the work between internal employees and subcontractors. Within the manning range permitted by such flexibility, the technology of the production process establishes a matrix of jobs whose vertical dimension reflects levels of job content. The mobility linkages between the jobs in this matrix and between the matrix and the external labor market are defined by the hiring, promotion, downgrading, transfer, and termination patterns already described.

If the process of filling vacancies in the job structure of the plant, from either internal or external sources of labor, were costless, the employer would be indifferent among the possible combinations of patterns of internal mobility and locations of entry ports. With every new hire, how-

ever, there are recruiting costs; and with both new hires and internal reassignments of employees, there are costs of screening and selection. With every new hire or internal reassignment, moreover, some training must occur as the employee becomes acquainted with the duties of his new job; and such training, even when provided on the job as is typically the case with production skills, has certain costs attached to it.

These training costs, often measurable only in terms of reduced productivity, wasted raw materials, damaged machinery, and the like, are a direct function of (1) the content of entry jobs and the differences in content among the job classifications which are grouped together for purposes of internal movement, and (2) the availability of particular labor-force skills or qualities on the external labor market.[17] Given the job structure of the plant, the profit-maximizing employer, excluding questions of equity and employee morale, will presumably attempt to establish a sequence of hiring and internal movement patterns which will permit him to fill vacancies in the job structure at the lowest cost. The process of designing jobs and of determining hiring and internal mobility patterns provides one of the primary mechanisms by which the costs of entry training and internal retraining are controlled within the plant.

Once the content of the jobs contained within the internal labor market is established, some jobs typically will be identified as entry ports because of the minimal entry training associated with them. Many of these entry jobs will necessarily be low-skilled, but more highly skilled jobs may also be entry ports when there is an expectation that workers possessing appropriate skills will be available on the external labor market. The remaining jobs in the internal market will be filled through upgrading, primarily because experience

---

[16] See Peter B. Doeringer and Michael J. Piore, "Labor Market Adjustment and Internal Training," *Proceedings of the Eighteenth Annual Meeting of the Industrial Relations Research Association*, December 1965, for a discussion of the nature of these costs.

[17] See Doeringer and Piore, op. cit.

and training acquired elsewhere in the internal job structure can be at least partially transferred to these jobs. The proportion of the jobs opened to the external market, therefore, will be substantially influenced by the skill mix and specificity of the internal job structure and by the relatedness of content among the jobs in that structure.[18]

JOB CONTENT RELATIONSHIPS

The dimensions of the patterns of movement within the internal labor market also are largely determined by internal job content relationships. For example, when specific progression ladders defining precise interjob mobility linkages are established, there is typically a logical relationship between the job progression pattern and the process of incremental skill development through on-the-job training. These lines of progression utilize prior internal training and experience to reduce the amount of additional training which must occur following a promotion.

LABOR MARKET FACTORS

Finally, the characteristics of the labor market in which a plant is situated will also provide an influence upon the location of the ports of entry into the plant's job structure. When the entry ports occur exclusively among job classifications with low content, the external labor market does not significantly affect the internal market structure. Plants which also find it practical, however, in terms of training costs, to hire into skilled maintenance or operating jobs, will find their ability to do so constrained by the external availability of the appropriate skills and experience.

This availability is a function of the "tightness" of the external labor market in which the plant is located. When external shortages of certain types of skill exist, the entry ports of the skills will cease to function, and the required skills will typically be developed internally.[19]

CUSTOM, TRADITION, AND EMPLOYEE PRESSURE

The forces of custom, tradition, employee pressure, and in many instances, unionism also impinge upon the operation of the internal market, occasionally to such a degree that the influences of the "economic" variables upon the structure of the market, described above, may be substantially reduced or even negated. The original causes of the patterns of movement within a plant may later become obscured; the observed structure of the internal market may then be viewed as a holdover from earlier causal economic influences or even historical accident, and so may be unrelated to the strict cost and efficiency requirements of the present internal market. Divergences from the least-cost internal market structures are, however, clearly limited by competitive pressures in the product market.

Employee pressures for employment and earnings security, union and employer bargaining objectives, and considerations of employee morale may also exercise a modifying influence upon the structure of internal labor markets. The observed grouping of job classifications for purposes of internal movement represents the product of the interests and pressures of the parties to the rules of the internal market. There is no presumption that such pressures, including sometimes even those of the employer, are necessarily related to the least-cost pattern for providing the internal labor market with the

---

[18] Particular job skills are plant specific when job content is unique to a plant in terms of the high proportion of orientation training to manual skill required, the idiosyncratic content of the job, or the difficulty encountered in adapting work habits acquired elsewhere on similar jobs to job performance in the plant.

[19] Depending on the production process, it may also be possible to subcontract some of the work performed within the plant to alleviate internal skill shortages.

appropriate skills required by the job structure of the plant. Nor is there any indication that these pressures of bargaining objectives must reflect an underlying community of worker, union, or employer opinion regarding "desirable" patterns of internal movement.

To the extent that these noneconomic variables modify the internal market structure, it is difficult to predict patterns of internal movement solely from the economic variables. Some of the diversity of hiring, promotion, and transfer patterns, found even among similar plants in this study, is probably attributable in some measure to such factors, since the immediate objectives prescribed by economic variables such as technology, product markets, external labor markets, training ladders, and the like, may be balanced against the noneconomic variables by adjusting the amount of internal training.

SUMMARY

The type of structure exhibited by an industrial internal labor market is initially a function of the economic forces of (1) the technology of the production process, (2) the quantitative and qualitative changes in product demand, and (3) the availability of various types and qualities of labor on the external labor market. The influence of these economic forces is frequently modified by noneconomic factors such as custom, bargaining, objectives, and employment and earnings security.

Since the internal labor market must not only operate efficiently in a static state but must also adjust efficiently to a dynamic economic environment, the influences of the economic determinants upon the internal market structure may be evaluated in terms of their effect upon the costs of obtaining the requisite skills. The costs of recruitment, selection, and skill development associated with various internal market structures are a function of the level, distribution, and plant specificity of the content of the job classifications within the internal job structure, the degree of transferability of skills and experience among these jobs, the amount of labor turnover, and the external availability of workers. These costs must be balanced against the pressures of equity and other noneconomic factors in the final determination of the internal market structure. When similar economic costs are associated with alternative internal market structures, considerable latitude is possible in the choice of structure, so that noneconomic considerations may be controlling. If significant economic cost differentials exist among alternative internal market structures, however, the competitive product market forces will limit the extent to which the internal market structure can be incompatible with the efficient operation of the plant.

Essay 6-2

Training and the supply of skills*

Lester C. Thurow

If, as I have suggested, we live in an economy where laborers acquire many of their cognitive job skills through informal training from other workers or from their immediate supervisors, we need a differently structured labor market than we would if the only purpose of the labor market were to allocate skills and establish equilibrium wages. A labor-training market must be so structured as to maximize the willingness of existing laborers to transmit their knowledge to new workers and to minimize every worker's resistance to acquiring new skills and accepting new technology.

Eliminating direct wage competition and limiting employment competition to entry jobs is a necessary ingredient in the training process. If workers feel that they are training potential wage or employment competitors every time they show another worker how to do their job, they have every incentive to stop giving such informal training. In that case each man would seek to build his own little monopoly by hoarding skills and information to make himself indispensable. Wage and employment insecurity also means that every man has a vested interest in resisting any technical changes that might reduce his wages or employment opportunities. To encourage training, employers must repress wage competition and build employment security. If they do not, the essential training processes within their plants come to a halt.

*Excerpted from Lester C. Thurow, *Generating Inequality: Mechanisms of Distribution in the U.S. Economy* (New York: Basic Books, 1975), pp. 81-86.

Conversely, in a job market where no one is trained unless a job is currently available (this is what on-the-job training means), where strong seniority provisions limit employment insecurity to a clear minority (the newly hired), and where there is no danger that some competitor with the requisite skills is going to be allowed to bid down wages, employees are going to be willing to transmit information to new workers and to accept new techniques. If anyone is to be made redundant by such techniques, it will be a clearly defined minority—new workers. The teacher does not injure himself by being willing to teach.

Consider the market for construction labor in the United States. To some extent it is the paradigm wage-competition labor market. An actual job shape-up exists so that workers do not have permanent jobs. In most areas, such as Boston, substantial short-run wage fluctuations occur. If unionized labor is in short supply, premiums will be paid in excess of union scales. If unionized labor is in surplus supply, union workers will leave the unionized sector and work for nonunion wage scales on nonunion construction. In terms of wage and employment competition, the construction labor market comes closer to the wage-competition model than any other. But what does it produce?

Severe restrictions are placed upon training, and the resistance to technical innovations is legendary. Let me suggest that construction workers and their unions exhibit the same responses and motivations as the rest of the population. Their attempts to build countervailing monopoly positions and their resistance to technical change are just what the rest of us would do if faced with the reality of wage and employment competition.

To illustrate the problem at close range, imagine that M.I.T. were to start hiring economics professors in the same way that construction workers are hired. Instead of the standard academic system of employment, M.I.T. institutes a shape-up. Every morning, all of the potential teaching candidates from the most illustrious professor to the most illiterate graduate student bid (bid on a quality-adjusted basis, or course) for the teaching jobs of that day. First, the process could be time-consuming and costly. Outside experts would be needed to determine the quality-adjusted prices that were being offered. There would have to be periodic evaluations of the knowledge possessed by each individual. Second, at the risk of libeling myself and my colleagues, I would be willing to bet that the education process would deteriorate. Each professor would have a vested interest in teaching false information or small amounts of information so that his students could not effectively bid against him. Every bright graduate student would be viewed as a potential threat. We would act to preserve our wage and employment conditions just as construction workers act to preserve their wage and employment conditions.

It is easy to say that bids could take into account the professor's willingness to teach the right information, but this is difficult and expensive to do in practive. An equally competent inspector would need to sit in every class to determine what was being taught. Classes would need two competent people—one teacher and one inspector—rather than one. There would also be the problem of how to accept bids for the job of "economics quality control inspector." Inspectors would be needed for inspectors. In some sense the static inefficiencies of the present tenure system promote the dynamic efficien-

cies of the present system. They minimize the resistances to spreading information and job skills.

A lack of wage competition is not peculiar to the United States. Even more repression of wage and employment competition can be seen in Western Europe and Japan. It is typically much more difficult to fire workers in Europe than it is in the United States. In Japan large industrial firms extend tenure to their employees in the same manner that U.S. universities extend tenure to their professors. Wages are even more heavily constrained by age and seniority as opposed to personal skills and merit. Although the absence of wage competition in the case of Japan may lead to static inefficiency, it certainly has not led to dynamic inefficiency. Japanese workers are held up as examples of a labor force being willing to accept technical change and to cooperate with each other to increase productivity. This is what we would expect from the perspective of job competition. If individuals can only raise their own incomes by raising the productivity of the entire enterprise, they have a direct incentive to increase training and to accept technical change. It cannot hurt their wage and employment positions and it should help.

As a result, the types of wage and employment competition that are the essence of efficiency in simple, static neoclassical models may not be the essence of efficiency in a dynamic economy where the primary function of the labor market is to allocate individuals to on-the-job training ladders and where most learning occurs in work-related contexts. Here, wage and employment competition becomes counterproductive.

No one quarrels with the proposition that flexible wages are necessary for an economy to maximize its current production (reach its static efficiency frontier), but an argument is being made that efforts to maximize current production may engender a slower future rate of growth of production (its dynamic efficiency frontier). Since the potential gains from maximizing long-run growth usually dominate the potential gains from maximizing current production, employers find it *profitable* to structure the labor market in order to maximize long-run growth at the expense of short-run output. Repressing wage and employment competition becomes a tool for increasing long-run productivity.[1]

This is why rigid wages and seniority rules are just as common in nonunion as in unionized sectors of the economy. In the long run it is profitable to limit wage flexibility. The real choice is between a market structure that maximizes current production and a market structure that maximizes the rate of growth of production. From this perspective lack of wage and employment competition is not an illustration of a "market imperfection" that produces inefficiency but rather represents a functional market adjustment that produces long-run efficiency. More knowledge is transmitted with it than without it.

MARGINAL PRODUCTS, INDIVIDUALS, AND JOBS

Since a job opening is the initial ingredient in the job-competition model, mar-

---

[1] Although direct wage and employment competition may not be pervasive, strong indirect wage and employment competition may occur if the product market is marked by high price elasticities of demand. If an industry or firm is marked by above-equilibrium wages, consumers force them back into line by shifting to alternative goods and services. The only comprehensive study of price elasticities, by Hauthakker and Taylor, found that out of 82 exhaustive consumption categories, 54 had price elasticities that were not significantly different from 0, 9 had price elasticities between 0 and 1, 8 had price elasticities between 1 and 2, and 11 had price elasticities in excess of 2. There is thus some scope for indirect wage and employment competition through the product market, but it is limited. In many areas it does not seem to exist.

ginal products are inherent in jobs and not in individuals. The individual will be trained into the marginal productivity of the job he is slated to hold, but he does not have this marginal productivity independent of the job in question. This is true even if the worker has managed to acquire the necessary job skills in some exogenous manner or if he has acquired the job skills on the job and has been laid off due to fluctuations in aggregate demand.

To keep the training process going, employers will not allow the unemployed to bid back into his old job at lower wages. For example, there is no reason why an unemployed pilot for Pan American could not bid to become a pilot for TWA or to undercut the remaining Pan American pilots. Everyone flies the same planes. Yet he is not allowed to do this because it would retard the long-run gains that are to be made by facilitating training. In other words, the short-run profits that are to be made by lowering pilots' wages are not worth the long-run costs. This example is taken from a unionized sector of the economy, but similar nonunion examples occurred in the early 1970s among unemployed aerospace engineers in New England who were not allowed to bid against those engineers who remained employed. Technically, the individuals had the necessary job skills, but they were frozen out of the market and thus did not represent an effective potential supply of labor. Their personal productivity and skills were irrelevant even though they existed. Similarly, manpower training programs report that they often have trouble placing trained workers since these workers are not allowed into the jobs for which they have been trained.[2]

The net result is the formation of a series of internal labor markets with limited

---

[2] See "Vocational Education," *Journal of Human Resources*, 3 (1963), pp. 1-140, supplement.

ports of entry.[3] Outside of these ports of entry jobs, the supply and demand conditions of the external labor market are

---

[3] For a more extensive discussion of internal labor markets see Peter B. Doeringer and Michael J. Piore, *Internal Labor Markets and Manpower Analysis* (Lexington, Mass.: D. C. Heath, 1971).

basically irrelevant. Because of the institutional need to facilitate informal on-the-job training, workers cannot regain employment opportunities by accepting lower wages. Technically, the individual may possess the necessary skills, but institutionally speaking he does not. His wage bid will not be accepted.

Essay 6-3

The internal wage structure*

E. Robert Livernash

The joint development of collective bargaining and personnel policies has disrupted the direct relation of many wage rates to hiring, so far as the labor market is concerned.[1] The wage rate is also a most inadequate and incomplete motivational explanation to account for an employee's willingness to remain in the employ of a given company.

The vast proportion of job vacancies in any plant or company is filled today, not by hiring from the outside, but by promotion from within the organization. There has been no sharp break with the past, for internal promotion has developed with the growing diversification and specialization of jobs. However, the growing importance of collective bargaining and modern personnel practices gave significant impetus to promotion from within.

---

*Reprinted from E. Robert Livernash, "The Internal Wage Structure," in *New Concepts in Wage Determination*, ed. George W. Taylor and Frank C. Pierson, pp. 143-72 (abridged). Copyright © 1957 by McGraw-Hill, Inc. Used with permission of McGraw-Hill Book Company.

[1] A closely related discussion is to be found in Clark Kerr, "Labor Markets: Their Character and Consequences," *American Economic Review*, vol. 40, no. 2 (May, 1950), p. 278. The distinction between the wage and employment function is an essential one.

The policy avoids criticism of holding back those already employed in favor of outsiders, and is a basic part of increasingly elaborate programs to build morale and security by encouraging a lifetime view of employment with a given organization.

This policy and practice of promotion from within restrict hiring to a relatively small number of what may be called "hiring-jobs." While the list of such jobs is not completely static over a period time, these jobs are at all times a small proportion of the total and are typically at the bottom of the wage scale. By contrast, some hiring-jobs are above the lowest wage level. This is true where an entire group of jobs, including the bottom job in the group, is above the lowest level and has not been integrated with other promotion sequences. It is also true for certain unique jobs requiring training not provided within the organization.[2]

The pattern of hiring-jobs is one aspect

---

[2] Variations in the extent and scope of internal promotion as contrasted with outside hiring are no doubt quite significant. Differences in the amount and type of training required on different jobs, differences in seniority units and customs, differences in management poli-

of the particular wage structure. In broad view, however, the pattern would show these jobs grouped at the bottom of the wage scale and spread throughout departmental and organizational units as entrance spots from which most other jobs are then filled.

Probably a worker would not decide to leave one employer simply on the basis of a higher wage rate in another plant. While seniority is a strong influence in promotion, its almost unqualified application to layoff brings greatly enhanced job security with continued years of employment. This security against layoff is given added meaning by protection against arbitrary discharge. Standards by which the equity of discharge is judged, consciously and unconsciously, give weight to length of service. Each year also finds increasingly elaborate benefit plans related in amount to length of service. In this world of seniority, an employee would certainly be peculiar if he judged his economic position only in terms of his wage rate. Even here, his alternative choice is with hiring-jobs elsewhere. Above all, job security with its hedge against "hard times" is a most important retention influence.[3]

Most particular wage rates are thus not directly or closely related to a local labor market from an employment point of view. Employees enter and leave plants from the lower-paying "bottom" jobs. Expansion brings more rapid promotion. Recession brings layoff or demotion and downgrading for low-service employees. While seniority patterns differ, layoff schedules illustrate the indirect connection between many jobs and the labor market.

Wage administration and wage inequities

Particular wage rates are set by administrative decision within the firm. Neither union nor management policies, attitudes, and objectives toward the wage structure can be regarded as simply an adjunct to the employment process. Managements have increasingly worked toward a stable structure frequently based upon job evaluation in the local plant. Unions have increasingly accepted a stable structure, but have worked to broaden the base of comparison and are more qualified in their acceptance of evaluation. Union skepticism toward job evaluation has many facets. Perhaps the greatest fear is of the use of evaluation to freeze unions out of the wage-differential area or to restrict wage-differential policy too narrowly. Related to this is fear of an overly scientific, as contrasted with a looser equity, approach.

SOME WAGE-STRUCTURE GENERALIZATIONS

The background considerations previously discussed tend to support the view that the wage structure requires special analysis as such. Each single wage rate is not simply a subcase of the general case of demand for, and supply of, labor for the firm. But how can the process of wage comparison be analyzed to place this process within a meaningful framework? Certainly it is not adequate to regard the wage structure as nothing more than a

---

cies, as well as other factors, make this a complex picture. Within the same industry some firms do more "outside" hiring than others. Differences also exist among different labor markets. The trend, however, is presumably toward broader integration of jobs and more extensive training and promotion.

[3] Statistics on labor turnover by length of service give clear support to this point of view. It would be difficult to maintain that ignorance of alternative employment opportunities is also a function of length of service. The resulting immobility is clearly a rational economic decision, though just how much immobility results is an open question.

There may, on the other hand, be some enhancement of mobility through the seniority advantage of getting in on the ground floor in new plants and expanding industries.

While seniority factors can be allowed for in explaining workers' job choices, they then obscure the explanation of wage differentials.

process of internal job-content comparisons. It is equally discouraging to attempt to relate each wage rate to the labor market. Finally, it is not possible to ignore labor-cost influence and restrict thinking about the structure to wage relationships without regard to cost significance.

As a starting point in developing an analysis, three propositions are advanced and then discussed. These propositions are themselves related and each proposition can be, and is, of different significance for different firms in different economic environments. Needless to state, the propositions also require supplementation in various ways. They are as follows:

1. In internal wage-rate comparisons of job content and job relationships, any given job is not related to all other jobs in an equally significant manner. Some jobs are closely related as to wage significance, others more remotely related. While such job relationships have no simple, single basis, the larger relationships develop around key jobs.

2. In the external comparison of job rates in the firm to labor-market rates, each job within the plant structure is not related to a market rate in an equally significant manner. Not only are there obvious variations in the "mix" of different types of plants and jobs in different labor markets but there is again no single, simple type of relationship. Joint integration to the market and to the internal structure, however, evolves around key jobs.

3. In relating the wage structure to labor cost, each job rate is not of the same significance as an element of labor cost. While most particular jobs are a small proportion of total labor cost, some are not, and employment at different wage rates varies widely in labor-cost significance— with the bulk of labor cost concentrated within a fairly narrow range of "production" rates.

The first two points are stated in terms of wage *comparison*. The significance of comparison is left open for development.

Internal comparison is advanced predominately as an equity concept inherited in large part from valuation in the market place, but applied in its wage-administration and job-content context to create "fair" wage rates. External comparison is also meaningful in an equity sense relative to wage rates paid elsewhere, but is in addition related to the opportunity to hire and select as applied to groups of jobs and to some individual jobs.

As a broad framework, forces influencing the general wage level for an industry or for a wage contour are assumed. Also assumed are forces influencing the general level for the particular plant within its industry and labor-market context.

Internal job comparisons and job clusters

The basic premise here is that internal job-content comparison as a basis for wage-rate determination is stronger, and of a somewhat different character, within certain groups of jobs than between them. It is difficult to give a single name to the job groups within which internal comparison is most significant, but they may be called job clusters.[4]

As an elaboration of the basic premise, there are broad job clusters containing narrower clusters. Broad groups may be illustrated within manufacturing as (1) managerial—executive, administrative, professional, and supervisory; (2) clerical, and (3) factory. Within each broad group, narrower groups are obvious.[5] Within the factory group are maintenance, inspection, transportation, and production. Within production are certain smaller groups,

---

[4] The term *job cluster* follows Dunlop; the broad outline of this approach has been jointly discussed over a number of years.

[5] Broad and narrow groups are somewhat arbitrary, but the distinction is essential relative to different types of structural wage changes. For example, for some structural problems one might find no need to break down the clerical group into narrower groups; for other problems, the subdivisions would be of primary importance.

varying with the nature of the industry.

Job-content comparison as a basis for wage-rate determination is felt to be strong within narrow clusters, somewhat weaker between narrow functional groups, and of least significance in relating broad clusters. An added notion must be introduced to this. Each cluster contains a key job, or several. Wage relationships within a narrow group and among such groups revolve around key jobs. Within clusters the primary determinant of non-key job rates is the job-content comparison with the key job. Among clusters, the basic consideration is the relationship among the respective key jobs.

Relationships among key jobs, and hence among clusters, cannot be outlined in simple form. The view has been stated that job-content comparison is somewhat weaker among narrow groups than within them, and weaker yet among broad groups. This does not necessarily imply that external forces become stronger as internal determination of wage differentials becomes weaker. In a broad way this is felt to be true, but the relationship between internal and external considerations is a separate, though related, question, heavily dependent upon the particular environment. What is meant is that in so far as internal comparison continues to be the basis for wage determination, the relative compensation among broad groups is less rigorously determined by job-content comparison but depends more upon general judgment as to the appropriate relationship.

The nature of narrow job clusters

There is no single basis of classification for narrow job clusters. Geographical location within a plant, organizational pattern and common supervision, related and common job skills, common hiring jobs and transfer and promotion sequences, as well as a common production function, tie jobs together. The notion of a com-

mon production function deserves some emphasis, however. Departments frequently signify separate job groupings as they relate to different phases of production, thus constituting a functional group of related jobs.

Special job clusters

There are, however, at least the following meaningful special types of job clusters falling within the broad managerial, production, and clerical groupings:

1. The departmental functional group. This is illustrated by the departmental association of jobs with their respective hiring-jobs and transfer and promotion patterns.

2. The skill family. This is illustrated by (a) a craft job as in a steel plant with its apprentice scale and progression, then the job starting rate and class, the intermediate rate, and finally the full journeyman rate and class; and (b) many occupationally based jobs—typists, stenographers, semicraft machine operators, locomotive engineers, and so forth—with simple or complex levels and types of skill.

3. Related types of work. Frequently inspection and assembly jobs in a factory are so diverse in character that they are not in any true sense an occupation or skill family, but are closely related for wage purposes and treated somewhat as though they were such a family. Various professional jobs—the "engineering" categories, for example—are closely related. Maintenance jobs constitute a similar category. Accounting and bookkeeping jobs might be described in part as a skill family and in part as related jobs. In various ways, jobs are thus pulled together through the performance of related kinds of work.

4. The work crew or closely knit work group. One of the clearest examples of such a group is a crew working on some large type of equipment—the open hearth

crew, the rolling mill crew, the paper machine crew, the printing press crew. The jobs on an open hearth—including first, second, and third helpers, the charging machine operator, the cranemen, the pourer, the stacker, and others—are clearly related by joint responsibility, level of responsibility, and the technical integration of work. Even small equipment frequently has operators, feeders, take-away men, and other kinds of specialized workers. A conveyor may create a closely knit work group. Various "gangs" may work at separate or remote locations. In an office, payroll jobs might constitute a closely knit work group.

In the above categories, the departmental functional group and the work crew or work group are, in wage terms, both "horizontal" and "vertical" in character. The skill group is predominately vertical and the related-job group can be either vertical or horizontal, but some of its most interesting impacts are horizontal. No exhaustive typing is possible, and there are groups within groups, as well as overlapping and tie-in relationships.

There can be no rigid classification of narrow job clusters. Sometimes a department is so large and diverse that it does not constitute a meaningful wage group. A related work group or a skill family may cut across departmental lines. In other cases, departments, skill groups, and related jobs may reinforce a single relationship. There is reality, however, in the concept of degree of wage relationship and job-content comparison in terms of groups of jobs.[6]

Job clusters and wage relationships

Within a narrow job cluster, wage relationships are predominately based upon a technical, though not necessarily formal,

job-content comparison. The skill required (including job knowledge) is the primary differentiating factor,[7] but there are modifications in job placement relative to responsibility, working conditions, and physical effort (in the sense of heavy or light work). These relationships are influenced somewhat by custom and tradition and are mutually interdependent with promotion and transfer sequences. A wage differential of 5 cents per hour between two jobs within such a group is typically quite meaningless in terms of ability to hire or retain employees in a market sense and is also insignificant in terms of labor cost.[8]

Close association of employees on cluster-type jobs creates an environment that forces close comparison of jobs and allows a type of direct comparison more meaningful than where jobs are less closely integrated. Within such a job group, evaluation typically works out with reasonable precision and normally preserves a high proportion of existing wage relationships. Job content does not, however, create a completely rigid hierarchy.[9] Minor differences in placement can and do exist among the same jobs in different companies. Complete agreement as to the proper relationships would not be expected. These differences, however, serve only to emphasize the common-sense patterns in the major outlines of the relationships and the reliance upon judgment as to the relative wage significance of job content.

Normally there are one or a few key jobs within a job-cluster group. A key job may simply be a "good" cross-comparison job, because of similarity of job content,

[6] Job-evaluation labor grades conceal the kind of job groups discussed and may appear to give an artificial simplicity to the relationships among jobs.

[7] In some process-type industries it may be debated whether skill or responsibility is the primary differentiating factor.

[8] It is related, however, to the previously mentioned, and difficult to define, concept of the promotion-incentive factor.

[9] Technological change is a constant disruptive factor.

but usually a key job has significance because of its importance as to number of employees or key skill.

Primarily, key jobs are the more important jobs, the dominant jobs, within a group. Nonkey job relationships are built around key jobs. A nonkey wage rate may be adjusted with minor or major social disturbance within the group, but with little or no impact outside the group. This is a significant limiting aspect of wage relationships. Adjust a key job, and it may well pull all or most of the nonkey jobs with it; and there will typically be repercussions outside the particular cluster—major or minor, depending on the strength of the ties with one or more other groups.

Internal comparison between key jobs in different clusters tends to be less precise and of a somewhat different character than comparisons within a group. As comparison is made among jobs that are very different in type and kind of job content, the area of judgment as to the "correct" relationship widens. Consciously and unconsciously, judgment leans more upon external market relationships or established internal relationships as the differences in job content and "social distance" increase.

Relationships among key jobs, and hence among clusters, must be qualified to admit differences in the strength and character of the association. Some relationships may be quite close in binding together internal groups. Two rival crafts forming key jobs in two groups may create a very close association. In other situations, the employees on one key job may hardly be aware of the existence of a second key job. The number of employees in particular groups, the traditional social position of a group, and other such considerations play a role in the relative strength or weakness of these relationships. Internal relationships may be reinforced or weakened by the existence and strength of external wage relationships.

Cost considerations are also involved, as discussed later.

Key jobs and market comparison

While recognizing these differences among key-job relationships, the general point may be illustrated by the common procedure in applying job evaluation. The problem of rating the key jobs is quite different from rating the nonkey jobs. The first step, creating the "skeleton" by placing key jobs within the evaluation scale, is much more difficult than filling in jobs once the skeleton is created. Where, for example, should the key maintenance jobs or the key office jobs be placed relative to the key production jobs? In the case of office jobs this direct question is typically avoided, since a different evaluation plan is almost always used. With the maintenance jobs there is a considerable area of judgment.

Putting the question even more broadly, certain jobs are "key" jobs from a market comparison point of view. This list of key jobs is not necessarily identical with the list of internal key jobs. Some wage structures are keyed to the labor market at only a few points. Not all companies or plants are in an identical market position. In a high-paying industry, reference to the labor market may be almost exclusively to other companies and plants within the industry. The steel industry inequity program appears to be a case in point. In a high-paying plant within an industry, existing plant relationships may be accepted as established relationships. In lower-paying plants and industries, market comparisons may be more directly related to local hiring conditions. But with all these relationships, the close association with job content becomes a weaker basis for wage determination.

Broadly speaking, there is, of course, a strong tie among all jobs in a plant. Stability of differentials, once established, is quite firmly maintained. Economic forces, both cost pressures and hiring considerations, apply in a major sense to the structure as a whole. A plant contemplating expansion from 20,000 employees to 40,000 in a city of modest size will have a different view of its "ability to hire" than will a small firm requiring an insignificant proportion of new entrants on the labor market to maintain normal employment. At the other extreme, the placement of one particular job is adjusted from time to time primarily with changes in job content. There are, however, adjustments of groups of jobs, such as all maintenance jobs, all office jobs, etc., demonstrating a degree of independence for broad and narrow clusters. This group movement of jobs is clearly shown under the impact of job evaluation. Study of such job-rate changes will demonstrate group realignment and a significant degree of preservation of narrow internal group relationships. Group adjustment is also shown in the historical evolution of particular wage structures. "Inequity" negotiations and the grievance procedure bring out responses between and within clusters.

While these various types of wage changes do not lend themselves to simple representation, they seem sufficiently clear to support the general proposition that all job rates, viewed through internal comparison standards, are not related with equal or similar significance, but are composed of a system of broad and narrow groups organized around key jobs. In rough outline, these groups can be analyzed in terms of joint demand and supply for particular types and kinds of labor. Perhaps, more appropriately, one should say that they reflect adaptations to labor-market conditions in which wage comparison and hiring considerations are blended. As part of this process, they change with modifications of job content as broad production processes are modified. No easy "causal" statement is possible; nonetheless, group wage movements are a significant aspect of the wage-determination process.

Wage-structure adjustment to market-rate influence

The influence of the labor market upon the wage structure can best be approached by a descriptive type of analysis. Individual firm and industry variations in the general level of wages are assumed to be a major source of rate dispersion. Consider in this setting the degree of dominance of particular market rates and the source of such dominance.

To start with some simple examples, in a small city one inquires of a high-paying firm what they pay an industrial nurse and why. The explanation is given that the job is evaluated and comes out at x dollars. Upon further discussion, we find that the personnel man feels that, in truth, the evaluation is definitely on the low side; but, after all, they're paying 25 percent more than the local hospitals. In a low-paying firm, we find that they pay the switchboard operator the identical rate paid by the telephone company. We ask whether that isn't high in terms of their other office jobs. The answer is yes, but they always hire a trained operator; the rate is really quite independent of other office rates; and it causes no "trouble." Consider an over-the-road trucking rate in a low-paying mill. Do they meet the trucking-firm rate? No, but they aren't organized yet and they do have the rate up so high that they would hate to have to argue it with some of their skilled production workers. In fact, they're not at all sure that they shouldn't sell their trucks and contract the work.

In all these examples the wages in question constitute peripheral rates for the companies discussed. These rates tend to be paid for hiring-jobs and they do not constitute internal key-job rates for significant clusters within the company (the trucking rate could be a key job in a warehousing department). They also have in each instance been pulled out of "consistent" internal alignment by market-rate influences. The market-rate influences are dominated by segments of industry in which the rates discussed are part of the central core of the general rate structure and subject to general rate influences in those industries. Consider a broader example: a paper box plant in Detroit in which the general rate structure is low by Detroit standards. How will this plant get maintenance and office employees and what will they be paid? We find that maintenance employees constitute a "tougher" problem than do office workers, but both are more difficult to obtain than the predominately female production employees. In this case, both maintenance and office rates are, the managers feel, on the high side relative to the firm's general level of wages. In fact, they have had to make "major" concessions to get and hold a maintenance staff.

In thinking of examples of market-rate influences, a series of considerations arises relating to how necessary it is to meet or at least come close to market rates and how difficult it is in terms of mutually interdependent wage relationships and cost effects within the firm. The pull of internal consistency through internal key jobs must be taken into account. This pull is around the central core of the general rate structure. There is also the pull of the market, which may be over a broad general group or quite specific as to a single job. The pull of the market may be essentially an equity comparison or quite directly related to hiring.

Certain market rates may be highly structured within a community, ranging from a single rate to a narrow band. Other market rates are much more diffuse, covering a wide band with no central identifiable dominant source. A rate may be part of the central core of the general wage level, a key job in a broad cluster, a key job within a narrow cluster, or a peripheral, semi-independent rate. The position and meaning of the same job rate vary from industry to industry and company to company. The rate may be closely or more remotely connected to hiring.

Among these various wage examples, consideration must be given to firms and industries insignificantly influenced by "local" labor-market conditions. An oil refinery in a town or city may be slightly interested in local rates but not meaningfully so. The managers make "equity" comparisons within the industry, but there are no local-market rate compulsions. Their general rate structure is simply high enough to create an internally determined structure subject to equity comparison within the industry. The basic steel structure, as previously mentioned, was similarly relatively uninfluenced by rates outside the industry.

The diversity of actual markets in terms of geographic location, industrial mix, size, degree of union organization, and other characteristics explains the fact of rate dispersion. Employees are closely attached to particular companies, and hiring in most cases is predominately related to vacancies rather than closely to rates. Nevertheless, market-rate influences upon a wage structure do exist. The problem is one of formulating this influence in reasonable balance with other forces. The influence runs predominately by groups and categories of jobs through key jobs. It must be stated relative to the general level of wages for the firm, as associated with its industry, and to the total wage pattern in a community.

Only confusion results from attempting to draw a hard and fast distinction between market influences and internal-rate relationships. But there are differences in degree of influence. Internal relationships are strongest within narrow functional groups, though even here the amount of the wage differential is more a part of a broader picture than is the rank order of jobs. Among clusters, the internal ties are stronger: (1) in relating a narrow group to a larger group of which it is a distinct part; (2) within roughly comparable skill bands; and (3) where closely comparable or identical jobs are found in several functional groups. As concerns comparisons and ties between broader clusters, the internal forces grow weaker and the market ties, including historically established relationships, become stronger.

The influence of labor cost and broad market contours

The influence of labor cost is exerted primarily through the general level of wages. Within this context, jobs vary in their labor-cost significance. Jobs must be considered as to both their cost and wage relationship.

The general level of wages may be commonly associated with a fairly well-defined modal group of "production" employees and jobs. In manufacturing it consists frequently of a group of semiskilled machine operators, assemblers, and other workers of this type. While for any one job within this skill band there is room for debate and adjustment without meaningful cost significance, total labor cost is fixed in large measure by the level of this band of rates. In other wage structures, the general level and modal group are associated with certain skilled jobs. In a printing establishment recently studied, the modal group and general level are clearly formed by the journeyman rates for the various crafts. Some structures may be bimodal and, indeed, some may have a single occupational rate as the key point in the general level. The general level is analytically related to the modal employee group and the concentration of labor cost. Wage-structure relationships are built around this central cost point.

Without exploring the ramifications of labor cost, it is clear that some industries

and some firms are more confined by labor cost than are others. We recognize for industries and segments of industries the influence of differences in rate of expansion, variations in the proportion of labor to total cost, the degree of price competition in the product market, the greater or lesser strategic influence of labor cost within the product competition framework, and other factors.

Each firm is related by labor cost to a product and industry reference. Within any industry, the position of each firm varies; though there appears to be greater opportunity for independence in some industries than in others. However, in all industries some firms gain leadership positions by marketing performance, product and methods research and innovation, factory efficiency, and other ways. This leadership creates cost latitude within which they may respond to the labor market. While this side of the coin is a "permissive" factor, frequently allowing a favorable position in the local labor market, the reverse of the coin is not. Firms in an adverse position within their industry, particularly in industries tied by competitive cost to a low general level of wages, are frequently forced into an adverse labor-market position. These forced differences in the general level of wages override in large measure the weaker equalizing tendencies for most particular job rates. Broad differences within a rate band for a job can commonly be associated with general-level differentials of this character.

THE MEANING AND SIGNIFICANCE OF JOB EVALUATION

In approaching job evaluation here, the primary question is the relation of the evaluation process to the internal and external wage forces under discussion.

Job evaluation is not a rigid, objective, analytical procedure. Neither is it a meaningless process of rationalization. If a group of people with reasonable knowledge of certain jobs rate them, for example, on the basis of minimum required training and experience, there will be frequent small differences of opinion, some major differences as well, but also a high degree of general agreement. The application of group judgment through the rating process normally produces an improved rate structure, but extreme attitudes as to the accuracy of rating are difficult to defend.

Job evaluation must produce acceptable results. The results may be judged from two levels: wage relationships among key jobs or relationships within clusters. As to the first, job evaluation is tested by the degree of correlation achieved between points for key jobs and accepted wage relationships among the jobs. If this correlation does not work out in a reasonably satisfactory way, weights and points have to be adjusted. If the correlation is satisfactory as a general relationship, some few jobs may still present a problem. Suppose a key job with an agreed-upon rate falls some distance away from the line of relationship between points and rates. Which is to give way, the points for the job or the agreed rate? Neither can be regarded as the supreme standard, and judgment is likely to result in some jobs being dropped as key jobs, where points are accepted as controlling, and in other jobs being rescored where the evaluation is thought to be less satisfactory than the agreed rate. There is nothing wrong with this kind of trial-and-error testing; job evaluation does not automatically resolve debatable relationships among key jobs, particularly when there is a conflict between internal standards and external comparisons or when strongly held traditional relationships exist.

Within narrow groups, gross disturbance of existing relationships is not likely to be found. Creating a simplified system of labor grades, with one wage rate or rate range for each labor grade, gives rise to

many small wage changes as part of the simplification process, but the rank order of job placement within narrow funcional groups will not typically be changed significantly, except for some small proportion of out-of-line rates. These out-of-line rates are most frequently associated with past technological change of a "deskilling" character. They may also result from overly successful grievance adjustments or from poor judgment in decentralized wage administration.[10]

In reviewing the results of a typical job evaluation, one is likely to find some major changes in relations among key jobs and clusters: day workers may advance substantially relative to incentive workers; skilled groups, such as maintenance, may gain relative to the semiskilled; particular "low-wage" departments may increase in relative position. Within narrow groups, most past relationships will remain, with a minority of clear-cut out-of-line rates being meaningfully corrected. Also, with the many small simplification wage changes, jobs may go up or down slightly and, in process, achieve a somewhat more consistent placement, particularly with respect to the degree of wage recognition given to unfavorable working conditions.

What significant points for wage determination can one draw from the practice of job evaluation? The following may be singled out:

1. Job evaluation was created as an administrative response to a social environment allowing freer union and employee criticism. In this environment authority and secrecy of rates no longer held criticism in check, and piecemeal adjustments of rates provided no lasting solution. Thus standards and policies for the wage structure as a whole had to be developed to meet the changed social environment.

2. Job evaluation probably strength-

---

[10] The remarks in this paragraph do not imply a high order of accuracy in job placement. Reasonable men can frequently disagree within a range of plus or minus one labor grade.

ened and broadened the influence of internal comparison. In part this may have produced an overemphasis on logical relationships. In part it reflected the union representatives' enlarged scope of interest, as contrasted with employee feelings of injustice, and introduced the "over-all" point of view of the wage specialist. In particular cases job evaluation has been part and parcel of the process of removing interplant differentials in multiplant firms and geographical differentials within an industry.

3. Job evaluation can and typically does accomplish a reasonable adaptation to internal and external forces at the time it is introduced. Can this adaptation remain appropriate over a period of time? There appears to be no general answer to this question, but it should be examined in terms of the relationships among and within clusters.

As to the relationships among clusters, the answer to our question will depend upon the particular economic and labor relations environment of the plant, changes in that environment, and upon the particular type of adjustments that are made to the environment. Suppose, for example, that in a semiskilled wage structure with a high concentration of employees in the lowest labor grades, general cent-per-hour wage increases are given in an amount determined appropriate for semiskilled employees but that, in process, the skilled employees suffer a relative decline in comparative differential in the labor market. Such a process could create a strain upon the evaluation plan leading to its partial abandonment. There are obviously great differences in various local economic environments and, over any postulated period of years, changes in an environment may be mild or quite drastic. An evaluation plan, however, cannot logically be presumed to be immune from whatever changes do in fact occur.

Within clusters, the stability of an evaluation plan over a period of time depends upon the administrative principles adopted, upon the degree of their genuine acceptance by employees, possibly upon the character of the plan being used, and upon the impact of process and product changes upon job content. Interesting questions, which cannot be dogmatically answered, arise in this area. The frequency, scope, and nature of technological change as associated with a particular plan and its administration can lead to continued acceptance of revised job relationships, to a succession of reevaluations, or to demoralization of the entire plan.

The initial introduction of a plan, even though well executed in the sense of building morale rather than creating a social revolution, cannot be assumed to continue without some degree of adaptation through administration and revision. This statement does not imply the doom of evaluation; it emphasizes continued study to determine the most appropriate administration and the type of revision necessary in the light of particular internal and external changes influencing wage relationships.

On the whole, job evaluation appears to reflect—in its introduction, in its problems and adaptations, and by its absence—the wage forces described in this essay. In its formal approach, evaluation does not recognize the substructure character of wage relationship; it hides it by the administrative grouping of jobs into labor grades. But under the surface, the jigsaw puzzle of relating job groups is involved. Internal relationships can be proclaimed as primary wage policy in certain wage environments, whereas by contrast such a policy in other areas results in rough sailing. Adjustments over a period of time require study to clarify the kind of adaptations which are developing.

SUMMARY

The heavily descriptive material in this essay was intended to create at least a loose analytical framework with respect to the nature and influence of internal comparison and external relationships. Perhaps, also, the impact of labor cost has been given some added structural perspective. In addition, some questions have been raised as to the wage significance of methods of payment. Collective bargaining has not been adequately discussed. Variations in union policies and variations in patterns of behavior in different collective-bargaining situations raise many difficult questions. Above all, the view has been emphasized that individual wage rates in particular plants must be analyzed, not as standing alone, but as part of a complex structural entity in a given economic and labor relations environment.

The simple outline of structural influences can be stated in this fashion. One office job, or any other job, cannot be paid at a rate anywhere within a diffuse range of rates found by a survey for that job in the local labor market. A much narrower range is typically established by the position of the job within its internal job cluster. As we move to wage relationships among job clusters, the internal comparison narrows to a consideration of one or a few key jobs in the respective groups. At this point a question arises: How strong are the internal ties between these two groups? They may be quite strong or relatively weak. If strong, job-content comparison meshes the two groups. If they are weak, a wider range of internal tolerance is created.

External forces as a structural influence clearly vary with the economic situation and the labor relations environment. The basic peg points of structure—the effective minimum hiring rate, the level of the modal group of semiskilled rates, the top skilled rates—are related to both structural and general-level considerations. In turn, the nature and extent of more particular external influences depend upon the general level of wages and upon the particular environment.

To what extent can the kind and range of structural wage forces discussed in this essay be dignified by the term "wage theory"? Perhaps not to any great extent in a strict sense. On the other hand, the concept of the internal wage structure interlocks internal and external and general-level and particular wage-rate forces. It is not exclusively employment-oriented, in that administrative and wage-policy variables are implied and various patterns of collective-bargaining behavior are recognized. The problem does not seem to be that individual wage rates are indeterminate within a wide range but rather that the significant variables must be encompassed.

Commentary

Custom and tradition only explain relationships and practices in terms of conformance to previously existing relationships and practices, they do not explain the origin of those relationships and practices. Job evaluation, as described by Livernash, provides a means to the identification of customary wage structure relationships and for perpetuation of those customary relationships; it does not identify or explain the origins of these relationships. Although not specified explicitly by the previous authors, we might infer that characteristics of the wage structure will reflect characteristics of the internal labor market, the structuring of career ladders in terms of the number of different career ladders and the number of different steps specified in each; the more elaborated the structure of assignments in the internal labor market, the more elaborated we might expect the wage structure to be. Two interesting examples of internal labor market structuring appear in the steel and brewing industries. The steel industry collective agreement specifies a number of different career ladders to which individuals can advance from the labor pool of recruits, carefully sequenced job assignments within each career ladder, and a structure of wage rates associated with assignments. Common practice in the brewing industry, on the other hand, permits open bidding among employees in staffing job openings; no career structure is specified for advancement from one job assignment to another. Consistent with these differences in internal labor market structure, we noted earlier that a single rate tends to prevail within brewing firms with no wage differentials among jobs. This comparison suggests that jobs which are hierarchically ordered according to some accepted criterion should also be hierarchically ordered in terms of wage rates, the hierarchical criterion in this instance reflecting succession patterns.

The essays which follow address specifically the development of wage structures and specific criteria and/or processes in hierarchically ordering jobs for wage structure differentiation. Essay 6-4 by Thurow continues the development of implications of his job competition model and elaborates upon the phenomena described by Livernash. Thurow argues that the utility of compensation varies critically with *relative* compensation rather than *absolute* compensation, that individuals judge wage rates relative to other wage rates. He goes on to point out, like Katz in an earlier essay, that labor supply is multidimensional and varies with the willingness of individuals to perform beyond the minimal task performances required. A structure of relative wages perceived as equitable by the employees is necessary to elicit this cooperation. Thus, the equity or acceptability of the wage structure is a critical influence of this dimension of labor supply. Thurow argues that the tests of equity in a wage structure dictate that rewards must be proportional to costs and that equal rewards must be associated with equal costs. He does not specify the components of cost but implies that these are sociological in origin, not individual, and reflect the particular value orientation of society.

Essay 6-5 from Adams elaborates a structural model of equity based upon concepts of distributive justice, a model analogous to that sketched by Thurow. Equity, in this formulation, is a relative judgment based upon social comparisons, self with another, rather than a judgment based upon comparison with some absolute standard. Judgments of equity are personal and individual rather than societal in nature. They are derived from comparison of perceptions of what an individual receives from an exchange relationship (outcome) relative to the individual's inputs when compared with the outcome/input relationship of some relevant "other" person. Interestingly, Adams develops this model in the formulation of inequity rather than equity, equity being defined implicitly as the absence of inequity. Adams' model is intuitively appealing as a rationale for job evaluation—the ratio of rewards (compensation) to inputs (skill, effort, experience) is equated among jobs by relating compensation directly to measures of job characteristics. However, Adams' model provides no rationale for any specific measures of compensation, inputs or relevant comparison persons, and indeed, research applying this model has found that selection and perception of these variables are subjective and individualistic, varying among individuals and circumstantial influences. Individual assessments of equity within the framework of this model do not demonstrate the stability required for operationalization of the model in the determination of equitable wage structures. Investigations employing the equity model have demonstrated that judgments of equity can be important influences of work behavior, however, and current inability to operationalize variables within the model should not detract from recognition of the importance of equity considerations in compensation.

Elliott Jaques (Essay 6-6) proposes a criterion of equity of compensation derived from extensive research at the Glacier Metals Company and presents a theoretical rationale for that criterion. The criterion proposed is the "time span of discretion" in a job, a measure of what Jaques terms the level of work performed in a job. This criterion of equity of wage payment emerged from studies at Glacier Metals where Jaques was searching for some system of job evaluation acceptable to the employees involved, some means of identifying the amount of compensation employees would accept as "fair pay" for the job. As conceptualized by Jaques, time span of discretion measures "the longest period of time which can elapse in a role before the manager can be sure that his subordinate has not been exercising marginally substandard discretion." Every job requires incumbents to take actions which may not be reviewed by the individual's supervisor for some period of time ranging from hours to years. The length of time span of discretion varies with the type of action taken (composition of a letter, adjustment of a machine, acceptance of bids, development of a new product), the information and control systems available, and closeness of supervision. Jaques would characterize each job in terms of the longest time span of discretion associated with the various tasks in the job, a measure obtainable only from the supervisor. Jaques reports that measures of time span of discretion of jobs correlate highly with assessments of fair pay for the job—by job incumbents, a relationship that has been replicated in other studies. Jaques' model, in contrast with the models of Thurow and Adams, proposes an absolute rather than relative standard for the determination of equitable compensation, equitable compensation is a function of the job itself rather than a function of social comparison. By implication, Jaques' model is applicable throughout society and is not limited to equitable wage structure considerations within the internal labor market; the ordering of payment for jobs throughout society on the basis of time span of discretion in those jobs would result in a structure of wages accepted by all employees as equitable. The norms of equitable payment are considered generalizable and not limited to a single organization, occupation, or labor market.

Essay 6-7 by Mahoney reviews various approaches taken in the judgment of equity in compensation and suggests that we lack any generally accepted criterion of equity in compensation and that the determinants of an equitable internal wage structure are subjective and subject to change with change in social values. The flat wage structure in the brewing industry and the highly differentiated wage structure in the steel industry are each equally acceptable in the different industry environments suggestive of different value orientations in these two societies. Other evidence of change in the criteria of compensation equity with change in social values appears in the judgments of the equity of differential compensation related to personal characteristics such as race and sex. Differentially compensating job holders on the basis of race and sex was accepted as equitable at one time but has since been judged to be inequitable and is prohibited by legislation reflective of changing values. Other job or jobholder characteristics such as age, education, and skill now associated with equitable pay differentials also may be challenged as inequitable at some future date as values continue to change. The development of an administrative approach to wage structure determination which insures the reflection of employees' values in the structuring of wages thus is more critical in the maintenance of an equitable wage structure than are the specific characteristics considered in job evaluation. No system for job evaluation is likely to generate wage structures judged as equitable over time unless modified and adapted as employee perceptions, values and judgments change over time.

Essay 6-8, also by Mahoney, examines compensation structures within the specific context of managerial organization structures, the relationship between compensation structure and management organizational hierarchy. He reviews several models of managerial compensation and empirical evidence concerning these models. One model by Herbert Simon posits a regular proportional differential of compensation between two adjacent managerial ranks which is expected and accepted as equitable by managers. Consistent with the internal labor market model, Simon hypothesizes that compensation for entry level managerial jobs reflects market rates determined by bidding for employees, and the compensation for successively higher levels in the organization is determined by application of the proportional compensation differential to this base rate of compensation. Elliott Jaques also proposes a compensation structure for managerial ranks based upon his research into time span of discretion; successively higher levels in the managerial organization are characterized with successively longer time spans of discretion and, consequently, larger amounts of compensation required for equitable pay. The evidence assembled by Mahoney suggests that a compensation differential of approximately 30 percent is considered appropriate for the higher of two managerial organization levels and that hierarchical level in the organization is a key determinant of judgments of equitable pay for managers. There is no obvious corollary to organization level in the nonmanagerial workforce for which we can infer a similar relationship although the evidence is suggestive that hierarchical ordering according to some criterion is predictive of equitable structuring of compensation throughout the workforce.

Essay 6-4

The sociology of wage determination*

Lester C. Thurow

Within the wage-competition framework there are three cases in which the marginal productivity distribution cannot hold: (1) If there are economies of scale in production, paying each factor its marginal product more than exhausts total output. In that case the output to pay marginal products does not exist. (2) If there are diseconomies of scale in production, paying each factor its marginal product leaves some extra output. Who is to get it? (3) If goods or services are produced in a joint production process in which each factor is absolutely essential to production, marginal productivities cannot be determined. Output drops to zero when any one factor is removed. In none of these cases is there an economic theory of distribution. Some principle other than marginal productivity must determine factor returns. Since there is no economic principle of distribution, bargaining and sociology must operate in the vacuum left by economics.

Although these three cases are important exceptions to marginal productivity, there is an even more fundamental problem, one that affects the possibility of paying people their marginal products in the wage-competition model and paying jobs their marginal products in the job-competition model. Marginal-productivity payments implicitly assume that individuals look only to their own wages and productivity to determine whether or not they are fairly paid. Yet they often look at their neighbor's wages. Preferences are

interdependent rather than independent. Utility depends upon relative income rather than absolute income.

As we have seen, a wide variety of more recent evidence points to the existence of interdependent preferences. Over the past three decades, the Gallup poll has asked, "What is the smallest amount of money a family of four needs to get along in this community?" The 17 answers to this question have all fallen between 53 percent and 59 percent of the average income of the year in which the question was asked.[1] The responses are consistent with respect to the average income in the year in which the question was asked but grow in absolute terms as average incomes grow. Lee Rainwater has shown that when people are asked to categorize others as "poor, getting along, comfortable, prosperous, or rich," they do so rather consistently relative to average incomes.[2] A University of Pennsylvania economist, Richard Esterlin, has reviewed the evidence as to how happiness is related to income in different countries of the world.[3] He finds that happiness (utility?) is almost completely dependent upon one's relative income position within one's own country and almost not at all dependent upon whether one is located in a high-income country or a low-income country.

Actually, utility functions seem to be

*Excerpted from Lester C. Thurow, *Generating Inequality: Mechanisms of Distribution in the U.S. Economy* (New York: Basic Books, 1975), pp. 104-13. © 1975 by Basic Books, Inc., Publishers, New York.

[1] Lee Rainwater, *Poverty, Living Standards and Family Well-Being*, Joint Center for Urban Studies of MIT and Harvard, Working Paper no. 10, p. 45.

[2] Ibid., p. 49.

[3] Richard Esterlin, "Does Money Buy Happiness?", *The Public Interest*, no. 30 (Winter 1973), pp. 3-10.

heavily, if not completely, determined by relative incomes and interdependent preferences rather than absolute incomes and independent preferences. Sociologists call interdependent preferences "relative deprivation," labor economists refer to wage contours, psychologists talk about envy. But whatever the name, interdependent preferences seem to be a widespread phenomenon.

To say that utility functions are highly interdependent, however, is not to say that men are going to be able to implement their interdependent preferences in the labor market. What allows individuals to exercise their interdependent preferences in the labor market? My utility may depend upon the income of my neighbor, but this would not influence my own wages or productivity in the standard wage-competition model. Like it or not, each individual would be paid his marginal product.

The lack of interest in interdependent preferences flows from two factually incorrect assumptions implicit in the wage-competition model. First, individuals are wrongly assumed to have fixed marginal products—skills—that they sell in the labor market. In fact, depending upon their motivations, individuals have a variety of possible marginal products. An unhappy worker can lower his productivity, often in such a manner that it is difficult and expensive to determine whether or not he has in fact done so. Although a worker's happiness or utility is irrelevant if he has a fixed marginal product, it is highly relevant if he has a variable marginal product. Employers need to set a wage structure that elicits voluntary cooperation and motivates their work force. The net result is an avenue whereby interdependent preferences can influence the wage structure.

Second, individuals are wrongly assumed to be interchangeable parts in the production process. In fact, most production processes require a degree of team-

work that can only be acquired through on-the-job experience and a high degree of internal harmony. A production team that has a revolving membership and is unhappy with its wage structure has a lower productivity than a team that is satisfied with its wage structure and has a stable membership. There is a high degree of truth in an old aphorism, "There is no institution that cannot be brought to its knees by working to rule." Efficient economic production is not possible if everyone does just what is required or what is compelled. The net result is an avenue whereby group preferences about a "just" wage structure can have a major impact on production. Because it can have an impact on productivity, it must be taken into account by the employer.

Economists have ignored the problem of getting individuals and groups to produce, but industrial psychologists have made this their key problem.[4] They ask how wages and other incentive systems can be used to promote maximum productivity. Economists see the work decision as a go-no go decision according to which the individual either does or does not sell his time and a fixed productivity for the offered bribe. Industrial psychologists see the work decision as a more continuous decision. A person decides to work, but he also decides how much effort and cooperation to provide. Economists might respond that workers can always be fired if they are not producing at the agreed upon level, but this ignores the costs of hiring and firing, the costs of determining whose productivity is below the norm, and the costs of disrupting the production team. Although there is a limited role for inspection and punishment, productivity in the final analysis depends upon voluntary cooperation, and this requires a wage structure that is in

---

[4] See Edward E. Lawler III, *Pay and Organizational Effectiveness: A Psychological View* (New York: McGraw-Hill, 1971).

harmony with the interdependent preferences of the work force.

The variability of individual and team production functions creates problems for the marginal-productivity theory of distribution since there is not *a* distribution of marginal products but *many* potential distributions of marginal products. If an employer attempts to pay a group its marginal products and these run counter to the interdependent preferences of the group, the employer may find a completely different set of marginal products from what he originally found. What is worse, an employer who attempts to impose a marginal-productivity distribution of earnings on a contrary set of interdependent preferences may find that productivity substantially decreases in the process. Interdependent preferences lead to a situation in which group and individual performances depend upon having a set of relative wages that the group itself regards as fair and equitable.

Employers are anxious to establish wage structures that their employees regard as equitable since their profits depend upon it. There is a profit-maximizing wage structure, but it need not be a marginal-productivity wage structure. Individual marginal products may have little to do with the structure of wages, for the structure of wages is dependent upon the structure of interdependent preferences rather than upon the structure of marginal products. Employer and employee interests in establishing an equitable distribution are easy to find in the economy. Bargaining about relative wages is at least as pervasive as bargaining about absolute wages. Perhaps the best recent example occurred in Sweden, where college workers struck to increase their pay *relative* to noncollege workers. Their demand was not for more income but for wider wage differentials.

Interdependent preferences combined with self-controlled individual and team production functions reinforce the employer's and employee's interest in reducing or eliminating wage and employment competition above the entry level. Direct wage and employment competition becomes counterproductive in the production environment since wage increases for one worker show up as real wage (utility) reductions for other workers. This loss in utility causes them to lower their own productivity and to disrupt team activities. Given the need for production teamwork and the existence of interdependent preferences, wages are negotiated and set on a team rather than an individual basis. Unions formalize and perhaps strengthen this process, but they do not cause it. Nonunion profit-maximizing employers have the same interest, and nonunion wage structures do not differ noticeably from union wage structures.

Team wage structures lead to different wages for the same skill (one of the major deviant puzzles). Some workers with a particular occupational skill work on high-productivity teams, whereas others work on low-productivity teams. Raw unskilled labor makes a very different wage, depending upon whether it works for General Motors or for a Mississippi plantation. The two workers have exactly the same skill, but they are effectively segregated from each other. The low-wage Mississippi farm worker is not allowed to make a bid for the job of the unskilled auto worker. One's employer becomes an important element in determining one's wages in a way that could not occur under simple wage competition. The net result is a structure of wages that is often more homogeneous within firms or industries than it is within occupations.

Although the wages for particular jobs may be heavily conditioned by the structure of interdependent preferences, this does not prevent each job from being paid in accordance with its marginal product. Within each job category employers hire workers until the marginal productivity of that job is driven down to the level given by the exogenous wage. Each job is paid in accordance with its marginal product, but the distribution of earnings is not determined in a process by which wages are used to clear markets or in which wages are necessarily equal for different employers. Marginal productivity still exists, but it has become a theory of employment rather than a theory of wages. It tells you how many people will be hired, but it does not tell you the wage rate for each skill.

Analytically, the problem is to know what factors produce and alter inderdependent preferences and group norms of industrial justice. Sociologists have extensively studied this process under the title of "relative deprivation."[5] Their studies indicate that individuals feel strongly that economic benefits should be proportional to costs (i.e., effort, hardships, talents, and the like) but that equals should be treated equally. Since there are various "costs" and rewards (income, esteem, status, power, etc.) in any situation, the problem immediately arises as to how equals are defined and how proportionality is to be determined.

This leads to the difficult problem of "reference group" determination. To what group do you belong and to what groups do you compare yourself when trying to determine whether or not you are being treated equally and proportionally? In any historical situation it is relatively easy to describe the different reference groups that exist, but it has proven difficult, or impossible, to find general principles that govern reference group formation.

Reference groups seem to be both stable and restricted. People look at groups that are economically close to themselves and require great social shocks, such as wars and economic depressions, to change their specifications of relative deprivation.

---

[5] For a good discussion of relative deprivation and the source of the following few paragraphs see Walter Garrison Runcimen, *Relative Deprivation and Social Justice* (London: Routledge and Kegan Paul, 1966).

Conceptions of what constitutes proportionality and equality tend to be heavily determined by history and culture. The distributions of the past are considered fair until proven unfair.

This explains why inequalities in the distribution of economic rewards that are much larger than inequalities in the distribution of personal characteristics seem to cause little dissatisfaction, and why people tend to ask for rather modest amounts when asked how much additional income they would like to be making. The happiest people seem to be those who do relatively well within their own reference group rather than those who do relatively well across the entire economy.

The importance of social shocks can be seen in the income changes caused by the Great Depression and World War II. In the Great Depression an economic collapse provided the mechanism for change. Large incomes simply had farther to fall than small incomes. In World War II there was a consensus that the economic burdens of the war should be relatively equally (equal sacrifice") shared, so the federal government used its economic controls over wages to achieve more equality. Wage policies during World War II were a manifestation of the change in the sociology of what constitutes "fair" wage differentials or relative deprivation. As a consequence of the widespread consensus that wage differentials should be reduced, it was possible to reduce wage differentials deliberately. After the wage differentials of the Great Depression and World War II had become embedded in the labor market for a number of years, they became the new standard of relative deprivation and were regarded as "just" even after the egalitarian pressures of World War II had disappeared. Basically, the same differentials exist to this day, 30 years later.

It is important to note, however, that the new standards were not imposed by government on a reluctant population but were imposed on the labor market by popular beliefs as to what constituted equity in wartime. No one knows how to engineer such changes in less extreme situations. Indeed, some sociologists have concluded that only wars can cause changes in norms of relative deprivation.

The labor economics literature discusses the concept of relative deprivation under a different name—wage contours.[6] As in relative deprivation, workers see themselves as belonging to a particular wage contour that has some fixed wage relative to workers in other contours. Over time, relative wages are very stable across contours.

From the perspective of the wage-contour hypothesis, wage and price controls can play an important role in controlling inflation. One of the major elements leading to wage inflation is the leapfrogging that occurs when wage structures accidentally get out of line with historical wage contours. One group gets ahead of its historical position and other groups attempt to reestablish their historical position, or even to get ahead so as to "get even" for the initial violation of "equity." As with relative deprivation, the wage-contour theory runs into problems. Thus, it seems to be impossible to find general principles that explain why specific wage contours exist. This makes it difficult to know how to alter reference groups or wage contours, but it in no way diminishes their importance to the structure of wages.

If utility functions are interdependent and conditioned by experience and history, relative wages may be rigid regardless of changes in the underlying supply and demand conditions. The historical wage differentials have the sanction of time and are assumed to be just until proven unjust. Moreover, the longer they exist, the more they condition workers' beliefs about what constitutes justice and

injustice.[7] The high degree of stability in the post-World War II wage structure is probably more an indicator of stable interdependent preferences than it is an indication of stability in the underlying distribution of technology.

To say that relative earnings are conditioned by interdependent preferences is not to say that relative earnings are immutable. Slow changes in relative earnings might be accepted since they never seem to challenge the accepted norms. Relative deprivation does, however, stop short-run wage changes from being used as a market-clearing mechanism. The static benefits to be gained by clearing markets with wage changes simply are not large enough to offset the losses from the labor disruptions that would follow.

Relative deprivation reinforces the employer's interest in reducing wage and employment competition. The desire to promote training and the acceptance of technical change is the carrot leading to reduced wage and employment competition; the consequences of violating the norms of relative deprivation are the stick preventing competitive wage and employment policies. The net result is a rigid structure of wages that provides little opportunity to bid into a job by being willing to accept lower wages.

Thus, if we are to understand the structure of earnings and the factors that produce changes in it, we shall need a sociology or psychology of interdependent preferences. Lacking a consistent theory of reference group determination, the sociology of wage determination is in a rudimentary form, but this does not diminish its importance. Workers' views about what constitutes an "equitable" wage structure

---

[6] John Dunlop, *Wage Determination under Trade Unions* (New York: Kelley, 1950).

[7] If, for example, hiring policies use educational degrees as a selection procedure, equitable structure of wages will probably begin to take these requirements into account. They become part of the costs to be considered. Higher wages must be paid for higher requirements.

have an important role to play in the determination of wages. Relative deprivation, wage contours, interdependent preferences, and envy all mean that economic stratification is man-made but that it is, to a large extent, self-perpetuating and autonomous.

Essay 6-5

Inequity in social exchange*

J. Stacy Adams

The existence of relative deprivation necessarily raises the question of distributive justice, or of the fair share-out of rewards; for deprivation is perceived relationally. The concept is not new, having been explored by political philosophers and others from the time of Aristotle. In the hands of Homans (1950, 1953, 1961) and of his colleagues (Zaleznik et al., 1958), the concept of distributive justice has taken on the articulated character of what may be more properly called a theory. As fully developed by Homans (1961), it is a theory employing quasi-economic terms. According to him, distributive justice among men who are in an exchange relationship with one another obtains when the profits of each are proportional to their investments. Profit consists of that which is received in the exchange, less cost incurred. A cost is that which is given up in the exchange, such as foregoing the rewards obtainable in another exchange, or a burden assumed as a specific function of the exchange, such as a risk, which would include not only potential real loss but the psychological discomfort of uncertainty as well. Investments in an exchange are the relevant attributes that are brought by a party to the exchange. They include, for example, skill, effort, education, training, experience, age, sex, and ethnic background.

Schematically, for a dyad consisting of A and B, distributive justice between them is realized when:

$$\frac{\text{A's rewards less A's costs}}{\text{A's investments}}$$

$$= \frac{\text{B's rewards less B's costs}}{\text{B's investments}}$$

When an inequality between the proportions exists, the participants to the exchange will experience a feeling of injustice and one or the other party will experience deprivation. The party specifically experiencing relative deprivation is the one for whom the ratio of profits to investments is the smaller.

Making explicit that it is the relation between *ratios* of profits to investments that results in felt justice or injustice is a distinct contribution that takes us beyond the concept of relative deprivation. To be sure, an individual may feel deprived, but he feels deprived not merely because his rewards or profits are less than he expected or felt was fair. Many men, when comparing their rewards to those of another, will perceive that their rewards are smaller, and yet they will not feel that

    *Reprinted from J. Stacy Adams, "Inequity in Social Exchange," in L. Berkowitz (ed.), *Advances in Experimental Social Psychology*, vol. 2 (New York: Academic Press, 1965), pp. 272-83 (abridged).

this state of affairs is unjust. The reason is that persons obtaining the higher rewards are perceived as deserving them. That is, their rewards are greater because their investments are greater. Thus, for example, if being of the male sex is perceived as a higher investment than being of the female sex, a woman operator earning less than a man doing the same work will not feel unjustly treated. The proportionality of profits to investments is comparable for the woman and for the man. Similarly, a young instructor usually does not feel that his rewards, low as they may be, compare unfairly with those of an associate professor in his department. As Homans notes, "Justice is a curious mixture of equality within inequality" (1961, p. 244).

The theory of distributive justice also addresses itself to the case of two or more persons, each of whom receives his rewards from a third party: an employer, for example. In such an instance, each of the persons is in an exchange with the employer, as in the simple dyadic situation discussed; but, in addition, each man will expect that the employer will maintain a fair ratio of rewards to investments between himself and other men. This, of course, is the perennial dilemma of employers, and it almost defies a perfect solution, though it is capable of better solutions than are often developed. One difficulty with finding neat solutions is that A's perception of his rewards, costs, and investments are not necessarily identical with B's perception of A's situation. To complicate matters, two persons, though they might agree as to what their investments are, may disagree as to the weight each investment should be given. Should age count more than sex? Should education be given as much weight as job experience? The psychometrics of this has not yet received much attention.

The relationship of distributive justice to satisfaction is treated only briefly by Homans, but it is nevertheless the subject of a formal theoretical proposition. If a state of injustice exists and it is to a man's disadvantage—that is, the man experiences deprivation—he will "display the emotional behavior we call anger" (Homans, 1961, p. 75). Here Homans is overly influenced by Skinnerian rhetoric. He means, plainly, that dissatisfaction will be felt or expressed. If, on the other hand, distributive justice fails of realization and is, to an observer at least, to a man's advantage, he will feel guilty. This aspect of the proposition is more novel and is substantiated by observations by Jaques (1956, 1961a) and by laboratory experiments by Adams (1963a) that will be discussed later. Homans also implies that the thresholds for displaying dissatisfaction and guilt are different when he remarks that "... he (the guilty man) is less apt to make a prominent display of his guilt than of his anger" (1961, p. 76). This suggestion, also made by Adams (1963a) and deducible from observations made by Jaques (1956), implies that distributive justice must fail of realization to a greater extent when it is favorable to an individual before he reacts than when it is to his disadvantage.

Others have stated formal propositions that obviously refer to the same phenomena as encompassed by the theory of distributive justice. The propositions listed by two writers are especially noteworthy because they were expressed in terms similar to those of Homans. Sayles (1958, p. 98), discussing the manifestation of dissatisfaction in industrial work groups, surmised that factory workers "compute" the fairness of their wages as follows:

$$\frac{\text{Our importance in the plant}}{\text{Any other group's importance}} = \frac{\text{Our earnings}}{\text{Their earnings}}$$

When the equality obtains, satisfaction is experienced. An inequality between the ratios causes pressures for redress, accompanied by dissatisfaction. "Importance in the plant" may be taken as equivalent to the perceived investments of group members, including skills and type of work performed, length of service, and such. This is made explicit in his model of the "economic world of the worker in his work group." According to this analysis, men are portrayed as comparing their jobs to other jobs and asking the questions, "Are these higher paying jobs actually more skilled than our own?" and "Do we earn *enough more* than the lower rated jobs to compensate for the skill difference?" The term "earnings" is, of course, comparable to Homans' rewards but is a less comprehensive term, excluding other outcomes such as intrinsic job rewards. It also subsumes less than the concept of profit or net reward, since it makes no provision for negative outcomes or costs, such as unfavorable work conditions or tyrannical supervision. Nevertheless, it is clear that Sayles conceives of justice as being a function of the perceived equality of ratios of investments and of rewards.

Using the terms of Festinger's theory of cognitive dissonance (1957), Patchen postulates that workers making wage comparisons make a cognitive relation of the following type (1961, p. 9):

$$\frac{\text{My pay}}{\text{His (their pay)}}$$

compared to

$$\frac{\text{My position on dimensions related to pay}}{\text{His (their) position on dimensions related to pay}}$$

This formulation is similar to Sayles' but more explicit, for dimensions related to pay are specified as being attributes such as skill, education, and seniority. These are clearly the same as Homans' investments. Patchen differs somewhat from Homans in his conceptualization, however, in that he also includes job interest among his "dimensions" related to pay. This is not so much an investment as it is a reward, either with positive or negative valence. When, according to Patchen, an inequality results from the comparison of the two proportions, cognitive dissonance

is experienced. In turn, dissatisfaction is manifested. However, dissonance and the attendant dissatisfaction are not necessarily a bad state of affairs from the point of view of the individual. Patchen points this out in an interesting departure from dissonance theory. Although consonant comparisons may be satisfying, they provide no basis for mobility aspirations, whereas dissonant comparisons unfavorable to the person permit a man to think that he is more deserving, that he merits higher pay or status. In effect, then, Patchen suggests that the motivation to attain consonance may be dominated by achievement motivation, and that under these circumstances dissatisfaction resulting from dissonant comparisons may be tolerated. Parenthetically, it may be pointed out that the pitting of these two motivations may partially explain why researchers have been unable to replicate some experiments that offered support for dissonance predictions (see Conlon, 1965, for example).

Relative deprivation and distributive justice, as theoretical concepts, specify some of the conditions that arouse perceptions of injustice and, complementarily, the conditions that lead men to feel that their relations with others are just. But they fail to specify theoretically what are the consequences of felt injustice, other than dissatisfaction. To be sure, Sayles (1958) mentions the use of grievance procedures and strikes to force redress, Homans (1961) cites a study by Clark (1958) in which a female employee reported slowing her pace of work as a means of establishing a more just relation with a co-worker, and Patchen (1961) gives evidence of dissonance reduction when wage comparisons are dissonant. However, these are more or less anecdotal and are not an articulated part of a theory. Men do not simply become dissatisfied with conditions they perceive to be unjust. They usually do something about them. In what follows, then, a theory will be developed that will specify both the antecedents of perceived injustice and its consequences. It is not a new theory. There are already too many "little" theories in social psychology. Rather, it builds upon the work previously described, and, in addition, derives a number of major propositions from Festinger's theory of cognitive dissonance (1957).

INEQUITY

Inequity exists for Person whenever he perceives that the ratio of his outcomes to inputs and the ratio of Other's outcomes to Other's inputs are unequal. This may happen either *(a)* when he and Other are in a direct exchange relationship or *(b)* when both are in an exchange relationship with a third party and Person compares himself to Other. The values of outcomes and inputs are, of course, as perceived by Person. Schematically, inequality is experienced when either

$$\frac{O_p}{I_p} < \frac{O_a}{I_a}$$

or

$$\frac{O_p}{I_p} > \frac{O_a}{I_a}$$

where $O = \Sigma O_i$, $I = \Sigma O_i$ and p and a are subscripts denoting Person and Other, respectively. A condition of equity exists when

$$\frac{O_p}{I_p} = \frac{O_a}{I_a}$$

The outcomes and inputs in each of the ratios are conceived as being the sum of such outcomes and inputs as are perceived to be relevant to a particular exchange. Furthermore, each sum is conceived of as a weighted sum, on the assumption that individuals probably do not weight elemental outcomes or inputs equally. The work of Herzberg et al. (1959) on job "satisfiers" and "dissatisfiers" implies

strongly that different outcomes, as they are labeled here, have widely varying utilities, negative as well as positive. It also appears reasonable to assume that inputs as diverse as seniority, skill, effort, and sex are not weighted equally. Zaleznik et al., in attempting to test some predictions from distributive justice theory in an industrial corporation, gave equal weight to five factors which correspond to inputs as defined here—age, seniority, education, ethnicity, and sex—but were unable to sustain their hypotheses. In retrospect, they believe (Zaleznik et. al., 1958) that weighting these inputs equally may have represented an inadequate assumption of the manner in which their respondents summed their inputs.

From the definition of inequity it follows that inequity results for Person not only when he is, so to speak, relatively underpaid, but also when he is relatively overpaid. Person, will, for example, feel inequity exists not only when his effort is high and his pay low, while Other's effort and pay are high, but also when his effort is low and his pay high, while Other's effort and pay are low. This proposition receives direct support from experiments by Adams and Rosenbaum (1962), Adams (1963a), and Adams and Jacobsen (1964) in which subjects were inequitably overpaid. It receives some support also from an observation by Thibaut (1950) that subjects in whose favor the experimenter discriminated displayed "guilty smirks" and "sheepishness." The magnitude of the inequity experienced will be a monotonically increasing function of the size of the discrepancy between the ratios of outcomes to inputs. The discrepancy will be zero, and equity will exist, under two circumstances: first, when Person's and Other's outcomes are equal and their inputs are equal. This would be the case, for example, when Person perceived that Other's wages, job, and working conditions were the same as his and that Other was equal to him on such relevant dimensions as sex, skill, seniority, education, age, effort expended, physical fitness, and risk incurred (risk of personal injury, of being fired for errors committed, for instance). Secondly, the ratios will be equal when Person perceives that Other's outcomes are higher (or lower) than his and that Other's inputs are correspondingly higher (or lower). A subordinate who compares himself to his supervisor or work group leader typically does not feel that he is unjustly treated by the company that employs them both, because the supervisor's greater monetary compensation, better working conditions, and more interesting, more varied job are matched on the input side of the ratio by more education, wider range of skills, greater responsibility and personal risk, more maturity and experience, and longer service.

Although there is no direct, reliable evidence on this point, it is probable, as Homans (1961) conjectured, that the thresholds for inequity are different (in absolute terms from a base of equity) in cases of under- and overreward. The threshold would be higher presumably in cases of overreward, for a certain amount of incongruity in these cases can be acceptably rationalized as "good fortune" without attendant discomfort. In his work on pay differentials, Jaques (1961b) notes that in instances of undercompensation, British workers paid 10 percent less than the equitable level show "an active sense of grievance, complaints or the desire to complain, and, if no redress is given, an active desire to change jobs, or to take action . . ." (p. 26). In cases of overcompensation, he observes that at the 10 to 15 percent level above equity "there is a strong sense of receiving preferential treatment, which may harden into bravado, with underlying feelings of unease . . ." (p. 26). He states further, "The results suggest that it is not necessarily the case that each one is simply out to get as much as he can for his work. There appear to be equally strong desires that each one

should earn the right amount—a fair and reasonable amount relative to others" (p. 26).

In the preceding discussion, Person has been the focus of attention. It should be clear, however, that when Person and Other are in an exchange interaction, Other will suffer inequity if Person does, but the nature of his experience will be opposite to that of Person. If the outcome-input ratio discrepancy is unfavorable to Person, it will be favorable to Other, and vice versa. This will hold provided Person's and Other's perceptions of outcomes and inputs are equivalent and provided that the outcome-input ratio discrepancy attains threshold level. When Person and Other are not engaged in an exchange with one another but stand in an exchange relationship with a third party, Other may or may not experience inequity when Person does. Given the prerequisites mentioned above, he will experience inequity if he compares himself to Person with respect to the same question as induces Person to use Other as a referent (e.g., "Am I being paid fairly?").

REFERENCES

Adams, J. S. "Toward an Understanding of Inequity." *J. Abnorm. Soc. Psychol.* 67 (1963a), 422-36.

Adams, J. S., and Jacobsen, Patricia R. "Effects of Wage Inequities on Work Equality." *J. Abnorm. Soc. Psychol.* 69 (1964), 19-25.

Adams, J. S., and Rosenbaum, W. B. "The Relationship of Worker Productivity to Cognitive Dissonance about Wage Inequities." *J. Appl. Psychol.* 46 (1962), 161-64.

Clark, J. V. "A Preliminary Investigation of Some Unconscious Assumptions Affecting Labor Efficiency in Eight Supermarkets." Unpublished doctoral dissertation (Grad. Sch. Business Admin.), Harvard University, 1958.

Conlon, Elizabeth T. "Performance as Determined by Expectation of Success and Failure." Unpublished doctoral dissertation (Dep. Social Psychol.), Columbia University, 1965.

Festinger, L. *A Theory of Cognitive Dissonance.* Evanston, Ill.: Row, Peterson, 1957.

Herzberg, F.; Mausner, B.; and Snyderman, Barbara B. *The Motivation to Work.* New York: Wiley, 1959.

Homans, G. C. *The Human Group.* New York: Harcourt, Brace, 1950.

Homans, G. C. "Status among Clerical Workers." *Hum. Organiz.* 12 (1963), 5–10.

Homans, G. C. *Social Behavior: Its Elementary Forms.* New York: Harcourt, Brace, 1961.

Jaques, E. *Measurement of Responsibility.* London: Tavistock, 1956.

Jaques, E. *Equitable Payment.* New York: Wiley, 1961a.

Jaques, E. "An Objective Approach to Pay Differentials." *Time Motion Study* 10 (1961b), 25–28.

Patchen, M. *The Choice of Wage Comparisons.* Englewood Cliffs, N.J.: Prentice-Hall, 1961.

Sayles, L. R. *Behavior of Industrial Work Groups: Prediction and Control.* New York: Wiley, 1958.

Thibaut, J. "An Experimental Study of the Cohesiveness of Underprivileged Groups." *Hum. Relat.* 3 (1950), 251–78.

Zaleznik, A.; Christensen, C. R.; and Roethlisberger, F. J. The Motivation, Productivity, and Satisfaction of Workers. A Prediction Study (Grad. Sch. Business Admin.) Harvard University, 1958.

Essay **6-6**

Equitable payment*

Elliott Jaques

We may attempt to construct a more precise definition of employment work. It is *the application of knowledge and the exercise of discretion within the limits prescribed by the immediate manager and by higher policies, in order to carry out the activities allocated by the immediate manager, the whole carried out within an employment contract for a wage or salary.* Two concepts appear in this definition. They are the concepts of the prescribed content and the discretionary content of responsibility. They constitute two of the foundation stones of our definition and measurement of work.

There are always to be found two different aspects to the responsibilities which

a manager sets out to be discharged. He sets them out partly in prescribed terms; that is to say, in such a manner that his subordinate will be in no doubt whatever when he has completed his task, and completed it as instructed. And he sets them out partly in discretionary terms; that is to say, in such a manner that his subordinate will have to use his own discretion in deciding when he has pursued the particular activities to the point where the result is likely to satisfy the requirements of his manager. In the case of the prescribed content of the responsibility, the subordinate knows when he has done his job because the result to be achieved or the regulations to be adhered to have been established in objective terms such that anyone would know when the work had been done as required. In the case of the discretionary content of the responsibility, no one can know definitely if the work

*Reprinted from Elliott Jaques, *Equitable Payment* (New York: John Wiley and Sons, 1961), pp. 71–84, 99, 123–33 (abridged). Copyright © 1961 John Wiley and Sons, Inc. Reprinted by permission.

has been done as set out by the manager, until that manager himself—or someone else officially on his behalf—has reviewed the results of the work and accepted it as satisfactory or rejected it as substandard.

The prescribed content of responsibility is laid down. It exists in external reality. It can be observed independently by any number of observers. It refers to the genuine rules and regulations; but it does not include so-called rules which are not really meant to be rigorously adhered to; such, for example, as those rules in the rule books of many enterprises which, if strictly worked to, would lead to the shutting down of the enterprise. In order for an aspect of work to be prescribed, there must be an externally defined and observable control such that a departure from regulations is immediately apparent without the exercise of judgment. These prescriptions may be given by means of physical controls, such as jigs, or railway tracks; mechanical controls such as automatic temperature regulators, or signals such as a light or a bell which do not require to be interpreted; administrative controls such as explicitly laid-down procedures to be followed, perhaps on or by specified dates; technical controls which require a particular technique to be employed in doing a job; or policy controls such as the delimitation of particular markets or customers or categories of customer with whom business is to be done.

If the external control eliminating choice for any particular aspect of an instruction cannot be objectively identified, then that aspect is not prescribed but is discretionary. Thus, for example: make sure you buy enough stamps; use the best method in the circumstances; design advertisements with public appeal; keep a satisfactory standard of finish; select the most capable of the applicants. All such instructions are prescribed in the sense only that they tell a subordinate to do *something* about stamps, best methods, appealing advertisements, satisfactory fin-

ish, or capable applicants. In the absence of any further and objective definition of what the manager intends by these terms, the meaning of the instruction and the sense of what would constitute its being carried out properly are left for the time being to the discretion of the subordinate. He must judge his manager's requirement on the basis of his previous experience of the work combined with his know-how or sense of what is required in that particular job.

It is impossible for any manager to issue an instruction that has no prescribed limits. There are always prescribing policies, limits, results to be achieved. On the way to achieving these results, however, some discretion must be used, since it is only the end result which is prescribed. Therefore, there is no such thing as an executive instruction which does not incorporate both prescribed and discretionary elements.

At minimum, the person doing the work must use his discretion on how it is to be organized and on the pace to be maintained in order to get the work done on time. Thus, for example, a manager may instruct his subordinate to carry out a series of chemical analyses on a certain material so as to determine its composition. He may, having decided in his own mind on the likely composition, specify precisely which tests he wants done and in which order. He leaves the pace of work and possibly certain judgments of observation to the discretion of his subordinate. Or he may simply instruct his subordinate to analyze the material, laying down no particular test, but perhaps setting certain limiting conditions such as ascertaining all the components present in amounts of 0.5 percent or more, but leaving smaller traces unanalyzed. With such an instruction, it is left to the judgment of the subordinate to determine the range of tests he will use, as well as the organization and sequence of the tests.

The performance of the prescribed content of responsibility demands knowledge. The person doing the job must have been taught, or must otherwise have learned, the particular routines, or the signals, or the tests, or the policies, or the techniques, which he has been instructed to use in carrying out his assigned activities.

In contrast to the prescribed content, the performance of the discretionary content of responsibility demands know-how, wisdom, gumption, *nous*. The person doing the job must exercise his own control and judgment from within himself. He himself must decide, choose, judge, feel, sense, consider, conclude just what would be the best thing to do in the circumstances, the best way of going about what he is doing. He may take his knowledge and previous experience into account, but knowledge and experience are not in themselves sufficient. They are insufficient in the sense that they cannot be automatically applied. They can be used only as guides when new features in a situation call for slight or radical variation on past activities, or sometimes for entirely new solutions based on hunch and guesswork, solutions for which there may be little precedent, or no precedent whatever.

The essential difference between the prescribed and the discretionary content may thus be noted. In the case of the prescribed content, a person's assessment and control of his working activity can be achieved by reference to objective standards external to himself; in the case of the discretionary content, assessment and control of his working activities must be achieved by reference to intuitively sensed standards within himself. The prescribed standards, since they exist in external reality, can be described in concrete terms; the discretionary responsibilities, since they refer to standards which a manager has in his mind, can be described only in subjective terms. If, therefore, a person were carrying out a prescribed series of tests and he were to be asked why he was

doing them, he would reply that he had been told to. Sitting quite still, he would be able accurately to enumerate which tests, and in what order, so that anyone else who had knowledge of that field of work would himself know precisely what tests to do if he were given that job.

In the case of the discretionary content, however, a very different pattern of behavior can be observed. If the same question were asked of a person who had been given the job of analyzing certain materials—which tests he did and in which order being left to his discretion—the answer would be something to the effect that he was doing a series of tests which he thought would be the best method of analyzing the material he had. If asked why, he might say that the color of the material, or its surface characteristics, or its feel, led him to suspect certain elements. He might have started with certain other tests, but on balance he thought that the particular sequence of tests he was using was most likely to give him the most accurate results most quickly. If pressed to explain why the color or surface characteristics or feel gave him the impression he had received, he might get some way towards putting his impression into words, but there would come a point at which words would fail him and he would be reduced to vague references to experience, or hunch, or simply to the fact that it just felt right. Meanwhile, he would be seen to be unwittingly moving his arms and hands in that kind of eloquent pawing into space which is substituted for words which are simply not there to express the touch and feel of intuitive judgment in doing a job. It is like the imitative gesture which inevitably accompanies a skilled worker's attempt to describe what he means by putting "just the right amount of force" into tapping delicately with a hammer, or applying a tool.

The use of this gesture for the purpose of filling in gaps in speech is uniformly characteristic of descriptions of the use of discretion. Whenever, in interview, a person begins to use his hands rather than words to explain how and why he does particular aspects of his work, then it can be taken for certain that he is talking about a discretionary aspect. The essence of the use of discretion is that it is intuitive, touch and feel, the sense of the job. It is nonverbalized knowledge—the kind that is carried in one's bones.

If we now ask what it is that an enterprise seeks when it employs a person to work in its executive organization—what is it that it pays a wage or salary *for*—we get a two-fold answer. First, it employs that person's capacity to carry out the prescribed responsibilities and to conform to them: he must know enough to do so. Second, it employs his ability to exercise sufficient discretion on his own account to cope with uncertainties, the vicissitudes, the unknowns, in the job: he must have enough capacity and experience—the know-how or the *nous*—to do so. It has seemed to me that one of the most intriguing and telling findings revealed by our social-analytic studies[1] was that it is the second of these responsibilities—the exercise of discretion—which is mainly connected with the sensation of the amount of responsibility in a job. We appear to derive our sensation of level of work or responsibility from the discretion we are called upon to exercise, and not from the regulated or prescribed actions which have been set and which we have learned and can carry out automatically.

As he carries out the discretionary part of a job, an employee must rely upon his own skill and *nous.* The skill and *nous* employed determine how well or how poorly his work is done. I am using skill and *nous* in a manner which I wish precisely to define. *Skill* is the capacity of a person to exercise sensory and perceptual

judgment in carrying out the discretionary aspects of his work. *Nous* is his capacity to exercise mental judgment for the same purpose. Skill is made up of the capacity to respond intuitively to the sense of touch, sight, hearing, taste, smell, or balance, and physically to guide and manipulate one's work according to the sense or feel of the job in the course of doing it. *Nous* is made up of the capacity to weigh up available information, to sense what other information, if any, ought to be obtained, and mentally to proceed on the basis of what feels like the best course of action where many factors in the situation are only unconsciously assessed, and some of the factors—perhaps even the most important ones—are simply unknown.

It is precisely this element of uncertainty, of having to rely on our own judgment, to guide our own actions, without knowing the result until the work has been completed and reviewed, that makes the feeling of weight of responsibility come from the discretionary content of the work. By contrast, the prescribed content leaves no room for uncertainty and makes no such demands.

The question remains, however, of how the extensiveness of the uncertainty in work is to be determined. An answer to this question was suggested by the most important of the findings presented in *Measurement of Responsibility.* It was simply that the longer the period of time that discretion had to be exercised in a role without the results of that discretion possibly coming to the attention of the immediate manager, then the greater was the psychological effort required for the work. In short, the longer you have to tolerate and stand up to uncertainty and yet keep on with your work, the greater is the responsibility. Looked at the other way round, the longer the employing organization leaves a member to carry on exercising his own discretion in his work, making decisions based on that discretion and committing resources of the firm in so do-

[1] See Elliott Jaques, *Measurement of Responsibility* (London: Tavistock, 1956).

ing, then the greater is the reliance of the firm upon him and the greater is the responsibility allocated to him. As I have previously reported, there is evidence to confirm the view that the length of this span of time corresponds with the financial value of the losses which would be caused by substandard discretion.

* * * * *

TIME-SPAN OF DISCRETION

To summarize, we may define the *time-span of discretion* as the period of time during which marginally substandard discretion could be exercised in a role before information about the accumulating substandard work would become available to the manager in charge of the role.

NORMS OF EQUITABLE PAYMENT

The most significant evidence showing that what is experienced by a person as level of work could be measured in terms of time-span, was the totally unexpected finding of a regular connection between time-span and the sums of money which individuals stated would, in their estimation, constitute fair payment for their work. Regardless of the actual wage or salary they might have been earning, regardless of type of occupation (accounting, engineering, shop management, manual or clerical work, purchasing, research, etc.), regardless of position (from shop floor work to top management), and regardless of income tax paid, individuals in jobs whose range of level of work as measured in time-span was the same, privately stated a very similar wage or salary bracket to be fair for the work they were doing. I now wish to call the pattern of differential payment so derived the *equitable work-payment scale.*[2]

This finding has been described in detail in *Measurement of Responsibility* for results obtained from analyses carried out with members of the Glacier Metal Company. I have since been able to obtain data in respect of over one thousand jobs, with confirmatory findings from a heavy engineering firm, a food factory, a bank, a woodworking concern, and a chemical works.

The results suggest the existence of an unrecognized system of norms of fair payment for any given level of work, unconscious knowledge of these norms being shared among the population engaged in employment work. It is because of these intuitive norms that I have had recourse to the concept of equity in describing the scale of felt-fair differential payments. I am using the term equity to express the notion of differentiated treatment rather than equal treatment of individuals, in accord with the differential circumstances affecting those individuals—in this case, differential levels of work or responsibility to which they are called upon to apply themselves. I shall want to return later in the course of our argument to consider how these standards of equity are unconsciously established and carried in the minds of individuals.

The character of the equitable work-payment scale is shown in Figure 1.[3] A number of features of this graph require comment and explication.

A. The earnings refer to total emoluments; that is to say the wage or salary plus any other fringe benefits such as, for example, use of car, assistance with purchase of house, provision of canteen meals, etc.

B. There is an artifact in the horizon-

---

[2] In *Measurement of Responsibility* I used the phrase "general wage and salary structure" to refer to this scale.

[3] The curves on this graph have been made by plotting the time-span felt-fair pay data from just over 1,000 analyses. For any given time-span, the deviations between individual statements of felt-fair pay range are of the order of ± 5 percent, with standard deviations of the order of 2 to 3 percent.

Figure 1: The equitable work-payment scale

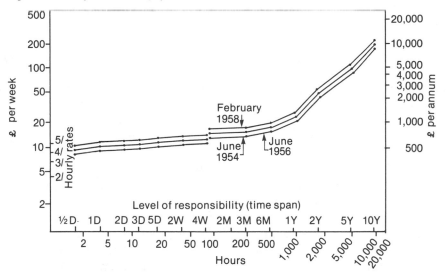

tal scale of time-span. In order to get a continuous scale from hours to days to weeks to years, I have taken one day to comprise eight working hours, a week to comprise five working days, a month to comprise four working weeks, and a year to comprise 12 working months.

C. During the five years I have been collecting data about felt-fair payment and level of work, the standards of what constitutes equitable payment have moved upwards. Percentage-wise this upward movement has conformed closely to upward movements in the wages index.[4] This finding is illustrated in Figure 1 by the three curves showing the equitable levels as they were in June 1954, June 1956, and February 1958. In these periods the wages index moved 1.10 percent and 1.07 percent respectively, and the equitable payment levels took a corresponding percentage rise. In the course of the same periods the cost of living

index[5] moved by 1.06 percent and 1.1 percent.

It is not surprising that these shifts in standards of equity should follow movements in the wages index rather than shifts in the cost of living. For equity is concerned with the relative treatment, within any given economy, of individuals compared with one another, rather than with any absolute standard of living—a factor determined by the degree of prosperity of the economy as a whole. Let me elaborate this point. In an expanding economy the mere fact of an individual increasing his standard of living does not necessarily represent personal progress. If his personal increase is identical with the average national increase, then he may feel that he is better off in the sense of sharing with others in the national prosperity, but without being any better off in the sense of having made personal progress in his career relative to others. Per contra, in a period of economic con-

---

[4] The Ministry of Labour wages index derived from the current average of negotiated and standard minimum wage rates for manual work: it is an index of the average national minimum wage for a normal working week.

---

[5] The cost of living index (the retail prices index) is derived from the current average prices of a standard list of consumer goods.

traction or depression, an individual's standard of living may be decreasing and yet at the same time he may be making individual progress in his career, in the sense of receiving merit increases which cancel out some of what would otherwise be a bigger drop in living standard.

We may note, therefore, that our findings are suggestive of the fact that the standards of what constitutes equitable differential payment tend to move in unison throughout the population, in terms of percentage proportional movement. The effect is that the differential pattern of payment for different levels of work has remained fixed. It is important to note, of course, that my data have been obtained during a few years only. A much longer time will be required to discover whether in fact there has been any genuine shift in the differential pattern, i.e., a closing or opening of the gap.

D. The norms of equity are independent of the amount of income tax paid by individuals. The independence of these norms from income tax probably reflects the commonly held view that it is unsatisfactory for employers to have to decide upon the relative needs of different employees and their families. These are matters for society as a whole to decide, and to express through government. Equitable payment levels can be maintained regardless of an employee's family and other commitments or absence of such commitments, leaving for taxation policy, national insurance, and welfare legislation to regulate how much of that income a person shall keep.

ACTUAL AND EQUITABLE PAYMENT

A point which calls for the most emphatic enunciation is that I have so far been talking about norms of *equitable differential* payment—of felt-fair payment—and have not said anything about the *actual* payment received, other than

to report that the earnings considered to be fair were independent of the actual wage or salary being earned by the person concerned. Norms of equitable payment are connected with level of work as measured by time-span. They appear to be uninfluenced by the fact that a person might never have received actual earnings which conformed to equity.

If individuals engaged in employment work do possess these shared norms of what constitutes fair pay for any given level of work, we may then ask whether these norms of equity influence a person's feelings about his actual pay. There is strong evidence to show that this influence does in fact exist. A person's attitude towards the wage or salary bracket paid for his work appears to be fundamentally influenced by the extent to which that bracket is consistent with what would be equitable for the range of level of work in his job, or deviates from equity either upwards or downwards. The following findings were obtained.

The results of individual discussions about actual pay in the course of the social-analytic work to which I have referred have been illuminating. A degree of consistency has emerged that has made it possible to predict individual feelings about actual payment brackets, if the actual and the equitable payment brackets are known. And conversely, it is possible to guess a person's actual payment bracket within a five percent degree of accuracy, if the equitable payment bracket and his feelings about his actual payment bracket are both known. These results can be briefly summarized.

Individuals react to conformity or nonconformity between their actual earnings and equitable payment in a characteristic manner. If the actual salary bracket for a person's role coincides with equity, he expresses himself as being in a reasonably paid role. If his actual payment bracket has fallen below the equitable bracket, he expresses himself as dissatisfied with the financial recognition for his role. If, on the other hand, his actual payment bracket has risen above the equitable bracket, then he reacts with a sense of being paid within a rather higher range than he can ever hope to maintain. The intensity of his reaction varies with the size of the discrepancy between the actual and equitable brackets.

More specifically, this trend of reactions of individuals to deviations between actual and equitable earnings is as follows. Individuals whose actual payment bracket remains within ± 3 percent of equity, tend to express themselves as feeling that their role is being reasonably paid relative to others. They may be dissatisfied for other reasons—they may not like that type of work, or their general working conditions, or they may think they could carry higher responsibility either within the same bracket or in another role, or they may just be dissatisfied with life in general— but they will, nevertheless, state that their pay is within a bracket that is reasonable enough for their work.

A person whose actual payment bracket falls 5 percent below equity feels moderately retarded, and states that the employing organization is treating him to some degree unfairly. If his actual payment bracket is 10 percent below equity, he feels he is definitely being treated unfairly; he may appeal to his manager; or if he does not feel his security of employment is strong enough to allow him to appeal, he will harbour ill-will. A fall in payment bracket greater than 10 percent below equity is accompanied by an employee's beginning to consider the possibility of getting satisfactory financial progress by seeking another job. If the employment situation in his occupation and his personal circumstances are such as to permit a change of employment, he will tend toward seeking such a change if the deviation reaches 15 percent, and the likelihood of his making the change becomes high if the deviation moves toward

a 20 percent discrepancy. If the employment conditions in his occupation, or his personal circumstances, are such as to make a change of job impossible, then at the 10-20 percent discrepancy range he will tend towards a state of mind in which he swallows his resentment and carries on with his job, but in what I can best describe as a depressed way: that is to say, he will tend to do his job more or less competently, but with an absence of that zest and enthusiasm which makes for high efficiency and personal satisfaction in work. Even under the conditions of full employment that have obtained in recent years, these latter circumstances have occurred in some types of employment, as, for example, in roles within some types of manual work and within the lower levels of accounting and general office work.

If a person's actual payment bracket moves to more than 5 percent above equity, he considers that he is getting more than a fair deal in his role as compared with his fellows in other roles. At the 10 percent level, compulsive elements begin to enter into his attitude. He may often have some anxiety about being able to maintain the high level of earnings; this anxiety increases with the length of time the earnings are received, the extra earnings themselves being treated as not secure and not to be counted upon. He experiences feelings of guilt with regard to others who are not doing so well. But guilt may be warded off by a devil-take-the-hindmost attitude. He may express resistance to change in the content of his work, to the introduction of new methods, or to transfer to other jobs. Greed and avarice may be stimulated, with a resulting antisocial grasping for further relative gain regardless of the consequences for the common good.

It may be useful to add that the reactions I have described apply equally at all executive levels. They are not confined to any particular group of people—high income, medium income, or low income.

Essay 6-7

Justice and equity in compensation*

Thomas A. Mahoney

The disarray of wage and compensation theory has been recognized widely for nearly two decades. Economic in origin and orientation, the theories dominant in the 1950s provided relatively little guidance to the administration of wages and compensation. Wage phenomena were explained as functions of market and institutional forces, and compensation administration had a relatively small role.

Many models and hypotheses concerning compensation developed since then give the impression that compensation administration can now be supported on a strong theoretical base. Most of these new models are products of behavioral scientists, however, and tend to be instrumental in nature; they stress the role of compensation as an instrument to influence behavior and performance of the workforce. Being instrumental in orientation, they would appear to provide the theory base to compensation administration that had been felt lacking. But this isn't necessarily so.

Developments in compensation theory in recent years largely ignore a basic issue—the issue of distributive justice. Also, compensation theory and administration today lack an accepted criterion of justice. And without an accepted criterion of distributive justice, the instrumental models of compensation offer little long-run potential.

Changing concepts of "just" wages

Concern over justice in the satisfaction of human wants has a long history. The two basic issues of economic theory—what should be produced with limited resources, and how this production should be distributed—are issues of justice, and historical developments in the theory of political economy reflect attempts to establish justice in the production and distribution of goods and services. For example, the origin of the "just wage" doctrine is ascribed to attempts by workers to exploit the labor market advantages of scarce labor relative to demand. A schedule of "just" wages was proclaimed by the state with the support of the church, and employers and employees alike were forbidden to rely upon market processes in the determination of other wage rates. These "just" wages tended to reflect traditional social class structures and thus perpetuated the status quo. The market was explicitly denied as a test of justice or equity, and social norms were employed instead.

More traditional economic theory traces its origins back to the ideas expressed by Adam Smith, who addressed the question of justice in terms of value and sought to identify the basis of value of goods and services including labor. Smith identified three conceptual bases for value, all of which he employed at one time or another:

1. Exchange value or simply the price arrived at in a competitive market; something is worth whatever a buyer is willing to pay for it.

2. Use value or the value ascribed to the consumption of something.

3. Labor value or the cost of the embodied labor; the labor consumed in the production of the item.

Use value and market value are employed constantly today in economic decisions—for example, when a farmer decides to feed his corn to his pigs rather than sell it in the corn market.

Despite his discussion of the different concepts of value, most of us today attribute to Smith the development of exchange or market value as the true and just measure of value. The labor market thus replaced tradition and social class as the determinant of justice in wage determination; the just wage following Smith was the market wage.

Some years later Karl Marx reintroduced Smith's different concepts of value. He observed wages as being determined by the labor market—the exchange value of labor. Following Malthus and Ricardo, Marx also reasoned that competition in the labor market forced this exchange value down to the level of subsistence for labor. He argued, however, that the use value of labor was greater than this exchange value, thus giving rise to the concept of surplus value that accrued to the capitalist. Marx carried his analysis further, but this application of Smith's concepts of use value and exchange value provided the basis for questioning the justice of wages based upon *exchange* value.

Whatever the motivation of various contributors to the development of marginal analysis, the marginal productivity theory provided a theoretical rationale for exchange value as the true measure of economic justice. The marginal productivity theory, with its assumptions of competitive markets and long-run general equilibrium, rationalized the market mechanism as the instrument for determination of justice in both the production and distribution of goods and services. Compensating each resource proportionately to its contribution to the satisfaction of consumer desires achieved optimal allocation of resources and thus equated use value and exchange value. Just compensation for labor as well as other resources was the *use* value which, given the structure of the theory, was equivalent to *exchange* value.

The theory of the firm as developed in marginal analysis thus provided a theoretical basis for exchange value (market value) as the measure of distributive justice; just wages are those wage rates that result from free competition in the labor market. Specific guides for wage administration provided by the theory were few, but the market test of justice was a significant contribution. We find this market test of justice applied today in resistance to union demands for wage rates above the market rate; in resistance to socially determined rates for minimum wages, welfare payments, and social security; and in reliance upon market surveys to justify wage rates offered employees.

Current challenges

The relevance of the marginal productivity theory for determination of just wages is severely questioned today. The restrictive assumptions of the theory are challenged by the prevalence of nonmarket exchanges such as defense contracting, by the recognized market power of large industrial organizations, and by the market distortions brought about by governmental subsidies and related supports. John Kenneth Galbraith has clearly stated the significant divergences of our economy from that of the marginal productivity model. It is not surprising that questions of justice and differences between use value and exchange value are being voiced. Cesar Chavez, for example, challenges the justice of wages for lettuce pickers, and women liberationists challenge the justice of sex discrimination in wages and employment opportunities. In a very real sense we are rejecting the labor market as the determinant of just wages and are seeking a new standard of justice to apply in wage determination.

Current concern for justice in compensation can be observed on two fronts. One set of concerns for justice questions the equity of distribution among occupations and socioeconomic groups in society, the equity of welfare payments, the equity of wage comparisons between teachers and craftsmen, and the equity of male-female or white-black wage comparisons. A second set of equity issues concerns more limited wage comparisons such as the equity of wage differentials within the firm or the equity of differential criteria for wage improvement within the firm. The marginal productivity theory with its assumptions of competitive markets and long-run general equilibrium provided the same criterion of justice for both types of concerns; the market wage was justified as the just wage in all instances. The two sets of justice or equity issues can no longer be linked to a single criterion once we remove the assumptions of competitive markets and long-run general equilibrium.

Development of concepts of dual labor markets in recent years evidences recognition of the inadequacy of marginal productivity theory to explain satisfactorily wage phenomena both within the firm and in the broader labor market. Observations about wage clusters and the concept of Balkanized labor markets have been developed into the concept of an internal labor market, an administrative unit that performs the same pricing and allocation functions within an organization that have been attributed to the competitive labor market in past models. Employees are recruited from the external labor market through selected entry ports and are assigned jobs and compensated at later stages in their careers on the basis of administrative rules rather than traditional market processes. The only link between wage rates paid by the firm and wage rates in the external market occurs at entry jobs where the employer is competing with other employers. Wage rates for jobs other than entry jobs may be established on grounds other than market comparisons since they are filled through promotion from within the firm.

Although not always recognized explicitly, compensation administration has recognized this distinction between the internal and external labor markets in wage determination for some time. A wage structure is developed through job evaluation that relates jobs one to another in the internal market, and it is priced by relating rates for key jobs with market rates.

Limitations of job evaluations

Job evaluation provides an administrative mechanism for determination of wage rates in the internal labor market with only limited reliance upon external market processes of wage determination. It provides a procedure for the determination of just wage rates, but it does not provide a criterion of justice; rather, it can be applied with any criterion of justice. Further, job evaluation does not address the issues of justice in compensation beyond the boundaries of the internal labor market.

Market wage rates inferred from wage surveys among firms employing job evaluation cannot be interpreted as the wage rates that would emerge from competitive market processes. They represent only the wage rates paid by other firms, wage rates arrived at through administrative pricing mechanisms. Recognizing the increasing irrelevance of the concept of a competitive market wage as a criterion of just wages, it becomes increasingly difficult to justify sex and race differentials in wage rates and employment opportunities, wage rates that provide earnings associated with poverty levels of income, and wage increases for construction workers proportionately greater than wage increases for teachers.

Wage and salary administration is in the curious position of appealing to the market criterion of justice in compensation and at the same time tailoring compensation practices to accommodate nonmarket influences. We talk about paying "what a job is worth," implying measurement of the use value of labor, and then consult surveys of market rates on the implicit assumption that exchange value and use value are equated. Additional criteria for compensation differentials—criteria such as seniority—are then accommodated. These accommodations often become so widespread that they appear in market surveys although they do not reflect the market rate that would emerge in a free market economy. Compensation differentials based upon seniority probably are just as noneconomic in basis as differentials based upon education, sex, color, or other related measures.

Characteristics of recent compensation models

Wage and compensation models developed in recent years tend to assume implicitly the existence of dual labor markets and are related primarily to motivation and behavior in the internal labor market. These behavioral science models also appear to be motivated by a desire to explain motivation and behavior and thus provide a basis for development of administrative programs to influence behavior. Issues of justice or equity are central to relatively few of these models.

The most widely known recent models are characterized by concepts of expectancy; individuals select actions based upon outcomes associated with the actions and expectancies or probabilities of these outcomes. Behavior is channeled by manipulation of outcomes associated with actions and by manipulation of expectancies of outcomes. In simple form, these

models are not dissimilar from the economist's model of individuals acting to maximize net advantage or the probabilistic decision-making model with individuals acting to maximize expected value.

Another model, the equity model, relates more directly to issues of justice and equity. In substance, it suggests that the contribution of parties to an exchange relect the anticipated or perceived equity of exchange, the equity of relationships of rewards, costs, and investments of parties to the exchange. This model has been the subject of considerable research, the results of which indicate that perceptions of inequity are significant in motivating behavior. Unfortunately, the equity model does not appear to be very predictive of the direction of this motivated behavior, and the implications for compensation administration are not apparent.

Motivation theory recognizes two distinct issues in motivation that often are merged in consideration of compensation and motivation. The first issue concerns arousal of the individual to a choice situation and energizing the individual to take action; the second issue concerns the direction of the action and behavior after arousal.

There is no reason to suppose that arousal and direction of behavior are interdependent other than in sequence; feelings of inequity arouse an individual to take action, but that subsequent action is dependent upon perceived outcomes and expectancies of outcomes.

Considerations of equity, or perhaps more correctly considerations of inequity, appear to be central to compensation theory and administration. Unfortunately there is little base in theory or practice for the determination and justification of any equity criterion. The traditional criterion of market rate can no longer be justified on theoretical grounds and is challenged increasingly as a practical criterion. The expectancy and equity models from the behavioral sciences relate to processes of choice and determination of equity but offer no guides to the content of equity criteria.

Job evaluation also offers a process for the determination of equitable relationships, but it cannot justify the content dimensions of equity criteria. One model proposed by Elliott Jaques in *Equitable Payment* does specify the content of a criterion for equity in compensation—the time span of discretion in work. Few scholars or practitioners accept Jaques' rationale, however, leaving us without a generally acceptable criterion of equity or justice in compensation.

The determination of equity or justice in compensation and distribution remains an empirical issue, and we have no accepted guides for public policy on compensation and distribution or for compensation administration in the internal labor market. Lacking any accepted guides, it /ould appear that issues of equity or inquity in compensation and distribution will plague compensation administration as norms of equitable payment shift with changing social values. The communist norm of ". . . to each according to need" probably is just as defensible today as the norm of "equal pay for equal work."

Essay 6-8

Organizational hierarchy and position worth*

Thomas A. Mahoney

Hierarchical relationships in formal organizations are phenomena of interest to varied scholars of organizations. These hierarchical relationships constitute phenomena to be explained by organization theorists concerned with organization structure, and phenomena with varied implications for status, power, and influence of concern to scholars of organizational behavior. Hierarchical relationships are perceived as instrumental in the coordination of efforts and as determinants of power and status in social relationships.

Early analyses of organization structure explained hierarchical relationships as a consequence of limited span of supervision necessary for coordination; pyramidal organization structures of supervision and reporting relationships were derived

from this concept of limited span of supervision. Hierarchical relationships in formal organizations reflect influences other than supervision, however, and strict pyramidal structures are uncommon. Rather, hierarchical level in formal organizations reflects power, influence, and status derived from sources other than merely supervision of subordinates. Hierarchical levels depicted in organization charts and job titles possess meaning apart from the implied supervision as evidenced by the assumed hierarchical equality of positions with similar titles reporting to a single supervisor regardless of the number of subordinates or subordinate levels of these positions. A vice president is a vice president regardless of the size of subordinate organizations.

Expectations of relationships between hierarchical level in formal organizations and salary are commonplace since both reflect status and worth in some sense. Per-

*Adapted from Thomas A. Mahoney, "Organizational Hierarchy and Position Worth," *Academy of Management Journal* (forthcoming).

haps because of these common expectations, there has been relatively little investigation of the nature of the relationships. Rather, the compensation of organizational executives has more commonly been analyzed in relation to job content or function than in relationship to organizational hierarchy. We examine here relationships of executive compensation and hierarchical level in formal organizations for insights into assessments of worth of hierarchical levels and for insights into the influence of hierarchical norms upon compensation levels.

RELATED THEORY AND RESEARCH

A formal theory of chief executive compensation based upon hierarchical influences was developed by Herbert Simon as an alternative to explanations based upon concepts of marginal productivity inferred from organization size and sales (Simon, 1957). Working from reported empirical relationships between the compensation of corporate chief executives and annual sales of corporations, Simon reasoned that sales and number of employees likely were related, and that the compensation of chief executives probably varied positively with employment in the organization. Assuming a competitive market for management trainees (e.g., MBAs) corporations would tend to pay similar salaries for management trainees regardless of organization size. Given some limited span of supervision, the number of hierarchical levels in a corporation should vary positively with total employment, larger organizations being characterized with more distinct hierarchical levels. Simon hypothesized some customary or traditional salary differential between any two adjacent levels in the hierarchy, a differential, b, which he hypothesized as a constant proportional difference. The compensation of the chief executive, C, can then be expressed as

$$C = A b^{L-1}$$

where

A = salary for management trainees,
b = proportional compensation differential between hierarchical levels,
L = number of levels in the organization.

Similar relationships ought hold for each level in the organization, L varying as the number of the organization level of concern measured from the entry level. Simon did not estimate b, the ratio of salary at one level in the management hierarchy relative to salary at the next lower level, directly, but suggested that it might vary from one organization to another depending upon average span of supervision. The hypothesis that there exists a customary or traditional proportional relationship between salaries at two adjacent levels in the organizational hierarchy, b, does imply an imputed worth to organization level, however, irrespective of job content or function.

Empirical estimation of b is difficult in any large organization because of the difficulties in equating organizational levels in different divisions and subsidiaries or across different chains of command. Fragments of evidence relating to the size and consistency of accepted relationships of compensation between any two adjacent hierarchical levels in formal organizations are available from several sources, however. Surveys of executive compensation by McKinsey and Company and the National Industrial Conference Board, for example, report compensation of the second and third highest paid executives in organizations as proportions of the highest compensation in the organization (Patton, 1951; Fox, 1966). These ratios vary somewhat from one industry to another, but are reported to be reasonably consistent over time, indicative of customary relationships which persist and which are reflective of industry characteristics. Averaging the ratios reported in these surveys across industries, it appears that the chief executive typically is paid 1.37–1.41 times the salary of the second highest paid position and 1.69–1.71 times the salary of the third highest paid position. Assuming both the second and third highest paid positions hold the same hierarchical level in the organization, the chief executive tends to be paid 1.55 times the average compensation at the next lower level in the hierarchy.

Elliott Jaques has proposed a model of executive compensation related to considerations of hierarchy based upon his investigations into fair pay and time span of discretion (Jaques, 1965). He reports that employee assessments of fair pay for a job vary directly with supervisory estimates of time span of discretion in the job, the maximal time elapsing in a task before supervisory review of performance. He also reasons that supervisory hierarchies reflect time span of discretion, each supervisor performing tasks with longer time spans of discretion than exist in the jobs he supervises. Structures of compensation parallel structures of organizational hierarchy, according to Jaques, because both are reflective of time span of discretion. He recommends, based upon consideration of time span of discretion, compensation relationships of 1.33 between adjacent managerial levels except at entry levels of management where 1.25 is the recommended relationship. Compensation differentials of this magnitude between adjacent hierarchical levels would be accepted as fair differentials, according to Jaques.

A methodological approach to the study of the influence of structural aspects of organizational positions upon perceptions of worth of positions was proposed by Kuethe and Levenson and applied in an exploratory study involving students in Sociology classes (Kuethe and Levenson, 1964). Kuethe and Levenson developed a measurement approach in-

volving organization charts depicting reporting relationships among positions in an organization where the salary of one position was fixed, and respondents indicated what they considered to be appropriate salaries for the other positions. Eleven different organizational configurations were employed, varying the number of total positions and hierarchical levels. Relationships among the top three positions were constant in all configurations (see Figure 1 for an illustration), two positions B and C reporting to a single position A, and the salary of position B was fixed at $10,000. There was one hierarchical level subordinate to position B in all configurations, the number of direct subordinates varying from one to three, hierarchical levels subordinate to position C varied from none to three and the number of subordinates varied from none to three. Kuethe and Levenson reported median salaries assigned the different positions in each configuration and results of analyses of these medians as functions of number of echelons and direct and indirect subordinates. They indicated, for example, that number of subordinate echelons influenced the median salary assigned position A more than did the number of positions in the organization.

While Kuethe and Levenson did not investigate directly compensation relationships between adjacent hierarchical levels, we can estimate these relationships from their reported data. Ratios between compensation at one hierarchical level (L) and the next lower level $(L+1)$ are calculated for each configuration and averaged across the 11 structural configurations to provide the estimates in Table 1 (line 3). These ratios, estimates of Simon's b, vary from 1.20 between organization levels 4 and 5 to 1.72 between levels 1 and 2, comparable with Jaques' estimate of 1.33 and with survey estimates of 1.55 for the ratio between levels 1 and 2.

The exploratory study of Kuethe and

Figure 1

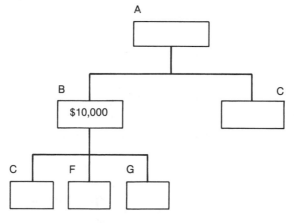

Illustrative organizational configuration from questionnaire, J. L. Kuethe and Bernard Levenson, "Conceptions of Organizational Worth," *The American Journal of Sociology* (November 1964), pp. 342-48.

Table 1

	L_1/L_2	L_2/L_3	L_3/L_4	L_4/L_5	L_5/L_6	L_6/L_7	L_n/L_{n+1}
1. Salary surveys	1.55						
2. E. Jaques.	1.33	1.33	1.33	1.33	1.33	1.33	1.25
Survey samples							
3. Sociology students	1.72	1.43	1.48	1.20			
4. Business students	1.56	1.40	1.35	1.31			
5. Compensation administrators	1.52	1.32	1.31	1.31			
6. Canadian managers	1.29	1.28	1.28	1.29	1.42		

Ratios of compensation for adjacent levels in a managerial hierarchy reported in surveys (McKinsey, NICB), hypothesized (Jaques), and obtained from surveys of appropriate or fair compensation. Hierarchical levels are ordered from the top, L_1.

Levenson has been replicated with two different samples, (1) upper division students in Business Administration ($n = 98$), and (2) corporate compensation administrators ($n = 58$) (Champlin, 1976; Lindberg, 1975). The salary assigned position B in these replications was changed from $10,000 to $20,000 to correspond more closely with current compensation levels, but the instrument was unchanged otherwise. Mean and median compensation assigned the different positions were virtually identical, so means were employed in the calculation of compensation ratios comparable to the ratios calculated from the Kuethe and Levenson study (lines 4 and 5 in Table 1). The compensation ratios derived from these two samples are much more restricted in range than those derived from judgments of the sociology students and are quite comparable between the two samples. With the exception of the compensation differential between levels 1 and 2, the remaining ratios also compare closely with Jaques' estimate of a 33 percent differential between adjacent managerial levels. Interestingly, the compensation differential between levels 1 and 2 is greater than the differentials between other adjacent managerial levels in all three samples, suggesting that the difference between levels 1 and 2 is qualitatively different than differences between other levels. Also, interestingly, the compensation differential associated with levels 1 and 2 by the business students and the compensation administrators (52-56 percent) compares reasonably closely with the 55 percent differential between corporate chief executives and the next two lower paid positions estimated from salary survey data.

The relatively closer agreement between judgments of the business students and the compensation administrators than between either and the sociology students may reflect somewhat greater awareness of the status implications of organizational level and hierarchy in business organizations within these two samples. The comparability between differentials of estimated worth for these two samples and the estimates derived from Elliott Jaques and from executive compensation surveys also suggest the possible influence of knowledge of corporate compensation practices upon estimates of worth. It is unlikely, however, that the business students, juniors and seniors taking a first course in Personnel, were as familiar with compensation practices as were the compensation administrators. Rather, the relatively close agreement among these estimates and judgments of differential compensation associated with organization levels might be interpreted as reflective of shared norms regarding the appropriate distance between organizational ranks, a salary differential of 30-40 percent being

necessary to distinguish between adjacent levels in the managerial hierarchy, and a salary differential of somewhat more than 50 percent being necessary to distinguish the top position.

While position title and function were not indicated in the organizational configurations used in assessing worth, certain positional characteristics other than level also varied across the configurations and influenced judgments of organizational worth, characteristics often associated with level. For example, level in an organizational hierarchy can be inferred from characteristics of the organization subordinate to a position or from characteristics of reporting and peer relationships of a position. Positions B and C both report to position A and have common peer and reporting relationships which were constant in all 11 configurations. Characteristics of the organizations subordinate to these two positions varied considerably in the different configurations, however. There was always one level of positions subordinate to position B, the number of subordinate positions varying from one to three, and the number of both subordinate levels and positions subordinate to position C varied from none to three. Position B was always one level removed from top and bottom of the chain of command, while position C varied from the bottom to three levels removed from the bottom in the chain of command. Despite these variations, the salary assigned position C relative to the fixed salary of position B averaged 95 to 98.6 percent with a relatively narrow range about the mean (see Table 2). This constancy of C's salary

Table 2

	Mean	S.D.	Range
Sociology students . . .	.95	.084	.8-1.1
Business students	.986	.035	.91-1.02
Compensation			
administrators.	.985	.028	.93-1.02

Distributions of compensation for position C relative to position B in 11 organizational configurations.

relative to position B suggests that hierarchical reporting level is a primary influence of positional worth. Positional characteristics of supervision exercised, direct and indirect, appear to influence worth, but only within some range associated with reporting level. The proportional differentials associated with supervisory characteristics of positions (about 15 percent) are considerably less than the salary differentials associated with organization level (about 30-40 percent). Hierarchical organization level thus appears to influence judgments of positional worth independent of other positional characteristics within the samples reported here.

Further evidence relating to compensation differentials associated with managerial organizational hierarchy is derived from a survey of managers employed in two divisions of a large Canadian manufacturing firm ($n = 310$ managers) (Mahoney and Weitzel). These managers were organized in a formal administrative hierarchy of five levels within each division—Section manager, Department manager, Manager, Director, and Division general manager which reported to a Group vice president. The surveyed managers were asked to assume that nonsupervisory employees reporting to the Section managers earned $10,000 and to then indicate the amounts they would consider to be fair compensation for each of the managerial ranks through Division general manager. Ratios between average fair compensation for each of the managerial ranks were calculated and are reported in Table 1 (line 5). These ratios of fair compensation are amazingly consistent from level to level, 1.28-1.29. The reasonably close correspondence between ratios of compensation obtained in this survey and those obtained in the earlier surveys is particularly interesting in light of the fact that managers in this survey probably considered implicitly job characteristics associated with the different managerial levels, information not available to respon-

dents in the earlier surveys. The major exception to the usual differential of 28-29 percent occurred in the comparison of fair compensation of Section managers with the $10,000 compensation arbitrarily assumed for nonsupervisory employees; a differential of 42 percent was indicated for Section managers relative to $10,000. This differential may have resulted from managers basing judgments of fair pay for Section managers upon current hiring rates for those positions, as hypothesized by Simon, and ignoring the rate of compensation assumed for nonsupervisory employees; alternatively, the general distance relationship appropriate to distinguish between ranks in the managerial hierarchy may be inadequate for the distinction between managers and nonsupervisory employees just as it appears inadequate for distinguishing the chief executive position. The notable breaks in this general distance relationship at both ends of the managerial hierarchy are interesting and suggestive of criteria other than rank influencing judgments of fair pay.

INTERPRETATION AND DISCUSSION

The evidence concerning differentials in compensation judged appropriate for different managerial levels in the organizational hierarchy reported here are fragmentary and drawn from a variety of sources. Various inconsistencies appear, due possibly to differences in samples and nature of the data obtained from each. The relative consistency of the evidence is particularly striking in view of the variety of sources and is suggestive of a general phenomenon relating distinctions in organizational rank or level with equivalent distances on a continuous scale of compensation, a difference of one rank or level being equivalent to approximately a 30-40 percent difference in compensation. This general relationship parallels relationships reported from psychophysics research into. stimulus discrimination. Weber-Fechner relationships from psychophysics research indicate that the amount of increase in stimulus level necessary to be noticeable or distinguishable from the previous level is some constant proportion of the previous level of stimulus (Torgerson, 1958). In our context, the amount of increase in compensation necessary to distinguish a higher from a lower organization level is a constant proportion (approximately 33 percent) of the compensation associated with the lower organization level. Studies of just noticeable increases in compensation indicate that considerably smaller proportional increases (3-4 percent) are needed to distinguish between amounts of compensation, so it would appear that the 33 percent proportional increment is related to distinction between ranks in the organizational hierarchy and not to distinction between amounts of compensation (Hinrichs, 1969).

One possible explanation of the reported differentials of compensation appropriate for different managerial levels might be that judgments of appropriate compensation reflect actual rates of managerial compensation. Ratios of actual compensation levels in the Canadian manufacturing firm, for example, were 1.22 and 1.23 for the L_2/L_3 and L_3/L_4 comparisons and 1.31 and 1.34 for the L_4/L_5 and L_5/L_6 comparisons. We noted earlier, however, that the sample of business students were not likely to be as familiar with rates of managerial compensation as were the compensation administrators, yet responses of the two samples were reasonably close together. Rather than inferring that survey responses reflect corporate compensation practices, it appears more reasonable to infer that corporate compensation practices are reflective of social perceptions of differences in rank and that corporate compensation differentials evolve to a structure of relationships consistent with social norms of rank differentials.

Another possible explanation of the evidence concerns dimensions of job content which might be inferred from organizational hierarchy, all observers inferring the same dimensions of job content (e.g., time span of discretion) from hierarchical relationships and basing judgments of appropriate compensation upon these inferred differences in job content. Job evaluation practices, for example, attempt to measure dimensions of job content and base compensation differentials upon difference in job content. The only apparent positional characteristics other than hierarchical level in the surveys of students and compensation administrators could not account for the differentials in appropriate compensation, and this explanation would have to assume other, unknown dimensions of job content as the basis for judging worth, dimensions which could be inferred only from hierarchical level. In order to explain the observed differentials in appropriate compensation, equivalent differentials of some unknown dimension of job content must have been inferred from hierarchical level, an argument supportive again of the general distance relationship concept. Equal proportional differences of whatever dimension is employed are required to appropriately distinguish between adjacent levels in the managerial hierarchy.

The evidence presented here is more relevant to the development of a general theory of hierarchical order than to the determination of compensation of corporate executives. That evidence suggests that organization level hierarchies imply clear distinctions of worth among the different levels of the hierarchy, distinctions of approximately 33 percent measured on a continuous scale of monetary compensation. Lesser differentials (e.g., 10 percent) appear inadequate to distinguish between adjacent levels and greater differ entials (e.g., 70 percent) are suggestive of distinctions greater than one level. The scale appropriate for distinguishing among organizational positions on dimensions other than hierarchical level (e.g., subordinates supervised) is different and inadequate to account for the differentials associated with organization level. Organization level of a position, whatever it connotes regarding position content, clearly is a significant influence of the worth or status of positions in organizations.

REFERENCES

Champlin, Fred. "An Analysis of the Effects of Organizational Structure on Perceptions of Appropriate Pay." Unpublished paper, University of Minnesota, 1976.

Fox, Harland. *Top Executive Compensation.* New York: National Industrial Conference Board, 1966.

Hinrichs, John. "Correlates of Employee Evalua-

tions of Pay Increases." *Journal of Applied Psychology* 53 (1969), 481-89.

Jaques, Elliott. "Preliminary Sketch of a General Structure of Executive Strata," in *Glacier Project Papers*, ed. Wilfred Brown and Elliott Jaques. London: Heinemann, 1965.

Kuethe, James L. and Levenson, Bernard. "Conceptions of Organizational Worth." *The American Journal of Sociology*, (November 1964), 342-48.

Lindberg, Charles A. "An Empirical Study of the Influence of Structural Variables on Conceptions of Position Worth." Unpublished paper, University of Minnesota, 1975.

Mahoney, Thomas A., and Weitzel, William. "Secrecy and Managerial Compensation." *Industrial Relations* 17 (1978), 245-51.

Patton, Arch. "Current Practices in Executive Compensation." *Harvard Business Review* 29 (1951), pp. 56-64.

Simon, Herbert A. "The Compensation of Executives." *Sociometry* 20 (1957), pp. 32-35.

Torgerson, Warren S. *Theory and Methods of Scaling.* New York: John Wiley & Sons, 1958.

Commentary

The preceding essays addressed the phenomenon of wage structuring within an organization from quite different vantage points. Each author considered wage structuring and wage differentials as important issues for consideration, but none related these issues to employee behavior or dimensions of labor supply in any clear, direct fashion. All related wage structuring to judgments of equity, but did not relate these judgments of equity to employee behaviors. Most considered equity judgments of wage structures within the context of the internal labor market rather than the external labor market suggesting inferentially that considerations of wage structure are of more relevance to existing employees than to prospective employees. Consistent with the internal labor market model, it would appear that wage level of the employing organization is more relevant in the attraction of labor supplies than is the structure of wages within the organization. Wage structure influences dimensions of labor supply other than the attraction of prospective employees.

These essays viewed equity and inequity as post hoc evaluations rather than as anticipations; equity and inequity are experienced rather than anticipated. They also indicated that judgments of inequity are disturbing and arouse the individual to seek change of, or escape from, the conditions viewed as inequitable; no such action orientations are associated with conditions of equity which are pleasurable. Equity comparisons were not developed as criteria for choice among alternative actions (an anticipatory model), rather, they were developed in explanation of reactions to experienced conditions. In this context, perceived inequity can be viewed as an arousal element in the total motivational process, arousing individuals to the desirability of change rather than as the criterion for choice among alternatives. Inequity is an energizing element in motivating a desire for change to escape the inequity conditions, but perceived inequity does not direct choices among alternative actions. A variety of actions including seeking transfer or promotion, absenteeism, protesting the inequitable conditions, and termination might alleviate the inequity experienced by the individual and choice among these alternatives involves some sort of expectancy model. This distinction between concepts of equity and choice parallels the distinction between concepts of satisfaction and choice made by March and Simon in Chapter 2; dissatisfaction and inequity arouse individuals to seek alternatives, but choices are made among the best alternatives, none of which may result in equity or satisfaction. Perceptions of equity and satisfaction emerge from this examination as equilibrium or stabilizing conditions, conditions necessary in the maintenance of labor supplies although not particularly motivating in the attraction of labor supplies.

Labor supply to the organization is composed of various components including the attraction of individuals to the organization (the decision to join) and the maintenance of the work force through avoidance of turnover (the decision to leave). The discussions in this chapter and in Chapter 8 suggest that the decision to join and the decision to leave an organization are distinctly different, that the decision to join is essentially selection of the most favorable alternative available, while the decision to leave often is more a rejection of the situation than attraction to an alternative. The decision to join an organization also tends to be more a function of readily comparable characteristics of the employment exchange such as wage level and opportunities for employment, while the decision to leave tends to be more a function of perceived equity of specific employment exchanges within the internal labor market. Admittedly the two decisions are interrelated as evidenced by the observation that voluntary turnover rates vary directly with opportunities for alternative employment expressed in relatively low unemployment rates; individuals are less likely to decide to leave an organization if opportunities to join other organizations are relatively meager. Equity considerations presumably determine the inclination of individuals to seek alternatives, while actual termination is influenced also by perceptions of the probability of finding improved alternatives. While equity judgments may reflect a variety of job characteristics, wage structure considerations probably predominate in equity judgments, wage structure being judged relative to comparable structures of status, skill, responsibility, and related job characteristics.

The elements of wage structure, wage rates associated with different jobs in the organization, also provide direction in the allocation of labor services among jobs. Just as wage level characterizes the inducements to join the organization, so wage rate characterizes the inducements to accept specific job assignments within the organization. Wage level, in this context, characterizes membership pay, payments for belonging to the organization, and wage rate characterizes job pay. Descriptions of internal labor market structures in this chapter suggest that career paths within the organization are relatively structured and that individuals exercise relatively little choice among job assignments other than possible rejection of an assignment. Thus it is more important that the structure of job wage rates conform equitably with employee perceptions of job and career structures in order to obtain acceptance of job assignments than it is for wage rates to provide incentives to seek specific job assignments. Equity of job wage rates within the wage structure is a necessary condition for securing acceptance of job assignments and the allocation of labor services but, given the structured practices of the internal labor market, it is not critical to the direction and motivation of choice. Individuals typically are assigned to specific jobs within the internal labor market and perceived equity of the wage structure is important in securing acceptance of these assignments and thus maintaining desired supplies of labor services for individual jobs.

With the exception of Jaques' hypothesis, the discussions of wage structure and equitable payment did not advance any specific criteria for judging the equity of wage structure, particularly the structure of wages for non-managerial jobs. Rather, Livernash, Adams, and Mahoney indicated that judgments of equity are based upon social norms, norms which are subject to change over time as values and attitudes change, but which can take the form of tradition. Tradition, reflective of wage differentials which persist over time, would appear to be an important influence in the legitimizing of a wage structure and in the determination of equitable relationships. Comparison of the single rate wage structure in the brewing industry with the relatively minute wage differentials observed among jobs in other industries testifies to the role of social norms and tradition in determination of the norms of equity; a wage structure judged equitable in one industry setting would be rejected as unfair in another industry setting. The real test of job evaluation, as noted by Livernash, is the acceptability of the resulting wage structure, not the content and weighting of the factors or dimensions employed. This is not to argue, however, that the content and weighting of job evaluation factors can be approached whimsically; the face validity of the job evaluation approach may be critical in establishing acceptability of the wage structure and, over time, may contribute to the development of social norms within the work force for the judgment of the equity of the wage structure. The key test of any system of wage structuring is the acceptability or equity of the resulting structure to those affected by the structure. Lacking any clear criterion of equity of outcomes, the equity of outcomes often is inferred from judgments of equity of the decision-making process, the specific criteria employed and the degree of participation or representation of those affected by the decisions. Employee participation in the design and administration of any system of job evaluation can be expected to enhance the acceptability of the resulting wage structure. The process of job evaluation can serve to establish, reinforce and legitimize custom and tradition as determinants of an equitable wage structure.

CHAPTER 7
TASK PERFORMANCE, MOTIVATION, AND COMPENSATION

T ask performance constitutes a third dimension or aspect of the supply of labor services. The first dimension considered was the supply of individuals seeking employment in the organization, the attraction of individuals to the organization and their decisions to join. Choice models of individual decision making were analysed as a basis for understanding and influencing individual behaviors in seeking out and accepting employment or membership in the organization. Our analysis in previous chapters suggests that individuals are attracted to employing organizations, not to specific jobs in the organizations which tend to be staffed through internal labor market processes. The attraction to and decision to join an organization thus is based upon an overall characterization of employment opportunities with the organization, rather than characteristics of specific jobs other than entry or hiring jobs. Wage level was proposed as the most relevant overall characterization of compensation inducements in the attraction of labor services. Wage level characterizes "membership pay" or compensation inducements for accepting employment in the organization. The labor force attached to an employing organization also is a function of maintenance of membership. Employee turnover or decisions to leave the organization were considered to be distinctly different from decisions to join; they reflect rejection of the organization more than attraction to another organization and, as such, probably are influenced more by considerations of inequity in the internal wage structure than by considerations of wage level.

A second dimension of supply of labor services relates to the staffing of individual jobs within the organization. Staffing assignments within the internal labor market are primarily a function of managerial decisions rather than individual applications and choices. Individuals may reject or seek to avoid assignments they dislike, but are limited in opportunities to seek out desired opportunities. The compensation characteristics important in the allocation of individuals among job assignments relate to "job pay" or wage rates for different jobs reflected in the wage structure, the compensation inducements related to specific jobs.

Task performance, the third dimension of supply of labor services, relates to the specific behaviors of an individual within a job assignment. The personal behaviors of concern are those likely to vary among individuals within a single job, behaviors such as compliance with directives, diligence of performance, absenteeism, and level of effort expended on the job. Just as these desired contributions are more specific than those considered in the concept of the employment exchange relevant in joining the organization, so too the related inducements also are more specific and relate to "person pay," the variations in compensation related to individual behaviors. The first section of this chapter examines alternative models of motivation as applied to task performance, and the second section examines specific issues in the compensation of task performance.

A: Motivation of task performance

The concept of motivation, although used in everyday discussions, is relatively complex and abstract. Motivation is a construct inferred from observable behavior, but never itself observed; it is a construct we employ as a cause in the explanation of observed behavior. In general, our conceptualization of motivation refers to an emotional state which serves to arouse and energize, direct, and maintain behavior. Many theories or models of motivation exist, some directed toward explanation of social behavior and others directed toward explanation of learning, child development, and physiological response behaviors; only a relatively few of these are directly relevant to our examination of work behaviors and need concern us here. Additionally, some motivation theories address principally issues of arousal (equity theories) while other theories are more concerned with decision making and choice (Smith, Vroom), and still others concentrate upon issues of developing and maintaining behavior patterns. Decisions to work or not work, occupational choices, decisions to accept employment and to terminate employment are easily conceptualized as decision making or choice behaviors. The motivation models examined earlier relate most clearly to these behaviors. There are other relevant work behaviors which are not as clearly conceptualized as choice behaviors, behaviors such as level of effort expended on the task, care and concentration upon task performance, and degree of observance of work rules. Motivation models relevant to these behaviors are reviewed in this section.

Theories of motivation or motivated work behavior typically fit either of two general classes, process theories or content theories. Process theories of work motivation address the basic question "*how* is work behavior motivated?" while content theories address the question "*what* motivates work behavior?" Process models attempt to explain the sequence of causal influences upon work behavior, the sequential stages of development terminating in a behavior of interest. The earlier essays by Rottenberg, Vroom and Adams exemplify analyses of the process of motivation, each specified a general model applicable regardless of the specific motivational content elements relevant to an individual. Content theories attempt to explain the substantive nature of motivating influences and are exemplified by Smith's detailing of employment characteristics of interest to individuals, Vroom's examination of the motivational bases of work, and Jaques' hypothesis specifying time-span of discretion as the critical element in judgments of equitable compensation. The motivation theories examined in this chapter tend to focus upon the process of motivation rather than the content elements in motivation.

Two theories often applied in the analysis of the process of motivation of work behavior are (1) the reinforcement or conditioning theory, and (2) the expectancy theory. Reinforcement or conditioning theory is analyzed in Essay 7–1 by Hamner, and expectancy theory is analyzed in Essay 7–2 from Lawler. Reinforcement theory views behavior as a function of learned or conditioned associations between stimulus, behavior, and consequences. An individual experiences reward or punishment associated with specific behaviors performed in specified situations leading over time to extinction of the punished behavior and repetition of the rewarded behavior. Thus individuals are discouraged from smoking in specified work areas through disciplinary punishment, and encouraged to submit suggestions through the awarding of prizes. Behavior at any point in time is a function of associations experienced in the past, and future behavior can be modified through change in the associations of stimulus, behavior, and consequences. Considerable research has been directed toward the discovery of the behavioral implications of different reward schedules or contingencies between behavior and consequences; Hamner reviews the results of this research and suggests implications for managerial practice including compensation administration.

The expectancy theory of motivation was presented earlier in an essay by Vroom; the selection from Lawler elaborates upon that model and applies it in the analysis of more specific work behaviors. Lawler compares expectancy theory with reinforcement theory and notes that while both support similar predictions about behavior, they differ in the explanation of this behavior and thus differ in suggestions of how to modify behavior. He notes, for example, that expectancy theory is cognitive in orientation and that behavior results from decisions made on the basis of anticipated consequences, anticipations derived from many sources other than past experience. Lawler also develops a concept of instrumental outcomes, an outcome with no intrinsic valence but which is attributed valence based upon the valence of associated ultimate outcomes and the expectancies of achieving these ultimate outcomes with the instrumental outcome. Thus, for example, compensation is attributed valence based upon the valence of other outcomes such as status, consumer goods, or a child's education, and the expectancy of attaining these outcomes through compensation. Compensation, in this context, is analogous to, but distinctly different from, the concept of conditioned reinforcer in the reinforcement model; the valence attributed to compensation in the expectancy model is a function of cognitive analysis rather than mere conditioning.

The reinforcement and expectancy theories share many elements in common, yet differ in several significant aspects. Note both the commonalities in these models as well as differences, and speculate regarding those behaviors and situations where each model appears to provide a more relevant explanation. We return to a comparative examination of the models following the essays.

Finally, Essay 7–3 from Locke focuses upon a specific element in the motivation of work behavior, the role of intentions or goals. Although not cast in terms of expectancy theory, Locke's analysis complements the treatment of expectancy theory by Lawler. As in expectancy theory, Locke's model emphasizes the role of cognition and anticipations in motivation. Locke does not consider how individuals establish goals or intentions, but does argue that individuals consciously specify goals which then influence both the level and direction of consequent behavior. Goals, in this analysis, influence behavior independently of anticipated outcomes. In this context, desire for achievement serves in the motivation of behavior; given commitment to a goal, individual performance varies with the level of effort required to achieve the goal.

Essay 7-1

Reinforcement theory and contingency management in organizational settings*

W. Clay Hamner

TWO BASIC LEARNING PROCESSES

Before discussing in any detail exactly how the general laws or principles of reinforcement can be used to predict and influence behavior, we must differentiate between two types of behavior. One kind is known as *voluntary* or *operant* behavior, and the other is known as *reflex* or *respondent* behavior. Respondent behavior takes in all responses of human being that are *elicited* by special stimulus changes in the environment. An example would be when a person turns a light on in a dark room (stimulus change), his eyes contract (respondent behavior).

Operant behavior includes an even greater amount of human activity. It takes in all the responses of a person that may at some time be said to have an effect upon or do something to the person's outside world (Keller, 1969). Operant behavior *operates* on this world either directly or indirectly. For example, when a person presses the up button at the elevator entrance to "call" the elevator, he is operating on his environment.

Operant conditioning[1]

The basic distinction between classical and operant conditioning procedures is in terms of the *consequences* of the conditioned response. In classical conditioning, the sequence of events is independent of the subject's behavior. In operant conditioning, consequences (rewards and punishments) are made to occur as a consequence of the subject's response or failure to respond. The distinction between these two methods is shown in Figure 1.

In Figure 1, we see that classical conditioning involves a three stage process. In the diagram, let S refer to *stimulus* and R to *response*. We see that in stage 1, the unconditioned stimulus (food) elicits an unconditioned response (salivation). In stage 2, a neutral stimulus (bell) elicits no known response. However, in stage 3, after the ringing of the bell is repeatedly

[1] Operant conditioning is also known as instrumental conditioning and Skinnerian conditioning.

Figure 1: Classical versus operant conditioning

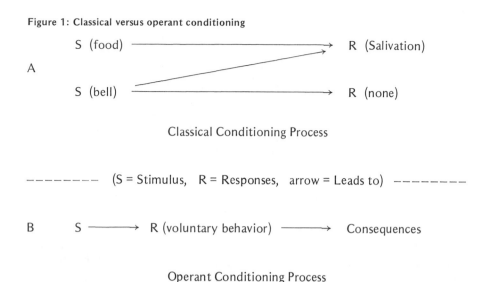

S (food) ————————————————→ R (Salivation)

A

S (bell) ————————————————→ R (none)

Classical Conditioning Process

———————— (S = Stimulus,   R = Responses,   arrow = Leads to)   ————————

B   S ————→ R (voluntary behavior) ————→ Consequences

Operant Conditioning Process

paired with the presence of food, the bell alone becomes a conditioned stimulus and elicits a conditioned response (salivation). The subject has no control over the unconditioned or conditioned response, but is "at the mercy" of his environment and his past conditioning history.

Note however, that for voluntary behavior, the consequence is dependent on the behavior of the individual in a given stimulus setting. Such behavior can be said to "operate" (Skinner, 1969) on the environment, in contrast to behavior which is "respondent" to prior eliciting stimuli (Michael and Meyerson, 1962). Reinforcement is not given every time the stimulus is presented, but is *only* given when the correct response is made. For example, if an employee taking a work break, puts a penny (R) in the soft drink machine (S), nothing happens (consequence). However, if he puts a quarter (R) in the machine (S), he gets the soft drink (consequence). In other words, the employee's behavior is *instrumental* in determining the consequences which accrue to him.

The interrelationships between the three components of (1) *stimulus* or envi-

ronment, (2) *response* or performance, and (3) consequences or *reinforcements* are known as the *contingencies* of reinforcement. Skinner (1969) says "The class of responses upon which a reinforcer is *contingent* is called an operant, to suggest the action on the environment followed by reinforcements" (p. 7). Operant conditioning presupposes that human beings explore their environment and act upon it. This behavior, randomly emitted at first, can be constructed as an operant by making a reinforcement contingent on a response. Any stimulus present when an operant is reinforced acquires control in the sense that the rate of response for that individual will be higher when it is present. "Such a stimulus does not act as a *goad*; it does not elicit the response (as was the case in classical conditioning of reflex behavior)[2] in the sense of forcing it to occur. It is simply an essential aspect of the occasion upon which response is made and reinforced" (Skinner, 1969; p. 7).

Therefore, an adequate formulation of the interaction between an individual and his environment must always specify three

_____
[2] Parentheses added.

things: (1) the occasion upon which a response occurs, (2) the response itself and (3) the reinforcing consequences. Skinner holds that the consequences determine the likelihood that a given operant will be performed in the future. Thus to change behavior, the consequences of the behavior must be changed, i.e., the contingencies must be rearranged (the ways in which the consequences are related to the behavior) (Behling, et al., in press). For Skinner, this behavior generated by a given set of contingencies can be accounted for without appealing to hypothetical inner states (e.g., awareness or expectancies). "If a conspicuous stimulus does not have an effect, it is not because the organism has not attended to it or because some central gatekeeper has screened it out, but because the stimulus plays no important role in the prevailing contingencies" (Skinner, 1969, p. 8).

Arrangement of the contingencies of reinforcement

In order to *understand* and *interpret* behavior, we must look at the interrelationship among the components of the contingencies of behavior. If one expects to influence behavior, he must also be able to manipulate the consequences of the behavior (Skinner, 1969). Haire (1964) reports the importance of being able to manipulate the consequences when he says,

Indeed, whether he is conscious of it or not, the superior is bound to be constantly shaping the behavior of his subordinates by the way in which he utilizes the rewards that are at his disposal, and he will inevitably modify the behavior patterns of his work group thereby. For this reason, it is important to see as clearly as possible what is going on, so that the changes can be planned and chosen in advance, rather than simply accepted after the fact.

After appropriate reinforcers that have sufficient incentive value to maintain stable responsiveness have been chosen,

the contingencies between specific performances and reinforcing stimuli must be arranged (Bandura, 1969). Employers intuitively use rewards in their attempt to modify and influence behavior, but their efforts often produce limited results because the methods are used improperly, inconsistently, or inefficiently. In many instances considerable rewards are bestowed upon the workers, but they are not made conditional or contingent on the behavior the manager wishes to promote. Also, "long delays often intervene between the occurrence of the desired behavior and its intended consequences; special privileges, activities, and rewards are generally furnished according to fixed time schedules rather than performance requirements; and in many cases, positive reinforcers are inadvertently made contingent upon the wrong type of behavior" (Bandura, 1969, pp. 229–30).

As we have said, operant conditioning is the process by which behavior is modified by manipulation of the contingencies of the behavior. To understand how this works, we will first look at various *types* (arrangements) of contingencies, and then at various *schedules* of the contingencies available. Rachlin (1970) described the four basic ways available to the manager of arranging the contingencies—*positive reinforcement, avoidance learning, extinction,* and *punishment*. The difference among these types of contingencies depends on the consequence which results from the behavioral act. Positive reinforcement and avoidance learning are methods of strengthening *desired* behavior, and extinction and punishment are methods of weakening *undesired* behavior.

Positive reinforcement. "A positive reinforcer is a stimulus which, when added to a situation, strengthens the probability of an operant response" (Skinner, 1953, p. 73). The reason it strengthens the response is explained by Thorndike's (1911) Law of Effect. This law states simply that behavior which appears to lead to a positive consequence tends to be repeated, while behavior which appears to lead to a negative consequence tends not to be repeated. A positive consequence is called a reward.

Reinforcers, either positive or negative, are classified as either: (1) unconditioned or primary reinforcers, or (2) conditioned or secondary reinforcers. Primary reinforcers such as food, water, and sex are of biological importance in that they are innately rewarding and have effects which are independent of past experiences. Secondary reinforcers such as job advancement, praise, recognition, and money derive their effects from a consistent pairing with other reinforcers (i.e., they are conditioned). Secondary reinforcement, therefore, depends on the individual and his past reinforcement history. What is rewarding to one person may not be rewarding to another. Managers should look for a reward system which has maximal reinforcing consequences to the group he is supervising.

Regardless of whether the positive reinforcer is primary or secondary in nature, once it has been determined that the consequence has reward value to the worker, it can be used to increase the worker's performance. So the *first step* in the successful application of reinforcement procedures is to select reinforcers that are sufficiently powerful and durable to "maintain responsiveness while complex patterns of behavior are being established and strengthened" (Bandura, 1969, p. 225).

The *second step* is to design the contingencies in such a way that the reinforcing events are made contingent upon the desired behavior. This is the rule of reinforcement which is most often violated. Rewards must result from performance, and the greater the degree of performance by an employee, the greater should be his reward. Money as a reinforcer will be discussed later, but it should be noted that money is not the only reward available. In fact, for unionized employees, the supervisor has virtually no way to tie money to performance. Nevertheless, other forms of rewards, such as recognition, promotion, and job assignments, can be made contingent on good performance. Unless a manager is willing to discriminate between employees based on their level of performance, the effectiveness of his power over the employee is nil.

The arrangement of positive reinforcement contingencies can be pictured as follows:

$$\text{Stimulus} \rightarrow \begin{array}{c}\text{Desired} \\ \text{response}\end{array} \rightarrow \begin{array}{c}\text{Positive} \\ \text{consequences}\end{array}$$

$$(S \rightarrow R \rightarrow R^+)$$

The stimulus is the work environment which leads to a response (some level of performance). If this response leads to positive consequences, then the probability of that response being emitted again increases (Law of Effect). Now, if the behavior is undesired, then the supervisor is conditioning or teaching the employee that undesired behavior will lead to a desired reward. It is important therefore that the reward administered be equal to the performance input of the employee. Homans (1950) labels this as the rule of distributive justice and stated that this reciprocal norm applies in both formal (work) and informal (friendship) relationships. In other words, the employee *exchanges* his services for the rewards of the organization. In order to maintain desired performance, it is important that the manager design the reward system so that the level of reward administered is proportionately contingent on the level of performance emitted.

The *third step* is to design the contingencies in such a way that a reliable procedure for eliciting or inducing the desired response patterns is established; otherwise, if they never occur there will be few opportunities to influence the desired behavior through contingent management. If the behavior that a manager wishes to strengthen is already present, and occurs with some frequency, then contingent applications of incentives can, from the outset, increase and maintain the desired performance patterns at a high level. However, as Bandura (1969) states, "When the initial level of the desired behavior is extremely low, if the criterion for reinforcement is initially set too high, most, if not all, of the person's responses go unrewarded, so that his efforts are gradually extinguished and his motivation diminished" (p. 232).

The nature of the learning process is such that acquiring the new response patterns can be easily established. The principle of operant conditioning says that an operant followed by a positive reinforcement is more likely to occur under similar conditions in the future. Through the process of *generalization*, the more nearly alike the new situation or simulus is to the original one, the more the old behavior is likely to be emitted in the new environment. For example, if you contract with an electrician to rewire your house, he is able to bring with him enough old behavioral patterns which he generalized to this unfamiliar, but similar, stimulus setting (the house) in order to accomplish the task. He has learned through his past reinforcement history that, when in a new environment, one way to speed up the correct behavior needed to obtain reward is to generalize from similar settings with which he has had experience. Perhaps one reason an employer wants a person with work experience is because the probability of that person emitting the correct behavior is greater and thus the job of managing that person simplified.

Avoidance learning. The second type of contingency arrangement available to the manager is called escape, or avoidance learning. Just as with positive reinforcement, this is a method of strengthening desired behavior. A contingency arrangement in which an individual's performance can terminate an already noxious

stimulus is called *escape learning.* When behavior can prevent the onset of a noxious stimulus the procedure is called *avoidance learning.* In both cases, the result is the development and maintenance of the desired operant behavior (Michael and Meyerson, 1962).

An example of this kind of control can be easily found in a work environment. Punctuality of employees is often maintained by avoidance learning. The noxious stimulus is the criticism by the shop steward or office manager for being late. In order to avoid criticism other employees make a special effort to come to work on time. A supervisor begins criticizing a worker for "goofing off." Other workers may intensify their efforts to escape the criticism of the supervisor.

The arrangement of an escape reinforcement contingency can be diagrammed as follows:

| Noxious stimulus | $\rightarrow$ | Desired response | $\rightarrow$ | Removal of noxious stimulus |

$$(S^- \rightarrow R \not\Rightarrow S^-)$$

The distinction between the process of strengthening behavior by means of positive reinforcement techniques and avoidance learning techniques should be noted carefully. In one case, the individual works hard to gain the consequences from the environment which result from good work, and in the second case, the individual works hard to avoid the noxious aspects of the environment itself. In both cases the same behavior is strengthened.

While Skinner (1953) recognizes that avoidance learning techniques can be used to condition desired behavior, he does not advocate their use. Instead a Skinnerian approach to operant conditioning is primarily based on the principles of positive reinforcement.

Extinction. While positive reinforcement and avoidance learning techniques can be used by managers to strengthen desired behavior, extinction and punishment techniques are methods available to managers for reducing undesired behavior. When positive reinforcement for a learned or previously conditioned response is withheld, individuals will continue to exhibit that behavior for an extended period of time. Under repeated nonreinforcement, the behavior decreases and eventually disappears. This decline in response rate as a result of nonrewarded repetition of a task is defined as *extinction*.

The diagram of the arrangement of the contingency of extinction can be shown as follows:

(1) Stimulus → Response → Positive consequences

$$(S \to R \to R^+)$$

(2) Stimulus → Response → Withholding of positive consequences

$$(S \to R \to R^+)$$

(3) Stimulus → Withholding of response

$$(S \not\to R)$$

The behavior which was previously reinforced because *(a)* it was desired or *(b)* by poor reinforcement practices is no longer desired. To extinguish this behavior in a naturally recurring situation, response patterns substained by positive reinforcement (Stage 1) are frequently eliminated (Stage 3) by discontinuing the rewards (Stage 2) that ordinarily produce the behavior. This method when combined with a positive reinforcement method is the procedure of behavior modification recommended by Skinner (1953). It leads to the least negative side effects and when the two methods are used together, it allows the employee to get the rewards he desires and allows the organization to eliminate the undesired behavior.

Punishment. A second method of reducing the frequency of undesired behavior is through the use of punishment. Punishment is the most controversial method of behavior modification, and most of the ethical questions about operant methods of control center around this technique. "One of the principal objections to aversive control stems from the widespread belief that internal, and often unconscious, forces are the major determinant of behavior. From this perspective, punishment may temporarily suppress certain expressions, but the underlying impulses retain their strength and press continuously for discharge through alternative actions" (Bandura, 1969, p. 292). While Skinner (1953) discounts the internal state hypothesis, he recommends that extinction rather than punishment be used to decrease the probability of the occurrence of a particular behavior.

Punishment is defined as presenting an aversive or noxious consequence contingent upon a response, or removing a positive consequence contingent upon a response. Based on the Law of Effect, as rewards strengthen behavior, punishment weakens it. This process can be shown as follows:

(1) Stimulus → Undesired behavior → Noxious consequence or withholding of positive consequence

$$(S \to R \to R^-)$$
$$(\quad \text{or} \not\to R^+)$$

(2) Stimulus $\not\to$ Undesired behavior

$$(S \not\to R)$$

Notice carefully the difference in the withholding of rewards in the punishment process and the withholding of rewards in the extinction process. In the extinction process, we withhold rewards for behavior that has previously been administered the rewards because the behavior was desired. In punishment, we withhold a reward because the behavior is undesired, has never been associated with the reward before, and is in fact a noxious consequence.

The use of aversive control is frequently questioned on the assumption that it produces undesirable by-products. In many cases this concern is warranted. Bandura (1969) states that it depends on the circumstances and on the past reinforcement history of the reinforcement agent and the reinforcement target as to whether punishment or extinction should be used. He says:

Many of the unfavorable effects, however, that are sometimes associated with punishment are not necessarily inherent in the methods themselves but result from the faulty manner in which they are applied. A great deal of human behavior is, in fact, modified and closely regulated by natural aversive contingencies without any ill effects. On the basis of negative consequences people learn to avoid or to protect themselves against hazardous falls, flaming or scalding objects, deafening sounds, and other hurtful stimuli. . . . In instances where certain activities can have injurious effects, aversive contingencies *must* be socially arranged to ensure survival. Punishment is rarely indicted for ineffectiveness or deleterious side effects when used, for example, to teach young children not to insert metal objects into electrical outlets, not to cross busy thoroughfares. . . . Certain types of negative sanctions, if applied considerately, can likewise aid in eliminating self-defeating and socially detrimental behavior without creating any special problems (p. 294).

An argument for positive reinforcement

Most workers enter the work place willingly if not eagerly. They have a sense of right and wrong and have been thoroughly conditioned by their parents and by society. By the time they reach adulthood, it can be assumed that they are mature. For these reasons, it is argued here as well as by others (Skinner, 1953; Wiard, 1972), that the only tool needed for worker motivation is the presence or absence of positive reinforcement. In other words, managers do not, as a general rule, need to use avoidance learning or punishment techniques in order to control behavior.

Whyte (1972) says "positive reinforcers generally are more effective than negative reinforcers in the production and maintenance of behavior" (p. 67). Wiard (1972) points out, "There may be cases where the use of punishment has resulted in improved performance, but they are few and far between. The pitfalls of punishment can be encountered with any indirect approach" (p. 16). However, a positive reinforcement program is geared toward the desired results. It emphasizes what needs to be done, rather than what should not be done. A positive reinforcement program is result oriented, rather than process oriented. A well designed program encourages individual growth and freedom, whereas negative approach (avoidance learning and punishment) encourages immaturity in the individual and therefore eventually in the organization itself.

Schedules of positive reinforcement

The previous discussion was primarily concerned with methods of arranging the contingencies of reinforcement in order to modify behavior. Two major points were discussed. First, some type of reinforcement is necessary in order to produce a change in behavior. Second, a combined program of positive reinforcement and extinction are more effective for use in organizations than are programs using punishment and/or avoidance learning techniques. The previous discussion thus tells what causes behavior and why it is important information for the manager, but it does not discuss the several important issues dealing with the scheduling or administering of positive reinforcement.

According to Costello and Zalkind (1963), "The speed with which learning takes place and also how lasting its effects will be is determined by the timing of reinforcement" (p. 193). In other words, the effectiveness of reinforcement varies as a function of the schedule of its administration. A reinforcement schedule is a more-or-less formal specification of the occurrence of a reinforcer in relation to the behavioral sequence to be conditioned, and effectiveness of the reinforcer depends as much upon its scheduling as upon any of its other features (magnitude, quality and degree of association with the behavioral act) (Adam and Scott, 1971).

There are many conceivable arrangements of a positive reinforcement schedule which managers can use to reward their workers (Ferster and Skinner, 1957). Aldis (1961) identifies two basic types of schedules which have the most promise concerning possible worker motivation. These schedules are *continuous* and *partial reinforcement* schedules.

Continuous reinforcement schedule. Under this schedule, every time the correct operant is emitted by the worker, it is followed by a reinforcer. With this schedule, behavior increases very rapidly but when the reinforcer is removed (extinction) performance decreases rapidly. For this reason it is not recommended for use by the manager over a long period of time. It is also difficult or impossible for a manager to reward the employee continuously for emitting desired behavior. Therefore a manager should generally consider using one or more of the partial reinforcement schedules when he administers both financial and nonfinancial rewards.

Partial reinforcement schedules. Partial reinforcement, where reinforcement does not occur after every correct operant, leads to slower learning but stronger retention of a response than total or continuous reinforcement. "In other words, *learning* is more permanent when we reward correct behavior only part of the time" (Bass and Vaughan, 1966, p. 20). This factor is extremely relevant to the observed strong resistance to changes in attitudes, values, norms, and the like.

Ferster and Skinner (1957) have described four basic types of partial reinforcement schedules for operant learning situations. They are:

1. *Fixed interval schedule.* Under this schedule a reinforcer is administered only when the desired response occurs after the passage of a specified period of time since the previous reinforcement. Thus a worker paid on a weekly basis would receive a full paycheck every Friday, assuming that the worker was performing minimally acceptable behavior. This method offers the least motivation for hard work among employees (Aldis, 1961). The kind of behavior often observed with fixed-interval schedules is a pause after reinforcement and then an increase in rate of responding until a high rate of performance occurs just as the interval is about to end. Suppose the plant manager visits the shipping department each day at approximately 10:00 a.m. This fixed schedule of supervisory recognition will probably cause performance to be at its highest just prior to the plant manager's visit and then performance will probably steadily decline thereafter and not reach its peak again until the next morning's visit.

2. *Variable interval schedule.* Under this schedule, reinforcement is administered at some variable interval of time around some average. This schedule is not recommended for use with a pay plan (Aldis, 1961), but it is an ideal method to use for administering praise, promotions, and supervisory visits. Since the reinforcers are dispensed unpredictably, variable schedules generate higher rates of response and more stable and consistent performance (Bandura, 1969). Suppose our plant manager visits the shipping department on an *average* of once a day but at randomly selected time intervals, i.e., twice on Monday, once on Tuesday, not on Wednesday, not on Thursday, and twice on Friday, all at different times during the day. Performance will be higher and have

less fluctuation than under the fixed interval schedule.

3. *Fixed ratio schedule.* Here a reward is delivered only when a fixed number of desired responses take place. This is essentially the piece-work schedule for pay. The response level here is significantly higher than that obtained under any of the interval (or time-based) schedules.

4. *Variable ratio schedule.* Under this schedule, a reward is delivered only after a number of desired responses with the number of desired responses changing from the occurrence of one reinforcer to the next, around an average. Thus a person working on a 15 to 1 variable ratio schedule might receive reinforcement after 10 responses, then 20 responses, then 15 responses, etc., to an average of one reinforcer per 15 responses. Gambling is an example of a variable ratio reward schedule. Research evidence reveals that of all the variations in scheduling procedures available, this is the most powerful in sustaining behavior (Jablonsky and DeVries, 1972). In industry, this plan would be impossible to use as the only plan for scheduling reinforcement. However, Aldis (1961) suggests how this method could be used to supplement other monetary reward schedules:

Take the annual Christmas bonus as an example. In many instances, this "surprise" gift has become nothing more than a ritualized annual salary supplement which everybody expects. Therefore, its incentive-building value is largely lost. Now suppose that the total bonus were distributed at irregular intervals throughout the year and in small sums dependent upon the amount of work done. Wouldn't the workers find their urge to work increased? (p. 63).

An important point to remember is that to be effective a schedule should always include the specification of a contingency between the behavior desired and the occurrence of a reinforcer. In many cases it may be necessary to use each of the various schedules for administering

rewards—for example, base pay on a fixed interval schedule, promotions and raises on a variable interval schedule, recognition of above average performance with a piece-rate plan (fixed ratio) and supplementary bonuses on a variable ratio schedule. The effect of each of the types of reinforcement schedules and the various methods of arranging reinforcement contingencies on worker performance is summarized in Table 1.

The necessity for arranging appropriate reinforcement contingencies is dramatically illustrated by several studies in which rewards were shifted from a response-contingent (ratio) to a time-contingent basis (interval). During the period in which rewards were made conditional upon occurrence of the desired behavior, the appropriate response patterns were exhibited at a consistently high level. When the same rewards were given based on time and independent of the worker's behavior, there was a marked drop in the desired behavior. The reinstatement of the performance-contingent reward schedule promptly restored the high level of responsiveness (Lovaas, Berberich, Perloff, and Schaeffer, 1966; Baer, Peterson, and Sherman, 1967). Similar declines in performance were obtained when workers were provided rewards in advance without performance requirements (Ayllon and Azrin, 1965; Bandura and Perloff, 1967).

Aldis (1961) encourages businessmen to recognize the importance of a positive reinforcement program. He also says that experimentation with various schedules of positive reinforcement is the key to reducing job boredom and increasing worker satisfaction. He concludes:

Most of us fully realize that a large proportion of all workers hold jobs that are boring and repetitive and that these employees are motivated to work not by positive rewards but by various oblique forms of threat. . . . The challenge is to motivate men by positive rewards rather than by negative punishments or threats of punishments. . . . Businessmen should recog-

Table 1: Operant conditioning summary

Arrangement of reinforcement contingencies	Schedule of reinforcement contingencies	Effect on behavior when applied to the individual	Effect on behavior when removed from the individual
	Continuous reinforcement	Fastest method to establish a new behavior.	Fastest method to extinguish a new behavior.
	Partial reinforcement	Slowest method to establish a new behavior.	Slowest method to extinguish a new behavior.
	Variable partial reinforcement	More consistent response frequencies.	Slower extinction rate.
	Fixed partial reinforcement	Less consistent response frequencies.	Faster extinction rate.
Positive reinforcement		Increased frequency over preconditioning level.	Return to preconditioning level.
Avoidance reinforcement			
Punishment		Decreased frequency over preconditioning level.	Return to preconditioning level.
Extinction			

Adapted from Behling et al., reprinted with permission of the author from "Present Theories and New Directions in Theories of Work Effort," *Journal Supplement and Abstract Service* of the American Psychological Corporation.

nize how much their conventional wage and salary systems essentially rely on negative reinforcement.

Thus the promise of newer methods of wage payments which rely on more immediate rewards, on piece-rate pay, and greater randomization does not lie only in the increase in productivity that might follow. The greater promise is that such experiments may lead to happier workers as well (p. 63).

REFERENCES

Adam, E. E., and Scott, W. E. "The Application of Behavioral Conditioning Procedures to the Problems of Quality Control." *Academy of Management Journal* 14 (1971), 175-93.

Aldis, O. "Of Pigeons and Men." *Harvard Business Review* 39 (1961), 59-63.

Ayllon, T., and Azrin, N. H. "The Measurement and Reinforcement of Behavior of Psychotics." *Journal of the Experimental Analysis of Behavior* 8 (1965), 357-83.

Baer, D. M.; Peterson, R. F.; and Sherman, J. A. "The Development of Imitation by Reinforcing Behavioral Similarity to a Model." *Journal of the Experimental Analysis of Behavior* 10 (1967), 405-16.

Bandura, A., and Perloff, B. "The Efficacy of Self-Monitoring Reinforcement Systems." *Journal of Personality and Social Psychology* 7 (1967), 111-16.

Bandura, A. *Principles of Behavior Modification.* New York: Holt, Rinehart and Winston, Inc., 1969.

Bass, B. M., and Vaughan, J. A. *Training in Industry: The Management of Learning.* Belmont, Calif.: Wadsworth Publishing Company, 1966.

Behling, O.; Schriesheim, C.; and Tolliver, J. "Present Theories and New Directions in Theories of Work Effort." *Journal Supplement Abstract Service* of the American Psychological Corporation, in press.

Costello, T. W., and Zalkind, S. S. *Psychology in Administration.* Englewood Cliffs, N.J.: Prentice-Hall, Inc., 1963.

Ferster, C. B., and Skinner, B. F. *Schedules of Reinforcement.* New York: Appleton-Century-Crofts, 1957.

Haire, Mason. *Psychology in Management,* 2d ed. New York: McGraw-Hill, 1964.

Homans, G. C. *The Human Group*. New York: Harcourt, Brace, 1950.

Jablonsky, S., and DeVries, D. "Operant Conditioning Principles Extrapolated to the Theory of Management." *Organizational Behavior and Human Performance* 7 (1972), 340-58.

Keller, F. S. *Learning: Reinforcement Theory*. New York: Random House, 1969.

Lovaas, O. I.; Berberich, J. P.; Perloff, B. F.; and Schaeffer, B. "Acquisition of Imitative Speech for Schizophrenic Children." *Science* 151 (1966), 705-07.

Michael, J., and Meyerson, L. "A Behavioral Approach to Counseling and Guidance." *Harvard Educational Review* 32 (1962), 382-402.

Rachlin, H. *Modern Behaviorism*. New York: W. H. Freeman and Co., 1970.

Skinner, B. F. *Science and Human Behavior*. New York: The Macmillan Company, 1953.

Skinner, B. F. *Contingencies of Reinforcement*. New York: Appleton-Century-Crofts, 1969.

Thorndike, E. L. *Animal Intelligence*. New York: Macmillan, 1911.

Wiard, H. "Why Manage Behavior? A Case for Positive Reinforcement." *Human Resource Management* (Summer 1972), 15-20.

Whyte, W. F. "Skinnerian Theory in Organizations." *Psychology Today* (April 1972), 67-68, 96, 98, 100.

Essay 7-2

Motivation in work organizations*

Edward E. Lawler III

EXPECTANCY THEORY

Like drive theory, expectancy theory can be traced back to hedonism and the work of the English utilitarians. In the 1930s, however, expectancy theory began to develop a different thrust. At this point, Tolman (1932) began to talk about expectations and to argue for an approach that was more cognitively oriented, and Kurt Lewin (1935) presented a cognitively oriented theory of behavior that contained terms such as "valence" and "force." Out of this early work by Tolman and Lewin, a number of very similar motivation theories have developed. All of these theories include a concept of valence—that is, the attractiveness of an out-

come—and a concept of expectancy—that is, the likelihood that an action will lead to a certain outcome or goal. The theories also converge in that they see valence and expectancy combining multiplicatively to determine behavior; hence, these theories can be referred to as expectancy × valence theories of motivation.

A number of theorists have picked up the main points of the early work of Tolman and Lewin and have built their own motivation theories within the expectancy × valence framework. The more prominent of these theorists are listed in Table 1. All of the theorists maintain that the strength of a tendency to act in a certain way depends on the strength of an expectancy that the act will be followed by a given consequence (or outcome) and on the value or attractiveness of that consequence (or outcome) to the actor.

Vroom's theory (1964) is the only one listed in Table 1 that was stated specifi-

*From Edward E. Lawler III, *Motivation in Work Organizations* (Belmont, Calif.: Wadsworth Publishing Co., 1973), pp. 41-58 (abridged). Copyright © 1973 by Wadsworth, Inc. Reprinted by permission of the publisher, Brooks/Cole Publishing Company, Monterey, California.

Table 1: Expectancy theories of motivation

Theorist	Determinants of impulse to action
Tolman	Expectancy of goal, demand for goal
Lewin	Potency × valence
Edwards	Subjective probability × utility
Atkinson	Expectancy × (motive × incentive)
Rotter	Expectancy, reinforcement value
Vroom	Expectancy × valence, where valence is (instrumentality × valence)
Peak	Instrumentality × attitude (affect)

From *Pay and Organizational Effectiveness: A Psychological View* by E. E. Lawler. Copyright 1971 by McGraw-Hill Book Company. Used by permission of the publisher.

cally for the purpose of dealing with motivation in the work environment. Thus, his theory is the logical one to examine to see how expectancy theory can be applied to work motivation. For Vroom, valence (V) refers to affective orientations toward particular outcomes. An outcome is positive if a person prefers attaining it to not attaining it, neutral if the person is indifferent to it, and negative if the person prefers not attaining it. Valence can vary from $+1$ to -1: maximally positive outcomes are $+1$; maximally negative outcomes are -1; neutral outcomes are 0. Vroom emphasizes that valence refers to an outcome's anticipated reward value rather than an outcome's actual reward value when obtained.

Vroom defines expectancy (E) as a momentary belief about the likelihood that a particular act will be followed by a particular outcome. Hence, like other expectancy theorists, Vroom sees an expectancy as a response-outcome association. Expectancies can be described in terms of their strength: maximal strength, designated by the number 1, is subjective certainty that the act will be followed by the outcome; minimal strength, designated by the number 0, is subjective certainty that the act will not be followed by this outcome.

Like other expectancy theorists, Vroom argues that expectancy and valence combine multiplicatively to determine motiva-

tion or force. The multiplicative aspect of the theory is important; it means that unless both valence and expectancy are present to some degree, there will be no force. When either or both are 0, the product will be 0 and motivation will be 0. If, for example, a person wants to perform well but does not feel that his effort will result in good performance, he will have no motivation to perform well.

Any action may be interpreted as leading to a number of outcomes; hence, one must consider how the combination of the various outcomes influences behavior. Vroom's theory argues for multiplying the valence of each outcome times the strength of the expectancy that the act will lead to the attainment of the outcome and then taking the algebraic sum of all the resulting products. Thus, he writes his theory as follows: Force = $\Sigma (E \times V)$, where Σ means that the products for all outcomes are added to determine force. This is a key point in the theory, since it means that tying a valent reward, such as pay, to a desired behavior, such as good performance, will not be enough to motivate the desired behavior. Pay can be highly valued and can be seen as closely related to performance; but if negative consequences, such as feeling tired or being rejected by a work group, are also perceived as related to good performance, there may be no motivation to perform. Finally, according to Vroom, a person will be motivated to perform well in a situation only if performing well has the highest $E \times V$ force in that particular situation. Performing well can have a strong force, but if performing poorly has a stronger force, the person will not be motivated to perform well.

There is one area in which Vroom's theory—and indeed all the expectancy theories—gets into muddy water. This difficulty involves the distinction between acts and outcomes. As Vroom states, "the distinction . . . is not, however, an absolute one. Actions are frequently described in terms of particular outcomes which they affect" (p. 19). Vroom uses the term "action" to refer to behavior that is within the person's repertoire—for example, trying to perform well or seeking a job. Thus, the belief that an act (trying to perform well) will lead to an outcome (performing well) is an expectancy; the relationship between an outcome (performing well) and another outcome (a reward such as pay) is an instrumentality that affects the valence of the original outcome. Many expectancy theorists are even less clear than Vroom is about the distinction between actions and outcomes. Some have tended to ignore the fact that trying to perform an act does not always lead to performing it. In some situations, trying to perform an act is equivalent to performing it; in these situations, it is reasonable to argue that motivation is determined by the kind of outcomes to which performing the act leads, since expectancies are likely to be 1. In many other situations, trying to perform an act does not always lead to performing it. For instance, good job performance does not automatically result from trying to perform well; hence, beliefs—the person's subjective probability—about whether good performance will result must be taken into account to explain behavior.

EXPECTANCY THEORY COMPARED WITH DRIVE THEORY

Drive theory and expectancy theory are different in a number of ways; however, both theories make similar predictions. Also, they both contain many of the same concepts; both theories include the notion of a reward or favorable outcome that is desired, and both postulate learned connections within the organism. For expectancy theory this connection is a behavior-outcome expectancy, and for drive theory the connection is an S-R habit strength.

Some of the aspects in which the theories differ are not crucial for understanding motivation in organizations (for example, how the theories explain avoidance behavior and the degree to which they believe the effects of anticipated goals can be generalized). However, the theories differ in two respects that are crucial for understanding motivation in organizations. Expectancy theory stresses the importance of forward-looking beliefs about what will occur, while drive theory emphasizes the importance of learned stimulus-response connections.

Extensive research has been done on the relationship between job performance and beliefs about how valued rewards can be obtained in organizations. This research shows that verbal statements of attitudes about (1) the importance of rewards and (2) how rewards are obtained are directly related to performance. The research also shows that a multiplicative combination of these two kinds of attitudes is a predictor of performance. These findings are perfectly predictable from expectancy theory, which emphasizes the importance of knowing a person's response-outcome beliefs and of combining them multiplicatively with the perceived value of the outcomes. Drive theory, on the other hand, stresses the importance of $_RH_R$ and considers how $_SH_R$ combines multiplicatively with drive. It does not stress the importance of the awareness of response-reward connections; thus, it does not lead one to look at these connections in order to predict behavior. Working from drive theory, one would be much more likely to look at S-R habit strength than at response-outcome connections in order to predict behavior. Thus, while the research on response-outcome beliefs by no means disproves drive theory, it does provide one reason for preferring expectancy theory.

Expectancy theory gives very loose specifications of how response-outcome connections are built up, thus allowing for the possibility of these connections being formed in a number of ways. Drive theory, on the other hand, postulates that S-R habit strengths are built up through repeated associations of stimuli and responses, which seems far too rigid and restrictive. It may be that this process is the only way association can be established among animals, but the necessity of the process where humans are concerned is doubtful. In the case of humans, drive theory's process constitutes one way—but not the only way—that connections can develop. There is evidence that in humans these connections can be formed in a number of ways, including vicariously or by other symbolic means. Ayllon and Azrin (1965) have shown that a simple verbal statement of the existence of a behavior-outcome connection can radically change the beliefs and motivation levels of people toward performing certain behaviors. A number of studies of pay (for example, Atkinson, 1958) have shown that different degrees of motivation occur depending on how the relationship between pay and performance is described. People work harder when they are told pay depends on performance than when they are told pay does not depend on performance. Other studies have shown that people develop behavior-outcome associations from watching other people and from trying something only once. These findings are quite congruent with expectancy theory, since this theory allows for the possibility of expectancies forming in a number of ways.

On the other hand, the sudden changes that do take place in subjective response-outcome probabilities and the consequent changes in motivation are not congruent with drive theory. Drive theory has always emphasized the slow building of associations and the importance of previous experience and temporally close associations. Still, many of the points made by drive theory about how associations come about do appear to be generally valid. Expectancy theory, or for that matter any motivation theory, could profit by specifying some of the more obvious factors that influence response-outcome connections; however, as an overall theory, the expectancy approach seems to be the most useful one for studying motivation in work organizations.

AN EXPECTANCY MODEL

A number of developments in motivation theory have taken place since Vroom stated his expectancy theory in 1964. The expectancy model presented here draws on these developments to provide the best available model for understanding motivation in organizations. This model is based on four points that the previous overview of the research on human motivation suggests are valid.

1. People have preferences among the various outcomes that are potentially available to them.
2. People have expectancies about the likelihood that an action (effort) on their part will lead to the intended behavior or performance.
3. People have expectancies (instrumentalities) about the likelihood that certain outcomes will follow their behavior.
4. In any situation, the actions a person chooses to take are determined by the expectancies and the preferences that person has at the time.

Figure 1 presents an illustration of the expectancy model in diagrammatic form. It shows the major factors that influence the strength of a person's motivation to perform in a given manner. First, motivation is shown to be influenced by the expectancy that effort or action on the part of the person will lead to the intended behavior. Thus, expectancy is simply the person's estimate of the probability that he will accomplish his intended performance, given the situation in which he

Figure 1: Expectancy motivation model

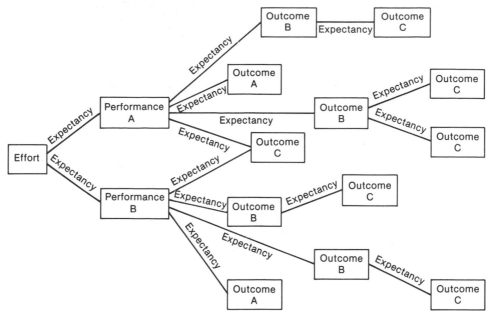

Performance A: The intended performance. A successful result from effort.
Performance B: Performance other than that intended. An unsuccessful result from effort.
Outcome A: An outcome sought as an end in itself.
Outcome B: An outcome sought as a prerequisite to other outcomes.
Outcome C: An outcome that can be obtained whether or not the effort leads to the intended performance.

finds himself. This can be labeled an $E \rightarrow P$ (effort $\rightarrow$ performance) expectancy. For example, a manager may think that he has a 50 percent chance of producing 2,000 cars a week in his plant if he tries. If we consider this kind of expectancy as varying from 0 to 1, the manager's $E \rightarrow P$ expectancy could be represented as .5. This kind of expectancy is typically more salient for complex and higher-level tasks than for simple tasks where little ability or skill is required.

Figure 1 also shows that expectancies about the consequences of task performance influence motivation. The model shows a number of expectancies, since successful task performance typically leads to a number of outcomes (as does unsuccessful performance). These expectations, which can be labeled $P \rightarrow O$ expectancies (performance $\rightarrow$ outcomes),

are subjective probability estimates and can vary from 0 to 1 in the same manner as the $E \rightarrow P$ expectancies. To return to the manufacturing manager example, he may be sure that if his plant does produce 2,000 cars a week he will receive a pay increase (his $P \rightarrow O$ expectancy equals 1). At the same time, he may also believe that there is a 50 percent probability that he will receive a promotion if he succeeds in producing 2,000 cars. In addition, he may see a number of other outcomes associated with producing 2,000 cars, and he may see still other outcomes associated with trying but failing to produce 2,000 cars.

In many instances where the $E \rightarrow P$ expectancy is less than 1, it is important to consider what outcomes a person connects with trying to perform in a given way and failing. In other words, where success cannot be assured, it is necessary to consider the person's perceived probability that performance other than the intended one will be the outcome. In the case of the manager, this would involve considering the possibility of trying to produce 2,000 cars a week and failing. In some situations, people obtain outcomes simply because they try to perform at a certain level. In these situations, a person will observe many of the same outcomes resulting from successful and unsuccessful performance, and he will realize that he will still receive a number of positive outcomes even though he fails to accomplish the desired performance. In some situations, many negative outcomes may be tied to failing to perform at the intended level, which may make trying very unattractive if failure is likely.

The model in Figure 1 also shows that only some of the outcomes are seen as leading to other outcomes. This factor is included to stress the point that some outcomes are sought as ends in themselves (for example, personal growth is sought as an end in itself), while others are sought because they lead to other outcomes (for example, money is sought because of what it will buy, not as an end in itself). The attractiveness of any outcome can be thought of as varying from very desirable (+1) to very undesirable (−1). As has been repeatedly stressed, there are two reasons why outcomes that are associated with performance may be valent: (1) they directly satisfy a person's needs, or (2) they lead to an outcome or set of outcomes that satisfy a particular need or set of needs.

Overall, then, the model illustrated in Figure 1 suggests that a person's motivation to perform in a particular way will be influenced by his expectancies about trying to perform in that way, his expectancies about the outcomes associated with performing at that level $(P \to O)$, and the attractiveness of the outcomes involved. These factors combine to produce a moti-

vational force to perform in the specified manner. For our hypothetical manager, this means that his $E \to P$ expectancy for producing 2,000 cars, his $P \to O$ expectancies for producing 2,000 cars, and the perceived attractiveness of the outcomes combine to determine his motivation to produce 2,000 cars.

Figure 1 does not show how the various expectancy factors combine to determine motivation. Most expectancy theories have operated on the assumption that the higher the $E \to P$ expectancy and the more closely performance is seen to be related to positively valent outcomes, the greater will be the motivation. Based on past research, this assumption seems generally valid. Motivation does seem to be greatest when $E \to P$ is high for successful performance and low for unsuccessful performance and when $P \to O$ is high for positive outcomes and low for negative outcomes.

In organizations, people are often forced to choose among a number of behaviors that are relatively attractive. Simply stated, the expectancy model predicts that people will choose to behave in whatever way has the highest motivational force. That is, people will choose to behave in whatever way has the highest $\Sigma [(E \to P) \times \Sigma [(P \to O)(V)]]$ score for them. In the case of productivity, this means people will be motivated to be highly productive if they feel they can be highly productive and if they see a number of positive outcomes associated with being a high producer. However, if for some reason they will receive approximately the same outcomes for being less highly productive, they probably will be low producers.

Managers often ask why their subordinates are not more productive. They seem to feel that people should be productive almost as if it is a question of morality or of instinct. The expectancy approach suggests asking a rather different question: Why should people be productive in a given situation? People are not naturally productive (or nonproductive). Thus, managers who wonder why their people are not more productive should start by comparing the rewards given to good performers with the rewards given to poor performers. Time after time, no real difference is found when this comparison is made. Thus, the workers' perception of the situation is that the good and the poor performers receive the same treatment, and this view is crucial in determining motivation. The example of an automobile assembly-line worker highlights this point. His pay is typically not affected by his performance, and his job is so simple that he receives no satisfaction from doing it well. Being highly productive does nothing more for him than to make him tired. Why should he be productive?

In summary, the expectancy model answers the two questions that were raised at the beginning of this chapter. It argues that both the attractiveness of the outcomes and the person's $E \rightarrow P$ and $P \rightarrow O$ expectancies influence which outcomes a person will try to obtain and how these outcomes will be sought. In order to answer one of these questions, it is necessary to answer the other, since they are so closely related. The choice of a behavior also implies a choice of which outcome will be sought, and the choice of an outcome partially determines what behavior will be attempted.

Determinants of $E \rightarrow P$ expectations

The single most important determinant of a person's $E \rightarrow P$ expectancies is the objective situation. Sometimes, of course, a person's perception of the situation is not accurate, and as a result the objective situation may not completely determine a person's $E \rightarrow P$ expectancies. However, it seems safe to assume that over time most people's $E \rightarrow P$ perceptions begin to fit reality reasonably well. Several of the other factors that influence $E \rightarrow P$ expectancies tend to encourage this. One of the

most influential of these factors is the communication of other people's perceptions of the person's situation. Other people's perceptions are not necessarily accurate, but more often than not they can be a corrective force when a person badly misperceives reality. This communication is most likely to be influential when the person communicating his or her perception is very experienced in the situation and is less emotionally involved in the situation. For example, the ski instructor can often effectively correct the new skier's misperceptions about the likelihood that the new skier can successfully negotiate a particular turn, since the ski instructor is a more objective and experienced observer. In many situations an older employee can effectively counsel a new employee about the difficulty of doing a job. Often a job looks much more difficult to the new employee than it in fact is, and the result is turnover or low performance.

Learning plays an important role in determining $E \rightarrow P$ expectancies, as well as helping to make these expectancies more accurate. As people gain more experience in a situation, they typically are able to develop more accurate $E \rightarrow P$ expectancies. After a number of trials at doing something, a person knows from his own experience what his ratio of successful to unsuccessful efforts is. From a straight statistical-sampling perspective, once a large number of trials have occurred, it is possible to estimate the likelihood of a particular event with great accuracy.

There is some evidence that personality factors can cause people's $E \rightarrow P$ probabilities to diverge from reality. Psychologists who have written about personality have emphasized that individuals have a self-image. Some time during infancy, human beings learn to distinguish themselves from their environment. They learn that they can influence the environment or act on it, and they get feedback about the effectiveness of these actions. Some things that people try to make happen do happen, while others do not happen. From this interaction with their environment, people develop a concept of themselves and of their competence in dealing with the environment. They learn what they can do and what they cannot do. They receive feedback from others about how they are perceived. Out of these experiences, people develop a knowledge of their existence and a self-image—that is, a view of what they are like. A crucial component of people's self-image is the beliefs they have concerning their response capabilities and their value and effectiveness. These beliefs are at the core of what is frequently referred to as self-esteem and are important for understanding the kinds of $E \to P$ expectancies people have.

Self-esteem can be influenced either positively or negatively depending on a person's effectiveness in dealing with his environment; but once a person has reached maturity, self-esteem—like a person's needs—appears to become relatively stable. There are large individual differences in self-esteem. Low-self-esteem people are generally poor estimators of their own ability to successfully carry out certain behaviors. They generally tend to underestimate the likelihood that they will be successful, although sometimes they are unrealistically high in their estimates. Nor surprisingly, people's self-esteem tends to be related to their $E \to P$ expectancies; as a result, motivating low-self-esteem people to perform well is difficult, since they are predisposed to believing that they cannot perform well. On the other hand, high-self-esteem people tend to have realistic $E \to P$ expectancies; thus, they respond more predictably and realistically to their environment. One way an organization can deal with this effect of self-esteem on motivation is by selecting only people who have high self-esteem, and another way is by trying to raise the self-esteem of the people already in the organization. The latter solution

presumably can be accomplished by providing the right kinds of jobs and leadership; however, the solution does not come easily, given the relative stability of people's self-esteem.

Figure 2 summarizes what has been said about the determinants of $E \to P$ expec-

Figure 2: Determinants of $E \to P$ expectancies

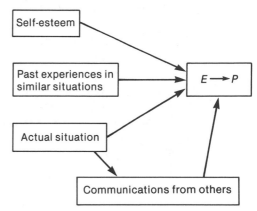

tancies, which are shown as being directly influenced by four factors: the person's self-esteem, his past experiences, the actual situation, and communications received from others. The figure also shows that the actual situation, in addition to directly influencing the person's $E \to P$ expectancies, influences what is communicated to the person, making it the crucial determinant of $E \to P$ expectancies. Because $E \to P$ expectancies are reality based, by changing the situation in which employees find themselves, organizations can influence employees' $E \to P$ expectancies—thus influencing motivation. As we shall see, job design has a strong influence on $E \to P$ expectancies and thus can influence motivation.

Determinants of $P \to O$ expectancies

Like $E \to P$ expectancies, $P \to O$ expectancies are strongly influenced by the objective situation, by people's past experiences in similar situations, and by what other people say about the situation. For example, one study has shown that people's perceptions of the probability that pay is related to performance are in accord with reality (Lawler, 1967). In this study, pay was clearly related to performance in one group of organizations where managers reported a strong relationship; managers reported a weak relationship in another group of organizations, and evidence supported their perception.

There is a great deal of evidence that verbal reports by co-workers can strongly influence a worker's $P \to O$ expectancies. Whyte (1955), in his work on incentive plans, has shown how workers are influenced by other worker's reports on the consequences of performing well. For example, workers can be convinced that if they are highly productive, the pay rate will be reduced, even though they have never seen it happen, and even though the company says it won't happen. Workers believe the event will happen because the event has been predicted by their fellow workers, who represent a high credibility source. Whyte also shows that workers develop other beliefs about the consequences of high productivity (for example, that high productivity will lead to rejection by other workers) even though they have never experienced such consequences.

Like $E \to P$ expectancies, $P \to O$ expectancies tend to be accurate, although there is evidence that under certain conditions $P \to O$ expectancies may be distorted. Raiffa (1968) has shown that people's subjective probabilities are generally related to actual mathematical probabilities. However, it has also been found that subjective probabilities tend to be larger than actual probabilities at low values and smaller than the actual probabilities at higher values. Thus, it seems that people tend to underestimate the possibility of a "sure thing" and to overestimate the possibility of a "long shot." Some sources have commented that evidence of the latter is present in the betting

and gambling habits of most Americans.

Some research suggests that $P \to O$ probabilities are influenced by the nature of the outcomes. One group of studies has shown that, to most people, positive outcomes seem more likely to occur than negative ones. Other studies have suggested that people see very positive outcomes as less likely to be obtained than less positive ones. Thus, people exhibit a general tendency to downgrade the possibility that very positive things will happen to them; people also downgrade the possibility that negative things will happen to them.

Some of the research on achievement motivation has suggested that $E \to P$ probabilities can influence certain $P \to O$ probabilities. Specifically, when the $E \to P$ probability is around .5, the achievement motive is aroused, and $P \to O$ expectancies having to do with achievement-type outcomes are affected. Apparently, when $E \to P$ is very high or very low, people do not see successful performance on their part as leading to feelings of achievement or competence, as they do when $E \to P$ is around .5.

Figure 3 summarizes what has been said so far about the determinants of $P \to O$ beliefs. It shows that $P \to O$ expectancies are influenced by past experience, communicated probabilities, $E \to P$ expectancies, the attractiveness of outcomes, and belief in internal versus external control. It also shows that the actual situation influences what is communicated as well as directly influencing the person's $P \to O$ expectancies.

REFERENCES

Atkinson, J. W. "Towards Experimental Analysis of Human Motivation in Terms of Motives, Expectancies, and Incentives," in *Motives in Fantasy, Action and Society*, edited by J. W. Atkinson. Princeton: Van Nostrand Reinhold, 1958.

Ayllon, T., and Azrin, N. H. "The Measurement

Figure 3: Determinants of $P \rightarrow O$ expectancies

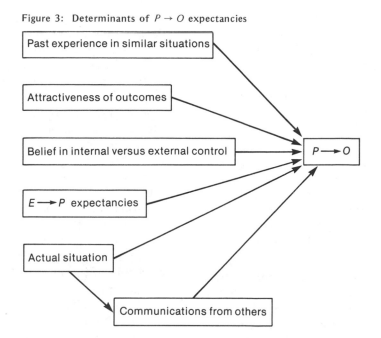

and Reinforcement of Behavior of Psychotics." *Journal of Experimental Analysis of Behavior* 8 (1965), 357-83.

Lawler, E. E. "The Multitrait-Multirator Approach to Measuring Managerial Job Performance." *Journal of Applied Psychology* 51 (1967), 369-81.

Lewin, K. *A Dynamic Theory of Personality.* New York: McGraw-Hill, 1935.

Raiffa, H. *Decision Analysis: Introductory Lectures on Choices under Uncertainty.* Reading, Mass.: Addison-Wesley, 1968.

Tolman, E. C. *Purposive Behavior in Animals and Men.* New York: Century, 1932.

Vroom, V. H. *Work and Motivation.* New York: John Wiley & Sons, 1964.

Whyte, W. F. *Money and Motivation.* New York: Harper and Row, 1955.

Essay 7-3

Toward a theory of task motivation and incentives*

Edwin A. Locke

In recent years, some psychologists have become dissatisfied with the limitations placed upon research and theory by the

*Reprinted from Edwin A. Locke, "Toward a Theory of Task Motivation and Incentives," *Organizational Behavior and Human Performance* 3 (1968), pp. 158-73 (abridged).

behaviorist dogma. A growing number of investigators have begun to study the effects of conscious goals, intentions, desires, and purposes on task performance. The basic (implicit or explicit) premise of this research is that man's conscious ideas affect what he does, i.e., that one of the (biological) functions of consciousness is the regulation of action (see Branden, 1966; Rand, 1964, for a fuller discussion of the nature and functions of consciousness).[1]

It is argued here, in agreement with Ryan (1958), that:

Tasks [intentions, goals, etc.] ... are to be treated as causal factors in behavior. By this I mean that a task is a *necessary* condition for most kinds of behavior. (To find and account for the exceptions is an empirical problem). .... I shall assert that a very large proportion of behavior is initiated by tasks, and that a very large proportion of tasks lead to the behavior specified by the tasks (p. 79).

It is the purpose of this paper to draw together and integrate the existing literature on the relationship between conscious goals or intentions and task performance. For our purposes the terms goal and intention will be used in their vernacular meaning as "what the individual is consciously trying to do." (Some distinctions between these two terms will be made later in the paper.)

It should be stressed that in the last analysis the content of a particular individual's goals and intentions must be inferred from his verbal report (based on his introspection). However, there are still a number of different procedures that may be used to study the relationship between conscious goals or intentions and task performance: (1) goals can be assigned by the experimenter before performance and the subject's acceptance of these goals (i.e., his decision to actually try for them) checked later by questioning; (2) subjects can be given a limited choice of goals before task performance and asked to choose one of them; (3) subjects can be

---

[1] There are important philosophical issues involved in the decision to use or not to use concepts referring to states of consciousness as explanatory terms. These issues are both epistemological, e.g., the problem of the privacy of conscious states, and metaphysical, e.g., the mind-body problem. Due to space limitations, however, the present paper is confined exclusively to a discussion of experimental findings.

allowed to set any goals they wish on the task and then asked to indicate what their goal was after performance. In addition, these methods can be used in various combinations; for example, results obtained using method (3) can be checked using method (1), i.e., by assigning the same goals to a new group of subjects that a previous group had set themselves. In the studies to be reported here, all three methods were used and all yielded substantial relationships between goals or intentions and task performance. Thus for our purposes, the advantages and disadvantages of the different procedures are not important (though in other contexts, it might be of interest to study them).

No attempt is made in the studies reported to specify the ultimate roots or causes of the particular goals or intentions an individual develops on a task. Our interest here is only in the relationship between these goals and intentions, once established, and subsequent behavior. Thus, we are not presenting a complete theory of task performance but only some foundations for a theory.

Turning briefly to the issue of nonintentional behavior, it is obvious that no individual is aware of or consciously intends every single action or movement he makes. But it remains to be seen just how much behavior can be explained with reference to conscious intent. For instance, Ryan (1958) argues: "The concept of *determining tendency* would suggest that the effect of a task [intention] may operate over such a time-span that it may produce an effect at a time when the individual is no longer aware of the task as such" (p. 82).

It may be instructive in this context to discuss four types of "unintentional" behaviors that occur frequently in everyday life in order to see to what degree these might be explained in terms of conscious intent:

1. *One category is behavior whose end is foreseen but in which each movement*

in the sequence that is the means to the end is not consciously initiated. For example, in returning an opponent's shot in tennis, an experienced player is not consciously aware of his footwork, backswing, or grip, but only of the intent to approach and return the shot. In such cases as this, the action leading to the goal has become automated through extended practice; each response automatically sets off the next response in the sequence. However, it should be recognized that the behavior sequence as a whole must still be *triggered* by a conscious intent (e.g., as "to return the shot" or "win the point" in the example above). Once the initial intent is abandoned, action ceases, e.g., if the tennis player suddenly decides not to try to return a shot, the usual action sequence will not occur.

Furthermore, automated behavior of this type is *initially learned* consciously and intentionally. This is true of any series of skilled goal-directed movements or actions taken by man (though such actions will involve physiological activities of which he may never be aware introspectively; see type 4 below).

2. A second category involves *behavior in which a different end occurs than is intended due to error or lack of ability.* For instance, one could try to return a tennis shot but hit the net instead. The behavior would be consciously initiated but the outcome would be imperfectly correlated with the intended outcome due to lack of knowledge or ability. Such behavior is usually described as "accidental." Clearly concepts other than conscious intent are required to explain accidents, but it should be recognized that accidents often involve very small deviations from the intended outcome (e.g., as when a tennis shot goes out of bounds by an inch). Thus conscious intent would be *one* factor in the explanation of the action sequence as a whole.

3. A third type of nonintentional behavior is *behavior in which the end that is*

foreseen logically entails another end that is not foreseen as such. For example, in a verbal "conditioning" or a free-association experiment, one might intentionally give only the names of "jewels" (rubies, emeralds, diamonds, etc.). In doing so one would also be giving "plural nouns." Plural nouns would not be consciously intended as such but would be logically entailed by the intention to list jewels. Dulany (1961, 1962) uses the term "correlated hypotheses" to describe subjects' hypotheses in verbal-conditioning experiments which are correlated with the "correct" hypothesis. One could similarly use the term "correlated behavior" to describe behavior which was not intended as such but which was logically correlated with intended behavior.

4. Finally, there is *behavior which is not and never was under direct conscious control, but may be indirectly controlled.* For instance, in the course of carrying out a voluntary act, many automatic, nonconscious physiological actions will occur (e.g., muscle contractions, neural activity, glandular secretions, etc.)—actions which one could not become aware of using the unaided senses. But by initiating certain molar actions one may indirectly control some of these molecular actions.

The key point to recognize in the above four cases is that all the actions in question were or could be *initiated* by a mental act, that they were or could be originally *set in motion* by a conscious goal or intention. In addition, the results or outcomes of the behaviors are ordinarily either the ones intended or are correlated with those intended (the size of the correlation depending upon the individual's capacity, knowledge, ability, and the situation).

The research to be reported here involves predominantly simple tasks in which learning complex new skills and making long-term plans and strategies is not necessary to achieve goals—tasks of the type in which effort and concentration are likely to have a relatively direct effect on output or choice.

This essay is divided into two parts. Part I (below) reports research dealing with direct relationships between goals or intentions and task performance. Part II (which is reprinted as Essay 7-5) is an extension of the theory to attempt to account for the motivational effects of external incentives on task performance. *An external incentive is defined as an event or object external to the individual which can incite action.* It is argued that if goals or intentions are a necessary condition for most kinds of behavior, then incentives will affect behavior only through their effects on goals and intentions and will have no effect independent of their effects on goals and intentions. Part II reports research relevant to this deduction.

I: GOALS, INTENTIONS, AND TASK PERFORMANCE

Goal difficulty and level of performance

The studies in this section are concerned with the relationship between the level or difficulty of the goal the subject is trying for and the quantitative level of his performance (amount of output, speed of reaction time, school grades, etc.). If goals regulate performance, then hard goals should produce a higher level of performance than easy goals, other things (such as ability) being equal.

Figure 1 shows the combined results of 12 studies on this topic by the present investigator and colleagues. In some of these studies goals were assigned to subjects by the experimenter and goal acceptance was checked by interviews. In other studies subjects set their own goals. In all cases goals were expressed in terms of some specific quantitative score that the subject was trying to achieve on each trial or on the task as a whole. Goal difficulty is expressed in Figure 1 in terms of the per-

centage of trials on which the subjects trying for a particular goal actually beat that goal. Performance level is expressed in terms of the within-study z-score for performance for the particular goal group in question. Thus each point represents a particular group (a particular goal) in a particular study; it indicates the probability of the subjects in that group reaching their goal and their mean output in relation to the other goal groups in that study.

The results are unequivocal: the harder the goal the higher the level of performance. Although subjects with very hard goals reached their goals far less often than subjects with very easy goals, the former consistently performed at a higher level than the latter. The rank-order correlation between goal difficulty and performance for all the points shown in Figure 1 is .78 ($p < .01$). (The one extreme point, circled in Figure 1, was not used, however, in calculating the slope of the function, as this would have given a misleading picture of the general relationship between the two variables.)

There have been a small number of studies by other investigators of goal difficulty and performance, and the findings have been similar to those reported above. Dey and Kaur (1965) using a letter cancellation task found hard (assigned) output goals to produce a higher level of performance than easy goals. Mace (1935) in a study of psychomotor performance found that subjects who were instructed to try to improve their scores 25 percent per day, improved at a faster rate than those instructed to improve at a rate of 5 percent per day. Siegal and Fouraker (1960), using an experimental bargaining task, asked some subjects to try for a specific quantitatively high profit and others to try for a specific quantitatively low profit. The former group actually negotiated higher profits than the latter. Locke (1966b) reanalyzed some data gathered by Fryer in a study of code learning, in

Figure 1: Output as a function of goal difficulty for 12 studies combined

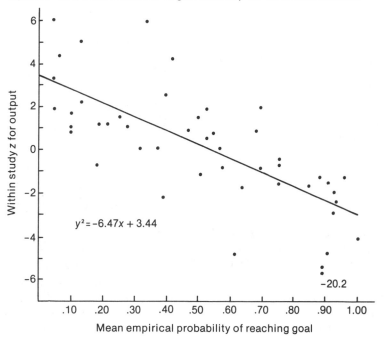

$$y^2 = -6.47x + 3.44$$

−20.2

which some subjects set goals before each trial and some did not. Locke found that those subjects who set high goals in relation to their previous performance performed better on the task than those who set comparatively low goals. Eason and White (1961) found that subjects who were instructed to try to stay on target in a pursuit rotor task for 0, 50, and 100 percent of the time, respectively, actually did so. Eason and White also found that subjects tracking a smaller target showed greater muscular control (greater precision of movement) than those tracking a larger target. (This is an example of category type 3 of unintended behavior discussed above: the subjects with smaller targets were not trying explicitly for greater muscular control than those with larger targets; this outcome was a logical correlate of the former subjects trying to "stay on" a smaller target.)

Stedry (1960), in a study of problem solving, demonstrated the importance of distinguishing between instructions and the subjects' personal goals. He told different groups of subjects to try to complete different numbers of problems in the time allowed. He also had subjects indicate their own personal levels of aspiration, either before or after the goals were assigned by the experimenter. He found that hard assigned goals led to a higher number of problems completed than easy goals only if the goals were assigned *before* the hard-goal subjects set their personal goals. If they set personal goals first, they tended to reject the assigned hard goals and performed quite poorly on the task.

Two previous studies have found significant relationships between students' grade goals and actual grade performance in school (controlling for scholastic ability). Uhlinger and Stephens (1960) and Battle (1966) used college freshmen and junior high school students as subjects, respectively. Unfortunately, however, the grade-goal questionnaires were administered near the end of the semester during which the grades were obtained, thus making the cause-effect relationship somewhat equivocal.

A study of "real life" goal-setting was carried out by Zander and Newcomb (1967). They studied the United Fund campaigns of 149 selected communities over a period of four years. It was found that communities who set monetary goals that were higher than their previous year's performance raised more money (in dollars per capita) in relation to their previous year's performance than communities who set goals that were lower than their previous year's performance. Further analyses supported the view that these goals were a cause rather than an effect of actual performance. (One exception to the former finding was that for communities with a history of failure to reach their fund goals, there was no correlation between goals and performance.)

In the industrial area, numerous investigators have observed that workers' output norms influence their level of production (e.g., Mathewson, 1931; Roethlisberger and Dickson, 1939; Smith, 1953; Whyte, 1955). The focus of interest in these field studies, however, was on the negative side of work norms and standards, on their effect in keeping *down* production. But a broader view of the issue should recognize that norms have a positive side; they also hold *up* production. A production norm is simply a work goal shared by a group of workers.

Relationship of qualitatively different goals to level of performance

The studies in this section are concerned with the relationship of qualitatively different goals to level of performance. Most of them deal with a comparison of the assigned goal of "do your best" with specific hard goals. The former was chosen for research by the present writer because it is used, explicitly or implicitly, in virtually all psychological experiments.

Yet, just what it means is not exactly clear. It was believed that such a goal did not necessarily lead to the highest performance possible. Thus it was decided to compare the output induced by a "do best" goal with that which could be produced by specific quantitative hard goals of the type used in the studies described in the previous section.

Eight studies comparing the effects of these two types of goals are considered. In six of the eight studies the subjects trying for specific hard goals performed at a significantly higher level than subjects trying to "do their best." Thus, a "do best" goal does not tend to produce (under the conditions of these studies) the highest possible level of performance.

Mace (1935) obtained a similar finding in a study of complex computation. He gave one group of subjects specific hard standards, geared to their ability level, to aim for in each work period, whereas other subjects were told simply to "do their best." The group with hard standards improved much faster than the "do best" group. Mace also analyzed the within-trial rates of the hard-goal and do-best groups and found that the difference between the groups was due entirely to the hard-goal group showing higher output toward the end of each 20-minute-trial period as compared with the do-best group. Both groups worked at the same pace early in each work period but the difference between them grew as the work period progressed. However, in one of the studies reported above (Locke and Bryan, 1966a) the superiority of the hard-goal groups was equally large during each segment of the work period (although in the latter study the periods were only 10-minutes long). On the other hand, in two other studies reported above (Locke and Bryan, 1967a) using single trials that lasted 1½–2 hours, Mace's finding was replicated. The difference between the groups increased steadily during the course of these long work periods. Clearly one reason that specific hard goals enhance performance is that they prolong effort during the latter portions of long work sessions.

In a study of a somewhat different nature, Henderson (1963) assigned fifth-grade children stories to read, but asked them to indicate what their *reading purposes* would be before they began. He found that children who formulated more complex, numerous, and creative purposes actually attained their purposes more fully and completely than did subjects who formulated fewer, less complex, and less creative purposes.

Finally, an industrial study by Meyer, Kay and French (1965) examined the effects of goal-setting during appraisal interviews on subsequent job performance. They found that of those performance items which were translated into specific goals, 65 percent showed subsequent improvement, while of those performance items that did not get translated into goals, only 27% showed subsequent improvement.

Behavioral intentions and choice

The designs of the studies reported in the preceding sections required all subjects to work at the same task (do the same thing) and the focus of interest was on how well they did it (i.e., output). The experiments to be reported in this section were designed so that subjects had a *choice* either as to the difficulty of the *task* they would work on or the particular kinds of *responses* they would give. The intention to make a certain task choice or to respond in a certain way will henceforth be called a *behavioral intention* (after Dulany, 1962).

Three studies conducted by the present writer and colleagues (Locke, Bryan, and Kendall, 1968) examined the relationship between behavioral intentions and task choice. The task in all cases was word unscrambling and subjects were allowed to

choose, on each trial, the length of the word (e.g., four letters, five letters, six letters, etc.) they would try to unscramble. Subjects had 45 seconds to try to solve each word chosen. Word-length choice was the dependent variable.

In the first study there were three blocks of ten trials each and subjects filled out a 5-point behavioral-intentions scale before each trial and before each block of trials. The scale asked the subject to indicate whether she intended to choose a "very hard word," a "hard word," a "moderately hard word," etc. on the next trial or block of trials. The intention ratings were quantified on a 5-point scale: 1 for the "very easy words" alternative, to 5 for the "very hard words" alternative. The mean within-subject correlation between word length choice and intentions across the 30 trials was .81 (median = .80). The mean within-block, between-individual correlation between block intention and mean word choice on that block was .60 ($p < .01$).

In the second study, the first block consisted of ten choices. Before trial 1, one third of the subjects were told to try to "succeed" as much as possible; one third were told to "get as great a sense of personal achievement as possible," and one third were told to try and "overcome the greatest possible challenges." Behavioral intentions were measured on a 5-point scale completed before the block began and were quantified on a 5-point scale as in the previous study (see above). The relationship between instructions, intentions, and mean word choice is shown in Figure 2. Clearly the "challenge" group developed the "hardest" intentions and chose the hardest (longest) words while the "success" group developed the easiest intentions and chose the easiest (shortest) words. The "achievement" group was in-intermediate on both variables. The correlation between instructions (quantified 5, 3, and 1 for the challenge, achievement and success groups, respectively) and

Figure 2: The relationship of instructions and intentions to word-length choice

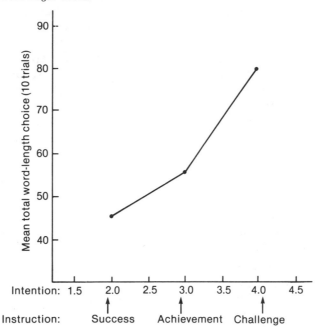

mean word-length choice on the ten trials was .67 ($p < .01$), while that between intentions and mean word-length choice was .88 ($p < .01$).

On block II, there were ten more trials but no specific instructions. The correlation between intentions and word-length choice was .81 ($p < .01$).

In the third study, subjects had five blocks of five choices each and they filled out an intention rating before each block. The within-block correlation between mean word-length choice and intentions were .78, .83, .79, .85, and .79 for the five blocks, respectively (all p's $< .01$).[2]

Let us turn now to studies in which all subjects had to work on the same task but had a choice of *responses*. These studies have all been in the "verbal-conditioning" area. Subjects are asked to free associate or to make up sentences and are "reinforced" (by the experimenter saying "good" etc.) for listing certain types of words or certain kinds of sentences. Dulany (1962) gave his subjects postexperimental interviews asking them to report their behavioral intentions and found highly significant correlations in three different studies between the subjects' behavioral intentions and the actual number of responses given in the intended category. For instance, subjects who intentionally tried to make up only sentences beginning with "I" or "We" actually made more such sentences than those who did not try to do this.

A study of a similar nature was conducted by Holmes (1966). Subjects who tried intentionally to give "I" or "We" sentences gave significantly more of them than those who did not try to do this, even when both groups were aware that "I", "We" sentences were the kind the experimenter was "reinforcing" them for giving.

---

[2] The blocks referred to here are not chronological (i.e., 1st, 2nd, 3rd, 4th, 5th) but refer to blocks in which all subjects received the same incentive, either 1, 2, 3, 4, or 5 cents. The effects of incentives on choice are discussed in Part II (Essay 7-5).

Two later studies by Dulany (1968) reported correlations of .94 and .90, respectively, between behavioral intentions and responses on a task where the subject was to select, on each trial, one of two sentences presented to him.

Finally, a field study by Leventhal and Niles (1964) showed subjects films which demonstrated the danger of smoking and its relationship to lung cancer. Afterwards, they asked each subject to indicate how much *desire* he had to get a chest X-ray. The stronger the desire to get an X-ray the more likely the subject was to actually have one taken.

REFERENCES

Battle, Esther S. "Motivational Determinants of Academic Competence." *Journal of Personality and Social Psychology* 4 (1966), 634-42.

Branden, N. "The Objectivist Theory of Volition." *The Objectivist* 5 (1966), no. 1, 7-12.

Dey, M. K., and Kaur, G. "Facilitation of Performance by Experimentally Induced Ego Motivation." *Journal of General Psychology* 73 (1965), 237-47.

Dulany, D. E., Jr. "Hypotheses and Habits in Verbal 'Operant Conditioning'." *Journal of Abnormal and Social Psychology* 63 (1961), 251-63.

Dulany, D. E., Jr. "The Place of Hypotheses and Intentions: An Analysis of Verbal Control in Verbal Conditioning." In C. W. Eriksen (ed.), *Behavior and Awareness.* Durham, North Carolina: Duke Univ. Press, 1962, pp. 102-29.

Dulany, D. E., Jr. "Awareness, Rules and Propositional Control: A Confrontation with S-R Behavior Theory." In D. Horton and T. Dixon (eds.), *Verbal Behavior and General Behavior Theory.* Englewood Cliffs, New Jersey: Prentice-Hall, 1968, pp. 340-87.

Eason, R. G. and White, C. T. "Muscular Tension, Effort, and Tracking Difficulty: Studies of Parameters Which Affect Tension Level and Performance Efficiency." *Perceptual and Motor Skills* 12 (1961), 331-72.

Henderson, E. H. "A Study of Individually Formulated Purposes for Reading in Relation to Reading Achievement Comprehension and Purpose Attainment." Unpublished Ph.D. dissertation, Univ. of Delaware, 1963.

Holmes, D. S. "Verbal Conditioning or Problem Solving and Cooperation?" Midwestern Psychological Association, 1966.

Leventhal, H., and Niles, P. A. "A Field Experiment on Fear Arousal with Data on the Validity of Questionnaire Measures." *Journal of Personality* 32 (1964), 459-79.

Locke, E. A. "A Closer Look at Level of Aspiration as a Training Procedure: A Reanalysis of Fryer's Data." *Journal of Applied Psychology* 50 (1966), 417-20. (b)

Locke, E. A. "The Motivational Effects of Knowledge of Results: Knowledge or Goal-Setting?" *Journal of Applied Psychology* 51 (1967), 324-29. (b)

Locke, E. A., and Bryan, J. F. "Cognitive Aspects of Psychomotor Performance: The Effects of Performance Goals on Level of Performance." *Journal of Applied Psychology* 50 (1966), 286-91. (a)

Locke, E. A., and Bryan, J. F. "The Effects of Goal-Setting, Rule-Learning and Knowledge of Score on Performance." *American Journal of Psychology* 79 (1966), 451-57. (b)

Locke, E. A., and Bryan, J. F. "Performance Goals as Determinants of Level of Performance and Boredom." *Journal of Applied Psychology* 51 (1967), 120-30. (a)

Locke, E. A.; Bryan, J. F.; and Kendall, L. M. "Goals and Intentions as Mediators of the Effects of Monetary Incentives on Behavior." *Journal of Applied Psychology* 52, 1968.

Mace, C. A. "Incentives: Some Experimental Studies." Industrial Health Research Board (Great Britain), 1935, Report No. 72.

Mathewson, S. B. *Restriction of Output among Unorganized Workers.* New York: Viking Press, 1931, pp. 104-21.

Meyer, H. H.; Kay, E.; and French, J. R. P., Jr. "Split Roles in Performance Appraisal." *Harvard Business Review* 43 (1965), 123-29.

Rand, Ayn. "The Objectivist Ethics." In Ayn Rand (ed.), *The Virtue of Selfishness.* New York: Signet, 1964, pp. 13-35.

Roethlisberger, F. J., and Dickson, W. J. *Management and the Worker.* Cambridge, Massachusetts: Harvard Univ. Press, 1939.

Ryan, T. A. "Drives, Tasks, and the Initiation of

Behavior." *American Journal of Psychology* 71 (1958), 74-93.

Siegal, S., and Fouraker, L. E. *Bargaining and Group Decision Making.* New York: McGraw-Hill, 1960, pp. 61-70.

Smith, P. C. "The Curve of Output as a Criterion of Boredom." *Journal of Applied Psychology* 37 (1953), 69-74.

Stedry, A. C. *Budget Control and Cost Behavior.* Englewood Cliffs, New Jersey: Prentice-Hall, 1960.

Uhlinger, C. A., and Stephens, M. W. "Relation of Achievement Motivation to Academic Achievement in Students of Superior Ability." *Journal of Educational Psychology* 51 (1960), 259-66.

Whyte, W. F. *Money and Motivation.* New York: John Wiley, 1955.

Zander, A., and Newcomb, T. "Group Levels of Aspiration in United Fund Campaigns." *Journal of Personality and Social Psychology* 6 (1967), 157-62.

Commentary

The reinforcement or conditioning model presented by Hamner describes the development of patterns of behavior through experienced pairing of desired behavior with rewards and undesired behavior with punishment. This pairing of behavior and rewards conditions individuals to engage in desired behavior more frequently than nonreinforced or punished behavior. The conditioning of behavior develops habits and is termed learning; confronted with a familiar stimulus, the individual engages in behavior which has been reinforced previously in that situation. We are all familiar with application of the reinforcement model of motivation in the training of children and animals, and also can observe that many of our own habits developed because we found certain behaviors rewarding in some manner.

The evidence concerning different schedules of reinforcement reviewed by Hamner suggests that both learning and maintenance of learned behavior proceed differently under different reinforcement schedules. Ratio schedules of reinforcement appear to condition behavior without regard to time, while interval schedules tend to condition behavior as a function of time; regular reinforcement schedules appear to condition behavior more quickly than variable schedules, but learned behavior is maintained longer when learned under a variable schedule. Thus a piece-rate system of compensation (regular ratio schedule) would appear more effective in achieving desired levels of performance than hourly compensation (regular interval schedule), and periodic, unscheduled bonuses (variable interval schedule) would appear more effective in maintaining performance over time than special holiday bonuses (regular interval schedule). A variable ratio schedule, judged most effective in the maintenance of behavior is exemplified in gambling rewards or in commission payments to sales persons; insurance agents, for example, are trained to make sales presentations repeatedly with the knowledge that only some percentage of these will result in sales. Initial sales behavior may be trained under a regular ratio schedule when the trainee agent is under contract, and maintenance of this behavior is sought as the agent is assigned commissions and reinforced under a variable ratio schedule. Despite the differential effectiveness of different schedules of reinforcement, there is some question about whether or not the manipulation of reinforcement schedules is an acceptable element of the employment contract, an issue considered in later essays.

The expectancy model elaborated by Lawler also deals with work behavior, rewards and punishments. However, the expectancy model emphasizes the role of cognition and choice prior to the behavior, while the reinforcement model views behavior as an almost habitual response to a stimulus because of repeated pairings of that behavior and reinforcements. The expectancy model casts individuals in a situation where they confront a variety of potential actions from which a choice must be made. Each potential action is evaluated in terms of the outcome(s) associated with the act, the likelihood of the outcome(s), and the subjective value (valence or utility) of that outcome to the individual. The action with the greatest expected valence or utility is selected. Attempts to guide individual actions take the form of increasing the valued outcome contingent upon behavior and altering the individual's perceptions of the likelihood of outcomes contingent upon behavioral choices.

The reinforcement model and the expectancy model share many common characteristics. Both are concerned with the explanation of behavior and with channeling or influencing behavior; both also emphasize the role of rewards and punishments in channeling behavior. There are significant differences between the models, however. Behavior is conditioned according to the reinforcement model through experiencing paired associations between behavior and rewards or punishments; habitual behavior is developed through such conditioning. The expectancy model is cognitive in orientation, individuals reason about expectancies and make conscious choices among alternative behaviors. Further, expectancies may derive from many sources, not merely past experience, and rewards may be anticipated although never experienced. Thus, for example, occupational choices are made on the basis of reward anticipations based upon published information, career counseling, and observations of the experience of others. Similarly, the expectancy model provides for drastic and immediate changes in behavior in response to new information about rewards and/or expectancies; sales persons respond to an announced contest prior to experiencing the rewards. The expectancy model suggests that work behavior is more easily and quickly modified than is implied in the reinforcement model. The expectancy model focuses upon conscious, rational choice while the reinforcement model focuses upon relatively less conscious and habitual behavior, significantly different types of behavior. The expectancy model might apply most clearly to situations of occupational choice and decisions to accept employment, while the reinforcement model might apply most directly to habitual behaviors such as pacing of work throughout the day and the sequencing of activities performed at the task. The two models can be viewed as complementary, explaining different types of behavior, rather than as offering competing explanations of the same behavior.

The two models also differ in terms of implications for the administrator seeking to influence behavior. While both stress the roles of reward and punishment, the reinforcement model emphasizes the differences in experienced schedules of reinforcement and the expectancy model emphasizes the expectations of reward and punishment. While both models indicate that a regular reinforcement schedule has the most immediate impact upon performance, the maintenance of behavior under a variable ratio reinforcement schedule explained by the reinforcement model is unexplained by the expectancy model. The expectancy model states that the likelihood of behavior is a direct function of both the valence and probability of reward, and reward schedules which alter the probability of reward are anticipated to impact directly upon performance. The expectancy model appears most applicable in the explanation of initial choices of behavior and the reinforcement model appears most applicable in the explanation of maintained habitual behavior.

The different formulations of the reinforcement model and the expectancy model of motivation suggest that choice behavior and habitual behavior be distinguished and that different motivational models apply to these behaviors. Thus, for example, the expectancy model might most appropriately be applied in the design of compensation to affect choices such as the decision to work, occupational choice, choice of firm, and decisions regarding acceptance of job assignments, promotions, and transfers. The reinforcement model might most appropriately be applied in the design of compensation to influence behaviors such as reporting to work on time, methods of task performance, and the level of effort and attention devoted to task performance.

The essay by Locke stresses the role of intentions or goals for performance. He presents evidence suggesting that behavioral responses of workers to incentives cannot be predicted directly from the expectancy model, that performance does not automatically increase with the opportunity to gain larger rewards. Rather, there must be a prior decision and intent of the individual to achieve higher performance. Locke's theory with its focus upon rational decisions and intentions is consistent with the cognitive focus of expectancy theory. Locke would recommend greater focus upon the shaping of intentions of individuals as a condition of achieving performance than upon the manipulation of reinforcement schedules.

Neither the reinforcement model nor the expectancy model addresses directly the issue of arousal or energization in motivation. Both assume some stage of arousal prior to the initiation of behavior, yet neither explains the origin of this arousal stage. The reinforcement model, with its acognitive orientation, assumes implicitly that arousal derives from some deprivation (e.g., hunger) or from encounter with a stimulus associated in the past with rewarded or punished behavior (e.g., a hot stove or a birthday party). The occasioning of deprivation is beyond the power of most organizational administrators who must rely upon stimulus associations to elicit arousal. The concept of arousal associated with the expectancy model is less clear and appears to be merely the recognition of opportunity for choice, however occasioned. The most apparent means of arousal would appear to be the presentation of alternative behaviors calling forth the opportunity for choices. Although not addressed specifically by Locke, he recognizes implicitly the role of arousal when he argues that reward opportunities do not direct behavior in the absence of specific performance intentions. The formulation of intentions serves to arouse the individual to behavioral alternatives and, presumably, anything which directs attention to the need for specific intentions (e.g., MBO planning) can serve as a means of arousal.

One issue which will arise later in our examination of content models of motivation is relevant at this point and ought to be mentioned. This issue relates to the distinction between intrinsic and extrinsic rewards. The distinction between intrinsic and extrinsic rewards derives from the relationship between behavior and reward, not from any substantive or content difference. Intrinsic rewards are those rewards inherent in the behavior process whereas extrinsic rewards are those rewards mediated by a second party and not inherent in the behavior. Thus, examples of intrinsic rewards might include the fatigue occasioned by the behavior, emotions induced from the rhythm of behavior, and the sense of achievement or failure occasioned from the behavior. Examples of extrinsic rewards would include praise or criticism concerning the behavior, monetary rewards and penalties and similar prizes conditional upon some specified level of behavior. This distinction between intrinsic and extrinsic rewards relates to reinforcement schedules— intrinsic rewards are experienced in a regular reinforcement schedule whereas the schedule of extrinsic rewards depends critically upon the administrator of rewards. The administration of extrinsic rewards requires considerably more attention than is the case with intrinsic rewards. At the same time it is far easier to design and implement extrinsic reward systems than to design and implement intrinsic reward systems. Employee compensation is basically an extrinsic reward mediated by an administrative system, yet it can be designed to supplement intrinsic rewards as, for example, the specification of short term performance goals and the measurement of performance facilitates individual assessments of performance necessary to feeling a sense of achievement through performance. The relationships between extrinsic and intrinsic rewards are not as simple as indicated here, however, and we return to this issue in a later chapter.

B: Compensating task performance

All forms of employee compensation are contingent upon some behavior and can be viewed alternatively as incentives or rewards. Incentives are potential rewards offered to individuals contingent upon prior behavior, and expectations of these rewards are intended to influence individual choices and behaviors. Rewards are experienced following earlier contingent behavior and are intended to develop habit patterns of response conditioned by repeated pairings of behavior and rewards. Anticipated rewards constitute incentives, and incentives, once received, are experienced as rewards. Both the expectancy and reinforcement models of motivation involve behavior-reward contingencies, the one focusing upon anticipations and choice, the other focusing upon rewards and response patterns.

While various types of desired employee behaviors can be identified, we have distinguished among the behaviors associated with three aspects of labor supply: (1) employee membership in the organization represented by joining and staying with the organization, (2) supply of labor services to specific jobs represented by acceptance of job assignments and minimal task performance, and (3) individual task performance beyond minimal role requirements. Compensation contingencies associated with the first two of these have been examined in analyses of wage level and wage structure, membership pay and job pay. Compensation contingencies related to the third aspect, individual task performance, can be viewed as performance pay and are considered in this chapter, the pairing of inducements with relatively specific performance contributions in the employment exchange. Wage level characterizes rewards for membership in the organization and varies from one organization to another; job rate characterizes rewards for minimal job performance and varies from one job to another; so, too, individual rates characterize rewards for varying performance levels in the job and should vary from one individual to another.

Despite the fact that both the expectancy and reinforcement models involve behavior-reward contingencies, there are some distinct differences between the two models. The expectancy model analyzes behavior as a consequence of choice, cognitive choice based upon expectations and inducements are viewed as incentives to influence choice. Reinforcement theory analyzes behavior as conditioned through repeated pairings of behavior and rewards and thus appears most relevant in the establishment of habits for repetitive forms of behavior. The decision to join an organization, a relatively uncommon and nonrepetitive behavior for most persons, is usually associated with conscious choice and probably is best understood in that context; the concept of wage level is clearly interpretable as an incentive to influence choice. A similar analysis might be applied to the role of job compensation in the wage structure as an influence of job choices. While wage level and job rate have clear incentive value in the influence of choices, it is not as clear that receipt of a weekly or monthly paycheck serves effectively as a reward in the reinforcement model. Thus certain aspects of inducements probably are easily understood as incentives within the context of the expectancy model while others are more easily understood as rewards within the context of the reinforcement model. Similarly, certain employment behaviors such as choice of organization and job are more easily analyzed within the context of the expectancy model, while other behaviors such as checking errors in a column of figures or stopping work to gossip with a co-worker are less clearly functions of conscious choice and may be better analyzed within the context of the reinforcement model. It is for this reason that we introduced the expectancy model earlier in our examination of labor supply to the organization (Vroom) and now consider the reinforcement model as well in our analysis of specific performance behavior within the job assignment.

Three issues or concerns arise in any consideration of contingent rewards: (1) the criterion or prior condition upon which rewards are contingent, (2) the degree of relationship between criterion and reward represented in expectancy of reward or schedule of reinforcement, and (3) the amount or form of reward which influences the valence or reinforcement properties of the reward. Various criteria or prior conditions may be established for contingent rewards—joining and maintaining membership are necessary conditions for receipt of periodic paychecks, for continued coverage under insurance and pension programs, and for obtaining discounts on purchase of the organization's products; minimal task performance is a necessary condition for receipt of the compensation associated with the job and for receipt of perquisites associated with the job such as office furnishings, company car, and expense account. Similarly, performance criteria may be established for contingent performance pay, criteria such as rate of absenteeism and/or tardiness, quantity and/or quality of output, accepted suggestions for change in work procedures, training or educational programs completed, or supervisory assessments of loyalty and potential for advancement. Both the expectancy and reinforcement models would predict that choices and behavior patterns can be directed toward specific performance criteria, and both would agree that operational criteria rather than intended criteria will be induced by contingency compensation. That is to say that the effective criterion will be the specific measure employed as a contingency criterion, whatever the intended prior performance. The design of criterion measures is critical in the use of contingency rewards to influence performance. For example, tardiness measures obtained from time clock records as the criterion for contingency compensation may reduce measured tardiness as employees have others clock them in although actual tardiness is unchanged. Careful measurement and control of the intended criterion for contingency rewards thus becomes quite critical in the use of contingency rewards to shape behavior.

The second issue, introduced in the essay by Hamner, relates to schedules of reinforcement and expectancies of reward contingent upon performance. The reinforcement model would predict quicker conditioning or learning under a continuous reinforcement schedule, probability of reward given performance equal to 1.0, and slower learning but greater retention under a variable reinforcement schedule, probability less than 1.0. The expectancy model associates greater force with higher expected valence implying maximal force with the probability equal to 1.0, a continuous reinforcement schedule. Interestingly, piece-rate compensation, once common in industry, exemplifies the continuous reinforcement schedule and yet has been abandoned in much of industry because of resistance by employees and associated problems of administration. A more common approach to rewarding individual performance involves periodic, subjective judgments by supervisors as the basis for merit increases, performance bonuses, and other forms of contingency compensation. This shift from more objective to less objective criteria for compensation, from more frequent to less frequent rewards, and from continuous to variable reinforcement schedules is contrary to recommendations implicit in both the expectancy and reinforcement models, and yet apparently enjoys more acceptance by the employees involved. Piece-rate forms of compensation currently are more commonly employed in the compensation of sales persons and professionals engaged in entrepreneurial activity rather than in the compensation of plant and office employees.

The third aspect of contingency compensation relates to the amount or form of contingency reward. Both the expectancy and reinforcement models would predict that rewards valued highly by the individual are more effective in influencing choices and conditioning behavior than are less highly valued rewards. While monetary compensation has been the major focus of our attention, other characteristics of the employment exchange also are rewarding and can be structured as contingency rewards. Compensation itself, for example, takes many forms, each of which can be employed in different contingency relationships. Pension payments are contingent upon length of service, insurance coverage is contingent upon continued sevice, perquisites are contingent upon job assignment, and stock options are contingent upon judgments of performance contributions. People work for pay or monetary compensation and it is unlikely they would generally accept praise, interesting work, or share ownership in lieu of pay; it is not as obvious, however, that monetary compensation is the most valued reward for a change in level of performance. Neither is it apparent how rewarding and incentive aspects of pay vary with the amount of pay, the relationship between the amount of valence or utility and amount of compensation. Relatively little is known at present about the valence or utility associated with different forms of contingency rewards or the amount of such rewards.

Essay 7–4 illustrates research into the effects of different reinforcement schedules upon work performance. Yukl, Latham, and Pursell report an experimental application of reinforcement schedules in a work setting where persons were employed in planting tree seedlings. Workers were paid a minimum base rate of compensation and were offered performance bonuses beyond that base compensation. Two different schedules were employed in calculating the performance bonus: (1) a continuous reinforcement schedule analogous to piece-rate, and (2) a variable reinforcement schedule under which performance level qualified individuals for probabilistic rewards. Given the probabilities involved in the variable reinforcement schedule, expected earnings were higher than under the continuous reinforcement schedule and the expectancy model would have predicted higher performance; predictions of the reinforcement model are ambiguous. In fact, no differences in performance were observed although the workers expressed preference for the continuous schedule. The authors speculate to the effect that the religious, educational, and socioeconomic backgrounds of the workers may have influenced their preferences for the security of the continuous schedules and that the presence of a competing schedule (the hourly base rate) may have influenced the lack of any difference in performance under the two schedules. These potential influences of the impact of reward schedules upon performance will be present in any applied setting and make difficult the direct transfer of findings from laboratory research into field applications.

The selection from Locke (Essay 7–5) elaborates upon his earlier discussion of the role of goals or intentions in motivation and presents some interesting findings about performance relationships with goals and with incentive compensation. Locke varied the amount of piece-rate incentive provided for performance of a simple laboratory task and the level of performance goal assigned individuals, difficult goals being those with lower probability of achievement. In summary, he reports no relationship between performance and level of incentive provided and a striking positive relationship between performance and difficulty of performance goals. In the context of expectancy theory, performance increased as the expectancy of relationship between effort and performance declined, but did not vary as the amount of reward associated with performance increased. One interpretation of Locke's findings focuses upon the difference between the roles of goals and monetary compensation in motivation. The acceptance of performance goals provides the opportunity for intrinsic reward through goal achievement, an intrinsic reward which will vary directly with the difficulty of the goal; monetary compensation is an extrinsic reward, a reward which may in this instance appear quite inconsequential relative to the intrinsic reward of goal achievement. Locke does suggest that monetary compensation may influence the level of goal accepted as an intention for performance, but he attributes the resulting performance to the motivation provided by the intentions as goals.

In Essay 7–6 Pritchard and Curts build upon Locke's study and report results of an experiment which indicate that both intentions and contingency compensation influence performance independently. They confirm Locke's finding regarding the influence of intentions upon performance and demonstrate that contingency compensation of a larger magnitude than considered by Locke also influences performance. These findings suggest that schedules of extrinsic compensation (monetary) can be used in securing acceptance of difficult goals (as in MBO planning) to provide the opportunity for intrinsic rewards of goal achievement which might not be present in the absence of goal commitment. This combination of intrinsic and extrinsic reward opportunities apparently provides greater motivational opportunities than monetary compensation schedules considered alone.

Several studies in recent years have challenged the hypothesis that intrinsic and extrinsic motivations are additive and have argued that the linking of extrinsic rewards to performance diminishes intrinsic satisfactions from job performance. In extreme form, this hypothesis would suggest that what was considered play is changed into work when linked with extrinsic performance rewards. While an interesting hypothesis, the research evidence is far from conclusive and the evidence of Pritchard and Curts concerning the additive influence of goals and contingency compensation upon performance is more convincing.

The valence of alternative forms of compensation (salary, sick leave, bonus, dental insurance, vacation, pension) has been discussed in the design of compensation programs and has been investigated in various surveys. The issue arises in consideration of which form of compensation provides relatively more valence viewed either as incentive or reward. Forms of compensation structured in terms of individual preferences presumably provide greatest reward to individuals. Various surveys of compensation preferences indicate that preferences do not always parallel cost to the employer and that preferences vary widely among individuals and organizations; there appear to be few generalizable relationships about preferences which might be applied in all situations. Recognition of this wide variance in preferences underlies proposals for cafeteria-style compensation programs where individuals are permitted to exercise limited choice of the form of compensation, a proposal which has been implemented in a few organizations. Unless contingent upon achievement of specified performance levels, it would not appear that choice among alternative forms of compensation would have any direct relationship to task performance, however. The distinction between extrinsic and intrinsic contingency rewards discussed above probably has more relevance in consideration of task performance.

The issue of how varying amounts of contingency compensation influence performance was considered indirectly in comparison of the selections from Locke and from Pritchard and Curts. Pritchard and Curts provided relatively greater contingency compensation than Locke and reported performance relationships not obtained by Locke. Other things being equal, it would appear reasonable to assume that the motivational effect of contingency compensation opportunities would vary with the valence or utility associated with the amount of compensation offered as an incentive. While it is unclear how valence or utility is associated with varying amounts of compensation, economic theory typically assumes diminishing marginal utility of any good including money; equal amounts of increase in money provide less utility as the base against which the money is compared increases. Thus the valence or utility associated with an incentive of $2 would be expected to be less for a person earning $10 than for a person earning only $5. Common assumptions to the effect that equal proportionate increases are equivalent in valence or utility are consistent with the assumption of diminishing marginal utility but cannot be deduced from that assumption. Psychophysical research into stimulus discrimination provides evidence of a relatively constant function relating size of a just noticeable difference of stimulus level to the level of stimulus experienced previously for a variety of psychophysical stimuli. This relationship, titled Weber–Fechner relationship, indicates that the size of a just noticeable increase in stimulus level is a constant proportion of previous stimulus level. Despite obvious differences between compensation and stimuli such as noise level and temperature, it is tempting to infer a similar relationship between just noticeable increases in compensation and current earnings. Several studies investigating possible Weber–Fechner relationships between just noticeable increases in compensation and current earnings have been inconclusive; just noticeable increases expressed as a ratio of current earnings vary with level of earnings and also vary among individuals at the same level of earnings. Possible reasons for this reported variance relate to the appropriateness of current earnings as the base against which compensation increases are compared. Opsahl and Dunnette observed earlier that compensation and compensation increases symbolize many different things (status, recognition, achievement, standard of living) and the standards for judging a just noticeable increase may well vary from one to another. The selection from Krefting and Mahoney reports one investigation of just noticeable increases in compensation with results suggestive of multiple criteria and related bases for judging increases in compensation. Results of this study suggest no single criterion for establishing variable amounts of compensation increases; rather, they describe the inconclusiveness of current theory and research as guides to varying amounts of compensation increases.

The final selection (Essay 7–8) from Whyte discusses another issue concerning task performance and contingency compensation, an issue already raised by Livernash. Whyte examines contingency compensation, particularly piece-rate compensation, in terms of what it symbolizes to the individual. Whyte also reasons that employees commonly work in teams or groups and react to contingency compensation as members of the group rather than as individuals. His analysis suggests that contingency compensation for individual task performance provides pleasurable rewards in the form of additional compensation and recognition for performance, but also fosters competition within the work group, threatens disruption of established social relationships, and may even jeopardize the jobs of less productive workers. Thus contingency compensation for individual task performance symbolizes both pleasure and pain to the individual in a work group; the performance effects of contingency compensation depend upon circumstances which are associated with the compensation, not the reward system itself. Like Livernash, Whyte emphasizes the role of the social setting in determination of individual assessments of, and reactions to, compensation. For many of the reasons identified by Whyte, employees working in groups appear to resist contingency compensation based upon objective measures of individual performance, and contingency compensation based upon infrequent, more subjective measures of individual performance (merit increases) have tended to replace piece-rate types of compensation. Piece-rate types of compensation such as commissions are quite common, however, for employees working individually such as sales persons where the influence of group and social norms is not present.

Various issues regarding contingency compensation and task performance are raised in these readings, issues that are not easily resolved at this time. In summary, all of the readings point up the complexities involved in the application of contingency compensation for individual task performance. A relatively simple concept like "pay for performance" becomes complex in application as one considers the appropriate measures of performance, alternative schedules for relating performance and pay, the amount and form of contingency compensation to be provided, and the likely interpretation of contingency compensation in a particular work setting. Whyte's concern about the influence of social setting upon reactions to contingency compensation, although written in 1955, is particularly relevant today with the developing trends toward greater use of work teams, project teams, and related approaches to work organization as means of providing greater job enrichment. We return to this concern in a later chapter with examination of the Scanlon Plan as an approach to compensation based upon consideration of social influences upon performance.

Essay 7-4

The effectiveness of performance incentives under continuous and variable ratio schedules of reinforcement*

Gary A. Yukl, Gary O. Latham,
and Elliott D. Pursell

A fundamental assumption in operant conditioning (Skinner, 1938) is that motivation as defined by the frequency with which an individual makes a given response, can be understood in terms of two basic concepts, namely, reinforcement and schedules of reinforcement (Ferster and Skinner, 1957). A reinforcer is any object or event (e.g., an employee's smile or a supervisor's praise) that when given immediately or almost immediately after a specific behavior is emitted increases the probability that the behavior (e.g., coming to work) will be repeated. A reinforcer that has been found to be effective for increasing the performance of rural workers is money (Lawler, 1971). In fact, money is probably one of the most durable reinforcers for all individuals who are old enough to appreciate its use (Bijou and Baer, 1966).

The success with which a behavior is strengthened, maintained, or weakened is dependent in part upon the frequency (scheduling) with which the reinforcers are administered (Luthans and Kreitner, 1975). For example, if every time a child, a worker, a manager, or a union official shouted they got their way, the probability that these individuals would again emit this response under similar conditions would be increased. If, on the other

hand, these individuals had emitted alternative behaviors to yelling (e.g., wrote a memo or spoke in a quiet voice) and those behaviors had not been reinforced, the probability that those responses would be repeated would be quite low. Thus, a basic strategy for motivating an individual on the job, using an operant paradigm, is to (a) identify those variables that are reinforcing for specific behaviors; (b) make the reinforcer a consequence of these job behaviors; and (c) determine the optimum schedule for administering the reinforcer.

A reinforcer which occurs every time an employee emits a specific behavior is called a continuous schedule of reinforcement (CRF). An individual who is reinforced every "nth" time he engages in a specific behavior is said to be on a fixed ratio schedule. For example, if every eighth time an individual emitted a specific behavior he was reinforced, he would be on a fixed ratio 8 schedule (FR-8). The number 8 designates the ratio of quantitative responses to reinforcement.

A variable ratio schedule is one in which a reinforcer occurs after only some of the responses, and the ratio of reinforced responses changes within the same schedule from time to time. For example, a reinforcer might be administered after one response, then after three more responses, then after six, then after five, etc. However, a mean (average) number of responses for reinforcement is chosen. A variable ratio 4 schedule (VR-4) means that a specific behavior is reinforced on

*Reprinted from Gary A. Yukl, Gary O. Latham, and Elliott D. Pursell, "The Effectiveness of Performance Incentives under Continuous and Variable Ration Schedules of Reinforcement," *Personnel Psychology* 29 (1976), pp. 221-31.

the average one out of four times. The number 4 designates the *mean* ratio of quantitative responses to reinforcement.

Ferster and Skinner have found that the schedule of reinforcement may have a greater effect on response rate than the size or magnitude of the reinforcer. Unfortunately, much of the research that has been done in support of this finding has been restricted to laboratory, hospital, or school settings. One exception to this trend was a job simulation study by Yukl, Wexley, and Seymour (1972). Part-time workers (college students) were paid $1.50 an hour to score multiple choice examinations. The workers were then divided into three groups. Each individual in one group was told that he would receive a 25¢ bonus for every batch of examinations (a continuous schedule) that he graded. The second group of individuals was told that each of them would receive a 50¢ bonus contingent upon grading a batch of examinations and correctly guessing the outcome of a coin toss (a VR-2 schedule since the ratio of reinforcements to responses was ½ as determined by a coin flip). The individuals in the third group were told that each of them would receive a 25¢ bonus contingent upon grading a batch of examinations and correctly guessing the outcome of a coin toss (a VR-2 schedule where the magnitude of the reinforcer was the same as that given to the individuals in the first group and 50 percent less than that given to the individuals in the second group). The productivity of Group 2 was significantly higher than that of Group 1 even though the individuals in each group received the same amount of money over time (25¢ every time versus 50¢ half the time). The productivity of Group 3 equaled that of Group 1 even though the individuals in the third group were paid 50% less than the individuals in Group 1.

Unfortunately, what is true or applicable in one instance is not necessarily true or applicable in another instance. Yukl and Latham (1975) compared the results of continuous and variable ratio schedules of reinforcement on tree planters in the rural South. In one crew, workers were given a $2 bonus contingent upon planting a bag of trees. In a second crew, workers were given a $4 bonus contingent upon planting a bag of trees and correctly guessing the outcome of one coin toss. Workers in a third crew were given an $8 bonus contingent upon planting a bag of trees and correctly guessing the outcome of two coin tosses. Productivity was highest for the workers on the continuous schedule of reinforcement.

This was the first study to compare the relative effectiveness of pay incentives on productivity in industry using different reinforcement schedules. Unfortunately, several methodological problems in that study prevented the authors from drawing firm conclusions. The most serious limitation was the possibility that differences between reinforcement conditions were due to extraneous factors. The planters could not be randomly assigned to the crews (i.e., treatments), and the crews may have differed in several respects (e.g., leadership).

The present study was conducted one year later to determine if the earlier results could be supported, and to investigate worker preferences for different incentive plans.

METHOD

Sample

The subjects were 16 male and 12 female employees who planted pine seedlings in North Carolina. These workers differed from the marginal workers studied by Yukl and Latham (1975) in that the present subjects were semiliterate, they consisted of whites as well as blacks, and their productivity was considered adequate by management. Many of these workers were individuals who, due to local and national economic conditions, had been laid off from year-round jobs, and who had thus resorted to seasonal field work. As in the original study, the planters worked in pairs. The pairs were mixed by sex and race and they all worked in the same area for the same supervisor. The composition of the pairs varied occasionally from day to day.

Procedure

A repeated measures design with alternating incentive periods was used to compare employee performance under $2 continuous reinforcement, $8-VR4, $4-VR2, and no-incentive conditions, Money was used as a reinforcer because interviews indicated that it was highly valued by the workers.

The original plan was to obtain a no-incentive premeasure for each planter, and then to expose the planters to a series of alternating periods under CRF and VR schedules. However, a short planting season and loss of many planting days due to rain prevented us from using as many incentive periods as were desired. Moreover, unavoidable criterion contamination on some planting days (e.g., planting unprepared land, pairing experienced planters with new ones for rapid training) limited the number of days with comparable data ("usable days"). The final design consisted of the following consecutive study periods: (1) a no-incentive premeasure period with data for 12 usable days of a four-week interval; (2) a continuous reinforcement period with data for ten usable days of a four-week interval; (3) a VR-4 period with data for nine usable days of a two-week interval; (4) another continuous schedule of reinforcement period with data for all ten working days of a two-week interval; and (5) a VR-2 period with data for nine usable days of a two-week interval. The explanation given to the workers during each phase of the study was as follows:

a. Continous schedule: In addition to your hourly pay you will always receive a $2 bonus contingent upon planting 1,000 trees.

b. VR-4: We realize that work can be difficult and tiring. As a result we would like you to have a chance to earn more money and to have some fun in the process. From here on, you are going to have the opportunity to receive $8 every time you plant 1,000 trees. All you have to do is correctly guess the color of a marble, held in your supervisor's hand, two consecutive times. If you guess incorrectly you don't really lose anything because you will always receive your regular hourly pay.

c. Continuous schedule: We are going to discard the game with the marbles for the next few weeks. From here on you will receive a $2 bonus every time you plant 1,000 trees.

The final time period in this study called for the reintroduction of the VR-4 schedule. However, the workers so disliked this schedule (to be discussed later) that a compromise was reached by substituting a VR-2 schedule. In this condition a $4 bonus was made contingent upon planting 1,000 trees and correctly guessing the color of only one marble.

"Correctly guessing the color of a marble" was used to ensure that the administration of the reinforcement would be variable or intermittent rather than continuous, and to ensure that the employee would perceive that the presentation of a reinforcer was under the control of his own behavior and not the behavior of someone in management. Any incentive money earned by a pair of workers who were planting together was split between them. The number and value of the chips given to each planter was recorded by the supervisor. Each week the chips were redeemed with a check for the amount of money won the previous week.

More than 50 individuals worked in the planting crew over the course of the study, but many of them were only employed for a short period of time. Due to the high rate of turnover and absenteeism, only eight planters worked in all five time periods. In order to maximize the size and representativeness of the sample used in the data analysis, pairs of conditions were compared separately rather than comparing all the conditions simultaneously. Each analysis was based on data from all of the planters who worked a majority of the working days in both of the conditions being compared.

A major difference in the present procedure from the previous study (Yukl and Latham, 1975) was the measurement of performance. In the earlier study, each pair of workers had their own bag of trees, and the number of bags was counted. In this study, a change in company regulations required that the crew work out of a common bag. Each pair of planters had a tallymeter to count the number of trees he or she planted. Productivity, measured for each worker, was thus defined as the number of trees planted divided by the manhours worked. To prevent any serious exaggeration of the count by the worker, a total tallymeter count of the crew was compared regularly with the bag count.

RESULTS

The variable ratio manipulation was checked by computing the actual rate at which the planters were reinforced. The overall rate for the planters used in the data analysis was 51 percent in the VR-4 condition and 68 percent in the VR-2 condition, which is substantially higher than intended. An attempt to discover the reason for the discrepancy, including observations of the crew on several different occasions, was not successful.

Despite the problems of an excessive reinforcement rate and a short period of exposure to each VR reinforcement schedule, some interesting results were

found. The effect of introducing the initial continuous reinforcement (CRF) condition was examined first. Of the 20 planters who worked throughout most of the premeasure period and most of the first CRF period, 15 planters had higher productivity after the incentive was introduced. A binomial test indicated that this proportion was highly significant ($p <$ .02). Productivity remained the same or declined slightly for four of the planters. However, there was a very large decline for a fifth planter whose premeasure performance was the highest in the sample. This was due to the fact that this individual had usually been paired with a highly productive co-worker who left the job after the premeasure period. The mean productivity of the 20 planters was 117.1 trees per hour in the premeasure period and 120.5 trees per hour in the CRF period ($t = 1.70$, $df = 19$, $p < .06$).[1]

The amount of improvement in productivity on the continuous schedule of reinforcement was not very substantial (3%) compared to improvement (33%) obtained with the same schedule and the same reinforcer in the previous study. However, the smaller amount of improvement is not surprising in light of the high premeasure performance in the present study. Planting conditions were quite favorable during the premeasure period, and the crew appeared to be highly motivated. The premeasure mean in this study (117 trees/hour) was considerably higher than the premeasure mean of the CRF group in the Yukl and Latham study (89 trees/hour), and it was nearly as high as the mean performance of the CRF group in that earlier study when it was receiving incentive (119 trees/hour).[2] The pre-

---

[1] Data from the second CRF period was not used for this comparison because there may have been carryover effects from the intervening VR period; actually, the results are similar if these data are included ($t = 1.69$).

[2] The number of trees per bag varies somewhat, but was found to average 1,100 rather than 1,000 reported by Yukl and Latham (1975).

measure mean in the present study was also higher than the mean performance of Yukl and Latham's comparison group (112 trees/hour) who worked in the same location the previous year. Since there is obviously a physical limit to how quickly a pair of planters can correctly plant seedlings, there was not as much potential for performance improvement in this study as in the earlier one.

The continuous reinforcement condition and the variable ratio schedule of 51 percent (originally intended to be VR-4) were compared next. Sixteen planters worked during most of the VR-51 percent period and most or part of the two CRF periods. An individual's average performance in each of the three time periods was examined to see if a certain trend or pattern was typical. Eight of the 16 planters showed a V-shaped reversal pattern. That is, the workers' performance was lower in the VR-51 percent period than in either continuous reinforcement period. Three planters showed an upward linear pattern (first CRF $<$ VR-51% $<$ second CRF), two planters showed a downward linear pattern (first CRF $>$ VR-51% $>$ second CRF), and three planters showed a reversal pattern with higher performance under the VR-51 percent condition than in either the first or second CRF period. Assuming that the likelihood of the four patterns is equal according to chance, a binomial test revealed that the probability of finding this many cases of the V-shaped reversal pattern is only .02. Thus the dominant pattern was for planters to perform better under the two CRF conditions than under the VR-51 percent schedule.

The performance data for both CRF periods were combined and a matched t test was used to compare it with performance on the VR-51 percent schedule. This analysis included three planters who worked in the VR-51 percent period, but who had only worked in one of the CRF periods. The mean performance of the 19 planters was 117.2 trees per hour in the CRF condition and 111.7 trees per hour in the VR-51 percent condition ($t = 2.08$, $df = 18$, $p < .05$). These results are consistent with the preceding analysis. Performance was higher in the CRF condition despite the fact that the amount of money received for planting 1,000 trees was slightly less than half the average amount received in the VR-51 percent condition ($2.00 vs. $4.08) due to the inflated rate of reinforcement in the latter condition.

Since the reinforcement rate varied considerably in the VR-51 percent condition, it was possible to conduct a supplementary analysis to determine the effects of a VR schedule on performance. The seven planters with the lowest rate of reinforcement (averaging 38%) were comparable to the VR-4 crew in the Yukl and Latham (1975) study, which had a 34 percent rate of reinforcement. For this subsample, the difference between mean performance on the VR-38 percent schedule (105 trees/hour) and mean performance on the combined CRF schedules (118 trees/hour) was even larger than the difference found for the entire sample ($t = 3.31$, $df = 6$, $p < .01$). On the other hand, for the seven planters on the highest variable ratio schedule (averaging 62%), performance (122 trees/hour) was not significantly different from the combined CRF periods (119 trees/hour). The two subsamples were compared to assess the effects of a variable ratio schedule of 38 percent versus a variable ratio schedule of 62 percent. The subsample with the higher rate of reinforcement (VR-62%) had significantly higher productivity ($t = 2.05$, $df = 12$, $p < .05$). In other words, when the magnitude of the reinforcer ($8) was held constant, performance was higher for workers who received a higher rate of reinforcement.

Performance on the VR-51 percent schedule was also compared to performance in the premeasure period using the

13 planters who worked during most of the usable days In both perlods. The mean productivity of these planters on the variable ratio schedule (116.6 trees/hour) was not significantly different from their mean productivity in the no-incentive premeasure period (119.0 trees/hour).

There were nine planters who worked during most of the VR-51 percent period as well as during most of the VR-68 percent (originally intended to be VR-2) period. Mean productivity was 121.9 trees per hour in the VR-68 percent period and 111.6 trees per hour in the VR-51 percent period for these workers. The difference between conditions was significant ($t = 3.55$, $df = 8$, $p < .01$), and it is consistent with the difference found within the VR-51 percent condition between subgroups of workers with different rates of reinforcement. Thus, despite a higher average incentive earned by these workers for 1,000 trees in the VR-51 percent condition (51% of $8.00 = $4.08) than in the VR-68 percent condition (68% of $4.00 = $2.72), performance increased as the rate of reinforcement increased.

The same nine planters also worked during the second CRF period, and their mean productivity during this period was 121.8 trees per hour. There was no significant difference between productivity in the CRF and VR-68 percent periods for these workers, even though the average incentive earned for 1,000 trees was somewhat higher in the VR-68 percent condition ($2.72 vs. $2.00). This finding is consistent with the absence of a significant difference between productivity under CRF and variable ratio reinforcement for the subgroup of planters with a high rate of reinforcement (62%) in the intended VR-4 period.

Productivity for the VR-68 percent period (the intended VR-2 schedule) was also compared to premeasure productivity. Only eight planters worked during most of these two widely separated time periods. No significant difference was found.

The final analysis involved the preferences of planters for different pay plans. A short questionnaire, administered at the end of the study, requested the workers to indicate which of the following four pay plans they preferred: $2 CRF; $4 VR-2; $8 VR-4; or a 25¢ per hour increase in their hourly pay.[3] Eighteen of the 22 planters (82%) said that they would prefer a flat 25¢ hourly increase. A binomial test indicated that this proportion was significantly higher than that which would be expected by chance ($p < .01$). The planters were next asked which of the three contingent incentives they would prefer to work under. The preference expressed by 17 of the planters (77%) was for the $2 CRF incentive ($p < .01$ by a binomial test). Finally, the planters were asked to indicate which incentive condition they would least prefer; 17 workers (77%) specified the VR-4 incentive ($p < .01$) by a binomial test).

Comments made on the questionnaire suggested that the planters did not like the uncertainty of a VR schedule (e.g., "odds too great," "unfair—too much of a risk") and were disappointed when they didn't win ("it's a let-down to lose after you've planted 1,000 trees"). These comments and complaints were similar to those voiced to supervisors in the previous study (Yukl and Latham, 1975). The comments were made despite the fact that all of the workers actually made more money per 1,000 trees planted under the "inflated" VR schedules.

DISCUSSION

The present research by itself falls short of what one would call a well-controlled experiment. There undoubtedly were variables operating in an unknown fashion which affected the results. Nevertheless, the problems encountered are not atypical

---

[3] The 25¢ per hour increase is nearly equal to the average per hour increase in earnings under the CRF schedule.

of those found in field settings (Reppucci and Saunders, 1974). In spite of these difficulties, and particularly because of the supporting data from a previous study (Yukl and Latham, 1975), several conclusions can be drawn.

The preferences of the planters were consistent with the results for performance. That is, despite the larger average earnings in the VR conditions due to the inflated reinforcement rates, the planters preferred the continuous schedule of reinforcement and performed as well or better under this condition. These results are also consistent with the results from the previous study (Yukl and Latham, 1975). The two studies complement each other, since the major limitations of one are avoided by the other. The possibility in the first study that the treatment effects were due to systematic differences between the groups was avoided in the second study by using within-subject comparisons. The possibility in the second study that the differences in incentive effects were due to order of incentive conditions, changes in planting conditions over time, or inadequate exposure to the VR schedules was avoided in the first study. Thus we are now more confident about concluding that, for the type of workers used in these two studies, a variable ratio schedule is less effective for improving performance than a continuous reinforcement schedule.

Both studies, however, share a common limitation. A variable ratio schedule based on a coin toss or the correct selection of a colored marble may not deserve the same nomenclature as VR schedules which do not include this particular kind of operation.[4] In most operant conditioning studies a VR schedule is predetermined for each subject. At the present time no administratively feasible procedure has been found for doing this with employees when

the reinforcer is money. Establishing a predetermined VR schedule for each employee was impractical because the employees would not have accepted a procedure where their incentive appeared to be given on the whim of the supervisor.

A second limitation common to both studies is that the planters were working under two concurrent schedules. That is, the workers were reinforced for attendance (pay contingent upon number of hours worked) as well as for performance. Using a strict operant conditioning paradigm, the two schedules should not have been mixed if strict comparisons were desired between the continuous and variable ratio schedules of reinforcement for performance. Once again, satisfying this requirement was not administratively feasible.

The results from the two studies with tree planters were clearly different from the results obtained by Yukl et al. (1972) even though those authors used a coin toss and concurrent reinforcement schedules. As previously noted, performance increased more for the student-workers in that study who were paid 50¢ randomly on half of the occasions they completed a unit of output than for individuals who were paid 25¢ for each unit of output. The higher response rates under a variable ratio schedule in the study by Yukl et al. may reflect differences between tree planters and college students in education and cultural background. The difference in results may also reflect a difference in economic conditions. The experience of losing potential incentive earnings was probably less disturbing to middle-class college students working in a temporary, part-time job than to workers in a lower economic bracket who must do seasonal work to earn a living. The expressed preference for a flat hourly increase as opposed to even a continuous schedule of reinforcement is in agreement with research reviewed by Lawler (1971) which showed that less educated people who

---

[4] The authors are grateful to H. M. Parsons and Marilyn Quaintance for their insights in this area.

have strong security needs and who are not high in needs for advancement and responsibility are not in favor of having their pay based upon performance.

REFERENCES

Bijou, S. W., and Baer, D. M. "Operant Methods in Child Behavior and Development." In W. K. Honig (ed.) *Operant Behavior: Areas of Research and Application.* New York: Appleton-Century-Crofts, 1966.

Ferster, C. B., and Skinner, B. F. *Schedules of Reinforcement.* New York: Appleton-Century-Crofts, 1957.

Lawler, E. E. *Pay and Organizational Effectiveness: A Psychological View.* New York: McGraw-Hill, 1971.

Luthans, F., and Kreitner, R. *Organizational Behavior Modification.* Glenview: Scott, Foresman, 1975.

Reppucci, N., and Saunders, J. T. "Social Psychology of Behavior Modification: Problems of Implementation in Natural Settings." *American Psychologist* 29 (1974), 649-60.

Skinner, B. F. *The Behavior of Organisms.* New York: Appleton-Century-Crofts, 1938.

Yukl, G. A., and Latham, G. P. "Consequences of Reinforcement Schedules and Incentive Magnitudes for Employee Performance: Problems Encountered in an Industrial Setting." *Journal of Applied Psychology* 60 (1975), 294-98.

Yukl, G. A.; Wexley, K. N.; and Seymour, J. D. "Effectiveness of Pay Incentives under Variable Ratio and Continuous Reinforcement Schedules." *Journal of Applied Psychology* 56 (1972), 19-23.

Essay *7-5*

Goals and intentions as mediators of the effects of external incentives*

Edwin A. Locke

In a number of the experiments reported in Part I (Essay 7-3), goals were manipulated by instructions. However, in most of the studies conducted by the author subjects' *acceptance* of their assigned goals was corroborated by interviews. Thus these studies were legitimately described as dealing with the relationship between goals and performance rather than the relationship between instructions and performance.

As every experimenter and shop foreman knows, one of the most efficient ways to get somebody to do something is to ask him, i.e., to *assign* him a goal or

*Reprinted from Edwin A. Locke, "Toward a Theory of Task Motivation and Incentives," *Organizational Behavior and Human Performance* 3 (1968), pp. 173-89.

task. But it is important to recognize that instructions do not inevitably nor automatically affect an individual's goals or behavior. For example, in some of the studies reported in Part I, postexperimental interviews revealed that subjects did *not* accept their assigned goals. For these subjects there was no relationship between assigned goals and performance. Only when these subjects were reclassified according to the goals they actually reported working for did a relationship between goals and performance emerge (e.g., see Locke and Bryan, 1966b, 1967a).

Our theory suggests that instructions will affect behavior only if they are consciously accepted by the individual and translated into specific goals or intentions.

This applies equally well to the instruction by an experimenter to "try for quality in your answers" to the instruction by a shop foreman to "produce 400 portzeebies an hour." It is not enough to know that an order or request was made; one has to know whether or not the individual heard it and understood it, how he appraised it, and what he decided to do about it before its effects on his behavior can be predicted and explained.

There have been very few studies in which the effectiveness of instructions and intentions in accounting for behavior have been actually compared. However, in the second study (Study 4 in Locke et al., 1968) of word unscrambling discussed previously in Part I, subjects were instructed to choose words to unscramble which would provide either "success," "achievement," or "challenge;" instructions correlated significantly with word choice ($r = .67$, $p < .01$), but this correlation was completely vitiated when the subjects' own behavioral intentions (established after the instructions were given) were partialed out ($r_p = .08$). In other words, the instructions were correlated with choice only by virtue of their correlation with intentions and had no effect on behavior over and above their effect on intentions.

Stedry's (1960) study should also be recalled in this context. Subjects tended to reject hard goals assigned by the experimenter if they had already set their own personal goals.

In a memory experiment Eagle (1967) instructed different subjects to use either a rehearsal strategy or an associative strategy in memorizing a list of words. Eagle found that instructions per se had no effect on amount of recall; only when subjects were reclassified according to the strategy they *actually reported using* did a difference between groups emerge (in favor of those using the associative strategy).

Although instructions are the most commonly used incentive in everyday life, most psychological research has been focused on other types of incentives such as money, knowledge of results, participation, etc. Let us turn now to evidence concerning the dependence of their effects on goals and intentions.

Goals as mediators of the effects of incentives on level of performance

Money. In a study reported by Locke et al. (1968) subjects worked on a brainstorming task (giving uses for objects) for three blocks of seven trials each. Goal-setting instructions and amount of incentive offered for output were systematically manipulated. It was found that subjects who set their goals high on block III relative to block II improved their performance on block III more than those whose block III goals were not substantially higher than their block II goals. On the other hand, there was no main effect of incentive independent of goal level. Subjects who had the same output goals produced the same amount whether they were paid a bonus for reaching the goal or not. Using groups' means as the units of analysis, the rank order correlation between output and goal level was .85 ($p < .01$).

In a second study reported by Locke et al., 30 subjects worked for 50 minutes at a toy construction task. The subjects set output goals at the beginning and at the halfway point of the work period. Half the subjects were paid on a piece-rate system and half were paid only for participation. It was found that the mean output of the two groups did not differ significantly in either half of the work period. This finding was congruent with the fact that the mean goal level of the two groups did not differ significantly in either period. On the other hand, when all subjects were combined, there was a significant relationship between second-half performance and second-half goal level.

Numerous industrial studies of the effects of monetary incentives on performance have found that the effectiveness of piece-rate incentive systems depend on the particular production quotas that workers have (e.g., Mathewson, 1931; Roethlisberger and Dickson, 1939; Whyte, 1955). If the workers feel that their long-term self-interest (either in terms of inter-personal relations, effort, or job tenure) will be threatened by trying to go "all out" for piece-rate earnings, they will restrict production to what they consider to be a "safe" level (a level that will protect their jobs and/or keep the time study man from retiming the job and setting new rates, etc.).

One effect of a well-run incentive system is that (providing the workers value money) it will encourage workers to accept tasks and set goals that they would not accept or set on their own (i.e., for the intrinsic enjoyment of the work itself). Thus, money can serve to *commit* subjects to tasks which they would not otherwise undertake. The use of incentives to insure goal acceptance was a key element in Taylor's (1911) "scientific management" system.

Knowledge of score. The studies to be reported in this section are concerned only with the effects of knowledge of overall scores (KS) on a task or knowledge of score on a task where there are no right or wrong answers (e.g., reaction time). Thus, we are concerned with "motivational" knowledge as opposed to epistemic knowledge of the type that can be used to correct errors (e.g., visual feedback on a dart-throwing task).

An initial study by Locke and Bryan (1966b) compared the effect of KS vs. NoKS on a complex computation task. Some subjects were allowed to compute their scores after each trial and some were not. The subjects had six trials of 10 minutes each. No difference was found between the KS and NoKS groups in performance. However, when the subjects were reclassified according to their postexperi-

mental goal descriptions, a significant relationship of goals to performance was found.

Two subsequent studies manipulated goal-setting and KS independently using a 2 X 2 design (Locke, 1967b; Locke and Bryan, 1967c). In both studies subjects worked on five trials of irregular duration (mean = 12 minutes) at an addition task. Periodically half the subjects (KS group) were given their scores and half (NoKS group) were not. In the first study, half the subjects were given specific hard goals to aim for on each trial, while the other half were told to "do their best." In the second study, half the subjects were given easy goals to aim for and half were given hard goals. In both studies, the subjects with hard goals performed significantly better than those with easy or do-best goals, but no difference in performance was found between the KS and NoKS groups. The results for the Locke (1967b) study are shown in Figures 1A and B. The hard-goal group is clearly superior to the do-best group in performance whereas the KS and NoKS groups have very similar performance curves.

Another study (Locke and Bryan, 1967b) found that when KS does facilitate performance, it does so only *through* its effects on goal-setting. Subjects were given 16 5-minute trials on a complex computation task. One group of subjects was allowed to compute their scores after each trial and another was not. Subjects filled out goal description questionnaires before, during, and after performance. It was found that the KS subjects performed significantly better than the NoKS subjects on the last eight trials, and it was only on these trials that the KS subjects set harder goals than the NoKS subjects. When differential goal-setting was controlled by partialing, the relationship of KS condition to performance was vitiated.

The important thing about KS, then, is not merely whether it is given or not given

Figure 1: The relationship of goals and knowledge of score to performance

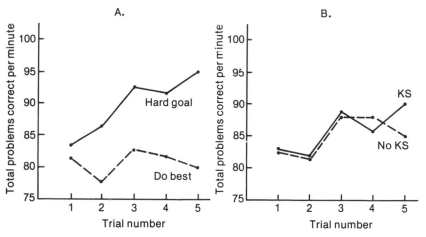

but how a subject interprets and evaluates it, and what goals he sets in response to it. The *form* in which KS in given, of course, can influence its effectiveness. For instance, if KS is given in such a form that it cannot be used to set goals or to judge one's progress in relation to a standard (as in Locke, 1967b; Locke and Bryan, 1967c) it will not affect motivation.

If, on the other hand, KS is given in relation to standards, the level of the standard can influence goal level. Locke (1967c) gave subjects feedback on a reaction-time task in relation to different standards; some subjects were told on each trial whether or not they had beaten their *best* previous score and others whether or not they had beaten their *worst* previous score. Positive feedback was given by means of a green light which signalled that a subject successfully beat the standard. In this study, subjects with the harder ("best") standards showed faster reaction times than those with easier ("worst") standards. To get green-light feedback, they had to try harder in the former case than in the latter. Thus giving knowledge in relation to the different standards in effect influenced the difficulty of the goals subjects tried for.

Time limits. Two studies by Bryan and

Locke (1967b) gave subjects different amounts of time to complete an addition task. One group of individuals was given just enough time to complete the problems (the number being geared to the subject's level of ability) while another group was given twice this amount of time. It was found that the subjects given an excess amount of time took longer to complete the task than those given a minimum amount of time. The subjects given an excess amount of time also set easier goals on the task than did those given a minimum amount of time. When time limits were removed and subjects were free to work at their own pace, both experimental groups set their goals at the same level and worked at the same pace. Thus, the effect of the different time limits appeared to be a function of the differing performance subgoals which they induced. Their effects did not extend to a situation where the work was self-paced.

The foregoing studies of time limits can be viewed as belonging to a wider class of studies concerned with the effect of task difficulty on performance. The difference between these studies and those discussed above is that in the present case no goals (other than completing the problems in the time allowed) were assigned as such; the subject was simply given a task and told how much time he had to complete it. The effect of the imposed time limits was a function of the goals the subjects set in response to them.

The above studies virtually exhaust the literature on the topic of goals as mediators of the effect of incentives on performance level. Our treatment of the next three incentives: participation, competition, and praise and reproof, is therefore confined mainly to a discussion of experiments in which goal-setting was mentioned only incidentally, or to discussion at the theoretical level.

Participation. A number of investigators have argued that employee participation in the decisions that affect them motivates better job performance (e.g., Maier, 1955; Likert, 1961; Viteles, 1953; Vroom, 1964), and there is research evidence that would appear to support this claim. However, the question that concerns us here is *how* participation serves to motivate job performance when it does so. In the typical field experiment on participation, many aspects of the job are likely to be changed: e.g., job method (method of performing the task), method of payment, rate of pay, quality and quantity of training, type of supervision, commitment of the worker to his assigned quota, the level of the quota, etc. Any one of these factors could affect subsequent production, but experimental research has not systematically tested the relative importance of each.

It will suffice for our purposes to point out that goal-setting, specifically a change in the production quota, has been an explicit element in many participation studies. For example, see the following description of Bavelas' study by Viteles 1953, p. 167):

. . . in the course of . . . [participation] meetings, the experimenter . . . talked about the greater ease of working together as a team; discussed in-

dividual production levels with the group; questioned its members as to the level of production which might be obtained if they worked as a team, and *asked if they would like to set a team goal for higher production* (italics mine).

In another study of participation by Lawrence and Smith (1955), the authors write:

Members of these groups were encouraged to use their own judgment in setting goals, but were reminded that *unless they set the goal a little above their present accomplishment they would be unable to determine the effectiveness of the group when working as a team* (p. 334, italics mine).

Similarly in a study of participation at General Electric reported by Sorcher (1967): "The employees were asked . . . to set quality goals for themselves, and to discuss how they might improve their performance so as to improve the quality of their output" (p. 16). In this study substantial improvements in work quality were obtained as a result of the group meetings.

Most revealing of all is a recent field study conducted by Meyer et al. (1965) where the effects of participation and goal-setting were more clearly separated. The authors found that: "While subordinate participation in the goal-setting process had some effect on improved performance, *a much more powerful influence was whether goals were set at all*" (p. 126, italics mine). In other words the content of the participation sessions was more important than the fact of participation itself.

The above quotes should not be taken to imply that participation has no motivational effect in and of itself. For example, Macoby (quoted in Viteles, 1953) suggests that participation may help to internalize motivation—to increase a subject's *commitment* to performance standards. The point is that goal-setting has been an integral part of previous studies of participation. Considering the amount of evidence there is (see Part I) that goals regulate performance, it must be concluded that the results of at least some of these studies can be attributed largely, if not entirely, to the goal-setting which was associated with, or induced by, the experimental design.

Competition. It is well known, both from experimental studies and from everyday experience, that competition can serve as an incentive to increase one's effort on a task. This phenomenon is an intrinsic part of athletics and business and is not unknown in academia. In the paradigm case of competition *another person's or group's performance is the standard by which goals are set and success and failure judged.* One reason competition in athletics is so effective is that winning requires that one surpass the performance of the *best* existing competitor. This typically results in the standard of success becoming progressively more difficult with time. Each time a record is broken, the level of performance required to win (against the record holder) is raised. Each competitor must then readjust his goal and his level of effort to the difficulty of the task. The result is progressively better performance. (Of course cognitive factors can facilitate performance improvement, i.e., discovering better methods of performing the task. But it is the individual's *goal* to win or improve that generally motivates the search for such innovations.)

The case is similar though not identical in business. (Unlike athletics, business is not a "zero-sum game," where one man's gain necessarily means another man's loss. In business, wealth is *created* and therefore everyone benefits in the long run). Competition will encourage the development of better and better products as long as there are firms who wish to increase their share of the market. Competition may also spur firms to increase their quality or lower prices in order not to lose business.

The effect of competition, both between individuals and between groups, depends upon the particular person or persons one is competing with and one's own values. In athletics, the goal is typically to beat the best other competitor. In business this is not always the case; typically, business firms are satisfied to surpass their own best previous performances. Students, if they are competing, will ordinarily pick other students with grades or abilities similar to their own to compete with, or else will try to surpass their own best previous grade-point average.

The case of an individual trying to improve over his own previous performance on a task can be considered a special case of competition: *self-competition.*

As with participation, competition may have other effects besides inducing goal-setting. Above all, competition probably encourages individuals to remain *committed* to goals that they might otherwise abandon in the face of fatigue and difficulty. For instance, if mile runners only ran against themselves or against a stop watch, the 4-minute mile might never have been broken.

In addition, competition encourages the setting of goals that might not have been set at all in the absence of the other party. For example, if the Ford Motor Company had not developed a mass-produced low-priced automobile, General Motors might not have thought of developing a similar (competing) model (at that particular time).

Praise and reproof. A recent review of the literature on praise and reproof (Kennedy and Willcutt, 1964) concluded that the effects of both incentives were highly variable though praise was generally more effective in improving performance. Most studies have found complex interactions between praise and reproof and such variables as: age, social class, race, sex, task, and intelligence.

As with all the other incentives discussed heretofore, the present theory suggests that the effects of praise and reproof will be a function of what goals the individual sets in response to them. It is clear from introspection and from everyday experience that sometimes the reaction to criticism is to clench one's teeth and try harder; at other times, the reaction is to give up (and "sulk") or to deliberately do badly (to "get even" with the critic). Similarly, praise sometimes leads to the setting of new and higher goals and at other times it is taken as a signal to "goof-off."

A theory explaining the precise circumstances in which praise and reproof will lead to the setting of higher and/or lower goals is beyond the scope of this paper. The important point is, however, that the effects of these incentives on performance should be a function of the goals the individuals set in response to them. The highly inconsistent results obtained by previous investigators may be attributed to their failure to control for differential goal-setting by subjects in the different experimental conditions.

The importance of goal-setting was implicitly recognized in one study, whose authors Kennedy and Willcutt (1964) paraphrase as follows:

The authors concluded that when the examiner's statements led subjects to assume that a particular level of performance is expected or that his performance is less satisfactory than that of other subjects, failure increases motivation; but when the examiner's statements only comment upon the subject's performance, failure lowers motivation (p. 329).

This implies that reproof will have a facilitative effect on performance when it is given *in relation to a standard*. Our previous discussion of knowledge of score suggested the same thing; giving scores in relation to a standard is one means of implicitly manipulating or encouraging goal-setting by a subject.

Another factor that has not always been controlled in studies of praise and reproof is that of success and failure. In some studies (e.g., Anderson, White, and Wash, 1966) subjects were given fictitious

test scores in relation to some (fictitious) norm and then praised (for high scores) or reproved (for low scores). Without two control groups given success and failure feedback alone, the relative contribution of praise and reproof as compared with task success and failure cannot be determined.

Let us turn now to the effects of incentives on choice.

Behavioral intentions and desires as mediators of the effects of incentives on choice

Money. Each of the three studies of word unscrambling described above (and reported in Locke et al., 1968) involved monetary incentives. In the first study, subjects were offered: 0 cents for successfully unscrambling their chosen word on the first block of ten trials; 2 cents for each word solved correctly (regardless of length) on the second block; and 10 cents for each word solved correctly (regardless of length) on the third block. It was found that subjects tended to choose easier words as the payment for success became greater. There was a correlation across blocks between amount of incentive and mean word-length choice of $-.51$ ($p < .05$). However, this correlation was vitiated ($r = .22$, ns) when the effects of intentions were partialed out, indicating that the money did not affect word choice independent of its effects on the subjects' intentions.

In the second study discussed above, subjects were given "success," "achievement," or "challenge" instructions on the first block of ten trials, but were offered no money for correct solutions. On the second block, subjects were given no instructions but were offered 4 cents for each word correctly solved regardless of length. The point biserial correlation, for all subjects combined, between mean word-length choice and incentive (coded 0 and 1 for blocks I and II, respectively) across blocks was −.48 ($p < .01$). However, when intentions were partialed out this r was reduced to a nonsignificant −.10. In contrast, intentions correlated .86 ($p < .01$) with word choice across blocks after incentive was partialed out.

In the third study in this series described above, subjects had five blocks of five trials each; on each block the subject was offered either 1, 2, 3, 4, or 5 cents for each word solved correctly on that block regardless of length. (The order was counterbalanced across subjects.) Again subjects tended to choose easier words when offered the higher incentive. The relationship of intentions and incentive to mean word choice is shown in Figure 2, where word choice is plotted as a function of incentive for each of three levels of intention. (Intention level 1.0 corresponds to the "very easy words" alternative on the intention scale; 2.0 corresponds to the "fairly easy words" alternative; 3.0 corresponds to the "neither too easy nor too hard" alternative; the few subjects who checked intentions harder than this are also included in this group.) It is clear that the effect of intention on word choice

Figure 2: Word-length choice as a function of incentive for three levels of intention

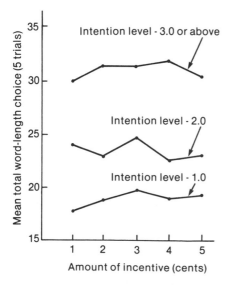

was considerable but there was no effect of incentive within any given intention level. As in the previous two studies, incentive had no effect on word choice independent of the subjects' behavioral intentions. (There was also a no-incentive comparison group in this study. The results were the same whether or not this group was included. For the complete report, see Locke et al., 1968, Study 5.) The overall correlation across blocks between intentions and word choice was .83 ($p < .01$); this correlation remained unchanged after partialing incentive. In contrast, the correlation across blocks of incentive with word choice after partialing intentions was .04 (ns).

Verbal "reinforcement." The previously discussed findings of Dulany (1962, 1968) and Holmes (1966) regarding behavioral intentions and verbal responses were obtained in studies of "verbal conditioning." The subjects in these studies were instructed to free associate or to make up sentences beginning with one of a number of pronouns, and the experimenter reinforced some arbitrarily designated class of words (e.g., plural nouns) or pronouns (e.g., I, or We) by saying "good" or "Mmm-hmm" after each response in that class. In the above three studies it was found that such "reinforcement" had no effect on responses independent of subjects' intention to give the "correct" response.

Another series of studies in this same area examined the effects of the subjects' conscious *desires* on behavior. In these studies subjects were asked to indicate the strength of their desire to get the reinforcement ("good," etc.) which the experimenter provided (e.g., DeNike, 1965; Spielberger, Berger, and Howard, 1963; Spielberger, Bernstein, and Ratliff, 1966; Spielberger, Levin, and Shepard, 1962). It was found that the frequency of emission of the "correct" response class was a direct function of the strength of the subject's desire to get the reinforcement (provided he knew what the "correct" response class was).

DISCUSSION

There is considerable evidence to support the view that goals and intentions are important determinants of task performance. It is argued that these long-neglected concepts are important enough so that any tenable theory of human motivation must take account of them. This conclusion is based both on the fact that consciousness is man's means of survival (Rand, 1964) and on the strong empirical relationships that have been obtained between goals and behavior.

The experimental findings also indicate that goals and intentions mediate the effects of incentives on behavior. It appears that a necessary condition for incentives to affect behavior is that the individual recognize and evaluate the incentive and develop goals, and/or intentions in response to this evaluation. A careful examination of the subjects' goals and intentions in research on incentives should produce more clear-cut results as well as providing a theoretical rationale for explaining how incentives affect action.

A highly simplified schematic showing the hypothesized sequence of events leading from events in the environment to action is given below:

Environmental			Goal-setting	
Event →	Cog- nition →	Evalu- ation →	Inten- tion →	Perfor- mance
(e.g., incentive)				
(1)	(2)	(3)	(4)	(5)

The present research examined only the relationships between stages 4 and 5, and between 1, 4, and 5. Cognition and evaluation were assumed to occur, but their contents were not specified. The focus of interest was on the *results* of these processes

(the goals or intentions established) and subsequent action. A complete theory of task motivation would, of course, have to deal with the processes of cognition and evaluation (and their determinants) as well as their outcomes.

It may be useful theoretically to classify the various incentives that were discussed in Part II. For our purposes the dimension of interest is the degree to which the different types of incentives suggest *specific* goals or intentions to subjects.

Instructions, of course, are the most direct means of manipulating goals and intentions. Instructions will influence behavior providing: (1) the individual accepts them, i.e., accepts the assignment as his own goal or intention, and (2) he is able to do what is asked (this will depend upon his knowledge, ability and the situation).

Giving an individual specific *time limits* is another fairly direct means of manipulating goals, given the same qualifications as for instructions. It was shown previously that individuals who accept different time limits will set different subgoals as well, but these were a result of their accepting the different time limits initially.

Two less direct means of manipulating goals are giving *knowledge of score* and providing *competition*. These incentives do not tell the subject directly what goal to try for, but if given in the right form, they may *suggest* specific standards to him. For instance, giving a subject his raw scores after each trial may suggest the goal of improvement (providing the trials are all the same length so that the trial scores are comparable). Similarly, giving KS in relation to some external standard is certain to imply a goal to the subject. Giving scores in relation to those of another person is a common way of combining KS and competition. Again the effects of both incentives will be dependent upon the subject choosing to use the KS to set goals or to try to beat the other individual. These two incentives are usually quite effective in experimental situations where the subject is actively looking for cues as to what he is supposed to do and is anxious to cooperate (Orne, 1962).

Money, praise and *reproof*, and *participation*, in contrast to the above incentives, are quite indirect means of manipulating goals. None of them directly suggests or implies that the subject should try for a *particular* goal as such. Offering an individual money for output may motivate him to set his goals higher than he would otherwise but this will depend entirely upon how much money he wishes to make and how much effort he wishes to expend to make it. It is useful in this context to recall the well-known sociologist Max Weber's observation that the introduction of high incentive pay may reduce output if the worker's income aspirations remain the same as before the incentive was introduced. Some workers would prefer to make the same money in less time than to make more money in the same amount of time. The most important role played by money is probably to get a subject to accept an assigned task or goal or to insure his commitment to a job.

Similarly participation as such will not necessarily suggest a higher output goal; this will depend on the particular *content* of the participation process (the particular nature of the decisions reached). The most direct effect of participation is probably to commit a subject to the decision reached (as with money), whatever that might be.

The effects of praise and reproof on goal-setting are also indirect. Praise and reproof per se represent only evaluations of the subject's past performance and do not imply what *he should do* in the future. A subject's reaction to these incentives will depend on such factors as whether he considers the comments just or unjust, the particular work context in which the comments were made, his liking and respect for the person making the comments, his own personality, etc.

In most real life work situations a combination of all of these incentives is employed. A worker is hired and *instructed* on what to do and *how fast* to do it; he is given or gets *knowledge of performance* either from others or from the task itself; he may *compete* with others for promotion; he is *paid* for working, he is *evaluated* by his supervisor, and sometimes he *participates* in decision making. All of these factors can be considered ways of (1) getting the subject to set or accept work goals, and (2) retaining his commitment to them and insuring persistence over time.

The issue of goal commitment has not been dealt with in any of the research discussed above, but it is no doubt an important factor in performance. The subject's degree of commitment to his goal may play an important role in determining how easily he will give up in the face of difficulty, how likely he will be to "goof off" when not being pressured from the outside, how likely he will be to abandon hard goals, and how prone he will be to "leave the field" (i.e., job) in the face of stress.

REFERENCES

Anderson, H. E.; White, W. F.; and Wash, J. A. "Generalized Effects of Praise and Reproof." *Journal of Educational Psychology* 57 (1966), 169-73.

Bryan, J. F., and Locke, E. A. "Parkinson's Law as a Goal-Setting Phenomenon." *Organizational Behavior and Human Performance* 2 (1967), 258-75. (b)

DeNike, L. D. "Recall of Reinforcement and Conative Activity in Verbal Conditioning." *Psychological Reports* 16 (1965), 345-46.

Dulany, D. E., Jr. "The Place of Hypotheses and Intentions: An Analysis of Verbal Control in Verbal Conditioning." In C. W. Eriksen (ed.), *Behavior and Awareness.* Durham, North Carolina: Duke Univ. Press, 1962, pp. 102-29.

Dulany, D. E., Jr. "Awareness, Rules and Propositional Control: A Confrontation with S-R Behavior Theory." In D. Horton and T. Dixon (eds.), *Verbal Behavior and General Behavior*

Theory. Englewood Cliffs, New Jersey: Prentice-Hall, 1968, pp. 340-87.

Eagle, M. N. "The Effect of Learning Strategies upon Free Recall." *American Journal of Psychology* 80 (1967), 421-25.

Holmes, D. S. "Verbal Conditioning or Problem Solving and Cooperation?" Midwestern Psychological Association, 1966.

Kennedy, W. A., and Willcutt, H. C. "Praise and Blame as Incentives." *Psychological Bulletin* 62 (1964), 323-32.

Lawrence, L. C., and Smith, P. C. "Group Decision and Employee Participation." *Journal of Applied Psychology* 39 (1955), 334-37.

Likert, R. *New Patterns of Management.* New York: McGraw-Hill, 1961.

Locke, E. A. "The Motivational Effects of Knowledge of Results: Knowledge or Goal-Setting?" *Journal of Applied Psychology* 51 (1967), 324-29. (b)

Locke, E. A. "The Effects of Knowledge of Results and Knowledge in Relation to Standards on Reaction Time Performance." American Institutes for Research (unpublished results), 1967. (c)

Locke, E. A., and Bryan, J. F. "The Effects of Goal-Setting, Rule-Learning and Knowledge of Score on Performance." *American Journal of Psychology* 79 (1966), 451-57. (b)

Locke, E. A., and Bryan, J. F. "Performance Goals as Determinants of Level of Performance and Boredom." *Journal of Applied Psychology* 51 (1967), 120-30. (a)

Locke, E. A., and Bryan, J. F. "Goal-Setting as a Determinant of the Effect of Knowledge of Score on Performance." American Institutes for Research (unpublished results), 1967. (b)

Locke, E. A., and Bryan, J. F. "Knowledge of Score and Goal Difficulty as Determinants of Work Rate." American Institutes for Research (unpublished results), 1967. (c)

Locke, E. A.; Bryan, J. F.; and Kendall, L. M. "Goals and Intentions as Mediators of the Effects of Monetary Incentives on Behavior." *Journal of Applied Psychology* 52 (1968), 104-21.

Maier, N. F. *Psychology in Industry.* New York: Houghton, 1955, pp. 137-80.

Mathewson, S. B. *Restriction of Output among Unorganized Workers.* New York: Viking Press, 1931.

Meyer, H. H.; Kay, E.; and French, J. R. P., Jr. "Split Roles in Performance Appraisal." *Harvard Business Review* 43 (1965), 123-29.

Orne, M. T. "On the Social Psychology of the Psychological Experiment with Particular Reference to Demand Characteristics." *American Psychologist* 17 (1962), 776-83.

Rand, Ayn. "The Objectivist Ethics." In Ayn Rand (ed.), *The Virtue of Selfishness.* New York: Signet, 1964, pp. 13-35.

Roethlisberger, F. J., and Dickson, W. J. *Management and the Worker.* Cambridge, Massachusetts: Harvard Univ. Press, 1939.

Sorcher, M. "Motivating the Hourly Employee." General Electric, Behavioral Research Service, 1967.

Spielberger, C. D.; Berger, A.; and Howard, K. "Conditioning of Verbal Behavior as a Function of Awareness, Need for Social Approval, and Motivation to Receive Reinforcement." *Journal of Abnormal and Social Psychology* 67 (1963), 241-46.

Spielberger, C. D.; Bernstein, I. H.; and Ratliff, R. G. "Information and Incentive Value of the Reinforcing Stimulus in Verbal Conditioning." *Journal of Experimental Psychology* 71 (1966), 26-31.

Spielberger, C. D.; Levin, S. M.; and Shepard, M. "The Effects of Awareness and Attitude toward the Reinforcement on the Operant Conditioning of Verbal Behavior." *Journal of Personality* 30 (1962), 106-21.

Stedry, A. C. *Budget Control and Cost Behavior.* Englewood Cliffs, New Jersey: Prentice-Hall, 1960.

Taylor, F. W. *The Principles of Scientific Management.* New York: Harper, 1911.

Viteles, M. S. *Motivation and Morale in Industry.* New York: Norton, 1953.

Vroom, V. H. *Work and Motivation.* New York: John Wiley, 1964.

Whyte, W. F. *Money and Motivation.* New York: John Wiley, 1955.

Essay 7-6

The influence of goal setting and financial incentives on task performance*

Robert D. Pritchard and Michael I. Curts

Locke and his associates have done a considerable amount of research on the topic of goal setting (see Locke, 1968, for review). One aspect of this research deals with the effects of financial incentives and goals on task performance. Locke, Bryan, and Kendall (1968) predicted that financial incentives have effects on performance only to the extent that they affect goal setting behavior, and that if goal setting behavior is constant, there will be no effects due to the magnitude of financial incentives. They concluded:

The results of the five studies reported here are consistent with the hypothesis that goals and intentions are . . . the mechanism by which monetary incentives influence behavior . . . (In) each of the five studies it was demonstrated that if goal or intention level was controlled or partialed out, there was no effect of amount of incentive on behavior. This was demonstrated in the studies of performance level by showing that the same goal level produced the same performance level regardless of whether incentives were offered for performance or not. (Locke, Bryan, and Kendall, 1968, p. 119.)

These results have important implications for organizational behavior. Specifically, they suggest that financial incentives will not influence performance unless goal setting also takes place.

This deemphasis on financial incentives is in direct contrast with other motivational approaches such as expectancy-valence models (e.g., Vroom, 1964; Graen, 1969; Porter and Lawler, 1968; and

*Reprinted from Robert D. Pritchard and Michael I. Curts, "The Influence of Goal Setting and Financial Incentives on Task Performance," *Organizational Behavior and Human Performance* 10 (1973), pp. 175-83.

Campbell, Dunnette, Lawler, and Weick, 1970). In fact, Lawler (1971) has recently presented an entire book on the importance of pay as an incentive in motivating job performance.

However, before we can say that the Locke et al. findings are really in conflict with the financial incentive tradition, several potential problems with the Locke et al. research must be considered. First, the financial incentives used by Locke et al. were quite small. The ranged from 2¢ to 25¢ per trial. Admittedly, there were a number of trials, but the effect of such small incentives on any given trial may have been small. Furthermore, it is reasonable to assume that other types of rewards operate in such goal setting experiments besides strictly financial rewards. Such things as feelings of achievement and pleasing the experimenter constitute rewards or incentives contingent on the subject's accomplishing the goals. To the extent that these incentives are powerful, the effects of small financial incentives may be washed out.

A second problem with the Locke et al. methodology is that in some of the experimental conditions subjects were told of the incentive and only then asked to set their own goals. With such a methodology it is difficult to separate the effects of goal setting from effects due to incentives. If a subject knows the incentive before he sets his own goal or before he accepts an assigned goal it is possible that the incentive influenced his goal setting behavior and thus his performance. In this situation it is possible that the actual goal setting itself had little or no direct influence on performance and the only effects could be due to incentives. Admittedly, the first two experiments of Locke et al. do not have this potential methodological problem. However, the last three could be so contaminated, and it is only these last three that dealt with the hypothesis that when incentive differences correlate with behavior differences, these differences will be accompanied by corresponding differences in goals or intentions.

The present study avoids this potential problem by offering incentives only after the goal has been set.

METHOD

Subjects

The subjects were 81 male and female students who signed up from the introductory psychology subject pool at Purdue University. They received experimental credit for participation as well as any money they earned during the experiment.

Task

A perceptual-motor task was used which required subjects to sort index cards into stacks according to the information contained on the card. They were told that the task was a type of information sorting task. Each card contained data from one person: sex (male-female), education (finished high school–did not finish high school), and income level (under $5,000, $5,000–10,000, over $10,000). Thus, 12 configurations of information (2 X 2 X 3) were possible. The subject's task was to read the card and place it on the one of 12 piles which corresponded to that pattern of information.

With this type of a task, performance could vary along both dimensions of quantity and quality. That is, measures of the number of cards sorted as well as the number of sorting errors are both measures of performance. Interpreting data

from such tasks is very difficult since it requires some decision rule about how many units of quantity are equal to how many units of quality. Interpretation of the data is greatly simplified if performance can only vary in terms of quantity. That is, quality variation is eliminated. To accomplish this, the cards the subjects sorted were each punched with three holes. One hole corresponding to the sex data on the card, one for the education level, and one for the income level. Thus, 12 unique patterns of three holes were generated, one pattern for each possible configuration of data. Furthermore, 12 corresponding patterns of metal spikes were attached to the sorting board. Thus, to correctly sort one card, the subject had to identify the pattern of data and fit the card on the correct set of spikes. If the subject made an error, the card would not fit on the spikes.

Procedure and conditions

Each subject reported to the experimental situation individually. The experiment was explained as a study of techniques to sort information that might be useful in clerical jobs. Every attempt was made to avoid making the task appear to be related to valued abilities such as creativity, intelligence, coordination, etc.

The task was explained to the subject and he was given a stack of 24 well-shuffled practice cards, two for each of the 12 positions, and asked to sort them. After answering any questions the subject had, he was given a large, well-shuffled stack of cards and told to sort them as quickly as he could. After ten minutes, the subject was told to stop, and the cards were removed. The subject was then given a rest period of approximately two minutes.

At this point, one of five experimental manipulations were given: goal setting—no incentive ($N = 21$); goal setting—50¢ incentive ($N = 20$); goal setting–$3 incentive

(N = 19); no goal setting—no incentive (N = 11); no goal setting—incentive (N = 10). In the goal conditions, subjects were told:

One of the things I am looking for is the improvement that a person shows on this type of a task over time. As you can guess, a person gets faster and faster at this type of a task as he learns it better. This is especially true when he first starts learning it and, in fact, we like to have people try to increase the amount of cards they sort by 30% the second try. What I would like for you to do is actually set a similar improvement goal for yourself and try to make that goal on the next set of cards. So, would you be willing to set a goal of a 30% improvement over your last attempt?

All subjects did give such a verbal commitment to the goal. This commitment was reinforced by the experimenter saying, "So, in other words, if you sorted 100 cards the last time, your personal goal this time would be 130, right?" Again verbal commitment was given by the subject.

The figure of a 30 percent increase was based on pilot work with the task and set such that 50 percent of the subjects, based on the pilot data, would reach the goal. The subjects were not told the number they had sorted on the first trial. This was done for all conditions so that subjects in the no goal conditions would not automatically set a goal of beating their first trial performance. This might be expected if they had been told the number of cards they had sorted.

After the subject had committed himself to the goal, he was given the incentive manipulation. In the zero incentive condition, nothing was said about incentives and the subject proceeded to sort for a second 10 minute period. In the 50¢ incentive condition, the subject was told: "If you do meet or exceed your goal of a 30 percent increase, in addition to the experimental points you will receive for participation in this experiment, you will also get 50¢." In the $3 incentive condi-

tion, a subject was offered $3 for reaching or exceeding his goal.

In the *no-goal conditions*, after the subject had sorted the first time, he was given the rest period, and for the incentive condition told: "Now I would like you to sort the cards for a second time, and, in addition to the experimental points you will receive for participating in the experiment, you will get 3¢ for every two cards you sort." This level of incentive was determined from the pilot work to be equivalent to the $3 incentive in the goal condition. This was accomplished by setting the piece rate so that if the performance in the piece-rate condition was equal to the performance under the $3 condition, the pay would be equal.

In the no goal—no incentive condition subjects were merely asked to sort the cards a second time.

After sorting the second time, subjects were given a short questionnaire, debriefed, paid, and dismissed.

RESULTS

The principal source of data in the experiment consists of changes in performance from trial one to trial two. The rationale for having two trials was twofold. First, such a design helps control for individual differences in ability by using each subject as his own control. Second, it was felt that having two trials would make setting a goal seem more reasonable to the subjects. Merely having them set a goal on their first trial when the experimenter had no idea of their ability to do the task might seem unreasonable to the subject.

Thus, relevant comparisons are the changes in performance from trial one to trial two in the various conditions. These data are presented in Figure 1. The data indicate that for the goal conditions there was no significant difference between the zero and 50¢ conditions, but the $3 goal condition resulted in significantly (p <

Figure 1: Differences in performance from trial
one to trial two as a function of experimental
condition

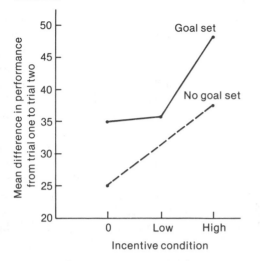

.05) greater increase in performance than did the zero incentive goal condition. The percentage of subjects who actually reached their goal in the zero, 50¢, and $3 condition were 42.9 percent, 55 percent, and 63.2 percent, respectively. In the no goal condition, the change in performance for the high incentive condition was significantly ($p < .02$) greater than for the zero incentive condition. Finally, there was a main effect due to goal setting with the goal setting conditions showing greater ($p < .05$) increase in performance than the no goal condition.

It is also of interest to examine the no goal conditions in more detail. It was felt possible that subjects in the no goal conditions might set their own performance goals for the second trial performance. To assess this, the postexperimental questionnaire asked subjects in the no goal conditions whether they had set a goal for their second trial performance. In the no incentive condition, 4 of the 11 subjects reported that they had set a goal, and 5 of the 10 subjects in the high incentive condition reported that they had set a goal.

The mean increase in performance for those subjects in the zero incentive condition who set a goal was 28.0, for those setting a goal in the high incentive condition it was 32.0. Respective figures for those not setting a goal were 24.7 and 43.3. Thus both for those subjects setting goals and for those not setting goals, the incentive conditions resulted in greater increase in performance.

It should be noted, however, that the self-set goals in the no goal condition were invariably phrased by the subjects (in the postexperimental questionnaire) in terms of sorting more cards on the second trial. Thus, they were not the specific, quantitative goals that Locke has found to have the strongest effect on performance (Locke et al., 1968).

One potential problem with the results is that the experimental group could have differed in initial ability (as reflected by their first trial performance) and that increases in performance would thus not be equally easy for all groups. In fact, the goal—$3 subjects did exhibit higher trial 1 performance than did the goal—0 subjects ($t = 2.74$, $p < .01$). However, if one assumes that subjects performing highly in the first trial would find it harder to increase their performance than subjects whose performance was lower in the first trial, we would expect groups of equal ability to support the present findings even more strongly. There were no differences in first trial performance between the zero and high incentive groups in the no goal conditions, no differences between who set and did not set a personal goal in the no goal condition, and no differences between subjects who set and did no set personal goals in the high incentive condition.

DISCUSSION

Taken as a whole, the results fail to confirm the hypothesis that incentives have no effect on performance outside of their effects on goal setting. Locke et al. (1968) point out that their hypothesis would not be supported if "different amounts of incentive should produce different levels of performance regardless of the level of the Ss' goal" (Locke et al. 1968, p. 107).

The findings of this study fulfill this condition. First, increases in performance were greater with the $3 incentive than with no incentive even though both groups of subjects set the same goal. Second, increases in performance under the piece rate condition were higher than those under the no incentive condition even though no goals were imposed and there were no real differences in personal goal setting. Finally, in the no goal condition those subjects who set a personal goal and were given an incentive increased their performance more than subjects who set a personal goal and did not receive an incentive; also, subjects who did not set a personal goal and who were given an incentive increased their performance more than subjects who did not set a personal goal and were not given an incentive.

One issue that must be considered, however, is the commitment of the subject to the goal. Locke et al. argue that one of the functions of an incentive may be to increase the subject's commitment to the goal. If it could be demonstrated that subjects offered the incentive were more committed to the goal, the Locke position would be supported in that the effects of the incentive would be operating through the mechanism of goal setting. To deal with this question, subjects were asked in the postexperimental questionnaire (given before they were told their second trial performance) to rate (a) how strongly they wanted to make their goal and (b) how important it was to them that they made their goal. Both of these ratings were made on nine-point Likert scales. Mean ratings for the strength of desire to make the goal for the goal-zero incentive, goal-low incentive, and goal-high incentive conditions were 7.52, 6.95, and 7.16, respectively. For the goal importance item these means were 7.19, 6.25, and 6.32. These data show that for both items, the subjects in the high incentive condition reported slightly lower commitment to the goal than did the subjects in the zero incentive condition. Thus, commitment to the goal due to the size of the incentive does not appear to be a factor influencing the results.

It is interesting to note that some of the Locke findings were indeed replicated. The data indicate that goal setting does have a positive effect on performance. More importantly, however, the Locke findings regarding the effects of incentives and goal setting were replicated in the 50¢ incentive condition. Specifically, when the incentive was 50¢ there was no difference in increases in performance between the goal-zero incentive condition and the goal–50¢ incentive condition. Thus, when the financial incentive is small, it appears to have no effect on performance over and above that due to goal setting. However, when the incentive is larger ($3) the incentive does effect performance over and above the effects of goal setting alone. It is quite possible, therefore, that the use of task instructions stressing creativity, coupled with low per-trial incentives such as those used by Locke et al. could tend to make the financial incentive effect quite weak and thus lead to the conclusion of no effect due to financial incentives.

The question remains, however, of how to explain the present results. We would argue that incentive effects and goal setting effects are both operating, and operating independently. Expectancy-valence models such as those presented by Vroom, 1964; Porter and Lawler, 1968; Campbell et al., 1970; and Lawler, 1971 would predict that as the valence of high performance increases by increasing the valence of outcomes associated with high performance, effort increases. Thus, the higher the financial incentive, the higher the effort and the higher the performance. Examination of the data within goal conditions supports this prediction in every case. Thus, we would argue that the anticipation of valued outcomes is influencing performance.

In addition, however, goal setting effects are also present. The subjects in the goal conditions clearly outperformed subjects in the no goal conditions. Thus, setting explicit goals does effect performance. What we are arguing is that the data indicate that the effects of goal setting are independent of the effects of financial incentives and that incentive effects as predicted by expectancy-valence models are supported when explicit goals are not set. In fact, the positive effects of goal setting could be predicted from expectancy-valence models. One could assume that successfully accomplishing the goal results in the satisfaction of such needs as achievement and recognition. The satisfaction of these needs are positive outcomes, and are contingent on high performance. Thus, the valence of high performance for subjects who set a goal is higher than for those subjects who do not set a goal. Expectancy-valence models would thus predict that subjects who set goals should exert more effort than subjects who do not set goals. This prediction is supported by the present data.

In terms of practical implications, the results of this study imply that while goal setting may enhance task performance, incentives can also have positive effects on task performance and that these incentive effects are in addition to rather than included in goal setting effects. Thus, while an organization may achieve positive effects on performance from goal setting procedures, these goal setting procedures should not replace financial incentives. In fact, the results of this study imply that the optimal strategy would be to use goal setting procedures in conjunction with financial incentives.

REFERENCES

Campbell, J. D.; Dunnette, M. D.; Lawler, E. E.; and Weick, K. E. *Managerial Behavior, Performance, and Effectiveness.* New York: McGraw-Hill, 1970.

Graen, G. B. "Instrumentality Theory of Work Motivation: Some Experimental Results and Suggested Modifications." *Journal of Applied Psychology* 53 (1969) 2, 1–25.

Lawler, E. E. *Pay and Organizational Effectiveness: A Psychological View.* New York: McGraw-Hill, 1971.

Locke, E. A. "Toward a Theory of Task Motivation and Incentives." *Organizational Behavior and Human Performance* 3 (1968) 157–89.

Locke, E. A.; Bryan, J. F.; and Kendall, L. M. "Goals and Intentions as Mediators of the Effects of Monetary Incentives on Behavior." *Journal of Applied Psychology* 52 (1968) 2, 104–21.

Porter, L. V. and Lawler, E. E. *Managerial Attitudes and Performance.* Homewood, Ill.: Irwin–Dorsey, 1968.

Vroom, V. H. *Work and Motivation.* New York: Wiley, 1964.

Essay 7-7

Determining the size of a meaningful pay increase*

Linda A. Krefting and Thomas A. Mahoney

Pay increases are important organizational rewards. Indeed, it is generally assumed that most employees see pay increases, rather than current level of pay, as the organization's reward for performance.[1] To be effective as rewards, they should be large enough to be meaningful. But how large is large enough? There are likely to be individual differences in this reward threshold. Compensation policies could be more efficiently designed and administered if the factors affecting these thresholds were understood and pay increases were geared to individual thresholds.

PREVIOUS RESEARCH

Although there is a great deal of research on pay related topics, much of it dealing with pay increases or differences in pay levels, most studies ignore the psychological meaning of pay or the question of pay increase thresholds.[2] The few studies which have focused directly on this threshold—i.e., on the smallest meaningful pay increase (hereafter referred to as SMPI)—indicate that some pay differences or pay increases seem too small to be meaningful to employees[3]—and that this threshold varies among individuals in a manner which may be related to their current pay levels.

Although these initial studies provide interesting insights into SMPI, they leave several issues unresolved: (1) SMPI has been viewed as a relatively constant percentage of pay, but the research estimates of this constant percentage vary greatly, from 3.5 to 11.5 percent. (2) The SMPI-pay relationship has only been tested indirectly by comparing SMPI to pay ratios. A much stronger test would be a direct measure of association between SMPI and pay. (3) Research efforts have concentrated on the single factor of pay as an influence on SMPI; other factors might also be feasibly considered.

---

*Reprinted from Linda A. Krefting and Thomas A. Mahoney, "Determining the Size of a Meaningful Pay Increase," *Industrial Relations* 16 (1977), pp. 83-93 (abridged).

[1] See, for example, Mason Haire, Edwin E. Ghiselli, and Lyman W. Porter, "Psychological Research on Pay: An Overview," *Industrial Relations* 3 (October 1963), 3-8; Robert L. Opsahl and Marvin D. Dunnette, "The Role of Financial Compensation in Industrial Motivation," *Psychological Bulletin* 68 (February 1966), 94-118; and David C. McClelland, "Money as a Motivator: Some Research Insights," *Management Review* 57 (Fall 1968), 23-28.

[2] For research on the effectiveness of monetary incentives, see Edward E. Lawler III, *Pay and Organizational Effectiveness* (New York: McGraw-Hill, 1971). For a recent review of equity research, see Paul S. Goodman and Abraham Friedman, "An Examination of Adam's Theory of Inequity," *Administrative Science*

Quarterly 16 (September 1971), 271-88. For research on the utility of pay increases, see Brian Giles and Gerald Ba rett, "Utility of Merit Increases," *Journal of Applied Psychology* 55 (April 1971), 103-109; and Jay R. Schuster, Jerome A. Collette, and Lyle Knowles, Jr., "The Relationship Between Perceptions Concerning Magnitude of Pay and Perceived Utility of Pay: Public and Private Organizations Compared," *Organizational Behavior and Human Performance* 9 (February 1973), 110-19.

[3] There have been three studies; Sheldon Zedeck and Patricia C. Smith, "A Psychological Determination of Equitable Payment," *Journal of Applied Psychology* 52 (October 1968), 343-47; W. Corbett and R. Potocko, "Economic and Psychological Determinants of the Comparability of Pay," *Proceedings* of the 77th Annual Convention of the American Psychological Association 4 (Part 2), 1969, pp. 711-12; John Hinrichs, "Correlates of Employee Evaluations of Pay Increases," *Journal of Applied Psychology* 53 (December 1969), 481-89.

ALTERNATIVE EXPLANATIONS OF SMPI

Because of the lack of theoretical work related to SMPI, previous researchers borrowed from the psychophysical and adaptation level literature which suggests that a subject evaluates an increase in the amount of some variable by comparing it with a base level.[4] SMPI researchers have assumed that employees evaluate pay increases in terms of a relatively constant function of current pay. Alternate possibilities—not so far considered—are that employees evaluate pay increases by comparing these with the amount they perceive as "normal" or "common" for pay increases or by examining the impact of these increases on their standard of living or consumption level.

The argument for *normal* pay increase as an influence on SMPI is best stated in terms of an adaptation level: those pay increases that the individual compares favorably with his notion of a range of accustomed pay increases are concrete indications of organizational recognition.[5] Pay increases that are perceived to be small relative to other pay increases do not suggest recognition and are probably not perceived as rewarding. According to this hypothesis, SMPI is the smallest pay increase within a range of normal pay increases based on the individual's pay experience and knowledge of the situation.

On the other hand, it can be argued that pay increases acquire meaning to the extent that they allow change in living standards.[6] If so, SMPI should be related to such factors as the individual's income (not pay), changes in the cost of living, and the cost of additional goods and services the individual would like to purchase.

Thus, arguments and research can be presented to support three alternative reference points—pay level, normal pay increase, and consumption—in the evaluation of pay increases and factors influencing SMPI. At the moment, there is insufficient evidence to determine which of these becomes the most important influence, particularly since two or even all three factors may influence SMPI simultaneously. Another possibility is that the relevance or salience of reference points may vary considerably among groups of employees; one group might rely on one reference point, while a second group uses another.

The meaning of a pay increase might determine which factor is most relevant as a reference point. If the meaning of a pay increase varies among individuals or groups, the factors influencing SMPI might also vary. For those who value pay increases for *recognition*, normal pay increases would have the greatest influence on SMPI, whereas for those who value pay increases for the *money*, consumption would have a greater influence. Within this framework pay itself has little inherent meaning and is thus unlikely to be the primary influence on SMPI.

It has also been suggested that satisfaction is related to pay expectations and demands and thus may also influence SMPI. For instance, it may take a larger pay increase to be meaningful to someone dissatisfied with current pay or with his job in general.[7] While job and pay satisfaction would not independently determine SMPI, they might supplement one of the other factors in explaining SMPI.

[4] E. Galanter, "Contemporary Psychophysics," in E. Galanter, ed., *New Directions in Psychology* (New York: Holt, Rinehart, and Winston, 1962); Harry Helson, *Adaptation Level Theory* (New York: Harper and Row, 1964).

[5] This argument can be found in Elliott Jaques, *Equitable Payment* (New York: Wiley, 1961) and McClelland, op. cit.

[6] The argument is stated most clearly by Saul Gellerman, *Management by Motivation* (New York: American Management Association, 1968).

[7] Lawler, op. cit., and Rober L. Opsahl, "Managerial Compensation: Needed Research," *Organizational Behavior and Human Performance* 2 (May 1967), 208-16.

RESEARCH DESIGN

The research reported here focuses on the issues raised concerning the smallest pay increase the individual finds meaningful. Specifically, the questions addressed are:

1. Does pay level, normal pay increase, or consumption best explain SMPI?

2. Would some combination of pay level, normal pay increase, and consumption variables explain SMPI better than a single factor alone?

3. How would the meaning of a pay increase affect the relationship between the alternative factors and SMPI?

4. Does job or pay satisfaction supplement the alternative factors in explaining SMPI?

DETERMINANTS OF SMPI

The individual contribution to SMPI of each of the three alternative factors was determined by regressing SMPI separately on pay level, the normal pay increase variables, and the consumption variables. These regression results are presented in the top part of Table 1. A comparison of the variance explained by each of the three regression equations suggests that all three factors could account for statistically significant but small amounts of variance in SMPI. Consumption was the most explanatory factor, explaining 15 percent of the variance, but it accounted for only 4 percent more variance than the least explanatory factor, pay.

Stepwise regression was used to determine (1) if a combination of pay level, the normal pay increase variables, and the consumption variables might explain SMPI better than a single factor alone and (2) if satisfaction could account for unique variance in SMPI. Four variables (income increment to keep up with the cost of living, last pay increase, expected pay increase, and pay satisfaction) contributed significantly to the explanation of SMPI. The fact that the variables in the equation represented more than one factor and could account for 26 percent of the SMPI variation indicates that a combination of factors can explain SMPI better than a single factor. The stepwise regression equation included a combination of normal pay increase, consumption, and satisfaction variables and could account for 11 percent more variance than the best single factor, consumption. The inclusion of pay satisfaction in the combination suggests that satisfaction has an independent influence on SMPI.

To assess the effects of the meaning of a pay increase, the sample was first divided into the "recognition" and "money" groups. SMPI was regressed separately on pay, normal pay increase, and consumption for each group to see which of the three factors could best account for SMPI, as shown in the bottom part of Table 1. For the recognition group, the normal pay increase variables explained considerably more variance (11 percent more) than either of the other two factors. For the money group, the consumption variables predicted SMPI better. These results are consistent with the initial expectations: normal pay increase variables are the most important influence on SMPI for the recognition group, consumption variables are the most important influence on SMPI for the money group.

Stepwise regression was used separately for each group to see if combinations of factors could improve prediction of SMPI within the two groups. The amount of SMPI variance accounted for in each group did improve when combinations of factors were considered. For the recognition group, a combination of normal pay increase and consumption variables explained SMPI better than normal pay increase variables alone (an improvement of 8 percent in explained variance). For the money group, a combination of consumption, normal pay increase, and satisfaction

Table 1: Regressions of smallest meaningful pay increase in various predictors

								Satisfaction			
		Last	Expected								
	Pay	pay	pay	Com-	In-						
Regressions	level	increase	increase	parison	come	COL†	SOL‡	Job	Pay	R^2	$\bar{R}^2$ §
All respondents											
(N = 203)											
Pay level	.33*									.11*	.11
Normal pay											
increase		.10*	.24*	.02						.14*	.13
Consumption					.20*	.29*	.02*			.16*	.15
Stepwise											
regression‖		.28*	.19*			.29*			−.15*	.26*	.25
Recognition group											
(N = 91)											
Pay level	.36*									.13*	.13
Normal pay											
increase		.14	.47*	−.10						.28*	.26
Consumption					.30*	.24	−.05			.17*	.15
Stepwise											
regression‖			.51*			.29*				.35*	.34
Money group											
(N = 95)											
Pay level	.31*									.09*	.09
Normal pay											
increase		.18	.21*	−.10						.12*	.10
Consumption					.06	.39*	.08			.22*	.20
Stepwise											
regression‖		.33*				.39*			−.20*	.32*	.31

*Significant at .05 level.

†Increment in income needed to keep up with the cost of living.

‡Increment in income needed to improve one's standard of living.

§ Because different regression equations differed with respect to the number of independent variables, and R^2 is known to be affected by the number of independent variables, a corrected estimate of explained variance, $\bar{R}^2$, was calculated. All equations were compared in terms of $\bar{R}^2$.

‖The stepwise regression procedure started with the variable contributing most to SMPI and continued to add variables to the regression equation until the contribution of the best of the variables excluded from the equation would not be statistically significant. The equation from the last step which includes all variables contributing significantly is presented here.

variables explained SMPI better than consumption alone (an 11 percent improvemen in explained variance). The factor expected to be most important in influencing SMPI was still most important in each group, but other factors could account for additional variance.

The best prediction of SMPI is obtained by using a different combination of predictors for the recognition and the money groups. Results show that a combination of factors led to better prediction of SMPI than single factors for each of these

groups or combinations of factors for the total sample.

The frequency distribution of reasons subjects consciously considered in responding to the SMPI question is presented in Table 2. Although the fixed responses provided the subject did not correspond exactly with the independent variables in the regression analysis, the results of the two approaches are quite consistent, especially with respect to the influence of inflation. Change in the cost of living was the most frequent reason sub-

Table 2: Reasons considered in answering SMPI question

Reasons	N	Percent of reasons	Percent of sample
My performance.	53	15.7	26.1
My last pay increase . . .	56	16.9	27.6
The last pay increase of others	11	3.0	5.4
Company policy on pay increases	43	12.8	21.2
Government guidelines. .	12	3.6	5.9
My current pay	50	14.8	24.6
Changes in the cost of living	93	27.6	45.8
Other.	19	5.6	9.4
Total	337*		

*Total number of reasons exceeds sample size ($N = 203$) because subjects were allowed to give more than one reason.

jects cited for the SMPI response. Similarly, the increment in family income to keep up with the cost of living was the only variable to contribute significantly to the prediction of SMPI in all of the combinations of factors. Level of performance, last pay increase, and company policy (all reasons associated in some way with customary pay increase practices of the organization) were also cited frequently.[8] In the regression analysis, at least one of the normal pay increase variables was significant in each of the combination of factors. Although pay level accounted for less unique variance in SMPI than consumption and normal pay increase variables, almost a quarter of the sample said they considered pay level in arriving at the amount they specified as SMPI.

DISCUSSION

The smallest pay increase an individual finds meaningful seems to be influenced by several factors; the exact factors depend on the significance of the pay increase to the individual. For the group

[8] Expected pay increase was not included in the set of fixed responses.

valuing pay increases as signs of organizational recognition, SMPI is a function of expected pay increase and anticipated changes in the cost of living. SMPI of those who value pay increases for the money is a function of expected changes in the cost of living, last pay increase, and pay satisfaction. Dividing the sample according to the meaning of a pay increase and using different factors for each group considerably improved the predictability of SMPI.

The fact that the best prediction of SMPI was obtained by using combinations of factors suggests two possibilities. Either the recognition and money groups included individuals influenced by different factors (i.e., some influenced by changes in the cost of living, others influenced by most recent or expected pay increase), or, more likely, individuals in each group were influenced by more than one factor. The average number of reasons cited for the SMPI question was 1.7. Individuals seemed to be aware that their answers were influenced by more than one fact so that combinations were consciously considered.

The need for an increment in income to keep up with the cost of living seems consistently to influence SMPI. It was the only variable to contribute significantly to the explanation of SMPI for both recognition and money groups (with almost twice as many individuals citing this factor as any other as the reason for their SMPI response). Even though the two variables are correlated, a pay increase need not equal perceived cost of living changes to be perceived as meaningful. The average amount given as the smallest meaningful pay increase was less than the average income increment viewed as necessary to keep up with the cost of living ($699 per year and $1,099 per year, respectively). Since the data were collected between July 1973 and January 1974 while the Consumer Price Index was increasing at a rate of about 8 percent per year, it should perhaps not be surprising that subjects were most concerned with inflation.

Both expected and most recent pay increases were important variables in explaining SMPI; each was important for one of the meaning groups. Among reasons given for SMPI responses, a number related to a normal pay increase: last pay increase was cited by 28 percent of the sample, current performance level by 26 percent, and company policy on pay increases by 21 percent. Thus the individual's own experiences, past and anticipated, help shape SMPI. The pay experience of others seems less important (it was not a significant factor in any of the regressions nor was it cited with any frequency by subjects as a reason for their SMPI response).

It is intriguing to note that pay satisfaction influenced SMPI for the money group but not the recognition group. Those in the money group who were satisfied with their pay required a smaller pay increase to be meaningful than those who were dissatisfied. One possible explanation stems from the fact that the money group was significantly less satisfied with pay than the recognition group. Pay satisfaction might only affect SMPI for generally dissatisfied groups.

Pay level was the only variable considered as a determinant of SMPI in previous studies; yet, in this study, pay level was not an important influence on SMPI. Alone pay could account for relatively little variance in SMPI (11 percent for the total sample), and it did not add to combinations of other factors in predicting SMPI. Previous studies compared mean SMPI/pay ratios across groups with different pay levels and did not measure the association between pay and SMPI directly. In this study, a direct measure of association was used and the two variables were not highly related. Thus it would seem that SMPI can be better predicted by considering combinations of factors which do not include pay.

In short, SMPI seems to be a complex function of consumption, normal pay increase, and satisfaction variables, with the relative importance of these three variables to any one individual depending on the meaning he or she gives to pay increases. These three factors explain about a third of the variance in SMPI. While this is a three-fold increase over the variance explained by pay level alone, a substantial amount of variance still remains unaccounted for. Further research to improve prediction of SMPI might concentrate on refining measures of the important variables, the search for additional variables affecting SMPI, and the examination of SMPI across time.

POLICY IMPLICATIONS

Although the results of this study are obviously not a sufficient basis for a redesign of compensation policy, they have some interesting implications. In particular, they suggest that designing a pay policy that simultaneously provides meaningful pay increases and minimizes costs seems to be an extremely complicated task.

Probably the simplest and most common policy is to set some constant percentage of salary as a minimum pay increase on the assumption that equal percentage increases have equal psychological meaning. The study casts doubt as to the wisdom of such a policy. Since current pay level is not an important factor in explaining SMPI, equal percentage increases are likely to have unequal psychological impact on different employees.

To insure psychologically meaningful pay increases, pay policy would have to specify that the pay increase received by the individual depends on the meaning of a pay increase, his or her perception of normal pay increases, his or her perception of changes in the cost of living, and his or her satisfaction with pay. Employees are not likely to accept these variations in the size of their pay increases as fair; pay increases are expected to be related to organizational contribution not to idiosyncratic perceptions. The design of a feasible yet fair pay policy that sets minimum pay increases roughly equal to SMPI for each individual seems virtually impossible.

Pay policy might specify some dollar amount for the minimum increase based on an amount that would be meaningful to most employees—a type of highest common denominator. The statistics for SMPI (an average of $699 per year, with a standard deviation of $496 per year) indicate that the minimum dollar increase needed to be perceived as meaningful to most would be quite large, thus costly. The optimal trade-off between meaningfulness of pay increases and the cost of pay policy may depend on the difference in behavioral and organizational consequences of meaningful and nonmeaningful pay increases. The nature of these consequences still remains conjectural.

Essay 7-8

The nature of incentive symbols*

William F. Whyte

We shall begin by examining the nature of these symbols and the theories of motivation on which they are implicitly based.

Piece rates are based upon a reward-punishment theory of motivation. We assume that the individual is encouraged to perform desirable actions through the offer of reward and is restrained from performing undesirable actions through the threat of punishment. Under piece rates the offering and withholding of money is at the heart of this reward-punishment system.

The theory assumes that man responds as an isolated individual to rewards and punishments. ... Let us now concentrate upon the relation between the individual and the incentive symbols.

The basic problem is that human behavior is a good deal more complicated than

*Abridged from William F. Whyte, *Money and Motivation* (New York: Harper and Brothers, 1955), pp. 194-217. Copyright © 1955 by Harper & Row, Publishers, Inc. By permission of the publisher.

this theory indicates. Psychologists and psychiatrists have demonstrated that a man's behavior cannot be understood simply in terms of the immediate rewards and punishments offered him. In fact, the very things he finds rewarding or punishing will be determined in large measure from his past experience. To cite an extreme example, we tend to take it for granted that physical pain is punishing and that therefore the individual seeks to avoid it. Nevertheless, throughout history there have been individuals and groups of people who have found it rewarding as a religious experience to submit to bodily pain.

But suppose we could overcome this difficulty. Let us assume that at least in the United States most people like money and consider the offering of it a reward and the withholding of it a punishment. Does that solve our problem?

Let us seek to answer this question by leaving the factory for a moment and consulting the findings of experimental psychologists.[1] While conditioning experiments have been performed primarily upon animals, they may provide us with some leads on human behavior.

It was the great Russian psychologist, Ivan Pavlov, who performed the classic experiments in this field. He worked with dogs, but other experimenters have achieved similar results upon other animals. In some of these experiments a piece of food served as reward and a mild electric shock as punishment. The sound of the bell was designed to indicate that food would shortly be offered, whereas a different sound signalized the approach of an electric shock. After only a few exposures to these auditory stimuli, the animal made the appropriate discriminations. When the bell sounded, and even before the food was offered, the animal would salivate and give other signs of anticipating a rewarding experience. For the other sound, it would crouch, lift up the leg that was to be shocked, or take some other apparently withdrawing or defensive reaction.

One condition should be noted in connection with its results. It has been found in various conditioning experiments that the animal does not continue indefinitely to respond in a vigorous manner to the stimuli. After repeated exposures, it reacts in a more lethargic fashion—as if losing interest in the whole business.

So far (if we overlook the condition just noted) the experiment seems to lend support to the reward-punishment theory. However, let us complicate the picture with reports on further conditioning experiments. In one case Pavlov presented to the animal two lighted disks of markedly different shapes. Upon presentation of one, food was forthcoming, whereas the other was followed by the shock.

When the conditioned reflex had been established—that is, when the animal responded consistently and appropriately to each of the two symbols—Pavlov began to modify the shapes of the disks so that they became more and more alike. At first the animal reacted much as before. As the symbols became more similar, it continued making the appropriate behavior discriminations but with increasingly marked signs of agitation. Finally a point was reached where the animal failed to respond to either disk in the accustomed manner; instead, it displayed such signs of agitation as barking, panting, cowering, struggling to escape, and so on. Furthermore, it was found that this reaction was not a momentary one. The animal that had so broken down in the experiment could not be led to respond to the experimental stimuli again until after a rest of some months or even years. Its behavior outside of the experimental situation also showed signs of abnormality.

Other researchers have repeated the experiment and achieved the same results. In fact, psychologists speak of such experiments as inducing an experimental neurosis.

We cannot safely reason from analogy concerning the behavior of animals in a laboratory to the behavior of men in a factory. Research must be done at many intervening points before we can make such a jump on the basis of scientific evidence. Nevertheless, certain analogies may be suggestive.

The first stage of the conditioning experiments suggests that consistent association of a given symbol with a reward establishes an appropriate response to that symbol, whereas consistent association of another symbol with punishment establishes an appropriate response to that symbol. However, we note that even consistent associations, when repeatedly made, seem to have a "wearing off" effect. We seem to see this effect in the factory also. We hear many complaints from

<hr>

[1] See H. S. Liddell, "Conditioned Reflex Method and Experimental Neurosis," in J. McV. Hunt, *Personality and the Behavior Disorder* (New York: Ronald Press, 1944), pp. 389 ff.

management that an incentive system that once stimulated a vigorous response seems now to be taken for granted and has little stimulating effect.

Our chances of eliciting desired responses with a reward-punishment approach depend upon our ability to establish a definite and consistent association between symbols that stand for rewards and the rewards themselves, and similarly in the case of punishments.

We have seen what happens when the animal becomes unable to discriminate between the reward symbol and the punishment symbol. When a given symbol can stand for either reward or punishment, the animal's behavior becomes disorganized.

It is the thesis of this essay that many piece-rate situations resemble much more closely the conditions of the experimental neurosis experiments than they do the experiments in which reward and punishment symbols are clearly differentiated.

We are not trying to say that factory workers are neurotic individuals. We are simply suggesting that many incentive systems place them in a conflict situation where they are unable to determine whether the symbols presented them stand for expected rewards or for expected punishments or for some combination of rewards and punishments. We feel that some of the defensive and aggressive behavior of workers must be understood in these terms.

We do not mean that money ceases to be a reward for workers in the situations we have discussed. We mean two things:

1. Money is only one of a number of possible rewards and punishments that may be involved in the incentive situation. Money is not the only thing to which the worker responds. He responds to the total factory environment, and we have been exploring some of the other aspects of this environment that have an effect upon him.

2. The effectiveness of the money symbol depends in part upon a direct connection between symbol, action, and reward (or, as the psychologists call it, reinforcement). In the animal experiments we find this connection established. The animal can get the reward only when the designated symbol is presented to him. This is often not the case in industry (we have described) some of the various possible forms of "cheating" which enable workers to get the money incentive without doing the work it is supposed to call for. This is not a unique instance. In our industrial research we have run across a number of cases where workers have made money by "writing" as well as by producing. In a situation of worker-management and union-management conflict, workers will still be motivated to make money, but if they can make it in other ways than through producing they will be content to do so. In fact, they may even derive special pleasure from being able to outsmart management in this way.

Confusion as to the behavioral meaning of the symbol also comes about because incentive symbols are so much more complex than the symbols that stand for food or electric shock in the conditioning experiments. It is not at all clear what connection there is between a given incentive symbol and reward or punishment as experienced by the individual. (Partly this is due to the fact that some people are much more interested in money than others. This aspect of the problem we shall explore later.) But even if we assume that all workers are interested in money, to some extent, we must note that it is not simply an amount of money that is offered. The dollar has meaning only as a price for a particular unit of production, and the attractiveness of the price depends upon the possibilities of production. This involves us in some difficult problems involving the determination of the nature of the symbols themselves.

* * * * *

ECONOMICS OF INCENTIVE RESPONSE

The proposition that everybody benefits through high production is almost an article of faith in the United States. To question this assumption may appear subversive and un-American. Nevertheless, we cannot accept the proposition on faith if we are to understand workers' response to incentive systems.

The high and rising standard of living of the United States might seem sufficient proof of the proposition, but here we must introduce a distinction between short-run and long-run results. We may agree that in the long run most people benefit from increasing production and yet in the short run an increase in production may involve hardships and difficult adjustments for quite a number of people. It has often been observed that man lives in the short run. He may, indeed, plan for a long-run future but he has to act and re-act to the situation that he meets on a day-to-day basis. To explain his reactions to incentive systems, we cannot be content with pointing out long-run results. We must examine speicfic situations.

Management's need to balance the production of the plant presents us with one limiting factor. Few incentive workers make a total product themselves. In nearly all cases the men in a given department simply produce parts of the total product. Suppose, for example, we are dealing with a plant that manufactures washing machines. Let us say that management plans its production in terms of 50 completed machines a day. Let us now give our attention to the men in the leg department. At four legs per machine, they will need to produce 200 legs in order to meet the daily quota of finished machines. Let's suppose they are on incentive and that they somehow decide to

abandon restriction of output and do as much as they can. They raise their production of washing machine legs up to 250 per day. Now management has a surplus of 50 legs each day, and washing machine legs by themselves, we assume, have no market value. So what does management do now? Management may be happy with this increased rate of output and yet it presents a problem that can be solved only by laying off some of the workers in the leg department or by transferring them to other departments. In this situation some workers stand to gain through increased incentive earnings but others will lose money or at least have an adjustment to make elsewhere. Perhaps under the circumstances it is better to keep production at the existing level and not go all out after the incentive. . . .

Apart from this problem of balancing the production of various departments, can we say that high production is good for everybody? We must recognize first that too low a rate of production leads in most cases to fewer instead of more jobs. If costs are too high, management may have to curtail operations within a department or perhaps close down an entire plant. But does an increase in production beyond any given point mean more jobs or at least the same number of jobs and more money for the workers? That depends upon the company's position in the market and the conditions of supply and demand for the company's product and also upon management's price policy.

* * * * *

Suppose we assume that as productivity goes up management decides not to cut its prices—and this in a situation where supply and demand are in balance at the existing price. Perhaps through a high-powered advertising campaign the company can sell more of its products without cutting prices. In other cases, however, we shall find the company putting out the same amount of production with some-what fewer workers. In such a case, then, we could have increased productivity on the part of workers leading to somewhat fewer jobs in this particular plant or department.[2]

There are other important factors that bear upon the relationships among productivity, prices, sales, costs, and profits, and level of employment. We do not go into them here because we are not attempting to present a comprehensive discussion of the economics of productivity. We are simply attempting to show that the relationship between worker productivity and the number of jobs available is not a simple one. Even if we agree that over the long run and for the economy as a whole increasing productivity leads to more rather than fewer jobs, we can point to many situations where there would be fewer jobs at least for the short run.

We are not assuming that workers make an economic analysis such as this, that they then decide that management's promises of more jobs with more production are not always true, and that they therefore decide to restrict production. We are concerned only with the relationship between the symbols of the incentive system and the experience that workers connect with these symbols. If the workers were firmly convinced that the symbols meant more earnings for everybody with more production, then we would not need to concern ourselves with the economic facts of the situation. However, worker interpretation of the meaning of these symbols depends upon the experiences they have actually had in industry. As it is, workers sometimes experience layoffs or transfers which they connect with too much production. (The economist might well point out in some

of these cases that the increase in production and the layoffs and transfers were coincidental instead of cause and effect. But this coincidental appearance of the two phenomena suggests a connection in the minds of those who experience or who might experience layoffs or transfers.) If more production were always a rewarding experience, we could assume that workers would respond much more strongly to the incentive system. The problem of management, then, is to create conditions where the incentive will be rewarding in an economic security sense as well as in other ways.

As we have seen, this does not simply involve the relationship between the individual worker and the management that offers him the incentive. It involves the relation of worker to fellow workers, of department to department, of the plant to the company, of the company to its competitors. All these relationships have a bearing upon the success of the incentive system.

CONCLUSION

As we examine the rate-setting process and the economic results of incentive production we are forced to conclude that the connections between the symbols and the promised rewards are neither simple nor consistent. This does not mean that the piece-rate symbol will evoke no response. It does mean that the response will be importantly influenced by the context of human relations within which the symbol is offered. Let us, then, examine further this human relations context.

THE INDIVIDUAL AND THE WORK GROUP

Man is not born loving money. He has to learn to love it. This learning takes place in varying degrees in various parts of the world. In economically underdevel-

---

[2] However, if the firm is only one among a large number of manufacturers in this line and supplies only a small fraction of the market, it may be possible to maintain prices and still increase production.

oped countries we find that the possibility of making more money does not lead people to do more work. On the contrary, they usually prefer to work a shorter number of days or hours to make the amount of money they have customarily earned. American and Western European businessmen have often been troubled by this phenomenon. Apparently the workers in these situations have not learned to want the consumers' goods that mean a rising standard of living. They are content to remain at the customary level. Factory work being unfamiliar to them anyway, they are quite happy to be able to maintain this standard of living by working a shorter time.

In our society too the response to money is a learned response; nor is it uniform. Americans in general, including factory workers, seem to have a stronger interest in making more money and in the things that money can buy than seems to be found in most other parts of the world. Even in the United States, however, among factory workers there are a great many variations in this response to money, as Dalton has so well demonstrated.[3] We must recognize also that money is not the only reward nor lack of money the only punishment available in any given situation. We can expect almost any American who is offered more money without any compensating dissatisfaction to respond to the money. The problem is that other rewards and punishments always go along with it. Different individuals strike different balances between rewards and punishments, including money.

The response to money in the factory, however, should not be considered as the response of an isolated individual. The factory worker reacts to management as a member of a group. The work group in the factory, like groups of people outside

the factory, tends to develop its own norms or standards of behavior. Not all the behavior to be observed in any given group is covered by the group's norms, but we can assume that the areas of behavior of greatest concern to the group will have established norms. In the factory, production is an important part of the activity of the group. Therefore, it is inevitable that certain understandings should arise as to the nature of a fair day's work. (It is not inevitable that these norms should be set low. Whether they are set low or high depends in large measure upon the relations between this group and the larger organization.)

While recognizing the importance of the work group in industry, we should not assume that every worker acts as a well-integrated member of some work group. Sociologists have pointed out that the individual does not necessarily identify himself with the people immediately around him. They speak of reference group theory to explain this phenomenon. The individual in the course of his social experience learns to respond to the norms of some group or groups, but he may find himself, for example at work, associating with people whom he does not consider part of his group at all.

Dalton has pointed this out in his discussion of the rate buster. There we found nine individuals in a department of some three hundred who did not abide by the group norms in production—and in various other forms of behavior. One of these men led an active social life outside the plant but associated with middle-class people and seemed to look upon fellow workers as beneath him and not worthy of any group loyalty. The other eight men were inactive socially outside the plant. For them the reference group seemed to be simply the family. Groups that they had been part of in the past had been drawn from a different social level from that represented by fellow workers and

[3] Melville Dalton, "The Industrial Rule Buster: A Characterization," *Applied Anthropology*, Winter, 1948.

they simply felt no compulsion to abide by the norms of such workers. Since these men had in effect declared themselves outside the work group, the customary forms of social pressure, including threatened ostracism, could hardly have any effect upon them. These men actually took pride in *not* being part of the work group.

Such men are extremely individualistic and highly acquisitive. Apparently they represent only a small minority even in such a supposedly acquisitive society as our own. Perhaps management would benefit if there were more people like this; on the other hand, the gains in production would have to be balanced against the extreme difficulties of building an organization with people who were determined not to fit into any organized group. It is idle to speculate as to what would happen if there were more rate busters. We should only note in passing that the theory on which the whole incentive program is based apparently applies to only a small fraction of the population.

Even as we observe most workers abiding by group norms of production, we should not assume that this acceptance of the norms is easily or happily accomplished. Dalton has presented us a picture of one factory department that may well apply to many others. There we see not one uniform response to the incentive, but people divided into three categories. The bottom producers, who hardly ever make incentive pay, have accepted the satisfactions of group membership and have renounced the incentive altogether. The rate busters have renounced the work group and devote themselves entirely to getting as much out of the incentive as they can. Most people fall between these extremes (50 out of 84 in Dalton's sample). They want to be part of the group and still they want to make more money. When they reach the ceiling on production established by the group norm they hold

back, but they hold back reluctantly. It is these people who chiefly experience the frustrations of the incentive system. Can it be only coincidental that Dalton found all his ulcer cases in this middle production group?

WHY RESTRICTION?

Our thesis here is that restriction of output under some circumstances contributes to the stability of relations among individuals in the work group. A group is not simply an undifferentiated aggregate of associating individuals. Groups have their own structures, with leaders and followers and varying levels of status or prestige separating them.

What are the sources of status in the work group? The job that a man holds is, of course, of prime importance. Jobs are ranked by management and workers in terms of their relative importance in the department. Even if we assume, however, that the people under discussion all hold the same job, we find at least two important sources of status distinction:

1. *Production performance.* What sort of worker the man is is important to fellow workers. They evaluate the skill, speed, and versatility with which he works.

2. *Interpersonal skill.* The leader in this area is a man whom others turn to for advice. It is he who brings up ideas that others act upon. It is he whom other people seek out for social or other discussions.

These two sources of status may fit together, but this will not necessarily be so. In fact, we may well find them pointing in different directions. Consider the following case, which, though not drawn from an incentive situation, will illustrate this point:

The department manufactures fine glassware. The men work in teams of from six to eight. This is a hand operation taking a high degree of skill and also requiring close cooperation among team members. The appointed leader of each team and the highest skilled man is known as the "gaffer." At the time we began our study, Paul DeSantis was recognized as the top prestige gaffer of the twelve who worked on two shifts in this department. He was a man in his mid-50s with more than 30 years' experience in the trade. He received the most difficult job assignments from management because he was recognized as the most skillful and versatile gaffer. However, he was also a rather slow worker.

This presented no problem as long as DeSantis was working on pieces which no other work team produced. However, as management introduced new pieces into production, some of the pieces that had been done by DeSantis' team exclusively were now assigned to the work teams of Jack Carter and Ralph Orlandella, two much younger men who had only recently attained the position of gaffer. These men had risen rapidly to the top in a period when production was expanding, so that the number of teams was doubled at a time when the old-time craftsmen were retiring or dying off. The old men in the department considered Carter and Orlandella as upstarts who were not really qualified glassworkers. The young men in the department, on the other hand, were encouraged to find men like themselves moving up and tended to gather around the young gaffers.

At first Carter and Orlandella had difficulty in doing the pieces that had been assigned to them from DeSantis' team, but in time they mastered the technical problem and developed the necessary skill and coordination of their team members. When they had mastered the jobs, they built up production to the level that had been attained by DeSantis and then began to move above his previous records. This was a conscious bid by the young gaffers for management approval (and possible pay increases) and for prestige among fel-

low workers. The young gaffers pointed out to their friends that they were showing that they could produce just as good pieces as DeSantis had turned out and more of them. DeSantis and other old-timers reacted against this challenge. Some of the old men refused to give technical advice that the inexperienced men badly needed, or gave misleading advice. The old-timers could not fail to acknowledge that the young men were getting good production but they deprecated this record by saying that the quality was poor and would never have been accepted when management in the old days had higher standards. Furthermore, DeSantis tried through intermediaries to get the young men to slow down. The argument they were to present was "Why do you want to kill the job? Seven an hour is a fair day's work."

Why this pressure to keep down production? DeSantis and his friends were talking just as do incentive workers when they warn their fellows that management will cut the rate if they produce too much. But there was no threat of rate cutting because there were no incentive rates. The rising production of the young men, furthermore, presented no possible economic threat to DeSantis because he was at the top of the rate range for the position of gaffer. He could go no higher except through general increases negotiated between union and management. On the other hand, long-standing company policy and the union contract protected him against wage cuts or layoffs, for his seniority was among the highest in the department.

He was saying in effect to the other men: If you work faster, management will expect everybody to work faster. There may, indeed, be some physical substance to this argument quite apart from the money to be gained or lost. There are important satisfactions in maintaining a customary work pace. However, the strong feelings manifested on both sides in this situation can hardly be attributed to questions of work pace and fatigue. The rise of the young men presented a threat to the status of DeSantis. He had held the unquestioned top prestige position. He was recognized as the most skilled and most versatile man. It was he to whom people turned for advice and it was he whom people watched when he had a particularly interesting job and they could take a moment from their work.

Now Carter and Orlandella were narrowing the gap in skill between themselves and DeSantis. They equaled DeSantis or even surpassed him in speed of production on certain pieces. Their status in the department rose. Especially the younger men gathered around them and followed their progress with interest. Thus we see that even in a department where skill is on a handicraft basis the speed of production can have an important effect upon the status of workers.

Let us turn from that actual example to a hypothetical situation in an incentive department in a mass production plant. In this department Al Collins holds the highest informal status. He is a man who is turned to for advice. He is respected also for his skill on the machine. At this time the group norm has established a ceiling of total earnings at 130 percent of base pay. Now let us make a completely impossible assumption: that without any other changes in this situation the ceiling is suddenly removed and each worker tries to see how much he can produce. Will Al Collins now turn out to be the top producer? Not necessarily so. Maybe he has the skill to turn out the highest quality product, but management is not now emphasizing quality except within certain limits set by inspection standards. Now Al Collins is a man who can perform what turns out to be a lot of unnecessary fancywork on the machine, but he is not a particularly fast worker. When the ceiling

goes off, he finds that, try as he will, he can only average about 130 percent, just 10 points above his former average. On the other hand, Tom Jones, who was formerly a mere nobody in the department, has no trouble in building his average up to 180 percent. Furthermore, he is not reluctant to let other people know how he is doing and even begins giving production tips to men who had formerly looked to Al Collins for advice.

Now, instead of being toward the top in production as he was under the ceiling, Collins finds himself in the middle. At the bottom are several workers who average about 110 percent. They are upset too because their performance did not look bad when everybody was keeping under 130 percent. But when a number of men are producing between 130 and 180, 110 looks poor indeed and these fellows feel that the foremen may be looking for ways to get rid of them even if they have seniority to protect them against layoffs.

Al Collins is not in such an economically threatened position. We can assume that his 130 percent average is quite satisfactory to management. However, the social balance in the department has been upset. The former leader of the men is shown up as only an average producer, while the top producer turns out to be someone who had little prestige in the department before.

This hypothetical example, together with the case from the glassworks, points out a function performed for the work group by restriction of output. It prevents the competition among the men which would disturb established interpersonal relations. If the ceiling on production is kept at a point where most workers in the department can reach it, then it is possible for a man like Collins to attain a leadership position in the department through exercising the sort of social skill that wins leadership outside the workplace.

* * * * *

CHAPTER 8

JOB SATISFACTION AND PERFORMANCE

J ob satisfaction is a continuing concern of managers, and concepts of job satisfaction figure prominently in various theories of compensation, motivation, and employee performance. Both the concept of satisfaction and the hypothesized relationships among satisfaction, compensation, and performance vary considerably from one examination to another, however. Satisfaction is viewed alternatively as a global affective variable and as a composite of numerous relatively independent facets; satisfaction is viewed as one pole of a bipolar satisfaction/dissatisfaction variable and as a variable independent of dissatisfaction. Similarly, satisfaction is conceived alternatively as an instrumental means to achieving employee performance and as a consequence or outcome of performance; satisfaction also is viewed at times as an end or goal to be sought independently of performance. Despite this rather confusing state of theory and knowledge concerning job satisfaction, we can hardly omit it from consideration in a review of perspectives of compensation and motivation. The selected readings which follow attempt a review of the varied considerations of job satisfaction, particularly as they relate to compensation and dimensions of labor supply to the employing organization.

Essay 8-1 by Schwab and Cummings presents a review of theories relating job satisfaction and performance. They identify three general classes of theory: (1) theories in which job satisfaction is viewed as a "cause" of performance, (2) theories in which the relationship between job satisfaction and performance is uncertain and moderated by other influences, and (3) theories in which job satisfaction is viewed as a consequence of performance. They criticize these theories for inadequate conceptualizations of both job satisfaction and job performance and direct attention to the question "what is job satisfaction?" prior to further conceptualization and research into relationships between job satisfaction and job performance.

Essay 8-2 by Locke examines directly the question "what is job satisfaction?" and develops a conceptual framework for the understanding and analysis of job satisfaction. Locke argues that job satisfaction and dissatisfaction, a bipolar concept, is an emotional response to the interaction of person and job; it derives from comparison of the person's perceptions of job characteristics (inducements and contributions) relative to valued amounts of these characteristics. Overall job satisfaction is a summary response to the varied reactions to specific job characteristics and thus depends upon the characteristics associated with the job, perceptions of and valuations of these characteristics. Change in any of these components of job satisfaction can occasion change in the level of overall job satisfaction of the individual.

Essay 8-3 from Lawler develops a somewhat different model of job satisfaction and examines relationships between satisfaction and measures of job performance. Like Locke, Lawler views job satisfaction as a composite of reactions to various job facets or job characteristics. Unlike Locke, Lawler suggests a definite structure of facets relevant to job satisfaction, a structure of facet dimensions imposed upon the job situation, whereas Locke specified no such structure. Lawler also indicates that the standard against which job facets are evaluated is some specification of "what should be" which is a function of perceived personal inputs and perceived inputs and outcomes of others, a social comparison process analogous to the equity model of Adams in Chapter 6. Locke, on the other hand, implies no such social comparison process in the valuation of job characteristics; values may be influenced from a number of sources.

Herzberg, Mausner, and Snyderman in Essay 8-4 present a strikingly different conceptualization of job satisfaction, a conceptualization which has aroused considerable controversy. They differentiate between job satisfaction and job dissatisfaction, viewing them as two separate factors rather than as two poles of the same underlying factor. Like Locke and Lawler, Herzberg et al. view satisfaction and dissatisfaction as composites of various facets; unlike Locke and Lawler, they argue that the facets or dimensions of satisfaction are different from the facets of dissatisfaction, and that the two factors of satisfaction and dissatisfaction are independent factors, not compensating elements of the same general factor. Elements or facets of job satisfaction relate to intrinsic aspects of task performance, achievement, and growth (motivating elements); and elements of dissatisfaction relate to the context surrounding the job (hygiene elements). Aspects of compensation contribute to both satisfaction and dissatisfaction, the actual pay received is a hygienic element related to dissatisfaction, and the sense of achievement reinforced by pay for performance is a motivating element related to satisfaction. Unlike Locke and Lawler, Herzberg et al. do not consider the origin of standards for valuation of job characteristics; they are more concerned with the content dimensions of satisfaction and dissatisfaction than with the process through which satisfaction and dissatisfaction are realized. Herzberg et al. imply that their motivating elements are both cause and consequence of job performance, and that dissatisfying elements are related causally with turnover and absenteeism although these performance relationships are not developed to any degree in their discussion.

A selection from March and Simon (Essay 8-5) presents their model mentioned in the Schwab and Cummings selection. They do not examine in detail the nature of job satisfaction, only indicating that it is a function of aspirations and rewards, a concept analogous to those of Locke and Lawler. Aspiration, however, is a function of previous rewards and tends to exceed previous reward levels; it is not conceived as a function of social comparisons nor does it appear as stable as Locke's values. Satisfaction, in this model, is conceived as a function of experienced rewards and dissatisfaction is conceived as a cause of search behavior, satisfaction connoting an equilibrium condition. Dissatisfaction is not a direct cause of performance, however; alternatives identified in the search process may indicate termination, absenteeism, or working to the rule. Choices among alternatives resulting from search are evaluated within the framework of the choice models presented in Chapter 3.

The final selection (Essay 8-6) by Mahoney attempts an integration and reformulation of models of job satisfaction and develops hypotheses concerning relationships between satisfaction and performance. No evidence relating directly to the proposed model is presented, and the empirical validity of the model is untested. It is consistent, however, with other models presented in this chapter and with reported evidence concerning those models.

Essay 8-1

Theories of performance and satisfaction: A review*

Donald P. Schwab and Larry L. Cummings

Unquestionably, it is the hypothesized connection between employee satisfaction and job performance which has generated the greatest research and theoretical interest. In the last 40 years, investigators have examined these two variables in a wide variety of work situations: (1) among organization members ranging from the unskilled to managers and professionals, (2) in diverse administrative and technological environments, (3) using individuals or groups as the unit of analysis, and (4) employing various measures of both satisfaction and performance. The methodologies employed in these studies, and their findings have been reviewed by Brayfield and Crockett; Herzberg, Mausner, Peterson and Capwell; and Vroom.[1]

Whereas earlier reviews have focused on empirical research, this paper reviews and evaluates *theoretical* propositions concerning the relationship between satisfaction and performance. Three major points of view are considered: (1) the view that satisfaction leads to performance, a position generally associated with early human relations concepts, (2) the view that the satisfaction-performance relationship is moderated by a number of variables, a position which gained acceptance in the fifties and continues to be reflected in current research, and (3) the view that performance leads to satisfaction, a recently stated position. Conceptualizations of satisfaction-performance relations which represent each of these positions are reviewed, even though several do not represent theories in any rigorous sense.

*Reprinted from Donald L. Schwab and Larry L. Cummings, "Theories of Performance and Satisfaction: A Review," *Industrial Relations* 9 (1970), pp. 408-30 (abridged).

[1] Arthur H. Brayfield and Walter H. Crockett, "Employee Attitudes and Employee Performance," *Psychological Bulletin* 52 (September 1955), pp. 396-424; Frederick H. Herzberg, Bernard M. Mausner, Richard O. Peterson, and Dora F. Capwell, *Job Attitudes: Review of Research and Opinion* (Pittsburgh: Psychological

Satisfaction → Performance

. . . management has at long last discovered that there is greater production, and hence greater profit when workers are satisfied with their jobs.

Service of Pittsburgh, 1957), pp. 107-11; and Victor H. Vroom, *Work and Motivation* (New York: Wiley, 1964), pp. 175-78.

Improve the morale of a company and you improve production.[2]

Historical perspective. The quotation from Parker and Kleemeir was almost certainly inspired by the Hawthorne studies, although the original investigators probably never stated the relationship so unequivocally. Roethlisberger, for example, in discussing the implications of the study for managers, noted that ". . . the factors which make for efficiency in a business organization are not necessarily the same as those factors that make for happiness, collaboration, teamwork, morale, or any other word which may be used to refer to cooperative situations."[3]

Yet, despite Roethlisberger's caveat, the early human relationists have been interpreted as saying that satisfaction leads to performance. Vroom, for example, argues that ". . . human relations might be described as an attempt to increase productivity by satisfying the needs of employees."[4] Strauss states that ". . . early human relationists viewed the morale-productivity relationship quite simply: higher morale would lead to improved productivity."[5] In the final analysis the interpretation is perhaps more significant than the original views expressed.

A current satisfaction → performance interpretation. The work of Herzberg and his colleagues provides perhaps the best illustration of current theory and research formulated on the view that satisfaction leads to performance. These researchers separate job variables into two groups, hygiene factors and motivators.[6] Included in the hygiene group are such variables as supervision, physical working conditions, regular salary and benefits, company policies, etc. These are viewed as potential sources of dissatisfaction, but not as sources of positive work attitudes. Among the motivators, Herzberg lists factors closely associated with work itself and its accomplishment, i.e., challenging assignments, recognition, the opportunity for professional growth, etc. These factors presumably contribute to work satisfaction and are the key factors associated with performance. Thus, Herzberg feels that low performance-satisfaction correlations obtained in other research studies can thus be explained since ". . . the usual morale measures are confounded . . . they tap both kinds of attitudes . . ." (i.e., satisfiers and dissatisfiers).[7]

In fairness to the original authors of *The Motivation to Work*, it should be recognized that the conclusion relating performance to the satisfiers but not to the dissatisfiers has escalated somewhat with the passage of time. In the original study, care was taken to report the actual percentages obtained and to at least raise alternative explanations of the findings.[8] These qualifications are not present in subsequent restatements of the original findings by Herzberg[9] or by other advocates of the two-factor theory.[10] In short, it appears that the satisfaction-performance findings of *The Motivation to Work* are being overinterpreted in the same manner as were Roethlisberger and

[2] Willard E. Parker and Robert W. Kleemeir, *Human Relations in Supervision: Leadership in Management* (New York: McGraw-Hill, 1951), p. 10.

[3] Fritz J. Roethlisberger, *Management and Morale* (Cambridge: Harvard University Press, 1941), p. 156.

[4] Vroom, op. cit., p. 181.

[5] George Strauss, "Human Relations—1968 Style," *Industrial Relations* 7 (May 1968), p. 264.

[6] Frederick Herzberg, Bernard Mausner, and Barbara Snyderman, *The Motivation to Work*, 2d ed. (New York: Wiley, 1959), pp. 59-83.

[7] Ibid., p. 87.

[8] Ibid., pp. 86-87.

[9] Frederick Herzberg, *Work and the Nature of Man* (Cleveland: World Publishing, 1966), p. 74; and Frederick Herzberg, "One More Time, How Do You Motivate Employees?" *Harvard Business Review* 46 (January-February 1968), 53-62.

[10] See, for example, David A. Whitsett and Erik K. Winslow, "An Analysis of Studies Critical of the Motivator-Hygiene Theory," *Personnel Psychology* 20 (Winter 1967), 391-415.

Dickson's findings in *Management and the Worker.*

Moreover, the evidence employed to support the premise that satisfaction leads to performance has been nonexperimental in design. As such, the studies obviously do not show causality. In fact, neither human relationists in general, nor Herzberg in particular, have provided an adequate theoretical explanation for the causal relationship which they postulated.

In sum, it is our view that the popular interpretation of human relations research has probably been detrimental to the understanding of worker motivation. An essentially unsupported interpretation was so quickly and widely accepted that the underlying theory was neither questioned nor refined. By assuming, without adequate analysis, that observed satisfaction-performance linkages were causally and unidirectionally related, subsequent researchers may well have misinterpreted the meaning of their data.[11] Ultimately, however, it was probably the human relationist's failure to develop a sufficiently sophisticated theory, combined with ambiguous, often contradictory research evidence, which led to other formulations of the relationship between these two variables.

Satisfaction—?—Performance

. . . high morale is no longer considered as a prerequisite of high productivity. But more than this, the nature of the relationship between mo-

rale and productivity is open to serious questioning. Is it direct? Is it inverse? Is it circular? Or, is there any relationship at all between the two; are they independent variables?[12]

The development of uncertainty. The statement by Scott (and others similar to it)[13] reflects perhaps more than anything else the pervasive influence of the previously mentioned review by Brayfield and Crockett. Their review of over 50 studies represents, depending on one's point of view, either a council of despair or a challenge for theory development and extended research. As we will illustrate, the latter (at least the theoretical dimension) seems to have prevailed.

Brayfield and Crockett hypothesized that employees govern their job seeking, job performing, and job terminating behavior by the law of effect, subsequently elaborated and relabeled by Vroom, and Porter and Lawler, as expectancy theory.[14] Regarding job terminating behavior, Brayfield and Crockett argued that: "One principal generalization suffices to set up an expectation that morale should be related to absenteeism and turnover, namely, that organisms tend to avoid those situations which are punishing and to seek

---

[11] Several findings of the Herzberg, et al., study suggest, for example, an alternative interpretation. They reported that 74 percent of satisfying and 25 percent of the dissatisfying sequences included feelings of achievement and/or recognition for successful or unsuccessful job performance. (Cf. Herzberg, et al., *The Motivation to Work*, pp. 72, 143.) In these instances, at least, it would seem plausible to argue that performance preceded, rather than followed, satisfaction. If one were to accept their conclusions about stated performance effects, it would seem appropriate to suggest a possible circular relationship between satisfaction and performance.

[12] William G. Scott, *Human Relations in Management: A Behavioral Science Approach* (New York: McGraw-Hill, 1962), p. 93.

[13] See also, for example, March and Simon who stated that "Attempts to relate these variables (morale, satisfaction, and cohesiveness) directly to productivity have failed to reveal any consistent simple relation." James G. March and Herbert A. Simon, *Organizations* (New York: Wiley, 1958), pp. 47-48. In the same vein, Carey, in commenting on the Hawthorne studies, noted ". . . the widespread failure of later (post-Hawthorne) studies to reveal any reliable relations between the social satisfaction of industrial workers and their work performance." Carey, op. cit., p. 403. Even Davis, an avowed human relationist, deferred to Brayfield and Crockett, conceding that one must ". . . recognize that high morale and high productivity are not absolutely related to each other." Keith Davis, *Human Relations in Business* (New York: McGraw-Hill, 1957), p. 182.

[14] Vroom, op. cit., and Lyman W. Porter and Edward E. Lawler III, *Managerial Attitudes and Performance* (Homewood, Ill.: Irwin, 1968).

out situations that are rewarding."[15]

Brayfield and Crockett encountered greater difficulty explaining satisfaction and job performance linkages through the simple application of the hedonistic principle. They suggested that satisfaction and job performance might be concomitantly rather than causally related. In addition, one ". . . might expect high satisfaction and high productivity to occur together when productivity is perceived as a path to certain important goals and when these goals are achieved. Under other conditions, satisfaction and productivity might be unrelated or even negatively related."[16]

Additional models. Three lesser known theoretical expositions of the satisfaction-performance relation further illustrate the influence of the mixed and uncertain research findings in this area.[17] Each suggests that both satisfaction *and* performance can be viewed as criteria of organizational effectiveness. Moreover, each suggests that relationships between satisfaction and performance need be neither direct nor particularly strong.

A theory of work adjustment. In the first of these, Dawis and his colleagues posit that work adjustment is a function of employee *satisfaction* and *satisfactoriness* (performance).[18] Satisfaction presumably results from the correspondence between the individual's need set and the organization's reinforcer system and has its major impact on individual decisions to remain with or withdraw from the organization. Satisfactoriness, alternatively, refers to the organization's evaluation (in terms of its goals) of the behavior of its members. It is assumed to be a function of the correspondence between the requirements imposed by the job and the abilities possessed by the employee and can result in one of several consequences, e.g., promotion, transfer, termination, or retention in present position. Incorporated in the Dawis et al. model is the possibility of a relation between satisfaction and satisfactoriness, although its form and strength are not developed. Moreover, their model allows one to explain variations in employee satisfaction without reference to performance (either as a cause or consequence).

Pressure for production as an intervening variable. In a related statement, Triandis has proposed a theory which shares with Dawis et al. the notion that satisfaction and performance need not covary under all conditions.[19] Triandis hypothesized that organizational pressure for high production influences both satisfaction and performance, but not in the same fashion. As pressure increases, job satisfaction is hypothesized to decrease irrespective of the concomitant variation in performance. Employee performance, alternatively, is hypothesized to be curvilinearly related to production pressure. At several locations within the typical range of employee satisfaction increasing pressure is hypothesized to result in increased performance, while at other locations the relation between pressure and performance is assumed to be negative. Triandis also hypothesized that satisfaction and performance may be directly linked in certain circumstances. Finally, satisfaction may also lead to moderate performance under the utopian condition of no pressure to perform. This would be the case

[15] Brayfield and Crockett, op. cit., p. 415.

[16] Ibid., p. 416. The tone of this quote anticipates a portion of the Porter-Lawler model to be discussed subsequently; namely that performance can lead to satisfaction when mediated by relevant goals (rewards in the terminology of the Porter-Lawler model).

[17] Rene V. Dawis, George E. England, and Lloyd H. Lofquist, *A Theory of Work Adjustment: A Revision* (Minneapolis: University of Minnesota, Industrial Relations Center, 1968), Bulletin 47; Harry C. Triandis, "A Critique and Experimental Design for the Study of the Relationship between Productivity and Job Satisfaction," *Psychological Bulletin* 56 (July 1959), pp. 309-12; and March and Simon, op. cit.

[18] Dawis, et al., op. cit., p. 8.

[19] Triandis, op. cit.

where a minimum level of performance is caused by intrinsic job satisfaction plus certain activity drives or needs for stimulus inputs and variation.[20]

Satisfaction and the motivation to produce. A model proposed by March and Simon perhaps best bridges the theoretical gap between the satisfaction → performance view of the human relationists and the performance → satisfaction view to be discussed in the following section.[21] The model suggests that both performance and satisfaction can serve as dependent variables.

Beginning with performance as the dependent variable, March and Simon hypothesized: "Motivation to produce stems from a present or anticipated state of discontent and a perception of a direct connection between individual production and a new state of satisfaction."[22] The hypothesis states that performance is a function of two variables: (1) the degree of dissatisfaction experienced, and (2) the perceived instrumentality of performance for the attainment of valued rewards.

Thus, the model suggests that a state of dissatisfaction is a necessary, but not sufficient, condition for performance. It is necessary because dissatisfaction of some sort is assumed to be required to activate the organism toward search behavior. It lacks sufficiency, however, because a dissatisfied employee may not perceive performance as leading to satisfaction or may perceive nonperformance as leading to greater perceived satisfaction.

March and Simon also specify conditions where performance may lead to satisfaction although the linkage appears weaker (moderated by a greater number

of variables) in their model than the satisfaction → performance linkage.[23] This is due to three factors. First, we have already noted that the hypothesized job satisfaction may result from the receipt of rewards which are not based on performance. Second, even if improved performance is the behavioral alternative chosen by the employee, satisfaction need not necessarily result since the actual rewards of performance may not correspond to the anticipated consequences. Third, in the process of searching for and evaluating the consequences of alternative behaviors, the worker's level of aspiration may be raised as much or more than the expected value of the rewards associated with the behavior. Thus, even if performance is chosen as the best alternative and its consequences are perfectly anticipated, the worker may find himself no more and perhaps less satisfied than before.

The models compared. The above three models can most easily be contrasted on the independent variables hypothesized to influence employee performance. The theory of work adjustment implies that the major determinant of performance is the structural fit between employee skills and abilities on the one hand and technical job requirements on the other. Thus, its implications for organizational practice are largely in the areas of employee selection, placement, and training. In contrast, March and Simon focus primarily on two motivational determinants of performance; namely, expected value of rewards and aspiration levels. Finally, Triandis

---

[20] For an elaborated treatment of the implications of activity drives or activation levels as correlates of task performance, see William E. Scott, Jr., "Activation Theory and Task Design," *Organizational Behavior and Human Performance* 1 (September 1966), pp. 3-30.

[21] March and Simon, op. cit.

[22] Ibid, p. 51.

[23] Because March and Simon hypothesize that in certain circumstances performance leads to satisfaction, their theory could have been included in the following major section. We include it here because they hypothesize that performance is not necessary for satisfaction, while dissatisfaction is necessary for performance. Porter and Lawler's theory, discussed later, also hypothesizes a circular causal connection between satisfaction and performance. It reverses the emphasis of March and Simon, however, since it concentrates on the performance → satisfaction linkage.

emphasizes the importance of pressure for production, an organizational variable. As such, the Triandis model ignores the impact of either skill and ability or motivational differences between individuals.

It is also interesting to contrast Triandis, March and Simon, and the Herzberg two-factor theory with regard to the circumstances leading to a causative linkage between performance and satisfaction. In the Triandis and March and Simon models, it is dissatisfaction which can have performance implications (negative in the former; positive in the latter). The two-factor theory alternatively suggests that it is predominately satisfaction which leads to high performance.

Performance → Satisfaction

...good performance may lead to rewards, which in turn lead to satisfaction; this formulation then would say that satisfaction, rather than causing performance, as was previously assumed, is caused by it.[24]

The performance → satisfaction theory represents an important departure from earlier views about the relationship between these two variables. Human relationists, not without some qualification, postulated that high levels of satisfaction would result in high levels of performance. Subsequent models focused on the complexity of the relationship, incorporating various intervening variables in an attempt to account for frequently ambiguous findings of empirical studies. The performance → satisfaction theory, while it retains the idea of intervening variables, stresses the importance of variations in effort and performance as causes of variations in job satisfaction.

The Porter-Lawler model.[25] Just as the

Brayfield and Crockett review significantly influenced subsequent theoretical developments on the satisfaction → performance issue, a later review published by Vroom in 1964 has apparently had a similar impact on recent theorizing. While noting the generally low correspondence observed between measured satisfaction and performance, Vroom nevertheless found that in 20 of 23 cases the correlation was positive and that the median correlation reported was +.14.[26] Porter and Lawler have cited this review and the generally positive nature of this association as a basis for suggesting that premature, pessimistic closure would be unwise and have expounded their model through a series of recent publications.[27]

Although the Porter-Lawler model posits circularity in the relationship between performance and satisfaction, the most direct linkage has performance as the causal and satisfaction as the dependent variable. That relationship is mediated only by rewards (intrinsic and extrinsic) and the perceived equity of those rewards. When performance leads to rewards which are seen by the individual as equitable, it is hypothesized that high satisfaction will result.[28] The model suggests that the generally low performance-satisfaction rela-

---

[24] Edward E. Lawler III, and Lyman W. Porter, "The Effect of Performance on Job Satisfaction," *Industrial Relations* 7 (October 1967), p. 23.

[25] The performance→satisfaction theory is attributed to Porter and Lawler because they have developed it most fully. As we have already noted, March and Simon

suggested conditions when performance could cause satisfaction. Vroom also suggests that performance as a cause of satisfaction is somewhat more tenable than the reverse (op. cit., p. 187).

[26] Ibid., p. 183.

[27] Edward E. Lawler III, and Lyman W. Porter, "Antecedent Attitudes of Effective Managerial Performance," *Organizational Behavior and Human Performance* 2 (May 1967), pp. 122-42; Edward E. Lawler III, "Attitude Surveys and Job Performance," *Personnel Administration* 30 (September-October 1967), pp. 3 ff; Lawler and Porter, "The Effect of Performance on Job Satisfaction"; Lyman W. Porter and Edward E. Lawler III, "What Job Attitudes Tell About Motivation," *Harvard Business Review* 46 (January-February 1968), pp. 118-36, and Porter and Lawler, *Managerial Attitudes and Performance.*

[28] The concept of equity does not play the central role in the Porter-Lawler theory as it does, say, in the works of Adams. See, for example, J. Stacy Adams, "Toward an Understanding of Inequity," *Journal of Abnormal and Social Psychology* 67 (November 1963), 422-36,

tionships observed in previous empirical research may result from rewards, particularly extrinsic rewards, which are often not closely tied to performance.[29]

For satisfaction to exert an influence on performance in the Porter-Lawler model, it must affect the value of the rewards received, which in turn interacts with the perceived effort → reward linkage to determine the level of actual work effort. Finally, effort moderated by role perceptions and abilities and traits determines performance. Because of the number of intervening variables involved, it seems unlikely that satisfaction (or dissatisfaction) has as much impact on performance as performance has on satisfaction.

A comparative evaluation. The March and Simon model probably provides the most salient comparison with the Porter-Lawler model because both explicitly postulate a circular performance-satisfaction relation. The theories can be contrasted regarding the conditions necessary to avoid entropy or the "running down" of the level of employee motivation. In the March and Simon model, the function is performed primarily by aspiration level. It is hypothesized that as the expected value of reward increases, level of aspiration increases, which in turn has a negative impact on satisfaction. Thus, the concept of aspiration level enables the model to be dynamic. That is, it is partially because of a rising aspiration level (resulting from the receipt of past rewards) that dissatisfaction is created, thereby leading to search behavior, one form of which can be performance.

Provision for the avoidance of entropy

is more tenuous in the Porter-Lawler model. To sustain effort and performance over time, it is necessary to assume that satisfaction experienced from the receipt of intrinsic rewards leads to enhanced value being attached to such rewards. One must assume, for example, that feelings of worthwhile accomplishment increase the attractiveness or valence of such achievement.[30] As the authors note, however, the relation between satisfaction and value of reward can be interpreted in contrasting ways.[31] There exists some physiological and psychological evidence to suggest that the greater the extrinsic reward satisfaction experienced, the less value attached to such rewards.[32] This would clearly lead to eventual entropy in the Porter-Lawler model. The point of contention between the two models on this issue centers on the causative factors in the continuity and preservation of behavior over time. Since both models are essentially based on need deprivation theories, some mechanism must be provided to prevent the system from attaining entropy.

Alternative sources of satisfaction. Porter and Lawler's model can be contrasted with both the March and Simon model and the theory of work adjustment on the question of the sufficiency of performance for satisfaction. The Porter-Lawler model implies that satisfaction results from rewards associated with performance. It does not, therefore, appear to take into account all sources of employee satisfaction. Consider, for example, an organization which bases its rewards on seniority or organizational longevity. For persons with relatively strong security needs and low task involvement, seniority

---

and "Wage Inequities, Productivity and Work Quality," *Industrial Relations* 3 (October 1963), pp. 9-16. In addition, at least one of the authors appears to have some serious reservations about the predictive utility of equity theory. See Edward E. Lawler III, "Equity Theory as a Predictor of Productivity and Work Quality," *Psychological Bulletin* 70 (December 1968), pp. 596-610.

[29] Lawler and Porter, "The Effect of Performance on Job Satisfaction," pp. 23-24.

[30] On this point, satisfaction or dissatisfaction having performance consequences, Porter and Lawler are clearly closer to Herzberg and the early human relationists than to March and Simon or Triandis.

[31] Porter and Lawler, *Managerial Attitudes and Performance*, pp. 39-40.

[32] Charles N. Cofer and Mortimer H. Appley, *Motivation: Theory and Research* (New York: Wiley, 1964), pp. 204-68.

may represent the most rational means to the attainment of valued rewards and satisfaction. That is, the performance → reward linkage is not a necessary condition for attainment of meaningful satisfactions. Nor is it necessarily a condition for organizational survival. There are industrial jobs where minimally acceptable levels of performance are sufficient conditions for sustained participation. If system rewards are based on participation rather than individual performance and if they are perceived to be administered equitably, then, logically, satisfaction may be evident. This possibility is accounted for in the theory of work adjustment through the correspondence between employee needs and the reinforcer system of the job. It is accounted for in March and Simon's theory by their explicit hypothesis that satisfaction may result from rewards associated with various forms of nonperformance.

Implications for administrative practice. The Porter-Lawler model is quite rich in terms of its administrative implications. For example, it shares with the theory of work adjustment implications for high performance through the modification of abilities and traits via selection and training processes. In addition, their theory more than the others suggests a role for performance appraisal and salary administration in increasing employee performance levels. Both activites presumably have the potential of influencing the effort → reward and performance → reward probabilities. Furthermore, salary level, and particularly salary structure, would appear to be important determinants of perceived equity of rewards.

Alternatively, the Porter-Lawler model does not explicity include supervisory and system pressure for high levels of effort and performance. These may be extremely important variables in some organizations. In this regard, Triandis' discussion is clearly more realistic. March and Simon's model also considers organizational pressure through its influence on the individual's evaluation of the perceived consequences of behavioral alternatives.

Discussion

Two broad problems suggested by our review of the theoretical literature are discussed in the present section. First, although we have noted some obvious differences and points of contrast between various theoretical viewpoints, rigorous comparison and evaluation is made difficult by the fact that there are few commonly defined constructs across various theories. Second, it appears questionable whether present theorizing has adequately accounted for the variety of relevant variables that may moderate satisfaction-performance linkages in any specific work environment.

Conceptual problems. In their review of empirical studies, Brayfield and Crockett observed: "Definitions are conspicuous by their absence in most current work in this area."[33] Much of the same conclusion can be stated after reviewing the theoretical literature, and the consequences are even more troublesome. In empirical research the measures employed ultimately define the variables. Thus, if operational procedures are adequately reported, one can identify the definitions and assess their appropriateness to the research question posed.[34] However, with regard to theory, it is impossible to ascertain the meaning of variables if the theoretician fails to define terms.

Satisfaction. The greatest ambiguity in theorizing about satisfaction-performance linkages has been in defining satisfaction. Three partially overlapping issues are

---

[33] Brayfield and Crockett, op. cit., p. 397.

[34] Evans recently identified five definitions of satisfaction generated by alternative measuring procedures. Martin G. Evans, "Conceptual and Operational Problems in the Measurement of Various Aspects of Job Satisfaction," *Journal of Applied Psychology* 53 (April 1969), pp. 93-101.

raised by the literature reviewed here. First, it is often unclear whether satisfaction is being used in a "narrow," need deprivation sense, or in a "broad," attitudinal sense. Second, it is generally not clear which needs or which attitudinal referents are being considered. Third, there is a question whether feelings of job satisfaction are generated with or without reference to conditions on other jobs. These issues make comparisons among theoretical positions risky.

Beginning with the need deprivation versus attitude issue, satisfaction-dissatisfaction may be thought of in the context of "elementary" motivation theory.[35] Needs, demands, or drives generate tensions (feelings of dissatisfaction). The individual engages in behavior designed to obtain goals or incentives to reduce the tensions (satisfy the need).

Alternatively, satisfaction-dissatisfaction can be thought of as the evaluative component of an attitude. A person may respond affectively (feel satisfied or dissatisfied) about an object or referent in his work environment. Peak has argued that an attitude toward an object is a function of the object's perceived instrumentality for obtaining a valued end.[36] Thus, an object (e. g., economic rewards)

could be positively valent (satisfying) in an attitudinal sense[37] while simultaneously deficient (dissatisfying) in a need sense. Illustrating these definitional differences, in the March and Simon model (dissatisfaction may lead to high performance), satisfaction appears to be defined in the need deprivation context.[38] Dissatisfaction (deprivation) in a sense, "pushes" the individual to behave. Satisfaction in the two-factor theory (satisfaction leads to performance), on the other hand, may refer to the affective feelings associated with certain job referents. A referent with positive valence may "pull" an individual to obtain it.[39]

Whether the theoretician chooses to work with needs or with attitudes, he must still identify the need types or attitude referents about which the individual feels satisfied or dissatisfied. There is evidence suggesting that global job satisfaction is made up of a least partially independent subcomponents.[40] Recent research at Cornell on the Job Description Index and other satisfaction measures, for example, has identified five subcomponents of overall satisfaction (work, pay, promotion, supervision, and co-workers) showing adequate convergent and discriminant validity.[41] The Minnesota Satisfaction Questionnaire has 20 factors which

[35] See, for example, David Krech and Richard S. Crutchfield, *Theory and Problems of Social Psychology* (New York: McGraw-Hill, 1948), pp. 40-43.

[36] Helen Peak, "Attitude and Motivation," in Marshall R. Jones, ed. *Nebraska Symposium on Motivation* (Lincoln, Nebraska: University of Nebraska Press, 1955), pp. 149-59. Note the similarity between attitude as defined by Peak and valence as defined by Vroom. In Vroom's model, motivation (force) is a function of valence (attitude) times the expectation that a particular behavior will lead to the desired outcome (op. cit., pp. 15-19). Porter and Lawler use attitudes to refer to valence as well as other antecedents of job performance (*Managerial Attitudes and Performance* and "Antecedent Attitudes of Effective Managerial Performance"). For quite a different formulation of attitude, see Daryl J. Bem, "Self-Perception: The Dependent Variable of Human Performance," *Organizational Behavior and Human Performance* 2 (May 1967), pp. 105-21. He argued attitudes result from behavior. For evidence on a similar theme, see Aaron Lowin and James R. Craig, "The Influence of Level of Performance on Managerial Style:

An Experimental Object-Lesson in the Ambiguity of Correlational Data," *Organizational Behavior and Human Performance* 3 (November 1968), 440-58.

[37] And hence be a necessary, but not sufficient, condition for motivation given Vroom's model.

[38] Unfortunately, March and Simon do not define satisfaction in their discussion. In fact, they do not explicitly distinguish between satisfaction, morale, or cohesiveness (*Organizations*, pp. 47-48).

[39] While Herzberg et al. employ the term job attitude when referring to satisfaction, they do not define it (Herzberg, et al., *The Motivation to Work*, pp. 5-12). More importantly, they do not discuss the mechanism whereby performance is perceived as the path to the attainment of the satisfying referent. In this context, see Vroom's discussion of expectancy (op. cit., pp. 17-18).

[40] For a review, see Vroom, op. cit., pp. 101-105.

[41] Lorne M. Kendall, Patricia C. Smith, Charles L. Hulin, and Edwin A. Locke, "Cornell Studies of Job

have shown only moderately high inter-correlations.[42] Hinrichs factored a 60-item satisfaction questionnaire and obtained nine fairly independent factors.[43]

Despite (or, perhaps because of) this type of research, little is known about the number of satisfaction objects, their interrelationship or their relationship to more global feelings of satisfaction.[44] With such basic questions about job satisfaction unanswered, it is imperative that theoreticians be specific about the satisfaction objects they have in mind. Performance implications may well differ depending upon the type of satisfaction under study.

The issues raised here do not exhaust those which might be considered when discussing conceptual problems associated with satisfaction. They do, however, serve to show that comparisons between different theories are difficult, if not impossible, without explicit definitions on the

part of the theorist. They also suggest that one might expect quite dissimilar relationships between satisfaction and other variables depending on one's definition of satisfaction.

Performance. In defining performance a fundamental issue pertains to the value of thinking in terms of some "ultimate" criterion as though it was a unidimensional construct.[45] This global approach is partially the result of efforts to arrive at operational measures of performance through overall ratings or rankings of the workers' effectiveness.[46] Recent theory and research severely questions the adequacy of this point of view.[47] Research has shown, for example, that alternative criterion measures are neither particularly stable over time[48] nor highly intercorrelated.[49] This suggests, of course, that relations between other variables and performance will vary depending upon the performance measure employed.

Despite this evidence, theorists interested in satisfaction-performance relations have generally treated performance as a

---

Satisfaction: IV The Relative Validity of the Job Description Index and Other Methods of Measurement of Job Satisfaction," unpublished paper, 1963. A recent thorough description of the development of the JDI can be found in Patricia C. Smith, Lorne M. Kendall, and Charles L. Hulin, *The Measurement of Satisfaction in Work and Retirement* (Chicago, Ill.: Rand McNally, 1969).

[42] David J. Weiss, Rene V. Dawis, George W. England, and Lloyd H. Lofquist, *Manual for the Minnesota Satisfaction Questionnaire* (Minneapolis: University of Minnesota, Industrial Relations Center, 1967), Bulletin 45, pp. 93-100. McCornack has shown how erroneous it may be to assume that because two variables correlate fairly highly with each other (e.g., two satisfaction measures) both will correlate about the same with some third variable (e.g., performance). Robert L. McCornack, "A Criticism of Studies Comparing Item-Weighting Methods," *Journal of Applied Psychology* 40 (October 1956), 343-44. See also Patricia C. Smith and Lorne M. Kendall, "Cornell Studies of Job Satisfaction: VI Implications for the Future," unpublished paper, 1963.

[43] John R. Hinrichs, "A Replicated Study of Job Satisfaction Dimensions," *Personnel Psychology* 21 (Winter 1968), 479-503.

[44] Weiss, et al., found that the factor structure of measured satisfaction varied across occupational groups (*Manual for the Minnesota Satisfaction Questionnaire*, pp. 22-23). While the factor structure was relatively constant across five subsamples in Hinrichs' study, differences existed in terms of the degree to which various factors correlated with an overall measure of satisfaction (op. cit.).

[45] For example, Bechtoldt defined the criterion as "... the performance of individuals on a success criterion." Harold P. Bechtoldt, "Problems of Establishing Criterion Measures," in Dewey B. Stuit, ed. *Personnel Research and Test Development in the Bureau of Naval Personnel* (Princeton: Princeton University, 1947), p. 357. At a somewhat more sophisticated level, Brogden and Taylor sought to quantify various performance dimensions on a single monetary continuum. H. E. Brogden and E. K. Taylor, "The Dollar Criterion—Applying the Cost Accounting Concept to Criterion Construction," *Personnel Psychology* 3 (Summer 1950), 133-54.

[46] Robert M. Guion, "Personnel Selection," *Annual Review of Psychology* 18 (1967), 191-216.

[47] For a brief but excellent discussion, see Marvin D. Dunnette, "A Note on *The* Criterion," *Journal of Applied Psychology* 47 (August 1963), 251-54.

[48] Edwin E. Ghiselli and Mason Haire, "The Validation of Selection Tests in The Light of the Dynamic Character of Criteria," *Personnel Psychology* 13 (Autumn 1960), 225-31, and Edwin E. Ghiselli, "Dimensional Problems of Criteria," *Journal of Applied Psychology* 40 (February 1956), 1-4.

[49] See, for example, Charles L. Hulin, "Relevance and Equivalence in Criterion Measures of Executive Success," *Journal of Industrial Psychology* 1 (September 1963), 67-78.

homogeneous variable.[50] This position is particularly troublesome when one thinks of measuring performance across different kinds of tasks, organizations, and occupations.[51] For example, on some jobs performance would appear to be heavily influenced by rule compliance and programmatic behavior, while on others problem solving and creative behavior are probably much more important. One might well expect differences in relationships between some satisfaction measure and these two types of performance.

---

[50] Moreover, definitions differ among theories. Porter and Lawler identify but do not distinguish (in terms of relations with satisfaction) between three types of performance measures: objective, subjective-supervisor, and subjective-self (Porter and Lawler, *Managerial Attitudes and Performance*, pp. 26-28). Performance is measured by self-evaluations in the two-factor theory (Herzberg, et al., *The Motivation to Work*, pp. 51-52). In the theory of work adjustment performance (satisfactoriness) is measured by the organization (Dawis, et al., *The Theory of Work Adjustment*, p. 9). While Triandis does not explicitly define the term, he appears to be emphasizing quantity of performance (Triandis, "A Critique and Experimental Design . . . ," see especially footnote 1, p. 309). March and Simon employ the term *motivation to produce* which appears to be more closely related to Porter and Lawler's effort than to any of the performance measures used (March and Simon, op. cit., pp. 52-53). With such variability in definitions, it is not surprising that hypothesized relationships between satisfaction and performance vary.

[51] In this regard, see Alexander W. Astin, "Criterion-Centered Research," *Educational and Psychological Measurement* 24 (Winter 1964), 807-22. He argued for the need to think of criteria in terms of relationships between the individual worker and his environment.

Conclusions

We close with a few recommendations for investigators interested in job satisfaction and performance. Although pleas for the use of standardized research instruments generally fall on deaf ears, we are unlikely to sample the necessary variety of work environments in a meaningfully comparable fashion unless there is greater utilization of common measures. We additionally urge researchers to obtain as much information about potential moderating variables as their data sources and methodological skills permit. Experimental studies obviously permit control and observation of potential moderators and should be employed more frequently than in the past. But additional survey research is also needed. Adequate controls can be obtained through subject selection and by the greater utilization of multivariate analytical techniques.

We are frankly pessimistic about the value of additional satisfaction-performance theorizing at this time. The theoretically inclined might do better to work on a theory of satisfaction *or* a theory of performance. Such concepts are clearly complex enough to justify their own theories. Prematurely focusing on relationships between the two has probably helped obscure the fact that we know so little about the structure and determinants of each.

Essay 8-2

What is job satisfaction?*

Edwin A. Locke

The present paper is focused around the following issues: the nature of emotions and their relationship to evaluation; the implications of this analysis for an understanding of the concepts of job satisfaction and dissatisfaction; and the relationship of this theory to other theories. Illustrative data are presented. A variety of related issues are also discussed.

The major theoretical orientation of the present paper, as will become evident, stems from Objectivist philosophy and psychology (see Rand and Branden references to follow; the interpretations and applications are strictly my own).

WHAT ARE EMOTIONS?

By introspection, man can observe that he experiences different degrees of pleasure or displeasure on different jobs and/or with different aspects of the same job. Job satisfaction and dissatisfaction are, then, complex emotional reactions to the job. Let us now discuss the nature of emotions.

Man's consciousness has three basic biological functions (i.e., potentialities for action): *(a)* cognition, the identification of existents (e.g., things, objects, actions, etc.); *(b)* evaluation, the estimate of the beneficial or harmful relationship of perceived existents to oneself; and *(c)* the regulation of action. (Trichotomies similar or related to the foregoing have been offered by a number of philosophers and theorists; the present theory is based on the analysis by Rand, 1964, and discussed

*Reprinted from Edwin A. Locke, "What is Job Satisfaction?" *Organizational Behavior and Human Performance* 4 (1969), pp. 309-36 (abridged).

in Branden, 1966a). For experiments bearing on the third function see Locke (1968).

The faculty of cognition (sensation, perception, conception) enables man to discover what exists, but it does not tell him what action(s) to take with respect to this knowledge. It does not reveal the *significance* to him of the existents he perceives. The survival of every living organism, however, requires action, and action requires a selection among alternatives. To maintain its life an organism must take actions which will fulfill its needs. It must *evaluate* the objects and conditions which confront it, using its own life as the standard.

The physical sensations of pleasure and pain are biologically programmed evaluations which inform an organism as to whether its present state or course of action is life-enhancing or life-negating. These sensations play a crucial role in protecting man's life, but they are not in themselves sufficient to guide his actions through the course of a lifetime. Past the level of sensations, man must discover what his life requires through a process of reasoning and the use of conscious foresight. He must *acquire* a code of values. (We will not be concerned here with the process of value acquisition in man. Suffice it to say that all men do acquire, by one means or another, an explicit or implicit code of values.)

A "value is that which one acts to gain and/or keep" (Rand, 1964, p. 15). "It is that which one regards as conducive to one's welfare" (Branden, 1966c, p. 1). The process of evaluation consists of estimating (consciously or subconsciously) the relationship between some object, action, or condition and one or more of one's values. Evaluation, the making of value judgments, is a process of subjective (i.e., private), psychological *measurement* in which a *value* is the standard. In making a value judgment one is answering the questions: "Does this object (action, condition) enhance or threaten my values? Is it for me or against me according to *my* code of values?"

It can be observed by introspection that man cannot hold all of his values in focal awareness simultaneously. The same is true of his knowledge. We refer to values and knowledge of which we are capable of becoming conscious but of which we are not now aware, as being subconscious.

When a man encounters a new object, situation, or problem, relevant knowledge and values ordinarily enter consciousness automatically. For example, when an unarmed hiker perceives a grizzly bear on the trail in front of him, he realizes, without the need for conscious reflection, the significance of the bear with respect to his own life and safety. He automatically appraises or evaluates the bear as dangerous. The emotional reaction he experiences is fear.

What then is the relationship of value judgments to emotions? Branden writes (based on a theory first presented in Rand, 1957, p. 947):

[Man's] emotional capacity is [his] automatic barometer of what is *for* him or *against* him (within the context of his knowledge and values).

The relationship of value-judgments to emotions is that of *cause* to *effect*. An emotion is a value-response. It is the automatic psychological result (involving both mental and somatic features) of a super-rapid, subconscious appraisal.

An emotion is the psychosomatic form in which man experiences his estimate of the beneficial or harmful relationship of some aspect of reality to himself (1966c, p. 5).

Branden argues that all value judgments do not result in emotions. However, for our purposes, the issue of when evaluations do and do not produce emotions is unimportant. Suffice it to say that emotions are the product of value judgments. Nor are we concerned here with the relationship between emotions and subsequent actions (for a discussion of this issue, see Branden, 1966d).

Man's most basic emotions are those of pleasure and displeasure, or joy and suffering. Pleasure is the consequence of (perceived) value achievement. "Happiness is that state of consciousness which proceeds from the achievement of one's values." (Rand, 1964, p. 28.) Displeasure or unhappiness proceeds from the (perceived) negation or destruction of one's values.

Because successful action is a requirement of man's life (a requirement of which he cannot help but be aware, implicitly or explicitly), in achieving his values he experiences his efficacy as a living being. "Happiness is the successful state of life" (Rand, 1964, p. 27).

EMOTIONS AND JOB SATISFACTION

How then do we define job satisfaction and dissatisfaction? Job satisfaction is the pleasurable emotional state resulting from the appraisal of one's job as achieving or facilitating the achievement of one's job values. Job dissatisfaction is the unpleasurable emotional state resulting from the appraisal of one's job as frustrating or blocking the attainment of one's job values or as entailing disvalues. *Job satisfaction and dissatisfaction are a function of the perceived relationship between what one wants from one's job and what one perceives it as offering or entailing.*

Note that there are three elements involved in the appraisal process (these elements are not experienced as separate during an emotional reaction but may be isolated by a process of abstraction): (1) the perception of some aspect of the job;

(2) an implicit or explicit value standard; and (3) a conscious or subconscious judgment of the relationship between (e.g., discrepancy between) one's perception(s) and one's value(s).

Let us illustrate the foregoing with some examples. (In these examples we will assume value importance is constant. More will be said about importance in a later section.) To predict a man's satisfaction with the length of his work week (divorced from the context of his job as a whole) we would have to know: (1) how many hours he (believed he) was working; (2) how many hours per week he wanted to work (ideally); and (3) the judged relationship (discrepancy) between these two figures. A sample function (using *anticipated* satisfaction as the dependent variable) is shown in Figure 1A. Thirty white-collar employees of a research firm in the Washington, D.C. area were asked to indicate their "ideal" work week length, and then to rate how satisfied they *would* feel with their actual work week if it were: *(a)* 50 percent longer; *(b)* 25 percent longer; *(c)* the same length as; *(d)* 25 percent shorter; and *(e)* 50 percent shorter than

this ideal length (all other factors, such as pay, remaining constant). The function indicates that there is an optimal length of work week with increasing deviations on either side of this figure being experienced as increasingly unpleasurable. (The shape of the function was the same for virtually all *S*s.)

This type of function, in which some optimal amount of a factor is most valued with quantitative deviations in either direction being increasingly disliked should hold for the great majority of job aspects (e.g., variety, task difficulty, temperature of workplace, attention from supervisor, travel required, etc.).

There are significant exceptions to this bell-shaped function, however. One of them is pay. In our culture at least there is no limit to the amount of pay that most men would like (ideally) to have.

However, individuals do not use infinite wealth as their sole standard in evaluating their pay. They also appraise it in terms of the perceived discrepancy between it and the *minimum* pay required to fulfill their present wants (or their pay relative to that of other people around them doing similar

Figure 1: Relationship of percept-value discrepancy to satisfaction for working hours and pay

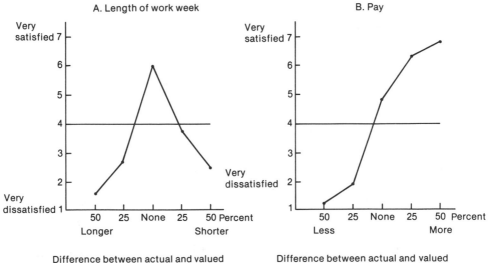

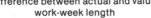

work). Their pay satisfaction results from comparing their actual pay with both their "practical ideal" (minimum adequate) and the amount that would fulfill *all* of their economic wants (ideal maximum).

Figure 1B shows a pay satisfaction function for the same 30 employees used above. They were asked to indicate their minimum adequate pay, given their present needs, and to rate how satisfied they *would* be with: *(a)* 50 percent less than this amount; *(b)* 25 percent less; *(c)* the same amount; *(d)* 25 percent more; and *(e)* 50 percent more than this amount.

In this case, the function is essentially linear. Getting less than the minimum leads to (anticipated) dissatisfaction. Getting the minimum amount of pay produces mild (anticipated) satisfaction; getting more than this amount produces increasingly greater satisfaction because it is closer to the ideal maximum.[1] (Virtually every subject in the above sample showed this linear function.)

Discrepancy-satisfaction functions with other shapes are possible. But the essential point is that in all cases an individual's evaluation of an object or situation will be a function of the perceived relationship between what he perceives and what he values.

Values are not intrinsic; they do not reside in things independent of their perceived effects on man. Nor are values subjective; they do not reside solely in man's consciousness independent of any facts. Values pertain to a relationship between man (or a living organism) and the facts of reality (Rand, 1967, pp. 21 ff). Value judgments are estimates of the significance of perceived facts against a man's value standards.

The causes of job satisfaction are not in the job nor solely in man but lie in the relationship between them. The prediction of job satisfaction necessarily requires an interactive approach—not because 20 or 30 correlational studies have "proved" it, but because of the *nature* of man and of the evaluation process.

PRESENT THEORY VERSUS RELATED VIEWS

The idea that job satisfaction is the result of an interaction between the person and his environment is not, in itself, new. In 1939, Roethlisberger and Dickson wrote that workers' attitudes towards objects in the work environment "can be referred to the relation between an organism and its physical environment . . ." (pp. 261-62). Likert wrote in 1961 that: "The subordinate's reaction to the supervisor's behavior always depends upon the relationship between the supervisory act as perceived by the subordinate and the expectations, values, and interpersonal skills of the subordinate" (pp. 94-95). Rosen and Rosen (1955) view job satisfaction as a consequence of the discrepancy between percepts and value standards. Views similar in certain respects to the above have been expressed by Katzell (1964), Morse (1953), Smith, Kendall, and Hulin (1969), and Vroom (1964).

Despite these apparent similarities, there are significant differences between the present view and those offered by most other investigators.

For one, most previous theorists have not used the concept of *value* consistently, if at all. Two concepts often used in place of or as synonymous with value are those of *expectation* and *need*.

The view that evaluations results from a discrepancy between what is perceived and what is expected (e.g., see McClelland, Atkinson, Clark, and Lowell, 1953) is based on a failure to distinguish between cognitive and evaluative concepts. Expec-

---

[1] In asking for ratings like this, one factor that has to be controlled is the individual's belief that too much pay would be *unjust* (and therefore dissatisfying). Though some individuals might well feel this way if overpaid, it is not relevant to the present issue where we are concerned with pay satisfaction all other factors being equal or held constant.

tation is a term denoting one's beliefs about what will occur in the future. What is expected, however, may or may not correspond to what is wanted. Conversely, what is valued may or may not correspond to what is expected. Dismissals, business failures, and demotions, if disvalued, produce displeasure whether they are expected or not. Promotions, raises, and achievements in one's work, if valued, produce pleasure whether they are expected or not. Empirically, values and expectations often coincide, because most people value only that which they have some reasonable chance of attaining. But when values and expectancies are separated experimentally, it is found that values rather than expectations determine satisfaction (Locke, 1967b; for an example of a clear recognition of the distinction between expectations and *desires,* see Rosenberg, 1957).

The experience produced by a discrepancy between what one gets and what one *expects* is *surprise.* If the outcome is in the direction of what one *values* ("better than expected"), it is a *pleasant* surprise. If the outcome is in the direction of what one *disvalues* ("worse than expected"), it is an *unpleasant* surprise. (It is possible, of course, for a person to value or disvalue the experience of surprise itself. But this does not contradict the above argument.)

Some investigators have argued that satisfaction is a function of the discrepancy between needs and outcomes. Schaffer (1953) claims that "Overall job satisfaction will vary directly with the extent to which those needs of an individual which can be satisfied are actually satisfied . . ." (p. 3). Morse (1953) and Porter (1962) view satisfaction as the result of the degree to which job needs are perceived as being fulfilled on the job.

Biologically the concept of need derives from the fact that living organisms require certain objects and conditions to maintain their physical health and survival. The analogous meaning of need at the psycho-

logical level would pertain to the conditions required for a healthy consciousness. In both cases the concept refers to the *objective* requirements of an organism's well-being.

A conscious living organism may or may not be aware of all its needs. Need frustration produces discomfort, but it does not automatically produce a conscious desire for the needed object. A man, for instance, must learn to recognize and interpret hunger and thirst sensations. There are more subtle needs such as that for certain vitamins and minerals which are identified only after hundreds of years of scientific investigation. There are complex needs such as self-esteem whose nature many men never become aware of explicitly.

The concept of need should be (but in common usage often is not) distinguished from the concept of *wish* or *value.* A value is that which a man *actually* seeks to gain and/or keep or considers beneficial. A value presupposes an awareness, at some level, of the object or condition sought. A need does not. Further, what a man wants or values may or may not be in his actual self-interest. Since men are neither omniscient nor infallible, they will not always seek values which in fact further and maintain their well being. Whether or not a man's values correspond to needs, it is his values which regulate his actions and determine his emotional responses. (The question of the difference in the quality of satisfaction produced by achieving rational and irrational values will be discussed in a subsequent section.)

A further difference between the present theory of job satisfaction and previous approaches concerns the failure of the latter to tie their claims to man's biological nature, i.e., to his need to take action in the face of alternatives. Previous investigators have not shown *why* value judgments were a requirement of man's life, nor have they recognized the relation between emotions and values. Thus, most insights about the nature of job attitudes have remained at the level of common sense hypotheses rather than being explicitly formulated causal principles.

This may explain why so few investigators have used the percept-value discrepancy model consistently to account for job satisfaction and dissatisfaction.

For example, Roethlisberger and Dickson (1939) evidently accept the interactionist view with respect to workers' evaluations of the physical environment but take a predominantly subjectivist position when it comes to explaining other attitudes. They emphasize the influence of the workers' hopes, fears, and fantasies irrespective of the environmental facts (see especially, p. 259).

One can also find research investigations based implicitly on the intrinsic theory of job attitudes. A book by Turner and Lawrence (1965), for example, attempted to find correlations between characteristics of the work task (or worker's perceptions of those characteristics) and job satisfaction without taking account of the worker's values. When the correlations failed to emerge as expected, the authors were forced to make far-reaching and often dubious inferences about individual differences in values in order to account for their results.

Another study (Zaleznik, Christensen, and Roethlisberger, 1958) attempted to predict job satisfaction from the workers' social status with equally disappointing results.

There have been numerous studies in which satisfaction has been correlated with such variables as age, tenure, pay, seniority, education, intelligence, ethnic group, and religion, etc. *None* of these measures indexes values or perceptions directly and infallibly; thus it is not surprising that the correlations have been both low and inconsistent from study to study.

Vroom (1964) has offered one of the most consistent interactionist models to date (since his view is similar to Peak's, 1955, the latter will not be discussed separately here). Nevertheless, there are significant differences between his model and ours. One difficulty with his model concerns the double usage of the concept of *valence*. On the one hand, the valence of an object or outcome is defined as one's *anticipated* satisfaction with something not yet attained (1964, p. 15). The term valence is also taken to be synonymous with one's *actual* satisfaction with objects which one *now* possesses (pp. 100-101).

Both usages of the term valence indicate that it refers to the *result* of an appraisal of some (anticipated or attained) object or situation. Vroom takes the individual's valence or liking for an object as the *starting* point of his explanatory scheme; a given valence is then explained in terms of other valences.

But there is no explanation of what an appraisal *is,* nor of where the *first* appraisal(s) or valences came from. Desires and satisfactions are not psychological primaries. They result from estimating the relationship between some perceived object or outcome and one's value standards. The causal concepts are perception, value, and value judgment; the resultants are emotions such as desire, satisfaction, attraction, etc.

It should be noted that one could properly explain *some* of a man's *values* (i.e., his instrumental values) in terms of his estimate of the other values to which they lead. *Note:* not all values are instrumental values. Some objects or actions are valued as ends in themselves (e.g., works of art, romantic love). To explain *why* a man *valued* a specific amount of pay for instance, one could examine the degree to which he saw this amount of pay as leading to other values (e.g., education, food, housing, vacations, travel, etc.). But this is a different matter from explaining a specific emotional reaction. To explain a man's *satisfaction* with his (present) pay, one would have to look at the relationship between his actual pay and his pay goal (i.e., value standard).

Vroom's model, in short, is not primarily intended to *explain* satisfaction at all (except in terms of other satisfactions). Rather its purpose is to account for choices and overt actions which stem from one's satisfactions and anticipated satisfactions.

An important distinction often overlooked by theorists (e.g., Vroom, 1960) is that between the *degree* to which a person values some particular amount of an element and the *amount* of that element he prefers. For example, two individuals could each prefer the same amount of participation in decision making but the importance of attaining this amount might differ in the two cases.

It will be helpful at this point to observe that every value has two attributes: *content* and *intensity* (see Rand, 1966 for further discussion of this issue). The content pertains to *what* the person wants to gain and/or keep; the intensity pertains to *how much* he wants to gain or keep it.

Porter measures satisfaction by subtracting (quantitative) percept ratings from "need" ratings. A problem with this procedure is that such scores do not reflect "need" importance, yet the latter also affects satisfaction. Furthermore, the discrepancy scores for different "needs" have no common denominator or attribute and thus are not directly comparable.

Katzell (1964) recognized the distinction between content and intensity in his theoretical treatment of job satisfaction. He argues that a given amount of object-value discrepancy will produce different degrees of satisfaction depending on the importance of the value to the individual. Katzell's basic formula is $S = 1 - (|X - V|)/V$ where S = satisfaction, X = the amount of stimulus, and V = the amount most desired.

Importance is taken into account by multiplying satisfaction by the impor-

tance rating. The present theory takes a somewhat different view of the way in which value importance is reflected in satisfaction ratings. This issue will be dealt with at length in a later section.

Aside from the fact that it will not explain attitudes toward pay,[2] there are two important critiques to be made of Katzell's model: *(a)* his formula is based on actual $X - V$ discrepancies whereas it is clearly the individuals' *perceived* discrepancies that determine affect; *(b)* Katzell's formula indicates that the more one wants of some element (holding importance constant) the less dissatisfying a given discrepancy will be. This is analogous to a Weber function for evaluation, e.g., the more of something one wants, the less "noticeable" will be a given amount of deficit. Katzell offers no evidence for this assumption, however; thus, there is no need to dispute it here.

FURTHER ISSUES

We have established the general principle that satisfaction is the result of value achievement and that the phenomenon can be studied experimentally. However, there are a number of problems to be solved before we will be able to account fully for a person's overall satisfaction with his job.

The dynamic character of values

Values differ in level of abstraction. A man's widest, most abstract values are his moral values, which in turn depend upon his morale code (Rand, 1966). An indi-

---

[2] If one were to use the individual's "minimum" pay goal in the formula, this would mean that getting more than the minimum would produce less satisfaction than getting the minimum itself: this is clearly fallacious. If, on the other hand, one were to plug in "infinite" pay, the formula would be insoluble. And if one plugged in a very large figure, e.g., a million dollars, the denominator of the right hand term would be so large in relation to the numerator that individual differences in pay satisfaction would be negligible.

vidual's specific values or goals are determined by his abstract values within the limits of what is available. One can distinguish, for example, between the value of money to a person and the specific amount of pay he will seek at a given time on a given job. The latter will depend on the former, and on the individual's estimate of his "market price" and/or his conception of a "just wage."

An individual's job satisfaction can be predicted and explained in the short range by taking account of his specific goals. To achieve this in the long run, however, one would have to consider his wider values. For these wider values determine what *future* goals a person will seek after achieving his *present* goals. For example, consider a man who values money highly and who has just received a desired raise. Although his immediate response will be one of satisfaction, he will not *remain* satisfied indefinitely with this amount of pay. He will soon set a minimal goal level that is higher than his present salary. Similarly, a person who values challenging work will not remain satisfied with repeatedly succeeding at a task that was *initially* difficult for him. He will eventually demand work which is more difficult than his present assignment.

The phenomenon of goal change can be observed on a small scale in certain level of aspiration experiments. In a recent study, Cartledge (1968) assigned 20 Ss specific, quantitative, end goals on an addition task. A total of 10, 6-minute trials were allowed to reach these cumulative scores. Those Ss who were assigned (and accepted) hard end goals ($N = 10$) set higher trial goals (subgoals) on the task than did Ss who were assigned (and accepted) easy end goals ($N = 10$). The setting of subgoals was governed by the subjects' long range purpose on the task.

Satisfaction with single trial performance in this study was a joint function of two factors: *(a)* the individual's perception of the *instrumentality* of his single

trial performance in achieving his end goal; and *(b)* his goal-performance discrepancy on that trial. This latter finding was due to the fact that individuals attained a sense of "achievement" from reaching their subgoals independent of their role in facilitating end goal attainment. ("Efficacy" was probably the wider value involved here.) The median multiple correlation, within Ss, between the above two variables and single trial satisfaction was .82. (This R was not calculated in Cartledge's original analysis.)

In a follow-up study[3] (incorporating methodological refinements), 20 Ss were given hard or easy cumulative end goals on a reaction time task (i.e., they had to accumulate a certain total amount of reaction time over a series of 20 trials). The median within-S multiple R between perceived subgoal-performance discrepancy plus perceived instrumentality, and single trial satisfaction was .89 (using data from the last 10 trials).

The dynamic character of job values can be observed every day in real life situations. In spite of this, the factors which affect changes in job goals have been given very little attention in job satisfaction research. Relevant studies would include: (1) identifying the relationship between the setting of specific goals and the individual's abstract values, in the context of his perception of the situation; (2) identifying factors which cause the individual to modify his abstract values. Especially crucial here would be the study of individual differences in methods of thinking (i.e., psycho-epistemology, Branden, 1964b).

Value hierarchies

Individuals hold their values in a hierarchy; they value some things more than others. If this were not so, men would be

---

[3] This study was run by Norman Cartledge and Claramae Stevens of the University of Maryland.

so overwhelmed by conflicts that they would be unable to act at all. Furthermore, men differ from each other in the degree to which they value things.

It was noted earlier that the same degree of discrepancy between perception and value could result in differing degrees of satisfaction depending on the importance of the value to the individual. Note that attaining and failing to attain a *more* important value produces more satisfaction and more dissatisfaction, respectively, than do the same outcomes with respect to a *less* important value.

Every experience of satisfaction or dissatisfaction reflects a dual value judgment: the *degree* of value-percept discrepancy and the relative *importance* of the value to the individual. Since both attributes of value, content, and intensity, are involved in determining emotional reactions, both must be considered when explaining such reactions.

It is important to recognize that value importance may vary as a function of the total amount of the value already possessed by the individual. In making actual choices people typically have to judge between the relative importance of *specific increments or decrements* of different values, *not* between the *total* amounts involved. For example, a man might consider pay an important value up to a certain minimum, but further pay increments might be valued less than, say specific changes in the work content. Conversely, there might be a salary so low that no amount of positive change in work content could compensate for it.[4]

Changes in importance should be re-

vealed by *changes* in the *slope* of percept-value discrepancy vs. satisfaction function. The overall slope of such a function would reveal only the *average* importance of the value to the individual, not necessarily the importance of obtaining some particular amount.

Overall job satisfaction

A job is not an entity but an abstraction referring to a combination of tasks performed by an individual in a certain physical and social context for financial (and other) remuneration. Since a job is not perceived or experienced as such, it cannot initially be evaluated as a single unit. Overall job satisfaction is the sum of the evaluations of the discriminable elements of which the job is composed.

There has been considerable controversy regarding how the separate evaluations should be combined to arrive at a valid sum (Ewen, 1967). A typical procedure is to have individuals rate their satisfaction with a fixed number of job elements (e.g., pay, work, supervision) and to sum the ratings, possibly weighting them according to their relative importance.

With respect to weighting, our previous analysis suggests that *importance is already included in and reflected by the satisfaction ratings* (to the extent that they are valid). Since value importance determines the degree of affect produced by a given amount of value-percept discrepancy, multiplying satisfaction scores by importance scores is redundant.

A valid overall index of satisfaction would, in the present view, be a sum of the evaluations of all job aspects to which the individual responds. It is important to note that all individuals may not seek the same *number* of values in their jobs. For instance, a surgeon will ordinarily seek a greater variety of values in his work than will a ditch-digger. A valid overall measure would still be a sum (*not* an average) of

---

[4] It would be misleading to assume that value importance necessarily decreases as an individual obtains more of a value. This opposite could as easily occur. Consider a man who saves for years in order to start a new business or to buy his own house. The *most* valued monetary increment in such a case will be the *last one*, the increment that makes possible the actual realization of his long range goal. By comparison the first increment saved in such a case would be valued very little.

the constituent satisfactions. Negative evaluations (dissatisfactions) would, of course, be subtracted from the total.

REFERENCES

Branden, N. "The Objectivist Theory of Volition." *The Objectivist* 5 (1966), no. 1, 7-12. (a).

Branden, N. "Volition and the Law of Causality." *The Objectivist* 5 (1966), no. 3, 8-14, p. 568. (b)

Branden, N. "Emotions and Values." *The Objectivist* 5 (1966), no. 5, 1-9. (c)

Branden, N. "Emotions and Actions." *The Objectivist* 5 (1966), no. 6, 7-11. (d)

Cartledge, N. "Some Determinants of Goal-Setting." Unpublished Master's Thesis, University of Georgia, 1968.

Ewen, R. "Weighting Components of Job Satisfaction." *Journal of Applied Psychology* 51 (1967), 68-73.

Katzell, R. A. "Personal Values, Job Satisfaction, and Job Behavior." In H. Borow (ed.), *Man in a World of Work*. Boston: Houghton-Mifflin, 1964, pp. 341-63.

Likert, R. *New Patterns of Management*. New York: McGraw-Hill, 1961.

Locke, E. A. "The Relationship of Success and Expectation to Affect on Goal-Seeking Tasks." *Journal of Personality and Social Psychology* 7 (1967), 125-34. (b)

Locke, E. A. "Toward a Theory of Task Motivation and Incentives." *Organizational Behavior and Human Performance* 3 (1968), 157-89.

McClelland, D. C.; Atkinson, J. W.; Clark, R. A.; and Lowell, E. L. *The Achievement Motive*. New York: Appleton-Century-Crofts, 1953.

Morse, N. C. *Satisfaction in the White-Collar Job*. Ann Arbor: Univ. of Michigan, Survey Research Center, 1953.

Peak, H. "Attitude and Motivation." In M. R.

Jones (ed.), *Nebraska Symposium on Motivation*. Lincoln, Nebraska: Univ. of Nebraska Press, 1955, pp. 149-88.

Porter, L. W. "Job Attitudes in Management: I: Perceived Deficiencies in Need Fulfillment as a Function of Job Level." *Journal of Applied Psychology* 46 (1962), 375-84.

Rand, Ayn. *Atlas Shrugged*. New York: Signet, 1957.

Rand, Ayn. "The Objectivist Ethics." In Ayn Rand's *The Virtue of Selfishness*. New York: Signet, 1964, pp. 13-35.

Rand, Ayn. "Concepts of Consciousness." *The Objectivist* 5 (1969), no. 9, 1-8.

Roethlisberger, F. J., and Dickson, W. J. *Management and the Worker*. Cambridge: Harvard Univ. Press, 1939.

Rosen, R. A. H., and Rosen, R. A. "A Suggested Modification in Job Satisfaction Surveys." *Personnel Psychology* 8 (1955), 303-14.

Rosenberg, M. *Occupations and Values*. Glencoe: Free Press, 1957.

Schaffer, R. H. "Job Satisfaction as Related to Need Satisfaction in Work." *Psychological Monographs* 67 (1953), no. 14.

Smith, P. C.; Hulin, C. L.; and Kendall, L. M. *The Measurement of Satisfaction in Work and Retirement*. Chicago: Rand-McNally, 1969.

Turner, A. N., and Lawrence, P. R. *Industrial Jobs and the Worker*. Boston: Harvard Univ. Graduate School of Business Administration, 1965.

Vroom, V. *Some Personality Determinants of the Effects of Participation*. Englewood Cliffs, New Jersey: Prentice-Hall, 1960.

Vroom, V. *Work and Motivation*. New York: Wiley, 1964.

Zaleznik, A.; Christensen, C. R.; and Roethlisberger, F. J. *The Motivation, Productivity and Satisfaction of Workers*. Boston: Harvard Univ. Press, 1958.

Essay 8-3

A model of job satisfaction*

Edward E. Lawler III

A MODEL OF FACET SATISFACTION

Figure 1 presents a model of the determinants of facet satisfaction. The model is intended to be applicable to understanding what determines a person's satisfaction with any facet of the job. The model assumes that the same psychological processes operate to determine satisfaction with job factors ranging from pay to supervision and satisfaction with the work itself. The model in Figure 1 is a discrepancy model in the sense that it shows satisfaction as the difference between *a,* what a person feels he should receive, and *b,* what he perceives that he actually receives. The model indicates that when the person's perception of what his outcome level is and his perception of what his outcome level should be are in agreement, the person will be satisfied. When a person perceives his outcome level as falling below what he feels it should be, he will be dissatisfied. However, when a person's perceived outcome level exceeds what he feels it should be, he will have feelings of guilt and inequity and perhaps some discomfort (Adams, 1965). Thus, for any job factor, the assumption is that satisfaction with the factor will be determined by the difference between how much of the factor there is and how much of the factor the person feels there should be.

Present outcome level is shown to be

*From Edward E. Lawler III, *Motivation in Work Organizations* (Belmont, Calif.: Wadsworth Publishing Co., 1973), pp. 74-77, 82-87. Copyright © 1973 by Wadsworth Inc. Reprinted by permission of the publisher, Brooks/Cole Publishing Company, Monterey, California.

the key influence on a person's perception of what rewards he receives, but his perception is also shown to be influenced by his perception of what his "referent others" receive. The higher the outcome levels of his referent others, the lower his outcome level will appear. Thus, a person's psychological view of how much of a factor he receives is said to be influenced by more than just the objective amount of the factor. Because of this psychological influence, the same amount of reward often can be seen quite differently by two people; to one person it can be a large amount, while to another person it can be a small amount.

The model in Figure 1 also shows that a person's perception of what his reward level should be is influenced by a number of factors. Perhaps the most important influence is perceived job inputs. These inputs include all of the skills, abilities, and training a person brings to the job as well as the behavior he exhibits on the job. The greater he perceives his inputs to be, the higher will be his perception of what his outcomes should be. Because of this relationship, people with high job inputs must receive more rewards than people with low job inputs or they will be dissatisfied. The model also shows that a person's perception of what his outcomes should be is influenced by his perception of the job demands. The greater the demands made by the job, the more he will perceive he should receive. Job demands include such things as job difficulty, responsibilities, and organization level. If outcomes do not rise along with these factors, the clear prediction of the model

Figure 1: Model of the determinants of satisfaction

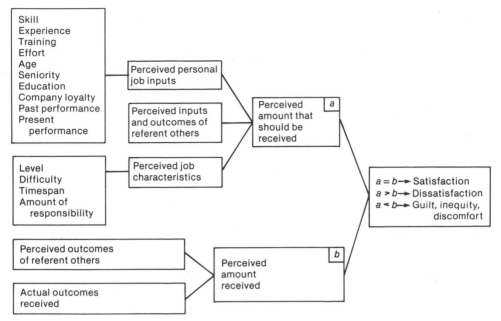

is that the people who perceive they have the more difficult, higher-level jobs will be the most dissatisfied.

The model shows that a person's perception of what his outcomes should be is influenced by what the person perceives his comparison-other's inputs and outcomes to be. This aspect of the model is taken directly from equity theory and is included to stress the fact that people look at the inputs and outcomes of others in order to determine what their own outcome level should be. If a person's comparison-other's inputs are the same as the person's inputs but the other's outcomes are much higher, the person will feel that he should be receiving more outcomes and will be dissatisfied as a result.

The model allows for the possibility that people will feel that their outcomes exceed what they should be. The feelings produced by this condition are quite different from those produced by under-reward. Because of this difference, it does not make sense to refer to a person who feels overrewarded as being dissatisfied.

There is considerable evidence that very few people feel overrewarded, and this fact can be explained by the model. Even when people are highly rewarded, the social-comparison aspect of satisfaction means that people can avoid feeling over-rewarded by looking around and finding someone to compare with who is doing equally well. Also, a person tends to value his own inputs much higher than they are valued by others (Lawler, 1967). Because of this discrepancy, a person's perception of what his outcomes should be is often not shared by those administering his rewards, and is often above what he actually receives. Finally, the person can easily increase his perception of his inputs and thereby justify a high reward level.

As a way of summarizing some of the implications of the model, let us briefly make some statements about who should be dissatisfied if the model is correct. Other things being equal:

1. People with high perceived inputs will be more dissatisfied with a given facet

than people with low perceived inputs.
2. People who perceive their jobs to be demanding will be more dissatisfied with a given facet than people who perceive their jobs as undemanding.
3. People who perceive similar others as having a more favorable input-outcome balance will be more dissatisfied with a given facet than people who perceive their own balance as similar to or better than that of others.
4. People who receive a low outcome level will be more dissatisfied than those who receive a high outcome level.
5. The more outcomes a person perceives his comparison-other receives, the more dissatisfied he will be with his own outcomes. This should be particularly true when the comparison-other is seen to hold a job that demands the same or fewer inputs.

Most theories of job satisfaction argue that overall job satisfaction is determined by some combination of all facet-satisfaction feelings. This could be expressed in terms of the facet-satisfaction model in Figure 1 as a simple sum of, or average of, all $a - b$ discrepancies. Thus, overall job satisfaction is determined by the difference between all the things a person feels he should receive from his job and all the things he actually does receive.

CONSEQUENCES OF DISSATISFACTION

Originally, much of the interest in job satisfaction stemmed from the belief that job satisfaction influenced job performance. Specifically, psychologists thought that high job satisfaction led to high job performance. This view has now been discredited, and most psychologists feel that satisfaction influences absenteeism and turnover but not job performance. However, before looking at the relationship among satisfaction, absenteeism, and turn-

over, let's review the work on satisfaction and performance.

JOB PERFORMANCE

In the 1950s, two major literature reviews showed that in most studies only a slight relationship had been found between satisfaction and performance. A later review by Vroom (1964) also showed that studies had not found a strong relationship between satisfaction and performance; in fact, most studies had found a very low positive relationship between the two. In other words, better performers did seem to be slightly more satisfied than poor performers. A considerable amount of recent work suggests that the slight existing relationship is probably due to better performance indirectly causing satisfaction rather than the reverse. Lawler and Porter (1967) explained this "performance causes satisfaction" viewpoint as follows:

If we assume that rewards cause satisfaction, and that in some cases performance produces rewards, then it is possible that the relationship found between satisfaction and performance comes about through the action of a third variable—rewards. Briefly stated, good performance may lead to rewards, which in turn lead to satisfaction; this formulation then would say that satisfaction rather than causing performance, as was previously assumed, is caused by it.

[Figure 2] shows that performance leads to rewards, and it distinguishes between two kinds of rewards and their connection to performance. A wavy line between performance and extrinsic rewards indicates that such rewards are likely to be imperfectly related to performance. By extrinsic rewards is meant such organizationally controlled rewards as pay, promotion, status, and security—rewards that are often referred to as satisfying mainly lower-level needs. The connection is relatively weak because of the difficulty of tying extrinsic rewards directly to performance. Even though an organization may have a policy of rewarding merit, performance is difficult to measure, and in dispensing rewards like pay, many other factors are frequently taken into consideration.

Figure 2: Model of the relationship of performance to satisfaction

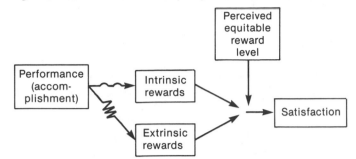

From E. E. Lawler and L. W. Porter, "The Effect of Performance on Job Satisfaction," *Industrial Relations* 7 (1967), 20-28. Reprinted by permission of the publisher, Industrial Relations.

Quite the opposite is likely to be true for intrinsic rewards, however, since they are given to the individual by himself for good performance. Intrinsic or internally mediated rewards are subject to fewer disturbing influences and thus are likely to be more directly related to good performance. This connection is indicated in the model by a semiwavy line. Probably the best example of an intrinsic reward is the feeling of having accomplished something worthwhile. For that matter any of the rewards that satisfy self-actualization needs or higher-order growth needs are good examples of intrinsic rewards [pp. 23-24].[1]

Figure 2 shows that intrinsic and extrinsic rewards are not directly related to job satisfaction, since the relationship is moderated by perceived equitable rewards (what people think they should receive). The model in Figure 2 is similar to the model in Figure 1, since both models show that satisfaction is a function of the amount of rewards a person receives and the amount of rewards he feels he should receive.

Because of the imperfect relationship between performance and rewards and the important effect of perceived equitable rewards, a low but positive relationship should exist between job satisfaction and job performance in most situations. However, in certain situations, a strong positive relationship may exist; while in other situations, a negative relationship may exist. A negative relationship would be expected where rewards are unrelated to performance or negatively related to performance.

To have the same level of satisfaction for good performers and poor performers, the good performers must receive more rewards than the poor performers. The reason for this, as stressed earlier, is that performance level influences the amount of rewards a person feels he should receive. Thus, when rewards are not based on performance—when poor performers receive equal rewards or a larger amount of rewards than good performers—the best performers will be the least satisfied, and a negative satisfaction-performance relationship will exist. If, on the other hand, the better performers are given significantly more rewards, a positive satisfaction-performance relationship should exist. If it is assumed that most organizations are partially successful in relating rewards to performance, it follows that most studies should find a low but positive relationship between satisfaction and performance. Lawler and Porter's (1967) study was among those that found this relationship; their study also found that, as predicted,

[1] E. E. Lawler, and L. W. Porter, "The Effect of Performance on Job Satisfaction," *Industrial Relations* 7 (1967), pp. 20-28. Reprinted by permission of the publisher, Industrial Relations.

intrinsic-need satisfaction was more close-ly related to performance than was extrin-sic-need satisfaction.

In retrospect, it is hard to understand why the belief that high satisfaction causes high performance was so widely accepted. There is nothing in the literature on motivation that suggests this causal re-lationship. In fact, such a relationship is opposite to the concepts developed by both drive theory and expectancy theory. If anything, these two theories would seem to predict that high satisfaction might reduce motivation because of a consequent reduction in the importance of various rewards that may have provided motivational force. Clearly, a more logical view is that performance is determined by people's efforts to obtain the goals and outcomes they desire, and satisfaction is determined by the outcomes people actu-ally obtain. Yet, for some reason, many people believed—and some people still do believe—that the "satisfaction causes per-formance" view is best.

TURNOVER

The relationship between satisfaction and turnover has been studied often. In most studies, researchers have measured the job satisfaction among a number of employees and then waited to see which of the employees studied left during an ensuing time period (typically, a year). The satisfaction scores of the employees who left have then been compared with the remaining employees' scores. Although relationships between satisfaction scores and turnover have not always been very strong, the studies in this area have con-sistently shown that dissatisfied workers are more likely than satisfied workers to terminate employment; thus, satisfaction scores can predict turnover.

A study by Ross and Zander (1957) is a good example of the kind of research that has been done. Ross and Zander measured the job satisfaction of 2,680 female workers in a large company. Four

months later, these researchers found that 169 of these employees had resigned; those who left were significantly more dis-satisfied with the amount of recognition they received on their jobs, with the amount of achievement they experienced, and with the amount of autonomy they had.

Probably the major reason that turn-over and satisfaction are not more strong-ly related is that turnover is very much influenced by the availability of other positions. Even if a person is very dissatis-fied with his job, he is not likely to leave unless more attractive alternatives are available. This observation would suggest that in times of economic prosperity, turnover should be high, and a strong rela-tionship should exist between turnover and satisfaction; but in times of economic hardship, turnover should be low, and lit-tle relationship should exist between turn-over and satisfaction. There is research evidence to support the argument that voluntary turnover is much lower in peri-ods of economic hardship. However, no study has compared the relationship be-tween satisfaction and turnover under dif-ferent economic conditions to see if it is stronger under full employment.

ABSENTEEISM

Like turnover, absenteeism has been found to be related to job satisfaction. If anything, the relationship between satis-faction and absenteeism seems to be stronger than the relationship between satisfaction and turnover. However, even in the case of absenteeism, the relation-ship is far from being isomorphic. Absen-teeism is caused by a number of factors other than a person's voluntarily deciding not to come to work; illness, accidents, and so on can prevent someone who wants to come to work from actually coming to work. We would expect satis-faction to affect only voluntary absences; thus, satisfaction can never be strongly related to a measure of overall absence rate. Those studies that have separated voluntary absences from overall absences have, in fact, found that voluntary absence rates are much more closely related to satisfaction than are overall absence rates (Vroom, 1964). Of course, this outcome would be expected if satisfaction does influence people's willingness to come to work.

ORGANIZATION EFFECTIVENESS

The research evidence clearly shows that employees' decisions about whether they will go to work on any given day and whether they will quit are affected by their feelings of job satisfaction. All the literature reviews on the subject have reached this conclusion. The fact that present satisfaction influences future absenteeism and turnover clearly indicates that the causal direction is from satisfaction to behavior. This conclusion is in marked contrast to our conclusion with respect to performance—that is, behavior causes satisfaction.

The research evidence on the determinants of satisfaction suggests that satisfaction is very much influenced by the actual rewards a person receives; of course, the organization has a considerable amount of control over these rewards. The research also shows that, although not all people will react to the same reward level in the same manner, reactions are predictable if something is known about how people perceive their inputs. The implication is that organizations can influence employees' satisfaction levels. Since it is possible to know how employees will react to different outcome levels, organizations can allocate outcomes in ways that will either cause job satisfaction or job dissatisfaction.

Absenteeism and turnover have a very direct influence on organizational effectiveness. Absenteeism is very costly because it interrupts scheduling, creates a need for overstaffing, increases fringe-benefit costs, and so on. Turnover is expensive because of the many costs incurred in recruiting and training replacement employees. For lower-level jobs, the cost of turnover is estimated at $2,000 a person; at the managerial level, the cost is at least five to ten times the monthly salary of the job involved. Because satisfaction is manageable and influences absenteeism and turnover, organizations can control absenteeism and turnover. Generally, by keeping satisfaction high and, specifically, by seeing that the best employees are the most satisfied, organizations can retain those employees they need the most. In effect, organizations can manage turnover so that, if it occurs, it will occur among employees the organization can most afford to lose. However, keeping the better performers more satisfied is not easy, since they must be rewarded very well. Although identifying and rewarding the better performers is not always easy, the effort may have significant payoffs in terms of increased organizational effectiveness.

REFERENCES

Adams, J. S. "Injustice in Social Exchange." In L. Berkowitz (ed.), *Advances in Experimental Social Psychology*, vol. 2. New York: Academic Press, 1965.

Lawler, E. E. "The Multitrait-Multirater Approach to Measuring Managerial Job Performance." *Journal of Applied Psychology* 51 (1967), 369-81.

Lawler, E. E., and Porter, L. W. "The Effect of Performance on Job Satisfaction." *Industrial Relations* 7 (1967), 20-28.

Ross, I. E., and Zander, A. F. "Need Satisfaction and Employee Turnover." *Personnel Psychology* 10 (1957), 327-38.

Vroom, V. H. *Work and Motivation.* New York: John Wiley and Sons, 1964.

Essay 8-4

The motivation to work*

Frederick Herzberg, Bernard Mausner, and Barbara Bloch Snyderman

This selection reports findings and interpretations of a study of attitudes of employed engineers and accountants. Individuals were asked in interviews to relate a sequence of events, either short run or long run, when they felt either exceptionally good (high) about their jobs or exceptionally bad (low) about their jobs. They were then asked to relate a second sequence of events different from the first, long run if the first had been short run and when they felt low if the first had been high; some individuals went on to relate three and four events when they had felt either exceptionally good or bad about their jobs. Categories of factors were induced from examination of the descriptions of incidents obtained in the interviews and these categories were then used to code job characteristics mentioned in the interviews. Summary results of the analysis of interview responses are presented in Figure 1. The percentage frequency of mention of a job factor in descriptions of particularly good and particularly bad incidents is indicated by the length of bars in the figure, the percentage frequency of mention in particularly good incidents to the right and in particularly bad incidents to the left of the figure. Thus, for example, achievement was mentioned in over 40 percent of the descriptions of exceptionally good incidents and in only 7 percent of the descriptions of exceptionally bad incidents. The width of

the bars represents the ratio of associations of the factor with long-run events to associations with short-run events; the wider the bar, the more frequently the factor was associated with long-run than with short-run events. The shading on the bars for achievement and recognition indicates that these factors were substantially more associated with short-run than with long-run events. These findings are interpreted to indicate that the job factors of working conditions, interpersonal relations, supervision, and company policy are dissatisfying factors which can occasion dissatisfaction but which do not contribute to extreme values of satisfaction. The factors advancement, responsibility, work itself, recognition, and achievement, on the other hand, are satisfiers which can occasion extreme values of satisfaction. The following discussion elaborates upon these findings and their interpretation.

Considering both frequency and duration of attitude effects, the three factors of work itself, responsibility, and advancement stand out strongly as the major factors involved in producing high job attitudes. Their role in producing poor job attitudes is by contrast extremely small. Contrariwise, company policy and administration, supervision (both technical and interpersonal relationships), and working conditions represent the major job dissatisfiers with little potency to affect job attitudes in a positive direction.

The differences shown in Figure 1 indicate another very basic distinction between the factors found in high job attitudes and those found in the stories

Figure 1: Comparison of satisfiers and dissatisfiers

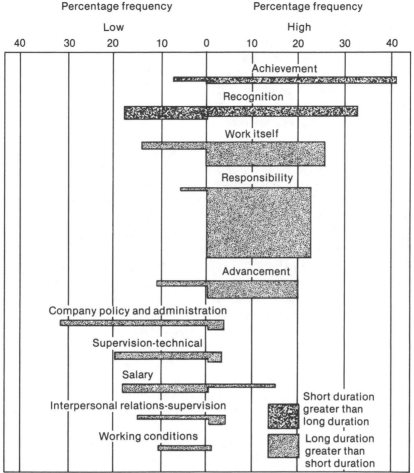

about low job attitudes. We have previously said that all the motivating factors focused on the job and that the factors that appeared infrequently in the high job-attitude stories could be characterized as describing the job context. It is just these job context factors, company policy and administration, supervision (technical and human relations), and working conditions, that now appear as the job dissatisfiers. We can expand on the previous hypothesis by stating that the job satisfiers deal with the factors involved in doing the job, whereas the job dissatisfiers deal with the factors that define the job context. Poor working conditions, bad

company policies and administration, and bad supervision will lead to job dissatisfaction. Good company policies, good administration, good supervision, and good working conditions will not lead to positive job attitudes. In opposition to this, as far as our data has gone, recognition, achievement, interesting work, responsibility, and advancement all lead to positive job attitudes. Their absence will much less frequently lead to job dissatisfaction.

SALARY

We are now ready to examine the factor of salary. It appears as frequently in the high sequences as it does in the low sequences. This is true, however, only when we compare totals, combining short- and long range attitude changes. We find that in the lows salary is found almost three times as often in the long-range as in the short-range sequences. For the high job-attitude stories salary is about equal in both durations. It would seem that as an affector of job attitudes salary has more potency as a job dissatisfier than as a job satisfier.

We can see that salary was associated with company policy and administration in about one half of the low sequences of events; in the high sequences it was most frequently associated with advancement and work itself. To be more specific, when salary occurred as a factor in the lows, it revolved around the unfairness of the wage system within the company, and this almost always referred to increases in sala- ries rather than the absolute levels. It was the system of salary administration that was being described, a system in which wage increases were obtained grudgingly, or given too late, or in which the differen- tials between newly hired employees and those with years of experience on the job were too small. Occasionally, it concerned an advancement that was not accom- panied by a salary increase. In contrast to this, salary was mentioned in the high stories as something that went along with a person's achievement on the job. It was a form of recognition; it meant more than money; it meant a job well done; it meant that the individual was progressing in his work. Viewed within the context of the sequences of events, salary as a factor be- longs more in the group that defines the job situation and is primarily a dissatisfier.

One systematic set of relationships did emerge both from our study of the litera- ture and from the findings [of this re- search]. It was noticed in the reviews of the literature that different results were achieved when the study design was con- cerned with what made people happy with their jobs as opposed to those studies directed toward discovering the factors that led to job dissatisfaction. The factors in our study that made people happy with their jobs turned out to be different from the factors that made people unhappy with their jobs. What does this finding imply for the general problem raised in the present section?

One of the basic habits of scientific thinking is to conceive of variables as operating on a continuum. According to this, a factor that influences job attitudes should influence them in such a way that the positive or negative impact of the same factor should lead to a correspond- ing increase or decrease in morale. Perhaps some of the confusion as to what workers want from their jobs stems from the habit of thinking that factors influencing job attitudes operate along such a continuum. But what if they don't? What if there are some factors that affect job attitudes only in a positive direction? If so, the presence of these factors would act to increase the individual's job satisfaction, but the fail- ure of these factors to occur would not necessarily give rise to job dissatisfaction. Theoretically, given an individual operat- ing from a neutral point, with neither positive nor negative attitudes towards his job, the satisfaction of the factors, which we may call the "satisfiers," would in- crease his job satisfaction beyond the neutral point. The absence of satisfaction to these factors would merely drop him back to this neutral level but would not turn him into a dissatisfied employee. Contrariwise, there should be a group of factors that would act as "dissatisfiers." Existence of these negative factors would lead to an unhappy employee. The satis- fying of these factors, however, would not create a happy employee. This basic dif- ference between "satisfiers" and "dissatis- fiers," which operate in only one direction in determining the job attitudes of work- ers, was one of the hypotheses of our study. In our own data, of course, we found that this unidirectional effect was truer of dissatisfiers than satisfiers.

There is still the possibility of a fluctuating "need hierarchy" operating within the group of satisfiers or dissatisfiers; or the order of importance of the components of these groups may be reasonably uniform for groups of workers who share certain common psychological characteristics. As we have seen, the data of our study do not permit us to draw any hard and fast conclusions on this point. Future research may be able to pinpoint the order of importance of the various satisfiers or dissatisfiers. Even better, we may be able to relate any given order of importance either to the situation or to the kind of people with whom we are dealing.

Be that as it may, our study has enabled us to lay down some lines of stability in the analysis of job attitudes. We are, therefore, a step beyond the fatalistic assumption that no secure conclusions can be drawn from a study of the needs people fulfill in their jobs. In the next section we examine at some length the implications for industry of the specific elements of lawfulness we have been able to introduce into this field.

* * * * *

MOTIVATION VERSUS HYGIENE

Let us summarize briefly our answer to the question, "What do people want from their jobs?" When our respondents reported feeling happy with their jobs, they most frequently described factors related to their tasks, to events that indicated to them that they were successful in the performance of their work, and to the possibility of professional growth. Conversely, when feelings of unhappiness were reported, they were not associated with the job itself but with conditions that *surround* the doing of the job. These events suggest to the individual that the context in which he performs his work is unfair or disorganized and as such represents to him

an unhealthy psychological work environment. Factors involved in these situations we call factors of *hygiene,* for they act in a manner analogous to the principles of medical hygiene. Hygiene operates to remove health hazards from the environment of man. It is not a curative; it is, rather, a preventive. Modern garbage disposal, water purification, and air-pollution control do not cure diseases, but without them we should have many more diseases. Similarly, when there are deleterious factors in the context of the job, they serve to bring about poor job attitudes. Improvement in these factors of hygiene will serve to remove the impediments to positive job attitudes. Among the factors of hygiene we have included supervision, interpersonal relations, physical working conditions, salary, company policies and administrative practices, benefits, and job security. When these factors deteriorate to a level below that which the employee considers acceptable, then job dissatisfaction ensues. However, the reverse does not hold true. When the job context can be characterized as optimal, we will not get dissatisfaction, but neither will we get much in the way of positive attitudes.

The factors that lead to positive job attitudes do so because they satisfy the individual's need for self-actualization in his work. The concept of self-actualization, or self-realization, as a man's ultimate goal has been focal to the thought of many personality theorists. For such men as Jung, Adler, Sullivan, Rogers, and Goldstein the supreme goal of man is to fulfill himself as a creative, unique individual according to his own innate potentialities and within the limits of reality. When he is deflected from this goal he becomes, as Jung says, "a crippled animal."

Man tends to actualize himself in every area of his life, and his job is one of the most important areas. The conditions that surround the doing of the job cannot give him this basic satisfaction; they do not have this potentiality. It is only from the performance of a task that the individual can get the rewards that will reinforce his aspirations. It is clear that although the factors relating to the doing of the job and the factors defining the job context serve as goals for the employee, the nature of the motivating qualities of the two kinds of factors are essentially different. Factors in the job context meet the needs of the individual for avoiding unpleasant situations. In contrast to this motivation by meeting avoidance needs, the job factors reward the needs of the individual to reach his aspirations. These effects on the individual can be conceptualized as actuating approach rather than avoidance behavior. Since it is in the approach sense that the term motivation is most commonly used, we designate the job factors as the "motivators," as opposed to the extra-job factors, which we have labeled the factors of hygiene. It should be understood that both kinds of factors meet the needs of the employee; but it is primarily the "motivators" that

serve to bring about the kind of job satisfaction and, as we saw in the section dealing with the effects of job attitudes, the kind of improvement in performance that industry is seeking from its work force.

We can now say something systematic about what people want from their jobs. For the kind of population that we sampled, and probably for many other populations as well, the wants of employees divide into two groups. One group revolves around the need to develop in one's occupation as a source of personal growth. The second group operates as an essential base to the first and is associated with fair treatment in compensation, supervision, working conditions, and administrative practices. The fulfillment of the needs of the second group does not motivate the individual to high levels of job satisfaction and to extra performance on the job. All we can expect from satisfying the needs for hygiene is the prevention of dissatisfaction and poor job performance.

Essay 8-5

Satisfaction and productivity*

James G. March and Herbert A. Simon

Few aspects of organizational behavior have been subject to as much speculation as have morale, productivity, and turnover. They are obviously important to the operating executive's day-to-day operations. Indeed, if we accept the economist's characterization of the administrator, productivity is one of the fundamen-

*Reprinted from James G. March and Herbert A. Simon, *Organizations* (New York: John Wiley and Sons, 1958), pp. 47-52. © 1958 John Wiley and Sons, Inc. Reprinted by permission.

tal secondary criteria (after profit) for his success. At the same time, propositions relating such achievement variables as productivity to the characteristics of the organization are basic to the student of organizations.

The model of individual behavior implicit in the "traditional" approach to productivity recognizes only those constraints on performance that have obvious machine analogues (Taylor, 1911). To organize efficiently is to define the physiological capacity of the human organism and to program activities to make full use of that capacity. More recently, students of individual behavior in an organizational setting have introduced into the model of organizational behavior a series of concepts like morale, satisfaction, and cohesiveness. Attempts to relate these variables directly to productivity have failed to reveal any consistent, simple relation (Viteles, 1953; Brayfield and Crockett, 1955). High morale is not a sufficient condition for high productivity, and does not necessarily lead to higher productivity than low morale. Somewhat reluctantly, theorists of industrial motivation have come to recognize that present satisfactions are often less important in influencing human behavior than perceived relations between present alternatives and future states.

Hence, it has become increasingly clear that important unanticipated consequences follow when the "machine" model of human organisms is used to stimulate production. It has also become clear that simple theories built on concepts of morale and satisfaction have had little or no success. In the remainder of this essay we will try to explain why this state of affairs exists and to indicate how the available research data can be used to outline a more adequate theory. In the first part we outline the relation between individual satisfaction and individual productivity, and in the second part we explore the important factors determining individual motivations to produce.

. . . there are important differences between two types of decisions by employees. The first is the decision to participate in the organization—or to leave the organization. The second is the decision to produce or to refuse to produce at the rate demanded by the organization hierarchy. The production decision is substantially different from the participation decision in that it evokes a significantly different set. At least some of the confusion

in the literature of morale and satisfaction stems from a failure to distinguish between turnover and productivity.

Consider the following general model:

1. The lower the *satisfaction* (3.34) of the organism, the more *search* for alternative programs (3.35) it will undertake [3.35:3.34].

2. The more search, the higher the *expected value of reward* (3.36) [3.36:3.35].

3. The higher the expected value of reward, the higher the *satisfaction* [3.34:3.36].

4. The higher the expected value of reward, the higher the *level of aspiration* (3.37) of the organism [3.37:3.36].

5. The higher the level of aspiration, the lower the satisfaction [3.34:3.37].

The system is summarized in Figure 1. With a few additional assumptions, we can translate the model into simple mathematical form. One possible translation goes as follows:

Let S = Satisfaction, A = Level of aspiration, L = Search rate, and R = Expected value of reward. The following equations correspond to the set of verbal propositions:

$$\frac{dA}{dt} = \alpha(R - A + a),$$ (1)

where

$$a > 0, \alpha > 0.$$

This interprets proposition 4 and adds to it an assertion about the dynamic process that leads to equilibrium. Since a is positive, at equilibrium the aspiration level will exceed the reward.

$$S = R - A.$$ (2)

This interprets propositions 3 and 5.

$$L = \beta(\bar{S} - S),$$ (3)

where

$$\bar{S} > 0, \beta > 0.$$

Figure 1: General model of adaptive
motivated behavior

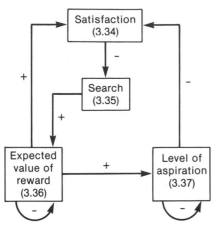

This interprets proposition 1. It also postulates a "desired" level of satisfaction, $\bar{S}$, at which search for increased satisfaction would cease.

$$\frac{dR}{dt} = \gamma(L - b - cR), \qquad (4)$$

where

$$\gamma > 0, \ b \geqslant 0, \ c > 0.$$

This interprets proposition 2. It postulates that a certain amount of search, $(b + cR)$, is required just to maintain the current level, R, of reward.

This system of equations determines completely the behavior of the dynamic system it describes. The system possesses a stable equilibrium.

Even without the mathematical statement, we can use the model to clarify the relations in which we are interested. Before doing so, however, some qualification is in order.

It is clear that the search behavior specified depends on an underlying belief on the part of the organism that the environment is benign and on the fact that search is usually reasonably effective. By our verbal hypothesis 2, we are alleging that such requirements are, in fact, met. Hypothesis 1 will be true only of organisms that do perceive the world as benign. If the environment is perceived as malevolent

and/or barren, search behavior will not necessarily follow from a decrease in satisfaction. Thus, aggression, withdrawal, and regression are certainly observable reactions to dissatisfaction that lead to frustration (Maier, 1949). These "neurotic" reactions are excluded from this model.

Similarly, hypothesis 2 will not be true if search is ineffectual. Ineffective search—cycling, stereotypy, etc.—is an important aspect of human problem-solving that is not included in the present model. Ultimately, we will require a set of hypotheses that deals with the switching from "normal" to "neurotic" reactions and from effective to ineffective search. For the present, we limit ourselves to the "normal" situation on both counts, although some special cases of "abnormalities" have already been considered in the bureaucratic models.

From this simple model of adaptive, motivated behavior we can see why the relation between satisfaction and individual productivity is complex. One would not predict that "satisfied" rats would perform best in a T-maze. Similarly, there is no reason for predicting that high satisfaction, per se, motivates a given individual to conform to the goals specified by the hierarchy.

Suppose a production employee is dissatisfied. We would predict that he would search for alternatives of action. What are the alternatives open to him? A rather large number of alternatives are likely to be evoked in such a situation, and a theory of motivation should specify the conditions under which these various alternatives are evoked. For simplicity, let us focus attention on just three key alternatives.

First, the employee can leave the organization. Observe that when satisfaction is low this alternative will frequently be evoked. The probability of accepting this alternative determines voluntary employee turnover.

Second, the employee can conform to the production norms of the organization.

Given the system of control in any complex organization, together with the general cultural climate within which an organization operates (at least in the United States), it is hard to imagine a situation in which this alternative is not at least evoked.

Third, the employee can seek opportunities for satisfaction without high production. He may "play politics" in the organization, or he may turn to nonorganizational or suborganizational groups and conform to their norms. These norms may deviate widely from those specified by the organization and may specifically limit production.

We will explore these and other alternatives in greater detail below. We assert that these three general types of alternatives are virtually always evoked and that they provide at least a first approximation to the employee's decision problem. Let us say then that an employee chooses either (1) to leave the organization, or (2) to stay in the organization and produce, or (3) to stay in the organization and not produce. Since the decision to leave the organization is considered [elsewhere], we will focus our attention at the moment on the decisions to stay inside the organization. Either decision (i.e., to produce or not to produce) can result in rewards that are perceived by the employee to be consequences of his behavior. That is, given either decision, under some conditions the employee will associate positive rewards with the behavior he has chosen; under other conditions the association will be much less strong or he will associate such behavior with outcomes he does not desire.

Individuals frequently perceive the rewards they receive as uncorrelated with their productivity, or as dependent on nonproduction variables and thus uncorrelated or negatively correlated with productive behavior. For example, if an employee operates to restrict productive effort in a manner dictated by subgroup norms and is subsequently rewarded by the subgroup (and without serious penalty from the organization), he will be motivated to restrict output.

From this we may conclude that high satisfaction, per se, is not a particularly good predictor of high production nor does it facilitate production in a causal sense. Motivation to produce stems from a present or anticipated state of discontent and a perception of a direct connection between individual production and a new state of satisfaction.

In this, we have not considered the extent to which high satisfaction facilitates high production, not by the satisfied individual himself but by others in the organization. Such a relation occasionally seems implicit in the literature of industrial relations. However, if there is no direct relation between individual high satisfaction and motivation to produce, it is not enough to show that high or low satisfaction is contagious in an organization. Rather, the theory must specify why and how the satisfaction level of one individual affects the productive habits of another.

Interpersonal factors in the relation between productivity and satisfaction have been too little studied to permit more than speculation. At the moment, psychological research is primarily directed toward "motivation to produce" rather than "productivity." As we shall see, there are important social factors impinging on the former, but current theory does not take account of interaction among persons in organized production except as it directly affects the goals of the individual participant.

REFERENCES

Brayfield, A. H., and Crockett, W. H. "Employee Attitudes and Employee Performance." *Psychological Bulletin* 52 (1955), 396-424.

Maier, N. R. F. *Frustration.* New York: McGraw-Hill, 1949.

Taylor, F. W. *The Principles of Scientific Management.* New York: Harper and Row, 1911.

Viteles, M. S. *Motivation and Morale in Industry.* New York: W. W. Norton, 1953.

Essay 8-6

Another look at job satisfaction and performance*

Thomas A. Mahoney

JOB SATISFACTION

Various reviews of the job satisfaction-performance literature have been published over the past 20 years, the most recent being Locke's review in 1976. (2) The review by Locke serves as a starting point in the analysis presented here.

Locke defines job satisfaction as "a pleasurable or positive emotional state resulting from the appraisal of one's job or job experiences," and notes that since a job is not a single entity, it must be analyzed in terms of its constituent elements. Job satisfaction, then, is some function of appraisals of these different constituent elements often termed facets or factors of job satisfaction. These elements have been the subject of more empirical analysis than conceptual formulation, and typical formulations of job elements are, to a large extent, functions of scaling techniques employed by researchers.

We begin with Locke's depiction of satisfaction as an emotional response to a judgment regarding an element or characteristic of the object of concern, a judgment involving comparison of perceptions of that element with some standard. Most conceptualizations of job satisfaction employ this same framework, perceptions of different elements of job satisfaction are evaluated relative to standards of desirability, and overall job satisfaction is a function of these summed evaluations. Locke also noted that the relationship between satisfaction and the percept-value comparison may vary among different

elements of job satisfaction; he noted for illustration that any percept-value discrepancy regarding length of work week is dissatisfying, while only deficiency percept-value discrepancies regarding amount of pay are dissatisfying. These relationships are depicted as functions A and D in Figure 1; function A is drawn with a maximum value of the function corresponding to percept-value congruence, whereas no maximum value is associated with function D. Satisfaction and dissatisfaction are conceived as poles of a continuum of a single construct. While no zero point is indicated on the satisfaction scale, such a point has conceptual meaning and is not merely a scaling issue; conceptually, this zero point is the point at which one begins to speak of degrees of dissatisfaction rather than degrees of satisfaction. While a number of functions are depicted in Figure 1 for comparative purposes, imagine a different zero point on the satisfaction scale for each function, that point on the satisfaction scale corresponding to percept-value congruence on the perception scale. In this context, then, function A applies to those elements of job satisfaction with which a concept of optimality is associated, elements such as hours of work, temperature and humidity of the workplace, and closeness of supervision. The degree of dissatisfaction experienced by the individual declines as perceptions of the level of these elements approach the optimal value assigned them and any discrepancy, deficiency, or overage, is ex-

Figure 1

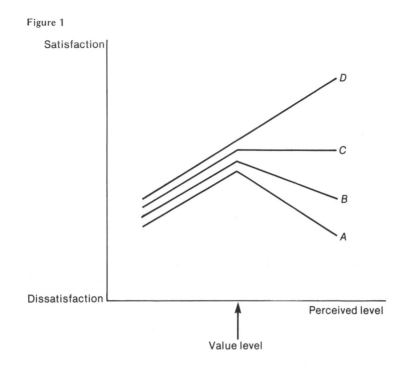

perienced as dissatisfaction. It is unlikely that the calculus of satisfaction is so precise that there is a single zero point on the satisfaction scale associated with percept-value congruence, however; rather, there likely is a zero range associated with a range of percept-value congruence, dissatisfaction being experienced only as the percept-value discrepancy approaches some threshold value. Satisfaction, conceived as the upper range of the satisfaction-dissatisfaction continuum, is achieved through percept-value congruence but is not capable of increase beyond that point. Also in this context, function *D* applies to those elements of job satisfaction for which no concept of optimality is appropriate, elements such as interesting work, skill development, and personal growth; the valued level of these elements is minimal rather than optimal. Percept-value deficiencies, in this instance, are dissatisfying while positive percept-value discrepancies are satisfying. The optimality value of function *A* implies an equilibrium concept of need, a specific value of the job element being

necessary for well being, while the valued level of function *D* implies a concept of minimal needs. Satisfaction values associated with function *A* merely connote the absence of need discrepancies while satisfaction, connoting a positive affect state with a range of values, is more easily associated with function *D* where positive percept-value discrepancies are pleasurable.

Two other functions, *B* and *C*, are illustrated also in Figure 1. Like function *A*, functions *B* and *C* also break at the point of percept-value congruence but they are not symmetrical functions as was function *A*. Function *B* is drawn to indicate that the relevance of percept-value discrepancies may depend upon the direction of the discrepancy, deficiencies being more disturbing than overages, and function *C* is drawn to indicate that only percept-value discrepancies are relevant to the satisfaction-dissatisfaction continuum. Function *B* might apply, for example, to elements judged against equity norms, elements such as relative compensation, relative rate of promotion, and relative severity of discipline. Function B suggests that inequitable treatment disadvantageous to the individual is more dissatisfying than inequitable treatment advantageous to the individual, although equitable treatment is most satisfying. Function C is drawn to illustrate the concept of satiation, percept-value deficiencies are dissatisfying while percept-value overages are of no relevance to the individual. Function C might apply to elements such as cleanliness of the workplace or amount of information provided through communication of policies. Lack of cleanliness or information is dissatisfying, but levels of these elements beyond the desired value are meaningless to the individual's satisfaction.

Most models of job satisfaction view overall satisfaction as a summed function of satisfaction with various job elements, the elements varying in terms of importance. Locke suggests that importance of any job element to overall satisfaction is not easily separated from the evaluative judgment of that element, and that importance of an element is reflected in the range of satisfaction values associated with the element. This concept is illustrated in Figure 2 in terms of the different slopes associated with functions X and Y, function X is appropriate for a job element more important to overall job satisfaction than the job element associated with function Y; percept-value discrepancies in function X occasion a wider range of satisfaction-dissatisfaction values than do identical percept-value discrepancies in function Y. This concept of importance also figures in the functions illustrated in Figure 1; function B, for example, indicates that percept-value deficiencies are more important than positive percept-value discrepancies. Importance thus may vary from job element to job element and from one form of percept-value discrepancy (deficiency) to another (overage).

Basic distinctions among the functions depicted in Figure 1 relate to the nature of the valued level of the element implied in the relationship of percept-value discrepancies and satisfaction. Functions A, B and C all imply an optimal value of job element, function D does not. Optimality, in this context, connotes equilibrium, a connotation not associated with the function D. This distinction parallels the distinction between satisfying job elements and dissatisfying job elements in the two-factor model of Herzberg, dissatisfying

Figure 2

Satisfaction

O

X

Y

Dissatisfaction

N

Level of job element

elements being characterized by functions *A*, *B* and *C*, and satisfying elements being characterized by function *D*. Percept-value discrepancies in functions *A*, *B* and *C* are associated with dissatisfaction and positive percept-value discrepancies may be associated with increasing levels of satisfaction only in function *D*. It is not necessary to conceptualize two independent factors of job satisfaction and dissatisfaction, however; we can employ concepts of satisfaction and dissatisfaction as poles of a single continuum and note that only certain job elements have relevance for the range of satisfaction values. The concepts of optimal value associated with functions *A*, *B* and *C* and minimal value associated with function *D* also parallel Maslow's distinction between lower order needs which can be fulfilled (functions *A*, *B* and *C*) and higher order needs such as self-actualization which are not capable of fulfillment (function *D*).

Two other concepts or dimensions of job satisfaction are suggested by the different functions in Figure 1 and by the difference between needs and expectancy models of job satisfaction. These concepts relate to deprivation and aspirational dimensions of job satisfaction. Following Locke's formulation, job satisfaction is conceived as a function of percept-value discrepancies of job elements. As indicated in Figure 1, there are a variety of functional relationships between satisfaction and percept-value discrepancies applicable to different job elements, optimal values are associated with certain elements and minimal values are associated with others. In accord with needs models of job satisfaction, we hypothesize need values for different job elements, need values which are either real or conditioned. Thus, for example, we conceive need values for comfortable working conditions, adequate supervision, equitable compensation and minimal sense of achievement, need values which may be optimal or minimal in nature. Need values

for job elements probably vary among individuals (e.g., temperature, noise level, cleanliness) and from one cultural setting to another (e.g., equity of compensation, interaction with co-workers and degree of supervision) and are relatively stable and resistant to change over time. Percept-need value discrepancies which are dissatisfying are suggestive of deprivation, a state most easily identified with functions *A*, *B* and *C* in Figure 1, although also related to percept-need value deficiencies in function *D*. Positive percept-need value discrepancies in function *D*, however, occasion increasing values of satisfaction. These positive discrepancies acquire meaning from some source other than need; they are valued for reasons other than relationship to need and suggest desires or expectancies rather than needs. The concept of aspiration rather than need is suggested by job elements with which minimal needs values are associated and where positive percept-need values are related to increasing values of satisfaction.

Aspirational concepts connote desires or goals, values likely to vary with an individual's experience and current achievement levels unlike needs values which are relatively more stable over time. Following the conceptualization of March and Simon as well as concepts of need achievement motivation, aspiration values for job elements are conceived as varying with current achievements and to generally exceed current achievements by some slight amount. (3) Aspiration values indicating desired or goal values can be associated with job elements in the same manner as needs values are associated with job elements. Thus we can conceive of two separate dimensions or components of job satisfaction, one related to percept-need value judgments (deprivational) and the other related to percept-aspiration value judgments (aspirational). Aspiration values for job elements are likely to coincide with needs values, given percept-need value deficiencies, and the distinction between needs value and aspiration value is largely irrelevant for job elements with optimal needs values (functions A, B and C). Aspiration values will be relevant for those job elements with minimal needs values, particularly under conditions of positive percept-need value discrepancies (function D). Percept-aspiration value deficiencies, like percept-need value deficiencies, are dissatisfying. Unlike need values, however, aspiration values vary with recent achievements and extreme values of aspirational dissatisfaction as well as satisfaction are short lived; the normal range of values of aspirational satisfaction also is more restricted than the range of values of deprivational satisfaction.

The concepts of deprivational and aspirational satisfaction associated with percept-value judgments are illustrated in Figure 3. Perceived job element values are indicated on the horizontal scale and deprivational and aspirational satisfaction values on the left and right vertical scales respectively. Need value for the job element is indicated at point N and will be relatively invariant with respect to perceived value of the job element; the zero point on the deprivational satisfaction scale is indicated at the intersection of

need value and the functional relationship between deprivational satisfaction and percept-value judgments. Two different perceived values of the job element, P_1 and P_2, occasion deprivational dissatisfaction and satisfaction respectively. Aspiration value varies with perceived level of the job factor, given deprivational satisfaction, and thus is indicated only for the perceived level P_2; aspiration value varies with achievements and thus the aspiration value A_2 exceeds the perceived level P_2 by some slight amount. The zero point on the aspirational satisfaction scale is indicated at the intersection of aspiration value and the functional relationship between aspirational satisfaction and percept-value judgments, O_2. An experienced level of the job element, P_1, occasions deprivational dissatisfaction; aspiration value is irrelevant or indistinguishable from needs value, and so aspirational dissatisfaction is indistinguishable from deprivational dissatisfaction. Change in the perceived level from P_1 to P_2 occasions deprivational satisfaction and momentary aspirational satisfaction. Given deprivational satisfaction, aspiration values become relevant to the individual and an aspiration value A_2 develops occasioning aspirational dissatisfaction. Deprivational satisfaction

Figure 3

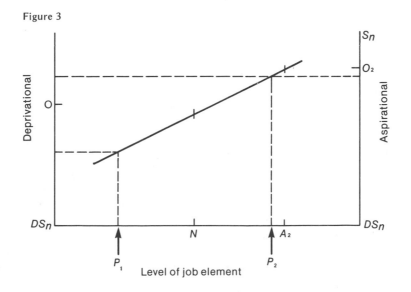

continues, however, as need level N remains relatively constant. The individual thus experiences both deprivational satisfaction and aspirational dissatisfaction at the same time.

To summarize, we propose two concepts of satisfaction, deprivational and aspirational, associated with job elements. Deprivational satisfaction is a function of percept-need value discrepancy and aspirational satisfaction is a function of percept-aspiration value discrepancy. Need values take the form of both optimal or equilibrium values and minimal values, each being appropriate for different job elements. A range of values of deprivational dissatisfaction is associated with percept-need value discrepancies where need value takes the form of an optimal or equilibrium value, while deprivational satisfaction in those instances is limited in range around the zero point of deprivational satisfaction; a range of both deprivational dissatisfaction and satisfaction values is associated with percept-need value discrepancies where need value takes the form of a minimal value, positive percept-need value discrepancies being satisfying. Aspirational satisfaction is distinguishable from deprivational satisfaction only as associated with job elements characterized by minimal need values and under conditions of minimal deprivational dissatisfaction. Aspiration values reflect past achievements and tend to exceed perceptions by some amount. Thus extreme values of aspirational satisfaction and dissatisfaction are likely to be short-lived and the range of aspirational satisfaction values is likely to be small with a mean value indicating minor dissatisfaction. Overall satisfaction with any job element is a function of both deprivational and aspirational satisfaction associated with that element. Overall job satisfaction is a summed function of satisfaction with the various job elements and, given the conceptualization of deprivational and aspirational satisfaction, will be influenced

most by deprivational satisfaction values. The possible values of aspirational satisfaction are restricted both in range and in terms of the number of elements for which aspirational values are appropriate. Nevertheless, the deprivational and aspirational dimensions of job satisfaction are maintained as separate dimensions since, as noted later, they have different motivational and behavioral connotations.

The distinction made between concepts of deprivational and aspirational satisfaction relates specifically to distinctions made between needs and expectancies models of job satisfaction, the needs models relating to deprivational satisfaction and expectancy models relating to aspirational satisfaction. The distinction between aspirational and deprivational satisfaction assumes different value standards for the percept-value judgments in job satisfaction and different functional relationships between satisfaction and percept-value discrepancies. A range of deprivational dissatisfaction may be experienced with any job element, while a range of deprivational satisfaction values is conceivable only for job elements characterized with minimal need values; aspirational satisfaction and dissatisfaction are relevant only relative to job elements characterized with minimal need values and in the absence of significant deprivational dissatisfaction. While a wide range of aspirational satisfaction values is conceivable, extreme values of aspirational satisfaction and dissatisfaction are likely to be short-lived. This formulation is consistent with data reported by Herzberg, Mausner, and Snyderman although the formulation differs from their interpretation. (4)

Those elements most frequently associated with dissatisfying events are elements for which optimal need values appear appropriate; percept-need value discrepancies will be dissatisfying and percept-need value congruence is associated with the zero point of deprivational dissatisfaction. Those elements associated with extremely satisfying events are elements for which minimal need values appear most appropriate and where positive percept-need value discrepancies will be associated with extreme values of deprivational satisfaction. The elements of salary and status are somewhat more complex; both minimal and optimal need values can be associated with each. Thus, for example, equity concepts implying optimal need values can be associated with salary as can minimal standard of living need values; any given salary may be deprivationally satisfying compared with one need value and deprivationally dissatisfying compared with the other. While Herzberg et al. inferred two independent dimensions of satisfaction and dissatisfaction from their findings, the findings can as easily be interpreted within the context of the different minimal and optimal need value concepts of our model. Similarly, their distinction between satisfying and dissatisfying events of long and short duration parallels our distinction between deprivational and aspirational satisfaction, extreme values of aspirational satisfaction and dissatisfaction being short-lived, and extreme values of deprivational satisfaction and dissatisfaction being capable of longer endurance.

The concept of overall job satisfaction is not uniquely determined in this formulation. Overall job satisfaction is conceived as some summary function of satisfaction with job elements, but at least two different functions are conceivable. Following Locke's logic, we view importance of the job element as incorporated in the assessment of the element rather than as an independent judgment to be combined with the assessment. However, we have specified two dimensions of satisfaction, deprivational and aspirational, involved in the assessment of job elements. The job element judgments which combine in overall job satisfaction can be illustrated with the three dimensional diagram in

Figure 4 associating the two dimensions of satisfaction with every job element. Two alternative formulations of overall job satisfaction are illustrated in equations (1) and (2) below where j refers to job element, a_j refers to aspirational satisfaction and d_j to deprivational satisfaction with element j. Identical measures of

$$S = \Sigma_j (a + d)_j \qquad (1)$$
$$S = \Sigma_j a_j + \Sigma_j d_j \qquad (2)$$

overall satisfaction are obtained from both formulations whether the aspirational and deprivational values are combined and summed across job elements or aspirational values and deprivational values are summed individually across job elements and then combined. We prefer the second formulation (2) which maintains the distinction between aspirational and deprivational satisfaction until the final operation because of different behavioral implications associated with these concepts; each individual can be characterized with aspirational, deprivational, and overall satisfaction values, not merely an overall satisfaction value. Given the logic of the model developed earlier, we would anticipate, for any individual, distributions of deprivational and aspirational satisfaction values of job elements as indicated in Figure 4. The distribution of deprivational satisfaction values will be positively skewed due to the fact that minimal need values are associated with only a subset of job elements; aspirational satisfaction values will be distributed more normally, but with restricted range and variance due to the adaptation of aspiration values to perception values. The combination of aspirational and deprivational satisfaction concepts at the level of job element as in Equation (1) would obscure any possible significance of overall aspirational satisfaction. We prefer to consider aspirational and deprivational satisfaction as related, but distinctively different, components of overall satisfaction, each implying differ-

Figure 4

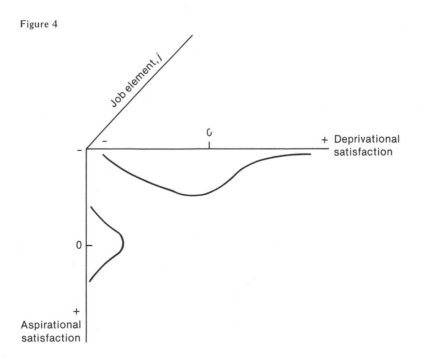

ent behavioral consequences. At any point in time, each individual might be characterized in terms of both aspirational and deprivational satisfaction, there being no necessary relationship between these two dimensions of overall satisfaction.

SATISFACTION-PERFORMANCE RELATIONSHIPS

Conceptualizations of performance in models of satisfaction-performance relationships have been even more ad hoc in nature than conceptualizations of job satisfaction. Performance has been conceived as both behavior and output and measured as turnover, absenteeism, and amount and quality of output. Performance behavior and output are distinctly different concepts, however; performance behavior is more easily conceptualized as a direct function of personal motivation than is performance output. Performance output is more realistically viewed as a function of task requirements and ability as well as

performance behavior. Because of this, it is not surprising that more consistent empirical relationships have been observed between job satisfaction and behaviors such as absenteeism and turnover than between job satisfaction and output measures; relationships with output are moderated by more contributing influences than are relationships with personal behavior. Conceptualizations of performance relevant to investigation of satisfaction-performance relationships thus probably ought to focus upon behavioral dimensions of performance subject to individual control rather than output dimensions which often are controlled by other factors.

A variety of behaviors relevant to the general concept of job performance can be identified, behaviors such as seeking and/or accepting employment, termination of employment, absenteeism or work attendance, following directions, registering complaints, submitting suggestions, exerting effort, and the pacing of behavior. It is by no means obvious that all of these behaviors ought to be subject to the same motivational influences; indeed, treatments by March and Simon and by Katz suggest that different work behaviors are subject to different motivational influences. (5) Thus relationships between job satisfaction and work behavior probably vary with the dimension of work behavior considered. Further, work behavior is conceptualized as behavior relevant to job performance whatever the motivational source, and certain work behaviors probably are influenced more by motivational influences outside the workplace than are others. Absenteeism on the first day of fishing season, for example, is influenced less by work motivations than by non-work motivations. It seems unlikely for these reasons that job satisfaction is consistently related to all work behaviors, and investigations of relationships ought to focus upon those behaviors linked conceptually with job satisfaction.

One approach to the conceptualization of performance behavior might differentiate behaviors on the basis of relevance to output. An alternative conceptualization distinguishes between habitual behavior and choice behavior. Elements of habitual behavior in work performance include pattern or sequence of task performance, timing of rests, time of reporting for and leaving work, and habitual level of effort expended in performance, behaviors that are repetitive and relatively standardized over time. Choice behavior in work performance includes behavior exhibited in relatively infrequent circumstances as well as changes from habitual behavior patterns, behaviors such as termination of employment, occasional absenteeism and tardiness, and change in level of effort expended at work. Habitual behavior is associated with concepts of satisfaction, whereas change in behavior involving choice is more easily associated with dissatisfaction. An individual is expected to continue to appear for work and perform at a usual level of effort as long as reasonably satisfied; given dissatisfaction beyond some threshold level, however, the individual might be expected to be alert to, and seek out, behavior changes which ought to prove more satisfying. Dissatisfaction, in this context, serves as the arousal stage in the motivational process; dissatisfaction motivates change, but does not determine the nature or direction of change.

Dissatisfaction with a job element in the earlier formulation is a function of discrepancy between the perceived and valued levels of the job element. Given some experienced level of dissatisfaction, the individual seeks a means of reducing dissatisfaction and/or achieving satisfaction. Consistent with expectancy models of motivation, choice among alternative behaviors is based upon perceived contingencies and expected outcomes. (6) The perceived or experienced level of any job element is more or less variable as a function of different behavior alternatives, however, and different behavior choices ought to be associated with dissatisfaction occasioned by different job elements. Thus, for example, certain job elements such as working conditions, company policies and practices, and closeness of supervision appear relatively constant for a particular job and the only behaviors which alter the level of those elements are behaviors such as termination and absenteeism which alter the level of the job elements actually experienced by the individual. The level of other job elements such as experienced fatigue, fun, and sense of achievement appear variable and controllable by individual behavior on the job. Deprivational dissatisfaction with job elements having variable values is unlikely to persist over time since the individual is able to determine the achieved or experienced value of those job elements; persistent and continuing deprivational dissatisfaction is likely only as related to job elements with constant values.

Reported empirical relationships between job satisfaction and performance are consistent with the conceptualization of job satisfaction and the conceptualization of satisfaction-performance relationships developed here. Reported relationships between job dissatisfaction and turnover and absenteeism, for example, would be hypothesized by the model. Persistent deprivational dissatisfaction is expected only where job element values are perceived as relatively constant and variable only in so far as the individual absents himself/herself from the job situation. The lack of consistent relationships between satisfaction and level of performance also is consistent with the conceptualization of job satisfaction and also explained partly by the fact that most investigations of satisfaction-performance relationships have been cross-sectional. Assuming the nature of deprivational and aspirational satisfaction developed earlier and traditional measures of job satisfaction as summed overall assessments of individual job elements, the resulting values most likely reflect deprivational rather than aspirational satisfaction. Typical performance measures probably also reflect habitual levels of task performance. Thus, for any given level of job satisfaction, we might observe quite different levels of task performance, each habitual for different individuals. Given these traditional measures, about all we might hypothesize is that individuals habitually performing at or above some minimal level of task performance would not express significant dissatisfaction with their jobs. This formulation of satisfaction-performance relationships is not unlike that of Herzberg where he suggests that dissatisfaction is associated with absenteeism and turnover, and that elimination of dissatisfaction is a necessary but not sufficient condition for achieving high levels of task performance. The job elements he classed as dissatisfiers are elements with which we associate concepts of optimal need value, elements where the range of dissatisfaction values exceeds the range of satisfaction values and where concepts of aspirational satisfaction are least relevant. They also are job elements for which perceived values are least controllable by the individual and where appropriate behavioral responses to persistent dissatisfaction involve absenting oneself from the job situation. Persistent deprivational dissatisfaction, in our context, is associated with avoidance and rejection behaviors such as termination and absenteeism which vary directly with dissatisfaction. The presence of deprivational satisfaction ought to be associated with behaviors of staying with the organization, appearing for work each day, and performing at some habitual level, but we have no basis for inferring a direct relationship between these behaviors and different values of deprivational satisfaction.

Change in work behavior is conceived as a joint function of dissatisfaction and perceived contingency relationships between behavior and job element values. Deprivational dissatisfaction which is persistent over time is conceivable only as related to job elements with relatively constant values; deprivational dissatisfaction related to job elements with variable values can be eliminated through appropriate behavioral choices to achieve a changed value of the job element. Continued motivation to change behavior following the achievement of deprivational satisfaction can be inferred from the concept of aspirational dissatisfaction. Aspirational dissatisfaction is conceived as independent of deprivational satisfaction only relative to job elements with minimal need values and only under conditions of minimal deprivational dissatisfaction. Under these conditions we argued that aspiration values adapt to perceived values and tend to exceed perceived values; thus some minimal aspirational dissatisfaction is normal in the presence of deprivational satisfaction. Job elements where this condition is likely to occur are associated with minimal need levels, elements not unlike Herzberg's satisfier or motivating elements, achievement, sense of responsibility, and intrinsic fun of the work itself. These job elements also are characterized by variable values, values directly related to individual behaviors such as level of effort expended. In a longitudinal analysis, we might expect aspirational dissatisfaction to be predictive of changed behavior and deprivational satisfaction a function of changed values of job elements resulting from this behavior.

This model of job satisfaction-performance relationships is summarized in Figure 5. Job elements are present for every form and level of performance behavior. The values of some job elements are relatively constant for a given job, elements such as working conditions, minimal task requirements, and membership rewards. The values of other elements vary within a given job contingent upon performance or some other variable, elements such as incentive compensation, fatigue, and elements intrinsic to task performance. Job satisfaction, an emotional response to all job elements, takes the form of deprivational and aspirational satisfaction and

dissatisfaction. Deprivational satisfaction is a function of judgment of perceived value of job elements relative to need value, importance of the element being reflected in the functional relationship. Need value of a job element may take the form of an optimal value, a satiation value, or a minimal value. Aspirational satisfaction is a function of judgment of perceived value of the job element relative to aspiration value, importance being reflected in the functional relationship. Aspiration value probably will be identical with need value for job elements with optimal or satiation need values, and for job elements with minimal need values when there exists a percept-need value deficiency. Aspiration value will exceed need value for those job elements with minimal need values when no percept-need value deficiencies exist; aspiration value, in this instance, will be a function of perceived value, always tending to exceed perceived value by some minimal amount. Summing across job elements, any individual will experience both deprivational and aspiration satisfaction or dissatisfaction with the job.

Given a lack of deprivational or aspirational dissatisfaction, habitual or custom-

Figure 5

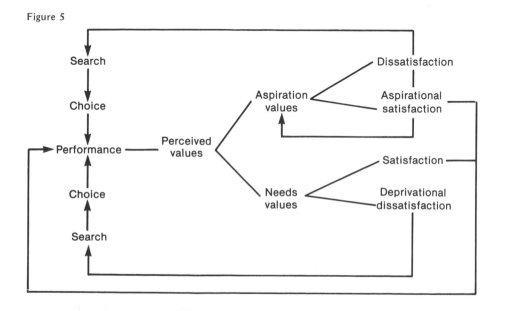

ary job performance will be repeated; there is no motivation to change behavior. Experiencing deprivational dissatisfaction, alternatives will be sought as a means of reducing or avoiding that dissatisfaction. Job elements where the value experienced is variable and contingent upon job performance offer opportunities for reducing deprivational dissatisfaction and we would anticipate changes in performance necessary to eliminate deprivational dissatisfaction. Deprivational dissatisfaction with job elements which have a constant value or which are not contingent upon job performance offer no such alternatives and dissatisfaction is likely to persist and to be accompanied with escape behaviors such as absenteeism and turnover. Aspirational dissatisfaction with a job element where deprivational dissatisfaction is experienced is likely to be indistinguishable from the deprivational dissatisfaction; aspirational dissatisfaction will be a significant independent motivating influence only under conditions of minimal deprivational dissatisfaction. Assuming some minimal deprivational dissatisfaction, any experienced aspirational dissatisfaction will occasion search for alternatives capable of achieving aspirational satisfaction. This dissatisfaction will be experienced relative to job elements characterized by minimal need values, job elements such as growth, fun, skill development and achievement, and behaviors will be sought which are expected to increase the experienced value of these elements. Behavior alternatives might include job transfer or promotion, higher level of task performance, or innovative behavior capable of providing greater achievement. Given the adapting level of aspiration values, extreme values of aspirational satisfaction and dissatisfaction are likely to be short-lived. Some minimal level of aspirational dissatisfaction is more common, assuming deprivational satisfaction. This aspirational dissatisfaction keeps the individual alert to opportunities for change, but is not asso-

ciated with the escape behaviors associated with extreme or persistent deprivational dissatisfaction.

The model of satisfaction-performance relationships developed here is consistent with, and builds upon, a variety of models of satisfaction-performance formulations as well as models of motivation. Job dissatisfaction is viewed as an arousal or energizing element in the motivational process; it does not provide an explanation of choice behavior. Choices made among alternatives are a function of path-goal expectancies expressed either as conditioned associations or in cognitive terms. Job satisfaction is a function of experienced levels of job elements, elements associated with performance in a job but which may be invariant for any specific job. In this sense, job satisfaction is a consequence of experience in job performance, not a cause of job performance. Overall job satisfaction is a function of two separable, although not independent, dimensions or components of job satisfaction, deprivational and aspirational job satisfaction. Experienced job satisfaction on either component is pleasing and conducive of repetition of habitual job performance; experienced dissatisfaction is displeasing and motivates effort to eliminate the dissatisfaction. As in the March and Simon model, dissatisfaction motivates search for alternatives. Dissatisfaction, rather than satisfaction, is predictive of change in behavior or performance consistent with empirical findings regarding relationships between dissatisfaction and absenteeism and turnover. Consistent with Locke's formulation, satisfaction is conceived as an emotional response to judgment of the perceived amount of a job element present relative to some standard, importance of the element being included in the functional relationship rather than figuring as a separate judgment. The distinction between deprivational and aspirational satisfaction relates to the distinction between needs and expectancy models of job satisfaction, deprivational satisfaction relating to need satisfaction and aspirational satisfaction relating to expectancy satisfaction. Need values, in this context, are relatively invariant with respect to recent experience while expectancy or aspirational values are a function of recent experience. Consistent with Herzberg's early findings, extreme values of aspirational satisfaction tend to be short-lived while values of deprivational satisfaction tend to be longer-lived, change in deprivational satisfaction being more a function of perceptions than of comparison levels. Need values which take the form of optimality values are distinguished from need values with the form of minimal values analogous with Maslow's distinction between lower order and higher order needs; lower order needs with optimality need values are capable of satiation; higher order needs, where aspirations beyond the minimal need values are relevant, are incapable of satiation. Aspirations, however, rather than need values, account for the continuing relevance of higher order needs in this formulation. The distinction between job elements for which optimal need values are appropriate and those for which minimal need values and aspiration values greater than need values are appropriate corresponds generally to the distinction between Herzberg's hygienic and motivator factors. Similarly, the behavioral implications he attributes to his dimensions of dissatisfaction and satisfaction correspond to the behavioral implications we attribute to deprivational dissatisfaction and aspirational dissatisfaction. The distinction between deprivational and aspirational satisfaction, however, permits us to attribute behavioral change to dissatisfaction mediated by motivational choice models rather than implying that performance is a direct function of satisfaction. High levels of deprivational satisfaction may be correlated with high performance, but performance level in this instance is a function of aspirational dissatisfaction and behavioral choices.

REFERENCES

1. Schwab, Donald P., and Cummings, Larry L. "Theories of Performance and Satisfaction: A Review." *Industrial Relations* 9 (1970), pp. 408-30.

2. Locke, Edwin A. "The Nature and Causes of Job Satisfaction," in Marvin D. Dunnette *Handbook of Industrial and Organizational Psychology.* New York: Rand McNally, 1976.

3. March, James G., and Simon, Herbert A. *Organizations.* New York: John Wiley & Sons, 1958, pp. 47-52, Chapter 4.

4. Herzberg, Frederick; Mausner, Bernard; and Snyderman, Barbara Bloch. *The Motivation to Work.* New York: John Wiley & Sons 1959.

5. March, James G., and Simon, Herbert A. *Organizations.* New York: John Wiley & Sons, 1958, Chapter 4; and Katz, Daniel. "The Motivational Basis of Organizational Behavior." *Behavioral Science* 9 (1964), pp. 132-46.

6. Vroom, Victor H. *Work and Motivation.* New York: John Wiley & Sons, 1964; and Lawler, Edward E. III. *Pay and Organizational Effectiveness: A Psychological View.* New York: McGraw-Hill, 1971.

CHAPTER 9

MOTIVATION, COMPENSATION, AND ORGANIZATIONAL BEHAVIOR

Organizational behavior is a much used and ill-defined term. It has been employed to refer to all individual and group behavior within organizations, to individual behavior relevant to organizational performance, and to behavior of organizations considered as units. We use the term to refer to those aspects of performance behavior broader in context than normally associated with the term task performance. Task performance, particularly as conceived in earlier readings, relates specifically to individual performance of established behavior routines. Katz, in an earlier essay, suggested different types of behavior essential for effectively functioning organizations: (1) joining and remaining with the organization, (2) dependable role (task) performance, and (3) innovative and spontaneous activity in achieving organizational objectives which go beyond the task specifications. This third type of behavior, while difficult to define, is no less critical than task performance in achieving organizational goals. Desired innovative and spontaneous activity would include cooperative, helpful behavior within a work team, maintenance of the workplace and tools, and taking safety precautions, making creative suggestions for improved processing, cooperating and assisting in the development and implementation of new technology, and self-training and development for improved performance or new assignments. These behaviors are not easily accommodated within the concept of task performance, yet are significant organizational behaviors. The essays in this chapter address these types of organizational behavior, the motivational bases for organizational behavior and wage payment schemes as they relate to this behavior.

The essay by Katz (9-1) elaborates upon his earlier essay which differentiated among types of organizational behavior. He now identifies six different motivational patterns observed within employing organizations and examines the implications of each relative to the different types of organizational behavior. The motivational patterns he identifies are (1) compliance to norms, (2) instrumental system rewards (analogous to membership pay), (3) instrumental rewards for individual performance (analogous to individual pay), (4) intrinsic satisfactions arising from role performance, (5) congruence of individual and organizational values, and (6) social satisfactions. Katz's analysis of motivational patterns encompasses many influences beyond those normally considered in the compensation of employees, motivational influences which may conflict with or reinforce the motivational influences of the compensation program of the employer.

Katz emphasizes a number of motivational influences present in an employment situation, influences deriving from employment compensation, disciplinary codes and norms of behavior, organizational goals and values, intrinsic aspects of task performance, supervisory review, praise and criticism of performance, social interactions with work team members, promotion and advancement practices, and supervisory and management style. Organizational behavior is a function of all of these interacting influences. All of these characteristics of the employment situation potentially enter into individual calculations of the "sum of the advantages and disadvantages" of the job and into the determination of individual satisfaction with the job. Each of these characteristics also serves to reinforce positively or negatively individual behavior depending upon individual valuation of the characteristic and the behavior with which it is associated. This network of motivational influences makes it difficult to identify specific consequences of different compensation practices and to prescribe compensation practices to achieve specified goals. The motivational effects of an attendance bonus, for example, may be counteracted by dissatisfaction occasioned through change in task requirements or hours of work. More critical, however, are the unintended effects of a compensation system upon motivational influences in the employment situation such as the effects Whyte observed of an incentive system upon the status hierarchy of the work group. Whyte noted that an incentive system intended to motivate higher levels of performance may in fact induce conflict and the imposition of performance bogeys when potential earnings under the incentive system conflict with the structure of earnings accepted as equitable within the work group. Behavior-compensation contingency relationships that appear simple in design often are quite complex when analyzed within the context of the full range of organizational influences upon behavior. Further, compensation programs designed to influence organizational behavior are not likely to be successful unless consistent with, and reinforced by, other motivational influences within the employment setting. Katz offers a framework for the identification and analysis of the full range of such influence.

The selection from Whyte (Essay 9-2) on the Scanlon Plan builds upon his earlier discussion of the meaning and importance of symbols in compensation; it also illustrates an approach to analysis of compensation practices within the context of the range of motivational influences identified by Katz. Whyte describes and analyzes the Scanlon Plan as an approach to the integration of compensation practices with other influences of organizational behavior. He views the Scanlon Plan as an attempt to motivate and reward organizational performance beyond minimal task performance by supplementing the influences of wage rate, wage structure, and incentive compensation for task performance; it is not viewed as a replacement for these more traditional characteristics of an employment compensation program. Briefly, the Scanlon Plan compensates employees for reductions in labor costs and shares these savings in labor cost with employees. Whyte points out that the Scanlon Plan is more than a formula for sharing savings in labor costs, however; successful implementation requires active employee participation in developing, reviewing, and implementing suggested approaches for reducing labor costs of production. Individual suggestions are reviewed by employee committees charged with continuing analysis of labor costs and with development of labor saving improvements. Individuals are not compensated directly for suggestions; any savings in labor costs effected are shared among all employees. This sharing of savings in labor costs is intended to achieve cooperation in the design and implementation of suggested changes and to supplement managerial recognition of unusual individual performance with group recognition of, and support for, individual performance which benefits all. The compensation system is aligned with, rather than opposed to, the system of informal rewards administered by the work group. Communication, trust, and cooperation also are promoted through open sharing of information and plans in the committee structure supporting the Scanlon Plan.

The Scanlon Plan of compensation is not widely employed despite Whyte's favorable review of the plan. A program to share savings in labor costs would be easier to design and administer in some organizations than in others; it would be relatively more difficult in an organization with rapidly changing product lines and product mix as well as in an organization with rapid technological change. Probably more critical, however, is the issue of fit or alignment of the participative aspects of the Scanlon Plan with overall management style and organizational climate. As Whyte's analysis indicates, successful implementations of the Scanlon Plan demonstrate the integration of a compensation plan with the social system of the work group and unsuccessful implementations demonstrate the lack of integration between requirements of the plan and managerial practices. In either event, the selection from Whyte illustrates the importance of integration of a compensation program with the total set of motivational influences in the workplace.

The final selection, Essay 9-3 from McKersie, considers "incentive methods of the future." He distinguishes between motivation and reward much as we differentiated incentive and reward earlier; an incentive specifies a goal or norm as an objective to be sought whereas rewards are experienced following performance. A theoretical ideal for relating incentives and rewards to the same norm is proposed. At the same time, McKersie notes that reward distribution is more flexible than incentives and that ad hoc rewards can be significant influences of organizational behavior. He urges flexibility and innovation in the administration of rewards for the varied forms of organizational performance beyond minimal task requirements, minimal task performance being compensated through more stable and predictable systems of compensation. Although written in 1963, McKersie's discussion is no less relevant today than it was at that time.

Essay 9-1

The motivational basis of organizational behavior: II*

Daniel Katz

TYPES OF MOTIVATIONAL PATTERNS

It is profitable to consider the possible motivational patterns in organizations under six major headings. Before considering their specific modes of operation and their effects, let me briefly describe the six motivational patterns which seem most relevant. These patterns are: (1) conformity to legal norms or rule compliance; (2) instrumental system rewards; (3) instrumental individual rewards; (4) intrinsic satisfaction from role performance; (5) internalization of organizational goals and values; and (6) involvement in primary-group relationships.

Rule compliance or conformity to system norms. Conformity constitutes a significant motivational basis for certain types of organizational behavior. Though people may conform for different reasons I am concerned here with one common type of reason, namely a generalized acceptance of the rules of the game. Once people enter a system they accept the fact that membership in the system means complying with its legitimate rules. In our culture we build up during the course of the socialization process a generalized expectation of conforming to the recognized rules of the game if we want to remain in the game. We develop a role readiness, i.e., a readiness to play almost any given role according to the established

norms in those systems in which we become involved.

Instrumental system rewards. These are the benefits which accrue to individuals by virtue of their membership in the system. They are the across-the-board rewards which apply to all people in a given classification in an organization. Examples would be the fringe benefits, the recreational facilities, and the working conditions which are available to all members of the system or subsystem. These rewards are instrumental in that they provide incentives for entering and remaining in the system and thus are instrumental for the need satisfaction of people.

Instrumental reward geared to individual effort or performance. System rewards apply in blanket fashion to all members of a subsystem. Individual rewards of an instrumental character are attained by differential performance. For example, the piece rate in industry or the singling out of individuals for honors for their specific contributions would fall into this category of instrumental individual rewards.

Intrinsic satisfactions accruing from specific role performance. Here the gratification comes not because the activity leads to or is instrumental to other satisfactions such as earning more money but because the activity is gratifying in itself. The individual may find his work so interesting or so much the type of thing he really wants to do that it would take a heavy financial inducement to shift to a job less congenial to his interests. It is

*Reprinted from Daniel Katz, "The Motivational Basis of Organizational Behavior," *Behavioral Science* 9 (1964), pp. 134-46 (abridged).

difficult to get professors in many universities to take administrative posts such as departmental chairmanships or deanships because so many of them prefer teaching and research. This motivational pattern has to do with the opportunities which the organizational role provides for the expressions of the skills and talents of the individual.

Internalized values of the individual which embrace the goals of the organization. Here the individual again finds his organizational behavior rewarding in itself, not so much because his job gives him a chance to express his skill, but because he has taken over the goals of the organization as his own. The person who derives his gratifications from being a good teacher could be equally happy in teaching in many institutions but unhappy as an administrator in any one. The person who has identified himself with the goals of his own particular university and its specific problems, potentialities, and progress wants to stay on at his university and, moreover, is willing to accept other assignments than a teaching assignment.

Social satisfactions derived from primary-group relationships. This is an important source of gratification for organizational members. One of the things people miss most when they have to withdraw from organizations is the sharing of experiences with like-minded colleagues, the belonging to a group with which they have become identified. Whether or not these social satisfactions become channelled for organizational objectives leads us to a consideration of the two basic questions with which we started: (1) What are the consequences of these motivational patterns for the various organizational requirements of holding people in the system, maximizing their role performances, and stimulating innovative behavior? and (2) What are the conditions under which these patterns will lead to a given organizational outcome?

MOTIVATIONAL PATTERNS: CONSEQUENCES AND CONDITIONS

Compliance with legitimized rules

In discussing bureaucratic functioning Max Weber pointed out that the acceptance of legal rules was the basis for much of organizational behavior (Weber, 1947). Compliance is to some extent a function of sanctions but to a greater extent a function of generalized habits and attitudes toward symbols of authority. In other words, for the citizen of modern society the observance of legitimized rules has become a generalized value. A great deal of behavior can be predicted once we know what the rules of the game are. It is not necessary to take representative samplings of the behavior of many people to know how people will conduct themselves in structured situations. All we need is a single informant who can tell us the legitimate norms and appropriate symbols of authority for given types of behavioral settings. Individuals often assume that they can control their participation with respect to organizational requirements when they enter an organization. Before they are aware of it, however, they are acting like other organizational members and complying with the rules and the authorized decisions.

The major impact of compliance with the legitimate rules of the organization primarily concerns only one type of organizational requirement, namely reliable role performance. The way in which any given role occupant is to perform in carrying out his job can be determined by the rules of the organization. But individuals cannot be held in the system by rule enforcement save for exceptions like the armed services. Nor can innovative behavior and actions beyond the call of duty be prescribed.

Though compliance with legitimate

rules is effective for insuring reliable role performance it operates to insure minimal observance of role requirements. In other words, the minimal standards for quantity and quality of work soon become the maximum standards. The logic of meeting legal norms is to avoid infractions of the rules and not to go beyond their requirements, for as Allport has pointed out (1934), it is difficult, if not impossible, to be more proper than proper. Why, however, cannot the legal norms be set to require high standards with respect to both quantity and quality of production? Why cannot higher production be legislated? It can, but there is an important force working against such raising of standards by changing rules. The rule which sets a performance standard in a large organization is also setting a uniform standard for large numbers of people. Hence it must be geared to what the great majority are prepared to do. If not, there will be so many defections that the rule itself will break down. Timing of jobs in industry illustrates this principle. Management does not want a loose standard, but if the standards are set so that many workers can meet them only with difficulty, management is in for trouble.

In the third area of behavior necessary for effective organizational functioning, namely innovative and spontaneous acts which go beyond the call of duty, rule compliance is useless by definition. There can be exceptions, in that rules can be devised to reward unusual behavior under specified conditions. The army, for example, will move the man who has pulled off a brilliant military exploit from a court martial to a court of honors. Though such exceptions may occur, organizations cannot stimulate innovative actions by decreeing them. In general the greater the emphasis upon compliance with rules the less the motivation will be for individuals to do more than is specified by their role prescriptions. The great weakness of a system run according to rules is the lack of the corrective factor of human enterprise and spontaneity when something goes wrong.

Conditions conducive to the activation of rule acceptance

Though compliance with rules can bring about reliable role performance, the use of rules must take account of the following three conditions for maximum effectiveness: (1) the appropriateness of the symbols of authority and the relevance of rules to the social system involved; (2) the clarity of the legal norms and rule structure; and (3) the reinforcing character of sanctions.

Appropriateness and relevance. The acceptance of communications and directives on the basis of legitimacy requires the use of symbols and procedures recognized as the proper and appropriate sources of authority in the system under consideration. The worker may grumble at the foreman's order but he recognizes the right of the foreman to give such an order. The particular directives which are accepted as legitimate will depend upon their matching the type of authority structure of the system. The civilian in the army with officer status, uniform, and unassimilated rank is not accepted by the enlisted man as the proper giver of orders. In a representative democracy a policy decision of an administrator may be rejected since it lacks the legal stamp of the accepted procedures of the system. An industrial company may have a contract with a union that changes in the speed of the assembly line have to be agreed to by both organizations. The workers accordingly will accept a speedup in the line if it is sanctioned by the union-management agreement, but not if it is the work of a foreman attempting to impress his superiors.

The acceptance of legal rules is also restricted to the relevant sphere of activity. Union policy as formulated in its authority structure is binding upon its members only as it relates to relations with the company. The edicts of union officials on matters of desegregation or of support of political parties are not necessarily seen as legal compulsions by union members. In similar fashion, employees do not regard the jurisdiction of the company as applying to their private lives outside the plant. And areas of private behavior and personal taste are regarded in our democratic society as outside the realm of coercive laws. The most spectacular instance of the violation of a national law occurred in the case of the Volstead Act. While people were willing to accept laws about the social consequences resulting from drinking, such as reckless driving, many of them were not willing to accept the notion that their private lives were subject to federal regulation.

Another prerequisite to the use of rules as the appropriate norms of the system is their impersonal character. They are the rules of the system and are not the arbitrary, capricious decisions of a superior aimed at particular individuals. The equivalents of bills of attainder in an organization undermine rule compliance. We speak of the officiousness of given individuals in positions of authority when they use their rank in an arbitrary and personal fashion.

Clarity. A related condition for the acceptance of legal norms is the clarity of authority symbols, of proper procedures, and the content of the legitimized decisions. Lack of clarity can be due to the vagueness of the stimulus situation or to the conflict between opposed stimulus cues. In some organizations, symbols of authority are sharply enough defined, but the relationship between competing symbols may lack such clarity of definition. One difficulty of using group decision in limited areas in an otherwise authoritarian structure is that group members may not perceive the democratic procedure as legitimized by the structure. They will

question the compelling effect of any decisions they reach. And often they may be right. Moreover, the procedure for the exercise of power may not be consistent with the type of authority structure. The classic case is that *of ordering* a people to be democratic.

Specific laws can be ambiguous in their substance. They can be so complex, so technical, or so obscure that people will not know what the law is. The multiplication of technical rulings and the patchwork of legislation with respect to tax structure means that while people may feel some internal compulsion to pay taxes, they also feel they should pay as little as they can without risking legal prosecution. A counter dynamic will arise to the tendency to comply with legal requirements, namely, the use of legal loopholes to defy the spirit of the law. Any complex maze of rules in an organization will be utilized by the guardhouse lawyers in the system to their own advantage.

Though our argument has been that legal compliance makes for role performance rather than for holding people in a system, the clarity of a situation with well-defined rules is often urged as a condition making for system attractiveness. People know what is expected of them and what they should expect in turn from others, and they much prefer this clarity to a state of uncertainty and ambiguity. There is merit in this contention, but it does not take into account all the relevant variables. The armed services were not able to hold personnel after World War II, and recruitment into systems characterized by rules and regulations is traditionally difficult in the United States. The mere multiplication of rules does not produce clarity. Even when certainty and clarity prevail they are not relished if it means that individuals are certain only of nonadvancement and restrictions on their behavior.

In brief, the essence of legal compliance rests upon the psychological belief that there are specific imperatives or laws which all good citizens obey. If there is doubt about what the imperative is, if there are many varying interpretations, then the law is not seen as having a character of its own but as the means for obtaining individual advantage. To this extent, the legitimacy basis of compliance is undermined.

Reinforcement. To maintain the internalized acceptance of legitimate authority there has to be some reinforcement in the form of penalties for violation of the rules. If there is no policing of laws governing speeding, speed limits will lose their force over time for many people. Sometimes the penalties can come from the social disapproval of the group as well as from legal penalties. But the very concept of law as an imperative binding upon everyone in the system requires penalties for violation either from above or below. Where there is no enforcement by authorities and no sanctions for infractions from the group itself, the rule in question becomes a dead letter.

Instrumental system rewards

It is important to distinguish between rewards which are administered in relation to individual effort and performance and the system rewards which accrue to people by virtue of their membership in the system. In the former category would belong piece-rate incentives, promotion for outstanding performance, or any special recognition bestowed in acknowledgment of differential contributions to organizational functioning. In the category of system rewards would go fringe benefits, recreational facilities, cost of living raises, across-the-board upgrading, job security save for those guilty of moral turpitude, and pleasant working conditions. System rewards differ, then, from individual rewards in that they are not allocated on the basis of differential effort and performance but on the basis of membership in

the system. The major differentiation for system rewards is seniority in the system—a higher pension for 30 years of service than for 20 years of service. Management will often overlook the distinction between individual and system rewards and will operate as if rewards administered across the board were the same in their effects as individual rewards.

System rewards are more effective for holding members within the organization than for maximizing other organizational behaviors. Since the rewards are distributed on the basis of length of tenure in the system, people will want to stay with an attractive setup which becomes increasingly attractive over time. Again the limiting factor is the competition with the relative attraction of other systems. As the system increases its attractions, other things being equal, it should reduce its problems of turnover. In fact, it may sometimes have the problem of too low turnover with too many poorly motivated people staying on until retirement.

System rewards will not, however, lead to higher quality of work or greater quantity than the minimum required to stay in the organization. Since rewards are given across-the-board to all members or differentially to them in terms of their seniority, they are not motivated to do more than meet the standards for remaining in the system. It is sometimes assumed that the liking for the organization created by system rewards will generalize to greater productive effort within the system. Such generalization of motivation may occur to a very limited extent, but it is not a reliable basis for the expectation of higher productivity. Management may expect gratitude from workers because it has added some special fringe benefit or some new recreational facility. The more likely outcome is that employees will feel more desirous of staying in an enterprise with such advantages than of working harder for the company for the next twelve months.

System rewards will do little, moreover, to motivate performance beyond the line of duty, with two possible exceptions. Since people may develop a liking for the attractions of the organization they may be in a more favorable mood to reciprocate in cooperative relations with their fellows toward organizational goals, provided that the initiation of task-oriented cooperation comes from some other source. Otherwise, they may just be cooperative with respect to taking advantage of the system's attractions, such as the new bowling alley. Another possible consequence of system rewards for activity supportive of organizational goals is the favorable climate of opinion for the system in the external environment to which the members contribute. It may be easier for a company to recruit personnel in a community in which their employees have talked about what a good place it is to work.

Though the effects of system rewards are to maintain the level of productivity not much above the minimum required to stay in the system, there still may be large differences between systems with respect to the quantity and quality of production as a function of system rewards. An organization with substantially better wage rates and fringe benefits than its competitors may be able to set a higher level of performance as a minimal requirement for its workers than the other firms and still hold its employees. In other words, system rewards can be related to the differential productivity of organizations as a whole, though they are not effective in maximizing the potential contributions of the majority of individuals within the organization. They may account for differences in motivation between systems rather than for differences in motivation between individuals in the same system. They operate through their effects upon the minimal standards for all people in the system. They act indirectly in that their effect is to make peo-

ple want to stay in the organization; to do so people must be willing to accept the legitimately derived standards of role performance in that system. Hence, the direct mechanism for insuring performance is compliance with legitimacy, but the legal requirements of the organization will not hold members if their demands are too great with respect to the demands of other organizations. The mediating variable in accounting for organizational differences based upon system rewards is the relative attractiveness of the system for the individual compared to other available systems in relation to the effort requirements of the system. If the individual has the choice of a job with another company in the same community which requires a little more effort but offers much greater system rewards in the way of wages and other benefits, he will in all probability take it. If, however, the higher requirements of the competing system are accompanied by very modest increases in system rewards, he will probably stay where he is.

Conditions conducive to effective system rewards

We have just described one of the essential conditions for making system rewards effective in calling attention to the need to make the system as attractive as competing systems which are realistic alternatives for the individual. In this context seniority becomes an important organizational principle in that the member can acquire more of the rewards of the system the longer he stays in it. The present trends to permit the transfer of fringe benefits of all types across systems undercuts the advantages to any one system of length of membership in it, though of course there are other advantages to permitting people to retain their investment in seniority when they move across systems.

Another condition which is important

for the effective use of system rewards is their uniform application for all members of the system or for major groupings within the system. People will perceive as inequitable distinctions in amounts of rewards which go to members by virtue of their membership in the system where such differences favor some groups over other groups. Management is frequently surprised by resentment of differential system rewards when there has been no corresponding resentment of differential individual rewards. One public utility, for example, inaugurated an attractive retirement system for its employees before fringe benefits were the acceptable pattern. Its employees were objectively much better off because of the new benefits and yet the most hated feature about the whole company was the retirement system. Employee complaints centered on two issues: years of employment in the company before the age of 30 did not count toward retirement pensions, and company officials could retire on livable incomes because of their higher salaries. The employees felt intensely that if they were being rewarded for service to the company it was unfair to rule out years of service before age 30. This provision gave no recognition for the man who started for the company at age 20 compared to the one who started at age 30. Moreover, the workers felt a lifetime of service to the company should enable them to retire on a livable income just as it made this possible for company officials. The company house organ directed considerable space over a few years to showing how much the worker actually benefited from the plan, as in fact was the case. On the occasion of a company-wide survey, this campaign was found to have had little effect. The most common complaint still focused about the patent unfairness of the retirement system.

The critical point, then, is that system rewards have a logic of their own. Since they accrue to people by virtue of their membership or length of service in an organization, they will be perceived as inequitable if they are not uniformly administered. The perception of the organization member is that all members are equal in their access to organizational benefits. Office employees will not be upset by differences in individual reward for differences in responsibility. If, however, their organization gives them free meals in a cafeteria and sets aside a special dining room for their bosses, many of them will be upset. In our culture we accept individual differences in income but we do not accept differences in classes of citizenship. To be a member of an organization is to be a citizen in that community, and all citizens are equal in their membership rights. A university which does not extend the same tenure rights and the same fringe benefits accorded its teaching staff to its research workers may have a morale problem on its hands.

Instrumental individual rewards

The traditional philosophy of the free-enterprise system gives priority to an individual reward system based upon the quality and quantity of the individual effort and contribution. This type of motivation may operate effectively for the entrepreneur or even for the small organization with considerable independence of its supporting environment. It encounters great difficulties, however, in its application to large organizations which are in nature highly interdependent cooperative structures. We shall examine these difficulties in analyzing the conditions under which individual rewards of an instrumental character are effective.

Basically the monetary and recognition rewards to the individual for his organizational performance are directed at a high level of quality and quantity of work. In other words, they can be applied most readily to obtain optimal role performance rather than to innovative and nonspecific organizational needs. They may also help to hold the individual in the organization, if he feels that his differential efforts are properly recognized. Nonetheless there is less generalization, or rubbing off, of an instrumental individual reward to love for the organization than might be anticipated. If another organization offers higher individual rewards to a person, his own institution may have to match the offer to hold him.

Individual rewards are difficult to apply to contributions to organizational functioning which are not part of the role requirements. Spectacular instances of innovative behavior can be singled out for recognition and awards. In the armed services, heroism beyond the call of duty is the basis for medals and decorations, but the everyday cooperative activities which keep an organization from falling apart are more difficult to recognize and reward. Creative suggestions for organizational improvement are sometimes encouraged through substantial financial rewards for employees' suggestions. The experience with suggestion systems of this sort has not been uniformly positive though under special conditions they have proved of value.

Conditions conducive to effective individual instrumental rewards

If rewards such as pay incentives are to work as they are intended they must meet three primary conditions. (1) They must be clearly perceived as large enough in amount to justify the additional effort required to obtain them. (2) They must be perceived as directly related to the required performance and follow directly on its accomplishment. (3) They must be perceived as equitable by the majority of system members many of whom will not receive them. These conditions suggest some of the reasons why individual rewards can work so well in some situations and yet be so difficult of application in large organizations. The facts are that most enterprises have not been able to use incentive pay, or piece rates, as reliable methods for raising the quality and quantity of production (McGregor, 1960).

In terms of the first criterion many companies have attempted incentive pay without making the differential between increased effort and increased reward proportional from the point of view of the worker. If he can double his pay by working at a considerably increased tempo, that is one thing. But if such increased expenditure means a possible 10 percent increase, that is another. Moreover, there is the tradition among workers, and it is not without some factual basis, that management cannot be relied upon to maintain a high rate of pay for those making considerably more than the standard and that their increased efforts will only result in their "being sweated." There is, then, the temporal dimension of whether the piece rates which seem attractive today will be maintained tomorrow.

More significant, however, is the fact that a large-scale organization consists of many people engaging in similar and interdependent tasks. The work of any one man is highly dependent upon what his colleagues are doing. Hence individual piece rates are difficult to apply on any equitable basis. Group incentives are more logical, but as the size of the interdependent group grows, we move toward system rather than toward individual rewards. Moreover, in large-scale production enterprises the role performance is controlled by the tempo of the machines and their coordination. The speed of the worker on the assembly line is not determined by his decision but by the speed of the assembly line. An individual piece-rate just does not accord with the systemic natue of the coordinated collectivity. Motivational factors about the amount of effort to be expended on the job enter the picture not on the floor of the factory but during the negotiations of the union and management about the manning of a particular assembly line. Heads of corporations may believe in the philosophy of individual enterprise, but when they deal with reward systems in their own organizations they become realists and accept the pragmatic notion of collective rewards.

Since there is such a high deree of collective interdependence among rank-and-file workers the attempts to use individual rewards are often perceived as inequitable. Informal norms develop to protect the group against efforts which are seen as divisive or exploitive. Differential rates for subsystems within the organization will be accepted much more than invidious distinctions within the same subgrouping. Hence promotion or upgrading may be the most potent type of individual reward. The employee is rewarded by being moved to a different category of workers on a better pay schedule. Some of the same problems apply, of course, to this type of reward. Since differential performance is difficult to assess in assembly-type operations, promotion is often based upon such criteria as conformity to company requirements with respect to attendance and absenteeism, observance of rules, and seniority. None of these criteria is related to individual performance on the job. Moreover, promotion is greatly limited by the technical and professional education of the worker.

It is true, of course, that many organizations are not assembly-line operations, and even for those which are, the conditions described here do not apply to the upper echelons. Thus General Motors can follow a policy of high individual rewards to division managers based upon the profits achieved by a given division. A university can increase the amount of research productivity of its staff by making publication the essential criterion for promotion. In general, where assessment of individual performance is feasible and where the basis of the reward system is clear, in-strumental individual rewards can play an important part in raising productivity.

Intrinsic job satisfaction

The motivational pathway to high productivity and to high-quality production can be reached through the development of intrinsic job satisfaction. The man who finds the type of work he delights in doing is the man who will not worry about the fact that the role requires a given amount of production of a certain quality. His gratifications accrue from accomplishment, from the expression of his own abilities, from the exercise of his own decisions. Craftsmanship was the old term to refer to the skilled performer who was high in intrinsic job satisfaction. This type of performer is not the clock watcher, nor the shoddy performer. On the other hand, such a person is not necessarily tied to a given organization. As a good carpenter or a good mechanic, it may matter little to him where he does work, provided that he is given ample opportunity to do the kind of job he is interested in doing. He may, moreover, contribute little to organizational goals beyond his specific role.

Conditions conducive to arousal of intrinsic job satisfaction

If intrinsic job satisfaction or identification with the work is to be aroused and maximized, then the job itself must provide sufficient variety, sufficient complexity, sufficient challenge, and sufficient skill to engage the abilities of the worker. If there is one confirmed finding in all the studies of worker morale and satisfaction, it is the correlation between the variety and challenge of the job and the gratifications which accrue to workers (Morse, 1953). There are, of course, people who do not want more responsibility and people who become demoralized by being placed in jobs which are too difficult for them. These are, however, the exceptions. By and large people seek more responsibility, more skill-demanding jobs than they hold, and as they are able to attain these more demanding jobs, they become happier and better adjusted. Obviously, the condition for securing higher motivation to produce, and to produce quality work, necessitates changes in organizational structure—specifically job enlargement rather than job fractionation. And yet the tendency in large-scale organizations is toward increasing specialization and routinization of jobs. Workers would be better motivated toward higher individual production and toward better quality work if we discarded the assembly line and moved toward the craftsmanlike operations of the old Rolls Royce type of production. Industry has demonstrated, however, that it is more efficient to produce via assembly-line methods with lowered motivation and job satisfaction than with highly motivated craftsmen with a large area of responsibility in turning out their part of the total product. The preferred path to the attainment of production goals in turning out cars or other mass physical products is, then, the path of organizational controls and not the path of internalized motivation. The quality of production may suffer somewhat, but it is still cheaper to buy several mass-produced cars, allowing for programming for obsolescence, than it is to buy a single quality product like the Rolls Royce.

In the production of physical objects intended for mass consumption, the assembly line may furnish the best model. This may also apply to service operations in which the process can be sufficiently simplified to provide service to masses of consumers. When, however, we move to organizations which have the modifications of human beings as their product, as in educational institutions, or when we deal with treating basic problems of human beings, as in hospitals, clinics, and remedial institutions, we do not want to rely solely upon an organizational control to guarantee minimum effort of employees. We want employees with high motivation and high identification with their jobs. Jobs cannot profitably be fractionated very far and standardized and coordinated to a rigorous time schedule in a research laboratory, in a medical clinic, in an educational institution, or in a hospital.

In addition to the recognition of the inapplicability of organizational devices of the factory and the army to all organizations, it is also true that not all factory operations can be left to institutional controls without regard to the motivations of employees. It frequently happens that job fractionation can be pushed to the point of diminishing returns even in industry. The success of the Tavistock workers in raising productivity in the British coal mines through job enlargement was due to the fact that the specialization of American long-wall methods of coal mining did not yield adequate returns when applied to the difficult and variable conditions under which British miners had to operate (Trist and Bamforth, 1951). The question of whether to move toward greater specialization and standardization in an industrial operation or whether to move in the opposite direction is generally an empirical one to be answered by research. One rule of thumb can be applied, however. If the job can be so simplified and standardized that it is readily convertible to automated machines, then the direction to take is that of further institutionalization until automation is possible. If, however, the overall performance requires complex judgment, the differential weighing of factors which are not markedly identifiable, or creativity, then the human mind is a far superior instrument to the computer.

The paradox is that where automation is feasible, it can actually increase the motivational potential among the employees who are left on the job after the changeover. Mann and Hoffman (1960) conclude from their study of automation in an electric power plant that the remaining jobs for workers can be more interesting, that there can be freer association among colleagues, and that the elimination of supervisory levels brings the top and bottom of the organization closer together.

Internalization of organizational goals and values

The pattern of motivation associated with value expression and self-identification has great potentialities for the internalization of the goals of subsystems and of the total system, and thus for the activation of behavior not prescribed by specific roles. Where this pattern prevails individuals take over organizational objectives as part of their own personal goals. They identify not with the organization as a safe and secure haven but with its major purposes. The internalization of organizational objectives is generally confined to the upper echelons or to the office personnel. In voluntary organizations it extends into some of the rank-and-file, and in fact most voluntary organizations need a core of dedicated people—who are generally referred to as the dedicated damn fools.

Now the internalization of organizational goals is not as common as two types of more partial internalization. The first has to do with some general organizational purposes which are not unique to the organization. A scientist may have internalized some of the research values of his profession but not necessarily of the specific institution to which he is attached. As long as he stays in that institution, he may be a well-motivated worker. But he may find it just as easy to work for the things he believes in in another institution. There is not the same set of alternative organizations open to liberals who are political activists and who are part of the core of dedicated damn fools in the

Democratic party. They have no other place to go, so they find some way of rationalizing the party's deviation from their liberal ideals.

A second type of partial internalization concerns the values and goals of a subsystem of the organization. It is often easier for the person to take over the values of his own unit. We may be attached to our own department in a university more than to the goals of the university as a whole.

Conditions conducive to internalization of system goals

Internalization of organization objectives can come about through the utilization of the socialization process in childhood or through the adult socialization which takes place in the organization itself. In the first instance, the selective process, either by the person or the organization, matches the personality with the system. A youngster growing up in the tradition of one of the military services may have always thought of himself as an Air Force officer. Similarly, the crusader for civil liberties and the American Civil Liberties Union find one another.

The adult socialization process in the organization can build upon the personal values of its members and integrate them about an attractive model of its ideals. People can thus identify with the organizational mission. If the task of an organization has emotional significance, the organization enjoys an advantage in the creation of an attractive image. If the task is attended by hazard, as in the tracking down of criminals by the FBI, or of high adventure, as in the early days of flying, or of high service to humanity, as in a cancer research unit, it is not difficult to develop a convincing model of the organization's mission.

The imaginative leader can also help in the development of an attractive picture of the organization by some new conceptualization of its mission. The police force entrusted with the routine and dirty business of law enforcement carried out by dumb cops and "flatfeet" can be energized by seeing themselves as a corps of professional officers devoted to the highest form of public service. Reality factors limit the innovative use of symbols for the glorification of organizations. Occupational groups, however, constantly strive to achieve a more attractive picture of themselves, as in the instances of press agents who have become public relations specialists or undertakers who have become morticians.

Internalization of subgroup norms can come about through identification with fellow group members who share the same common fate. People take over the values of their group because they identify with their own kind and see themselves as good group members, and as good group members they model their actions and aspirations in terms of group norms. This subgroup identification can work for organizational objectives only if there is agreement between the group norms and the organizational objectives. Often in industry the norms of the work group are much closer to union objectives than to company objectives.

This suggests three additional factors which contribute to internalization of group objectives: (1) participating in important decisions about group objectives; (2) contributing to group performance in a significant way; and (3) sharing in the rewards of group accomplishment. When these three conditions are met, the individual can regard the group as his, for he in fact has helped to make it.

Social satisfactions from primary-group relationships

Human beings are social animals and cannot exist in physical or psychological isolation. The stimulation, the approval, and the support they derive from interacting with one another comprise one of the most potent forms of motivation. Strictly speaking, such affiliative motivation is another form of instrumental-reward-seeking, but some of its qualitative aspects are sufficiently different from the instrumental system and individual rewards previously described to warrant separate discussion.

The desire to be part of a group in itself will do no more than hold people in the system. The studies of Elton Mayo and his colleagues during World War II showed that work groups which provided their members social satisfactions had less absenteeism than less cohesive work groups (Mayo and Lombard, 1944). Mann and Baumgartel (1953) corroborated these findings in a study of the Detroit Edison Company. With respect to role performance, moreover, Seashore (1954) has demonstrated that identification with one's work group can make for either above-average or below-average productivity depending upon the norms of the particular group. In the Seashore study the highly-cohesive groups, compared to the low-cohesive groups, moved to either extreme in being above or below the production standards for the company.

Other studies have demonstrated that though the group can provide important socioemotional satisfactions for the members it can also detract from task orientation (Bass, 1960). Members can have such a pleasant time interacting with one another that they neglect their work. Again the critical mediating variable is the character of the values and norms of the group. The affiliative motive can lead to innovative and cooperative behavior, but often this assumes the form of protecting the group rather than maximizing organizational objectives. So the major question in dealing with the affiliative motive is how this motive can be harnessed to organizational goals.

REFERENCES

Allport, F. H. "The J-Curve Hypothesis of Conforming Behavior." *J. Soc. Psychol.* 5 (1934), 141-83.

Bass, B. M. *Leadership, Psychology, and Organizational Behavior.* New York: Harper, 1960.

Mann, F. C., and Baumgartel, H. J. *Absences and Employee Attitudes in an Electric Power Company.* Ann Arbor, Mich.: Institute for Social Research, Univ. of Michigan, 1953.

Mann, F. C., and Hoffman, R. L. *Automation and the Worker.* New York: Holt, Rinehart and Winston, 1960.

Mayo, E., and Lombard, G. *Teamwork and Labor Turnover in the Aircraft Industry of Southern California. Business Res. Studies No. 32.* Cambridge, Mass.: Harvard Univ., 1944.

McGregor, D. *The Human Side of Enterprise.* New York: McGraw-Hill, 1960.

Morse, Nancy. *Satisfactions in the White Collar Job.* Ann Arbor, Mich.: Institute for Social Research, Univ. of Michigan, 1953.

Seashore, S. *Group Cohesiveness in the Industrial Work Group.* Ann Arbor, Mich.: Institute for Social Research, Univ. of Michigan, 1954.

Trist, E., and Bamforth, K. W. "Some Social and Psychological Consequences of the Long Wall Method of Coal-Getting." *Hum. Relat.* 4 (1951), 3-38.

Weber, M. *The Theory of Social and Economic Organization.* Glencoe, Ill.: Free Press, 1947.

Essay 9-2

The Scanlon Plan*

William F. Whyte

The Scanlon Plan consists of two basic parts: (1) a social process whereby suggestions for productivity improvements can be made and carried out; (2) a formula for sharing the fruits of productivity improvements on a plant-wide basis.

THE INCENTIVE BONUS PLAN

Scanlon and his associates argue that

NOTE: This chapter is based primarily on the following: George P. Shultz, "Worker Participation on Production Problems," *Personnel*, November 1951; George P. Shultz and Robert P. Crisara, "The Lapointe Machine Tool Company and United Steelworkers of America," National Planning Association, November 1952; Russell W. Davenport, "A Case History of Union-Management Cooperation," in Paul Pigors and Charles Myers, *Readings in Personnel Administration* (New York: McGraw-Hill Book Company, 1952), p. 461. Parts of this chapter, especially the section on suggestion plans, are based on a manuscript by Savies and Strauss.

*Abridged from William F. Whyte, *Money and Motivation* (New York: Harper and Brothers, 1955), pp. 166-88. Copyright © 1955 by Harper & Row, Publishers, Inc. By permission of the publisher.

there is really no such thing as the Scanlon Plan in the sense of a universal formula that is applied to every plant. They point out that the sharing formula must be devised to fit the particular operating conditions of the plant in question. They also argue that the formula by itself produces no results. It is the reorganized activity of people that pays off. . . .

The Scanlon Plan objective is to devise a formula which will most adequately reflect the productive efforts of workers and management people as a whole. It may help us to concentrate on one example, the Lapointe Machine Tool Company, in illustrating one possible formula.

* * * * *

At Lapointe the Plan grew out of the initiative of the local union president and his committee, who sought out Joseph Scanlon and persuaded him to meet with them and management to propose a new cooperative approach. The possibility of reexamining and even changing the formula from time to time provides a further field for union involvement even in this narrow area involving the financial formula.

... In the Lapointe case management argued that labor costs over the months preceding the introduction of the Plan in 1947 were unduly inflated by World War II conditions. Management proposed and the union, a local of the United Steelworkers of America, accepted as a base a ratio of labor costs to sales value 3 percentage points below that which had existed in the base period. ...

"For each 1 percent of increase in productive efficiency as reflected in production value, a 1 percent participating bonus will be paid to each employee working under the Plan."[1] Thus 100 percent of the labor cost improvement is paid out to participating members. ... Management expects to make its gains through spreading its overhead over increased production.

In Lapointe all employees of the company, with the exception of top management, share in the bonus. This means that foremen, superintendents, engineers, and other managerial people have a recognized part in the Plan. ... The top executives share in a bonus system of their own, based on sales.

The bonus is paid in terms of a percentage of the participants' regular pay. If the bonus is 20 percent for a given month and the production worker's regular earnings in that month were $400, he would receive an $80 bonus. Similarly, the engineer who had a salary of $600 for that month would receive $120. ...

The many Lapointe workers who had been on piece rates were guaranteed their regular hourly rate plus their average incentive earnings prior to the time that the Plan went into effect. In other words, the company was gambling that these men would produce at least as much as they had under piecework even after the direct individual incentive was withdrawn. ...

The Plan at Lapointe provides for possible changes in the ratio of labor costs to production value. The agreement envisages several possible conditions that may make such a change desirable. Management might introduce substantial technological improvements that would lower labor costs "without any increase in productive efficiency on the part of the participants." Increases in wage rates might justify a change. Increases or decreases in sales prices would affect the ratio. A major change in the product mix might affect the ratio, and so on. The agreement makes no attempt to anticipate all such possible conditions. It simply opens up possibilities for union and management to negotiate a new ratio. Three such changes were negotiated in the first four and a half years of the Plan's existence. On the other hand, Shultz reports that there have been some major technological changes without a change in the ratio.[2]

* * * * *

The Lapointe Plan establishes a reserve fund to meet fluctuations in labor costs. This was not included in the original plan, but the machine tool industry is naturally subject to wide fluctuations in its volume of business. A month when business was down might show not only no bonus to be paid, but might reveal an actual deficit. The union agreed in negotiations with management that is would only be fair to meet such deficits out of a reserve fund. It was therefore agreed upon that one-half of the first 15 percent of any bonus earned in any month should be set aside as a reserve. Any unused portion of this reserve by November of the given year should be paid out in December and a new reserve fund established.

---

[1] Shultz and Crisara, op. cit., p. 71.

[2] Letter to W. F. Whyte.

SUGGESTION PLAN: OLD STYLE

The system for developing and implementing suggestions is one of the basic parts of the Scanlon Plan. In order to see the significance of the Scanlon approach to suggestions, it may help us first to examine suggestion systems as they are generally applied in industry today.

Years ago there were probably many foremen and other management people who took the attitude toward workers represented in the statement, "You're paid to work. I do the thinking around here." No doubt such attitudes still exist in industry even though few people would give them such blunt expression. However, it is coming to be more and more realized that workers do think about their jobs, that they are capable of making suggestions that would lead to improvements in efficiency. In fact, many management people are convinced that there is a veritable gold mine in these ideas. The problem is to develop a plan that will systematically bring these ideas to management's attention.

Suggestion plans exist in many companies. They generally operate in this manner: The individual who has an idea tears off an entry form from the stack conveniently located in his department above a suggestion box. He writes his suggestion on this slip of paper and either signs his name or identifies himself by his clock number. He then drops his entry into the box. These slips are collected periodically from various departments and studied by a suggestion committee appointed by management. Departmental management is consulted before committee decisions are made.

For every idea accepted a cash award is made. For cases where no cash savings can be shown, the accepted suggestion draws a nominal award of perhaps $5 or $10. Where a savings in labor costs can be shown, management makes an effort to

estimate the amount that can be saved in six months or a year and pays the employee some predetermined percentage of this figure. In some cases these payoffs are substantial. The top award in some companies may run into several thousand dollars.

Where such plans are well administered (within their own logics) and where the company is really prepared to offer substantial rewards for valuable suggestions, there is no doubt that such systems provide management with practical ideas worth far more than the costs of administering the suggestion plan. In other words, if such a suggestion plan were withdrawn—and no alternative presented—management would lose and at least some employees would lose an opportunity of supplementing their earnings and expressing their ingenuity. Nevertheless, we find that many such suggestion plans are made little use of by employees, and even in the cases of the best of such plans we suspect that they do not begin to tap the storehouse of ideas actually possessed by workers, let alone those ideas that workers and management people together could develop if they devised more effective ways of stimulating such ideas.

There seem to be important limitations actually inherent in suggestion plans as commonly practiced. Often management only pays what workers regard as ridiculously small amounts for valuable suggestions. Even if we assume that management is prepared to pay generously for suggestions, there are other stumbling blocks, which are discussed below.

1. The traditional suggestion plan puts its emphasis upon the contribution of the *individual*. He is offered an individual reward for his individual idea. In many cases a cost-saving idea will involve the readjustment of jobs and people in the department. Such changes may be looked upon by other people as a threat to their position and security. Thus the individual who

makes such a suggestion may win money and yet stir up the resentment of fellow workers. Under such conditions many people would rather keep their suggestions to themselves.

2. *Foreman-worker relations.* Many foremen look upon a successful suggestion submitted by a worker in their departments as a reflection upon their own competence. They fear that higher management might say, "Why didn't the foreman think of that himself?" Many workers recognize this and fear that the foreman will retaliate against them if they submit suggestions. Even when the worker prefers to withhold his name in the contest, the foreman is likely to have a pretty good idea as to which of his men might be putting in suggestions.

This problem can be met to some extent if management takes pains to give the foreman recognition for suggestions coming out of his department. For example, management is advised to have the foremen present the awards and with a maximum of fanfare and publicity, especially if the award is a substantial one. However, even these measures may not eliminate worker fear of retaliation if no other changes are made in the foreman-worker relations.

3. *Problems in the ownership of ideas.* The standard suggestion approach assumes that a good idea is devised by a single individual—though sometimes two individuals may sign their names to a suggestion. This assumption is contrary to experience and to research observations. We saw in examining Donald Roy's experience that the workers in his department had many production ideas that were unknown to management.[3] No doubt some of these ideas were developed full blown by a single individual, but even in those cases the ideas had been shared with the rest of the shop. Some of these ideas had been around for a

---

[3] William F. Whyte, *Money and Motivation,* chapters 3, 5 and 7.

long time, so that it would be quite impossible to determine who had invented them. There were also, of course, ideas originated by one individual but modified and improved upon by one or more others. This same observation can be made in many other factory situations.

Now suppose some individualist decides to take one of these ideas and put it in the suggestion box. Then we hear from fellow workers, "It was really my idea, but that bastard stole it from me and cashed in on it," and similar expressions of resentment. Thus the individual incentive on suggestions may stimulate conflict within a department.

4. *Complex ideas and human relations.* We generally find that the most valuable ideas for the improvement of efficiency are not those limited to one machine or to one productive operation. Such ideas may involve changes in the relations of machines to each other, in the relations of worker to worker and of workers to management people. In such a situation the individual worker is not in a position to see all parts of the problem that are necessary to the working out of a practical plan. The individual may have the initial idea but a group process may be required before the idea can be put into practical form. This calls for consultation among a number of people. However, the individual suggestion award discourages such consultations. The emphasis is upon individual ownership of the idea, and many people naturally fear to talk their idea over with other people lest they lose some claim on its ownership.

5. *Paper communication versus social interaction.* The standard suggestion system is a depersonalized operation. It is only at the point of making the awards, especially in some of the larger cases, that a personal element enters in. The communication of the suggestion is in writing and the suggestion committee studies these written documents. Furthermore, many

workers who have good ideas find it difficult to express them in writing. The writing requirement thus serves as a barrier to communication.

We once heard a personnel man say that he considered the suggestion plan "the most valuable form of communication between workers and management." This sort of paper communication may pay off in dollars saved, but it is one of the elementary observations of social research that if we wish to change the attitudes or behavior of people we will find that face-to-face interaction has far more powerful effects than written communication.

SUGGESTION PLAN: SCANLON STYLE

The Scanlon suggestion plan is a marked contrast to traditional systems.

In the first place, there is no individual payoff. This means that the Scanlon approach relies on a completely different type of motivation. The individual is expected to contribute his ideas for the benefit of everyone. He is rewarded, of course, but in a less tangible way. We assume that where the system works the individual must receive a good deal of recognition from fellow workers, union officers, and management. Since he does not stand to gain on an individual financial basis, he is not caught between a desire to benefit himself and the possible adverse reactions of his work group.

Furthermore, the Scanlon suggestion system is not left to the initiative of isolated individuals. A definite structure is set up for the discovery, development, and implementation of suggestions. The structure operates through union and management. In every department a union production committeeman is appointed or elected. This committeeman and the foreman constitute the production committee of the department. They meet together at least once a month to discuss possible suggestions for improvement. This suggestion

activity is separate from grievance handling, but the grievance committeeman is invited to sit in on discussions if he cares to do so. The production committeeman may also call in one or two employees from the department in connection with problems with which they are particularly familiar.

Above the departmental production committee level there is an administration or screening committee composed of three management and three union representatives. It is hoped that many suggestions brought by the production committeemen to the foremen can be put into effect within the department without further discussion. However, there will necessarily be other suggestions which require higher level consideration. These are referred to the screening committee. There will also be suggestions that originate at the screening committee level, since they involve interdepartmental problems.

Each departmental production committee is expected to keep minutes of its meetings, giving details on the suggestions made and on the action taken with them. These minutes are transmitted to the screening committee as a means of keeping that group informed about all developments.

According to the formal program, the screening committee is not a decision-making body. It simply presents recommendations to management. The fact is, of course, that higher management officers sit on this committee, so we can assume that a recommendation from the committee will receive most serious consideration.

The bare outline of the Scanlon Plan calls for suggestions to be put in written form by the production committeemen and for certain regularly scheduled meetings. This formal approach, of course, represents only the minimum foundation of the plan. Insofar as such an approach is successful, it must be supplemented by a good deal of informal discussion between production committeemen and workers, committeemen and foremen, committeemen and screening committee members, and so on. Even if suggestions are written, we assume that at least at the departmental level many items are discussed without being put into writing. Nor should the discussions be limited to those who hold formal offices in the cooperative program. The formal structure described above simply provides the channels through which suggestions are processed. These channels are supposed to provide a means for involving everyone—worker or management—in the cooperative system. If the cooperation is limited to the official functionaries, we cannot expect the results that have been achieved in some cases.

Just how do people become involved in this cooperative system? Some cases may tell the story better than any general discussion can.

1. *Eliminating resistance to change.* This example comes from a printing plant:

One of the pressroom employees pointed out that wastepaper was now being crumpled up and thrown in a basket in preparation for salvage. Everyone conceded that, if this paper could be salvaged in flat form, its value would be much higher. Management had been aware of this possible saving but had been unable to enlist the cooperation of the employees in keeping the stock flat. A committee member pointed out the reason for the lack of cooperation: workers felt the foreman was trying to check on them to see how much paper they wasted. Consequently, through various subterfuges they made it impossible for him to police his system. With the suggestion and impetus coming from the employees themselves, however, there was no trouble in getting the wastepaper placed in flat form on pallets located at appropriate places in the pressroom.[4]

Here it is not the idea that is new, but the way of carrying out the idea. The idea in itself was fairly obvious, but relations between management and workers within the department were such that it could

_____
[4] Shultz, op. cit., p. 6.

not be carried out. When the cooperative program got under way it became possible for workers to bring about the changed behavior.

2. *Improving management plans.* This case involves the installation of conveyor systems in the printing plant before and after the development of the cooperative program.

Before the cooperative program began, management introduced a conveyor system into one of the departments in the traditional management manner. The planning department developed the plan without assistance of other groups. The conveyor system was explained to the superintendent and foreman involved, and a blueprint was placed on a bulletin board of the department. However, no explanations were given to the employees and they had no opportunity to express their thoughts and feelings on the matter.

The new conveyor system immediately ran into trouble. Instead of pitching in to help out in this situation, the employees were delighted with the apparent failure of the change. Production dropped below previous average figures and remained down for ten months, until management decided to junk the system.

Shultz describes the second conveyor case in this manner:

In contrast to this experience is the installation of a conveyor system after the plan had been in operation for two months. As in the former case the Planning Department had an idea for the rearrangement of the machines and the use of a conveyor to facilitate certain transport problems. In this case a blueprint was made and posted on the bulletin board, but the employees stated that they could not read the blueprint and that, therefore, they could make very few, if any, suggestions about the proposed plan. Consequently, a small-scale model or templet of what the layout would look like under the new plan was placed at a central location in the department. The employees still, however, made practically no suggestions about the new plan.

One afternoon a member of the planning group happened to be in the department and started discussing the proposed layout with a few of the employees. After he had criticized the proposal in a number of respects, a great many comments were made both by the foreman and by the employees. These comments were gathered together and a Production Committee meeting was held attended by the Industrial Engineer responsible for the proposals. At this meeting the employees and the foreman joined together in strenuous criticism of the conveyor part of the plan. After about two and one-half hours' discussion, the Production Committee agreed that the rearrangement of the machines would be beneficial but wanted the engineer to reconsider several aspects of the conveyor system.

About a week later, another meeting was held and the Production Committee agreed to a modified version of the conveyor system, with the understanding that it would be installed in such a manner that they could make changes fairly easily. Subsequently, the Production Committee did make several important changes, especially in the manning of the new system. The drastic revision in the department layout and the revised conveyor system are now accepted as an improvement by the workers and the foremen concerned and the productivity of the department has been increased by about 20 percent.[5]

Here we see that management has not abandoned its customary managerial function of planning for technological and process changes. The difference is that management now consults the people who are most directly involved in the changes. This has two effects. On the one hand, it reduces or eliminates resistance to the change. On the other hand, it makes possible the modification of the plan so that it will be more efficient in its technical as well as in its social sense.

3. *Joint discussion of complex problems.* Shultz presents this case again from the printing plant:

The long-term problem in the Press Room was loss of work to outside manufacturers who, because of their superior equipment, could presumably turn out the work more cheaply. One of the chief losses was the approximately two million workbooks a year contracted for by an outside

press. With their own bread and butter at stake, the Press-Room Committee investigated the relative cost of doing the work at the plant as against sending it outside. They found that the outside price was $15.90 per hundred for a particular order and that the Planning Department figured the cost of doing this job in the plant was $21.55 per hundred, a differential of $5.65 for each 100 workbooks. Then the Production Committee showed management how the plant costs could be brought down to $17.65 per hundred. This tremendous saving was the result of two factors: (1) the elimination of unnecessary operations, and (2) reductions in the estimated time requirement on the operations that were performed. By further investigation into other books of this type, the Production Committee found that certain administrative costs that were properly incurred by the company were not allocated to outside work. Finally it was found that the reduction of inplant overhead cost per unit resulting from the possible increased volume was not being considered. When all these factors were taken into consideration, it was found that a specific 50,000 workbook order could be produced at the plant for 50¢ per hundred cheaper than it could be printed outside—a figure 28 percent under management's original cost estimate.[6]

* * * * *

We see that the workers and union representatives are not simply concerned with problems of improving a particular machine. They become involved with management in problems that go to the heart of the business: the relationships among productivity, costs, prices, and profit. The cost situation presents a goal for them to shoot at. If people did not know what the cost problems were, they would have no particular motivation for developing such complicated plans for improvement. Now, the costs and the company's competitive position provide the goals around which the cooperative activity is organized. Apparently this searching inquiry into the cost situation can be initiated on the union's side by a challenge or it can be initiated when management asks for union

---

[5] Ibid., pp. 7-8.

[6] Ibid., p. 8.

help in examining possibilities for reducing costs on a particular order.

4. *Teamwork on technical improvements.* Here let us turn to two cases presented by Shultz and Crisara from Lapointe:

Start—grind—stop—wait—"mike." And start all over again. That is the way to grind round broaches. Start the machine, grind off a little stock, press the stop button, wait for the machine to coast to a stop, then "mike" the broach. Learn to set up and operate the machine, read blueprints, dress the abrasive wheel, get the "feel" of micrometers. These skills are required of a cylindrical grinder.

Where was the problem? Production and quality were good. The foreman was satisfied. The company was satisfied. But a worker thought the job could be done better. For him there was too long a wait between pressing the stop button and being able to "mike" the broach. He had a vague idea that applying some kind of electrical brake on the machine would make it stop faster and therefore speed up production. His foreman liked the idea. But together they were unable to go any further with it.

They suggested it to management, but were told that it would cost $1,200 to buy a speed control, and that the present speed reducer which cost $450 would have to be scrapped. This was considered too expensive.

But neither the worker nor the foreman gave up. In a chat with an electrician they got further information and, in a few days, what seemed to be a practical solution. The results, as told by the electrician, were:

"This didn't require a major change in the machine, because we found a way of supplying a source of d.c. current directly to the motor windings and using a shot of d.c. as a brake. The time saving is so great that, after we put it on the first one, they applied it to 17 other machines. They tell me this saves one hour a day per machine. It cost only $1.25 for the fuse block, about $14.00 for a relay, plus a couple of hours for the maintenance man to install."[7]

In the above case it was a worker who took the initiative on the suggestion, but the plan finally carried out was a joint product of worker, foreman, and electrician. . . .

* * * * *

5. *Real versus paper control.* Shultz presents this case again from the printing plant:

One of the departmental Production Committee's most vigorously-pressed suggestions concerned the scheduling of jobs. Workers complained that they often set up their equipment as scheduled, only to find that the particular paper needed for that job was not yet on hand. Though paper for other jobs was apparently available, they could not make a switch since setup time was generally great. This complaint involved people outside the department, however, so the Production Committee could do little about it themselves. They passed it on to the top Screening Committee, a group which included the company president.

The head of the scheduling department, of course, felt particularly concerned with this complaint, and so he did some "homework" in preparation for the meeting. For each job, the worker turns in to the scheduling department a time slip on which is tabulated the total elapsed hours in terms of "running time," "delays," and so on. The department head examined the file of these slips thoroughly and found that there was actually very little delay due to "insufficient paper." When the question came up in the meeting, he triumphantly produced these "facts" and discounted the complaint as of minor importance. This disclosure was greeted with an embarrassed silence. After a long half-minute, one of the workers spoke up: "Those time slips are way off. We fill them out. We were told by the foreman that he would get in trouble if we showed that delay time, so we usually added it to the running time. We've been doing it that way for years. We had no idea you were using the slips as a basis for planning."

Further discussion brought out that the schedulers were using the time slips, not just as a check on coordination between paper storage and production departments, but also as a basis for calculating the running times on different types of jobs. Now, with a newly reliable source of information, the scheduling department is able to work much more effectively.[8]

---

[7] Shultz and Crisara, op. cit., pp. 49-50.

[8] Shultz, op. cit., pp. 8-9.

This case illustrates a problem that is general in management in many plants. Management establishes control systems for two purposes: (1) to plan production efficiently and (2) to evaluate the performance of various individuals and units of the plant. From the standpoint of foremen and workers there is a possible conflict between these two objectives. To protect themselves from the impact of higher management evaluations, workers and foremen often seek to present a picture of operations that looks good or at least looks stable. If they can eliminate large fluctuations from the record, they will be subjected to less pressure from above. The records they fill out, therefore, are often a combination of facts and fiction in such proportions that no one outside the department can know which is which. If management uses these records to plan its production and work-flow scheduling, these plans are built upon the shaky foundation of semifictional information.

Really effective control depends upon the availability of accurate information. In a conflict situation the workers, and even foremen, see to it that higher management is supplied with highly misleading information. People at low levels in management may realize that the information is misleading, but they are in no position to do anything about it. For the nature of the information provided depends in part upon the functioning of the social system. When more cooperative relations are established, it becomes possible to strip away the fictions and provide more accurate information. The fictions can be eliminated only when they no longer serve a function for the people who have created them. When workers and foremen no longer have such a need to protect themselves from higher management, it becomes possible to achieve a degree of management control of the production process that has not hitherto existed.

6. *Involving the total organization.*

What happens under the Scanlon suggestion plan when there is no payoff? This occurred 16 times in 58 months at Lapointe.

The first three months brought bonuses of 24.5, 20.1, and 12.6 percent. Then followed three no-bonus months, one with 4.7 percent, and then two more barren months. How did the people meet the crisis? Shultz and Crisara tell the story in this way:

What happened later on when production dipped and there were no bonuses? The cause was simple and well-understood (though not excused) by everyone. They had "worked themselves out of a job." Management did not anticipate the effect on production of the new arrangement and consequently the backlong of business that had looked big was shortly dissipated. What should the parties have done? It might have been possible to maintain bonus figures in the period that followed by means of heavy layoffs. On the other hand, why should a few men earn bonuses while others earned nothing? And what about the delays and training costs involved in the future when the expected business developed? After considerable discussion of the reasons for the problem and the prospects for the months to follow, union and management agreed that the work force should be held together. This meant no bonus during the lean period. In the meantime management concentrated on the job of increasing sales. While some orders for standard equipment got them back to a small bonus in June, the bulk of the job-lot type of business typical of Lapointe could not be put directly into the shop; it had to go through the engineering department first. With July vacations coming up, another crises appeared in the offing. But even before they were propositioned about it, the engineers decided to postpone their vacations in order to process the work. With this added payroll and relatively little production, July figures looked bad; however, by September production was rolling again.[9]

The story is interesting from two points of view. It shows that people are willing to accept reversals without losing faith in the plan, providing they are thoroughly

_____
[9] Op. cit., pp. 36-37.

and personally involved in carrying it out. Under these circumstances, the information provided will be accepted and acted upon. A mere management handout of information, however accurate, would not suffice to maintain confidence.

Here we also see the importance of involving the total organization in the plan. After all, it is the total organization that accomplishes the results that lead to the payoff. If the engineers in this case had not been involved in the plan and had gone off on vacation at the customary time, it is likely that the whole cooperative program would have died at this point.

NEW VERSUS OLD SUGGESTION PLANS

Let us review the suggestions discussed in the preceding examples. Could any of them have been provided management through the functioning of a traditional individual reward suggestion system?

Only in the first case is it reasonable to conceive of this happening. A worker might well have put in a suggestion that costs could be cut if wastepaper were piled flat instead of crumpled up. However, the idea was not the problem in this case at all. The problem was to get the people to accept and put the idea into effect. Under the individual suggestion plan, such a suggestion regarding the handling of wastepaper might have been made, and yet that in and of itself would have done no good.

We should also note that some of these problems involved not a single suggestion, but a combination of many. The emphasis here is not upon a specific suggestion, but rather upon the solution of a problem.

Perhaps the closest example to the type of suggestion that could come up through an individual plan is that which was involved in the electric brake case. We note that the worker had a germ of an idea but was not able to carry it out without the help of foreman and electrician. If this had happened under an individual plan, would the suggestion have actually been developed? Perhaps the worker would fear that if he took the suggestion up with the foreman, the foreman might take credit away from him. And if the electrician was called in on the suggestion, it would then become a real problem as to whose suggestion it was. The electrician could certainly claim ownership of the suggestion. Under such circumstances the worker might feel that it would be foolish to consult the electrician at all. Thus, the idea would probably have been stillborn.

The Scanlon approach seems to bring forward the type of suggestion that is available through other suggestion plans, but it also seems to tap a field that is totally outside the reach of such plans. We noted earlier that some of the most valuable suggestions involved changes in the relations of machines to each other, of men to machines, of workers to supervisors, and so on. It is exceedingly unlikely that the individual worker will have enough knowledge and experience to be able to present that kind of suggestion. Such a suggestion is traditionally thought of as in the realm of management planning; but we have seen in the case of the conveyor that when changes of this nature are made, without any involvement on the part of workers and supervisors, all sorts of dislocations develop. We can therefore conclude that the Scanlon approach taps a reservoir of ideas that would not be reached with the traditional approach at all. Perhaps reservoir is not a good simile because it assumes that the ideas just lie there waiting to be tapped. The cases described clearly indicate that for the most important suggestions this is not the case. People contribute much more in the way of valuable suggestions when they are stimulated to shoot for new goals by a social system that makes such activity possible.

We also see a contrast in the actual number of suggestions and particularly in the number of acceptable suggestions made. In the first four and a half years of the Scanlon Plan's existence in the Lapointe plant, 1,506 suggestions were made. During this period the plant grew from 294 employees to 1,085. If we average the quarterly figures of the number of employees on the payroll, we get a figure of just under 500 employees as an average for this 4½-year period. That means that the average employee submitted about three suggestions within this period. Of course, there were some who submitted no suggestions and some who submitted many more than three. However, Shultz and Crisara point out that new employees have fitted into the system and are contributing suggestions at a surprisingly rapid rate. For the final 12-month period recorded by them (October 1951-September 1952) there were 637 suggestions, of which 178 came from people who had never previously made a suggestion. Twenty-eight percent, then, of the total volume came from these first-time people.

Even more impressive, however, is the proportion of suggestions that have been accepted and put into practive. Specialists on individual suggestion plans warn management that it should be prepared to find that a large proportion of the suggestions will be impractical. One expert states, "On an average 75 out of every 100 suggestions are turned down."[10] He then goes on to advise management as to how it should deal with these turned down suggestions.

Shultz and Crisara report that 80 percent of these 1,506 suggestions made at Lapointe have been accepted and put into operation. Another 5 percent were still under consideration and only 15 percent had been rejected.

How can we explain this striking contrast between 75 percent rejected and 80 percent accepted? On the basis of the data

given we cannot be sure of the answer, but an examination of the suggestion-making process in the two cases gives us our best clues. We have noted that the Scanlon suggestion program involves a good deal of informal discussion among workers and between workers and management people. It is probably at this stage that impractical suggestions are weeded out. The man who has an idea checks with other workers and perhaps tries to get advice from management people. At this point he may either get the help he needs to put his suggestion in practical form or else he may decide that it is not worth submitting. In the case of the individual suggestion plan, on the other hand, the employee is not likely to have the benefit of this consultation. He feels he had better keep the idea to himself in order to retain possession of it. Under these circumstances it is natural that a large proportion of the suggestions coming up in such a program will be impractical.

RESULTS ACHIEVED

Our story has already indicated some of the results achieved under this cooperative approach. Using the Lapointe case as an example, we can summarize them in this way:

1. *The growth of cooperation.* The union was organized at Lapointe in late 1944. Toward the end of the first year of its existence there was an 11-week strike. During the next several years, relations between the parties improved, but there was still a good deal of difficulty over some grievances. With the institution of the cooperative program at the end of 1947, worker-management and union-management relations changed markedly in the direction of cooperation. Shultz and Crisara report that grievances have practically disappeared.

2. *Strengthening of the company's competitive position.* The company not

---

[10] Herman W. Seinwerth, "Suggestion Plans—The Value to the Personnel Relations Program," reprinted in Paul Pigors and Charles Myers, op. cit., p. 459.

only has grown on a scale that might have been impossible without the cooperative program, it has improved its competitive position in a most impressive manner.

3. *Elimination of output restriction.* On the basis of previous studies, we have been accustomed to assuming that restriction of output exists anywhere and everywhere. Apparently in some of these Scanlon cases it has been well-nigh eliminated. The union president cites an example of a grinder at Lapointe who had been averaging $76.40 a week on his incentive rate. In four days after the Plan was instituted, he turned in enough work so that it would have amounted to $184 under the pre-existing incentive plan. This is only a single example and is certainly not enough to allow us to assume that no restriction remains at all. However, it does suggest that the tight ceiling on production has been eliminated. With no more individual incentive rates there is no longer any threat of rate cutting, and the worker can contribute to the goal of the total organization without incurring the enmity of fellow workers.

4. *The payoff to workers.* What are workers getting out of it? The most tangible results are shown in the bonuses paid over the four and a half years reported by Shultz and Crisara. Between December 1947 and September 1952 the bonus has ranged between 0 and a high of 52.1 percent. Sixteen of these 58 months showed no bonus and 20 showed 20 percent or over.

HOW WERE THE GAINS WON?

We shall need a good deal more research before we reach a full understanding of the spectacular results gained in some Scanlon Plan plants—and also of the failures encountered in other attempts, for there have been failures and we can learn from them too. The following analysis must be considered tentative.

1. *A new management approach.* Suc-

cess of an activity such as is involved in the Scanlon Plan requires a veritable revolution in management's conception of its functions and in its behavior in relation to workers and union representatives. The management preoccupied with protecting its prerogatives had best not consider the Scanlon Plan at all.

* * * * *

It is fashionable for management people to say that participation on the part of workers is important. But often they give themselves away by saying that the worker "must be made to feel he is participating." This synthetic sense of participation they seek to provide perhaps by distributing financial statements to workers and in other ways telling them how the business is getting along. But real participation involves changes in the behavior and activity of people. It involves getting workers to initiate changes in the behavior of management people. If management is unwilling to make any significant changes, then it is futile to start on such a program.

2. *Reciprocity in initiating action.* We have noted that in order for the cooperation program to succeed, management people must be willing to respond to action initiated by workers and union representatives. As we look over the cases above, it becomes evident that this initiation is not one-sided. We see cases where management has called upon union officers and workers to take action in solving management problems. If management simply sat back and waited for union people to come up with ideas, the cooperative program would soon peter out. Management is expected to take the initiative in the solution of manufacturing problems, but in these cooperative cases management learns to take the initiative in a different way. Instead of simply initiating through giving out orders, management makes clear to the participants in the program the real problems of production that management faces. In this way manage-

ment enlists skill, understanding, and intelligence that otherwise are little utilized.

3. *Ability of management to make changes.* The program requires not only a receptivity on the part of management people, but also an ability to make changes. The two do not necessarily go together. We have fragmentary information on one case where the Scanlon Plan has failed to achieve the sort of spectacular results noted at Lapointe and in some other cases. The union's international representative gives this explanation of the situation: He points out that the company manufactures large pieces of equipment. As these units move through the factory, there are often times when numbers of workers are standing idle waiting for the next unit to arrive. The union representatives on production and screening committees have argued vigorously that management must improve its production scheduling before any substantial improvements in labor costs will appear. This management has not done.

It is unclear from our data whether management has been unreceptive to ideas in the production scheduling field or simply has found it impossible to make basic improvements. It is, of course, easier to balance production and keep all workers occupied most of the time when the factory manufactures a large number of small units than is the case when large units of varying types move through the plant. However, some of the large broaching machines manufactured by Lapointe present the same problem, and there the problem was solved. Whether it is unreceptiveness to what is proposed or inability to make changes, the result seems to be the same. It is difficult to stimulate workers to bring forward suggestions that would result in relatively small savings when they see the thousands of dollars that are wasted in the waiting time.

4. *Involvement of the total organization.* The Scanlon approach provides for a remarkably widespread involvement of people in the discussion of production problems. Workers become involved, but not only workers. We see engineers, production schedulers, accountants, and so on contributing their specialized knowledges. In fact, the work of the modern factory is so complex that the solution of any given problem often involves the specialized knowledges of several different types of functionaries. The Scanlon Plan provides for this flexible sort of involvement. At the same time, the involvement is not left completely to chance and spontaneous development in the various parts of the plant. A formal system is provided to bring suggestions up from department to screening committee and to management for action. The formal framework does not determine success, but it does provide a set of procedures through which the widespread informal activity can be organized and brought to a successful conclusion.

Essay 9-3

Wage payment methods of the future*

Robert B. McKersie

INCENTIVE METHODS OF THE FUTURE

As a general matter it is impossible to identify the best wage payment method. While some of the strengths and weaknesses of each wage payment method are inherent in the system itself, most are contingent upon the environment within which the method is installed. The selection of the best approach depends upon the peculiar characteristics of each situation. With this reservation in mind, some of the salient characteristics of wage payment methods, that will be most appropriate in the years ahead, will be identified.

The ideal incentive system should have these characteristics:

1. It will combine employee and employer interests. Theoretically this conjunction of employee and employer interests is attainable. The three concepts of *participation, achievement* and *rewards* provide a way of thinking about this integration. Ideally an incentive system should bring about a *participation* on the part of employees in the vital problems of the business, be it the participation of a piece worker who concerns himself with problems of work flow, breakdowns, and material defects, or a group of Scanlon Plan employees who turn their attention to increasing teamwork and attacking common problems. This involvement should stimulate motivation and thereby elicit extra *achievement.* Due to this additional

performance the organization can share *rewards.* In turn the rewards reinforce participation and achievement. A type of feed-back or closed-loop system exists. In effect, participation becomes the mediating device for translating the primary goal of the employer, achievement, and the primary goal of the employee, rewards, into mutually shared goals.

2. For people to *participate* effectively they have to know the problems of the business. Management must communicate the concerns so people can focus their attention on important problems. As has been mentioned several times, effective participation requires teamwork and co-ordination, both vertically and horizontally, in the organization. Certain structural devices are needed to facilitate this involvement, such as committees, meetings, communications, etc.

3. Performance standards are needed to elicit and to reward achievement. But a standard which is effective for eliciting motivation may not be appropriate for rewarding accomplishment. To be effective in motivating people a standard needs to contain the problems of the business, to be expressed in simple terms, to remain unchanged as long as possible, to measure input over a short time period, and to be applied to small groups. If these criteria are met, then the standard should have some "pull" or stimulus. On the other hand, to allocate equitable rewards a standard needs to reflect stable conditions, to adjust for changes in volume, product mix and other underlying variables, to be altered frequently, to measure input over a long time cycle, and to be applied to large

*Reprinted from Robert B. McKersie, "Wage Payment Methods of the Future," *British Journal of Industrial Relations* 1 (1963), pp. 208-12.

groups. Clearly, the two sets of criteria are different.[1]

The Scanlon Plan meets the requirements of a good *motivating* standard. Under this approach, standards are gross, they embody the essential problems around which people can focus their attention, and they are long term in nature. But the Scanlon Plan does not always pay equitable rewards. As mentioned earlier, it allocates rewards for "one shot" accomplishment, for volume windfalls, and improvement over an historic norm.

Contrastingly, profit sharing meets the requirements of a good *rewarding* standard. It allocates equitable rewards since achievement is defined by a norm that represents competitive conditions. Achievement is measured against the current market and rewards are only paid when performance is obtained that is better than could be normally expected in the light of current operating conditions.

But the profit and loss statement does not provide a good *motivating* standard. It measures results after the fact, rather than providing targets; it usually measures long run results rather than discreet tasks; and it reflects many exogenous influences, rather than just portraying the conditions that are within the control of the work force.

One solution would be to combine the strengths of the Scanlon Plan with the strengths of profit sharing; namely, to use one type of standard for motivating employees and another one for rewarding employees. While theoretically this may seem like the best of both systems, it does weaken the linkage between participation, achievement, and rewards. It would appear like a sleight-of-hand to motivate employees with one set of standards and reward them with another.

However, there remains a better approach, one which meets both sets of criteria. It stands as an intriguing possibility, as a juncture between the internal emphasis of the Scanlon Plan and the external emphasis of profit sharing. This is the use of "market" quotations as bench marks. In today's economy, almost any task or group of tasks can be subcontracted. Companies constantly face "make or buy" decisions. They are searching around for the most economical means of producing each component. These competitive prices (the bid price at which a given operation can be done on the outside) could be used as performance norms, both for defining and rewarding achievement.

The subcontracting quotation resembles an "internal" standard in several respects: it states a norm in terms of costs and it usually can be obtained from small groupings of tasks or operations. On the other hand, it resembles an "external" standard, since it is based on the "test of the market" and reflects competitive conditions.

To date, however, subcontracting referents have not been incorporated into formal incentive plans. In the case of the B. & O. Plan, a job security incentive was invoked but no cash rewards were paid. Currently, many managements use subcontracting quotations as a check on their own efficiency or as a threat to send work out should efficiency not improve.[2] But these same managements have not used these bench marks for defining and paying

---

[1] In this discussion we have been attempting to make a distinction between the *stimulus* that comes from the task itself and the *reinforcement* that comes from receiving extra earnings. For the initial stimulus to be present, the task has to be something people can "see"—something with which they can identify. For the reinforcement to be present the extra earnings must be related to extra effort. Clearly, the two concepts are related since rewards feed back and influence participation or effort (in the manner discussed earlier in this section). But for purposes of analysis it is helpful to indicate when a standard is functional for motivating and when for rewarding effort.

[2] "The ready availability of outside contractors provides a useful comparison or base point for evaluating internal costs. Without this competitive resource, internal costs could get out of line." Margaret K. Chandler and Leonard R. Sayles, *Contracting-Out* (New York: Graduate School of Business, Columbia University, 1959), p. 28.

rewards. Executives talk generally about the challenge of competition but rarely do they translate these exhortations down to the level of specific operations and into terms which specify the targets.

4. *Rewards* can be allocated in a number of ways. Ad hoc or one-shot rewards have a certain appeal. They do not lock the organization into any plan which is difficult to abandon. One of the characteristics of the ideal incentive arrangement is that it should be easily abandoned. Abandoning one plan and adopting another provides the opportunity for "new beginnings." These gains are substantial and incentive plans must be supersedable.

Ad hoc rewards can involve something as simple as ceremonializing a breakthrough. For instance, in the oil industry they frequently knock off for the afternoon and have a party when a new field is brought in.

One-shot rewards also might be paid for rapid assimilation of change. Such an approach might do something about the following problem that occurs during a technological changeover.

From the point of view of the workers, all during the period when they went home with the greatest degree of mental and nervous fatigue, and when management expected their utmost cooperation, financial incentive for working, as the record shows, was the lowest—at first "no bonus" over and above base pay, and then for a time small incentive earnings. Later, with far less effort or anxiety, their incentive was at a maximum, rising at times to 35 and 40 percent above base pay.[3]

Krulee has made a similar point that traditional incentive systems overlook an important area of accomplishment when they discourage people from learning.[4]

_____
[3] Charles R. Walker, *Toward the Automatic Factory* (New Haven: Yale University Press, 1957), pp. 138, 163.

[4] Under such circumstances (individual piece-rate), the output of an individual is primarily a measure of his expenditure of energy but not of his creativity or ability to learn from experience. Learning becomes quite liter-

The efficient handling of a changeover can be one of the most important contributions that employees can make. It might be desirable to establish a changeover or learning curve and to pay rewards for any shortening of the duration.

Rewards can also be paid on a regular and prearranged (formula) basis: the sharing of cost savings as in the Scanlon Plan or profits as in profit sharing arrangements. Rewards should be distributed uniformly throughout the achieving group. By distributing them as a percentage of base pay, wage and salary relationships are preserved. Different individuals may contribute differently to the reward pool, but the distribution should be uniform in order to emphasize the team approach.

The reckoning period should be as short as possible so that people can associate rewards with accomplishment. The year-end payout of profit sharing plans is not as meaningful as the monthly reward of Scanlon Plans. On the other hand, the payout period should be long enough to attenuate the variations that occur when incentive payments are made on a task by task basis. Since many jobs have a long cycle of accomplishment, and since it is difficult to establish accurate standards for these jobs, the payout interval may need to be quarterly or even semiannually.

The size of the achieving group should be as small as possible.[5] In many situa-

_____
ally someone else's responsibility, namely, that of the industrial engineers or other specialists who set rates." (Material in parenthese added.) Gilbert K. Krulee, "Company-Wide Incentive Systems," *Journal of Business* 28 (January 1955), p. 41.

[5] But note should be taken of the fact that plant-wide schemes can exert considerable "pull" in large plants. Stromberg Carlson has employed upwards of 10,000 employees and its Scanlon Plan has operated effectively.

The profit sharing plan at American Motors appears to be exerting a stimulus:

At the annual meeting stockholders heard an unsolicited statement by the president of our largest local union at Kenosha, Wisconsin, with some 12,500 members. He said: ". . . this new concept of management-labour relations . . . has done more to improve the quality of the product than any other item . . .

tions it is possible to group employees into small clusters. The thrust of decentralization and regionalization has brought about the establishment of smaller manufacturing units. The movement in the direction of establishing profit centers may provide the means for identifying smaller groups of people.

5. The endorsement of group incentive

plans should not be interpreted to mean that all individual incentives are outmoded. On the contrary, recognition of the individual is extremely important. For the reasons given earlier, individual rewards, such as promotional opportunities and merit awards, need to be strengthened in order to help close the motivational gap.

The emphasis of this paper has been on wage *payment* systems. For this aspect of compensation, arrangements should apply more to groups than to individuals. However, the wage *structure*, which has not been considered in this paper, should provide the necessary incentives for eliciting and rewarding individual accomplishment.

I think it has proven out and will continue to prove out. It has made everyone in the Kenosha plant—every employee—feel that he is part of the family. It has given him the kind of loyalty that has been lacking in the past and we know that under this progress-sharing plan, it will keep improving and the results will be beneficial not only to management and labour but also to the consumers and the stockholders." Edward L. Cushman, "Implications of Progress Sharing," remarks before the Canadian Club of Toronto (March 5, 1962).

CHAPTER 10
TOWARD AN INTEGRATED THEORY OF COMPENSATION

Readings presented in this book are labeled "perspectives" of compensation and reward because they represent a variety of views towards compensation and reward issues. As perspectives, these views often are oriented towards somewhat different phenomena and often originate from different vantage points. Like the fabled blind men describing an elephant, these perspectives often appear unrelated and occasionally inconsistent although each may be an accurate presentation of a specific point of view and useful for specific purposes. As noted in the introduction, we concentrated wherever possible on the presentation of theoretical or conceptual models relevant to compensation and rewards; empirical research was introduced as relevant to these models, but we deliberately neglected descriptive presentations of or advocacy of specific compensation and reward practices. Instead, our intent was to contribute to the development of a theoretical framework useful in the analysis of compensation and reward issues, a theoretical framework currently lacking. We attempt in this chapter to develop at least the skeleton of a theoretical framework for the integration of different perspectives presented in earlier chapters.

Several threads which run through most of the different perspectives in earlier chapters relate to compensation as an element in an exchange relationship, a means of making whole or balancing other elements in the exchange. In the context of the employment exchange, rewards or inducements are provided as compensation for contributions by the individual. Whether viewed as incentive or reward, compensation is intended to effectuate an exchange of labor services. Assuming voluntary exchanges, this compensation or balancing is a prerequisite for exchange; individuals do not willingly enter into exchanges which occasion a net loss to that individual. This does not mean, however, that all voluntary exchanges must be regarded as fair or equitable by both parties, only that no net loss is suffered and that the exchange appears as the best feasible alternative. Since at least two parties are involved in any employment exchange, both parties must concur on the desirability of the exchange, the employee must feel compensated for labor services and the employer must feel the labor services are worth the compensation provided. The compensation perspectives reviewed relate both to employer valuation of labor services provided and to employee valuation of labor services sought.

Viewed instrumentally, compensation inducements in the employment exchange are intended to elicit, direct, and maintain specific labor services sought by the employing organization. The overall supply of labor services varies along several dimensions (e.g., people, hours, skills, effort) which can be analyzed in terms of individual behavior models. The individual behavior involved in affecting each of these dimensions was analyzed from the stand-point of individual decision making and choices. As indicated in Figure 10-1, individuals choose to work or engage in alternative activity, select an occupation in which to qualify and work, select among alternative potential employers, exercise choice in accepting specific job assignments with the employing organization, and determine the level of performance provided within the job assignment. Although presented in a sequential process in Figure 10-1, actual choices are not always as discrete as indicated. A decision to work, for example, may be contingent upon employment opportunities

Figure 10-1: Behavioral dimensions of supply of labor services

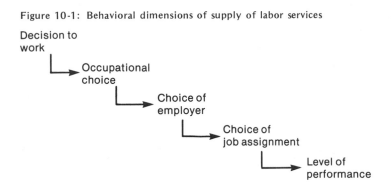

within an occupation and/or employing organization already selected by the individual. For analytical purposes, however, it is convenient to consider each choice individually and to proceed from decisions regarding general dimensions of labor services (size of labor force) to decisions regarding more specific dimensions of labor services such as choice of job and level of performance. Certain of the decisions indicated in Figure 10-1 are made relatively infrequently by an individual (decision to work and occupational choice) and other decisions such as job choice and level of performance are made relatively more frequently; the level of effort expended in job performance thus is a more variable dimension of labor services than the number of persons qualified in an occupation. Also, although each behavioral dimension of the supply of labor services is cast in the framework of choice decisions, certain dimensions are more obviously functions of cognitive decision making than others. Occupational choice, for example, is more easily analyzed within the context of a decision-making model than is level of job performance. The degree to which cognitive decision making characterizes each of these dimensions of supply of labor services probably varies with the infrequency of decisions and the range of potential consequences of the decisions. Thus while a single decision-making model can be applied in the analysis of all of these behavioral dimensions, it is not unlikely that the relevance of the model and of specific variables in the model vary from one behavioral dimension to another.

Individual decisions to work and occupational choices determine the number of persons available for employment in any occupation and thus the size and composition of the labor force available to all employers; they influence only indirectly the supply of labor services to any individual employing organization. These summed decisions made by individuals are most easily understood as influenced by the sum of employer inducements rather than as influenced by the employment inducements of any individual employer. While individuals may decide to work and make occupational choices in response to individual employer offers of employment, overall behavior of the labor force responds to the sum or average of summed employer offers. Behavioral dimensions of choice of employer, job choice, and level of performance represent those behaviors of most direct interest to an employer and those behaviors most directly influenced by the employer's inducements.

The distinction between behavioral dimensions deterministic of the size and composition of the labor force and those which determine more directly the supply of labor services realized within the organization parallels the distinction between external and internal labor markets in our analysis. Employers compete with one another in the attraction of individuals to join the organization and, through this competition, influence indirectly individual decisions determining the size and composition of the labor force. Individuals attracted to join a specific organization are removed from competition in the broader, external labor market and subsequent decisions and behavior are more a function of influences within the organization than of competing influences in the external labor market. Individuals are recruited into the employing organization through a limited set of entry jobs from which they advance over time and are allocated to different job assignments within the organization. Employees of an organization are a differentiated labor force in the sense that their mobility among job assignments within the organization typically is greater than their mobility among employers. Individual employers seek to attract and hold quality employees within the internal labor force, induce willing acceptance of job assignments, and achieve high levels of job performance. Employer compensation strategies thus reflect primarily consideration of the influences of compensation upon these specific aspects of labor supply, and our analyses of labor supply focused upon the attraction of employees to the organization, maintenance of the internal labor force, acceptance of job assignments, and level of performance analyzed in terms of employee behaviors.

Ability to pay compensation and remain profitable is an obvious constraint upon employer compensation strategies, which aids in understanding observed compensation phenomena and in the determination of individual employer compensation strategies. Briefly, labor costs rather than compensation are constrained by profit considerations. Labor costs may be defined to include the cost of all inducements provided in the employment exchange; direct compensation, fringe benefits, and other attractions offered employees. Since it appears that the level of other inducements tends to vary directly with compensation, we can subsume the full package of inducements under the concept of compensation although accounting analyses of ability to pay ought to be more specific. Realization of profit from production dictates that the average cost of labor be constrained to a level less than the average revenue product of labor minus all costs other than labor. Average revenue product is a function of the physical productivity of labor determined largely by nature of the product and production technology and a function of market price of the product determined largely by the elasticity of consumer demand and pricing competition among producers. The ability to pay compensation conceptualized as average net revenue product of labor thus varies from one industry to another depending upon production technology, consumer demand, and product pricing competition. Average net revenue product conceptualized as ability to pay compensation serves to constrain the average cost of labor or wage level, not specific rates of compensation paid individual jobs. While wage level is an average of wage rates, it can be considered as a parameter in the determination of wage rates and the composition of the set of inducements offered for employment rather than as a summary statistic reflective of these structure and composition decisions. Considerations of ability to pay thus constrain wage level or average cost of labor which in turn constrains decisions about wage structure and compensation forms only to the extent that they must be compatible with this wage level parameter. This wage level parameter can be estimated directly from accounting data and employed as a guide in other compensation decisions, or, as noted in our analysis, specific compensation measures reflective of industry competitors can be employed in making wage decisions under the assumption that, other things equal, similar compensation structures result in similar wage levels. Given the assumed similarity of product, technology, raw materials costs, and product prices among industry competitors, any individual producer might infer ability to pay labor costs from compensation surveys of industry competitors. Wage contours reflective of industry or product market groupings thus have a basis in economic analysis and are not merely a consequence of fad or convenience.

Wage level or average cost of labor thus serves as a general economic constraint upon employer compensation strategies. There is, however, considerable opportunity for variation in compensation structure, schedules, and form or composition—variables analyzed as they relate to specific dimensions of labor supply behaviors of interest in the development and maintenance of a labor force. A general model of motivation and/or behavior was employed in our analyses of specific dimensions of labor supply behaviors, a general model which was elaborated somewhat differently in each analysis depending upon the specific relevant influences. That model, sketched in Figure 10-2, views behavior or performance at any point in time as a consequence of either cognitive choice and decision making or previously established

Figure 10-2: General model of motivation/behavior

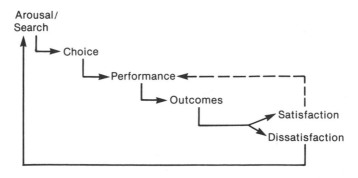

behavior patterns analogous to habit. Outcomes experienced in association with any performance are perceived as satisfying or dissatisfying to the individual. While outcomes include directly contingent consequences of performance, they are not limited to these consequences; they also include elements in the context surrounding performance and indirectly contingent consequences. Sentiments of satisfaction are pleasing to the individual, reinforce the previous behavior, and encourage repetition of that behavior. Sentiments of dissatisfaction, on the other hand, are disturbing and stimulate the individual to be alert to, and seek out, ways of reducing that dissatisfaction. Opportunities for change in behavior are generated through this search or through arousal to alternatives occasioned through stimuli external to the individual such as nomination for promotion, transfer, or reassignment. Change in behavior or performance is viewed as a consequence of cognitive choice and decision making among alternative behaviors; an individual may opt to change behavior or not depending upon evaluation of the available alternatives. Maintenance of a repetitive performance pattern is viewed as a function of satisfaction with the outcomes of previous performance as well as rejection of alternatives considered in the decision making stage. Much observed behavior, particularly stable and continuing behavior patterns, will be reflective of habit based upon decisions made in the past, while changes in behavior will be reflective of specific, immediate choices.

Various motivational perspectives analyzed earlier can be integrated within this general model of behavior. The concepts of reinforcement and conditioned behavior, for example, are relevant in the analysis of behavior maintenance through the satisfaction/performance link, and the cognitive models of choice and decision making are relevant in the analysis of, and choice among, behavior alternatives. Viewed in this context, these different motivational perspectives are complementary rather than competing, they each relate to different aspects or phases of the general behavior model. The more specific model of aspirational and deprivational satisfaction developed in Chapter 8 also can be incorporated within this general model as can the motivational perspectives relating to equity considerations which presumably influence the values employed in assessments of certain outcomes of performance.

This general behavior model, when applied to analysis of behaviors of accepting and terminating employment, acceptance and performance of job assignments, highlights the specific compensation issues related to attraction and maintenance of a labor force and to achievement of desired levels of task performance.

Attraction of a labor force. The attraction of a labor force to an organization involves employers competing with one another in the broader, external labor market. Once employed within an organization, individuals develop specific ties with the organization in the form of specialized qualifications, rights based upon tenure and rewards contingent upon continued employment, all of which tend to vary directly with organizational tenure and reduce employer mobility of the individual. A labor force differentiated from the broader labor market and tied in one way or another to the organization, develops a labor force less responsive to competing opportunities with other employers. Major competition among employers in the labor market thus centers upon the attraction and recruitment of individuals for expansion and maintenance of the organizational labor force.

Potential sources of applicants for employment with an organization include unemployed persons seeking employment, new entrants to the labor force, and persons employed in other organizations. Applicants will be most easily attracted from the unemployed and new entrants; only employed persons who are dissatisfied with their current employment and seeking new opportunities are likely applicants from among the employed. Satisfied employees with other organizations typically are not seeking alternative employment and considerable effort is required to make those persons aware of and interested in alternative employment opportunities. Most potential applicants for employment will be desirous of and seeking employment opportunities; successful recruitment of these persons requires that they receive information about employment offers available with the organization and judge these offers attractive.

Decisions to apply to, and accept employment with, an organization involve cognitive comparison of the employment exchange offered with either some generalized norm of expectations or specific alternative employment exchanges. In either event, the evaluation involves expectations reflecting both the level of outcome and probability of outcome. Wage rates of entry jobs and expectations of employment, anticipated opportunities, are clearly factors in the attraction of applicants for employment; either can be manipulated to make the organization appear more attractive as a source of employment. Employment outcomes beyond the entry job also may be relevant in the attraction of employees; some assessment of the average level of compensation paid and expectations of advancement within the internal labor market probably are employed in evaluation of longer run outcomes of employment. Characterizations of the employer's wage structure available in the labor market are not likely to be very accurate and probably are more reflective of hiring rates than of the internal wage structure; similarly expectations of advancement probably are more reflective of hiring opportunities than of actual advancement rates.

Our analysis indicates that both wage level of entry jobs and anticipated opportunities for employment are significant influences in the attraction of a labor force. An organization known as a high wage employer and/or a hiring employer is more likely to attract applicants than would otherwise be the case. Payment of high wage rates for entry jobs relative to the wage rates of competing employers would attract relatively more applicants from the available labor force easing recruiting, permitting greater selectivity, and reducing the need to vary wage rates as production and demand for labor varies. To the extent that greater selectivity is permitted, the relatively higher wage rate influences positively the potential productivity of recruits, a particularly relevant consideration if the internal labor market is structured such that higher skilled jobs are staffed primarily through promotion from entry jobs. These considerations influence an employer to utilize any ability to pay higher wages in offering wage rates for entry jobs comparable with, or higher than, entry job wage rates of competing employers in the labor market. The capability to offer relatively high entry wage rates may stem from several sources. A high wage industry employer located in a labor market where competing employers operate in low wage industries permits such capability; wage rates within the organization also may be structured such that relatively high entry job wage rates are balanced by relatively low wage rates for jobs staffed through internal labor market processes, thus controlling average labor cost.

In summary, comparisons with product market competitors indicate maximum wage rates that an employer can offer and remain competitive and comparisons with labor market competitors indicate minimum wage rates an employer can offer and attract the necessary labor force. Wage rate comparisons with labor market competitors are more critical for entry jobs than for advanced career jobs staffed through promotion from within; wage rates for advanced career jobs are considered below in the maintenance of a labor force as an issue regarding wage structure.

Maintenance of a labor force. Consistent with the general model of motivation and behavior, the decision to accept employment with an organization is viewed as continuing until reexamined as a consequence of experienced dissatisfaction. Continued employment with the organization is a normal consequence of the initial decision to join, not a consequence of repetitive decisions to stay with the organization. Continued employment may result at times from rejection of opportunities for termination, but more commonly it reflects continuing, unquestioned acceptance of the initial decision to accept employment with the organization. The general behavior model also suggests that awareness of alternative employment opportunities is in large part a function of search initiated by experienced dissatisfaction. Thus decisions to terminate employment typically proceed from dissatisfaction rather than from alternative attractions luring an individual away from the organization. This hypothesis is consistent with observations that most employees have faulty perceptions of wage levels paid by other employers and observations that relatively few employed persons are active participants in the external labor market, only those persons who are dissatisfied with their current employment participating to any degree in active search within the labor market. In general, it appears that individuals accept employment with an organization, withdraw from active participation in the labor market and develop commitment to the employing organization. They only reengage in active search of the labor market as they experience dissatisfaction and develop a desire to leave.

While dissatisfaction may stimulate search for more satisfying alternatives, it need not result in decisions to terminate employment. Decisions to terminate employment are a function of both level of alternative rewards and the probability of these rewards. Thus termination rates vary inversely with the level of unemployment or directly with the probability of alternative employment. A dissatisfied employee may choose to remain with the organization because of lack of alternatives.

The compensation issues related most directly to maintenance of an organizational labor force are those which influence employee dissatisfaction and desire to leave and those which influence decisions to terminate when alternative employment is considered. Decisions to terminate employment may be either decisions to accept specific other employment opportunities or decisions to terminate and then seek alternative employment, depending in part upon generalized expectations about the ease of finding alternative employment and the ease with which the individual can engage in labor market search while still employed. Decisions of the first type involve comparison of two specific employment alternatives, while decisions of the second type involve comparison of current employment with some generalized concept of the alternatives thought to be available in the labor market. Rewards contingent upon continued employment and tenure such as seniority rights in job assignment, length of service compensation, and pension rights can be structured to make it relatively costly for the individual to terminate employment and thus influence decisions to stay. Similarly, expectations of future rewards indicated in the internal structure of compensation rates, career ladders in the internal labor market, and expectations of promotion influence the relative attractiveness of the current employment and thus decisions to stay or leave. Individual employees might desire to leave for a more attractive alternative and yet remain with the organization because of anticipated rewards or perceived costs of terminating employment.

Desire to leave the organization is viewed as a direct function of experienced dissatisfactions, most likely deprivational dissatisfaction associated with job characteristics the individual is incapable of changing. While deprivational dissatisfaction might be experienced with any of a number of job characteristics, the compensation characteristics with the most apparent relevance to deprivational dissatisfaction probably concern those associated with equity considerations. Persisting perceptions of inequity in compensation are easily associated with dissatisfaction and desire to leave the organization. The structure of wage rates or compensation differentials within the organization was examined as a significant element in judgments of equity of compensation although other elements such as compensation schedule and the structure of compensation differentials of individuals within a single job probably also influence equity judgments as well. While various possible indicators of an equitable wage structure were examined, the ultimate test of an equitable structure of compensation is that of acceptability by the affected employees. It appears that job characteristics, personal characteristics of job incumbents, social norms, custom, and tradition all influence the perceived equity of any structure of compensation differentials and that specific influences vary from one organization to another. The administrative approach of job evaluation provides a means of identifying operational criteria of equity in the structuring of compensation differentials within a specific setting and, perhaps equally important, a means for rationalizing and/or influencing customs regarding the criteria to be employed in judging the equity of the wage structure. To the extent that the structure of compensation differentials in the organization is judged to be equitable, we would expect reduction of dissatisfaction and desire to leave as a consequence of compensation.

The structure of compensation differentials within the organization, considered primarily in terms of equity considerations, influences dissatisfaction and desire to leave but does not appear particularly relevant in the motivation of desired behavior within the organization. The provision of an equitable compensation structure is a necessary, but not sufficient, condition for the motivation of task performance. Perceived equity of the compensation structure may influence job choice and willingness to accept specific assignments, however, as well as desire to leave, and thus affect this aspect of the supply of labor services. Individuals experience inequity of compensation in specific job assignments and seek to avoid that inequity through avoidance of those job assignments. Other things being equal, employees attached to an organization are expected to accept willingly promotions within career ladders of the internal labor market, but only if these promotions are perceived to be compensated in an equitable fashion. Thus perceived equity of the structure of compensation differentials contributes to maintenance of the desired allocation of individuals among job assignments as well as maintenance of the overall labor force of the organization.

While equity of the compensation structure does not appear to contribute to positive job satisfaction and thus balance other dissatisfying job elements, other compensation characteristics such as wage level and implied achievement recognition may contribute to positive job satisfaction and thus motivate continued employment and advancement within the organization. These characteristics are considered in more detail in the next section which deals with performance dimensions of labor supply behaviors.

Job performance. Job performance is a complex, multidimensional concept that has been inadequately conceptualized and analyzed. Different types of performance and their associated behaviors probably should be identified and analyzed separately; for example, behaviors such as absenteeism, rule violation, sabotage, working to rule, striving to exceed quotas, and suggesting innovations in task performance may well be quite different in terms of motivation and require different models in their explanation. For purposes of analysis here we shall distinguish between three general types or levels of task performance, performance of minimal task requirements, performance below, and performance beyond the level of minimal task requirements. As in Chapter 8, we also distinguish between two patterns of performance, the maintenance of previously established levels of task performance, and change in the level or type of task performance. Briefly, maintenance of previously established levels of task performance is viewed as a function of satisfaction experienced with that performance and its outcomes, whereas change in level of task performance is viewed as a function of dissatisfaction with the previous performance and the associated outcomes, and as a function of anticipations of satisfaction which might be experienced with a change in performance. The level of task performance resulting from a change is conceived as a function of decision making based upon expected reward contingencies associated with alternative behaviors.

The general concept of an exchange of inducements and contributions in an employment contract has been applied throughout our analysis, the individual employee providing contributions of work behavior in exchange for employer inducements including compensation. An individual accepting employment within the context of an inducements-contributions exchange is normally expected to provide the minimal performance specified as contributions in the exchange. The inducements-contributions exchange can be viewed as an employment contract specific to the individual and job assignment or, more realistically, as a linked sequence of exchanges, each more specific than another. We can, for example, consider a general employment contract related to accepting employment and membership in the organization and another, more specific, employment contract related to performance in a specific job. Individuals accept employment in an organization expecting to advance through job assignments over time, yet knowing only general requirements for continued membership (disciplinary code, attendance), minimal performance required on the entry job assignment, and immediate compensation rewards reflective largely of rewards for organizational membership. Specific inducements and contributions associated with assignment to other jobs in the organization only become known through continued employment and advancement to other assignments within the internal labor market; these later inducements-contributions exchanges elaborate and refine the more general exchange for membership and relate to performance in specific job assignments. Details of these more specific exchanges also change over time with changes in task composition of jobs and with supervisory expectations. Performance of minimal organizational and task requirements is normally expected in acceptance of the employment contracts for membership in the organization and for specific job assignments, a performance level we would expect to be maintained as long as the individual experiences satisfaction with the employment exchange. Change in performance to a level either exceeding or falling below the level of minimal organizational and task performance implies prior experience of dissatisfaction and choice of the new performance pattern as potentially more satisfying.

Different types of behavior are clearly associated with performance levels below and above minimal requirements. Performance below the level of minimal task requirements is associated with withdrawal types of behavior, the withholding of effort through absenteeism, loafing, and lack of attention, while performance above the minimal level required is associated with the exertion of extra effort, attention and commitment. These differences in behavior suggest differences in either or both the nature of dissatisfaction experienced and the resulting evaluation and choice among alternative behaviors. The model of satisfaction and performance developed in Chapter 8 can be utilized in analysis of the compensation issues related to these different performance behaviors. We distinguished in that model between aspirational and deprivational concepts of satisfaction, the first reflecting achievements relative to aspirations and the second reflecting performance outcomes relative to felt needs or "necessary" outcomes. Need values for compensation can be inferred from considerations of budgets necessary to maintain living standards and from considerations of equity, equity relative to others in the community, other jobs in the organization, and others performing the same job assignment. Aspiration values for compensation can be inferred relative to desired living standards and the status, recognition, and achievement symbolizations of compensation. We observed in Chapter 8 that some minimal aspirational dissatisfaction is common due to changing aspirations, but that aspirational dissatisfaction is unlikely to be large and persist over long periods of time. Deprivational dissatisfaction, on the other hand, may be significant and persisting if opportunities to correct it are not easily found.

The condition normally expected for most employees is one in which the individual experiences compensation outcomes associated with minimal performance which achieve the level of outcomes considered necessary and no deprivational dissatisfaction with respect to compensation is experienced; the compensation provided provides the necessary living standard and is considered equitable relative to other employers, other jobs within the organization and other persons performing in the same job. Some aspirational dissatisfaction is normal and the employee will be alert to behavior changes which would result in increased compensation for instrumental use or symbolic of achievement and recognition. Contingency relationships between performance and compensation will be considered and the indicated behavior selected if the net result is anticipated to provide favorable results. Some level of performance will be achieved at which point further change is considered unproductive and we would expect this performance level to be maintained until changed conditions result in more favorable anticipations of consequences of alternative behaviors.

What we term deprivational dissatisfaction is associated with job elements perceived as below some minimal necessary level (e.g., minimal standard of living) or as discrepant from some optimal level (e.g., equity). A minimal necessary level may be associated with the amount of different forms of compensation such as salary, vacation, medical insurance, or anticipated pension. Optimal levels may be associated with equity considerations relative to others in the community, other jobs in the organization, or other employees in the same job. Like aspirational dissatisfaction, deprivational dissatisfaction stimulates search for alternatives which would prove more satisfying; unlike aspirational dissatisfaction, it is less likely to be diminished by modification of values felt to be necessary. Contingency compensation relationships perceived to be instrumental in the reduction of deprivational dissatisfaction are expected to influence behavioral choices. Thus performance at a level necessary to achieve need levels of compensation might be expected, and the level of performance realized would depend upon need levels of the individual and the contingency relationships between performance and compensation. The behavioral implications of deprivational dissatisfaction reflecting perceptions of inequity in compensation are less predictable, however. They include the initiation of complaints and grievances, request of job transfer, or rejection of an offered assignment, or withholding of effort to restore equity. What appears to be performance at a level less than minimally acceptable may well be a consequence of perceived inequities of compensation where withholding of effort is viewed as instrumental in restoring equity. The establishment of equitable compensation relationships would, in such an instance, be a necessary condition for achieving minimal required task performance.

The general behavior model summarized in this section has been applied in the analysis of compensation issues and we have largely ignored other motivational influences of behavior. While the model might be applied in the analysis of other motivational influences, that is beyond the scope of this treatment. Compensation represents only one set of inducement elements in the employment contract, however, and the motivational implications of some aspect of compensation may in practice be obscured by the motivational implications of other characteristics of the employment contract. For example, an employee may behave in an undesirable manner due to unpleasant co-workers regardless of the equity of compensation relationships in the organization.

Attempts to direct performance behavior through compensation influences appear in contingency relationships established between behavior and compensation; compensation is made contingent upon the desired performance. While conceptually simple, compensation contingency relationships may in fact be quite complex due in part to the various symbolizations of compensation and in part to the distinction between aspirational and deprivational aspects of satisfaction. We observed in Chapter 9 how incentive compensation might be viewed as instrumental in achieving greater compensation and/or recognition and thus serve aspirational purposes and, at the same time, threaten the maintenance of equitable compensation relationships and occasion deprivational dissatisfaction. In a sense, all compensation is contingent upon some prior qualification and contingency relationships ought to be examined carefully in any application to identify unintended contingencies and consequences which may accompany the intended contingencies and consequences. These unintended aspects of employee compensation often are more potent in directing behavior than the intended aspects.

The models employed in our analyses were oriented toward the individual; individual motivation and behavior was the focus of analysis. The same holds true for most theory and research concerning motivation and behavior. Most work behavior, however, occurs within a group or social setting and we know relatively little about the effects of the social setting upon individual motivation and behavior. Compensation is a source of potentially rewarding outcomes, but the meaning and significance of those outcomes depends in large part upon the social system within which those outcomes are experienced. Certain of the interactions between compensation characteristics and the social system of the work group were discussed in earlier readings, but they did little more than alerting one to considerations of the influence of the social system in the analysis of compensation issues. Again, until there is more analysis of the influence of the social system upon individual behavior within groups we can do little more than stress the importance of consideration of the social system in the design and administration of compensation approaches.

We must recognize also that compensation is only one of many potential sources of rewards associated with work performance. The social system of the work group, the tasks performed at work, and the full range of organizational and supervisory practices are three major sources of other outcomes of work behavior. It is difficult at this stage to generalize concerning the relative motivational influence of outcomes of these different sources. We can infer, however, that behavior-outcome contingencies controlled by one source of outcomes will be relatively less effective as an influence of behavior when it competes with alternative behavior-outcome contingencies controlled by another source. Competing behavior-outcome contingencies probably are, in fact, dysfunctional to the extent that they introduce uncertainty and confusion. The specification of performance-compensation contingencies is likely to be most effective in influencing performance when it reinforces related contingency relationships present within the organizational, supervisory, and social systems. In this sense, compensation probably is better viewed as a handmaiden to these other sources of motivational influence rather than as a powerful, independent source of motivational influence upon work behavior.

EMERGING ISSUES

Any attempt to integrate or synthesize conceptualization about a topic is almost inevitably reflective of past thought rather than oriented towards an unpredictable future. This book also reflects past theory and practice regarding employee compensation as evidenced in the various perspectives reviewed here. Given these perspectives, we can speculate about future developments in compensation theory and practice, particularly given certain assumptions about developing trends in society and work organization.

Apparent trends in American society include increasing levels of education of the population, increasing affluence and concern for leisure and consumption, increasing numbers of families with multiple jobholders, and increasing concern for values other than the Protestant work ethic, values relating to environmental quality, quality of work life, and quality of social relationships. Evidence of these trends as they affect work and compensation appears in increased professionalization and skill levels of the work force, career planning by individuals and employers, disinclination of employees to accept relocation particularly if it involves a job change for spouses, experiments with flexitime and shortened work weeks, and efforts to redesign jobs and tasks to provide more interesting and challenging work.

The organization of work and jobs also is changing partly in response to changes in society and the work force and partly in response to changing technology of production. The division of labor into very specialized, routine and repetitive tasks as exemplified by the assembly line is giving way in many instances to team organization with rotating assignments, enlargement of jobs to include more tasks, and more frequent alteration of job content through the addition and elimination of assigned tasks. Very specific and stable structures of tasks in jobs are giving way to broader classes of jobs with flexible and changing content.

One of the implications of these trends for compensation administration relates to what we termed earlier "job pay" or compensation variations related to specific job assignment. The replacement of a finely graded structure of stable and specific jobs with broad classes of jobs with flexible and varying task content calls for parallel modification of wage structures; specific job content can no longer serve as the basis for fine distinctions among rates of compensation. Rather, we might anticipate development of compensation structures with relatively fewer job related differentials and relatively more differentials associated with individuals in the same job class. Organizational forms such as matrix organization and project organization illustrate the type of development anticipated. In project organization, for example, engineers with a certain specialization and skill level are assigned to work as team members on specific projects and any individual may work on several projects during a year, projects involving different types of tasks. Under such an arrangement, engineers of the same specialty are grouped together in a common skill class and assigned as appropriate to different projects. The structure of compensation differentials is based first upon skill class and then upon specific levels of project performance by individual engineers. Similarly, we might anticipate development of broad skill classes of other employees as the basic element in structuring compensation differentials, and consideration of individual performance as a second element in structuring compensation differentials among employees in a single class. Relatively more of the range of differential compensation would be associated with individuals and relatively less with classifications than is the case today.

The administration of compensation differentials among individuals within broad job or skill classes would appear to alter somewhat the incentive and reward aspects of compensation. The criteria for individual compensation differentials are not as apparent or objective as the criteria associated with job differentials suggesting that the conditions responsible for individual compensation differentials may have to be learned through experience rather than through observation of the compensation structure and associated job characteristics. Individual compensation differentials thus would appear more analogous to rewards than to incentives.

We might also anticipate greater employee participation in the design and administration of individual compensation differentials as these differentials account for relatively more of total variation in the overall structure of compensation. Concern for the maintenance of equity in compensation relationships may well lead to greater involvement in individual evaluation just as participation in job evaluation is employed in securing acceptance of the equity of the resulting structure of compensation differentials among jobs. Equity considerations suggest that acceptance of a system of individual evaluation will become as critical as acceptance of a system of job evaluation is today.

Provision of opportunity for choice among alternative forms of compensation already is being advocated and is the subject of experimentation in some organizations. At the same time, the proportion of compensation paid in the form of fringe benefits increases constantly. More flexibility for individual choice of forms of compensation probably will be provided in the future as a means of controlling the costs of compensation and yet permitting greater opportunity for individuals to attain perceived necessary levels of specific forms of compensation such as insurance, pension, and vacation. Opportunities for the exercise of choice may well be made contingent upon length of service or skill level thus providing some incentive for desired behavior.

A final observation regarding the development of compensation theory and practice relates to integration of compensation considerations and the full range of organizational, administrative, and motivational concerns for work and the employment contract. Compensation is a major element in the employment exchange, although by no means the only significant element. A variety of other motivational influences also exist within the job situation. Employee compensation is a more potent influence of work behavior in so far as it complements these other influences. Complementary associations between compensation administration and other administrative practices will become more common as we learn more about the motivation of work behavior and continue development of a more general theory of rewards and motivation in work organizations.